SHOTS HEARD ROUND THE WORLD

Winning Independence: The Decisive Years of the Revolutionary War, 1778–1781

Apostles of Revolution: Jefferson, Paine, Monroe, and the Struggle Against the Old Order in America and Europe

Whirlwind: The American Revolution and the War That Won It

Jefferson and Hamilton: The Rivalry That Forged a Nation

Independence: The Struggle to Set America Free

The Ascent of George Washington: The Hidden Political Genius of an American Icon

Almost a Miracle: The American Victory in the War of Independence

Adams vs. Jefferson: The Tumultuous Election of 1800

A Leap in the Dark: The Struggle to Create the American Republic

Setting the World Ablaze: Washington, Adams, Jefferson, and the American Revolution

John Adams: A Life

The First of Men: A Life of George Washington

Struggle for a Continent: The Wars of Early America

A Wilderness of Miseries: War and Warriors in Early America

The Loyalist Mind: Joseph Galloway and the American Revolution

SHOTS HEARD ROUND THE WORLD

AMERICA, BRITAIN, AND EUROPE IN THE REVOLUTIONARY WAR

JOHN FERLING

BLOOMSBURY PUBLISHING

NEW YORK · LONDON · OXFORD · NEW DELHI · SYDNEY

BLOOMSBURY PUBLISHING
Bloomsbury Publishing Inc.
1385 Broadway, New York, NY 10018, USA
50 Bedford Square, London, WC1B 3DP, UK
Bloomsbury Publishing Ireland Limited,
29 Earlsfort Terrace, Dublin 2, D02 AY28, Ireland

BLOOMSBURY, BLOOMSBURY PUBLISHING, and the Diana logo are trademarks of
Bloomsbury Publishing Plc

First published in the United States 2025

ISBN: HB: 978-1-63973-015-5; EBOOK: 978-1-63973-016-2

LIBRARY OF CONGRESS CATALOGING-IN-PUBLICATION DATA IS AVAILABLE

2 4 6 8 10 9 7 5 3 1

Typeset by Westchester Publishing Services
Printed and bound in the U.S.A. by Berryville Graphics Inc., Berryville, Virginia

To find out more about our authors and books visit www.bloomsbury.com and
sign up for our newsletters.

Bloomsbury books may be purchased for business or promotional use. For information on
bulk purchases please contact Macmillan Corporate and Premium Sales Department at
specialmarkets@macmillan.com.

For product safety–related questions contact productsafety@bloomsbury.com.

For Keith Pacholl
Historian, tech helpmate, and above all my good friend

CONTENTS

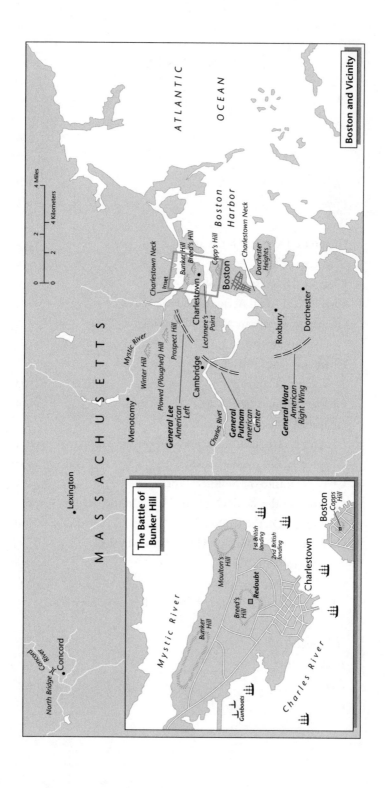

Boston and Vicinity

ATLANTIC

OCEAN

Boston Harbor

4 Miles

4 Kilometers

Charlestown Neck

Bunker Hill

Breed's Hill

Inset

Copp's Hill

Charlestown Neck

Dorchester Heights

Boston

Charlestown

Lechmere's Point

Mystic River

Winter Hill

Plowed (Ploughed) Hill

Prospect Hill

General Lee
American
Left

Cambridge

Charles River

General Putnam
American
Center

General Ward
American
Right Wing

Roxbury

Dorchester

Menotomy

M A S S A C H U S E T T S

Lexington

Concord River

North Bridge

Concord

The Battle of
Bunker Hill

Mystic River

Moulton's Hill

Bunker Hill

Breed's Hill

Redoubt

1st British landing

2nd British landing

Charlestown

Boston

Copps Hill

Charles River

Gunboats

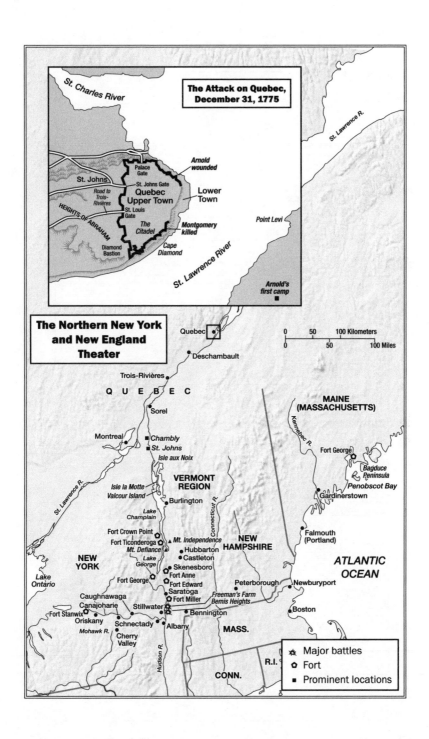

The Attack on Quebec, December 31, 1775

St. Charles River

Arnold wounded

Palace Gate

St. Johns Gate

St. Johns

Quebec Upper Town

Lower Town

Road to Trois-Rivières

HEIGHTS OF ABRAHAM

St. Louis Gate

The Citadel

Montgomery killed

Point Levi

Diamond Bastion

Cape Diamond

St. Lawrence River

Arnold's first camp

St. Lawrence R.

The Northern New York and New England Theater

Quebec

Deschambault

Trois-Rivières

QUEBEC

Sorel

Montreal

Chambly

St. Johns

Isle aux Noix

MAINE (MASSACHUSETTS)

Kennebec R.

Fort George

Bagduce Peninsula

Penobscot Bay

Gardinerstown

Isle la Motte

Valcour Island

VERMONT REGION

Burlington

Connecticut R.

Lake Champlain

Fort Crown Point

Fort Ticonderoga

Mt. Defiance

Mt. Independence

Hubbarton

Castleton

Lake George

NEW HAMPSHIRE

Falmouth (Portland)

NEW YORK

Skenesboro

Fort Anne

Fort George

Fort Edward

Saratoga

Fort Miller

Peterborough

Freeman's Farm

Bemis Heights

Newburyport

ATLANTIC OCEAN

Lake Ontario

Caughnawaga

Canajoharie

Stillwater

Bennington

Boston

Fort Stanwix

Oriskany

Schenectady

Albany

MASS.

Mohawk R.

Cherry Valley

Hudson R.

R.I.

CONN.

0   50   100 Kilometers
0   50   100 Miles

✳ Major battles
⬠ Fort
■ Prominent locations

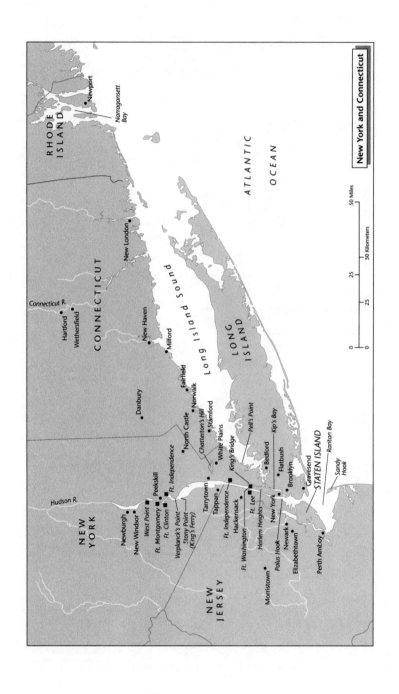

New York and Connecticut

RHODE ISLAND

Newport

Narragansett Bay

ATLANTIC OCEAN

CONNECTICUT

New London

Connecticut R.

Hartford

Wethersfield

New Haven

Milford

Danbury

Fairfield

Norwalk

North Castle

Chatterton's Hill

Stamford

White Plains

Long Island Sound

LONG ISLAND

Pell's Point

Kip's Bay

King's Bridge

Bedford

Flatbush

Brooklyn

Gravesend

STATEN ISLAND

Raritan Bay

Sandy Hook

Hudson R.

NEW YORK

Newburgh

New Windsor

West Point

Peekskill

Ft. Montgomery

Ft. Clinton

Ft. Independence

Verplanck's Point

Stony Point (King's Ferry)

Tarrytown

Tappan

Ft. Independence

Hackensack

Ft. Lee

Ft. Washington

Harlem Heights

New York

Paulus Hook

Newark

NEW JERSEY

Morristown

Elizabethtown

Perth Amboy

50 Miles

50 Kilometers

0   25   50

0   25   50

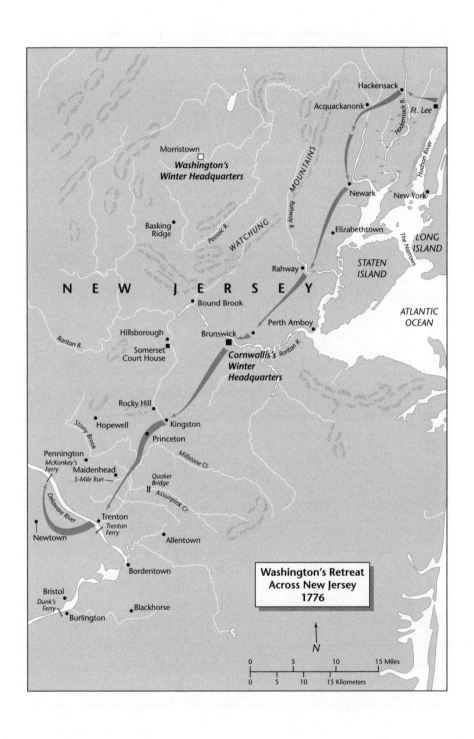

Hackensack
Acquackanonk
Ft. Lee
Hackensack R.
Hudson River
Morristown
*Washington's
Winter Headquarters*
Newark
New York
WATCHUNG
Rahway R.
MOUNTAINS
Basking
Ridge
Passaic R.
Elizabethtown
LONG
ISLAND
STATEN
ISLAND
Rahway
N E W J E R S E Y
Bound Brook
Perth Amboy
ATLANTIC
OCEAN
Raritan R.
Hillsborough
Brunswick
Somerset
Court House
*Cornwallis's
Winter
Headquarters*
Raritan R.
Rocky Hill
Stony Brook
Hopewell
Kingston
Princeton
Pennington
*McKonkey's
Ferry*
Millstone Cr.
Maidenhead
5-Mile Run
*Quaker
Bridge*
Assunpink Cr.
Delaware River
Trenton
*Trenton
Ferry*
Newtown
Allentown
Bordentown
Bristol
*Dunk's
Ferry*
Blackhorse
Burlington

**Washington's Retreat
Across New Jersey
1776**

N

| 0 | 5 | 10 | 15 Miles |
| 0 | 5 | 10 | 15 Kilometers |

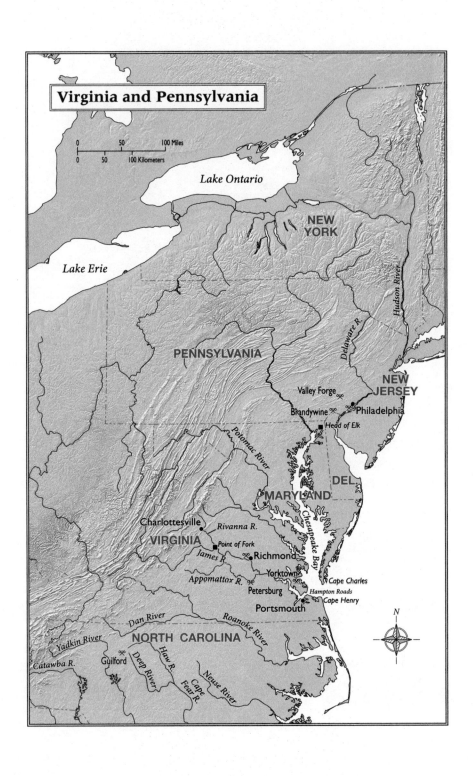

Virginia and Pennsylvania

0   50   100 Miles
0   50   100 Kilometers

Lake Ontario

NEW YORK

Lake Erie

PENNSYLVANIA

Delaware R.

Hudson River

NEW JERSEY

Valley Forge

Brandywine
Philadelphia
Head of Elk

Potomac River

DEL

MARYLAND

Charlottesville
Rivanna R.

VIRGINIA
Point of Fork
James R.
Richmond
Yorktown
Chesapeake Bay
Cape Charles
Appomattox R.
Petersburg
Hampton Roads
Cape Henry
Portsmouth

Dan River
Roanoke River

Yadkin River
NORTH CAROLINA

Catawba R.
Guilford
Deep River
Haw R.
Cape Fear R.
Neuse River

N

The Carolinas and Georgia

Roanoke River

Dan River

Yadkin River

Guilford

Hillsborough

Haw River

Deep River

Neuse River

Catawba River

Salisbury

NORTH CAROLINA

Cowen's Ford

Gilbert Town

Ramsour's Mill

Charlotte

Cross Creek

Cape Fear River

Moore's Creek Bridge

Cowpens

King's Mtn.

Waxhaws

Wilmington

Fishing Creek

Camden

Hobkirk's Hill

Great Pee Dee River

Saluda River

Winnsboro

Broad R.

Wateree River

Little River

Ninety Six

SOUTH CAROLINA

Congaree R.

Kettle Creek

Edisto River

Santee River

Georgetown

Augusta

Savannah River

Monck's Corner

ATLANTIC OCEAN

Briar Creek

Charleston

Ogeechee River

GEORGIA

Savannah

Tybee Island

N

0   50   100 Miles

0   50   100 Kilometers

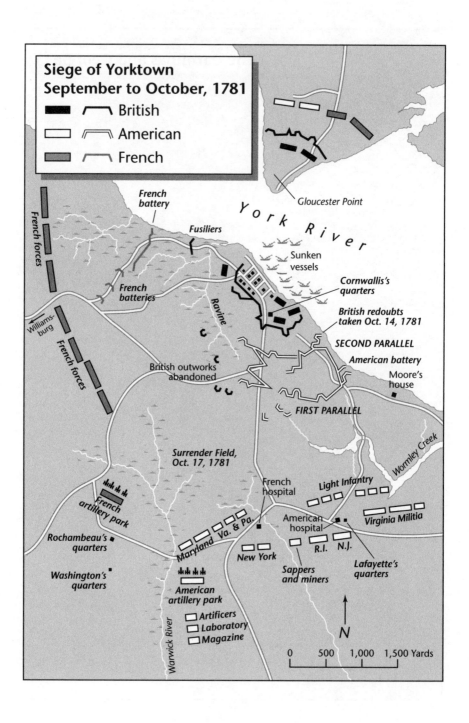

Siege of Yorktown
September to October, 1781

- ◼ ⌐ British
- ☐ ⌐ American
- ◼ ⌐ French

French battery

Fusiliers

York River

Gloucester Point

French forces

Sunken vessels

French batteries

Cornwallis's quarters

Ravine

Williamsburg

British redoubts taken Oct. 14, 1781

SECOND PARALLEL

French forces

British outworks abandoned

American battery

Moore's house

FIRST PARALLEL

Surrender Field, Oct. 17, 1781

Wormley Creek

French hospital

Light Infantry

French artillery park

American hospital

Virginia Militia

Rochambeau's quarters

Maryland, Va. & Pa.

New York

R.I.

N.J.

Washington's quarters

Sappers and miners

Lafayette's quarters

American artillery park

N

Artificers
Laboratory
Magazine

Warwick River

0   500   1,000   1,500 Yards

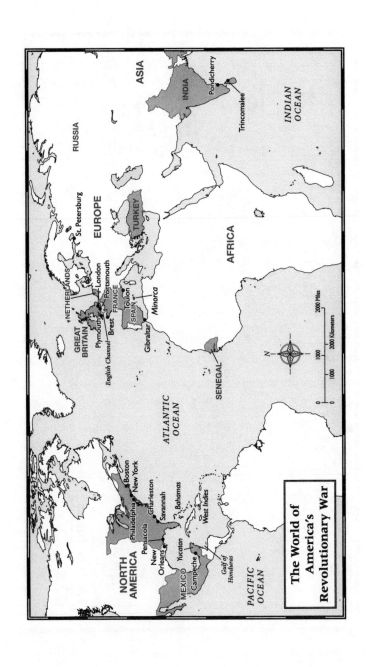

The World of America's Revolutionary War

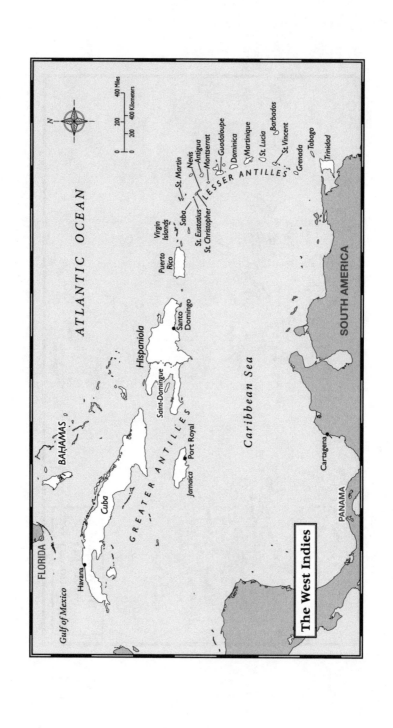

The West Indies

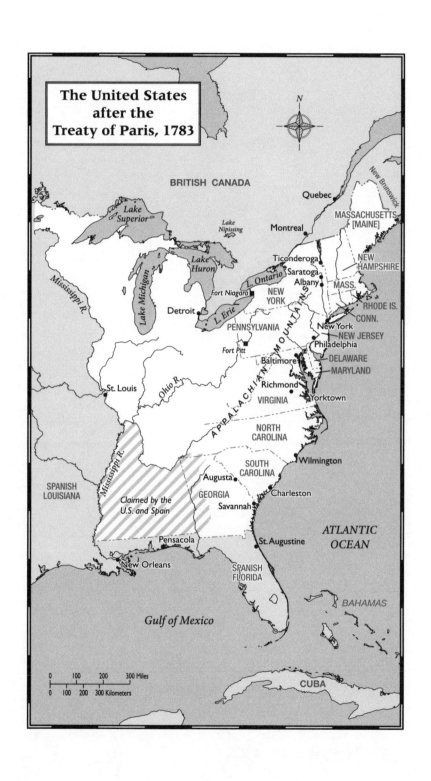

The United States
after the
Treaty of Paris, 1783

N

BRITISH CANADA

Lake Superior

Lake Nipissing

Quebec

New Brunswick

MASSACHUSETTS [MAINE]

Montreal

Lake Huron

Lake Michigan

Mississippi R.

Ticonderoga

Saratoga

L. Ontario

Fort Niagara

NEW YORK

Albany

NEW HAMPSHIRE

MASS.

RHODE IS.

CONN.

Detroit

L. Erie

PENNSYLVANIA

New York

NEW JERSEY

Philadelphia

Fort Pitt

Ohio R.

Baltimore

DELAWARE

MARYLAND

St. Louis

Richmond

VIRGINIA

Yorktown

APPALACHIAN MOUNTAINS

NORTH CAROLINA

Mississippi R.

SOUTH CAROLINA

Wilmington

Claimed by the U.S. and Spain

Augusta

GEORGIA

Charleston

SPANISH LOUISIANA

Savannah

Pensacola

St. Augustine

ATLANTIC OCEAN

New Orleans

SPANISH FLORIDA

BAHAMAS

Gulf of Mexico

0   100   200   300 Miles

0   100   200   300 Kilometers

CUBA

PREFACE

NOW THAT AMERICA WILL be commemorating the semiquincentennial—the 250th anniversary—of its War of Independence, what pops into your mind as you hear or witness references to that conflict? Perhaps it is Paul Revere's ride, Benedict Arnold's treason, the weaponry of that war, or the guerrilla bands that formed in the South. Maybe you think of a famous person, possibly George Washington or Benjamin Franklin, Betsy Ross or John Paul Jones. Is it the image of America's Revolutionary War officers in their buff-and-blue coats and British troops in their gaudy red uniforms? Given the popularity of Emanuel Leutze's painting of Washington crossing the Delaware and William B. T. Trego's rendering of America's ragged soldiers tramping through the snow in *The March to Valley Forge*, are you struck by thoughts of a battle or the plight of the men in the Continental army?

Would you think of Comte de Vergennes or Bernardo de Gálvez, Comte de Grasse, Comte de Rochambeau, Conde de Floridablanca, Lord North, George III, Louis XVI, or Carlos III? They, too, were major players in the war, a conflict that was not confined to North America but was international in scope. That this was a war featuring many countries and far-flung fields of battle has not dominated the literature on the War of Independence or the popular culture celebrating the conflict. In fact, when General Washington in 1783 said goodbye to his army and later spoke to Congress when surrendering his commission, he said nothing about the help America had received from France and Spain.

When I was young—before I became a historian and taught and wrote about the Revolutionary War—the American Revolution and the War of Independence were not on my mind, and I knew little about either. The usually sad exploits of the Pittsburgh Pirates, the escapades of TV's Ralph Kramden, and the adventures of Mike Hammer, Mickey Spillane's fictional New York private eye, occupied much of my thinking. In Texas, where I grew up, the Texas Revolution of the 1830s grabbed more attention than the American Revolution, and Sam Houston was emphasized more than Sam Adams. I knew something about the battles at the Alamo and San Jacinto and next to nothing—and maybe nothing—about Saratoga and Brandywine. I don't recall Ms. Buchhorn, my high school American history teacher, spending nearly as much time on the American Revolution as she did on the Civil War, which I recall her referring to as the "War of Northern Aggression." Until I took American history in college I didn't even know where Yorktown was located. It sounded as if must be in New York.

I do recollect being assigned to read Ralph Waldo Emerson's poem "Concord Hymn" in an American literature class when I was in 10th grade. Emerson had been asked to write the poem for the July 4, 1837, celebration of American Independence in Concord, Massachusetts, a village west of Boston that had been a site of fighting on the first day of the Revolutionary War. The poem was read and then sung by a local choir to the tune of a favorite hymn, "Old Hundred." Emerson wrote that the New England yeomen who fought that day were "heroes" who had risked death in order to "leave their children free." The day's festivities in Concord, he said in the poem, were being held 62 years after the event so "That Memory may their deed redeem."

The first stanza of the poem is the best remembered, or at least it is what sticks in my mind:

> By the rude bridge that arched the flood,
>   Their flag to April's breeze unfurled,
> Here once the embattled farmers stood,
>   And fired the shot heard round the world.

If my memory is accurate, the part I picked up on was "embattled farmers." As my grandfather owned a farm about 50 miles outside of Pittsburgh, I thought maybe the farmers who had taken up their muskets and risked life and limb that bloody day lived and worked more or less as he did. I am sure that the part about "the shot heard round the world" did not register with me.

It does now. America's Revolutionary War, and how "the world" responded to that faraway conflict in Britain's colonies in North America, is what this book is about. Years before "the shot heard round the world" was fired, France had sent secret agents to America to learn if the colonial protests against British policies might someday, somehow, turn into a revolution. Soon after learning of fighting between colonists and British regulars at Lexington and Concord, on April 19, 1775, France sent another agent to Philadelphia to assess the colonists' ability to wage and sustain a war, and to discover whether the insurgents needed and wanted assistance. They did, and in 1777 shiploads of French war materials arrived in America. Soon, too, vessels sent by Spain docked in America with essential provisions for the rebels. All the while, clandestine shipments of arms and ammunition, and a thousand and one other items needed for America's war effort, were being channeled from European seaports though a Dutch colony in the Caribbean, where American merchants procured the cargoes and delivered the goods to America's coastal towns and cities. In 1778 France entered the war as an American ally, and the following year Spain went to war with Britain as a cobelligerent of the United States.

Shots Heard Round the World is a book about this long, grim war. It dragged on for eight years and was America's longest war before the Vietnam conflict. Unlike World War II, the outcome could not be foreseen until the final great battle in America in 1781. A British victory seemed likely in the early years of the war. Thirty months into hostilities a British defeat seemed probable. By 1779 the war had become a stalemate. From that point onward the civil and military leaders of every belligerent country knew that victory was possible, but defeat was not out of the question. At the outset of 1781, seven long years after the shots rang out at Lexington and Concord, Sir Henry Clinton, commander of Britain's army in America, was more optimistic than General Washington. Indeed, a year before the decisive and climactic siege of a British army at Yorktown, Washington admitted that he had almost given up hope that America could gain its independence. When the war was finally won, Washington said that America's victory was nothing short of miraculous.

The miracle could not have occurred without the help of the French and Spanish. These two autocratic and royalist nations that came to the aid of American rebels who, after 1776, were waging a republican revolution, seeking an egalitarian society, and—for some at least—hoping to establish a democratic political system. The war itself was dangerous for France and Spain, both of which had suffered disastrous defeats at the hands of Great Britain only a dozen years earlier. But aiding revolutionaries and risking the possibility of unleashing the radical republican spirit at the heart of the American rebellion was also threatening to European monarchies and the aristocracies that bolstered them.

This is a book about the war. It does not focus exclusively on generals, military strategies, and battles. It considers the home fronts in America and Great Britain, and of the European belligerents. It delves into decisions made by civil leaders in the countries at war and in neutral nations impacted by hostilities, always focusing on what they knew at the time, not what we know today. It examines the diplomacy pursued by the nations touched by the armed conflict and the diplomats trusted with statecraft.

Of course, *Shots Heard Round the World* analyzes the war in America. At the outset it considers why the war occurred. It goes on to appraise the strategies of every belligerent. It shows why Britain had the means to crush the American rebellion during the first 30 months of fighting, and it assesses why it failed to do so. It evaluates the military and civil leaders on both sides, the choices they faced, and the reasons for their most crucial decisions.

The book explores why monarchs in old, still-feudal Europe ran the peril of becoming enmeshed in a war of liberation waged by republican insurgents thousands of miles away in America. It asserts that they understood the risks they were running and the benefits they believed could be reaped through intervening to aid the Americans. It demonstrates why their intervention was a fateful step for themselves, for that generation, and for generations to come.

It is a rare war that has no surprises. America's Revolutionary War, and the responses to it, resulted in rude awakenings for every belligerent. The British went to war thinking that the conflict might last only days or weeks and that the fighting might be restricted to Massachusetts. Soon Britain was scrambling to find troops that it had never imagined would be needed. The delegates in America's Continental Congress, or at least a majority of them, went to war in 1775 thinking that the colonists' resolve and a spirited resistance on the field of battle would force Britain to make war-ending concessions within a year or so. The French and Spanish in 1776 believed that secret aid for the rebels would be sufficient to force Britain to relinquish its American colonies. When France's leaders in 1778 learned that clandestine assistance was insufficient, it committed a large navy, thinking that would turn the tide and bring the war to a satisfactory conclusion. Far from it! *Shots Heard Round the World* looks into why so many steps went so wrong and what those missteps meant for the course of the war. The book ponders, as year after year rolled by and the war continued, what the stalemated war meant for each belligerent from 1779 onward, including how the deadlock shaped military strategies, diplomacy, civilian morale, relations between the American and French allies, the link between the Bourbons, and the durability of both Britain's commitment to continuing the war and France's staying power.

As this book is an international history of America's Revolutionary War, it assesses not only the war in North America (including lands far to the north, south, and west of the 13 states) but also hostilities in the Caribbean, Europe, and Asia and on the high seas. Portions of the book are centered in the handsome offices of civil leaders in London, Madrid, Versailles, and assorted neutral nations in Europe. It was in those offices that fateful decisions were made concerning entering the war, waging war, continuing hostilities, determining the leadership and size of the armies, and diplomacy, including the peace negotiations that followed the decisive engagement at Yorktown.

This is not a book solely about well-known generals, famous founders, monarchs, prime ministers, and diplomats. This war, like every war, was fought by soldiers. Regardless of the army, soldiers led a harsh existence. Theirs was a life of lonely toil, deprivation, discipline, draconian punishments, and episodic danger. A great many did not live to see the end of this war. The war also touched every American on the home front and most in Great Britain. For a great many who never soldiered, the war meant abundant sacrifices, including the loss of income or a job, doing without familiar commodities, and long, lonely stretches of anxious waiting for the return of a loved one on the front lines. Some at home in America faced danger, whether from nearby soldiers or diseases that spread from armies to civilians. The book examines each army in this war and the Indigenous warriors who fought with and against them.

This was a long war that gripped many nations, numerous leaders, countless thousands of soldiers, and millions of civilians, some of whom lived in countries at peace yet were touched by hostilities, some who resided in nations at war and experienced repercussions from a conflict that began at faraway Lexington and Concord, Massachusetts. Among other things, *Shots Heard Round the World* seeks to explain why nations fought, along with their war aims, strategies, and diplomacy; the war's outcome; the human toll of the conflict; the making of the peace settlement; and the unexpected consequence of the war.

The semiquincentennial of the American Revolution and its War of Independence comes at a parlous time for American democracy, one of the most dangerously uncertain times it has faced during the past 250 years. As the nation celebrates the long, desperate struggle to win the war, and the sacrifices made by the soldiers and civilians on the home front to gain that victory, hopefully today's citizenry will remember what spurred that long-ago generation to fight—and for years to fight on and on—against incredible odds. Thomas Paine, America's foremost pamphleteer during the American Revolution, frequently wrote that it was the "spirit of '76" that inspired the perseverance and sacrifices made by the Revolutionary generation. That spirit was an ethos that stirred a passion to break free of royal, aristocratic, and autocratic domination and establish a democratic republic grounded on the sovereignty of the people.

CHAPTER I

DECISIONS FOR WAR

AMERICA'S REVOLUTIONARY WAR MIGHT have been avoided, but it wasn't, and the American insurgency might have been crushed within a year or so of fighting, but it wasn't. What began as a civil war within the British Empire continued until it became a wider conflict involving nations in Europe and affecting peoples and countries far from Great Britain and North America. Long after the soldiers laid down their arms, future generations in America and in distant corners of the world were touched—sometimes favorably, sometimes adversely—by the American Revolution and the fallout from its war.

The stirrings that led to the conflagration were set in motion in the 1760s, when Great Britain embarked on a striking departure in its colonial policies. It was a multifaceted divergence that stepped on many toes, including those of the most powerful residents in the 13 North American colonies. Britain tightened its regulation of imperial trade, hoping to eliminate smuggling by urban merchants who trafficked in outlawed foreign commodities and sought to avoid paying duties on legitimate commerce. Imperial authorities also mandated a temporary halt to western migration beyond the Appalachian Mountains, antagonizing land speculators—mostly wealthy and influential colonists—and land-hungry farmers. With the Stamp Act, in 1765, Parliament for the first time sought to levy taxes on its American subjects. It subsequently turned to other forms of taxation. To many colonists it seemed, as it did in 1774 to the Virginia planter and businessman George Washington, that Great Britain was pursuing "a Systematic ascertion of an arbitrary power" in violation of "the Laws & Constitution of their Country, & to violate the most essential & valuable rights of mankind."[1]

Many colonists harbored grievances other than those concerning regulations and taxes. Some people in some provinces were unhappy with having to pay tithes to the established Church of England. Restlessly ambitious colonists resented the fact-of-life limitations that faced colonials. Confronted with an unspoken but all-too-real second-class rank within the British Empire, aspiring colonists recognized that the door was closed to their sitting in Parliament, gaining ministerial and diplomatic posts, or rising to the loftiest ranks in the British army or the Royal Navy. Britain had fought three wars in the three-quarters of a century down to 1763, and the American colonists had been dragged into each conflict. Many colonists viewed these as Europe's wars that were of little concern to them, and they were eager to escape the talons of faraway leaders who made the wars and expected the participation of the American colonists. Doubtless, too, there were a great many ordinary colonists such as Levi Preston, a farmer in Danvers, Massachusetts, who in 1775 expressed in crystal-clear terms what troubled him: "we had always governed ourselves and we always meant to," but the British government "didn't mean we should."[2] Like Preston, a great many colonists thought the time had come for Americans to control their own destiny.

Widespread protests against Britain's new colonial policies flared in the 1760s. Colonists remonstrated with petitions, pamphlets, economic boycotts, and sometimes violence. A succession of British governments during the next several years backed and filled. Some measures were repealed; others were recalibrated. However, Parliament held intransigently to the position that it possessed the power to legislate for the colonies "in all cases whatsoever."

In 1768, convinced that Massachusetts was the epicenter of the turmoil, London redeployed three regiments of its army from the western frontier to Boston to cope with the unrest. Long since convinced that standing armies were tools of oppression and toxic threats to liberty, some colonists interpreted the arrival of the troops in Boston as yet another indicator that the British government was in the clutches of brutish tyrants. There was talk of armed resistance when the British regiments landed in the city, but nothing came of it. In fact, tensions eased after 1770 when Britain again repealed some of its troubling legislation and removed most of its troops from Boston, housing them in barracks outside the city. Tranquility coincided with the creation of a ministry headed by Frederick, Lord North. In his late 30s when he became the prime minister, North was astute, witty, anything but haughty, and given his unflattering and uninspiring bearing—one observer described him as "booby-looking"—scarcely charismatic. He had sat in Parliament and the ministry for years. Economic matters were his primary concern. Colonial affairs were of secondary interest to him, and during his early years as prime minister he sought to keep the Americans quiet by avoiding new inflammatory measures, dreamingly hopeful that subsequent generations could discover a peaceful solution to the imperial dilemma.[3] North's passivity worked for a time. However, in 1773 surging protests erupted once again, this time against a tax on tea, a parliamentary measure that antedated North's ministry and had been neither enforced nor rescinded. When North's government found reasons for implementing the legislation, three colonies—Pennsylvania, New York, and South Carolina—prevented ships carrying dutied tea from docking and unloading their cargoes. Protest leaders in Massachusetts, having failed to stop the vessels bound for their colony, staged the Boston Tea Party in December 1773, dumping today's equivalent of several million dollars' worth of tea into Boston Harbor. The extent of colonial defiance, and the wanton destruction of private property, brought the possibility of war to the forefront.

Such rage swept across England that further appeasement was out of the question. "[W]e must risk something," Lord North avowed.[4] His government contemplated an assortment of responses, including the use of force to crush the American rebels. Although the ministers foresaw little trouble in suppressing the insurrection, in 1774 they opted instead for peaceful coercion, something that had hardly been tried previously. Singling out Massachusetts for punishment, the ministry hit the colony with the Coercive Acts, measures that included a fine, closure of Boston Harbor until restitution for the tea was made, significant changes in the province's 80-year-old charter, and an act that authorized sending arrested colonists outside the colony for trial.

The colonists learned the details of the acts in the spring. Although the legislation applied only to Massachusetts, it sparked outrage elsewhere. Many thought that London was pursuing a policy of divide and conquer. Today Massachusetts would taste repression; tomorrow it would be the turn of another colony. Though many outside Massachusetts disapproved of Boston's destruction of the tea, a ubiquitous fear existed that if a faraway imperial government could alter the charter of one colony, it could transform the charters of all colonies. Such a step could radically change the structure of the provincial governments and even endanger cherished religious traditions. Anger and apprehension were plentiful, but every American activist understood that to defy the Coercive Acts in all likelihood meant war. The point of no return had come. Parliament held inflexibly to the position that it could make any law that it wished for the colonies. American insurgents just as unwaveringly maintained that there were limits to Parliament's power over the colonies, and some colonists insisted that Parliament had no power over the colonists. They recognized only the authority of the British Crown. It appeared to activists on both sides that the time had arrived when the alternatives were colonial submission or war.

Samuel Adams, Boston's flinty, tireless, undaunted, and never-overawed popular leader, advocated that each colony embargo British imports until the Coercive Acts were repealed. However, a majority of provincial assemblies urged a conclave of all the colonies to determine a uniform American response. Such a body, they reasoned, was necessary to discover whether the will existed to implement a national embargo. Moreover, if defiance led to war, only a national assembly could determine if there was sufficient unity among 13 separate colonies to wage war with Great Britain. It was the prospect of hostilities more than any other factor that led the colonies to agree to meet in Philadelphia in September 1774 in what came to be called the First Continental Congress. It would determine how to respond to the Coercive Acts and answer the question of whether armed resistance was feasible. Some even saw a congress as the best hope of escaping war, thinking that a demonstration of colonial unity might cause London to back down again.

Every colony but Georgia sent delegates. The congressmen convened at a Philadelphia tavern on September 5, but quickly moved to Carpenter's Hall, where they met several days a week for seven weeks. It was soon evident that the "Commencement of Hostilities is exceedingly dreaded here," as John Adams, a delegate from Massachusetts, put it. Many congressmen were "fixed against Hostilities and Ruptures," he said, unless they "become absolutely necessary, and this necessity they do not yet See." War, those delegates believed, "might rage for twenty year, and End, in the Subduction of America, as likely as in her Liberation." Dread of war led to differences over how resolute Congress could afford to be. Some delegates, convinced that the colonies must continue to have "the Aid and Assistance and Protection of the Arms of our Mother Country," held stubbornly to the belief that "we must come to Terms with G. Britain." But a majority agreed with Congressman George Washington. He believed that the colonies should never under any circumstances "submit to the loss of those valuable rights & privileges which are essential to the happiness of every free State." The divisions led the delegates "to steer" what John Adams called a "middle Course between Obedience . . .

and open Hostilities." Congress refused to create an army or acquire arms and munitions, though it encouraged the colonies to ready their militias for the possibility of war. It also agreed to an immediate national boycott of British imports and a year later, if necessary, a suspension of colonial exports within the British Empire. In a major concession by the hard-liners, Congress agreed that Parliament might regulate imperial commerce. Otherwise, Congress resolved that Parliament was powerless to legislate for the colonies. Congress concluded by addressing the king, George III, telling him that it sought peace and reconciliation and urging him to prevent hostilities.[5]

Some delegates, convinced that Congress had laid the groundwork for war, were gloomily apprehensive as they left Philadelphia. Others, like Samuel Adams, were delighted by Congress's determined stand. The delegates, he said, had manifested "the Spirit of Rome or Sparta." Few, if any, thought the steps taken by Congress would bring an end to the imperial crisis, and a great many likely would have agreed with John Adams's assessment: "We are . . . at the Brink of a Civil War." Every delegate knew that the decision for war or peace now rested with Great Britain, and in all probability most shared Washington's outlook: If London pushed "matters to extremity," more "blood will be spilt" than in all of America's previous wars combined.[6]

LONDON, 3,000 MILES AWAY, anxiously awaited word of what the Continental Congress had done, but British officials were not the only ones keeping watch on events in North America. French authorities had kept a sharp eye on Britain's American provinces since the earliest colonial protests. France had fought a series of wars with Britain during the past 75 years, and the last one, the Seven Years' War, had ended disastrously for the French in 1763. Since then, France's monarch and officials in the foreign ministry had sought redemption and retaliation.

During the Seven Years' War, Britain had destroyed the French navy, seized French forts in the Ohio Valley and northern New York, and utterly defeated France's armies in Canada. France, long a dominant power in Europe, was reduced to a shadow of its former self. At the peace table, it lost Nova Scotia, Acadia, Quebec, all that it had held east of the Mississippi River, some but not all of its West Indian colonies, and Senegal and assorted African slave-trading posts. France, in numbed despair, also watched as its commanding share of the Newfoundland fisheries was reduced to a minuscule level. It was an especially painful blow. As early as 200 years before, some 500 French ships were engaged in the Newfoundland fisheries, an enterprise that for generations had produced jobs, wealth, and experienced seamen for the navy. The war left France prostrate at the feet of Great Britain, for given their crippled navy, the French were incapable of defending their overseas possessions, regaining those they had lost, or maintaining crucial maritime interests in the Mediterranean. Furthermore, France's economy was in disarray, laden with heavy war debts and the reduction of its colonial trade to one-seventh of what it had been prior to the war.[7]

Late in the war, Carlos III, the recently crowned king of Spain, agreed to the Third Family Compact, an alliance with Louis XV, the Bourbon monarch in Versailles to whom he was related. Entering hostilities had not been a wise decision. Spain was ill prepared and lost Havana and Manila in the fighting. Britain ultimately returned both in exchange for Florida, which in those days consisted of the present state together with the lower portions of today's Alabama and Mississippi, including Mobile and Pensacola. France ceded Louisiana, including New Orleans, to Spain in order to secure its agreement to end hostilities before even more was lost. Even so, Spain lost Uruguay to Portugal and granted Britain timber rights in Central America, but the loss of Florida was the heaviest blow inflicted on Madrid. Britain's presence in the Gulf of Mexico jeopardized the Spanish convoys that annually carried home silver extracted in Spanish America, a prize of huge importance, as it amounted to 20 percent of the total revenue in Spain's treasury. The acquisition of Louisiana was a balm for Spanish losses, providing Madrid with connections to its colonies in today's Texas, New Mexico, and California.

Still, the war shocked the Spanish no less than the French, and it led Carlos III to embark on a wide-ranging program of reforms. Rebuilding the navy commenced immediately, and attempts were made to revamp the army along the lines of the more modern structures of most European powers, including opening officer ranks to those outside the aristocracy. He additionally introduced administrative and economic reforms throughout the Spanish Empire and opened some ports to foreign commerce. Above all, the Spanish king learned a newfound wariness in foreign affairs, especially with regard to another war with Britain.[8]

Following its disastrous war, France abandoned its long-held dreams of becoming an American colonial power. Its first, and indispensable, postwar goal was to see to its security in Europe, where France was somewhat isolated. It therefore looked on the Family Compact as a vital factor in the protection of French interests on the continent. Even before the Seven Years' War ended, France embarked on its second step—rebuilding its navy. The undertaking was presided over by the middle-aged but boyish-looking Étienne François, Duc de Choiseul, a former soldier who simultaneously served as foreign minister and naval minister. Choiseul coped with a depleted treasury in his struggles to remake France into a first-class power. The economy was beyond his reach, but Choiseul ushered in changes in the army, improving discipline and enhancing administrative efficiency. While presiding over the French navy, he added ships, reformed naval administration, and created Europe's initial professional corps of shipbuilders, an elite group that through innovative engineering sought to make French ships superior to those in Britain's Royal Navy. Choiseul also dispatched naval engineers to Spain to help his ally modernize its navy. The plan of the Bourbon monarchs was to construct a combined fleet of 140 ships of the line, giving them the numerical superiority necessary to wage war with Britain, even to invade England. Work dragged on year after year. It was unavoidably exacting and time-consuming, and the French in particular had to be careful to avoid provoking London. In 1771, not only did France briefly suspend its naval overhaul in the midst of a dangerous crisis with Britain, but Louis XV dismissed the rabidly anti-British Choiseul as a means of reducing tensions. A decade after the Seven Years' War, French naval prowess remained strikingly inferior to that of the Royal Navy.[9]

Obeisance fueled France's sulfurous hatred for Great Britain. French leaders were mortified by the drubbing sustained in the Seven Years' War and throughout the postwar years often felt humiliated by the treatment experienced at the hands of their more powerful rival. France desperately sought a restoration of its once grand stature and with almost a feral savagery it ached for revenge. "England is the declared enemy of your power and your state, and she always will be," Choiseul had told Louis XV in 1765. He added, "Only the revolution which will occur some day in America, though we shall probably not see it, will put England back to that state of weakness in which Europe will have no more to fear of her."

It was axiomatic at Versailles that British dominance stemmed from its "colonial possessions in America," as the wealth derived from the American colonies was thought to propel Britain's "power and ambition." Choiseul was still in office when the first signs of insurgency appeared in America. He counseled that France and its Spanish ally must not remain "idle spectators." He and others saw the colonial unrest as a heaven-sent opportunity to reduce British power, a window that in all "probability would never occur again." Choiseul was even willing to "run the risk" of "fomenting the conflict and making it inextinguishable" by aiding the colonial rebels. In the mid-1760s he sent three agents to America to determine the outlook of the colonists. Reporting widespread resentment of Britain's new colonial policies, they believed that a rebellion was imminent. One who visited Williamsburg heard a defiant Virginian exclaim, "Let the worst come to the worst, we'll call the French to our succor." Wishing for more information, Choiseul dispatched Johann Kalb, a German-born officer in the French army, on a similar exploratory mission. After touring from Philadelphia to Boston, Kalb concluded that an American rebellion was someday inevitable but that it would not occur until America's population exceeded that of England's, and at the moment England's population was five times that of its 13 colonies. The "present condition of the colonies is not such as to enable them to repel force with force," Kalb added with meaningful clarity. A bitterly disappointed Choiseul took no steps to stir the pot in America. By 1774 Choiseul had been dismissed, but in the final days of that year another set of officials in the French foreign ministry awaited word from America, this time eager to discover what the Continental Congress had done.[10]

ONCE ENGLAND LEARNED IN the summer of 1774 that an illegal American congress would meet, some officials foresaw the inevitability of war. That was how George III saw things. The "dye is now cast," the monarch said, adding, "Blows must decide whether they are to be subject to this country or independent." He also advised Lord North, who at times needed bolstering, that "we must not retreat." Official word from Congress itself at last reached London early in December 1774, but acting on the instructions of the king, who counseled that the decision of how to respond must be one of "reason not passion," North's ministry waited a month before beginning its deliberations. Throughout those 30 days most English newspapers truculently assailed the Continental Congress's defiant stand.[11]

The ministers took up the American question in January. Their discussions spun out for several days, but from the first it was clear that the overwhelming majority felt the time for negotiations and concessions had passed. The prevailing mood was to crush the insurgency by force. Few anticipated much trouble coping with the rebels, who possessed neither a national army nor a navy. Every colony had a militia system, but it was presumed that untrained and inexperienced militiamen could not put up much of a fight against Britain's professional soldiers. Nearly all thought the war would be short. Some believed the colonists would capitulate the minute they understood that Britain was prepared to use force. Most anticipated a battle or two, but expected the colonists to lay down their arms once they tasted defeat. A lengthy war was not foreseen. Even if the colonists somehow persisted after a couple of thrashings, which nearly all looked on as unimaginable, the Americans lacked the manufacturing capacity and financial wherewithal to sustain a protracted struggle. With fewer than 3,000 gunsmiths in the colonies, they could not even put a sufficient number of guns in the hands of their militiamen. Vital resources such as gunpowder were virtually nonexistent. Besides, as the colonists had seldom cooperated with one another in earlier wars, it was unlikely that all 13 provinces would act in concert. If they did, it was presumed that solidarity would collapse when confronted with adversity. The ministers clutched to the belief that most colonists remained loyal and that outside New England, and especially beyond Massachusetts, little sentiment existed for the rebellion. Some potentially troubling possibilities were raised. A lengthy conflict accompanied by heavy rates of attrition would cause acute distress, for heavy losses would necessitate finding more and more replacements, and that, in turn, could bring on social and economic troubles. However, virtually no one envisaged prolonged hostilities. Others wondered whether the army could successfully campaign in the American backcountry, but most thought the capture of coastal cities would bring the colonists to heel. Of greater concern was the possibility that France and Spain might aid the colonists or enter the war against Britain, but most thought hostilities would be over before the Bourbons could act.[12]

Throughout the crisis set in motion by the Coercive Acts, the ministry had received excellent advice from General Thomas Gage, who was both the royal governor of Massachusetts and commander of Britain's army in America. Now in his mid-50s, Gage had soldiered for more than 30 years and had seen combat on numerous occasions. He had a solid education and when chosen to be a colonial chief executive in 1774 was looked on as honest, prudent, and discerning. Given his position as the army's commander, a post he had held for the past decade, Gage was in the best position of any royal official in America to see the big picture. In a series of reports to London he warned that the rebellion was widespread, the colonists were preparing for war and might be capable of fielding a large and worthy military force, and backcountry residents would "attack any Troops who dare to oppose them." He also cautioned that New England's soldiers would not be "rabble." They would be "freeholders and farmers of the country," and they would be "numerous." As a consequence, he would need "a very respectable force" to cope with armed resistance. In communiqués that reached London before Lord North's government learned of the steps taken by the Continental Congress, Gage spoke often of the "violent party" and "hot leaders" in Massachusetts who were "spiriting up the people . . . to resistance." At the very moment that Massachusetts's congressional delegates set off for Philadelphia, Gage wrote that "the popular fury" within the province "was never greater" than at present. He added that while nonviolent coercive measures may have succeeded in the initial period of the colonial insurgency, "the people [are now] more lawless and seditious." The time for "reasoning is over; nothing can be done but by forcible means," he told London.

Despite his earlier admonitions, Gage, in the aftermath of Congress, still hoped against hope that war could be avoided. He advised that if London sent additional troops and arrested the "most obnoxious" rebel leaders, "the government will come off victorious," possibly without having to use force. However, if the ministry chose war, it must send quite a large army to America. Britain's army, in 1774, totaled nearly 50,000 men, but Gage possessed a mere 3,400 troops in Boston. In October, he told London that if he could have 20,000 men, it would save Great Britain both "Blood and Treasure." Gage also cautioned that the first engagement would be crucial. If the British force was too small to perform effectively, American defiance would stiffen. But if he possessed the numbers to utterly destroy the rebel army in the initial engagement, America's will to continue fighting would crumble.[13]

Toward the end of January 1775 the ministry made the momentous decision to use force. It voted to send Gage 3,000 additional troops, far fewer than he had warned would be needed, and with the knowledge that reinforcements could not possibly reach America before the first blow was struck. However much the ministers may have been influenced by Gage's counsel, they clearly ignored his sage advice to defer hostilities until Britain's army possessed the strength to overpower whatever military forces the insurgents could field.

North then directed the American secretary, the Earl of Dartmouth, one of the few ministers who had opposed the decision for war, to draft the order to Gage to use force. Dartmouth's communiqué of January 27 ordered "a vigorous Exertion of . . . Force." Gage was not to shrink from sending men into the backcountry and he was to arrest the "principal actors & abettors" of the rebellion in Massachusetts. Summarizing what his fellow ministers had been saying in coming to this decision, Dartmouth told his commanding general that any resistance offered by the rebels "cannot be very formidable," as they were "a rude Rabble without a plan, without concert." Hostilities should end with "a single Action," he predicted. Even so,

Dartmouth added that a cavalry regiment, three infantry regiments, and 700 marines were being sent.[14]

Less than a month later, Dartmouth notified Gage that "should it become necessary," four regiments from Ireland, an additional 1,700 men, could be sent.[15]

Near the time that Dartmouth's order to use force went out, Richard Henry Lee, a leader of Virginia's insurgency, wrote that "all N. America is now most firmly united and as firmly resolved to defend their Liberties" should Great Britain "attempt to take them away."[16]

War, dreaded by some, welcomed by others, and seen as inescapable by most, was about to explode.

CHAPTER 2

WAR

A MONTH AFTER LORD Dartmouth's order was sent, Lord North finally addressed Parliament. Already the Earl of Chatham, William Pitt, an iconic figure in England given his heroic leadership in guiding Britain to victory in the Seven Years' War, had spoken against war. A week before Dartmouth drafted his message to General Gage, Chatham, old and infirm, afflicted with rheumatism, gout, depression, and probably cardiac issues, appeared before the House of Lords and spoke while leaning on a cane for support. Chatham gallantly urged Parliament to acknowledge the right of the colonists to legislate for themselves in internal matters and to embrace the American Congress's willingness to accept London's regulation of imperial trade. He urged his colleagues to choose "concord . . . peace, and happiness," and by all means to avoid hostilities. To go to war would be to embark on a fool's errand, he said, adding that Britain could not win the war. The army could seize towns and colonies, but it would never have the numbers to control "the country it left behind" as it tramped from province to province. He warned that America was 1,800 miles long and filled with "valorous" citizens who cherished liberty and could never be brought to heel. France and Spain, he added, were watching and "waiting for the maturity of your errors" before they pounced. "[L]et us retract when we can, not when we must," beginning with the immediate recall of Britain's army.[1]

North went before Parliament on February 20 to speak at length about the American crisis, but he divulged neither that his government had decided on war nor that the order to use force had gone out. Even so, it was generally presumed that the ministry was committed to war. Weeks before North spoke, Edmund Burke, a young Irishman who a year earlier had made the principal speech in the Commons in opposition to the Coercive Acts, correctly advised correspondents in New York that the government would "embrace no conciliatory measures." The king had already opened the session in January by urging a "firm" response to American defiance, a stance that members of North's faction in Parliament parroted. Some even insisted that taking a hard line did not mean war. It was "romantic to think the colonists would fight," they maintained, given that American men were "cowardly."[2]

North spoke frequently that winter, but his initial speech set the tone. If the colonists refused to accept the sovereignty of Parliament, he promised, "we can meet no compromise." He burnished his tough talk with a feigned "peace plan." He told the king in private that the purpose of his sham offer was not to peacefully resolve the crisis but to build support in England for the war that was coming. But he postured before Parliament as the author of a serious proposal that would meet the colonists' grievances and avert war. He proposed giving the colonists the opportunity to determine what kind of taxes to levy, although Parliament would decide when to tax and how much each colony must raise. Fully expecting the colonists to spurn his offer, North sent additional troops to America and moved to restrict the trade of all the colonies, not solely Massachusetts. One of his admirers proclaimed that the prime minister's statesmanship would "render Ld. North's name immortal in our English history." However, fearing that increased taxation at home would foster opposition to the coming hostilities, North had already reduced the navy. In 1775, he turned a deaf ear to the entreaties of the Earl of Sandwich, the First Lord of the Admiralty, who urged wartime mobilization of the Royal Navy. Expansion of the navy would not begin until October 1776 and comprehensive mobilization was not launched until January 1778.[3]

North's actions brought on the final prewar parliamentary debate on the American crisis, and once again it was Burke who made perhaps the most important speech against going to war. He had moved from Ireland to England years earlier to study law, but politics became his calling and by 1775 he had sat in the Commons for 10 years. Portly, with dark wavy hair, and habitually in debt from living above his means, Burke had long since become a luminary among the foes of Britain's American policies. Echoing Chatham, Burke in March told the Commons that it was madness to pursue "peace through the medium of war." Peace must be "sought in the spirit of peace." If force was used, there was "no further hope of reconciliation" and Britain would lose America, where the "fierce spirit of liberty is stronger . . .

than in any other people of the earth." He hinted at refashioning the British Empire along the lines of a commonwealth system in which the nearly autonomous colonists were bound by loyalty to the king. It was a radiant and rational address, and it largely fell on deaf ears.[4]

GENERAL GAGE, IN BOSTON, had been busily preparing for war since he'd learned that an American congress was to meet. The arrival of a smidgen of reinforcements, as well as units that he'd redeployed from Halifax, Philadelphia, and New York, had brought his troop strength up to roughly 6,000 men by the spring. Aware that many of his men were young and inexperienced—one-third had served for less than three years and next to none had ever experienced combat, prompting one senior officer to moan that this was an "army of children"—Gage stepped up training exercises. He had his men on the drill field each day, even when the slate-gray sky spit snow. He staged field days on Boston Commons when entire regiments practiced assaults on an entrenched adversary or learned the proper response to an ambush.[5] He also set his men to fortifying the city and on more than one occasion dispatched parties to sequester the king's powder stored in distant magazines, always taking pains to avoid a "bloody" incident. When one such mission to Salem in February came within a whisker of provoking armed resistance, Gage confessed that the undertaking had been a "mistake."[6] Thereafter, he abandoned these initiatives. He desperately wished to avoid responsibility for triggering hostilities. It would be better if the decision to fire the first shot was made in London and even better if the American rebels were the first to open fire. Gage's long wait for a war that he suspected was inevitable ended on April 14 when HMS *Nautilus* arrived bearing Dartmouth's order to vigorously exert force. Gage had earlier prepared a plan for this eventuality, a strike against a rebel arms depot in Concord, about 20 miles west of Boston. He chose that target because its proximity to the city meant the operation could be concluded rapidly before many Massachusetts militiamen responded, but also because he wanted to get his hands on two insurgent ringleaders, Samuel Adams and John Hancock, who were known to be in Lexington, which lay astride the road to Concord.

Military plans are notorious for going awry, and Gage's went off the rails. He knew that surprising the colonists was essential to the success of the undertaking, but the insurgents' spy network in Boston had learned of his plan. Before the British soldiers moved out, dispatch riders, including Paul Revere, galloped into the hinterland to warn as many village militia units as possible that the regulars were about to march on Concord. Gage also contributed to the looming disaster by sending too few men. He chose companies of grenadiers and light infantry, the cream of his army, but fewer than 900 men were dispatched, barely 15 percent of the troops in Boston.

The march was uneventful until the troops reached Lexington. Upon entering the hamlet, they discovered that the local militia company awaited them. Heavily outnumbered, the militiamen offered no resistance, but when ordered to disperse, a shot rang out. No one knew who fired that shot or whether it was accidental or deliberate. But in the tension-packed atmosphere on Lexington Green, that gunshot precipitated a burst of shooting that spilled blood on both sides. No British soldier was mortally wounded, though for the first time colonists had fired on the king's troops. Seven militiamen were killed, two in the first volley and five others before British officers reestablished control of their frenzied troops.

The incident in Lexington was over quickly, and the British force continued its march. Forewarned, the Concord militia had also mustered during the night, though they took up a position on a hill far from the center of town, where they remained for several hours while the regulars went about their task of destroying the armory. All the while, militiamen from far and wide arrived and joined their Concord comrades. But it was not until near noon, by which time the colonists' armed force had swelled to about 500 men, that the militiamen advanced on their foe. To reach the center of town, and the regulars, the Americans had to cross the Concord River. The North Bridge that spanned the river was defended by about 100 British soldiers. The militiamen proceeded resolutely. The British did not budge. As at Lexington, men on both sides were edgy, and before long a jumpy regular fired on the colonists. At the sound of the gunshot, other regulars instinctively discharged their muskets. Militiamen returned the fire. Men on both sides were hit. Three of the king's soldiers were killed.[7]

Gage had soldiered long enough to anticipate trouble, but he never imagined the cataclysm that was about to occur. The return march to Boston—a trek down a thoroughfare that henceforth would be known to the Yankees as "Battle Road"—was a bloodbath. Minutemen, militiamen who were to be ready to take the field on a minute's notice, arrived throughout the day and joined the fight. The ranks of the rebel soldiery swelled to over 1,000, including numerous men from the already bloodied Lexington militia. European armies of that age typically clashed in set-piece battles that featured unconcealed rows of soldiers on unobstructed landscapes. But the American militiamen were hidden behind stone walls, trees, barns, and haystacks. Many emerged just long enough to squeeze off a shot before moving to another hiding spot, where they reloaded and fired again. The British responded with flanking parties to root out their enemy farther up the road, but they were largely unsuccessful. As Gage later acknowledged, his soldiers were "fatigued," having been awake for 36 hours and already marched more than 20 miles, and they were subjected to one ambush after another. Nor was it solely militiamen who attacked the regulars. Some civilians fired on the redcoats from what they mistakenly thought was the safety of their homes.[8]

A British captain was startled to learn that the "country is all in arms" and the colonists were not "great cowards." He and his fellow soldiers faced "one incessant fire" from the moment they departed Concord. By the time the British force reached Lexington, it had suffered heavy casualties.[9] The regulars might never have gotten to Boston had not reinforcements awaited them in Lexington, men who had been summoned following the day's first bloodshed nearly eight hours earlier. British casualties continued to mount in grim fighting that raged until the harried soldiery reached Boston.

The myth subsequently lingered that soldiers in the Revolutionary War displayed a chivalrous manner unseen in more modern wars. Chivalry was sometimes evident among officers, but war then, as always, was gruesome, and some men in the feverish passion of battle acted fiendishly. Defenseless men on both sides along Battle Road were shot out of hand. Nor was altruism in evidence when the British stormed houses whose owners had acted as snipers. Seen as partisans, those residents faced a harsh reckoning. A militiaman who entered one house after the fighting found bodies everywhere as he walked through "Blud . . . half over [my] Shoes."[10]

The carnage of that day was startling. Fifty Americans were dead and another 44 were wounded or missing. The British paid a heavier price. The colonial "rabble," as Lord Dartmouth had represented them, had dauntlessly faced up to British regulars, inflicting 272 casualties, a number roughly equivalent to one-third of those who had departed Boston in the quiet, peaceful darkness of the previous night. Sixty-five British soldiers were dead. Gage, in a striking understatement, said his men had been "a good deal pressed" and admitted his astonishment at the "Surprizing Expedition" with which the militiamen had responded.[11]

The next day was no less startling to Gage. He awakened to find that thousands of armed men from all four New England colonies had arrived during the night and taken up positions around Boston. Newspapers labeled the force the "Grand

American Army" and others called it the "Camp of Liberty." It swelled to 16,000, though in a few days it leveled off at about 12,000. The soldiers were more or less under the command of General Artemas Ward of Massachusetts, a Harvard-educated farmer, assemblyman, and judge who had been a lieutenant colonel of militia in the Seven Years' War and was appointed brigadier general of the Massachusetts militia in 1775. Ward took his orders from the Massachusetts Provincial Congress, an illicit body that the insurgents created when the assembly was shut down by the Coercive Acts. The siege army was posted in a long arc on the north, west, and southern sides of the city. One young lieutenant, who probably spoke for many, acknowledged that he did not know the "right or wrong" of the conflicting British and insurgent positions.[12]

Gage hunkered down, anxiously awaiting the promised reinforcements. Instead, late in May, HMS *Cerberus* sailed into Boston Harbor bearing three British generals, each destined to play a substantive role in the war. William Howe would in a few months succeed Gage as commander of the army, and years later Sir Henry Clinton would succeed Howe. John Burgoyne would be a pivotal figure in 1776 and 1777. Gage was happy to get the brain trust, but he would have been happier had the generals been accompanied by several regiments. Two months after the war's first day, Gage had gotten only 226 marines and an artillery regiment, which he supplemented by recruiting about 100 Loyalists. His reports to London took on an air of desperation. "We wait with impatience for reinforcements," he wrote, adding that all of New England and New York were in "open rebellion" and his army must be tripled in size. Several governors in other provinces also advised London that royal government had been "entirely overturned" or was "drawing to an end," and implicitly urged London to commit a larger army.[13]

Gage was so heavily outnumbered that he could give no thought to taking the offensive. He focused instead on defending Boston, although he somehow neglected to secure the heights that overlooked the city. They were not ignored by the Massachusetts Provincial Congress, which, against the wishes of General Ward, ordered the occupation of the hilly farmland across the Charles River from Boston at Charlestown. Ward complied, directing Colonel William Prescott of Pepperell, a combat veteran, to take 1,200 men and construct fortifications at a suitable location. Prescott reckoned his force would be nearly invincible if well fortified on Bunker Hill, but 57-year-old Israel Putnam was the senior officer and celebrated in New England for his well-publicized feats in the previous war. Putnam chose Breed's Hill, which almost everyone subsequently concluded was a poor choice.

Overnight on June 17, Prescott's men, mostly farmers accustomed to physical labor, fashioned a redoubt and entrenchments that extended 50 yards eastward. Prior to sunrise, and before work was completed, a British army patrol discovered what was afoot. Gage had to act. The rebels atop Bunker Hill (as everyone thereafter mistakenly referred to the site) possessed eight artillery pieces. Suddenly, rebel artillery commanded Boston Harbor, the British army's lifeline to Great Britain. The dilemma facing Gage was not whether to fight but how.

Gage summoned a council of war. Two options were pondered. General Clinton, whose strategic thinking had been shaped by experience and reading the likes of Thucydides and Caesar, always preferred to avoid frontal assaults. In this instance, Clinton advocated flanking movements and, as the Royal Navy was unchallenged, he also proposed landing 500 men on the isthmus at the northern base of Charlestown peninsula to seal off the rebels' lane of retreat. The rebels would be trapped. Gage would not only score a relatively bloodless victory but also expose the amateurism of his foe, leading other colonists to see the futility of further military resistance.[14] Gage personally overruled Clinton's idea, preferring a frontal assault, an option advocated by General Howe and a majority of officers. His appalling experience on Battle Road notwithstanding, Gage continued to look on the colonial militiamen with disdain, and he and others also lusted to avenge the earlier loss of comrades. Gage also felt that a thorough drubbing of the crude enemy force would demonstrate to insurgents throughout America the foolhardiness of fighting the king's army.

Gage gave Howe 2,300 men and orders to take Charlestown Heights. Howe, in his mid-40s, had studied at Eton, but, like Gage, had turned to soldiering while an adolescent and the army was his classroom.[15] Neither a painting nor a reliable description of Howe exists, other than that he was a man of few words and—according to universal agreement—a courageous and daring soldier. More than once in the Seven Years' War he had been selected to lead risky and arduous missions, and while this undertaking was not expected to be especially difficult, battles were always filled with surprises and hazards. In fact, while crossing the Charles River, Howe discovered that more colonials were on the hill than he had been led to believe, and he called for reinforcements. He would go into battle with about 2,600 men.

The British plan was simple. The navy was to shell residences and shops in Charlestown on the west side of Bunker Hill, setting fires that would flush out snipers. The army was to land in the southeast corner of the peninsula, which splayed out to the Mystic River and was secured by the navy. Most of the American defenders were in the redoubt and entrenchments at the crest of the hill, 500 yards from Howe's landing site, but some colonials were positioned between the town and redoubt. As British artillery posted on the beach at the landing site hammered the American defenses, infantrymen were to advance up the treeless and sometimes sloping, sometimes steep hillside. This was farmland and bucolic pastures; meadows and fallow land overgrown with waist-high grass dotted the landscape, with stone walls and wooden fences coursing here and there.

While British officers organized their men, mortars fired from Copp's Hill at the north end of Boston and the navy's big guns pounded Charlestown with incendiary shells that ignited "great pyramids of fire." Meanwhile, Howe was confronted by an unwelcome surprise. The chief of artillery had sent the wrong size cannon balls. The British were reduced to firing grapeshot, and a British colonel later acknowledged that the king's artillery "had no effect."[16] Howe also made a dire mistake of his own. He could have had the navy run armed vessels up the Mystic River to shell the colonial force hunkered down behind the fences and stone wall east of the breastwork. Had that step been taken, he might have been able to rapidly turn the enemy's flank and envelop the colonial forces on the summit of Bunker Hill. But Howe stuck to his brazen plan for a frontal assault.

It was well into the afternoon—on a bright, uncommonly hot day for so early in the summer—before Howe's men began their advance. He dispatched two regiments to take on the colonials west of the redoubt, defenders who for the most part were sheltered by low walls or trees in an orchard. Howe divided his remaining force. He led half the men to attack where 500 rebels with two artillery pieces were posted. General Robert Pigot, with the other half of the force, was to take the redoubt.

No one, including General Putnam, ever knew how many colonial soldiers were on Bunker Hill. Some regiments that Ward dispatched never arrived, and some of the men who appeared did not stick around for the fighting. A good guess is that when the shooting started there were about 2,500 in the American force. They were for the most part farmers and were wearing the wide-brimmed hats and homespun shirts they donned while tending their fields. Some may have been eager to be a part of the grand adventure of soldiering and fighting, but the ranks included those who were less than ecstatic about facing battle. One, who was probably not alone, seethed at the "treachery" of the colonial leaders who had gotten him into this pickle "so that we were brot [here] to be all slain."[17] Some of these men had doubtless exuded bravado in previous days. Now, although surrounded by comrades and friends, each man felt terribly alone. As they watched the British troops advance toward them, sun glinting off their bayonets and the ringing commands of hard and determined enemy officers filling the air, it is likely that nearly every soldier atop Bunker Hill quaked with gut-wrenching fear. As is nearly always true of inexperienced soldiers on the cusp of their first battle, men trembled, vomited, prayed, cried, and soiled themselves.

Dread and apprehension racked soldiers on both sides, and like men in other wars, not a few probably thought it "seemed unreal" that they had suddenly come face-to-face with such peril.[18] Time seemed to stand still. The British had hundreds of yards to climb and fences to surmount. They kept coming, slowly but inexorably, white-faced soldiers led by grim-faced officers. The muskets in the hands of the soldiers on both sides were notoriously inaccurate when trained on a faraway target, but they were deadly at short range, and the American officers told their men not to fire until the king's soldiers had closed to within 50 yards. One rebel later recalled that he "distinctly heard [Putnam] say, 'Men, you are all marksmen—don't one of you fire until you see the white of their eyes.'" Others remembered him urging the men to "Reserve your fire," "Aim at the handsome coats," and "Pick off the commanders."[19]

Howe's division, on the Americans' left, came first. They hoped that a fusillade and bayonet charge would turn the enemy's flank. Their officers cried out, "Push on! push on!" They were 200 yards away, then only 100 yards from the American line, close enough for the rebels to clearly see the faces of the men they would try to kill. They waited to fire until the enemy closed to within 50 yards. Then they "gave them . . . a hot fire," as Colonel Prescott said later. Men fell in droves. But others kept coming. The Americans fired again. More British soldiers fell; some had been hit numerous times. The regulars fell back, regrouped, and resolutely advanced again. The Americans could hear enemy officers "goad[ing] forward their men." As before, the British forged ahead into a withering fire.[20]

These failed attempts to reach the American lines caused Howe to pull back and reassemble his men. Meanwhile, Pigot's men drew closer to the redoubt. At 300 yards they came under artillery fire. They kept coming. At 25 yards they experienced even more carnage than Howe's men had encountered. The men in the redoubt fired salvos that seemed to some regulars "a continual sheet of flame" and to others an "uninterrupted peal of thunder." The regulars also faced a withering crossfire from Americans on their right and left. General Burgoyne, who had fought in

Europe in Britain's last war, said this was "one of the greatest scenes of war" he had ever seen. He added that the "horror" on this American hillside was "beyond any thing that ever came to my lot to witness."[21]

Howe, though "exceedingly soldierlike" in the words of an eyewitness, was stunned. A fight against the callow colonials was not supposed to go this way. Howe said later that the calamity he had led his men into confronted him with "a Moment that I had never felt before."[22] Hundreds of his men, including many of his staff officers, had been killed or wounded and he had not come close to securing his objective. Even as some of his officers appealed to him to call off the attack, Howe summoned reinforcements and stubbornly persisted. It was a part of his nature. Furthermore, Howe had urged what even he must now have seen had been a mistaken battle plan, and he could not bear the disgrace that would come from having been repulsed. Once reinforcements arrived late in the afternoon, Howe, with four infantry regiments, ordered another advance. Yet again, the regulars ascended this blood-soaked hill, stepping over the bodies of friends and comrades.

Howe did not know that the colonial defenders were low on ammunition. Some had only one round left. Yet they remained in place to discharge that last shot. The British had ample ammunition and were well disciplined, and despite suffering an appalling rate of casualties, they kept coming. This time they reached the entrenchments and redoubt, mostly because of the colonists' shortage of ammunition. It was now the colonials who faced a bloodbath. Men were shot, bayoneted, bludgeoned, and cut to pieces with swords. One British officer later described what he called the "Horror of the Scene." The redoubt "'twas streaming with Blood & strew'd with dead & dying Men, the Soldiers stabbing some and dashing out the Brains of others." Many rebels took flight down the hill toward the isthmus that Clinton had wanted to seal shut. Some were shot in the back as they fled. One who fell was Joseph Warren, a prominent Boston physician and head of the Provincial Assembly's Committee of Safety, who senselessly had come to the redoubt as an observer. He was cut down by a gunshot to the head before he had run more than a few yards down the hill.

Most who had bolted reached the isthmus and safety, but nearly 150 Americans lay dead and at least 271 had been wounded. The overwhelming majority of casualties occurred after the British penetrated the colonists' entrenchments. The rebel soldiers had performed capably while protected by fortifications, and it is conceivable that Howe might never have taken Bunker Hill, at least through frontal assaults, had his adversary possessed ample munitions.[23]

The British casualty toll was far more horrific. Ninety British officers—40 percent of those in Boston—died or were wounded, and fully 50 percent of the regulars who had been led into this disaster were victims, many on their first day of combat. Altogether, 226 redcoats were dead and 928 were wounded. Nearly 20 percent of Gage's force in Boston had been lost on one warm and golden afternoon.

Technically, Britain had won the battle. But Howe acknowledged privately that his "success" had been "too dearly bought," and with refreshing candor Clinton later remarked that another such victory would ruin the British army in America. Gage did not divulge his losses in his report to the ministry in London, though he admitted they were "greater than we can bear." He preferred to stress his men's "perseverance under heavy fire," the "great numbers" of colonial victims, and how the "action has shown the superiority of the King's troops." His most honest revelation was that the enemy soldiers were "not the despicable rabble too many have supposed them to be." They were well led, possessed talented military engineers, and, if entrenched, would fight with "an uncommon degree of zeal and enthusiasm." Their commitment to a cause they believed in led them to "Shew a Conduct" that they had never demonstrated in the Seven Years' War.[24]

The best appraisal of what had occurred was offered by a young British officer and was never seen by anyone in Lord North's ministry. The "gross ignorance" of the army's leadership had "murdered" hundreds of British soldiers by concocting a senseless battle plan, he said privately. He thought Howe had acted "from an absurd and destructive confidence, carelessness, or ignorance." He was aware of the alternative strategy that Clinton had urged, and noted that had Gage and Howe listened, they could have "shut them [the rebels] up . . . as in a bag."[25] Instead, Gage and Howe, in their hubris and lust for revenge, had turned a deaf ear to Clinton, and a disaster that need never have occurred was the result.

The legacy of the calamity was profound, especially on Howe's thinking. In the day's final rays of sunlight he walked across the battlefield, steeped in blood and flush with appalling suffering. The stench of death abounded, and Howe heard the forlorn "cries and groans" of the "poor wretches in their dying moments." He was a professional soldier who had previously experienced the dreadful butchery and carnage of battle, but he bore a heavy responsibility for the cataclysm on Bunker Hill. The "horror"—his term—that he had unleashed mangled his spirit. By his own admission, it was a burden he had never previously borne, and he was never the same soldier again.[26] Once daring, once willing to unhesitatingly put at risk the lives of the men he commanded, Howe would thereafter be a far different leader, a general who rarely again exhibited the dauntless audacity that had brought him distinction within the British army.

Events between April and June 1775 also had a profound impact on the colonists. Many saw Britain's use of force as a heinous betrayal. A "Brother's Sword has been sheathed in a Brother's breast," George Washington exclaimed when word of Lexington and Concord reached Mount Vernon. John Adams discovered that a "military Spirit" now "runs through the Continent," a sharp contrast to the dread of war that had pervaded the First Continental Congress. The new mood sprang from the hardened attitude toward Britain that was brought to life by war, but it was also due to the realization that American soldiers could with success face off against Britain's professional warriors. "Never was there such a Spirit," exalted Adams.[27]

CONGRESS HAD A WAR on its hands when it reconvened in May 1775, a couple of weeks after Lexington and Concord, but six weeks prior to Bunker Hill. It was quickly apparent that every congressman wished to respond to Britain's use of force with armed resistance. But what would they be fighting for? Was it reconciliation with the mother country on America's terms? Or was this a war to secure independence from Great Britain? A sizable minority favored independence, but as hostilities mandated "unbroken Harmony," as one delegate put it, the more radical congressmen were compelled to accept what the reconciliationist majority favored. The radicals reluctantly agreed to yet again petition the king to intervene on behalf of his "faithful colonists." In July they consented to a declaration explaining that the colonists had not taken up arms with the design "of separating from Great Britain." For the next 15 months Americans fought to remain within the British Empire. They continued to recognize the authority of the Crown, but not that of Parliament.[28]

The First Congress had been created to decide how to respond to the threats posed by the Coercive Acts and to formulate a statement of American rights. Managing the war effort would now be Congress's overriding task, and nearly everything it would do during the next several years was somehow related to the war. Congress rapidly purchased military supplies and urged or sanctioned the readiness of provincial forces. But weeks passed before it created a national army, though a motion to do so had been offered five days after it convened.[29]

Congress finally acted in June after learning that separate armies raised by Connecticut and Massachusetts under Ethan Allen and Benedict Arnold had captured Fort Ticonderoga, occupied by a tiny garrison of largely inattentive British regulars. Although that uncoordinated operation had succeeded, Congress knew that chaos would ensue if each colony undertook whatever military steps it desired. Some central direction was essential. Congress was also pressured by New England to create a national army, as it alone was bearing the burden of supporting the Grand American Army. Besides, the officers in that army were mostly political appointees, and some were out of their depth. It was deemed essential to have a national army led by capable officers.

On June 14, three days before Bunker Hill, Congress created the Continental army. John Adams immediately recommended that George Washington be commissioned its commander in chief. Congress discussed the matter for several hours. There may have been some opposition to replacing Artemas Ward, and some may have worried that the Yankees who composed the existing army would not follow a non–New Englander. But much of the time was likely devoted to learning as much as possible about Washington from Virginia's delegates. In particular, Congress wished to learn whether Washington was an impulsive sort and if there were hints in his character that pointed to wantonness.

Washington had commanded Virginia's army for five years in the Seven Years' War. Now 43, he was old enough for the job, but not too old. He looked like a leader of men. He was rugged and sinewy, trim and in good health; and at nearly six feet four inches, he stood about eight inches taller than the average fully grown adult male of that day. Washington was private and taciturn, though many saw that and his dignified and formal manner as virtues. He had made hard decisions in the earlier war, including hanging some men, revealing a steely toughness deemed essential for a military commander, especially one who would have to revamp the army he would inherit outside Boston. A wealthy planter who had served in Virginia's assembly for 17 years and had attended both congresses, Washington was comfortable in social situations and understood the ways of the legislators and governors with whom he would have to deal. Some in the First Congress, feeling that the day would come when a commander of an American army would be chosen, had met at length with Washington, hoping to get a feel for what he was like. He struck most as a sober, calm, steady individual, and they discerned nothing that disqualified him. It was true that Washington had never commanded a large army, but in the earlier war he had spent enough time with two British armies to get a feel for how European-style armies operated. Nor did Congress have to plead with Washington to take on the assignment. He had worn his old Virginia Regiment uniform to every session of Congress, his hardly abstruse manner of lobbying for the position. On June 15, Washington was approved and commissioned "to command all the continental forces, raised, or to be raised."[30]

The next day Washington addressed his fellow congressmen, telling them he would not accept the whopping $500-a-month salary that Congress offered, preferring to serve without pay and to be compensated at war's end for the expenses he had incurred. His pronouncement disturbed some, who feared he was setting a precedent that would disqualify talented leaders from middling backgrounds, but most happily approved his "noble and disinterested" proffer. It also rang loud and clear with the citizenry, who viewed it a virtuous act.[31]

Washington's selection had not been vexing. Choosing the other general officers was more difficult, and Congress stumbled a bit, though it probably did as well as could be expected. Congress planned to fill eight slots, but to mollify some colonies that pushed for favorite sons, it appointed a dozen men to assorted general officer ranks. Washington asked for and got the appointments of Charles Lee and Horatio Gates, former British officers who had immigrated to Virginia. Most of the remainder had soldiered in the Seven Years' War, though some were largely devoid of military experience. Some in this batch of officers would shine. Some would not.

Congress and Washington wanted an army that would be organized along the lines of the traditional European armies of the day. Two weeks after Washington's selection, Congress enacted the Continental Articles of War, a martial legal system patterned on what had long existed in the British army. Punishments included flogging—up to a maximum of 39 lashes—and capital punishment for desertion in combat and passing vital information to the enemy. Later in the year Congress added treason to the list of capital crimes. Savage by today's standards, the American version was less draconian than its British counterpart. Washington, of course, was obligated to adhere to the Articles of War, and Congress also instructed him to convene a council of war composed of his available general officers when faced with a far-reaching decision. He was not obliged to adhere to their advice, however. He was the commander in chief and the final decision was his to make.[32]

Congress agreed to voluntary enlistments for a period of one year. The people everywhere were "as Spirited in the Cause as in New England," one congressman more or less accurately concluded, and recruiting that summer was smooth and easy.[33] Farmers and artisans were drawn to serve by patriotism, a longing for adventure, and the hope of heroism. Some were persuaded to enlist after hearing their pastors and local luminaries, who for the most part would remain safely at home, exhort them to take up arms.

A week after his selection as commander, Washington departed for Boston. Having experienced countless troubles during his stint as Virginia's commander in the French and Indian War, Washington knowingly remarked that he was embarking on a "tempestuous Ocean" with "no safe harbour."[34]

ONCE LONDON RECEIVED THE wholly bleak news of the British army's losses in the war's two engagements, Lord North advised the king that this conflict "must be treated as a foreign war." The casual nonchalance that had characterized the ministry's decision to use force only a few months before was gone. Britain faced a major war that required a more Herculean effort than had been foreseen. General Gage was removed from command three days after word of Bunker Hill reached London. Soon thereafter Howe was appointed his successor. During the summer the ministry, after meeting repeatedly, took a step that Gage had recommended prior to going to war. It agreed to raise and send more British soldiers to America. The ministers also wanted their Native American allies in Canada and along the frontier to go on the warpath, a move that would tie down colonial militiamen and hopefully discourage support for the insurgency. The Royal Navy was to blockade New England and as much of the coast south of those colonies as possible, a step taken to erode civilian morale and hamper the colonists' acquisition of provisions from abroad. While the navy could act relatively quickly, most of the other measures would take time. The ministry was looking toward the campaign of 1776, which could not start before winter ended, fodder for the army's horses became available, and the primitive roads of that day were once again passable. Gage had recommended shifting Britain's emphasis to New York, citing the problems involved in driving "the rebels from their entrenchments" outside Boston, and London concurred. Once the campaign of 1776 was set in motion, Britain's long-term strategic objectives would be to capture Manhattan and Long Island, destroy Washington's army, and detach New England—still thought by many to be the driver of the rebellion—from the other nine colonies.[35]

George III, untroubled by gnawing doubt, wholeheartedly embraced the ministry's plans. In October he told Parliament that the colonies were in "open rebellions" and pledged his support of the "utmost endeavors to suppress such rebellion and bring the traitors to justice."[36] All the while, North was working to implement the decisions made by his cabinet, including bringing its army in America up to 35,000 by the following summer, more troops than Gage had ever requested. North encountered snags, but came close to filling the ranks by redeploying troops from wide and far, and revamping the customary requirements and inducements for enlistments.

To reach the desired manpower total, Britain ultimately had to hire foreign troops, a commitment the government did not reveal to the public until those soldiers had been garnered. Nearly every country in Europe engaged mercenaries in their 18th-century wars, but in 1775 Britain found it difficult to secure them. Russia and the United Provinces of the Netherlands were approached and refused. London next turned to the German territories and duchies. Some of these also declined, but eventually subsidy treaties were concluded with six German principalities. The largest was Hessen-Kassel, and the Americans thereafter referred to all the Germans they fought as "Hessians." The terms of the accords obligated the German rulers to furnish men and equipment, and required Britain to provide the German soldiers with the same pay, provisions, and medical care allocated to the British soldiery. Altogether, 12,200 German mercenaries were to be furnished by the summer of 1776 and another 5,000 were to come later. There was a dash of opposition to hiring foreign soldiers when word of the transactions was finally made public in England. Some of the dissent arose from the high cost involved—in excess of three million pounds—while others thought it unseemly that the colonists would be set upon by foreign soldiers or worried that the German soldiers would desert in droves.[37]

North also made a key personnel change. Lord Dartmouth, the dovish American secretary, was ousted and Lord George Germain, a hawkish member of the House of Commons, was put in his place. Germain had been an intransigent foe of appeasing the colonists and, after the Boston Tea Party, an advocate of coercion. A former soldier who had twice suffered severe wounds in combat in the Seven Years' War, Germain was thought by many to be the best choice for understanding a distant war and overseeing strategy and the army. Tall and muscular, with a commanding presence and impressive intellect that beamed omniscience, he nevertheless had many detractors. Not only was he so formal and withdrawn that many thought him snobbish, but following a court-martial on charges of cowardice in the Battle of Minden in 1759, he had been dismissed from the army. Many could neither forget nor forgive that stain on his character, and intolerant homophobes treated him with incivility for his well-known sexual preference. Tenacity was one of

Germain's strengths. He had clawed his way back, winning a seat in the Commons and achieving a reputation for perceptivity among the hard-liners. On the cusp of his 60th birthday, Germain took office in November 1775 as the American secretary. Wired for redemption, he offered spirited talk of winning the war in 1776. With the exception of issues related to finance, Lord North was more of a cabinet manager than its leader, opening the door for Germain to immediately play a commanding role on matters related to the war in America.[38]

Howe succeeded Gage in October, and many of his communiqués hardly differed from those of his predecessor. He told London that the army was safe from attack in Boston—indeed, he wished the enemy "would attempt so rash a step and quit those strong entrenchments"—and he, too, recommended centering the next year's campaign on taking New York. He proposed that in the interim he transfer his army to Halifax, where he would await reinforcements and train his green soldiers. Gage had spoken of his troops' inexperience and so did Howe, divulging that many of his new men lacked "the smallest confidence as soldiers." The worst were Irish Catholics, he added, as they were "certain to desert if put to hard work."[39]

DUC DE CHOISEUL HAD long since been ousted and no longer shaped French foreign policy. In June 1774, at the same moment that word of the Coercive Acts reached Boston, 54-year-old Comte Charles Gravier de Vergennes became France's secretary of state for foreign affairs, a post he would hold throughout the Revolutionary War. The scion of a humble noble family in Dijon, young Vergennes studied law before entering the diplomatic service. After stints in Germany and Lisbon, and a brief stay in Versailles, Vergennes was appointed France's minister in Constantinople, a post he held for 16 years. While there he married a commoner, a French widow of a Turkish physician. His choice provoked frowns and ripples of scandal through class-conscious Versailles, and both it and policy differences between himself and Choiseul contributed to his recall from his post in 1768. For three years Vergennes idled impatiently and largely in isolation on his sprawling estate in Burgundy, a home that included a vast château and lavish gardens, canals, and fountains. In 1771 Comte de Maurepas, the chancellor and real power in the ministry, brought him back and sent him to Stockholm as France's ambassador. Three years later, after smallpox took the life of Louis XV, the new king, 21-year-old Louis XVI, was drawn to Vergennes, whom he saw as temperate, trustworthy, and accomplished, a virtuous man who was devoted to his wife and children. Attracted by Vergennes's "sense of order," experience, sagacity, competence, and reputation for circumspection, the new monarch thought him the ideal choice for completing the task of restoring French power and prestige. The young king wrote to Vergennes of the "good that I hear spoken of you from all sides," including word of "your diplomatic skill," and asked him "to come as soon as you can" to head the foreign ministry.[40]

Vergennes was a devout Catholic who took the teachings of the Church seriously, though some at Versailles, shaped by Enlightenment rationalism, looked on him as a *Tartuffe*, a hypocrite who surely feigned his piety. Love had drawn Vergennes to his wife, and because of his abiding love for her, as well as his spirituality, he was one of the few ministers at Versailles who never took a mistress. Deeply conservative, he remained unmoved by the writings of Enlightenment philosophes, did not question the time-honored Bourbon foreign policy, and faithfully served his monarch, for whom he felt genuine respect. Louis XVI never wavered in his admiration of Vergennes, and the two maintained a long and superb working relationship.

Although born into the nobility, Vergennes hailed from a family far from the top of the social hierarchy, and many at Versailles responded to him with snobbery, looking down on him as hopelessly provincial and bourgeois, even seeing him as a "foreigner," as one supercilious official put it. Vergennes was all too conscious of the disdain of those who were nobles of the sword, and it shaped his behavior. He habitually deferred to his social betters, anxious to please them and avid to win their approbation. He grew to be a workaholic, worried endlessly over the stability of his ministerial position, and suffered frequent stress-related illnesses. Thomas Jefferson, who met often with Vergennes in the 1780s, found him to be agreeable, not the devious sort he had been led to expect, a man of calm authority who was strictly regulated and well organized, a diplomat who functioned with the efficiency of a well-oiled machine. His manner was grave and formal, and nearly everyone saw him as methodical. Vergennes struck others as honorable and high-minded, tireless, serious, prudent, reserved, solemn, and not given to the dissolute habits that characterized many of the French nobility. In time, too, the outsider grew to be nearly unrivaled in his skill as a player in court politics.[41]

The new monarch emphasized his wish to avoid war. Vergennes, too, sought peace, at least until the restoration of the French navy was completed, which he believed would take about four more years. In 1774 the Royal Navy possessed

142 ships of the line, of which 72 were instantly ready for service. Against this, France had 64 ships of the line, of which perhaps fewer than half could immediately be pressed into service. Vergennes waited patiently as Antoine-Raymond-Gaulbert-Sartine, whom the king had recently elevated from superintendent of the Paris police to the office of naval minister, labored tirelessly to improve and strengthen France's navy.[42]

Down the road, when the navy was strong again, Vergennes saw war with Great Britain as inevitable. He advised the king that England was "greedy, restless, more jealous of the prosperity of its neighbors than awake to its own happiness, power-fully armed and ready to strike on the instant." Furthermore, it "looks with envy" on France's colonies in the West Indies. Vergennes yearned to avenge the humiliating losses that France had suffered in the Seven Years' War and the "arro-gance and insults" that Britain had directed toward France over the past decade. But for the immediate future, peace was essential. That necessitated patience and restraining France's ally Spain, which was threatening war with Portugal, a conflict that would inevitably embroil France and Great Britain. Vergennes succeeded in holding back the Spanish, at least in part by convincing them that both Bourbon nations might in time benefit from the problems that Britain was having with its rebellious American colonies.

Hostilities in America were still a year away when Vergennes became the foreign minister, but storm clouds had gathered. He came to power understanding that if Britain went to war with its North American colonists, it could well be the means of realizing his cherished goal: the "elevation of [Louis XVI's] soul and the gran-deur of . . . [his] power." He understood that Britain would be seriously, perhaps fatally, diminished if it lost its American colonies and the commerce, wealth, and naval strength that those provinces helped make possible. News arrived in Versailles in the summer of 1775 that Britain and its colonies were at war. This could be a godsend for France, all the more so as the French ambassador in London was advising that the British army could not suppress the American insurgency. Word also reached Vergennes's desk that French businessmen in England had learned from Arthur Lee, an American living in London, that Virginia would trade tobacco for French munitions and other military provisions. Vergennes, fully aware that France was not yet ready for war, needed more information. It was necessary, he thought, to send an agent to America to take "a good look at [the colonists] politically and militarily." Achard de Bonvouloir, a French army officer who was familiar with America from earlier travels, drew the assignment. Bonvouloir was directed to assess the mood of the colonists and assure them of French compassion. In October 1775, he sailed for Philadelphia aboard *Charming Betsy*.[43]

WASHINGTON ASSUMED COMMAND OF the inchoate Continental army outside Boston on July 2. His letters that summer were filled with many of the same woes his foes across the Charles River in Boston were expressing: He had too few troops, and those that he had were wretchedly inexperienced. He faced additional problems that were not headaches for Howe. Discipline in the ranks that Washington inherited was somewhere between lax and nonexistent, and Washington soon concluded that not a few of his officers were unfit. Congress had foreseen some of the army's shortcomings and told Washington before he left Philadelphia to "new model" the army—make the necessary changes that would transform it into an effective fighting force. He could not touch the general officers, but he broke several lower-ranking officers, including two colonels and a major, elevated others who had performed valorously in the two earlier battles, and imposed a harsh disciplinary regimen on his army. He sought to create élan within the officer corps and esprit de corps among the troops by designing uniforms and insignias. Colored ribbons were to distinguish the ranks of the loftier officers (the commander's was blue), and cockades festooned with a designated color denominated lower-ranking officers. As in Britain's army, each regiment was to adopt its own distinctive colored coat. All the while, Washington put his men to building what he—and Gage and Howe—thought were impenetrable defensive lines. In July and August, he worried incessantly about a British attack. By September he was more confident, both because his army was improved and, as he correctly assumed, the enemy had concluded that the Continentals were too well entrenched to risk an attack.[44]

Nevertheless, with a force of British regulars just across the river that any day might possibly receive substantial reinforcements, Washington felt that he faced a perpetual crisis. In fact, he did face a series of very real crises that summer and fall. The first was his discovery of a dearth of weaponry and powder. New Hampshire could furnish only one man in four with a musket. Worse still was word that Massachusetts possessed hardly any powder. According to one observer, Washington was so stunned that he "did not utter a word for half an hour." Massachusetts had only 82 barrels of powder after the fighting along Battle Road and even less in the aftermath of Bunker Hill. Washington advised Congress that his soldiers possessed "not more than 9 Rounds a Man."[45]

Over the next few months several provinces, including rebel sympathizers in Bermuda, sent powder to Washington's army. Those were not the army's major source, however. In 1775, and again in 1776, considerable military hardware was shipped by Dutch merchants. The United Provinces, also known as the Dutch Republic, a deeply divided confederation of seven provinces, was tied to Great Britain both by its vast holdings in the English public debt and through ancient treaties that obligated it to support England with troops and a naval squadron if its homeland was attacked. Historically, the Dutch proclaimed neutrality in Europe's wars while seeking to garner wealth from the hostilities. Britain's problems with the American colonies offered them yet another chance for making money, and a year before the war began, the Dutch were already selling powder to the colonists.

The British ambassador in The Hague reported in 1774 that Massachusetts and Rhode Island were purchasing gunpowder from an Amsterdam firm, and he allowed that the Dutch Republic was "the common sewer of Europe thro' which all the filth [of military hardware] circulates." General Gage and the royal governor of New York had also reported an illicit trade between merchants and the Dutch. Britain responded by declaring the shipment of "warlike stores" to be contraband and threatened retaliation. The Dutch officially prohibited such commerce, though that hardly ended the traffic. The proscribed Dutch shipments now sailed from France, Spain, and Portugal, as well as from smaller ports and unfamiliar estuaries. Dutch merchants also turned to smuggling. They sent vessels loaded with cargoes labeled as tea, coffee, flour, sugar, and rice but that actually consisted of arms and ammunition—much of which the merchants acquired in what now is Belgium—to St. Eustatius, a Dutch colony in the Leeward Islands, as well as to French Martinique in the Windwards. Yankee merchants in particular had long utilized these entrepôts to skirt around Britain's restrictive trade policies, and once the Revolutionary War was underway, they swapped tobacco, rice, and indigo for war materials in the island ports. Patriotism and ideology played little role on either side in the brisk trade. These were merchants enticed by what has forever enchanted businessmen—profits.

The British attempted to stop the shipments by blockading American seaports, stepping up measures to intercept contraband payloads off the European coast, and threatening the Dutch Republic. Nothing worked. Meanwhile, Congress did what it could to facilitate the trade. In September 1775 it created the Secret Committee and tasked it with acquiring powder, 10,000 muskets, and 40 field artillery pieces. Congress additionally contracted with agents in the West Indies and Europe who were to obtain military supplies in return for the colonists' cod, grains, tobacco, and rice. In 1775, and again the next year, the Americans acquired more arms and powder from the Dutch than from any other source.[46]

The first signs of autumn were visible when Washington faced a second jarring emergency. His soldiers' enlistments began expiring in October and virtually every man went home. Some even took their precious weapons with them. Nearly all were Yankee yeomen eager to tend their farms. Besides, they felt that they had done their duty and it now was someone else's turn. Washington offered cash bonuses, furloughs, and appeals to patriotism to stem the tide. Nothing stopped the exodus. In private the commander in chief, who owned scores of slaves who tended his farm at Mount Vernon, seethed at the New Englanders' "dearth of Public Spirit, & want of Virtue." Haunted by fear that the enemy would take advantage of his lack of manpower, Washington later said he had spent many sleepless nights that fall. Awash with gloomy apprehension, he told a confidant that had he understood the full measure of the challenges he would face, "no consideration upon Earth should have induced me to accept this Command." He even claimed that if his conscience would sanction it, he would resign and, if necessary, move to the backcountry and live in a "Wig-wam." That he got through the predicament was due to the four New England governors rushing in militiamen, frenzied recruiting in several provinces, and Congress's decision to make it possible for men to enlist for as little as six months. Although Washington often despaired at "how Slow this important work goes on," he had 8,500 men by Christmas and in February the same number he had begun with in July.[47]

Sheltering his men presented Washington with another quandary, as tents were available for only a small portion of the soldiery. Some men rigged their own tents with sailcloth or made rudimentary shelters from stone and earth, and large numbers were housed in barns and abandoned houses, and even in buildings on the Harvard College campus. A tiny percentage of the soldiers were quartered in private residences. In time, tents arrived from several colonies, and Congress helped by purchasing large quantities of tent cloth in Philadelphia and New York. With the harsh New England winter approaching—Boston's first snow that year was on November 17—Washington for the first and last time in the war sought to have large barracks constructed for his army. The plan was to build 16-by-96 feet units, each to house 100 men. Given a shortage of skilled workers, not a single barrack had been completed by Christmas and a great many men spent the harsh winter of 1775–1776 in cold and often damp tents.[48] On the other hand, Washington's men largely escaped food scarcities. Victuals were obtained from the scores of nearby New England farming villages. Unlike virtually every other winter in the war, the men ate reasonably well throughout the army's nine-month stay on the periphery of Boston.

Washington, an experienced soldier, knew that proper sanitation was crucial for the health of his soldiery. But his best efforts to maintain hygienic standards could not prevent the outbreak of camp diseases, including dysentery and smallpox. The maladies raced through the siege army and spread into neighboring hamlets. A contagion that took the life of John Adams's younger brother, Elihu, a militiaman in the siege lines, spread to the Adams household in nearby Braintree and countless other villages. At times, eight or more residents died weekly in Braintree, including Adams's mother-in-law and a beloved family servant. Abigail Adams, John's wife, and one of the couple's children fell desperately ill but survived. Records are too incomplete to know for certain, but the civilian death toll that year may have exceeded the mortality rate within the army.[49]

Washington never had an adversarial relationship with Congress, but throughout the war differences separated the two. The first instance arose that fall when Washington, watching his soldiers go home, implored Congress to enlist soldiers for three years or the duration of hostilities. He sought to avoid an annual recruiting emergency, but he also knew that veteran soldiers were better soldiers. Congress wanted no part of a standing army, which it feared would become a vehicle for despotism, as had often happened throughout history. Standing armies were also thought to be inevitably composed of what John Adams called society's "meanest, idlest, most intemperate and worthless" men. Congress sought an army that was broadly representative of society's freemen.[50]

Congress was Washington's boss and he unhappily assented. Among the greatest virtues that Washington demonstrated was his ability to work with Congress, an attribute that in part was derived from his years in the Virginia assembly, service that had provided him with an understanding of how legislators thought and acted. Nevertheless, there were dustups, the first of which came that October when Congress sent a delegation to confer about the manifold concerns Washington had raised during his first months as commander. Discussions were cordial and the congressmen agreed to seek remedies for the problems, but on the third day they crossed a line that Washington could not tolerate. They told him that Congress "much desired" that the army attack the British in Boston. Washington knew that catastrophe lurked should Congress, far from the front and inexpert in military matters, dictate strategy. He handled this problem by summoning a council of war, which recommended against an attack, in essence saying it would be America's Bunker Hill. The committee accepted that, and later in the fall Congress resolved that the question of attacking Boston was best left to Washington.[51]

There were times when Congress took steps that Washington thought were best not taken, but he wholeheartedly approved of Congress's midsummer decision to invade Canada. The First Continental Congress had appealed without success to the citizens of Quebec to send delegates to Philadelphia. Immediately following the outbreak of hostilities, Congress again urged the Canadians to "join with us." The entreaty did not elicit a response. A few weeks later Congress, impelled by numerous motives, authorized the invasion. It believed that most Canadians, who until recently had been French citizens, would assist the rebel army. Congress also incorrectly imagined that General Guy Carleton, the royal governor of Quebec, was planning to invade New York or New England, or both. Furthermore, many congressmen felt that taking Canada would secure New England from British and Indian attacks, and it might provide the necessary leverage to nudge London toward an acceptable accommodation.[52] Not a few in Congress, as well as many powerful figures in the northernmost colonies, were enticed by the possibility of acquiring the verdant stretches of land that beckoned in Canada. An invasion was attended with risks aplenty. To think that a new and untried army supported by a jerry-built supply system could succeed against targets hundreds of miles away was daring, perhaps foolhardy. However, optimism was stoked by the belief that most Canadians would welcome the invaders and an awareness that there were few British regulars in Canada.

Congress created the Northern Department within the Continental army and named New York's Philip Schuyler, one of the general officers it had earlier selected, as commander in that sector. The invasion plan was for Schuyler's army to advance down Lake Champlain and into Canada, and ultimately proceed eastward to Quebec. Schuyler had soldiered about as long as Washington in the Seven Years' War, though his background was mostly in dealing with logistical issues. During the summer of 1775 he proved adept at acquiring provisions and vessels of seemingly every shape and size. But Schuyler lacked experience in offensive operations, and soon enough he displayed fatal signs of indecisiveness. From the outset, many thought success hinged on acting rapidly and wrapping up the campaign before Canada's menacing winter closed its grip and British reinforcements arrived. Weeks passed, then two months, and not a soldier had taken a step toward Canada.

The army did not move out until late August, and then it was Schuyler's second-in-command, General Richard Montgomery, who ordered it to advance. Montgomery, a former British army officer who had immigrated to New York, was one of the general officers that Congress had chosen. He had taken command of the army when Schuyler was felled by illness. With nighttime temperatures already hinting that piercingly cold weather was just around the corner, he put the army in motion. Washington, like Montgomery, was also frustrated by Schuyler's inaction and had stepped into the breach to create a second force that would advance on Canada through Maine. Washington thought the additional manpower would help guarantee success, but he also hoped its departure would stir Schuyler to act. Washington chose the young colonel Benedict Arnold—intelligent, tenacious, aggressive, and authoritative—to lead that invasion force.[53]

Little time elapsed before harbingers of pending disaster appeared in each of the advancing American armies. Montgomery had 1,700 inexperienced and undisciplined troops, some of whom were more skilled at plundering isolated farmsteads than in soldiering. In no time, Montgomery remarked that his army overflowed with "pusillanimous wretches."[54] Two months were required to take the first obstacle, St. Johns on the Richelieu River above Lake Champlain, a British fort garrisoned by a force one-third the size of its attackers. Washington, learning of the victory, exclaimed that now there was "little Doubt the entire Reduction of Canada" was assured. Montgomery was probably less sanguine. In the course of the siege, he had sent parties far and wide to harvest the Canadians who were supposedly eager to serve in the invading army. No takers were found.[55]

It was nearly November when Montgomery at last advanced again, heading for Montreal, 50 miles away. On some days, sprits of snow were visible. Within a few more days, a heavy snow fell and the roads froze. When the snow and ice melted, the roads turned to a fetid ooze. General Carleton chose not to defend Montreal, wishing to save his 750 men for the defense of Quebec. Montgomery took the tiny hamlet on November 11, but he was in deep trouble. Desertion had been a constant problem, and in mid-month the men from Connecticut quit the army the moment their enlistments expired. Most were sick of army life and not a few had come to see this campaign as a misbegotten venture. But Montgomery persevered, and on learning that Arnold's force had reached Quebec, he moved out quickly.[56]

Arnold's force had assembled outside Boston in August. It was composed of 1,050 volunteers who claimed to be "active Woodsmen." Few actually fit that description, and they were about to embark on one of the most severe trials faced by

American soldiers in this or any war. They arrived in Maine late in September. After pausing to construct bateaux that would carry men and provisions over the region's many swiftly flowing rivers, the soldiers embarked on September 25, with Arnold's resounding "To Quebec and victory" ringing in their ears. Disaster struck quickly. Numerous bateaux were destroyed by swirling rapids or overturned because of the inexperienced hands manning them. Nearly a quarter of the army's food was lost. Rain and mud seemed to be constant companions, and 19 days out the season's first snowstorm struck, followed a few days later by a hurricane. An entire battalion of 450 sapped and disheartened men deserted on October 25, and they took their provisions with them. The remainder of Arnold's cold, wet, weary men plodded on through forests heavy with the tang of rotting autumn leaves, sometimes carrying their bateaux for miles between portages. Every man was afflicted with skin disorders and many fell victim to dysentery. Hunger drove them to eat the unfortunate dogs that had accompanied the army, even to gnaw on rawhide and devour their lip salve and hair grease. One of Arnold's soldiers said, not unfairly, that the grueling endeavor was the "equal [of] Hanibal's [crossing] over the Alps." Through it all, Arnold, a hot mass of passion, ambition, and resolve, exhibited undoubted qualities of leadership, pushing his men onward.

They trudged on through what one trooper described as "hideous swamps and mountain precipices" and "execrable bogmire[s]" thick with "impenetrable . . . shrubs." Finally, early in November, the army came upon a town inhabited by French settlers who fed them. A few days later, in the creeping light of early morning, they spotted the St. Lawrence River and Quebec. Sixty-five days had passed since they departed the environs of Boston, but there was no sign of Montgomery's army. Nevertheless, as evening deepened into darkness, Arnold and his men crossed the wide, placid river and made camp about 20 miles from Quebec. A scouting party soon found Montgomery in Montreal and alerted him to Arnold's arrival. Nearly four weeks after Arnold's men first glimpsed Quebec, the two forces—now totaling 1,325 men, about half the number that had set off from New York and Massachusetts—rendezvoused under dark and heavy clouds with a surge of relief and joy.[57]

The men had faced terrible ordeals and now they were confronted with the fearful prospect of attempting to take Quebec. Montgomery knew the immense peril that awaited. He was also aware that he must act soon, as nearly his entire army would melt away when enlistments expired on January 1. Carlton's force, holed up inside Quebec, was not about to come out and fight. Montgomery, obdurately bent on accomplishing his mission, first tried to gain his adversary's surrender through a siege. But Carlton had sufficient supplies to see his army through it. On December 31 Montgomery tried the only alternative short of terminating the campaign. He attacked in the midst of what one of his soldiers described as "a violent storm of snow." The assault was a disaster not unlike that which had befallen the British on Bunker Hill. After leading his men to the entrance of the town, along the way "with his own hands" cutting down and pulling up one obstacle after another, Montgomery was decapitated by a blast of gunfire from a redoubt. Arnold was badly wounded, though somehow he managed to continue urging his troops forward "in a cheering voice." Some 60 rebel soldiers were killed or wounded, and 426 were taken prisoner and marched to an uncertain fate. Barely one-third of those who had embarked on the ill-fated campaign in August remained. A few survivors whose enlistments had not expired remained camped outside Quebec maintaining a lifeless siege. Joy prevailed inside Quebec's walls. The city, said one of the king's soldiers, had been "freed from a swarm of misguided people, led by designing men [who were] enemies to the libertys of their country."[58]

The invasion of Canada had failed spectacularly. It probably had always been a calamity waiting to happen, and disaster struck on the final day of 1775.

THE CRUCIAL FIRST YEAR of war had wound down. The British army remained trapped in Boston, powerless to fight its way out and, due to a lack of Royal Navy transports, unable to relocate to Halifax, as Howe wished. His soldiers glumly endured a long, glacial, sickly winter in Boston without adequate fuel, blankets, winter clothing, and sustenance. The paucity of food was so great that meat was allocated only to the seriously ill.[59]

Washington, who by nature had an affinity for action and was troubled by the belief that some in Congress had grown restless with an inert army, toyed with taking the offensive. In September, he had proposed an attack on the fortified redcoats in Boston, a notion that his horrified generals wisely dissuaded him from taking. But Washington's frustration at his inactivity festered, as he felt that his army's idleness would continue as long as it lacked a powerful artillery arm.

During the several months of the siege, a 25-year-old artillerist had caught his eye. Henry Knox, a rotund prewar Boston bookseller who appeared to have spent more time reading about military history and gunnery than selling books, impressed the commander with the job he had done laying out the siege lines in Roxbury.

Besides, Knox had the backing of Samuel and John Adams, whose influence in Congress was not to be ignored. In November, Washington named Knox to command the army's tiny artillery regiment. Washington and a congressional committee had previously discussed retrieving the artillery captured at Fort Ticonderoga, and Congress subsequently authorized such a step. The first job that Washington gave Knox was to travel to Ticonderoga and bring the guns to the army outside Boston. Success was far from assured. The installation was 300 miles away from Boston and rivers and mountains lay between the two sites.[60]

That autumn Washington often noted in his correspondence, "Nothing of Importance hath happened." But by Christmas, he knew that something of great substance was happening. He had heard from Colonel Knox, who was en route to Boston with 14 mortars, two howitzers, 39 cannon, and shells and iron from which cannonballs could be made.[61]

As December ebbed, Howe waited impatiently for the transports that would allow his army to escape Boston, and Washington anxiously anticipated the arrival of artillery that might make possible an attack on his fortified enemy. At the same moment Washington heaved a sigh of relief at having gotten through his first year as commander, telling the president of Congress, "It is not in the pages of History perhaps, to furnish a case like ours; to maintain a post within Musket Shot of the Enemy for six months together . . . and disband one Army and recruit another." He added that should another army be successfully recruited, "I shall think it the most fortunate event of my whole life."[62]

CHAPTER 3

SUCCESS AND FAILURE

ACHARD DE BONVOULOIR, THE French army officer dispatched by the foreign ministry to garner information on the military capabilities of the American insurgents, arrived in Philadelphia just before Christmas in 1775. He had visited the city earlier in the year and, through intermediaries, arranged to meet with Congress's Secret Committee soon after *Charming Betsy* docked. The committee, whose five members included Benjamin Franklin, wanted to keep the meetings secret. As Congress was now meeting in the Pennsylvania State House, known today as Independence Hall, the talks with Bonvouloir were conducted at night in Carpenter's Hall, where the First Congress had met. So great was the committee's stealth that not all members of Congress were aware of what was occurring.

Bonvouloir insisted that he was acting on his own, not as a representative of the French government, a fiction that hardly fooled the committee members. The congressmen quickly asked if France would sell arms and other military supplies to the Americans and provide "two able engineers" to help the Continental army. Bonvouloir promised to pass along the requests to the foreign ministry. Soon after the meetings concluded, Pierre Penet and Emmanuel de Pliarne arrived. Representing a Nantes mercantile firm that was already doing business with Willing, Morris, and Company, perhaps Philadelphia's largest commercial company, the two Frenchmen also met with the Secret Committee and proposed a deal: American whale oil and tobacco in return for arms and munitions. Discussions dragged until word arrived of the American military disaster at Quebec. The news prompted the committee to immediately conclude contracts with the French businessmen.[1]

Bonvouloir had advised Congress not to send an envoy to France. He feared that if Britain discovered what was afoot, France might back away from providing help. But Congress, rocked by the dreadful news from Quebec, which arrived soon after Bonvouloir departed, did not listen. It dispatched one of its former members, Silas Deane, to Paris. Deane, who before the war had been a successful lawyer and merchant in Wethersfield, Connecticut, was instructed to pose as a businessman. Franklin furnished the names of acquaintances that might act as go-betweens in arranging a meeting with Comte de Vergennes and Parisian merchants. If Deane succeeded in gaining an audience with the foreign minister, he was to request "Arms for 25,000 Men, with a suitable Quantity of Ammunition & 100 field pieces." He was additionally to seek "Linens & Woolens" for the soldiery and "other Articles" to be used in bribing the Indians to remain neutral. Deane was also to gauge France's likely response should America declare independence. Deane was on his way by early April.[2]

While Deane was getting his instructions, Congress sought to bolster the remnants of its woebegone army outside Quebec. It sent additional Continentals to Canada, including some new recruits—the first to be raised through cash bounties—and replaced General David Wooster, General Montgomery's successor, with General John Thomas. Wooster was in his mid-60s and thought to be too decrepit to cope with the demands of his post. Thomas, another of the original general officers chosen the previous June, had once been a physician in Kingston, Massachusetts, served in the Seven Years' War, and impressed Washington with his performance during the siege of Boston. Congress also dispatched two of its members, Franklin and Samuel Chase of Maryland, together with two non-congressmen, to Canada. They were to determine the degree of support in Quebec for the American insurgency and assay the condition of the rebel army. Congress, which early in the war appeared at times to live in a fantasyland, radiated confidence. Its presiding officer, John Hancock, predicted that the replenished army would seize control of Quebec before winter ended.[3]

It soon was evident that Hancock's optimism was misplaced. Thomas found that he had fewer men, field pieces, and kegs of powder than he had been promised. Meanwhile, Franklin and Chase discovered that the American rebels had "few friends . . . here." The two congressmen first reported that a larger American army was needed if Quebec was to be taken and held, but after a few more days of scrutiny they decided that the Canadian enterprise was beyond redemption. The military operation was afflicted with so many irresolvable problems that not even a larger army could succeed. Many officers were "unfit," the men were undisciplined, and the supply system had broken down completely, if it had ever functioned properly. In light of these troubling afflictions, the commissioners recommended a withdrawal from Canada before it became an even greater pit of despair.[4]

The troubles that the commissioners foresaw soon spiraled into catastrophe. In May, well before the report sent by Franklin and his comrades reached Philadelphia, the first of the British reinforcements raised by Lord North arrived in Quebec. General Carlton remained the commander in chief, with General John Burgoyne, who commanded the newly arrived troops, serving as the second-in-command. Carleton didn't hesitate to act. He emerged from his lair and led what now was his 5,000-man army against the handful of rebel besiegers. A "panic so violent" instantly seized the callow American troops. They fled, leaving behind weapons, powder, and comrades too sick to run for their lives. Thomas succeeded in restoring order within a couple of days and organized a structured retreat. His objective was to pull back to the vicinity of Montreal, where he planned to make a defensive stand. But Thomas succumbed to smallpox during the withdrawal and Congress appointed General John Sullivan as his successor. A New Hampshire lawyer who had no real military experience prior to the war, Sullivan was the archetypal political appointee, and it soon became apparent that he was in over his head. Brimming with fevered optimism, he hurried to Canada thirsting for glory. On assuming command, Sullivan jettisoned Thomas's planned defensive. Instead, he ordered an advance that took his men into peril. At Three Rivers, halfway between Montreal and Quebec, Sullivan ran upon his adversary, a force three times larger than his own. Nevertheless, Sullivan attacked, a decision that General Burgoyne, a professional soldier, characterized as "preposterous." To boot, Burgoyne added, the assault was "executed with timidity." Not surprisingly, a portion of the rebel army was mauled. All of it might have been destroyed had Carlton responded aggressively. Instead, he held back, enabling Sullivan to retreat, just about the only wise decision the rebel commander made during the campaign. What was left of the American army fell back to Isle aux Nois, a mosquito-infested island above Fort Ticonderoga on the Richelieu River. Droves of Sullivan's men died in June, principally from smallpox and dysentery.[5]

The Canadian venture, which Congress had authorized a year earlier in a burst of misconceived conviction, was over. Thousands of men had been poured into the vortex and about 10 percent of them had died or were languishing in captivity, and still more were so badly crippled by wounds and disease as to be unfit for further military service. Two armies had been pummeled, two generals had perished, and, following the Continental army's initial test under fire, serious doubts existed about the competency of Generals Schuyler, Wooster, and Sullivan, one quarter of the initial general officers chosen by Congress. Furthermore, the reports of Franklin and Chase, who had observed firsthand the fatal deficiencies in America's war effort, caused some in Congress to wonder whether the American rebellion could survive 1776 without massive foreign assistance.

BONVOULOIR'S REPORT REACHED VERGENNES'S desk in Versailles in late February, about the time that the foreign minister heard from the French chargé d'affaires in London that the Americans "can no longer hold their ground" and soon would have "no choice but to surrender." Bonvouloir's assessment could not have been more different, in some measure because he wrote prior to learning of the rebels' Canadian debacle. His report bulged with fanciful optimism. "Every one here [in the American colonies] is a soldier," he said, adding that the troops were "well clothed, well paid and well led." He claimed that the rebels could field an army of 50,000 and call on limitless numbers of militiamen. The members of Congress had resolved "to fight to the end for their freedom and the enemy will have to chop them to bits" to win the war. More grimly, and more accurately, he divulged that the rebels had no navy and their army lacked arms, ammunition, blankets, tents, and seemingly every other sort of provision needed by a military force. Vergennes, who did not yet know that the Canadian invasion had gone off the rails, had expressed doubts about Britain's ability to crush the American rebellion. Bonvouloir's assessment of American zeal, determination, and abilities seemed to confirm the foreign minister's optimism.

Shortly thereafter another report concerning America's Revolutionary War reached Vergennes, this one from Pierre-Augustin Caron de Beaumarchais, a commoner who had become France's best-known playwright following his hit *The Barber of Seville*. Beaumarchais's fame opened doors to the king and the foreign minister, both of whom utilized him on assorted missions. While in London in 1775, Beaumarchais had become friends with Arthur Lee, the Virginian who practiced law in the city and, on the side, did what he could for the American insurgency. Lee told Beaumarchais that the Americans were eager to trade with France and could field far more troops than Britain, and that American independence would be an economic and national security godsend for France. But Lee acknowledged that to achieve independence the rebels needed abundant French aid. Beaumarchais immediately sniffed the possibility of personal profit if France provided assistance, and he was chosen to play a role in getting the materials into the hands of the Americans.

Beaumarchais responded by writing to Louis XVI. (His missive was sent to Vergennes but addressed "to the King alone.") Aware that the young monarch desperately wished for peace, at least for the foreseeable future, Beaumarchais proposed a plan that would keep Britain at war while France remained at peace. The best course for France to follow was to keep the conflict in America going as long as possible, he contended, and that could be achieved only if France provided assistance for the colonial insurgents. He recommended just enough backing to put the Americans "on an equal—but not a superior—level of strength with England." You "cannot have the peace you desire unless you prevent at all costs peace between England and America," he told the king. He concluded with the claim that he was the man who could carry out "the arrangement" of assistance to the Americans, as he was "persuaded that my zeal will supply my want of talent" in such matters.[6]

With reasons of his own for wishing to aid the Americans, Vergennes felt that it was now or never if France was to benefit from Britain's imperial troubles. Because of the Americans' long-dependent status as colonists, the foreign minister understood that they unavoidably lacked the resources needed for waging war against a powerful adversary. Before taking the matter to the king, Vergennes first sounded out Spain, his Bourbon ally. In March, at nearly the moment Silas Deane embarked for Paris, Vergennes wrote to Pablo Jerónimo Grimaldi y Pallavucini, Spain's foreign minister, laying out the case for aiding the American rebels. Grimaldi quickly agreed, hopeful that Britain would remain occupied in the Northern Hemisphere while Madrid tended to its concerns in the Southern Hemisphere and in the North American borderlands. Grimaldi also saw assistance to the American rebels as a means of drawing out hostilities and utterly exhausting both Great Britain and the Americans, both of which he believed posed a menace to Spanish interests.

Soon after the reports of Bonvouloir and Beaumarchais reached Versailles, Vergennes submitted two memoirs to the Conseil de Roi, the king's advisory council and the supreme organ of the state. In "Considerations," Vergennes sought to convince the king that providing arms to the Americans would be carried out secretly so as not to provoke Great Britain. He additionally argued that France would be the beneficiary by tying down the British in America during the next couple of years while

France completed the rehabilitation of its navy, readied its army, and enhanced its defenses in the Caribbean colonies.

In "Reflections," his second memoir, Vergennes candidly stressed how France would benefit from a prolonged Anglo-American war and from American independence. With a view quite unlike that of Grimaldi (and Beaumarchais), Vergennes depicted American independence as beneficial. France, he wrote, would acquire much of the American trade that Britain lost, and the Royal Navy would be weakened as it suffered the loss of American seamen and materials needed in the construction of naval vessels. Vergennes concluded with the recommendation that France "give to the insurgents secret assistance in munitions and in money." He again emphasized that the aid must be "cloaked and hidden and only appear to be commercial in nature." Vergennes had outlined a plan for a proxy war. The Americans would do the fighting and dying, and with secret French assistance they would hopefully win their independence. His foremost objective, however, was French security, which at this point he believed could be enhanced without French bloodshed.

One minister on the king's council, Anne-Robert-Jacques Turgot, Baron de l'Aulne, the recently appointed comptroller general, opposed aiding the American rebels. He sympathized with the plight of the Americans, but believing that Britain could never quash the colonial insurgency, Turgot maintained that France could profit from its enemy's woes without intervening. Principally, however, Turgot cautioned that another round of warfare would impede his efforts to carry out economic reforms necessary for reducing France's persistent and steadily increasing indebtedness, changes that he insisted were "crucial to the prosperity of the state and the relief of its inhabitants." Turgot knew that France had not been solvent for more than a generation. He believed that French indebtedness, like a dagger poised at the heart, was life-threatening to the ancient régime. Turgot attributed France's economic problems, at least in some measure, to its chronic warfare. He was not alone in reaching this conclusion. Voltaire grasped the danger and around this very moment warned that more "than half the money in circulation in the kingdom" had been frittered away in recent conflicts. The nation had been at war nearly half the time since 1672, and each war was more costly than its predecessor. At the conclusion of the War of Austrian Succession in the 1740s the debt totaled upwards of 200 million livres. When the Seven Years' War ended in 1763 the debt exceeded 520 million livres, and thereafter 60 percent of annual revenues were consumed in repaying interest charges. Nearly all countries carried some debt, but

France, as Turgot understood, was dogged by an archaic financial system and in particular a manner of taxation that in the words of one scholar was "decrepit, incoherent, complicated, unequal, and unjust." The French complained of high taxes, but among the entitlements enjoyed by the ruling nobility was a considerable means of tax avoidance. The financial system was rife with perfectly legal means for the aristocracy and the more affluent to evade paying taxes. By the time Turgot took up his duties, French indebtedness was six times greater than the annual revenue, and it stubbornly increased annually. Without economic reforms, and peace, Turgot knew that adequate revenue for meaningfully reducing the debt would be unavailable. As it was, France borrowed to pay off the indebtedness accrued through earlier borrowing, a feature that led the Dutch ambassador to Versailles to exclaim that French finances "are not on a good foot."

The state of French finances was a closely guarded secret, but Turgot knew the score and in private warned that involvement in another long war could destroy the French economy and possibly France and the Crown along with it. He preached the strictest economy and the need for reforms leading to a dependable flow of revenue through a recalibrated system of taxation. As the maintenance of peace was a crucial element in his plans, Turgot cautioned that Vergennes's call for assisting the insurgents would inevitably lead to war with Great Britain. Warning that the "first gunshot will drive the state to bankruptcy," he characterized another war as "the greatest of evils" as it would risk reducing France to a permanently weakened condition.

The French king had other reservations about assisting the Americans. He said that he "disliked the precedent of one monarchy giving support to a republican insurrection against a legitimate monarchy." Vergennes dodged that argument, emphasizing that the assistance to the rebels was "not so much to terminate the war between America and England as to sustain and keep it alive to the detriment of the English, our natural and pronounced enemies." Louis XVI was ultimately persuaded, and on May 2 a majority of his ministers approved providing one million livres for covert arms shipments to the American insurgents through Beaumarchais. Vergennes immediately advised Beaumarchais that Spain would provide him with an equal sum, and he told the playwright to "establish a large commercial house and, at your [financial] risk, supply America with arms, munitions, equipment, and all other necessary matériel for carrying on a war." Beaumarchais was not to ask the Americans for any money and was warned that the "operation must afterward feed and support itself" through reciprocal trade arrangements. Aware that the acquisition, loading, and transporting of the war materials could not be achieved rapidly, Vergennes understood that the American rebels would be on their own during the campaign of 1776. France's commitment would be useful only if the insurgency survived the coming test of arms. Meanwhile, Louis XVI agreed to additional funding for rehabbing the navy, with an eye toward soon having 37 ships of the line ready to sail.[7]

With a French loan worth millions of dollars in today's money in his pockets, Beaumarchais created Roderigue Hortalez et Compagnie. It had offices in Paris and a staff of six, none of whom had a background in business. That spring and summer, Beaumarchais traveled about France in search of provisions and the vessels that would transport them to America. By happenstance, he was in Bordeaux when Silas Deane disembarked following his long but safe transatlantic crossing. The two met, though both men so carefully hid their intentions that neither learned the other was also on a mission to procure weaponry for the Americans. A month later Vergennes, after meeting with Deane, took the necessary steps to get him together again with Beaumarchais. Deane thought his counterpart was "a man of wit and genius," and also a tough negotiator. In September, after lengthy discussions, the two concluded a contract for the acquisition and delivery to America of 1,600 tons of muskets and cannon, in addition to powder, ammunition, tents, spades, axes, blankets, and clothing.

While Beaumarchais acquired the goods and arranged their transport to French ports, Deane handed out some 60 commissions to adventuresome French army officers who were eager to assist the Continental army. Although he had no authority to allocate commissions, by year's end some of the French volunteers had already begun crossing the Atlantic. At the same moment, Beaumarchais's activities were paying dividends. In December, *Amphitrite*, the first vessel laden with goods for the Continental army, sailed from Le Havre. By March 1777, eight more vessels were on the way, and when they returned to France, their cargo holds bulged with timber essential for France's shipbuilding industry as well as an assortment of commodities that included tobacco, sugar, and grains. Beaumarchais's dream of profiting from the American war was on the high road.[8]

BEFORE THE PROVISIONS GARNERED by Beaumarchais and Deane crossed the Atlantic, General Washington had already received some 10,000 muskets and one million pounds of gunpowder from abroad. Furthermore, in January 1776, a year before *Amphitrite* sailed, he was the recipient of a colossal stockpile of goods, including artillery, delivered by Henry Knox from Fort Ticonderoga. In a war filled with exceptional achievements, Knox's performance stands out. He had supervised a force of 300 soldiers and civilians that loaded 43 hefty cannon, 16 mortars, and ponderous barrels of powder, lead, and flints onto 42 sleds. Altogether, the total weight of the freight exceeded 120,000 pounds and was pulled by 160 oxen and numerous horses. Inescapable problems hindered operations. A "want of snow" delayed the operation. Once it did snow, a quick and "cruel thaw" made transit impossible for a spell. On finally reaching Albany, the cache had to cross the icy Hudson River. One cannon broke through and sank to the bottom of the river. Knox was so angry that he cheekily admonished General Schuyler, a superior officer, for his "careless manner" in conducting the river crossing. But all was not lost. The gun was salvaged with the assistance of "the good people of the city of Albany." Once across the river, the expedition faced the hazards of crossing the wind-scoured Taconic Mountains in the dead of winter. The sleds, animals, men, and priceless military stores had to traverse winding icebound mountain roads, ascend tall hillocks, and, even worse, survive downgrade plunges into deep valleys. Fortitude, muscles, and block and tackle got the job done without the loss of life or weapons. At the end of the third week in January the party reached the eastern side of the range. All that remained was an easy sprint to the siege lines outside Boston.[9]

While Knox's men struggled with the ordnance, Washington spent considerable time contemplating how to use the prizes they were bringing. Feeling pressure from Congress, more imagined than real, and uneasy with the passive role that had been forced on him, Washington wanted to act. He saw three options: assault the entrenched British army in Boston, the option a council of war had earlier rejected; attempt to retake Bunker Hill; or occupy Dorchester Heights west of Boston, high ground that also commanded the city and that General William Howe had puzzlingly not secured. Washington preferred the first option, without a doubt the riskiest of the three choices, and in mid-February presented it to another council of war together with an admission that it would be "attended with considerable loss." His horrified generals saw things in a more sober light. A series of forts along ridgelines and naval vessels sporting an abundance of firepower guarded access to the city. Besides, the generals said, the army lacked sufficient troops for "Offensive War." But if Washington's generals opposed an attack, they, too, wished to act. They recommended stealthily taking Dorchester Heights and inviting Howe to run the risk of attacking and suffering another Bunker Hill. Washington consented.[10]

Two weeks of meticulous preparations followed for what was expected to be a bloody battle with casualties running as high as 2,000. On March 3, Washington ordered the guns that Knox had brought to open up on the city, barrages that were designed to prevent the redcoats from spotting the pending operation. On March 5 the rebels occupied the heights. It was an unseasonably mild night and far brighter than Washington had hoped for. It was also the sixth anniversary of the Boston Massacre, an incident in which a squad of British soldiers had fired into a crowd of protesters at the Customs House. In peacetime, insurgent leaders had annually commemorated the event with rousing oratory in the Old South Church. That, of course, was impossible in 1776, but before the operation began, Washington spoke to his men and reminded them that British soldiers had killed several Bostonians on that memorable night in 1770. He exhorted his troops to "avenge the death of your brethren" as well those who had perished thus far in this war.[11]

The first rebels to go up the hill were 800 soldiers dragging carts and wagons loaded with tools for digging entrenchments. A couple of hours later, 1,200 stout workers, chosen presumably because of their fitness for hard labor, ascended the heights and spent the evening digging fortifications or straining to get the hefty artillery up the hill and in place. At 4:00 A.M., two hours before sunrise, these tired, sweaty men came off the hill and were replaced by 3,000 soldiers, a larger force than that which had occupied Bunker Hill. They took up positions in the entrenchments and awaited battle. Luckily for the rebels, a soft, kindly breeze carried the noise created by all this activity away from the city.[12]

The operation on March 5 took the British by surprise. For a second time during the siege, Britain's commander awakened at dawn's golden light to discover rebel artillery overlooking Boston Harbor. This time, the number of rebel artillery pieces far exceeded those that had been positioned atop Bunker Hill nine months earlier. Washington was ready for battle. It was now Howe's call. Though acutely scarred by the catastrophe on Bunker Hill, Howe immediately ordered an attack and had five regiments loaded onto transports that would convey them to Dorchester. He had probably bowed to pressure brought by officers who lusted for another go at the rebels. But an attack did not make much sense. Howe at last possessed sufficient transports to extricate his army from Boston, which all along had been his objective. Besides, while Howe could bloody Washington's army, his own army would pay a considerable price that might prove detrimental in the far more important summer campaign he foresaw in New York. Delays in loading the transports gave Howe a reprieve. He called off the afternoon attack and rescheduled it for the next day. But the next morning was stormy, forcing another cancelation. Given time to ponder the matter, Howe opted not to attack. He told his officers that he had canceled the operation because the storm had given the rebels additional time to prepare their defenses, making success "very doubtful." It was a cover story. He had decided to get out of Boston, though his army could be safely extricated only if Washington permitted. It would take time to load thousands of troops and an abundance of guns and equipment onto ships in the harbor, and all the while Continental artillery could pour down a deadly fire.[13]

Howe was not without leverage. He advised Washington that his army would raze Boston if the rebels resisted its departure. The American commander faced a difficult choice. He might so seriously damage his adversary's army that Britain would have second thoughts about continuing the war. On the other hand, if Boston was destroyed, leaders in New York, Philadelphia, and Charleston might lose their appetite for continuing hostilities. Washington wisely chose to let Howe go. Contingents within the American army entered the city the moment the British army sailed away, setting off a tumult of celebration by jubilant residents. The British army's occupation that had begun eight years earlier was over and, as one Bostonian declared, the city was rid of "a set of men whose unparalleled wickedness, profanity, debauchery, and cruelty is inexpressible." The public cheered Washington as well. Unaware that Howe had all along planned to leave Boston, most believed that Washington's daring occupation of Dorchester Heights had forced the British to depart. Washington, who was in the dark with regard to Howe's plans, did his part to spread the notion that his action had liberated the city. "[O]ur possessing Dorchester Heights . . . put them in a most violent hurry to Imbark," he boasted.[14] If Washington reaped laurels that he did not fully deserve, he warranted the honors heaped on him for having successfully carried out the siege of Boston, an operation whose success at times was far from assured.

While Bostonians celebrated, the enemy soldiers sailed from frigid Boston to raw and damp Halifax, where Howe planned to await the reinforcements that would enable him to launch the campaign for New York. The notion of transferring Britain's focus from Massachusetts to New York had first been broached by General Gage, though he had wanted to leave a force in Boston that could tie down parts of the Continental army and Yankee militiamen. Howe in his first week as commander in October had largely concurred with the notion of campaigning to take New York, though he preferred the "entire evacuation" of Boston and the usage of some of those troops to take Newport, Rhode Island. He indicated, too, that he wished to open the New York campaign in April, for which he would need 20,000 men while another 10,000 seized and occupied Newport. Around Christmas 1775, Howe learned of an impediment to his plans. London wanted a portion of the reinforcements that would be crossing the Atlantic to be sent to North Carolina. The American secretary had been advised by the royal governor of that colony that 3,000 Loyalist troops could be raised to reestablish royal control there. Once that seemingly simple errand was accomplished, those men could join Howe's army in New York, but that meant the New York campaign could not begin until much later than April.[15]

As British reinforcements slowly trickled into Halifax, Howe pondered the looming New York campaign. His overall thinking did not differ radically from Gage's. Both foresaw numerous advantages from securing New York. Taking the Hudson River—which flowed from the Adirondacks above Albany to New York Harbor and the Atlantic—would substantially sever New England's ties to the other colonies. Furthermore, Britain's possession of Manhattan would provide gateways for the invasion of New England, assist in suppressing the rebellion in neighboring New Jersey, and deliver a superb harbor to the Royal Navy. Howe further believed that his campaign in New York would lead to his long-awaited showdown with Washington's army. If the colonial rebellion somehow survived following Britain's victories in New York, Howe would next squeeze New England at strategic points. He painted a picture of rapid and vigorous actions, adding that he had "every reason to flatter myself" that the strikes he unleashed would "have the most intimidating effects upon the minds of those deluded" colonists. Lord Germain, the new American secretary and a proponent of aggressive warfare, welcomed word of his general's energy and lively spirit. As he rarely communicated with Howe at this juncture—unlike Dartmouth, who had sent instructions to Gage every three weeks or so—it was apparent that Germain believed he had found the man who could do the job and required neither advice nor prodding. Germain saw his role as one of furnishing Howe with sufficient troops. Howe's job was to use those troops wisely and forcefully.[16]

Howe waited impatiently in Halifax for reinforcements and provisions as March, April, and May slid by. Germain confessed to Howe that recruitment of the troops had been difficult and that the general would find many of the men unseasoned and "of little use to you" without considerable training. Finding the warning to be true, Howe set to unremittingly drilling each batch of men who arrived, almost all of whom were newcomers to military service. Reveille sounded at daybreak and tattoo at sundown, and in between there were three daily drill sessions. Early in June, after weeks of training, Howe pronounced his soldiers to be in "high order."[17]

AS A RESULT OF the tardy arrival of provisions sent from England, and the need to make repairs to several vessels that had crossed the Atlantic with reinforcements, Howe's army remained in Halifax until deep in June. Even then, the Hessians had not arrived, and General Henry Clinton, together with about 1,500 troops that had spent the miserable winter in Boston, was not with Howe. When ordering the operation in North Carolina, Germain directed five infantry regiments and two companies of artillery in Ireland to cross to the southern province. The squadron was commanded by Commodore Peter Parker. Germain told Howe to select one of his officers to command the army that would gather in North Carolina. Howe chose Clinton, who was to proceed to North Carolina and rendezvous with the force that Parker was bringing.

North Carolina's royal governor, Josiah Martin, writing from a cruiser off the coast after having been forced to flee his colony, had advised London that the province teemed with Loyalists eager to overthrow the "oppressive" rebel government and restore royal rule, but they needed arms and military stores. Lord Dartmouth, in his last days as American secretary, frankly told Martin, "I think you are too sanguine in your expectation," but he bowed to pressure and sent 10,000 muskets and six artillery pieces, which were packed into the vessels that Commodore Parker commanded. Germain, more optimistic than his predecessor, expected success. He ordered Clinton to pardon those who laid down their arms, but to arrest those who refused and to destroy their property and any town that supported them. Once royal rule was restored in North Carolina, Clinton was to proceed to Charleston, and if it "refuses to admit the King's forces, you will attack it and ... reduce it." Not for the last time in this war, London, and especially Germain, were swayed by the excessively upbeat claims of Loyalists.[18]

Every aspect of the Carolinas campaign failed. Clinton arrived off Cape Fear in March and discovered that a Loyalist force gathered by Governor Martin had been destroyed by a smaller army of rebels in December at Moore's Creek Bridge. A Tory army no longer existed. Dartmouth had been spot-on in questioning the rosy picture that Martin had painted. Nor was Parker's squadron anywhere to be seen, though it was supposed to have sailed in December. Like Howe, who spent the spring marking time, Clinton waited week after week for Parker to arrive. He spent his idle time plotting the best strategy to pursue when the fleet finally appeared. Clinton accepted the premise that a considerable population of Loyalists resided up the Cape Fear River in eastern North Carolina, but he now believed it best—crucial in fact—that henceforth any Loyalist armed force must take the field only when acting in concert with British regulars. Consequently, Clinton wished to establish two British bases on the Chesapeake. Guarded by British frigates, each would be an asylum for the Loyalists. Provided with the arms that Parker was bringing and provisioned by the Royal Navy, the armed Tories could reside safely in their Chesapeake posts until Howe's army arrived later in 1776, fresh from its victories in New York. Thereafter, the regulars and Tories, acting jointly, would reestablish royal rule in the lower South.[19]

Parker's fleet finally arrived in mid-May, 90 days later than anticipated, its tardiness caused by unavoidable delays in departing and an agonizingly lengthy Atlantic crossing. Parker's outlook for the coming operation differed from Clinton's. Aware of Germain's interest in capturing Charleston, Parker was also armed with intelligence provided mostly by Loyalists and displaced royal officials that the city's defenses were in an "unfinished state." He proposed scrapping Clinton's Chesapeake plan and sailing for South Carolina. It was Clinton's call. He was a superb strategist and his Chesapeake plan had merit. Furthermore, he was a stickler about not opening campaigns until every scrap of detailed information had been gathered, and he and Parker had only a scant knowledge of Charleston and its defenses. But when a letter from Howe arrived in which he spoke of Charleston as "an object of importance to His Majesty's service," Clinton against his better judgment acquiesced.[20]

Clinton later said that as if "blindfolded" he and Parker sailed for what one historian characterized as the "most heavily fortified city in America." Charleston's leaders had long since seen to the city's defenses, and they worked to upgrade them once the war with Britain began. Furthermore, early in 1776, when the rebels learned that Clinton had sailed from Boston for points south, Congress created the Southern Department within the Continental army and named General Charles Lee as its commander. Ultimately, Lee would command some 6,500 men, half of them Continentals and the remainder militiamen. He trained them while providing advice and direction on last-minute defensive preparations. Lee also used his authority to compel white men to perform manual labor that in Charleston was customarily the lot of enslaved people.

The British arrived in June with 2,200 troops and an armada of 50 ships. But their lack of knowledge about the geography and tides in Charleston Harbor and about the city's defenses proved crippling. Clinton and Parker's objective was to trap and capture the American defenders ensconced in Fort Sullivan on Sullivan's Island, which guarded the entrance to Charleston Harbor. It was to be a joint operation. Clinton knew that his men could not make an amphibious landing on the island's northern end, as it was defended by a large rebel force. Instead, his infantrymen were to cross Breach Inlet from Long Island and come ashore after wading across a channel where the water was purportedly 18 inches deep. All the while, Parker's heavy ships, with a total of 270 guns, were to bombard the rebel fort.

Little time elapsed before the British leaders' lack of information caught up with them. The shallow channel was in fact seven feet deep, and strong winds that day forced in more water. To his "unspeakable mortification," as Clinton later put it, the army could not land and "share in the attack." Parker went into the fray thinking he could get his ships within 70 yards of the shore. But shoals and contrary tides prevented the vessels from getting closer than 500 yards. The navy pounded away from that distance, but their cannonballs could not penetrate the thick walls of the fort, constructed of soft absorbent palmetto logs. All the while, the guns in the fort flailed away at Parker's squadron, causing enormous damage to several ships. One sailor said his vessel turned into a "slaughterhouse." He did not exaggerate. In all, the British suffered 80 casualties, Parker among them, as he was wounded twice, though not fatally. The royal governor of South Carolina, aboard one of the vessels, was killed and so, too, was the captain of a ship. Clinton later recalled that all were "brave and gallant men" whose blood had been "fruitlessly spilt." By the end of the encounter, the navy had fired 7,000 rounds and used up 12 tons of powder, and had suffered a calamitous defeat. The rebels had lost 38 killed and wounded, and had successfully defended Charleston. The Americans had displayed incredible courage, but in the end, according to General Lee, it was the "stupidity" of the British that turned the tide in the engagement. One of Britain's army officers attributed the outcome to a series of unfortunate "little accidents." Clinton was nearer the truth when he said the debacle was due to "delusive information."[21] It was not the last time in this war that Clinton made decisions based on misinformation, but he never again went into an action as blindly as he did on this occasion.

When the shooting ended, Clinton pressed Parker to "lose no time" in conveying his troops to New York to join Howe in retaking the royal province, a campaign that as far as he knew might have already begun.[22]

CHAPTER 4

PIVOTAL ACTIONS
AND INACTIONS

JUNE 28, 1776, WAS A busy, even epochal, day. General Clinton's attempted landing on Sullivan's Island went awry that morning. Some 800 miles to the north, the first Continental army soldier was executed in this war, hanged before a crowd of 20,000 curious onlookers in New York City. Later that day an army sentinel, squinting through a spyglass, spotted a sea of masts and sails off Long Island, a squadron of 400 transports and more than 70 warships, including 30 ships of the line (vessels that mounted over 60 guns). The enormous fleet so startled one observer that he thought "all London was afloat."[1] The armada carrying General Howe's somewhat reinforced army was approaching New York for what many on both sides expected to be the moment of truth in the Revolutionary War.

Lord North had spent the winter and spring finding reinforcements. Badly shaken by Britain's heavy losses in the war's initial engagements, North often fell prey to despondency. He told a friend in private that he now doubted that the American insurgency could be suppressed by force, though he never suggested that Britain's defeat was inevitable. Expecting a longer war than he had previously imagined, the prime minister feared the conflict would be harmful to Britain's economy, social fabric, and institutions of government, including Parliament and the monarchy. North was not the only one jolted by word of the fighting on Battle Road and Bunker Hill. Opposition newspapers were filled with gloomy essays and letters lashing out at the "absurdity and madness" of war against a "united, active,

able, and resolute" enemy on the other side of the Atlantic. Some predicted more
Bunker Hills for Britain's armed forces.[2]

Throughout the summer and fall of 1775 the ministry had been inundated with
thousands of petitions, roughly half of which questioned the war. The public divide
somewhat mirrored the political cleavages that would exist throughout hostilities.
As a general rule, the squirearchy—the wealthy elite—supported the war, while
artisans and shopkeepers hoped for concessions to the American rebels that would
restore peace. Within Parliament, opponents of the conflict looked on hostilities as
a civil war and embraced the colonial insurgents as brethren who were defending
liberty and freedom against the menace of authoritarianism. Some were convinced
that if the government suppressed liberty in the colonies, it was only a matter of time
before autarchy prevailed in England. Not all foes of the war took that stance. The
views of some sprang from hatred of the higher taxes that accompanied hostilities.
By November, the government had imposed a four-shilling land tax, and further
levies were anticipated. Some questioned whether Britain could militarily suppress
the rebellion, and others saw dangers in the expansion of Britain's army and navy.
Some cautioned that the "unjust, felonious war" might be "fatal and ruinous to our
country," particularly if the Americans were driven into the arms of France and
Britain was confronted with a wider, more dangerous war. The cities and countryside were largely quiet, though a vocal anger toward the government's recruiting
efforts was apparent in some quarters, and riots occurred here and there when the
navy began impressing mariners into its ranks.

Supporters of the war argued that the survival of the British Empire hung in
the balance. This made it a cause worth fighting for, they insisted, as the loss of the
American colonies would lay waste to Britain's maritime supremacy, the pivot
on which national security and continued prosperity rested. They brushed aside
the sting of the 1775 disasters in Massachusetts. "Reducing America to a just
obedience . . . is not without difficulties," some acknowledged, but they added that
"a great people" can overcome great challenges. Many who backed the war asserted
that the early setbacks were due to having gone to war with "too small a force," but
an army of adequate size would "deprive [the rebels] of all idea of resistance."
Throughout 1775 and 1776 the war hawks opposed concessions to the colonial
insurrectionaries. Some answered those who lamented the heavier wartime taxation with the argument that once the rebels were put in their place, assessments at
home would decrease as revenue was derived from the collection of taxes on the
colonists.[3]

Meanwhile Lord North searched for a means of ending hostilities, including a stab at subterfuge. His government leaked the contrived claim that the Bourbon powers had proposed saving London from a long, ruinous war through a partition treaty that would divide America between themselves and Britain. Charles Inglis, an Anglican cleric in New York, and a Tory, rushed a pamphlet into print early in 1776 that spread the tale. "I can whisper a secret," Inglis wrote in revealing the supposedly inside information. He confided that London was considering returning Canada to France and what the British called East and West Florida to Spain in exchange for their neutrality. "Let no man think this chimerical or improbable," he added. "The independency of America would be so fatal to Britain, that she would leave nothing in her power undone to prevent it." Not a few Americans, including some hard-core rebels like Samuel Adams, saw such behavior as business as usual for the scheming Europeans, who were famous for swapping or dividing territories. After all, four years earlier three monarchical nations had partitioned Poland. Lord North's endgame was to convince the colonists that concluding the war and remaining within the British Empire was preferable to French entrenchment on New England's northern border or a Spanish presence on the periphery of South Carolina and Georgia.[4]

However, North believed the best shot at peace in 1776 was through offering a generous peace proposal. Aware that Congress yet remained committed to reconciliation, North hoped to offer pardons to the rebels and send peace commissioners to America to conduct negotiations.[5] But neither George III nor the hard-liners in the cabinet favored conciliatory steps at this juncture, though the king was amenable to granting pardons and sending commissioners to superintend the transition to royal rule. North was soon aware that his wish to extend a meaningful peace offering was out of the question. One can only guess at the outcome had Britain extended genuinely placatory terms while the reconciliationists still controlled Congress. It may have delayed the decision to declare independence, and given the military woes the rebels experienced in the summer and fall of 1776, Congress may have been more willing to make peace. In fact, four weeks before independence was declared, John Dickinson, a Pennsylvania congressman and leader among the deputies who sought reconciliation, predicted that if Britain launched serious negotiations, it would find "Many Friends" here. Three weeks after independence was declared, Robert Morris, a powerful member of Congress, still thought that if Great Britain "offer[ed] peace on admissible terms I believe the great majority of America wou'd still be for accepting it."[6]

In 1775, the king, according to tradition, was to open the autumn session of Parliament with an address. Lord Germain appears to have been the official who most influenced the monarch's thinking. Throughout the decade of imperial troubles, Germain had opposed appeasement, and he now steadfastly pushed for an aggressive military policy, certain such a course could annihilate the insurgency in 1776. He opposed anything that would drag out hostilities, fearful that public support would wither in a protracted conflict and that the danger of French belligerency would increase if the war was prolonged. The king respected Germain and listened to him, though the monarch required little arm-twisting. He, too, opposed negotiations.[7]

On October 26, George III rode from St. James's Palace to the Palace of Westminster to make his speech. His huge carriage rattled slowly through London's streets, lined with an estimated 60,000 citizens drawn to the spectacle. As the posh carriage shuddered to a halt at Westminster, cannon blasts welcomed the king's arrival. Members of the House of Lords escorted him to the throne at the head of the compact chamber, a room so small that scores of onlookers had to remain standing. The king spoke in a commanding tone. He was uncompromising. The colonists "now openly avow their revolt ... for the purpose of establishing an independent empire," he declared, and he affirmed his support for the "most decisive exertions" to suppress the rebellion. He revealed that "certain persons" would be sent to America to issue pardons and "receive the submission" of the colonies. North had wished to negotiate with rebel leaders. George III made no mention of negotiating. Those "commissioned to restore" peace, he said, were being sent to accept America's surrender.[8]

Part of the ritual was for both houses of Parliament to answer a monarchical address, and the king had hardly departed before acrimonious debates erupted in both the House of Lords and the House of Commons on the nature of the responses. Those who defended the stance taken by the king resolutely insisted that victory was not in question, though some admitted that as many as 60,000 troops might have to be sent to America. Other delegates believed that conciliation was necessary to resolve the crisis but urged continued military action in order to "put us upon a proper footing to negotiate" with the rebels on some future day. Opponents of the king's harsh message maintained that "evil counselors" had "poisoned the ear of the sovereign." The war, they said, was "cruel, unnecessary and unnatural." They blasted North as "the blundering pilot who had brought the nation" to the point of "a butchery of his fellow subjects." Not a few portrayed the colonists as waging "a noble and glorious struggle ... for what they conceive to be their liberties, and the natural rights of mankind." Those who were dead set against the war were a power-less minority. Parliament and the monarch had decreed that there would be a military campaign in 1776.[9]

North attended nearly every session and spoke frequently, and he brought the debate on the House of Commons' answer to the king to a close with an address of his own. Concealing his pessimism, the prime minister advised that a powerful military force was being sent to America together with commissioners armed "with offers of mercy upon a proper submission." This "will shew we are in earnest" in seeking "an honourable reconciliation," he said, and it would demonstrate that Britain was "prepared to punish, but ... ready to forgive." Throughout his lengthy speech, North said nothing about the commissioners' latitude to negotiate.[10]

The identity of the commissioners and the authority given them would be hashed out by a ministry that was unwilling to consider conciliation. In fact, North's government soon obtained passage of a further coercive measure, the American Prohibitory Act. The legislation extended the naval blockade to all 13 rebellious colonies and authorized the confiscation of cargoes and impressment of colonial merchant sailors into the Royal Navy.

Between February and May 1776, North's ministry wrangled over whom to appoint as commissioners. There was support for Admiral Richard Howe—brother of the general and recently named commander of Britain's naval arm in North America—to serve as the lone commissioner. Germain balked. Aware that Howe had often sympathized with the colonial protesters, Germain pushed for a three-member commission that would include two undersecretaries of state who could be counted on to oppose any concessions. The imbroglio was resolved by naming General William Howe to serve alongside his brother. But the commissioners' instructions still had to be determined. Nearly all agreed that the colonists must acknowledge Parliament's legislative authority "in all cases whatsoever." Germain pressed for having the colonists submit to unlimited parliamentary power as a prerequisite for any steps taken by the commissioners. North was more flexible, and rancor between the two grew so intense that when the American secretary hosted a grand ball that spring, he invited seemingly all of London's elite except the prime minister and Lady North. After weeks of bruising contention, the final settlement was essentially a victory for Germain. With most ministers assuming that nothing would be done until after British arms had vanquished the insurgents, it was agreed that once a colony recognized Parliament's sovereignty, the commissioners could issue pardons, restore royal government, superintend the demobilization of rebel military forces, and oversee the dissolution of illegal political bodies. After a colony had taken those steps, the commissioners were to see that assembly elections were held and legislation enacted to compensate the Loyalists for lost property.[11]

Meanwhile, the reconciliationists in America's Continental Congress were buoyed by the king's revelation that peace commissioners would be crossing the ocean. Unaware of the limited leeway the commissioners would possess, these congressmen eagerly awaited their arrival, praying they would "come with proper Powers" that would produce a "mutually beneficial Accommodation." Not every congressman shared their expectations. John Adams looked on the king's mention of commissioners as little more than a "fatal delusion," just another instance of "Knaves imposing upon Fools."[12]

ON THAT EVENTFUL JUNE 28, perhaps at the very moment that the army's lookout sighted the British squadron off Long Island, a congressional committee in hot, humid Philadelphia handed Congress's presiding officer a draft of a document declaring American independence.[13] The reconciliationists' stranglehold on Congress had gradually diminished during 15 months of war, and early in June the delegates, ready at last to seriously contemplate severing ties with Britain, voted to create a committee "to prepare a declaration of independence."[14]

A flurry of activity had led to Congress's decision to create the committee. On June 7, Richard Henry Lee, thought by many to be the most influential member of Virginia's delegation, introduced a resolution calling for American independence. Lee's motion replicated a resolution recently enacted by the provincial assembly in Williamsburg. Virginia had proclaimed that the 13 colonies were "free and independent States . . . absolved from all allegiance to the British Crown." Lee had added passages that called on Congress to take "effectual measures for forming foreign Alliances" and preparing a "plan of confederation."[15]

The next day, a Saturday, Congress debated whether the time had come to declare independence. The foes argued that several congressional delegations had not been authorized by their provincial assemblies to declare independence, military necessity did not require such a step, and the colonies would enjoy a more peaceful and prosperous future within the British Empire. Some warned that as not every colony favored independence, taking such a step might sunder America's wartime unity. Others cautioned that France and Spain not only would never adequately aid the United States, but they also might even join with Britain to partition America, each taking a section.[16]

The numbers of those who championed an immediate declaration of independence had grown steadily as the war hardened attitudes toward Britain, and in June the proponents of an immediate break with Britain were helped by the grim news just reaching Philadelphia of the ill-fated rebel army in Canada. Many believed that military necessity required that Congress declare independence, as it was apparent that foreign aid was essential for effectively waging war. France's forthcoming secret aid would be insufficient, they said. Meaningful amounts of assistance hinged on breaking all ties with Great Britain.[17]

At the end of the exhausting Saturday session, Congress decided to defer a final decision on independence for three weeks. On Monday, June 10, it created what came to be known as the Committee of Five—composed of Benjamin Franklin, John Adams, Virginia's Thomas Jefferson, Roger Sherman from Connecticut, and Robert R. Livingston of New York—and charged it with preparing a declaration of independence by July 1.[18]

To this point, Congress had waged war to remain within the British Empire on its own terms. In 1774, Congress had recognized no parliamentary authority over the colonies save for its right to regulate trade. That, too, fell once hostilities erupted, and thereafter fealty to the Crown had been the colonists' sole link to Great Britain. Congress had now come to the brink of severing that last tie.

The removal of France from North America after the Seven Years' War had caused some colonists to question whether British protection was any longer necessary, though it was London's new colonial policies that provoked many to rethink America's presence—and subordinate status—in the British Empire. But nothing radicalized as many colonists as did the war. The long-held belief that Britain was a loving and benevolent parent state died once the British army killed colonists on Battle Road and Bunker Hill, and the government sent over more soldiers to kill more colonists. The Royal Navy's October 1775 shelling of Falmouth, Massachusetts (now Portland, Maine), a bombardment that completely destroyed the hamlet and left the residents homeless as another grim New England winter approached, was the breaking point for others. A few weeks later many southerners were gripped with terror and outrage on learning that Virginia's royal governor, Lord Dunmore, had offered freedom to rebel-owned slaves willing to bear arms in the fight against the rebels. In no time, some 1,600 enslaved persons, half of them women, fled to Dunmore, and many bore arms in what he called the "Ethiopian Regiment." A cascading fear surged among slave owners who foresaw the loss of their labor force, while many who owned no chattel quaked at the prospect of armed Black people bent on revenge and rampaging across the countryside. Shortly before Christmas 1775, Edward Rutledge, a South Carolina congressman, spoke of the sulfurous rage that Dunmore had provoked, noting that he had done more "to work an eternal separation between Great Britain and the Colonies, than any other expedient, which possibly could have been thought of." [19]

The appearance of *Common Sense*, a pamphlet written by Thomas Paine and published in Philadelphia on January 9, 1776, furthered sentiment for independence. Although congressmen had secretly discussed breaking with Great Britain, no writer before Paine had dared to openly urge independence. Paine, a native of England, was steeped in the ideas of a vibrant English reform movement that sought to broaden suffrage rights, make Parliament more representative of society, limit monarchical powers, and rectify an unfair and unequal system of taxation that fell heavily on the lower social orders. In 1774, at age 37, Paine had reached a crossroads in his life in England. He knew that if he remained in England he was likely to spend the rest of his life plying his trade as a stay maker. He wanted more than a lifetime of hunching over a workbench. He may not have had an alternative firmly in mind, but like many another down-at-the-heels Englishman, Paine immigrated to the colonies in search of something better. Soon after settling in Philadelphia he began writing newspaper essays, some of which readily revealed his sympathy for America's cause. Paine's lucid compositions captured the attention of influential Philadelphians and advocates of independence in Congress, and late in 1775 some urged him to produce a tract denouncing reconciliation and advocating American independence. [20]

Common Sense was the result, a pamphlet like no other among the scores published in the previous decade of upheaval. Earlier discourses, largely the product of lawyers, were mostly ponderous, legalistic works brimming with Latin phrases that had reached small audiences of well-educated readers. Paine, in contrast, wrote for a wide audience—and he found one. Some 150,000 copies of *Common Sense* were sold in three months, and that was only the beginning. [21] It was America's first bestseller. Previous pamphleteers had mostly defended Britain's constitution as the world's best, but claimed that Parliament had violated it by imposing unprecedented and unconstitutional policies on the colonists. Paine, however, was a true revolutionary. He did not wish to compel Parliament to adhere to Britain's constitution. He called that constitution "rotten," charged that British monarchs were despots and warmongers, and portrayed the ruling titled aristocracy as a cruel and uncaring oligarchy.

Paine not only wished to sever all connection with Great Britain, he sought to transform the colonial protest into an American Revolution that would turn the 18th century's political and social world upside down. The purpose of government, he trenchantly argued, was to provide for freedom, happiness, and security, not to serve as a bulwark for the ruling order. Under republican governance the people would be the source of authority, and as a consequence, the lives of ordinary people would be substantially improved. He challenged the reconciliationists' argument that the colonists would be better off by remaining within the British Empire. An independent America, Paine wrote, would no longer be dragged into Britain's wars, and Americans could trade with whomever they pleased. Independence meant peace, freedom, and prosperity. The new American nation would be a lodestar for people everywhere. It would become the "asylum for mankind" seeking to escape an "old world . . . overrun with oppression." In a grand flourish, Paine proclaimed, "We have it in our power to begin the world over again." American independence would be nothing less than the "birthday of a new world."[22]

Nearly a quarter of Paine's pamphlet dealt with the war, and much of it consisted of exaggerated claims of America's military capabilities. Even so, Paine warned that America lacked the means to fight a protracted war. Published just as word arrived of Montgomery's failed campaign to take Quebec, *Common Sense* was seen as prophetic in its assertion that America badly needed help from potentially friendly nations in Europe, countries like France and Spain, which were Britain's traditional enemies. But, wrote Paine, there was no incentive for those nations to aid the colonists so long as America's objective was reconciliation with Britain. However, American independence would enable those countries to open trade with America and their national security would be enhanced as a result of Britain's loss of its colonies, the primary source of London's power.

Britain's use of force, Dunmore's proclamation, and *Common Sense* were crucial elements in the radicalization of colonists, and so too was word that Britain had hired foreign mercenaries, news that reached America while many were reading Paine's pamphlet. The German mercenaries that the colonists insisted on calling Hessians were reputed to be vicious, ruthless soldiers, and their utilization provoked fears that they would "plunder" and "destroy us." It also added credence to the insurgents' message that Britain was bent on "the most compleat and barbarous conquest of the Country." Until the Hessians were hired, many who cherished reconciliation held intransigently to the notion that the king cared deeply for the colonists. But George III's complicity in hiring mercenaries ruined his standing in America. Many now thought him a "Tyrant" for his "infamous" act of retaining "butcher[s]" to "Slaughter us."[23]

At nearly the same moment, as spring blossoms appeared on trees in 1776, America learned of the Prohibitory Act that embargoed every colony's foreign commerce. Massachusetts congressman Elbridge Gerry said that it yet again revealed how Britain's ministry knew "so little of our feelings or character. . . . Have they not yet ascertained that we know our rights?" More than one congressman proclaimed that the measure "made the Breach between the two Countries so wide as never more to be reconciled." Others thought that Britain's latest "cruelty & injustice" made an "eternal separation" from the mother country a necessity.[24]

Like a row of falling dominoes, these war-related occurrences demolished the luster of reconciliation. By May, Virginia was prepared to declare independence, and most of New England was not far behind. Late that month John Adams thought Maryland, the Carolinas, and Georgia were also close to being ready to take the plunge. The reconciliationists were strongest in the four mid-Atlantic provinces that once had substantial economic ties to the mother country, although Adams attributed their resistance to independence to the fact that they had not yet "tasted the bitter Cup" of war. At the beginning of June, Adams knew there was "infinitely greater" support for independence than ever before, but he also understood that "Unanimity in this Time of Calamity and Danger" was imperative. War required solidarity. Had it not been for the unending stream of dire tidings from Canada, the holdout provinces might have delayed a final break past the summer of 1776, possibly well past it. But the unsettling knowledge of America's dysfunctional military operations provided the cement required to gain unanimity for declaring independence. In June, when Congress created the Committee of Five, Richard Henry Lee summed up the brutal truth of where the American rebels found themselves: "we are certainly unequal to a Contest" with Britain "without any assistance from without." He added: "It is not choice then, but necessity that calls for Independence, as [it is] the only means by which foreign Alliance can be obtained" and sufficient war materials secured.[25] With the vanquished northern army in shreds on Isle aux Nois, Howe's army soon to land near New York City, and General Carleton's large army in Canada thought to be poised to invade New York, most leaders of the American insurgency understood that delaying independence could be fatal.

In June, while awaiting the draft of a declaration of independence, Congress took several crucial steps. It ordered several provinces to ready their militia for service with the Continental army in the coming campaign in New York, prodded all the colonies to hurry their production of powder, restricted exports of salt beef and pork (commodities the army needed), investigated the causes of the disasters in Canada, appointed General Horatio Gates to succeed John Sullivan as the commander of the northern army, created a committee to draft a constitution for the new nation, established the Board of War and Ordnance in hopes of bringing about greater efficiency in military administration, and ordered the raising of a "flying camp," a force of 10,000 to guard New Jersey and Pennsylvania and follow Washington's orders.[26] The colonies were busy as well. By the end of the month every province but New York had authorized its congressmen to vote for independence.

All along, the Committee of Five had been at work. Its first step was to choose Jefferson, who had a deserved reputation as a gifted writer, to draft the document. It was a wise move. Adams was a sparkling letter writer, but almost everything he wrote for publication was composed in dreary legalese that put off the average reader. Franklin wielded a glorious pen and would have prepared a readable list of charges against Great Britain, but there was little evidence that he saw what America was about to do as anything more than quit the British Empire. Sherman and Livingston would have been out of their depth. Jefferson was cut from different cloth. Years later he said that he had seen the Declaration of Independence as "the signal of arousing men to burst the chains" that had shackled them for centuries. He sought to write a declaration "pregnant with our own [fate] and the fate of the world."[27] Like Paine, Jefferson saw the American Revolution as the inauguration of a new age—what Paine later called the Age of Reason—a transformative time that would embody the loftiest ideals of the Enlightenment. It would be a period when humankind, guided by reason and at last able to govern itself, would sweep away the tyrannies, sophistries, and mythical delusions of the Age of Monarchy. For Jefferson, and many of his countrymen, the American Revolution was about more than severing ties with Great Britain. It was about creating a free and self-governing republican nation that would be a beacon for the rest of the world, and the light from that beacon would be switched on by the ringing words within the Declaration of Independence. In Jefferson's mind, the Declaration of Independence would give birth to a new world.[28]

Jefferson completed the draft in only five or six days, and nearly all that he wrote survived the committee's scrutiny. The document that Congress would consider was Jefferson's handiwork, although what Congress wanted beyond showing cause for severing ties with Great Britain was not clear. Jefferson justified the break with Britain in an arraignment of 27 specific charges that cataloged a "long Train of Abuses and Usurpations" demonstrating "a Design to reduce them [the colonists] under absolute Despotism." For the most part, he assailed the actions of the monarch, not Parliament, because for the past year Congress had recognized the Crown as America's sole tie to the empire. He also mentioned numerous appeals to "our British brethren" only to find that they were "deaf to the voice of justice & of consanguinity."[29] The charges that Jefferson compiled against the king and parent state were largely forgotten within a few years. That was not true of the draft's second paragraph, Jefferson's magisterial précis of the meaning of the American Revolution:

> We hold these truths to be self-evident, that all Men are created equal, that they are endowed by their Creator with certain unalienable Rights, that among these are Life, Liberty, and the pursuit of Happiness—That to secure these Rights, Government are instituted among Men, deriving their just Powers from the Consent of the Governed. . . .

The Committee of Five submitted the draft declaration on that crucial June 28. But before it could ponder the document, Congress first had to make its decision on independence. On Monday, July 1, Congress spent nearly the entire day in its sweltering chamber on what John Adams called "the greatest Debate of all"—whether or not to declare independence.[30] John Dickinson led off with a condemnation of independence. He wished to continue fighting, he said, but not to break away from Great Britain. He raised the specter of a partition treaty among foreign powers if the war dragged on, as it would if America sought independence, for Britain would throw everything it had into preventing the loss of the colonies. But if the colonists' goal remained reconciliation, said Dickinson, one or two American victories would compel Britain to offer satisfactory terms. In what had come to sound untenable to many, he insisted that the colonists should remain within the Britain Empire and reap its benefits, including generations of peace, security, and prosperity. Independence, on the other hand, would be a leap into dark, uncharted waters that could be fraught with myriad domestic and foreign dangers.

John Adams followed Dickinson and urged independence. No record of his speech has survived, but he was a capable orator, having honed his skills in years of arguing before Bay Colony juries. With a fierce conviction, he almost certainly emphasized what he had said in a recent letter to Patrick Henry: "The importance of an immediate Application to the French is clear." Adams stirred many of his listeners. A New Jersey congressman proclaimed him the "Atlas of Independence," and a Southern delegate exclaimed that "an angel was let down from heaven to illumine Congress."[31] The speeches by Dickinson and Adams took up most of Monday afternoon, but deep into that night nearly every other member of Congress spoke briefly on the issue.

The vote on independence would come the next day. A soft, cooling summer rain was falling when Congress convened on Tuesday. After tending to preliminaries, the delegates voted. Adams knew the motion would carry, presumably by a margin of "almost Unanimity." He was wrong. On July 2, Congress declared independence by a unanimous vote. Voting was by states and the final tabulation was 12–0. New York, still awaiting instructions from the provincial assembly, abstained. But it also voted for independence a few days later.[32]

Congress then turned to the draft declaration, and for roughly 10 hours over the three sessions between July 2 and 4, it edited the document. Congress ultimately reduced the draft by a third, though fortuitously Jefferson's second paragraph that gave meaning to the American Revolution survived intact. So, too, did passages aimed toward Europe. In assuming an "equal station" among "the powers of the earth," the Declaration stated, the new American nation wished "Trade with all parts of the world," would "hold the rest of mankind, Enemies in War, in Peace Friends," and possessed "full Power" to "contract Alliances [and] establish Commerce." Congress additionally left unchanged the final line in Jefferson's draft: "we mutually pledge to each other our lives, our fortunes, and our sacred honour." Though perhaps often overlooked by succeeding generations, the congressmen were making a resounding commitment to the American Revolution and a vow of unified dedication in support of the war. Their stout affirmations were directed at the American citizenry, Britain's leadership, and potential patrons in Europe.

While most that was crucial in what Jefferson had written remained, Congress tragically excised one item in the draft bill of indictment, a charge that might well have changed the trajectory of American history. Jefferson, who had previously supported an effort by the Virginia assembly to end the importation of African slaves and would subsequently support gradual emancipation within his state, had arraigned the king for having "waged cruel war" on the "sacred rights & liberties" of Africans by "captivating & carrying them into slavery." He hoped the Declaration of Independence would put America on the road to terminating slavery.[33] But congressmen from South Carolina and Georgia would not vote for a declaration that included such an obvious abolitionist statement, and for the sake of unity Congress bowed to their wishes.

Although John Adams had chafed at the reconciliationists' control of Congress, and the delay they caused in declaring independence, he expressed surprise that the break with Great Britain had come as quickly as it had. Independence had been declared 30 months after the Boston Tea Party, 22 months after the First Congress assembled, and 15 months after war erupted at Lexington and Concord. But Adams was all too aware that independence would have to be won on battlefields through a terrible cost of "Toil, and Blood, and Treasure."[34]

HOWE'S ARMY IN 1776 would total about 32,000 men, five times the number that Gage had possessed on the day hostilities began. But not all the troops had arrived when the huge British armada docked in New York. Clinton's force was on its way from Charleston, 1,000 Scottish Highlanders were also coming, and there were no Hessians. They had departed their respective territories in Germany months before but faced long marches to German or Dutch ports, followed by what was usually about a 10-day voyage to Portsmouth, England, from which they sailed for America. For the fortunate, an Atlantic crossing took four or five weeks at sea, though one unhappy German officer and his men spent 12 miserable weeks in what he called "a sort of imprisonment" on his ship. Most of the mercenaries had reached New York by August 15, though some would not see Manhattan until deep into autumn.[35]

The British army came ashore on Staten Island in early July, but Howe could not move until all his soldiers and shipments of camp equipage arrived. Forty supply ships had sailed from England during the winter; some had yet to appear, and the cargoes of some that had reached America were ruined in transit. Logistical issues in fighting a war 3,000 miles away had reared their head and would continue to be nagging problems for the British army. America's distance from the home islands was not the only hindrance. Eighteenth-century Britain was so administratively primitive that coordination between departments was virtually nonexistent. Supplying the large British army sent to America in the Seven Years' War had not been a paramount issue because the colonists had pitched in to help. But the

Americans would not be providing assistance in the Revolutionary War. And logistical concerns would not be Howe's only problem in the campaign of 1776. While he possessed a decent map of Manhattan and Long Island, prepared earlier by a skilled cartographer in London, there were no maps that detailed localized areas in the region. Furthermore, a viable intelligence system awaited creation.[36]

Howe was not alone in facing problems. Every general in this war coped with troubles, though few ever faced the mountainous difficulties that plagued General Washington in 1776. To "enumerate the particulars" of his adversities "would fill a volume," Washington remarked.[37] He was a relatively inexperienced commander who had spent most of his adult life as a farmer and businessman in Virginia. His corps of officers was even more callow, and only a handful of his troops that summer had ever faced the ordeal of combat. Washington's army would be numerically inferior, and half or more of the troops would be raw militiamen. Furthermore, as Beaumarchais's weaponry and powder destined for America had not yet been loaded onto transports in French ports, not every Continental possessed a firearm, and those who did were short of ammunition. Nor did Washington have any cavalry, having shortsightedly sent home his 500 dragoons. But perhaps the greatest problem facing Washington was in defending islands—Manhattan Island and Long Island—against an enemy that possessed the world's strongest navy. General Clinton, who had grown up in New York City, did not think the rebels could successfully defend the islands. Washington may have agreed, though he felt that he had no choice but to defend them. If the British took New York and the Hudson River, he said, "they can stop the intercourse between the Northern & Southern Colonies, upon which depends the safety of America." Besides, Washington was aware that Congress, with which he had met in May, expected him to defend New York, which the delegates understood was the "Key to the whole Continent." John Adams, a leader in Congress, could not have been more cogent when, in January, he told Washington: "No Effort to secure it [New York] ought to be omitted."[38]

In January, Washington had sent General Charles Lee to New York to formulate a plan of defense. Lee was not a military engineer, but he was a clever veteran officer with years of military experience. His objective was to make the enemy pay a terrible price for every square foot of territory that it took and to prevent the fall of New York City, which he and Washington saw as Britain's first step toward cutting "the Continent in twain." Lee put to work his 2,000 Continentals and New York militiamen, as well as every enslaved person and free laborer that levies could raise. They constructed fortifications in northern Manhattan and Brooklyn Heights, on the Long Island route to the East River and the entrance to New York Harbor, and at sites on the Hudson River. Lee also instituted draconian measures against the Tory residents, arresting some and disarming others. He ordered the steps, he said, lest "We shall weep repentance with tears of blood."[39]

After Lee was transferred to the southern theater, work continued through the spring and summer under the direction of others. In Brooklyn Heights, in particular, the Americans sought to design an impregnable defensive barrier. A mile-and-a-half-long chain of forts, many set on promontories formed by rock outcroppings, had been constructed, as had redoubts surrounded by generous ditches and connecting trenches that extended at both ends to the East River. In all, these installations housed 40 cannon. All brush had been cleared and trees felled for 100 yards to provide a clear view of the approaching enemy. A marker was placed 50 yards downrange in the open field to alert the defenders that the attackers were in the "kill zone." Washington arrived in New York in April, and by June he was persuaded that New York had been put into "a very respectable posture of Defence" and that his well-trained troops could stand up to their professional adversary. Clutching at straws, he added that as "our cause is just . . . Providence . . . will . . . afford its aid."[40]

Washington's counterpart, General Howe, was aware of myriad options for putting down the American insurgency that had been advanced in military and civilian circles. Some had thought a naval blockade could do the job, but the first year of the war had demonstrated that alone was not feasible; the American coast was simply too extensive even for the formidable Royal Navy. Others preferred pitiless measures against civilians and soldiers, but Howe spurned wanton cruelty as criminal. Some favored relentlessly pursuing and attacking the enemy's army. While in Halifax, Howe spoke of his eagerness to fight Washington in "the open field," but added that such a fight "will not readily be brought about." The rebels, he thought, would withdraw into the forbidding backcountry where a large regular army "cannot follow." By the time he landed in New York, Howe embraced the strategy of reestablishing British control of the major coastal cities through which the bulk of American exports and imports flowed. Once those ports were shuttered, rebel armies would face crucial shortages and civilian morale would deteriorate. Taking control of important rivers was a relatively similar strategy, in that it would impede communications and divide provinces, pushing some colonies into the backwaters of the war.[41]

Howe saw what he was up against when his army landed on Staten Island. His enemy was "numerous and very advantageously posted with strong entrenchments," he noted, and an abundance of artillery protected the city. As he contemplated how to take New York, Howe consulted with Clinton, the second-in-command, who proposed trapping the Continental army on Manhattan by severing all lanes of retreat. Clinton urged landing portions of the army at assorted sites in the northern reaches of Manhattan while the navy prevented the enemy's escape across the Hudson River. Clinton's plan was feasible, for on July 12 the Royal Navy succeeded in running three warships up the Hudson past the array of river obstacles the rebels had painstakingly constructed and Fort Washington, an installation that peered down on the river from a lofty precipice. Clinton was so confident that the enemy's force could be trapped and obliterated that he predicted he would be eating Christmas dinner at home in England. But Howe rejected Clinton's plan. He wanted to fight the Continental army. Regular warfare was what the British army was trained for, and a year into hostilities it had not yet had the opportunity to square off against its adversary in such an action. Besides, the destruction of Washington's army in all likelihood would end the colonial rebellion. Howe had long been wedded to first landing his army on Long Island. That choice was even more tantalizing once Howe realized that Washington, who had no idea where the British would land, had divided his army, posting more than half of his 20,000 men at sites in Manhattan and some 6,800 on Long Island. Howe glimpsed a showdown with his adversary, an opportunity he had thought he would never get. Even better, it would be a fight against a numerically inferior foe.[42]

Once Long Island was his, Howe would implement a strategy that had crystallized in his thinking over a period of months. First, he would take New York City and its magnificent harbor. Thereafter, he would simultaneously take New Jersey and Newport, Rhode Island, his launching pad for the invasion of New England. Before long, a campaign would begin to take control of the Hudson River, a step to be accomplished by his army, accompanied by the navy, as both struck north into the Hudson Highlands above Manhattan while General Carleton invaded New York from Canada.[43]

As Howe awaited the expected provisions and reinforcements, he conceived the plan for his Long Island offensive. Although he had spurned Clinton's recommendations regarding Manhattan, Howe accepted his plan for the Long Island campaign. Having personally reconnoitered the area, Clinton had found a pass on the Jamaica Road east of the rebel lines that Washington had left unguarded. Clinton proposed a feint at the western end of the American lines while the main army turned the rebels' eastern flank. A diversionary ruse in one sector followed by

a main thrust in another quarter was standard operating procedure among Euro-
pean armies, but none of the rebel leaders appear to have imagined they would face
such a thing. At dawn on the morning of August 22, 15,000 British troops under
Charles, Earl Cornwallis, landed unopposed at Gravesend, six miles below Brooklyn
Heights. They were "as merry as in a Holiday," said one of the king's soldiers. The
Americans troops were in equally "high sperits," according to a Yankee, and eager
for their foe to "come on" if they "dare." Washington was under the impression that
Howe was throwing only 9,000 men into his campaign, when in fact 24,464 British
troops were ready for battle in the two sectors on Long Island. Washington was
victimized by poor intelligence, a problem he compounded by moving 3,000 men
from their fortifications to a 10-mile-long ridgeline called the Heights of Guana, a
crest that was too long to be adequately defended by so few troops. The capstone of
Washington's amateurish folly was that he and his green officers were about to fall
for his enemy's hardly unconventional subterfuge.[44]

On August 27, at daylight, Cornwallis's diversionary force launched an attack.
During the preceding night Howe's main army, guided by a Loyalist, had circled
around the rebels' left flank and advanced undetected behind its adversary. After a
couple of hours of fending off Cornwallis, confidence soared among the heedless
Americans. But around 8:30 A.M. the king's soldiers burst from the woods behind
them. Some rebel soldiers and units fought valiantly—Howe subsequently praised
the Delaware and Maryland regiments—some surrendered, some were killed while
trying to surrender, and a great many of the unseasoned and startled men ran for their
lives. Roughly 80 percent escaped to the fortifications on Brooklyn Heights. The
others were not so fortunate. Many vainly sought safety in nearby thick forests, only
to be hunted down and killed or captured. Some tried to reach safety by swimming
across Gowanus Creek, as wide as a football field. Several drowned and several more
were shot by British soldiers leisurely perched on the banks. During the brief battle
roughly 1,500 Americans were killed, wounded, or taken captive, including two
rebel generals, John Sullivan and William Alexander, who called himself Lord Stirling. The sole failure in the British performance, wisecracked Howe's secretary, was
that the redcoats "could not run" fast enough to overtake the fleeing "Poltroons."
Meanwhile, Washington seethed at the "Shameful and disgraceful" showing made
by his troops, though their panic was in considerable measure the bitter harvest of
the maladroit leadership that had caused them to be taken by surprise.[45]

The British had won a rousing victory. Ahead of them stood the rebel redoubt
that guarded the approach to five forts and long lines of interconnecting

entrenchments in Brooklyn Heights. Howe had come to what historian William Smith characterized as the "key moment" of his career, though it might better be described as the first in a series of decisive moments the general faced. In the chaos following that first engagement, the American forces were scattered and in disarray, and a British frontal attack might have overwhelmed the rebels who remained on Long Island, close to one-third of what had been Washington's army at the start of the day. Clinton later said that had Howe attacked, "Not a [rebel] would have escaped" Long Island, but at the moment when the decision had to be made, Howe—like nearly every commander in every such situation—received conflicting advice. Some of his officers and his intelligence arm cautioned that an attack would result in nightmarish losses, and he was told that not even an army of 50,000 could overrun the enemy's lines. Other officers, convinced that the rebel defenses were manned by hundreds when thousands were needed, urged an attack. They asserted that even if the rebel defenders were more numerous than thought, their strength was diluted because they were scattered through several installations. Furthermore, in the earlier action that day, the enemy soldiers had hardly demonstrated that they were reliable warriors. Howe weighed the conflicting counsel and elected not to attack. (Clinton later said that had he been in Howe's shoes, he would have made the same decision.)[46] Subsequently, Howe acknowledged that a frontal attack would have succeeded, but "the loss that might have been sustained" would have been too great. He believed upwards of 1,500 men would have been casualties. Besides, Howe was confident that he had a foolproof alternative to storming the rebel lines. Success, he said, would soon be "ours at a very cheap rate" through a siege. While the navy blocked the rebels' escape across the East River, the army would keep the enemy soldiery pinioned in their forts. Soon or later, the snared enemy would have to surrender. The British would gain a bloodless conquest.[47]

According to Clinton, the British eventually determined that "at the very moment" when Howe opted not to attack, there were "not above 800" rebel defenders in the lines that "required at least 6000 to defend." That assessment appears to have been more or less accurate, as American officers that very day advised Washington that while the forts and redoubts were well constructed, the connecting entrenchments were incomplete, weakly defended, and vulnerable.[48] In retrospect, by not immediately attacking in the turbulent moments following the thrashing suffered by the Americans on Long Island, Howe missed a golden opportunity to inflict what might well have been the fatal blow to the American insurgency. There were good reasons for ordering an immediate attack and good reasons for settling for a siege operation, but that Howe ultimately shrank from a frontal attack was perhaps the legacy of the emotional scars he bore from the carnage on Bunker Hill. Likely spared a colossal defeat that could have turned around the course of the war, General Putnam put his finger on the rebels' good fortune in a pithy remark: "General Howe is either our friend or no General."[49]

On August 29, as Howe prepared a siege operation, a two-day storm with heavy rain and lashing wind hit New York, idling the Royal Navy because of the likelihood of damage from the gales. Washington faced a difficult choice, and like Howe two days earlier, he received clashing advice. Some of his generals, envisaging another Bunker Hill, urged that the troops be left in their forts and entrenchments to face a British attack. Some also warned that an attempt to bring off the men—they would somehow have to be transported to Manhattan through the swirling currents of the mile-wide East River, possibly in the face of the Royal Navy—would be more perilous than making a stand in Brooklyn. Others argued that the greater peril would be to leave the men in Brooklyn to contend against a vastly superior enemy. Washington could be indecisive and slow to act, but on this occasion he made a rapid decision. He would attempt to extricate the men in Brooklyn.

Washington assigned the task of mustering sufficient vessels to General William Heath, who before the war had been a Roxbury, Massachusetts, militia officer. Heath somehow got the job done in eight hours, collecting an armada that ranged from rowboats to sloops. Washington turned to Colonel John Glover, commander of soldier-mariners from coastal Marblehead, Massachusetts, to man the crafts and get the weaponry, baggage, men, and even cattle to safety. Glover and his men made 11 arduous trips across the river. The pelting rain and sable night were fortuitous for the rebels, who also caught a break when the wind shifted, enabling their sailing craft—which had been inoperable for the first three hours—to make the crossing. But the wind was capricious. It led to delays that caused the operation to take longer than anyone had imagined. With sunrise, the threat increased that the British navy would discover what was afoot or that Howe, aware of what his wariness had wrought, would strike those still on the other side of the river from Manhattan. But again, luck was with the rebels. A thick, yellowish fog crept over the river and Brooklyn Heights, obscuring the final stages of the evacuation. Some 13 hours after the withdrawal began, the last of the rebels, a contingent that included General Washington, crossed to Manhattan. The British learned that their prey, including men, munitions, and field artillery, was gone only when the fog burned off. It almost seemed as if the Providence that Washington believed would protect him had done just that, though in reality the American commander had acted boldly and at great risk.[50]

The events in late August provided an education for a shaken Washington, who to this point had thought his soldiers were sufficiently trained and disciplined to meet regulars in the fierce test of battle. He rethought his strategy, telling Congress that henceforth he would pursue a Fabian strategy. He would choose when and where to fight, and would avoid "a general Action" in which his entire army was put at risk. Instead, he would seek to bleed the British dry while preserving his army, dragging out hostilities in the expectation that eventually London would conclude the war's price was too great or that France would enter the hostilities. As for Howe, the realization that excessive caution had robbed him of a decisive victory should have been an object lesson. It wasn't.[51]

Howe paused before taking his next step. He and his brother, Lord Howe, were peace commissioners, and since their arrival in July they had sought to parley with the rebels. They had no luck in bringing Washington to the table, but in the aftermath of Long Island, Congress sent Benjamin Franklin, John Adams, and South Carolina's Edward Rutledge to Staten Island for talks with the Howes on September 11. Admiral Howe appears to have imagined that the negotiations could succeed, a hope grounded in a belief that the outcome of the battle on Long Island had made the rebels amenable to peace on Britain's terms. The three congressmen were escorted past an honor guard of grenadiers, which Adams thought looked "as fierce as the furies," and into the house that Lord Howe had appropriated. After a sumptuous meal with the admiral, the only peace commissioner present, the talks began. They ended quickly when the Americans learned that Howe was authorized to proclaim peace only "upon Submission" of the colonies. There was a surreal aspect to the conclave, for the Americans knew that if they lost the war, their genial host in all likelihood would turn them over to the hangman. Years would pass before the two sides again discussed peace. For the present, as one of Howe's staff scribbled that evening in his journal, "nothing remains but to fight it out against a Set of the most determined Hypocrites & Demagogues."[52]

Washington was aware that the resumption of fighting was imminent and that Britain's target would be Manhattan generally and his army in New York City in particular. However, the American commander was unaware where the enemy would strike and unable "to form our defense on some certainty." His troops were widely scattered. Some 3,500 under Putnam were posted in New York City at the southern tip of Manhattan, a second division was strung out over 14 miles on the east coast of the island, and batches of the remainder guarded an even greater length on the west side. What Washington understood with clarity was the need to evacuate the city, which he saw as a trap waiting to happen. He wished to "keep the Army together" between Harlem Heights, some 12 miles north of the city, and King's Bridge at the northern tip of Manhattan, his portal to escaping the island should it come to that. Congress quickly consented to abandoning the city, but a majority of the generals balked, and Washington would not act without their consent. Thereafter, he spoke with each general separately, a tactic that brought them around and enabled him to get his way, a stratagem he would often utilize in the future. The army's evacuation of the city began on September 12, the day after the failed peace talks on Staten Island, but it was attended by what the commander called "insuperable difficulties." Three days later, divisions from Howe's army landed at Kip's Bay, on the east side of Manhattan just above the city. Only stores and the sick had been removed from the city. Putnam's large force was still there, threatened with great peril.[53]

Clinton had urged a landing in the north to secure the King's Bridge and prevent the enemy's escape. He understood that his plan meant a long, bloody fight, but he believed—almost certainly accurately—that it would culminate in the destruction of nearly the entire rebel army.[54] Howe spurned Clinton's recommendation. Instead, he sought a less costly victory of smaller proportions. By landing at Kip's Bay, he hoped to ensnare the rebel troops still in the city. Howe appears to have believed that the capture of the city and Putnam's soldiery, coming atop the rebel debacle two weeks earlier on Long Island, would bring about the colonists' submission.

Howe anticipated stout resistance to the landing, followed by a counterattack from Washington. Given those conceivable dangers, perhaps most commanders would have prepared a plan similar to Howe's. Following the amphibious landing, his army was to secure the beachhead and establish defensive positions in the hilly terrain a quarter mile or so inland. Only then, and after all the troops had landed, would units of the army begin the two-mile advance across Manhattan to the Hudson River, in the process sealing off all roads leading out of the city.[55] A more daring commander would have ordered his light infantry to move with dispatch immediately upon landing, closing all exits from the city. Howe was no longer such a commander.

Around 11:00 A.M. on September 15 the first wave of longboats carrying the initial landing party of British troops set off while five British warships pounded the rebel lines on Kip's Bay. A terrified Yankee soldier in the entrenchments later said he "began to consider which part of my carcass was to go first." Deciding not to wait for the "rake of their guns" to zero in, he fled, as did almost all his comrades. Washington and Putnam, hearing the shelling, rode like the wind for Kip's Bay and sought to stymie the flight. There was no stopping it. The first wave of British troops, under the command of Clinton, came ashore "without the least opposition." Clinton ordered four battalions of Hessians to pursue the rebels who had bolted for safety while he led additional troops to the rolling inland area. Obeying Howe's orders, Clinton secured the sector and waited—and waited and waited—for the remainder of the invasion force and Washington's counterattack, a rebel onslaught that never came.

Meanwhile, Putnam spent hours seeking to restore order near Kip's Bay and did not return to the city until sometime in the afternoon. It was not until 4:00 P.M., nearly five long hours after the first invaders landed, that his troops began to move out. Another hour passed before a Hessian brigade closed off Bloomingdale Road, the route that Putnam's men, led by Major Aaron Burr, a young native of Manhattan, had taken on their long trek to Harlem Heights. The Americans had lost more than 350 men that day. Nearly all were troops that had been posted at Kip's Bay and failed to make good on their panicky attempt to escape. The troops in the city got away intact. For the second time in two weeks, a great prize had slipped though Howe's grasp.[56]

After the engagement on Long Island, Washington had advised Congress of his "want of confidence in the Generality of the Troops." Militiamen, he said, were incapable of "a brave & manly" performance under fire, and he suspected that their unworthiness had "Infected" large numbers of Continentals, ruining them as well. The sight of the men at Kip's Bay "flying in every direction and in the greatest confusion" hardly bolstered Washington's confidence. He did not say so, but he may have agreed with General Knox that the army was "a receptacle for ragamuffins" and that many lower-ranking officers were "ignorant, stupid men." In the aftermath of Kip's Bay, Washington stationed troops at sites on the Hudson and at King's Bridge, but the bulk of his army was with him in Harlem Heights. He anticipated a dark, foreboding future. He expected Howe to soon "land above or below" King's Bridge and "inclose us" on Manhattan Island, and he understood that when that occurred, he would be in desperate straits. Should the enemy succeed in blocking his retreat off the island, Washington acknowledged that he would have to "fight them on their own Terms or Surrender," the very opposite of what he said he hoped to avoid through his newfound Fabian strategy. Given the dire future that he foresaw in remaining on Manhattan Island and the grave choices that such a course portended, the best solution facing Washington was to abandon the island and escape the snare. Yet Washington made no attempt to escape the death trap that was Manhattan.[57]

Ten days before Kip's Bay, General Nathanael Greene, who in time would become the officer whose counsel Washington most trusted, had urged the abandonment of New York City as well as all of Manhattan. There was nothing to be gained and everything to lose by remaining on Manhattan, he maintained. A "speedy retreat," he went on, was the only way to "oppose the Enemy successfully and secure our selves from disgrace." He added that Washington's job was to protect the "General Interest of America," not that of New York.[58]

But Washington did not move off the island then or during the three dangerous weeks that followed. He remained entrenched in the ominous confinement of Harlem Heights. It was Washington's most mysterious conduct during the war. He told some that the "absurd interference" of Congress kept him rooted to this spot, though in fact Congress had sanctioned a withdrawal days before the British came ashore at Kip's Bay. It may have been that, like so many others he, too, had caught Bunker Hill fever and remained where he was in the hope that Howe would attack. He had also been "greatly inspirited" by the performance of his men in a small skirmish with the enemy in Harlem Heights on the day after Kip's Bay, and that action might have boosted his confidence to the point that it skewed his judgment. It is conceivable, too, that weeks of pressure and anxiety had taken their toll on Washington. Physically and emotionally exhausted, he appears to have sunk into a black hole of depression that left him confused and dangerously immobile. The endless crises and what he called his "perplexing circumstances" had deprived him of adequate sleep. His correspondence suggests that he had come to feel that the destruction of his reputation as a leader and soldier was inescapable. At times, he seemed to say that maybe it would be best if he died in a blaze of glory while leading his troops in battle. He confided that he would not wish his job on his worst enemy. He also admitted that he was unaware of "what plan of conduct to pursue." That was inaccurate. He had "resolved not to be forced from this ground while I have life."[59]

Washington's army remained inert, but he was not totally inactive. He sent spies into New York City, hoping to learn the enemy's plans. One who did not make it out gained posthumous fame. Nathan Hale was captured and executed on September 22.[60] Washington also solicited Congress's reaction to putting New

York City to the torch. "[O]ught It to stand as Winter Quarters for the Enemy?" he asked. Congress ordered him not to raze the city, but on September 21 a devastating blaze consumed one-quarter of the dwellings in New York. Even more would have gone up in flames had the wind not suddenly shifted directions. There can be no doubt that the inferno was a case of arson, as fires erupted nearly simultaneously at numerous points and the British captured several firebugs in the process of setting blazes. There also can be little doubt that some central planning and direction went into burning the city. To this day the head of the conspiracy remains unknown. General Washington steadfastly denied having dispatched the arsonists, though he had compelling reasons for bringing down infinite problems on his enemy and was well positioned to organize such a scheme. The British, after a careful inspection, concluded that the fire was "designedly set" and Washington was almost certainly "privy to the villainous act." Their judgment can't be accepted at face value, but in all likelihood the conclusion they reached was correct.[61]

While Washington's army on Manhattan remained motionless, Howe, too, was idle for a full month after Kip's Bay, wrestling with the best option for his next step. He even considered terminating his campaigning until the following year, telling London that Washington's army was "too strongly posted" in Harlem Heights "to be attacked." Unwilling to risk another Bunker Hill, Howe would consider only a siege operation, but he was also reluctant to take the option, fearing that winter's bad weather would make supplying the siege army an insoluble problem. Cold weather had in fact already arrived; at nearly this very moment, Washington wrote to Congress of his army's need of heavier clothing as winter was approaching, adding the "change of weather . . . we every day feel." Late in September, Howe advised Lord Germain that he had "not the smallest prospect of finishing the contest this campaign" in 1776. This would be discouraging news for the American secretary, as he had told Parliament that the insurgency would be crushed that year. Howe tried to soften the blow by saying that he would take Newport before year's end. It was widely regarded as the finest port in the northern provinces, and possession of Rhode Island was essential for an invasion of New England. Howe also unconvincingly advised Germain that the "much dispirited" colonists might abandon "all thoughts of further resistance" beyond 1776 should abundant British reinforcements arrive over the winter.[62]

Howe finally acted in mid-October, putting in motion a variance of the plan that Clinton had twice advocated—sealing off the northern exit from Manhattan. Howe chose Throg's Neck peninsula, a narrow spit of land above King's Bridge that protruded into Long Island Sound, for his landing site. If successful, he might trap Washington's stationary army in Manhattan and force it into the field to fight to avoid being pinned in during the approaching winter. If nothing else, Howe said, his action might coax many among the "desponding multitude" of colonial rebels to rethink their commitment to the rebellion.[63]

Howe positioned three brigades near Harlem Heights to somewhat limit Washington's freedom of action and gave command of the Throg's Neck mission to Clinton. The squadron of 80 ships carrying 11,000 troops sailed up the East River and into Long Island Sound before disembarking an advance party of 4,000 men on the morning of October 12. They came ashore without a hitch, as only 25 Continentals were posted in the vicinity of the landing site. But Clinton soon found that he was in trouble. Not only had the enemy destroyed a bridge and causeway that furnished the only passage through the conspicuously narrow Neck, but also the tapered landscape ruled out the possibility of sending out flanking parties. What is more, the sandy, marshy terrain inhibited the movement of artillery beyond the neck. Nevertheless, Clinton ordered his troops to proceed inland. Before long, they encountered the handful of rebels who had fallen back when they'd spotted the British armada and were now sheltered behind a jury-rigged breastwork devised from cords of firewood. Those men—some armed with deadly accurate rifles— stopped the British advance in its tracks. While Clinton regrouped, Washington rushed in reinforcements, bringing to 1,800 the number of Continentals that the British would have to fight through. General Putnam had earlier allowed, "Give an American army a wall to fight behind and they will fight forever." Washington may not have fully concurred, but he was aware that the area was "lined with Stone fences" and he was unlikely to ever find a better place to wage a defensive fight. One of his aides licked his chops at the prospect of the "considerable Slaughter" that loomed, and another thought that "if we cannot fight them here we cannot do it anywhere." Clinton, too, dolefully concluded that a tragedy was about to occur. Geography inhibited his ability to turn the enemy's flank and, as usual, he was loath to order a frontal assault. When Howe arrived, he discerned that given his lack of a detailed map, he had chosen an improper landing site. Five crucial days passed while he groped to find better spot and brought up reinforcements. A disgusted Clinton, who had never favored landing at Throg's Neck, called the affair "tweedledum business."[64]

Whether or not Washington knew it, the Continental army—and the American Revolution—was on the brink of the greatest crisis it ever faced. If Howe succeeded in springing his trap, the Continental army on Manhattan was doomed. But Washington made no move to escape during the several days before Howe's second landing. He might never have attempted to escape had not General Lee returned to his side. Lee had been in Savannah making preparations for a campaign against Loyalists in Florida when Congress summoned him. He arrived in Philadelphia five days before Clinton landed on Throg's Neck. Some in Congress had lost confidence in Washington; nearly all the others wanted Lee at Washington's side. He is more valuable than 10,000 soldiers, thought one delegate. Congress sent Lee to Manhattan before he had time to unpack his baggage. On October 14, 48 hours after Clinton's landing on Throg's Neck, Lee rejoined Washington. In an instant, Lee understood the treacherous situation the army faced and advised Washington to escape Manhattan. Washington trusted Lee and listened, but he would not act without the sanction of a council of war. Two more menacing days passed before the council met. Its members were aware that Howe's army was boarding the vessels anchored off Throg's Neck, probably for another landing at a more desirable site. On October 16, the council voted to try to outrun the British.[65]

Readying an army for a move requires time. While the commander reconnoitered the coast on Long Island Sound, hoping to discern Howe's most likely landing site, the army packed essential items and burned the rest. Fifty days after the miracle escape from Brooklyn Heights, and at the very moment that the British fleet weighed anchor and departed for Pell's Point, the Continental army began its getaway from Manhattan. "We are, I expect, upon the Eve of something very important; what may be the Issue: Heaven can tell. I will do the best I can, and the leave the rest to the supreme direction of Events," Washington wrote that day.[66]

Washington, uncertain of Howe's destination, had posted troops here and there. He had put 750 Continentals under Colonel Glover at Pell's Point, three miles above Throg's Neck, and the site that Howe had chosen for his second landing. The moment Glover glimpsed the Royal Navy's sails off the coast, he positioned his men behind the ubiquitous stone walls. Putnam's theory about the resolve of American soldiers fighting from behind a wall was about to be tested once again. It soon was demonstrated to be sound. Glover's men cut the British to pieces. The rebels fired, retreated behind another wall, fired again, and retreated again. The British kept advancing, but slowly. The stout rebel resistance bought time for the main American army, a few miles to the west, to make its escape from Manhattan. Glover and his men also inflicted a heavy toll on Howe's army. Hundreds of British and

Hessians were cut down that day, almost certainly more than had been lost on Long Island in August.[67]

The rebel army had jettisoned all that it could do without, and much that the men needed, in order to hasten the retreat to the hilly and safer terrain in White Plains. Howe set off after his prey, but he did not strip down his force, and his headway was additionally hindered by a dearth of horses, bad roads, and rebel pickets. Washington's army reached its destination in three days. Howe's shorter march consumed 10 days, and when he arrived he found 13,000 rebels in strong, hilly defensive positions. Howe possessed an equal number of troops and yet again he had a shot at a showdown against the main rebel army, a prospect for which he repeatedly said he yearned. Clinton advised against a frontal attack, reasoning that the enemy's flanks were secure and "their retreat practicable when they pleased." Howe may have reached the same conclusion, as he ordered an attack on Washington's right wing, strongly positioned on Chatterton Hill. The British took their prize late in the day after heavy fighting, losing some 350 men in the process. Howe's plan for the next day was different. He now vowed to throw his army into a frontal assault on the American lines, a course some of his generals had favored from the outset. But a heavy rainstorm forced a delay, which Washington utilized to withdraw farther north. He may have hoped his adversary would track him deeper into the backcountry, but Howe knew he would face forbidding hazards the deeper he plunged into the interior. The British packed up on November 1 and returned to Manhattan. Roughly 125 days had elapsed since Howe's arrival on Staten Island. His losses had exceeded 1,000 men, and Washington's army was still intact.[68]

What Howe might do next was a mystery, but Washington was "almost certain" that he would "make a descent . . . into Jersey." Washington and his generals agreed to divide the army to meet any eventuality. General Heath was given 4,000 Continentals with which to defend the Hudson Highlands. Washington, with 2,000 regulars and whatever militia he could scrape together, was to cross the Hudson and drop down into New Jersey. Lee was posted at New Castle with 7,000 men to defend against an invasion of New England or to sprint to the aid of Heath or Washington. Finally, it was agreed to leave the 3,000-man garrison at Fort Washington. When Washington soon thereafter learned that Carleton had opted not to invade New York that fall, he knew that more than 1,000 Continentals under General Gates at Ticonderoga could also help any threatened contingent.[69]

Aside from holding firm to his notion of sending General Clinton to take Newport, what Howe had in mind when he returned to Manhattan is not known.

But when intelligence reported that the rebels had left a large force at Fort Washington, he seemingly cast aside his gloomy memories of Bunker Hill and in a rare display of brio decided to attack. Given that his caution had resulted in the enemy's escape from Brooklyn, New York City, and Manhattan—and with the campaign of 1776 nearly over—he may have believed that he must attack. Four thousand Hessians sent by London, whose presence he had clamored for, had just arrived, and that, too, might have nudged him into action.[70]

Washington had ample time to abandon Fort Washington and withdraw his men to safety across the river, but General Greene, who commanded this sector, thought the post was defensible. It was Washington's call. If he successfully defended the fort against a British attack, the British might suffer a second Bunker Hill. If the British instead besieged the installation, Washington believed his force could break free from the investment and be saved. Washington wrestled indecisively with his decision for 40 hours.[71]

Howe attacked while Washington was still trying to reach a decision, and he gained his greatest victory. The Americans fought valiantly. The British and Hessians were no less stout-hearted, as they first had to ascend a steep, craggy precipice in the face of the enemy's deadly fire and thereafter assault a concealed enemy. Howe's men had a fourfold numerical advantage, and in the end they overwhelmed the defenders, inflicting the worst defeat that Washington would suffer in this war. The British lost 458 men. The Americans suffered 149 men lost in the fighting, but 2,870 rebel soldiers were taken prisoner, many of whom died in captivity.[72]

That wasn't the end of the American disaster. Three days later the suddenly energized Howe struck again. He sent General Cornwallis with 5,000 men to strike Fort Lee, a huge rebel supply depot across the river from Fort Washington. For inexplicable reasons, Washington had failed to order the fort's evacuation. Under cover of darkness, Cornwallis's assault troops climbed the tall, steep, rain-slick cliffs of New Jersey's Palisades. They found the rebel installation guarded by only a dozen "dead drunk" soldiers. They also discovered that Washington had made no attempt over the previous 72 hours to remove the treasure trove of stores within the fort. Already starved for weaponry and provisions of every kind, the rebels lost 30 cannon, 8,000 cannon-shot, 4,000 cannonballs, 2,800 muskets, 400,000 cartridges, 500 entrenching tools, 300 tents, and 1,000 barrels of flour. The British additionally took thousands of abandoned cattle in the meadowlands near Hackensack. In his report to Congress, filed the next day, Washington acknowledged that the "unhappy affair" of Fort Washington was followed by "further misfortunes," though he said that the disaster would have been greater had not most of the stores been removed before Cornwallis's arrival, a dodgy claim.[73]

Cornwallis set off immediately after Washington, who retreated through New Jersey. Cornwallis, in command of a reinforced army that had swollen to 10,000 British and Hessians, was cut from different cloth than Howe. Now 37 years old, he had soldiered from more than 20 years and had experienced combat in Germany in the 1760s. He volunteered to serve in America and arrived in the spring of 1776, after which he saw plenty of action in the New York campaign. Cornwallis had a reputation for valor, honesty, and compassion for those he commanded, but most of all he was seen as a soldier who epitomized aggressiveness, one who could be counted on to act resolutely, energetically, and zealously.[74]

Cornwallis's army was three times the size of Washington's minuscule force, and the disparity soon grew even more lopsided when Maryland and New Jersey militia brigades departed following the expiration of their terms of service. The rebels retreated below Hackensack 24 hours before Cornwallis arrived, setting what would be an unbroken pattern. Just as Washington's army had scurried faster than Howe's in the withdrawal to White Plains, the rebels now stayed ahead of their foe, in part because they took steps to slow Cornwallis's advance. The rebels destroyed bridges and felled trees across roads, and rear guards of riflemen and artillerymen harried the enemy. A British soldier said the rebels were "always above a day's march" ahead, but Americans spoke of their "terrible situation with the enemy close upon us." At one point Washington said the enemy was "in sight now."[75]

During the retreat, Washington informed Congress that "the situation of our affairs is truly critical." A few days later he characterized his predicament as "truly alarming" and acknowledged that "our force [is] by no means sufficient to make a stand against the Enemy, much superior in numbers." On November 30 when his army reached Brunswick, Washington warned that the "Enemy are still advancing" and it "is impossible to oppose them." His only hope appeared to be escaping across the Delaware River and throwing up defensive emplacements. But an army is seldom more vulnerable than when undertaking the painstakingly slow process of crossing a river. Indeed, five days were ultimately required to get the men, provisions, and heavy weaponry across the Delaware. The chase through New Jersey presented the British with yet another superb opportunity to score a decisive victory, and never more so than when they might have pinioned their adversary against the Delaware River and forced it to fight against heavily unfavorable odds.

But once again Howe failed to take advantage of what Washington called his "melancholy situation."[76]

Howe ordered Cornwallis "not to advance beyond Brunswick." Howe was aware of the plight of Washington's army and at one point had even acknowledged that had Cornwallis caught Washington, the rebel "army must inevitably have been cut to pieces." For his part, Cornwallis made a valiant stab at overtaking his adversary. Ordering a "forced march," his troops trekked 20 miles in a single day. But when Cornwallis reached Brunswick and obeyed orders to pause there, 48 hours remained before Washington's army could begin its time-consuming crossing of the Delaware River.[77]

In a summer and fall filled with curious decisions, the choices made by Cornwallis and Howe at this juncture are perhaps the most baffling. Cornwallis had been ordered to stop at Brunswick, though he subsequently acknowledged that he had the latitude to act if he believed that "a material stroke" would decimate his enemy.[78] His men had been on the move for 10 days and were exhausted. But so were Washington's men. They had been in the field far longer, and during the three weeks since beginning their march southward from above White Plains, not many days had passed when they had not been on the move, including the past 11 days of steady retreat. Both armies were drained. Arguably, the rebel soldiers were the more wearied. Cornwallis could have briefly rested his bone-tired men, forded the Raritan, and been on his way long before Washington's army began to cross the Delaware. Cornwallis did not always adhere to his commander's orders, but in this instance he did. His army remained in Brunswick.

One day before Cornwallis reached Brunswick, Howe wrote to Germain that he soon would possess all of eastern New Jersey, after which he would go into winter quarters. He said nothing about the possibility of trapping and destroying Washington's army. In fact, he waxed on about the next year's campaign. Late in November, Howe was satisfied with being in "possession of East Jersey." Three weeks later, in another communiqué to Germain, Howe explained that while his "first design" had been the pacification of eastern New Jersey, on joining Cornwallis in Brunswick on December 6 he glimpsed the possibility of crossing the Delaware and "getting to Philadelphia" before year's end. However, when the British army finally reached the river, it discovered that Washington's army had already crossed and the rebel commander had removed all boats in the vicinity. The "passage of the Delaware being thus rendered impracticable," Howe terminated operations for the winter.[79]

Unraveling Howe's bewildering thinking at this critical moment in the war is next to impossible. Even Washington found it perplexing. With "a little enterprise and industry," he later remarked, Howe could have destroyed "the remaining force which still kept alive our expiring opposition." Caution had been Howe's watchword throughout the campaign of 1776. However, given Cornwallis's overwhelming numerical superiority and the forlorn nature of Washington's force, it is difficult to comprehend his excessive wariness as November eddied into December. Perhaps he feared a sudden mobilization of militia forces that would strengthen Washington's hand, though intelligence gleaned from Loyalists, deserters, and intercepted rebel dispatches pointed to the militia's inactivity. Besides, if Howe worried along those lines, General Clinton had proposed a plan that should have allayed his concerns. Clinton wished to land a force at Perth Amboy—only some 15 miles from Washington's lane of retreat—and advance on the rebels from the east while Cornwallis came after them from the north. As Washington did not have the manpower to stop one adversary, he could hardly have coped with two. Washington anticipated that Howe would choose that tactic, and he knew that if it was carried out before his "little force" crossed the Delaware, he would be fatally threatened by the enemy "upon our Front" and in his "rear." Clinton knew that as well, and he was confident that through his plan the colonial rebellion would be "wholly crushed by the annihilation of [Washington's] corps." But Howe rejected the plan and instead dispatched Clinton with four brigades to reclaim Newport. It is conceivable that Howe believed the Continental army could not survive the winter. He knew of reports that the insurgency and rebel army were collapsing, even that the Continental army could not "keep together 'till Christmas." Howe's letters to Germain suggest that he wasn't that optimistic, but he may have concluded that sacrificing large numbers of his men in an attack on a spent enemy simply was not worth it.[80]

On the day before ordering Cornwallis to temporarily suspend his quest to overtake Washington, the Howe brothers, in their capacity as "Commissioners for Restoring Peace," had issued a proclamation offering pardons and a guarantee not to seize the property of all rebels who within 60 days took a loyalty oath to the Crown and pledged "to remain at peace." Admiral Howe was known to believe that kindness was the best means of reclaiming the loyalty of the "misguided part" of the king's "disaffected subjects." As it is difficult to escape the conclusion that General Howe was never intent on catching Washington's army, it may be that through some distorted logic he convinced himself that the rebellious colonists were more likely to accept a pardon if the sting of submission was ameliorated through the face-saving knowledge that their army had not been destroyed. If he embraced such a bizarre notion, virtually no one else in Britain's military in America shared the belief. Even Lord Howe's secretary was certain that peace was "coextensive with the Power of the Sword."[81]

WHAT THOMAS PAINE EVER after referred to as the "dark period" of the Revolutionary War had descended on the Americans. Morale was indeed crumbling in the wake of defeats and retreats, and spirits were further shredded when General Lee was captured in New Jersey while en route to link his army with Washington's. Not a few members of Congress now anguished that the Revolution "will be destroyed" by British "Fire and Sword." With gloomy apprehension some predicted that the rebellion soon would "perish in infamy." In December, while it was still presumed that Howe's target was Philadelphia, Congress fled to Baltimore, leaving a three-member executive committee in Philadelphia "to execute such continental business as may be proper and necessary." Congress gave Washington "full power"—in essence, dictatorial powers—to conduct the war in its absence.[82]

Congress was prepared to make any concessions necessary to induce France to "enter the War as soon" as possible. Pennsylvania congressman Robert Morris summed up the state of affairs: "Our situation is critical & does not admit of Delay." Unless France soon entered the war, he said, America must make peace with "her opressors." He further disclosed that at the war's outset "Every Man was then a bold Patriot," but now that "Death & Ruin stare us in the face," all too many "Shrink coward like from the Danger."[83]

To add to what Morris called "Calamities sufficient for any Country," faith in Washington's abilities had collapsed within some circles in the army. A lieutenant colonel raged that "less generalship never was shown in any war," and a colonel who wished that Lee commanded the army concluded that the "vast burthen" of command was "too much" for Washington's limited talent. Before his capture, Lee wrote to a friend that Washington's proclivity for "fatal indecision" guaranteed "eternal defeat" for America's cause.[84]

Washington feared for his survival as commander and for the cause, and some of the general officers shared his apprehension. One of them got the idea of utilizing Thomas Paine's amazing writing skill to restore public confidence. Luckily, he was available. In September, after about two months' service as a soldier in the flying camp, Paine had signed on as a secretary to General Greene. He ran errands and drafted some of his commander's orders and correspondence, and at times was under fire. Greene was likely the one who recommended putting Paine's magical pen to use, and a few days after the Fort Washington debacle the penman set to work on an essay. Legend has it that Paine used a drum as a table and, after nightfall, a campfire's illumination in order to write. It was slow going, leading to a command decision to send Paine to Philadelphia in hopes that his essay would appear before year's end. The strategy worked. Paine's squib, *The American Crisis*, hit the streets a week before Christmas. No writer ever composed a better hook as an opener:

> These are the times that try men's souls. The summer soldier and the sunshine patriot will, in this crisis, shrink from the service of their country; but he that stands it *now*, deserves the love and thanks of men and women.

Paine, with some truth and a daub of whitewash, proclaimed Washington's military capability. The commander's exemplary character came to the fore in the hour of great peril, said Paine, and it was among America's "public blessings" to have Washington leading the fight. Paine minimized the recent calamities and sought to rejuvenate support for the "glorious cause" by insisting that victory was possible. He also appealed to Congress to create a standing army composed of regulars, not soldiers who served for only one year.[85]

Washington had plans of his own. In the course of the retreat across New Jersey, he envisaged, if presented with a worst-case scenario, making haste for hilly and supposedly impregnable Morristown, New Jersey, and going into winter quarters. It was the choice he almost surely would have attempted had Clinton landed at Perth Amboy. But Washington's first preference had been to establish a defensive line at Brunswick, where he expected to be joined by Lee—who had been summoned with his soldiery from New Castle—and give battle. It likely was an unwise choice, but he was spared the fight he wanted when Lee's army was late in arriving. Washington then made what in the long run would prove to be the best choice among his options. He hurried to Trenton and the Delaware River, which his unmolested army slowly crossed while Cornwallis paused at Brunswick.[86]

Once in Pennsylvania, with a wide river separating his army from the enemy's, Washington was safe for the time being. But, for good reason, he was wracked with despair. His soldiers, described by a civilian onlooker as a "set of dirty, ragged people, badly clothed, badly disciplined and badly armed," were devoid of nearly every essential provision. The artist Charles Willson Peale, serving in the Pennsylvania militia, encountered his brother, a Continental, around this time and did not recognize him. He "was in an old dirty blanket-jacket, his beard long and his face full of sores . . . which disfigured him." Washington knew that his tiny, bedraggled army could not stop the British if they crossed the Delaware when it froze and advanced on Philadelphia. American "affairs are in a very bad way," Washington acknowledged, to which he added: the "game is pretty much up."[87] But he was not ready to give up. The urgency of that desperate moment and his will to fight pushed him to do something. Otherwise, when his soldiers departed, as they surely would when their one-year enlistments expired at the end of December, it would be impossible to lure new recruits into an army that had suffered major disasters and had finished the year by being chased out of New Jersey. What is more, the public's support for the war would utterly collapse. Washington also feared that his own reputation was in tatters. He began to contemplate recrossing the Delaware and assailing his adversary in New Jersey.[88]

Despite the gloomy state of affairs, every man under him could go into battle with a musket and 60 rounds, a bonanza due largely to more than a year of clandestine Euro-American trade.[89] Furthermore, the gradual arrival of Pennsylvania militia and some men from the armies of Gates and Lee increased Washington's army to a bit over 6,000 men. A plan took shape in his mind. Howe had put his army into winter quarters, scattering small divisions throughout New Jersey, despite Clinton's admonition that the chain of posts was "extended too much." Three cantonments were near the Delaware River. Bordentown and Burlington were downriver. Trenton, where 1,500 Hessians were garrisoned, was directly across from Washington's army. Three days before Christmas, Washington and his generals reached a decision. It was audacious and born of desperation. A rebel force would cross back into New Jersey on Christmas night and strike the Hessians in Trenton at daybreak on December 26.[90] There was a daring streak in Washington's character, and that trait put him on the path to gaining his greatest unilateral achievement in this war.

Under a wan and fading sun, Washington with 2,400 ragged men set off in midafternoon on Christmas Day. Half his men carried muskets made in France, Spain, and Liège in the Austrian Netherlands; the other half toted weapons fashioned in Britain or America. Washington's plan was to cross the river 10 miles above Trenton, while a second force of 1,800 crossed 12 miles below the hamlet and 800 militiamen traversed the river directly across from Trenton. Washington's force and the militia units were to strike the Hessians from opposite sides while the third rebel force circled around and blocked the escape routes.

Washington's division had hardly begun its march before the weather deteriorated. It rained, then sleeted and snowed, and all the while a razorlike wind lashed the men. The commander and the highest-ranking officers were astride horses, but the troops were on foot, and some were without shoes. After slogging several miles, the corps reached McConkey's Ferry on the ice-clogged river, where it would make the crossing that would put it in the lion's den with a river at its back. Eighteen field guns, 50 horses, and vast amounts of ammunition—cargo weighing 350 tons—made the river crossing on large ferries. The men were loaded into vessels ranging from small crafts to large Durham boats that ordinarily transported heavy loads of freight. A combination of experienced local rivermen and John Glover's Marblehead mariners got everyone and everything across safely. It was a stunning achievement. Three times during the year the army had accomplished seemingly impossible undertakings. Knox had transported unwieldy artillery from Ticonderoga to Boston, the trapped army had been rescued through a treacherous crossing from Brooklyn to Manhattan, and now this. Once across the river, the men faced another long, cold slog. One recalled Washington coming down the line and in a "deep and solemn voice" saying, "Soldiers, keep by your officers. For God's sake, keep by your officers!" The army reached Trenton close to sunrise, hours later than planned. But they had made it. Unbeknownst to Washington, the two other rebel forces had failed to get across the swiftly flowing icy river. Washington's force alone would make the attack.[91]

The Hessian garrison had not stirred. The enemy's sluggishness was not because they were sleeping off Christmas revelry, as was once imagined. Their commander, Colonel Johann Rall, had let down his guard. Contempt for the rebels partially accounted for his carelessness, though he had also been advised by the British that the rebels lacked the provisions needed for a surprise attack. To boot, Rall thought it unimaginable that an army could get across the icebound Delaware River on a stormy night.[92]

At 8:00 A.M., under a leaden, snow-filled sky, Washington cried out, "Advance and charge." Three divisions struck seconds after American artillery began pounding the slumbering enemy. Rall leaped from his bed and sought to organize an effective response, including a fallback into a nearby orchard. Some of his men fought and fought hard, though in the estimation of General Knox "the hurry, fright, and confusion" of the surprise attack crippled their response. The battle was over quickly. More than 100 enemy troops lay dead or wounded, and 900 were captured. Rall was among the dead. Washington had scored his first battlefield victory in this war and taken his first step toward redemption.[93]

When Washington learned a couple of days later that the Hessians in nearby Burlington and Bordentown had abandoned their cantonments and, in disarray, had taken flight, he persuaded a council of war to agree to once again cross the Delaware to go after them. Weather delayed the operation until December 31. When he reached Trenton, Washington learned that the Hessians were long gone and that Cornwallis, with about 8,000 men, was coming after him from Princeton. Another council of war voted to stay and fight. Washington posted his army on sloping ground behind the Assunpink Creek, which was flowing swiftly and could be crossed in only a few places. The rebels had brought over a vast amount of artillery and, in the wake of his men's performance at Throg's Neck, Pell's Point, and White Plains, Washington was willing to hazard all by putting his men in a strong defensive position.

Cornwallis arrived late in the afternoon of January 2. All he had to do was seal the exits in this bucolic area and Washington, yet again, would be trapped. But Cornwallis, a warrior through and through, never shrank from a battle. Besides, he possessed a considerable numerical superiority, 8,000 against 5,000, with 40 percent of his adversary's army consisting of militiamen. Cornwallis's thirst to fight on this day may also have been spurred by the relative ease of the British victories on Long Island and at Fort Washington, and frustration at having been denied the chance to fight during his pursuit of Washington through New Jersey.

Cornwallis ordered an assault at two crossings. Hessian grenadiers were the first to try to cross, advancing into what Knox called an artillery "salute" and a blast of small-arms fire that took a heavy toll, stopping the advance in its tracks. The survivors, stepping over comrades who lay in the cold, blood-soaked water, fell back. Cornwallis poured in shock troops. They, too, were cut down without getting across. He ordered attack after attack. Each failed. The horror was halted only when darkness draped the landscape. In an hour of mayhem 365 of the king's soldiers—5 percent of the men who had marched to the Assunpink—had been sacrificed to their commander's obstinacy. Cornwallis's bravado had not diminished, however. "We've got the Old Fox safe now. We'll go over and bag him in the morning," he exclaimed. His vow to "go over" suggests that he planned more bloody forays for the next day, but he did not get the chance. Washington's army slipped away that night, skirting Cornwallis's eastern flank. The force was led under cover of deep darkness by Colonel Joseph Reed, a Princeton graduate familiar with the region's back roads. (General Clinton later charged, with justification, that Washington "could not possibly have escaped . . . had only a single patrol been sent to feel for him.")[94] Washington's destination was Princeton, which he hoped to reach before Cornwallis learned of his flight. The rebels left campfires burning on the empty hillside throughout the night to deceive Cornwallis. The ploy worked. Cornwallis did not learn that the fox was gone until the next morning.

By then, Washington's army was approaching Princeton, where only a small British force remained. Washington hoped to catch them by surprise, but during the night Cornwallis had sent for more men to pour into the meat grinder on the Assunpink. At 8:00 A.M., in the dappled sunlight of the early winter morning, Washington's force ran into a 700-man British unit headed for Trenton. Though badly outnumbered, the British fought. When they made a bayonet charge, the sight of which often caused panic in the rebel lines, Washington personally rushed forward into the fray. At one point he was under fire from enemy troops only 50 or so feet away. The overwhelmed British soon broke and ran for nearby Princeton. For a change, it was the Americans who now pursued their enemy. The British mounted a stiff resistance in Princeton and the fighting continued until deep into the morning, but the rebels were more numerous and the king's troops were doomed to fail. When the engagement ended, 450 British had been killed, wounded, or captured. Thirty-seven Americans were dead and an equal number had been wounded. "It was a glorious day," wrote one of the unscathed rebel soldiers, a day "I would not have been absent from . . . for all the money I ever expect to be worth."[95]

The events of that pivotal week revived Washington's spirits. As he ended the campaign of 1776 by taking his army into winter quarters in Morristown, he could only hope that his sensational triumphs had boosted his countrymen's wilting morale. The reversals certainly caused concern in the enemy camp. Ambrose Serle, Howe's secretary, had in July referred to Washington as "a little paltry Colonel of Militia at the Head of a Banditti of Rebels." In August he had drolly reflected on the rebels' cowardice. In November Serle was convinced that the taking of New York City and Fort Washington had given rise to the "dying Groans of Rebellion." But in January, after Trenton and Princeton, his earlier panache gave way to an acknowledgment that Washington's triumphs would "revive the drooping Spirits of the Rebels."[96]

The British had lost about 2,000 men during the last disastrous week of the year's campaign. In the five months since landing on Staten Island, more than

3,500 British troops—a tenth of Howe's army—had been killed or wounded. Howe had taken New York City and all of Manhattan and Newport—which a Clinton-led expedition occupied in December—as well as a sliver of New Jersey. But Howe had not destroyed the Continental army.

The daring that Washington had exhibited had been handsomely rewarded. Howe, too, had scored a major victory when he had acted with audacity in assailing Fort Washington, but for the most part he had campaigned in 1776 in a feckless manner. Crushing the American rebellion had likely been within Britain's grasp in 1775 had the informed advice offered by General Gage been followed by the British government. Given the inexperience of the rebels' military leaders and soldiers, and the woeful shortages that plagued the Continental army, the British had an even better chance to crush the insurgency in 1776. But through sluggishness, misjudgments, and excessive caution, Howe permitted a series of propitious openings to slip through his fingers. Bunker Hill, to a greater extent than any other factor, had put Howe on a fast train toward failure. It pulled into the station in the campaign of 1776.

Shortly after Princeton, Thomas Paine, in the second installment of *The American Crisis*, posed a salient question to General Howe: "By what means, may I ask, do you expect to conquer America? If you could not effect it in the summer, when our army was less than yours, nor in the winter, when we had none, how are you to do it?"[97] It was a question that soon would also be raised in London, Versailles, and Madrid.

CHAPTER 5

EUROPEAN AID
AND PLANNING FOR
CAMPAIGN 1777

EARLY IN 1777 WASHINGTON learned of the arrival of French ships "deeply laden" with cargoes to assist the American war effort. There were muskets, mostly in "very fine" condition, as well as powder, uniforms, blankets, and shoes. American merchants and American privateers also delivered goods, including items that had long been scarce in civilian markets.[1]

Some of the more conventional commerce had its origin in deals concluded in Europe or the Caribbean by American agents under contract with Congress. In other instances, European merchants, usually from France or Spain, sent commodities that they hoped to trade for American products, chiefly tobacco. The first fruits of Spanish assistance arrived late in 1776, and by New Year's Day, New England longshoremen had already unloaded 100,000 flints, 45,000 pounds of lead for shot, and 1,000 blankets sent from Bilbao. Not everything sent by Spain landed in east coast ports. Some goods came through New Orleans, where they were purchased by American merchants and transported up the Mississippi and Ohio Rivers to Fort Pitt.[2]

By March 1777 five of Beaumarchais's vessels were at sea, their cargo holds crammed with sufficient arms and clothing to outfit an army of 30,000 men. As they plowed the ocean, additional ships were being loaded at French ports. Before summer 200 pieces of field artillery, 30,000 light flintlock muskets, and thousands of bayonets and tents had been transported by Beaumarchais's fictitious Roderigue Hortalez et Compagnie. When *Mercure*, the first of its vessels, docked in Portsmouth, New Hampshire, in March, three New England states descended like vultures on the cargo. That prompted Congress to take steps to assure that in the future there would be an orderly dispersion of the precious stores. When *Amphitrite*, the next Beaumarchais ship, also docked in Portsmouth, Congress ordered that its haul of 6,200 muskets and 52 cannon be delivered to the Springfield armory.[3]

Months before Beaumarchais's first ships reached America, Congress had appointed three commissioners to conduct American diplomacy in Europe. The move was in response to Richard Henry Lee's resolution urging not only independence but also that Congress take "effectual measures" to secure foreign alliances. While Thomas Jefferson drafted a declaration of independence, another committee prepared what came to be known as the Model Treaty, a guide for American envoys in Europe. John Adams was the workhorse on that committee, and the document it produced, which Congress adopted in September, sanctioned commercial treaties. It was silent with regard to alliances, a nod toward the deeply held belief that American independence was a step toward escaping European monarchs and their interminable wars. Congress also shied away from a treaty of alliance with France from fear that the French in return would demand territorial concessions in North America. In fact, Adams's prototype sought to have all European commercial partners recognize that the new United States would consist of all of British America, including Canada and every inch of territory to the Mississippi River. Above all, Adams and Congress understood that a commercial treaty would provoke Britain to declare war on France, and in addition to trade, getting the French into the war was their primary goal.[4]

Late in September 1776, following the abortive meeting with Admiral Howe on Staten Island, and near the time the British army landed on Throg's Neck, Congress selected its diplomats. Silas Deane, who had been in France since late spring, was an easy choice, as was Benjamin Franklin, the most renowned American and a man with diplomatic experience. Congress asked Jefferson to be the third member of the team, but he declined, pleading that he could not abandon his gravely ill wife. Congress then chose Richard Henry Lee's brother, Arthur Lee, who had spent much of the past 15 years in Great Britain earning degrees in medicine and the law, and serving as an agent for Massachusetts in London while funneling intelligence to Congress's Committee of Secret Correspondence.

Believing it "highly probable that France means not to let the United States sink in the present Contest," Congress instructed the diplomats to seek a commercial treaty and "to procure . . . either by purchase or loan" eight "well manned" ships of the line. The envoys were also directed to give Spain "the Strongest Assurances" that the United States had no designs on its "dominions in South America."[5]

All three commissioners were in Paris by Christmas, but as this was the age of sail and not a time of speed-of-light communication, the diplomats were unaware of the war crisis that had descended on the United States in the last weeks of 1776. It was not until March 1777 that the commissioners learned of Congress's frantic appeal to make whatever concessions were necessary to bring France into the war. The envoys lived in Paris for about 60 days, but late in February Jacques-Donatien Le Ray de Chaumont, a successful entrepreneur deep into the business of funneling supplies to America, invited all three envoys to reside in the Hôtel de Valentinois, one of the dwellings on his sprawling estate in suburban Passy. Deane and Franklin immediately moved in, though Lee chose to live separately. Deane and Franklin, who had known each other while serving in Congress, worked relatively well together. Lee was another matter. Suspicious of everyone and everything, Lee was spiteful and quarrelsome, and seldom heard a conspiracy theory he didn't like. Deane and Franklin grew to despise him. After a year of coping with Lee, an utterly exasperated Franklin warned him that his "Sick Mind" was leading him to think others "mean you ill, wrong you, or fail in Respect to you," an outlook that could only "end in Insanity." Before his diplomatic mission concluded, Franklin was certain that Lee was in fact insane.[6]

Three days after Christmas 1776 the commissioners met for the first time with Comte de Vergennes, a secret conclave in Paris, not Versailles, lest the British, who had spies everywhere, learned of the meeting. During the fall, when reports of Britain's military success on Long Island reached Vergennes, he had grown deeply alarmed about American capabilities. By December, his outlook had improved. He knew nothing of what had occurred recently, but he was buoyed by knowledge that Washington's army had survived into October as well as by Franklin's rose-tinted information that Congress would field an army of 68,000 men in the campaign of 1777. Vergennes was akin to a man on a tightrope. He wished to avoid war with England in 1777, but he also wanted to keep the war in America going in order to deplete Britain's strength and, possibly, compel London to grant American independence. Vergennes opened the meeting with the commissioners by pouring on treacle. He lauded Franklin for his many achievements, Deane for his good judgment and cooperation, and Lee for his zealous work in London on behalf of the insurgency. The meeting was cordial—he "treated us . . . with all civility," the envoys subsequently reported—though Vergennes refused both the Americans' request for a commercial treaty and several ships of the line. France must be "cautious of giving Umbrage to England," he confided, but acknowledged that French ports were open to commerce with the Americans in items not on Britain's contraband list. Vergennes also consented to a loan of two million livres and arranged for the Americans to meet with the Farmers General, an association of French bankers and businessmen. Seventy-five days later, negotiations with that consortium resulted in a contract for two million livres in exchange for 400 hogsheads of American tobacco. Before year's end the commissioners also met with Spain's ambassador to France, who they felt seemed "well dispos'd toward us." The Spanish envoy's hands were tied, given that Carlos III viewed "an approaching War with Reluctance." While the ambassador made no commitments, he allowed that the "Cry of [his] Nation is for us."[7]

Exuberant at their good start, Lee in February traveled to Spain and met the Spanish foreign minister in Burgos, halfway between the French border and Madrid. Spain, like France, was not ready for war, but it, too, was prepared to furnish more secret aid to the Americans. Out of this meeting, Diego María de Gardoqui, head of a mercantile company in Bilbao, became Spain's counterpart of Beaumarchais. With funds provided by the Spanish government, Gardoqui soon furnished money and supplies—including uniforms, munitions, muskets, shoes, and blankets—to the Americans, all of which was to be exchanged for "strong Virginia tobacco."[8]

Although French largesse had been nothing short of spectacular, the American envoys were bitterly disappointed by Vergennes's refusal to consent to a commercial treaty or to sell or loan the ships of war that could protect America's commerce. While Lee was away, Deane and Franklin debated whether to press the issue. Franklin favored a "patient perseverance, and to wait events." Deane argued for "warm and urgent solicitations." In the end Franklin acquiesced, perhaps because his colleague was more experienced in dealing with the French. Without greater military supplies, they told Vergennes in two memorandums, it might soon become "hardly possible" for the United States to wage war. Furthermore, if serious setbacks occurred due to a lack of supplies, the "Minds of the People" in America "may become more inclined to listen to terms of Accommodation" proffered by London. Should America opt for peace, they also warned, Britain would then turn "the War against France." On March 14 the three rebel envoys received their initial communiqués from home, including Congress's directive to do whatever was necessary to lure France into the war. Aware at last of the grave situation at home, the commissioners proposed a military alliance in return for a restoration of some of the American territory lost by France and Spain in the Seven Years' War. Vergennes spurned the offer, explaining yet again that France was not ready to enter into hostilities.[9]

Clearly, scare tactics would not move Vergennes. Events, good or ill, would dictate the course France would take. Thereafter, Franklin and Deane, often at variance with Lee, mostly waited and hoped that France would come around. Franklin at times has been depicted as having achieved the impossible in France. There is no question that he was wildly popular. He sat for portraits and his image appeared on dishes, medals, mementos, even chamber pots. He was lauded as "the most distinguished character in Europe," the "ornament of the New World," and the embodiment of American republicanism with all its hopes of transforming the sordid world. Franklin had been a self-promoter since his arrival in Philadelphia in 1723 as a nearly penniless 18-year-old. Once in France, he traded his powdered wig for a soft martin fur hat he had acquired during his mission to Canada early in 1776. The hat was the customary paraphernalia of American backwoodsmen, especially trappers, and Franklin took to wearing it indoors and out, a conscious effort to present himself as the denizen of primitive America, a land of rustics who were struggling in a cruel world to attain liberty and freedom. The French public was unaware that Franklin was living a life of affluence, waited on by nine servants, conveyed by a hired coachman, delighting in a wine cellar stocked with more than 1,000 bottles, and dining daily at a lavishly filled table.

Franklin's posturing charmed the French. He became, as historian Jonathan Dull observed, the "soothing public face" of the American Revolution and the new American nation, and he succeeded in arousing popular fervor for the American insurgency. That is not to say that the good will he inspired pressured Vergennes to act imprudently or that the skillful Franklin manipulated France's foreign minister. Vergennes was experienced, accomplished, and savvy, and his loyalty was to his king and France's national interest. He was not bamboozled by Franklin. Vergennes thought Franklin was impeccably honest, though there is no indication that he came to see him as an exceptional diplomat. Franklin was 70 when he arrived in France, and age, plus a host of physical ills, chiefly gout and kidney stones, at times took their toll on his energy and activities. He abhorred conflict—"I hate Disputes. I am old, and cannot have long to live, have much to do and no time for Altercation," he said in 1778—and that character trait led Vergennes to criticize him for not doing a better job of restraining his sometimes intemperate colleagues. Franklin's greatest flaws, however, were his trusting nature and his unawareness of the British spies all about him who at times took advantage of his heedlessness. The French understood this and were careful not to divulge any secrets to the American commissioners, a secrecy that hindered better relations. Franklin's diplomacy did not move mountains, but no American diplomat ever served at a more vital time in the nation's history, and during the pivotal year of 1777 he merited the trust placed in him by Congress.[10]

THE DISASTERS ON THE first day of the war and at Bunker Hill led Britain's press to prepare its citizenry for a long, bloody, and costly war. But news of Howe's capture of New York City and his sensational conquests of Forts Washington and Lee, as well as word of the miseries suffered by rebel soldiers, led the loyal press to report early in 1777 that the war could not last much longer and the coming campaign would be the final one. There was even a touch of sympathy for ordinary colonists beguiled by the "barbarous" Continental Congress and deceived soldiers who suffered agonizing privations of "common Necessaries." When accounts reached London that Washington had perished toward the end of 1776, one newspaper published a sympathetic obituary that lauded his courage and skill. Once it was discovered that Washington was very much alive, the press savaged him as a "tyrant" who had secured dictatorial powers. The pro-war segment of Britain's press contended that rebel military forces were destitute of every conceivable provision and could not last much longer. Once Philadelphia fell, which many anticipated would happen that winter, the war would be over, according to many press accounts. Newspapers proclaimed that the "three great incendiaries"—Franklin, Samuel Adams, and John Hancock—would pay the ultimate price for their folly and all others who had served in Congress would be exiled from the British Empire.[11]

The English public also anticipated good news from General Guy Carleton. By late summer 1776 it knew that he had driven the rebel army out of Canada. More successes were foreseen. Lord Germain shared those expectations. He looked forward to word that Carleton had kept moving through the autumn, taking Fort Ticonderoga at the southern narrows of Lake Champlain and advancing all the way to Albany. The American secretary envisaged 1776 ending with the "Rebel Army between two Fires." It would be snared betwixt Carleton's army in Albany and Howe's in Manhattan at the southern end of the Hudson River.[12]

That had not occurred. Carleton had missed opportunities in the spring of 1776 to destroy the tattered and retreating rebel army, though by June he had descended to Fort St. John on the Richelieu River, some 120 miles north of Ticonderoga. He paused there to construct warships and transports to convey his army up Lake Champlain. Meanwhile, the Americans, under General Philip Schuyler, commander of the army's Northern Department, were building their own fleet. By September, Carleton's vessels were ready, though he displayed scant optimism. The rebels had built a "considerable naval force," he moaned, and he suggested that the lateness of the season would likely prevent him from attacking Ticonderoga, much less advancing to Albany. The two hastily fashioned navies clashed on Lake Champlain in October. Carleton had 20 gunboats. The Americans, under Benedict Arnold, had 16. Arnold performed valiantly during the 24-hour fray, but British experience and numbers prevailed. Although both sides suffered damage and losses, the 10,000 British and German troops in Carleton's transports were unscathed.

Carleton now faced the decision of risking an attack on Ticonderoga, a fortress that long had been thought so impregnable that many called it the "Gibraltar of America." Generally accurate intelligence reported that there were upwards of 14,000 rebel defenders at Ticonderoga. (There were actually 12,000.) The two sides were about evenly matched in terms of numbers, although nearly every soldier under Carleton was a regular. Carleton ultimately decided against an attack or a siege, rejecting both alternatives on the grounds that if successful, it would be difficult to supply the troops garrisoned at Fort Ticonderoga throughout northern New York's long, fearsome winter. Not all his officers agreed. General William Phillips, head of Carleton's corps of artillery, believed an assault would succeed given the history of "very strong panic" displayed by the rebel soldiery since May. Phillips also insisted that "every art of war should be practiced upon these people, whose ignorance renders stratagem and surprise so easy to succeed." General Burgoyne, who had unsuccessfully advocated sending a "powerful" diversionary force from Lake Ontario via Oswego to pull away some of Ticonderoga's defenders, concurred with Phillips's "great displeasure" at Carleton's having not risked something. Since May, Carleton had been exceedingly cautious and he remained so at this critical juncture. After 13 days of brooding vacillation—and at around the same moment that Howe reined in Cornwallis in New Jersey, enabling Washington's army to escape across the Delaware—Carleton pulled his forces back to Canada. It was a decision that astonished "the whole army," according to a senior German officer.[13]

Word of Washington's victories at Trenton and Princeton, and news that northern New York had not been invaded, reached London at more or less the same time in late winter. The disclosures were discouraging, but the king, Germain, and the ministry remained staunch supporters of continuing the war. George III believed the public was willing to "bear the burden of another year of war," confident it would be the last year of hostilities. Lord North and his cabinet shared that confidence. With considerable armies in Manhattan and Canada, and additional ships on the way to Lord Howe, sweeping victories were anticipated in 1777 that would finally crush the American insurgency. North was aware that France was sending war supplies to the Americans and rebel vessels were carrying tobacco and other commodities to the Continent, but he believed Britain's stronger navy could largely suppress the clandestine trade that sustained the rebel resistance. He was also convinced that France would not enter the war in 1777.[14]

London's *Annual Register* reported that "a majority of the people gave at least a kind of tacit approbation" to the continuation of hostilities in 1777. The mood was one of sapping disappointment that the war had to go on, but the populace was resigned to one last year of fighting. Even the Rockingham Whigs, who had led the opposition to Lord North's American policy, reined in their public disapproval, though most still thought the war would end "fatally" for Great Britain once the public realized "the calamitous State we are in." Edmund Burke, a leader in the bloc, put it another way: "No good can come of any Event in this War."[15]

Despite Burke's frequent condemnation of the war in Parliament, two years of hostilities had left him overwhelmed with doubt concerning the American rebels' chances of success. Burke, in a private letter to Rockingham in January 1777, expressed astonishment that the colonial insurgency had survived this long and added that he had come to believe the days of American resistance were numbered. It was "now evident that they cannot look standing Armies in the Face," he said, adding that the rebels were "inferior in everything," their "grand Army" couldn't field more than 12,000 men, and their militia was "not wonderfully well composed, or disciplined." Washington shrank from "a general engagement, prudently enough," he went on, but at best such a strategy would only "delay their ruin." Burke was wrong in one regard. He believed the rebels would receive little foreign assistance. In fact, he thought the real purpose behind Congress's dispatch of Franklin to Paris was to negotiate with Britain's ambassador "on the Basis of a dependance on this Crown. This I take to be his Errand." If that was Congress's intent, Burke though it might succeed, as the Americans were "impaird but not perfectly ruind." He even considered going to France to meet with Franklin to learn if the Rockingham Whigs might "be made a sort of Mediatours of the Peace."[16] But his faction's leaders opposed such a trip and he did not cross to Paris.

Not everyone in England was happy with having to endure another year of war. Many merchants and manufacturers had done without their colonial trade for two years. Furthermore, during the past 12 months or so, American privateers had captured 90 British vessels at sea, ships valued at £576,000. The worth of the lost cargoes was incalculable, but surely enormous, and insurance rates had risen precipitously. Restiveness was also apparent in towns that sent fishing fleets to the Grand Banks. The loss of imports from the colonies made grain prices soar, causing concern. Interest rates were inching upward and shortages of capital were beginning to pinch. The landed classes in England were long accustomed to paying a land tax, but it had increased when the war began. Whereas about 12 percent of the government's revenue in peacetime came from the land tax, by 1777 it was approaching 25 percent. Like others, landowners also paid poor rates and levies for the state church, and those taxes had increased as well. Despite the squeeze they felt, these disparate elements continued to support the war, though many in all likelihood agreed with John Wilmot, who represented Tiverton in Devonshire in the House of Commons. One more year until victory, said Wilmot, but if victory was not secured in 1777, he could not support the continuation of a war that had already cost "twenty millions of money . . . and the too certain prospect of future calamities."[17]

While the belief abounded in England that 1777 would be the war's final year, General Howe planned his strategy for that decisive year. He was aware that London expected it to be the final year of hostilities and that northern New York had not been invaded in 1776. With these things in mind, Howe, on November 30, a month before Britain's misfortunes at Trenton and Princeton, sent his plan for the campaign of 1777 to Germain.[18]

It was cogent and bold. Howe called for multipronged strikes by his army while Carleton invaded New York and descended to Albany. Howe proposed that a force of 10,000 in Newport drive northward, seizing Providence and conducting devastating raids along the Massachusetts coast as it advanced toward Boston. A "defensive army" of 8,000 would meanwhile complete the pacification of eastern New Jersey. A third force of 10,000 would simultaneously move up the Hudson River, destroying rebel installations in the Highlands en route to linking with the army that had taken Albany. With the Hudson River in British hands, the ties between the four New England colonies and the remaining nine provinces would be severed. Following his successful summer campaign, Howe foresaw leaving 2,000 men in Newport and 5,000 in New York to protect those vital bases while the bulk of his army turned its attention toward Georgia and South Carolina. During the winter, he would stamp out the last vestiges of the colonial insurgency in those provinces. As his army was to be "much divided," Howe requested an additional 15,000 men. If necessary, they might be either Russians or Hessians.[19]

Wars are filled with unexpected occurrences, but even without reinforcements Howe's plan offered a realistic possibility of gaining the decisive victory that would crush the rebellion. The threats posed by the force in eastern New England and that which was ascending the Hudson might have drawn off sufficient Continentals and Yankee militia to enable the British force descending from Canada to take Albany. The army in New Jersey in all likelihood would have tied down militia in the mid-Atlantic provinces that otherwise would have been destined to join with Washington's army. Sometime that summer Washington's army—fighting along the Hudson River against a numerically superior foe supported by the Royal Navy—would be caught "between two Fires," as Germain had anticipated.

Germain did not receive the proposal until the end of December, by which time Howe had drafted another plan that he would turn to in the event that reinforcements were not being sent. His claim that the size of his army dictated whether his initial plan could be implemented is questionable. Given the unequivocal pressure from London to win the war in 1777, Howe likely had second thoughts about achieving that goal through his original plan. After all, the Canadian invasion army would have to capture Fort Ticonderoga, a task that most thought would be a prolonged undertaking. In fact, Howe in his new plan said, "We must not look for the northern army to reach Albany before the middle of September," after which it would have to be taken through battle or siege. Such a late date, or conceivably even a later one, would make it difficult—and probably impossible—to gain a decisive victory in 1777. London's expectations in all likelihood drove Howe to envisage a new plan, one that was radically different and, at least in part, conceived in the belief that the rebellion could be suppressed in 1777 only by crushing Washington's army.

Taking Philadelphia was to be Howe's primary objective in the second plan he dispatched to Germain. He thought he could accomplish the undertaking with an army of 19,000. He believed his new plan would guarantee the moment-of-truth engagement with Washington, for the rebel commander would have to defend Philadelphia, the home of Congress and a major port of entry for provisions being sent from abroad to sustain the rebellion. Writing prior to Washington's victories in Trenton and Princeton, Howe said that morale had ebbed among Pennsylvania's rebels and would be obliterated through the capture of Philadelphia. Howe now spoke of sending only a small diversionary force of 3,000 into the Hudson

Highlands to facilitate to "some degree" the southward advance of the British invasion army from Canada.[20] The talk of forming a junction with the Canadian army had vanished, as had most of the actions that were to have diverted rebel forces from defending against the invasion of New York and capture of the Hudson.

On January 20, not yet having learned of Germain's response to his initial plan but aware that rebel morale had rebounded in the wake of Washington's "unfortunate" victories in Trenton and Princeton, Howe composed a third plan, in which he elaborated on campaigning to take Philadelphia. He foresaw a two-pronged invasion of Pennsylvania, one force crossing the Delaware and advancing on Philadelphia from the north while a second force sailed up the Delaware River and threatened the city from the south. As Trenton and Princeton had "thrown us farther back" by guaranteeing rebel success in recruiting a larger army, Howe now asked for 20,000 reinforcements. He never mentioned the British army that would invade New York from Canada.[21]

In March, Howe received Germain's response to the first plan he had drafted 100 days earlier. The American secretary approved Howe's "well-digested" plan of numerous offensives, but said there was not the "least chance" that he could dispatch 15,000 additional troops.[22] Howe quickly responded with a fourth and final plan. Philadelphia remained his target and he would invade Pennsylvania by sea, though given the lack of reinforcements, New Jersey would have to be abandoned. What is more, the Canadian army would have to fend for itself. However, given the likely size of the invasion army and the large number of Loyalists that would take up arms for their king, that force should face "no difficult task" in seizing Albany.[23] The bold plan of November was gone. The hope of crushing the rebellion and ending the war in 1777 would now hang on two threads: the success of an unaided army in reaching Albany and Howe's ability to defeat Washington in an epic engagement outside Philadelphia.

On assuming office as American secretary, Germain had vowed that the commanders "serving on the spot . . . are the proper judges" of strategy and tactics.[24] He had adhered to his vow throughout 1776 and by year's end had been severely disappointed with some outcomes. He expressed his "great mortification" at Carleton's failure to do more to utterly destroy the rebel army in Canada or to attempt the conquest of Fort Ticonderoga. Similarly, Germain found Howe's failure to trap Washington's army in New Jersey and the costly losses at Trenton and Princeton to be "extremely mortifying."[25]

Given these misfortunes, Germain might have played a bolder role in shaping Britain's strategy for 1777, especially as he was able to meet with Generals Burgoyne and Clinton when both returned to London that winter to tend to personal and professional business. Germain, who had long harbored a cranky dislike of Carleton, stripped him of command of the army in Canada, though he left him in his position as governor of Quebec. The American secretary first turned to Clinton as Carleton's successor in commanding the invasion army from Canada. Although Clinton craved advancement and an independent command, he somewhat mysteriously declined the appointment, saying simply that Burgoyne was more familiar with the region. It was more likely that Clinton, who had long since remarked on the hazards of campaigning in the menacing American backcountry and had a good idea of Howe's plans, looked with foreboding on the venture. Germain then named Burgoyne to command that force. Burgoyne had previously met with both the American secretary and the king, and had outlined a plan for the invasion of New York in a lengthy written document. Aware only of Howe's initial plan, Burgoyne foresaw that "the sole purpose of the Canadian army was to effect a junction with General Howe."[26]

While Germain was digesting Burgoyne's plan, he conferred often with Clinton. Germain by then was aware that Howe not only had proposed a campaign to take Philadelphia but also no longer planned substantial diversions in the Hudson Highlands to assist Burgoyne. Germain asked if Clinton thought General Washington could be drawn into a set-piece battle of the sort that Howe foresaw. "[H]e was a fool if he did," Clinton answered. Germain then asked about the wisdom of taking Philadelphia. Clinton thought it imprudent. For one thing, securing the city after it was taken would immobilize a huge chunk of the army. Besides, the more important objective should be "a vigorous exertion of the two British armies on the Hudson." A campaign in which Burgoyne received no support from Howe, Clinton added, would be to "hazard . . . a miscarriage." Germain also asked if Clinton thought Howe could take Philadelphia and still have time to advance up the Hudson in support or Burgoyne's descent. Clinton did not think so.[27]

In March, after reading Howe's first three plans and consulting with Burgoyne and Clinton, Germain appeared unruffled. He approved Howe's third plan and— ignoring Clinton's opinion that Howe could not campaign for Philadelphia and advance up the Hudson in the same season—his orders to Burgoyne were unequivocal: "proceed with all expedition to Albany" to "join General Howe." There was no hint that Germain conceived of the potentially formidable obstacles that

Burgoyne might encounter. With "a view of quelling the rebellion as soon as possible," Germain added in his orders to Burgoyne that "it is become necessary that the most speedy junction of the two armies should be effected."[28] Inscrutably, Germain never issued such a stark directive to Howe.

Two years into the war, Germain cleaved to nearly the same tainted view of the rebels' military capabilities that had pervaded the ministry on the eve of hostilities. In March 1777, he allowed that the "military conduct of the rebels has been such as must infallibly make them appear contemptible in the eyes of a soldier."[29] His thinking was doubtless shaped by the rebels' poor showing on Long Island and at Kip's Bay, and the disastrous decision to defend Fort Washington. There was truth in what he said, but his thinking overlooked the experience that the rebel leaders had gained in two years of war. It also ignored that foreign assistance, which could not be hidden from the British, would leave American forces better armed and provisioned than ever before. Never wavering from his vow to leave strategic decisions to his commander in the field, Germain said that he trusted Howe as a "competent judge" of his chances of taking Philadelphia and in the same campaign season having "time . . . to cooperate with the army ordered to proceed from Canada" to Albany.[30] That assumption strained credulity. He should have listened to Clinton, who had two years of American campaigning under his belt. Clinton knew that invading Pennsylvania would be a formidable and time-consuming undertaking.

Opinion in Great Britain cried out for its military to bring an end to the American rebellion in 1777, and some believed the coming campaign would be nothing less than Britain's last chance to win the war. Germain was responsible for managing the war, formulating British military strategy, seeing to its execution, and in this instance coordinating a strategy that involved two armies operating in different theaters. As the implicit war minister, Germain failed egregiously in designing the approaching campaign. Britain's plans for the campaign of 1777 were built on quicksand.

AT THE OUTSET OF 1777 Washington informed Congress of his recent, and grand, victories at Trenton and Princeton. Not yet the Olympian figure he would become, and all too aware that some had recently questioned his leadership, Washington emphasized his roles in inflicting great damage on the enemy in Trenton, at the Assunpink, and in Princeton. In reporting on the loss of Fort Washington in

November, Washington had stressed that he acted on the "Advice of most of the General Officers," and especially on that of Nathanael Greene, whom he made the fall guy for the disaster. Now, however, Washington told Congress that his New Jersey triumphs came about because of "my expectation" and the actions that "I ordered."[31] If a bit hyperbolic, the final decisions had rested with Washington, and at great risk it had been his decision to cross back into New Jersey and engage the enemy. The hazards he ran had ended in successes that were crucial to America's cause.

Washington had no time to gloat. He faced problems on top of problems, the most immediate of which was to recruit men for his vanishing army. Few of those who had entered the Continental army for one year's service reenlisted. Washington had put his tiny army into winter quarters in Morristown, and it was safe. But the shortage of troops meant that he could do little more during that dismal winter than send out small detachments to remove horses, cattle, wagons, and grain in the vicinity of the British cantonments, and to harass British foraging parties. His great worry was that once the Delaware River froze, Howe might cross it and descend on Philadelphia, which Washington knew that he was powerless to defend with his "mix'd, motley crew." The "misfortune of short Inlistments, and an unhappy dependence upon Militia" tied his hands, he said. Congress had not heeded Washington's pleas for a standing army in 1775, but immediately after the trouncing the rebels suffered on Long Island, the delegates agreed to long-term enlistments. Yet recruiting was always a slow and uncertain process, and deep into the spring of 1777 Washington's army was in no position to take the field. Enveloped with despair, Washington wondered how "we shall be able to rub along till the New Army is raised." Grasping at straws, his answer was: "Providence has heretofore saved us in a remarkable manner, and on this we must principally rely."[32]

The army's often lamentable showing in 1776 had sent "A Shudder thro' the Continent," and Congress, as Ezra Styles, soon to be the president of Yale College, put it. Nearly every congressman now understood that "curs'd short inlistments" were ruinous. Only a standing army could develop "Able officers" who "are the Soul of any Army," said John Adams, adding that a "masterly Discipline" of the troops could be achieved only by "inlisting a permanent Body of Troops." "[S]hort inlistments has almost ruined us," said one congressman; a Virginia delegate thought that every state must now raise "new levies" of men committed to lengthy service. The new army was to consist of 88 battalions and 75,760 men, a bit more than Franklin told Vergennes would be raised in 1777.[33]

On the advice of William Tudor, the army's judge advocate, and Washington—who complained that the "Rules & Regulations of War" were "unfit... for the Government of an Army"—Congress also revised the Articles of War, incorporating many of the harsher practices that were allowed under the articles that governed the British army. Chiefly, the new articles provided for more draconian punishments. The maximum corporal punishment was increased from 39 to 100 lashes, and the number of capital crimes was drastically expanded. The original articles, adopted in 1775, authorized capital punishment only for desertion in combat and divulging information to the enemy. The new articles retained the two existing capital crimes and also permitted death sentences for desertion; inciting and engaging in mutiny; striking an officer; occasioning a false alarm; misbehavior before the enemy; casting away arms and ammunition; passing provisions, arms, and ammunition to the enemy; and forcing a commanding officer to surrender a post.[34]

Two weeks before his Christmas-night victory at Trenton, Washington had remarked that unless a new army was quickly raised, America's cause was hopeless. Throughout the winter, gloom pervaded his headquarters given the sluggishness with which recruiting proceeded. Time and again Washington lamented that he was in a position of "scarce having any Army at all." Saying that "Necessity obliges me," Washington in January raised the sensitive issue of conscription. The only way "to complete the new Levies [is] by draught, if they cannot be fill'd seasonably by voluntary inlistments," he said. He additionally justified taking the step by contending that with an adequate army he might inflict "a fatal stab" before reinforcements crossed the Atlantic. Conscription was not an idea that caught fire, and in April he anguished that the country would "never get any army assembled." That same month he told Congress, "I wish I could see any prospect of an Army," and he revealed to others that only the British army's lingering inactivity had prevented disaster. He rubbed along by persuading state governors to summon their militiamen to active duty, a step that most chief executives abhorred. "The Backwardness of the Continental levies obliges me, much against my Will, to call for a further Support from the Militia," Washington typically told one chief executive in April. With spring in bloom in May, he advised Congress that "we find ourselves greatly distressed for want of Men." A "strange unaccountable languor seems too generally to prevail" across the land, he exclaimed. In June, he said that if Howe took the field, it was "very unlikely, that any effectual opposition can be given" to the threat he posed. He also told Congress that the "shameful deficiency in all our Armies" gave him "disagreeable Apprehensions" about the coming campaign.[35]

Recruiting went forward, though it soon was clear that the army was nowhere near as large as Congress wished or Franklin had told Vergennes it would be. The notion of raising an army of 75,000 had been unrealistic, but it was reasonable to expect more than were finally raised. The ranks in 1777 topped out nearly 50 percent short of congressional expectations. But there were bright spots for Washington, including that in the end the army was roughly twice as large as in the previous summer. Congress also increased the number of artillery regiments and for the first time authorized Continental cavalry regiments, enabling Washington to raise 3,000 dragoons, or horse soldiers. During the winter lull, Washington, with Congress's approval, sought to reform the army's hospital system.[36]

Washington additionally readied his army for the summer's campaign by having the soldiery inoculated against smallpox, a deadly scourge that reached epidemic proportions during the first two years of the war. Inoculation had long been customary within the British army, and in 1775 Howe ordered his unvaccinated troops in besieged Boston to undergo the procedure. It could be risky, however, and Washington shrank from ordering it in the Continental army before 1777. But in February, aware that if unchecked the disease could have "calamitous consequences" for his army, Washington ordered that all unvaccinated men must be inoculated. He changed his mind a few days later, though after a week he reversed himself and again ordered the inoculation of his troops. He likely took the step because he learned that the fear of contracting smallpox in army camps was playing havoc with recruiting. The vaccine had been available for decades and long before the war enlightened colonists, including Franklin, Thomas Jefferson, and John Adams, had undergone the procedure, which involved days in quarantine but vested them with a lifetime immunity. Washington had no need for inoculation, having contracted smallpox in his teenage years. He had nearly died, but his tribulation paid off in that he, too, was immune thereafter. Finally resolving that his soldiery must be inoculated, Washington declared that necessity "require[d] the measure," for if the disease struck with its "usual virulence we should have more to dread from it than from the Sword of the Enemy." He also encouraged public officials to exhort civilians in their states to take the vaccine.[37]

Beginning in February, Washington's days were brightened by repeated tidings of the arrival of Beaumarchais's ships: A "French Vessel is arrived at Portsmouth with about Twelve Thousand Fire Arms . . . and other stores"; "A Brigg arrivd this day from Nantz her cargo consists of 272 chests of Arms" containing 6,800 muskets; "I congratulate you on the Arrival of a Vessel . . . from France, with eleven

Thousand Stand of Arms"; "A Vessell is just arriv'd at Boston with 12000 Stand of Arms 1000 Barls of Gun Powder &c &c from France." Occasionally privateers also brought captured British arms into American ports. "Glorious News," exclaimed Washington when he learned that two privateers had docked in Boston with dry goods worth £50,000.[38]

In May, however, Washington experienced an unprecedented problem. Silas Deane, in Paris, had without congressional authorization granted commissions in the Continental army to some 60 French officers. The first wave disembarked in America in the spring of 1777. Washington had little use for most of them, looking on them as officers of unproven capabilities who couldn't speak English. The greatest problem arose when Philippe du Coudray alighted in May accompanied by 18 other officers and 10 sergeants. He bore a commission as a major general that antedated that of three Continental army major generals: Sullivan, Greene, and Knox. If the commission awarded by Deane was adhered to, du Coudray would displace Knox as head of the army's artillery corps. All three American generals threatened to resign if Congress, which had the sole authority to appoint field grade officers, recognized du Coudray's commission. That dilemma was resolved when du Coudray fell into the Schuylkill River and drowned. But several other French volunteers remained. Already frayed by the stress of command, Washington told Congress that "skillful" engineers and artillerists would be "extremely useful," but otherwise he would be happy to see the remainder return home. It was Congress's problem to deal with. Congress understood that the presence of the officers could damage the army, but it also worried that the rejection of large numbers of French officers—some of whom were noblemen with friends in high places—could cause its French benefactors to sour on America's insurgency. Ultimately, Congress commissioned only four of the officers that Deane had sent, though it awarded commissions to six others dispatched by France's minister of war and the French army.[39]

One of the best that Congress accepted that year was Johann de Kalb, the secret agent that Duc de Choiseul had sent to America in 1768 to detect whether an American revolution was imminent. Congress commissioned him as a major general and he served with distinction until his death in battle three years later. The French officer taken on board that summer who would gain the greatest fame in this war was in many ways the least likely to achieve distinction. Marie-Joseph Paul Yves Roch Gilbert du Motier, Marquis de Lafayette, had met with Deane in December and, though five months shy of his twentieth birthday and with precious little military experience, was awarded the rank of major general. Lafayette arrived in

Philadelphia in July and was given the cold shoulder by the first several congressmen with whom he met. That ceased when Congress learned that Lafayette was from an eminent family that was close to the queen and his uncle was France's ambassador to Great Britain. When Lafayette said he wished no compensation and asked only to serve directly under Washington, Congress commissioned him as a major general. That very night Lafayette met Washington, who happened to be in Philadelphia, and the American commander welcomed the radiantly jaunty young man with kindness. Washington habitually looked on others in terms of what they could do for him and here was a young man who could be quite beneficial, possibly as a soldier, more assuredly through his contacts in Versailles. Lafayette, whom one scholar characterized as "an impressionable young man," in no time came to so admire Washington that he wanted "to think and act and speak like him" until in due course he "became a little like Washington."[40]

All winter and spring Washington wrung his hands over the enemy's intentions. In January and February he remained convinced that Howe would soon move against Philadelphia. "If he does not," Washington remarked late in February, he is "a Man of no enterprize." Puzzling over the mystery of why the British commander would "suffer us to remain unmolested," Washington guessed that it must be because Howe's army lacked sufficient horses. By March Washington had decided that Howe was waiting "for the Season to be a little more advanced," but expected him to strike "before we have an army to oppose 'em." A month later Washington speculated that Howe perhaps planned to attempt to link with Burgoyne's army in New York. Aware in late May that enemy troops were boarding transports in New York Harbor, Washington guessed that Howe's "first object" would be "possessing Hudson's River." If that wasn't the case, he must be about to sail to Philadelphia.[41]

It was neither, at least not at this juncture. "The Campaign is opening," Washington had said at the beginning of April. That had not been borne out. Now it was June. Five months had passed since Trenton and Princeton, and six months had elapsed since Howe called off Cornwallis's pursuit of Washington through New Jersey. All the while Howe had remained immobile. He offered an array of excuses for his inactivity. He was plagued by a lack of stores, tents, horses, and fodder for the equines. He also wished to await the return of Captain Nisbet Balfour, whom he had dispatched to London months before to attain firsthand information regarding the thinking of Germain and other officials. Balfour returned on May 8 with letters from Germain and word that the American secretary wanted Howe to act more aggressively, including launching raids on coastal Massachusetts and

New Hampshire, forays that would hinder rebel recruiting, erode morale, bottle up Yankee militiamen, and provide safeguards for British shipping. Germain's admonition did not nudge Howe into action. No coastal raids were conducted and another month passed before the army at last acted.[42]

On June 12, General Howe moved. The transports in New York Harbor delivered troops to Amboy on the Jersey coast. They quickly advanced to New Brunswick. There were now 18,000 enemy troops in New Jersey. Howe hoped Washington would assume that his objective was Philadelphia, a threat that might draw the Continental army into a set-piece battle or, if that failed, that the British could cut off some of the scattered Continental divisions. Sure that Howe was about to move on Philadelphia, Washington advanced from Morristown to Middlebrook to be nearer Howe's line of march toward the city. But Washington took up a safe position in the Watchung Mountains, moved his threatened divisions out of danger, and summoned reinforcements from Peekskill. Then he waited in the safety of his mountain den. He had more or less divined Howe's intent, and it led a high-ranking British officer to praise the American commander's "cool and prudent conduct." A week later, Howe tried again. He withdrew to Amboy, hoping the Americans would pursue his retreating army, a blunder that would enable the British to seal off Washington's retreat. Washington was fooled. But when he learned of skirmishing, he quickly withdrew to the safety of his mountain. That was enough for Howe. On June 26 he evacuated every British soldier in New Jersey.[43]

Howe's gambit was over and it left Washington mystified as to what his enemy had been up to. Perhaps Howe had sought to destroy portions of the American army. Maybe he had merely sought provisions. Possibly he had just wished to "plunder the Inhabitants & spread desolation." What was next on Howe's agenda? Washington did not know. He only knew that he likely would face "a very disagreeable dance."[44]

CHAPTER 6

THE CRITICAL MOMENT IS AT
HAND: THE 1777 CAMPAIGN

GENERAL JOHN BURGOYNE BOARDED *Apollo* in Portsmouth on April 2 for a voyage to Canada and the launching of the campaign of 1777. He lingered in Quebec briefly in early May before joining his army in Montreal. Burgoyne expected success on his venture up Lake Champlain and across land to Albany along the route that he and Lord Germain had agreed on.

Major General Burgoyne was 55 years old, 10 years older than General Washington. He had studied at Westminster School, a prestigious institution whose alumni included John Locke and numerous royal officials, and served with distinction in Britain's army for three decades, winning laurels in the European theater in the Seven Years' War. William Pitt had recommended Burgoyne as commander of the army's first cavalry regiment, created in 1758, and he had led the unit with courage and prudence. Throughout his life, Burgoyne had succeeded in nearly everything he had tried: He was happily married and his wife's dowry had furthered his advancement in the army; he had been elected to Parliament in 1762; he was drawn to the theater as a playwright, and his comedies about English society were popular; his good sense as a leader of men was widely acclaimed; and his luck as a risk-taker usually prevailed in war and at the gaming table, to which he was habitually drawn. Deep into middle age, Burgoyne remained strikingly handsome and impressively sophisticated and fashionable, an experienced officer who possessed all the tools, including self-confidence, to meet the challenges he was about to face.

Burgoyne was boundlessly optimistic. His encounters with the rebels in Canada the previous spring had convinced him that the adversary's amateurish leaders and callow soldiers were incapable of worthy opposition to a professionally led British army. Burgoyne's confidence had been bolstered by Germain's insistence that General Howe was to advance on Albany from the south as his invasion force descended from the north. It was a strategy designed to compel the enemy to divide its forces to meet the dual challenges. Before leaving London, Burgoyne was aware that Howe planned to campaign for Philadelphia and that Germain had approved the undertaking. But both the American secretary and Burgoyne expected Howe to take the field early in the spring, providing ample time for him to complete operations in Pennsylvania and strike into the Hudson Highlands during the summer. Burgoyne also anticipated that considerable numbers of Native Americans and New York Loyalists would assist his army, and that a diversionary force under Lieutenant Colonel Barry St. Leger would simultaneously invade New York farther to the west, taking some Continentals and many enemy militiamen out of the picture. St. Leger was to descend from Oswego on Lake Ontario, capture Fort Stanwix, and thereafter take the Mohawk River to its intersection with the Hudson, where he would unite with Burgoyne. So confident was Burgoyne that before leaving England, he had bet Charles James Fox 50 guineas that he would return victorious to London by the end of the year.[1]

Troubles piled up as Burgoyne prepared to set off, though he did not yet regret making the wager with Fox. His army was one-quarter smaller than he had expected. He had 7,300 men, not the 11,000 he had anticipated; instead of droves of Indian allies, only 400 warriors arrived. Faced with severe shortages of horses, wagons, tents, and baggage, he wrote to Germain that Governor Carleton had done little since the previous autumn to prepare for an invasion. These were surprises, though the greatest bombshell by far was his discovery that Howe did not plan to advance up the Hudson. Howe, in April, had notified Carleton that there would not be time for him to link up with Burgoyne. The notion that the armies of Burgoyne and Howe were to come together on the Hudson River had been the salient purpose of British strategy for 1777. That, now, was out of the question.[2]

Nevertheless, Burgoyne was hardly short of boldness or courage, and the gambler's streak in him persisted. He remained upbeat, his confidence boosted by the knowledge that nearly 1,000 Indians had rallied to St. Leger's side, Howe was leaving a force of some 7,000 in New York City under General Clinton that might provide help if needed, Carleton had found additional horses and wagons for him, and reinforcements from England had arrived in Quebec in early June. Both Burgoyne and his artillery commander, General Phillips, had believed that Fort Ticonderoga might have been captured in October. Now in possession of a larger army and stronger naval arm, both were confident that its fall was inevitable over the summer. Once that fortress, with its garrison, was taken, Burgoyne and Phillips felt that the push to Albany would be largely unimpeded. Phillips was so sanguine that he predicted an end to the "unhappy quarrel" with the colonists before New Year's Day.[3]

Burgoyne's army moved out during the second week in June. The first to shove off was an advance corps under Brigadier General Simon Fraser. The 48-year-old Fraser commanded the army's elite unit of marksmen, grenadiers, and light infantry. The bulk of the army followed. The right wing consisted of nearly 4,000 British troops under Phillips, a large, sinewy, tough, terrible-tempered veteran who tolerated no misconduct. On the left were some 3,100 Germans under 39-year-old Major General Friedrich Adolph Baron von Riedesel, whose wife of 15 years accompanied him on the expedition. The two wings reunited at Fort St. John, which Burgoyne had reclaimed from John Sullivan's retreating army a year earlier. At St. John, Burgoyne found his naval fleet of three heavy warships, a couple of schooners, four gondolas, and a large number of bateaux. Their ascent continued until June 17, when Burgoyne paused to regroup and to address his men. With plans on the table to attack Fort Ticonderoga, he proclaimed that it would be "our glory and preservation to storm" the stronghold. He enjoined his soldiers to rely "upon the bayonet," a tool "of the valiant" that would cause the amateurish rebels to take flight. Given their pronounced fear of bayonets, Burgoyne predicted that the rebels would "place their whole dependence in entrenchment and rifle pieces."[4]

Three days later, Burgoyne's armada dropped anchor at Cumberland Point, pausing to meet with the Indigenous braves who would accompany his army. Drawing on his theatrical background, Burgoyne donned his resplendent scarlet uniform and added every enhancement that officers customarily sported to amplify their authority. The Native Americans, likewise aware of the power of ornamentation, were adorned in war paint. Burgoyne urged them to "go forth in might and valor," but to exhibit restraint toward civilians. Given "your magnanimity of character," Burgoyne told them, he knew they would keep their scalping knives sheathed when encountering noncombatants. At the close of his energizing speech, the Indians shouted, "Etow! Etow!" They understood and would comply. Afterward, they performed a war dance and imbibed from Burgoyne's rum pot. While they

drained his liquor, Burgoyne drafted the "Proclamation to the American People."
He called the rebels "terrorists." In the same breath, he threatened to turn loose
"thousands" of Indians. Resistance to his advance, he warned, would result in
"Devastation, Famine, and every concomitant Horror" imaginable. Burgoyne's
force soon broke camp and moved south, with the Indians in their birch canoes in
the forefront.[5]

BURGOYNE EXPECTED VICTORY, BUT he also anticipated facing a demanding
challenge in taking Fort Ticonderoga, a post widely thought to be impregnable. In
fact, Fort Ticonderoga was somewhat less than indomitable. Twelve months earlier
rebel leaders discovered that the installation presented a "sorry sight." The British
had done little to maintain it following the removal of the French from North
America in 1763 and the Americans had done even less following its capture in the
spring of 1775. The threat posed by Carleton in 1776 stirred the Americans to
act, although General Anthony Wayne, who had taken command of the fort in
November, had only 1,413 men to put to work on tasks that required a vastly larger
number. Colonel Jeduthan Baldwin arrived in February 1777 and directed work
repairing the existing fortifications and building new ones. Although Baldwin had
constructed defenses during the Seven Years' War and siege of Boston, he was not a
trained military engineer. Colonel Thaddeus Kosciuszko, a veteran Polish officer
who had recently been commissioned in the Continental army as an "able engineer," arrived at Fort Ticonderoga in May 1777. He pronounced Baldwin's design
fundamentally flawed, in part because the defense of Mount Defiance, whose 853-
foot summit towered over the fortress, had been ignored.[6]

General Schuyler, who had commanded the army's Northern Department for
the past two years, was subsequently widely blamed for the woeful condition of
the fort. But he was chronically shorthanded. The fort was not threatened for
seven months after October 1776, and the Continental army—which melted away
as enlistments expired late in 1776—lacked the manpower to spare for a post that
was not menaced. From the fall of 1776 until the cusp of Burgoyne's arrival, never
more than 2,000 effectives garrisoned Fort Ticonderoga.[7]

While some in Congress worried that the fort might be fatally undermanned,
most remained convinced that the installation was unconquerable. It stood on a
promontory on Lake Champlain's quarter-mile-wide southern shore, a point
where any vessel that sought to pass was an easy target for the fortress's guns.

Furthermore, a boom composed of "sunken pieces of large timber" had been installed to connect the two shores and impede, or prevent, the progress of enemy ships seeking to run the gauntlet. Ticonderoga bristled with batteries, blockhouses, redoubts, and breastworks, some made of stone. Defenses had also been constructed on both Mount Independence to the southeast (which also commanded the lake and was actually a better choice as a defensive position than the fort itself) and Mount Hope on the northwest side. But no steps had ever been taken by the French, British, or Americans to keep an enemy from capturing lofty Mount Defiance, whose summit stood high above the passage between Lake Champlain and Lake George. Major General Arthur St. Clair, who took command of the fort in mid-June—just days before Burgoyne's arrival—was one of a long line of American commanders who thought Fort Ticonderoga was vulnerable, though not so much because Mount Defiance had been ignored. Aside from Kosciuszko, American officers held the prevailing view that the British could not get artillery up the rugged steep hill, and even if they accomplished that Herculean feat, their guns would not threaten the fort.

St. Clair was more worried about Baldwin's fortifications and his army's lack of manpower. Whereas 12,000 had defended Ticonderoga against Carleton's incursion the previous October, St. Clair had 2,089 infantrymen and 238 artillerists. Not only had recruiting lagged in this region as elsewhere, but Washington had the bulk of the troops, which he held on to through the winter and spring while he sought to learn Howe's intentions. Besides, throughout the spring Washington doubted that the army in Canada would invade New York. He was convinced it would sail southward to join with Howe. Nor did Schuyler think the British would come up Lake Champlain. He thought the enemy would descend the Mohawk River and bypass Fort Ticonderoga. Both were wrong, as St. Clair learned on nearly the very day in June that he assumed command.[8]

Schuyler complained incessantly about his dearth of troops, and he advised Washington that should an "Accident" or "Disaster" "befal us at Tyonderoga," the enemy would be able "to march where they please." In a series of letters, Schuyler added that "Inattention" to the Northern Department—by whom he did not specify—had left Fort Ticonderoga weakly defended, devoid of adequate provisions, and unlikely to be held in the face of a "serious attack."[9] On June 20, the day that Burgoyne addressed his Indian allies, Schuyler convened a council of war. He had learned a week earlier that an enemy force was approaching, but even then—and for the next eight days—he continued to think it was a feint and that the real contest would come elsewhere. But the council had to decide what to do if the British appeared. It was agreed that if faced with an attack, Fort Ticonderoga was to be evacuated and Mount Independence defended. Baldwin was put to work making additional improvements, and as many provisions as possible were moved to Mount Independence. Unless swarms of militia arrived, and soon, St. Clair doubted that the British could be stopped, though at times he appeared confident that the British could be made to pay such a heavy price that they would be prevented from reaching Albany that year.[10]

Washington, on July 2, responded to Schuyler that he could not imagine the post "can possibly fall into the Hands of the Enemy in a short Time." Disaster already beckoned when Washington dashed off his communiqué. Burgoyne had struck the day before. Fraser's light infantry and the navy had moved rapidly, taking Mount Hope and beginning to cut off the defenders' avenues of escape. Five days after striking, General Phillips—pronouncing that "Where a goat can go, a man can go"—got artillery to the top of Mount Defiance, the master stroke that most American leaders had not thought possible. That same evening, St. Clair ordered that the fort be abandoned, a decision that prompted derision among some British soldiers. After "all their pretended boastings of . . . choosing rather to die in their works than give them up," laughed one redcoat, the rebels had frantically withdrawn. Although St. Clair had conceived assorted plans for defending Ticonderoga, he had not made preparations for a retreat. Mayhem followed. St. Clair had some of the troops, but he did not know what had become of all his men.

For five days Schuyler—who was in Albany when he learned that Ticonderoga had fallen—had no idea what had become of his army. He would not know until nearly nine days later. All the while he feared that perhaps half or more of the men had been captured along with the post. He finally got word that most of the army was with St. Clair and was attempting to reach Fort Edward, a post about halfway between Ticonderoga and Albany. The word "disaster," which Schuyler had said might occur, was too mild a term for what in fact had occurred. After hardly firing a shot, Burgoyne had captured Fort Ticonderoga and, with it, scores of artillery pieces, thousands of muskets, invaluable provisions of all kinds, and a handful of prisoners.[11]

While Schuyler puzzled for days over what had become of his army, Burgoyne knew the direction in which at least some of the enemy had retreated, and he sent Fraser's light infantry and several German units under Riedesel to track them down. Fraser drove his men relentlessly and within 24 hours they caught up with the rear guard of St. Clair's army at Hubbardton, some 20 miles southeast of Mount Independence. The Americans had superior numbers when, on July 7, Fraser attacked. It was one of the bloodier engagements in this war. The Americans, firing "showers of balls mixed with buckshot," fought so well that Fraser had to summon help from Riedesel's Hessians. Their arrival forced the rebels to withdraw. The Americans lost 130 men in three hours, and at least as many were taken prisoner; their adversary's losses in killed and wounded were slightly higher.[12]

By then, Burgoyne was at Skenesborough, at the southern end of Lake Champlain, the site of the staging area for the invasion of Canada back in 1775. Burgoyne had pursued some of the rebels who fled Ticonderoga, but they were gone when he arrived, having fled to Fort Anne farther south. Their officers had spurred the retreat with repeated shouts to "march on, the Indians are at our heels." The Americans left behind a cornucopia of arms, munitions, stores, and vessels. Altogether, Burgoyne had taken possession of 128 indispensable artillery pieces at Ticonderoga and Skenesborough. On the same day that Fraser fought the rebels at Hubbardton, Burgoyne sent the Ninth Infantry Regiment to take Fort Anne, well down Wood Creek. The rebels had escaped, abandoning and razing the installation. Nonetheless, only 10 days had elapsed since the assault on Ticonderoga commenced and Burgoyne was now within 75 miles of Albany.[13]

Taking Ticonderoga was thought by some to have been a turning point in the war. On learning of Burgoyne's success, George III exclaimed, "I have beat them! I have beat all the Americans!" The monarch exaggerated, though his perspective hardly differed from that of the British troops on the expedition. A corporal spoke for many when, with a sigh of relief, he exalted that the soldiers' "toils . . . be nearly at an end" as Albany was "within their grasp."[14] In fact, in June a truly crucial moment had arrived. Burgoyne had expected a protracted siege of Fort Ticonderoga. Instead, his success had been "equally fortunate and rapid." Within a few days he achieved what he had thought would require weeks. However, his rapid success created a logistical problem. The disparate elements of his army that he had sent off after the fleeing rebels soon came together at Skenesborough, but his stores, weaponry, and munitions were back at Ticonderoga. Burgoyne had not planned for this. Eighteen long days passed, during which the scattered rebels were an army in name only, before he began his move on Albany from Skenesborough. It was not that Burgoyne was sluggish. Indeed, he acted prudently. Rather than have the tons of supplies and heavy guns at Ticonderoga brought to Skenesborough by land, he chose to have them transported up Lake George, from which they would ultimately portage 16 miles over relatively good roads to a site where they would rendezvous with the main army. But for sound security reasons Burgoyne did not wish to leave Skenesborough and begin his overland march to the rendezvous site—a 23-mile trek through a primordial wilderness—until the goods from Ticonderoga began their portage. Day after crucial day passed while he waited.[15]

There was another option that Burgoyne might have chosen. Given the enemy's all-too-apparent disarray, Burgoyne might have dispatched Fraser's corps, the cream of the army, to advance to Fort Edward on the Hudson. Fraser was a veteran soldier who had seen combat in two previous wars. His assault troops were the hardiest and most experienced and disciplined soldiers in the British army. They were adept at moving rapidly and living off the land. It had taken Fraser only about 36 hours to march from Mount Independence to Hubbardton, roughly the same distance as from Fort Anne to Fort Edward. For four days after July 9 only 2,000 rebels held Fort Edward, and two-thirds of them were poorly armed militiamen.[16] It is conceivable that Fraser could have taken Fort Edward. At the very least, his corps might have secured the route below Skenesborough before the rebels could obstruct it. However, Burgoyne had next to no information concerning the whereabouts of St. Clair's army or its size, or if it even still existed. Sending off Fraser would be risky. Burgoyne, the preeminent risk-taker, did not take the risk.

While he waited at Skenesborough, Burgoyne deployed some men to garrison Ticonderoga and others to guard what soon would be a lengthening lifeline between his army and Ticonderoga. He would ultimately begin his descent with 52 artillery pieces, over 500 wagons (30 of which carried Burgoyne's baggage and that of his staff), 50 teams of oxen, and hundreds of horses.[17]

During Burgoyne's long stay at Skenesborough, his rebel enemy was busy. Even as the British approached Fort Ticonderoga, Schuyler ordered the Springfield Armory to hurry cannon to the front. Oxen teams transported the artillery to Peekskill and from there the guns went up the Hudson. By August, 22 M1740 artillery pieces that had crossed the Atlantic on *Amphitrite* were with an American army camp just south of Saratoga. Washington had also acted. Early in July he sent four regiments to Ticonderoga, though they arrived well after the post was lost. For days after learning of the loss of Ticonderoga, Washington continued to plead that he could not spare any additional men, though Howe had yet to depart New York. It would be up to Schuyler, he said, to stop Burgoyne with whatever troops he had, including militiamen. However, Washington asked Congress to send Benedict Arnold to the Northern Department. He was "judicious & brave," knew that country well, and his presence would "animate the Militia greatly & spur them on to a becoming conduct."[18]

Schuyler's leadership in this war had left much to be desired, but in the July crisis he acted decisively. He vowed to "throw as many Obstructions in the Enemy's Rout as possible," and within five days of the retreat from Ticonderoga he dispatched New York and Massachusetts militias to fell trees across the path the enemy would take coming south, and to destroy bridges, drive off cattle, burn fields of grain, divert streams so that the enemy had to advance on foot rather than via bateau, and remove all weaponry, wagons, and stores from several storage depots en route to the Hudson. Schuyler sped tools and carpenters to Fort Edward, and once he located Kosciuszko, he put him to work constructing entrenchments at that post. He countered Burgoyne's earlier blustering proclamation with one of his own that alerted residents to purported British atrocities in the mid-Atlantic states and advised would-be Loyalists that General Howe had recently abandoned his Tory helpmates in New Jersey, leaving them to face rebels bent on retribution. A veritable whirlwind of activity, Schuyler continued to appeal to Washington, Congress, and the authorities in New York and New England for troops. His pleading with Washington finally paid off. On July 22, the commander in chief, aware of the anxiety among northern congressmen, ordered the 1,300 men in John Glover's brigade to march north, though it would be nearly August before they reached Albany.[19]

After July 12, Schuyler's army came together at Fort Edward by fits and starts. St. Clair's tattered force arrived, as did the Albany County militia and the brigade Washington had sent days earlier. On July 18, six days before Burgoyne began his descent and two weeks after Ticonderoga was lost, the American army at Fort Edward totaled around 4,000, about two-thirds of whom were Continentals, though Schuyler complained that many of the regulars were too old or too young to be of much help, and some were sick or unarmed. He pleaded for more men.[20]

Once the British artillery and supply train began the portage from Lake George to join with main army, Burgoyne moved south. The "toil of the march was great," he later said of the tramp from Skenesborough. It was July and stiflingly hot in the dark, airless forest. Each soldier carried about 60 pounds of equipment and provisions, "a burden which none except the old Roman veteran ever bore," exclaimed a British soldier. From the first, the British also encountered the handiwork of Schuyler's axmen. Huge trees had to be removed from the roads and more than 50 bridges repaired or rebuilt. A long causeway had to be constructed over one marsh, an endeavor that took a host of men several days of sweaty labor. Arachnids and insects, including "venomous swarms of musquitoes," tormented the men, and poisonous snakes abounded. Wagons and gun carriages broke down with regularity and had to be overhauled. The terrain was rugged, the underbrush thick, and frequent summer rainstorms often turned the earth so muddy that at times it was laborious to merely walk, much less to move heavy equipment. Burgoyne called the trek an ordeal of "great fatigue and labour," but after one week his army reached Fort Edward, which Schuyler had abandoned, retreating farther south to consolidate his forces.

Burgoyne was later censured for bringing along some 50 artillery pieces, but he felt that he had no choice. He expected to be outnumbered and knew his enemy would be entrenched. He knew, too, that they fought well when behind ramparts. He anticipated relentlessly hammering his foe to blast them out of their shelters. Burgoyne was also subsequently criticized for not having brought his entire army via the Lake George route, but the time consumed in taking his army back to Ticonderoga to join the supply train would have added several days to his journey to Fort Edward. As it was, 23 pregnant days passed after Fort Ticonderoga fell before Burgoyne's army reached Fort Edward, time well spent by his resourceful enemy. Already, Burgoyne was the victim not of his mistakes but of happenstance and the vicissitudes of campaigning against a resourceful adversary in the unforgiving American backcountry.[21]

Having just emerged from his arduous wilderness march, Burgoyne was largely unaware of his adversary's growing strength. He continued to exude optimism. He characterized his enemy's repeated retreats as signs of "desperation," anticipated soon being reinforced by St. Leger, expected some sort of diversion by Clinton in the Hudson Highlands, and looked forward to soon entering "country better adapted to manoeuvre." Not that Burgoyne was without problems, the chief of which was that he had not destroyed the American army. St. Clair's abandonment of Fort Ticonderoga, widely viewed as spineless treachery, had in fact saved the army. In addition, Schuyler's scorched-earth policy was already confronting the British with food shortages, few Loyalists had surfaced to augment the British regulars, and Burgoyne had found his Indian allies to be as troublesome as "spoiled children." They were mostly interested in plundering, he said, and while in the field were prone to inflict "enormities" on civilians, including "women and infants," that Burgoyne said were "too horrid" to describe. Indeed, as the army approached Fort Edward, an Indian war party captured and grotesquely slaughtered Jane McCrea, a frontier resident who lived near the post. General Horatio Gates, commander of the American army who soon would supplant Schuyler as head of the army's Northern Department, wrote an open letter to Burgoyne denouncing the murder. Although he had never met the victim, Gates described her as "a young woman lovely to the sight, of virtuous character and amicable disposition" who had been "Shot, scalp'd, strip'd & Butchered in the most shocking Manner." His published missive was a propaganda triumph that helped arouse Yankee militiamen to take up arms against the invader, men activated by vengeance against what they saw as a morally depraved enemy and an existential urge to protect home and hearth. American poets and antiwar writers in Britain also denounced McCrea's killing, filling in the gaps with lurid details of the outrage, and always depicting the Native American warriors as pawns in Burgoyne's all-too-ready eagerness to "turn savages loose upon society." In reality, many British officers were outraged by the atrocity and, like many patriot writers, depicted Indigenous Americans as racially prone to violence. One British officer characterized the Indians as "blood thirsty monsters" whom he would henceforth refer to as "Savages."[22]

Although Burgoyne remained confident, Benedict Arnold, who reached Fort Edward shortly before it was abandoned, surveyed the situation and concluded that "we shall be able to manage Genl Burgoyne" so long as Howe did not come up the Hudson.[23] Within a couple of weeks, Arnold's prophecy was borne out, for by then Burgoyne's campaign had begun to unravel. By mid-August, Burgoyne doubted that he would see St. Leger, who was bogged down in a siege operation at Fort Stanwix, an installation that blocked his access to the Mohawk River. St. Leger's investment lasted three weeks, but on August 22, discouraged by the arrival of rebel relief forces, he lifted the siege and retreated to Canada, clutching to the futile hope that he could reach Burgoyne via Lake Champlain. St. Leger and his men ultimately made it to Ticonderoga, but no farther.[24]

That was only the beginning of the "alarming truths" that Burgoyne acknowledged seeing with crystal clarity in August. He knew that Congress, early in August, had removed Schuyler as commander of the Northern Department. Many congressmen had long been disappointed with Schuyler's leadership, or lack thereof. The loss of Fort Ticonderoga, and the period that followed when Schuyler had no idea of his army's whereabouts, was the final affront. Burgoyne also knew that Gates had been appointed as Schuyler's successor, a transition that meant the British army now faced an enemy led by a former British army officer. Burgoyne was aware, too, that reinforcements were pouring into the rebel army, which was now about 25 miles below Fort Edward in Stillwater. Burgoyne was short on specifics, but New England militiamen were coming to Gates's army in droves, and Washington was detaching men from his army and units posted in the Hudson Highlands.

Atop those untoward events, Burgoyne's army had been in the field for some 60 taxing days, and the punishing slog to Fort Edward had incapacitated numbers of his men and sparked desertions. He paused at Fort Edward for two weeks to rest his men and stock up on supplies sent down from Ticonderoga. As he waited, he prayed for good news from St. Leger and Howe. None came. Burgoyne had begun to see the handwriting on the wall. Once he started south from Fort Edward, he would be taking his army into the maw of an enemy force "superior to mine in troops" and his supply line would be tenuous. Burgoyne had come to the key moment of his campaign. As August unfolded, he made three critical decisions. He moved south to Fort Miller, where he crossed to the east side of the Hudson, a choice he made because he would face no enemy resistance until he recrossed at Saratoga, after which he would have to fight his way through Gates's army to reach Albany. However, by moving across the river, he severed his ties to the supply line that ran back to Ticonderoga when he was already short of provisions. His initial decision necessitated a second. On August 4, Burgoyne dispatched a Hessian detachment of some 750 men under Lieutenant Colonel Friedrich Baum to Bennington, Vermont, the site of a rebel supply depot and pastures filled with grazing cattle. Baum, who was given fewer men than General Gage had sent to Concord on the first day of the war, was ordered to return with a month's supply of food. It would be a 200-mile round trip into the American backcountry that British officers going back to the war's first day had found to be forbiddingly dangerous. On August 6, for the first time since he'd arrived in Canada nearly 100 days earlier, Burgoyne heard from Howe. The communiqué confirmed what Howe had told Carleton back in April. He would not be coming north as his "intention is for Pennsylvania."[25]

Burgoyne now faced the third and most crucial of his three August decisions. As he knew incontrovertibly that Howe would not provide assistance, Burgoyne's best option would have been to return to Fort Edward for the winter—as he said that his supply line from there to Fort Ticonderoga was secure—or retreat to the safety of Fort Ticonderoga and resume the campaign in 1778. The next year might bring help from St. Leger, Carleton in Canada, Germain in England, and Howe in Pennsylvania. He knew that a large rebel army commanded by a capable professional officer stood between him and Albany, although he lacked good intelligence regarding the exact strength of Gates's army. He also knew that his own troops had already been in the field for three months and likely faced a lengthy further stretch of campaigning to reach Albany, if they reached it. Howe, to his detriment, had at key moments in 1776 acted with excessive caution. At this key moment Burgoyne threw caution to the wind. On August 20 he wrote to Germain that "duty" compelled him to move on Albany as soon as he gathered "25 days provisions."[26]

The poor showing by his adversary in Canada in 1776 and his easy conquest of Ticonderoga perhaps misled Burgoyne into thinking that the enemy in his path could never stop him. (Baron de Riedesel, at nearly this very moment, advised London that the campaign had been one of "Successes so rapid.") Burgoyne was possibly driven forward by his awareness that Carleton had been stripped of his command following his failure to attempt to take Ticonderoga the previous fall. Or perhaps the gambler streak in Burgoyne shaped his judgment and put him on the riskiest of paths. Whatever led to his decision, Burgoyne said that he expected to be in Albany within three weeks, a comment that adds credence to the belief that he seriously underestimated the capability of his enemy. His intriguing decision to continue was matched by his curious failure at this juncture to request assistance from Clinton in Manhattan.[27]

As Burgoyne was making his decision, Baum and his men advanced into a nightmare. Militia from Vermont, New Hampshire, and Massachusetts had been roused by the threat posed by Burgoyne's descent, and by early August they were commanded by Brigadier General John Stark, a Continental officer who had fought in the Seven Years' War and at Bunker Hill and beyond. Stark had vastly superior numbers. He commanded some 2,000 men, a great many of them armed with newly arrived French muskets. Stark's militiamen encircled and struck the Germans at Bennington on August 16, bringing on a disaster of the magnitude the British had experienced at Bunker Hill. Only 14 of Baum's soldiers escaped and another 250 in a relief party were lost. Burgoyne had lost 15 percent of his army. While the enemy's army was growing, Burgoyne's was shrinking, though he partially supplanted his losses by calling down men stationed along his supply route. Burgoyne understood his predicament, which he spelled out in a despondent letter to Germain four days after Bennington. Had St. Leger joined him and Baum not lost his detachment, and had a diversion been made up the Hudson, he would "have been before now at Albany," wrote Burgoyne. But he was not in Albany and his prospects for success were "less prosperous" now than they had been three weeks earlier.[28] The Bennington debacle gave Burgoyne another chance to scrap his campaign. But he soldiered on. Burgoyne was on a path to tragedy for himself and the thousands of men under him, and given the forlorn tone of his communiqué to the American secretary, he may have foreseen the outcome.

Two days after Bennington, Gates arrived in Albany and took command of an army of 5,888 men, a force slightly smaller at that juncture than the army Burgoyne possessed. Gates, now 50, was stooped, wore spectacles, and had long had gray hair, but if he struck some as over the hill or out of his element, looks were deceiving. Gates had been an officer in the British army for 15 years, including in America in the Seven Years' War, and he understood leadership, armies, and warfare. Infused with republican zeal, he quit England—which he called an "obstinate old slut"—and moved to Virginia in 1773, where he farmed until the war broke out. When Congress ousted Schuyler, Gates was appointed his successor.[29] The American force that he inherited had swelled during the past six weeks and was continuing to grow. Late in July, Washington pleaded that "Not a man more" of his could be sent north, but in mid-August he relented and dispatched more. He even sent off Daniel Morgan's corps of 578 riflemen, a contingent widely regarded as the crown jewel of the Continental army. By early September, Gates's army was larger than Burgoyne's, and it continued to grow. The Continentals under Arnold that had helped turn back St. Leger in the Mohawk Valley arrived along with additional militiamen. By the second week in September, Gates's army had ballooned to around 10,000.[30]

Three weeks after taking command, Gates led his army from Stillwater to Bemis Heights, a site chosen by Kosciuszko because it stood above the Hudson River and the road to Albany, and as dense woods to the west would inhibit Burgoyne's freedom of movement. Burgoyne, in June, had predicted that his enemy would fashion sturdy fortifications before he arrived to face them, and Kosciuszko had in fact laid out U-shaped entrenchments that stretched nearly a mile from the low-lying river to the forests in the hilly ground on the American left. The earthworks were anchored by three batteries overlooking the river road, the river, and the low country in the center of what was likely to be the battlefield. Work remained to be done, as Gates's left would be the least protected against an enemy strike. Nevertheless, the American lines bristled with French-manufactured cannon nestled in their singular red carriages.

Around the time that Gates moved north, Burgoyne resumed his march to the south. On September 14, the British army crossed back to the west side of the Hudson. Four days later, the two armies were only three miles apart. Gates's combat strength on the day of the looming battle would be 8,359, some 2,000 more than Burgoyne would take into battle. Furthermore, given the woods and hilly terrain on his right and the river on his left, Burgoyne would be able to put only 23 pieces of artillery in the field on the day of battle, a number the Americans could more than match. Nor did Burgoyne have the luxury of reconnoitering the area. He would go into the battle without a precise understanding of the terrain or where the enemy might be strongest and weakest. What Burgoyne did know, of course, was that he had to break through the Americans to reach Albany. His men were almost entirely regulars and, in his estimation, better soldiers than Gates possessed. But he knew that the Americans, and especially American militiamen, fought very well when protected by emplacements. Gates knew that too, and his plan, for the most part, was to keep his men in their defensive stronghold.[31]

On the cool fog-shrouded morning of September 19 the British army entered an area of Bemis Heights known as Freeman's Farm, and that rustic tract of pastures, meadows, and cultivated fields would lend its name to the ferocious battle that was waged there during the afternoon. The British advanced in three columns. Burgoyne's finest troops were on the right and would assail the enemy sector where the entrenchments were unfinished. If they succeeded in securing the high ground, they might flank the American left, opening the door for a British breakout. As the British moved forward, Arnold, the second-in-command, urged Gates to send forward his men and fight a set-piece battle before the enemy could bring its artillery to bear on the defensive emplacements. Gates rejected the idea. Only Morgan's riflemen and a small detachment of light infantry were sent out to "harass" the British.

The Battle of Freeman's Farm began with skirmishes around noon. More intense action soon followed, and what had been a farmstead was filled with cacophonous sounds of battle. Artillery erupted with thunderous fusillades and thousands of muskets discharged balls that zinged here and there, whacking trees and tearing into men and horses. "Such an explosion of fire I never had any idea of before," said a young British lieutenant, who added that the field guns sounded like "great peals of thunder" that "almost deafened us." By mid-afternoon the Americans in the field—confronted with "British troops repeatedly . . . [using] their bayonet with their usual success," according to one of the king's soldiers—were falling back. Arnold, sometimes on his own, sometimes with Gates's consent, rushed in reinforcements. From around three o'clock until dusk settled over the killing ground, the fighting was savage. Men grappled at close range, sometimes hand to hand. It was barbarous. War, and combat, brutalizes. A battle is a reversion to a state of nature and an ultimate existential crisis. One's life hinges on taking the life of another. In this engagement, as in every battle, the combatants were often disordered, even befogged, losing track of all but what was necessary to stay alive, and sometimes even that was elusive. What many of Burgoyne's survivors most remembered was the deadly fire that Morgan's riflemen rained down on them. The "Wagon Boy," as some troops secretly called Morgan, a reference to the days he had served the British army as a teamster in the Seven Years' War, moved his men about his sector by sounding orders on a turkey call, and these rough-hewn soldiers took up perches high in trees or squeezed off shots while sheltered behind tree trunks. They pinpointed officers and artillerists, and were largely responsible for taking out two-thirds of the men assigned to move and operate Burgoyne's field guns.[32]

There were times when the Americans recoiled in the face of an enemy charge and times when they counterattacked. The same was true, too, of the British, who at moments fought "amidst heaps of the dead." Burgoyne later said that throughout much of the brawl his force was "critically pressed by a great superiority of fire." Both Arnold and Burgoyne were in the thick of this fight, and their presence inspired the men under them. An American thought Arnold was "the life and soul of the troops." A British officer was awed that Burgoyne was "everywhere" and "shunned no danger." At one point, Arnold begged for reinforcements, certain he could envelop and destroy the enemy in the center of the field. But Gates continued to think that a wholesale abandonment of his defenses was imprudent, a decision that caused rancor with Arnold and subsequent criticism by contemporaries and some historians. As night approached, the Americans fell back to their defenses. Some redcoats thought the Americans had been saved by nightfall, but others believed the rebels' salvation was because heavy losses had "much weakened" Burgoyne's army. Whatever the case, Burgoyne had failed to fight through. He was no closer to Albany than he had been at sunrise, and he had lost about 460 of his men, about 8 percent of his army. The Americans suffered over 300 casualties. Arnold and Morgan, and their men, had played vital roles in the feral struggle, though Caleb Stark, a son of General John Stark who had fought that day in a New Hampshire militia regiment, found the heart of the matter in observing that by nightfall Burgoyne would have been on his way to Albany had it not been for the French muskets and artillery. Throughout the dark, mournful night that followed, the soldiers who had survived listened to the wrenching "groans of our wounded and dying," and unavoidably untended, comrades. As with the aftermath of nearly every engagement, the luckless victims lay through the night in grievous pain and hopeless anguish on the mangled, reeking farmland now littered with splintered trees and shredded clothing hanging from bushes. Their only companions were the bodies of dead men and horses.[33]

Burgoyne, in the wake of the battle, dug in behind strong redoubts that he ordered constructed. His options were limited to ordering another attack, waiting for Gates to assail him, or attempting to retreat from what now appeared to be a gathering snare. He was pondering his choices when two days after the engagement a letter arrived from Clinton in Manhattan. When penning the letter Clinton had no way of knowing the problems his old friend faced. The last letter that Clinton had received from Burgoyne was written prior to the Bennington disaster. Burgoyne had said he was in the "highest spirits," requested no help, and anticipated reaching Albany by August 23. Having heard nothing more, Clinton by the second week in September had concluded that Burgoyne had not reached Albany. Clinton divulged that his orders were explicit: His "principal object" was to maintain the "security" of Manhattan. Nevertheless, if "concurrent circumstances" suggested that Burgoyne required help, Clinton could make "a little diversion" up the Hudson, a step that might draw away some of the enemy forces that Burgoyne faced. He could step off, he said, within 10 days of hearing from Burgoyne. Burgoyne wasted no time in requesting that Clinton act immediately. "Do it, my Friend, directly," he wrote. If Burgoyne had seriously considered attempting to retreat to safety, Clinton's letter dissuaded him. He remained at Bemis Heights.[34]

Clinton received Burgoyne's plea for help on September 26 and within a week sailed up the Hudson with 3,000 men. Clinton's mission was a spectacular success as far as it went. On October 6 his men successfully stormed Forts Clinton and Montgomery, on the cusp of West Point, some 50 miles above Manhattan. A witness said that during the action Clinton "scaled the top the [adjacent] mountain, himself carrying the British colors, which he kept holding aloft, while his troops . . . carried the post[s]." Later that day, Clinton wrote to Burgoyne that he had done all he could with the limited number of troops at his disposal and hoped that his diversionary actions would be "serviceable."[35]

Given the communications lag and the failure of some messengers to make it through the enemy lines, Burgoyne remained in the dark with regard to what Clinton was doing. He waited and hoped as day after day passed. Meanwhile, the British army's food supply dwindled, compelling Burgoyne to "diminish the [men's] rations." He called two councils of war. The generals disagreed bitterly over the best course to take. It was left to Burgoyne to make the burdensome decision. He yet again refused to withdraw. He opted to take one more shot at breaking through to Albany. On October 7, he sent out a large reconnaissance force to search for the weakest point in Gates's defenses. Intelligence reports led Gates to conclude that the British planned to attack that day, and he responded boldly. He sent out several units to attack the British right flank, which soon collapsed, bringing on a disorderly retreat. Gates poured in reinforcements, which prevented Burgoyne from taking full advantage of the fortifications he had begun constructing 18 days earlier. Gates had a huge numerical advantage in the Battle of Bemis Heights, and early on in the engagement some in the British army understood that "all is irretrievably lost." Yet the fighting raged on for nearly three more hours. Casualties mounted on both sides. Arnold took a bullet in the same leg that had been wounded at Quebec two years earlier, and his leg sustained additional injuries when his disabled horse fell on it. Burgoyne was once again in the midst of the action, and a bullet "passed through his hat and another through his waistcoat," but somehow he was unscathed. Many high-ranking British officers were not so fortunate, including Simon Fraser, who was gut-shot by an elderly Albany militiaman wielding a long hunting gun. Some officers thought the loss of Fraser took all the fight out of Burgoyne. Not long thereafter, with the enemy sending in additional reinforcements and his army in danger of being encircled, Burgoyne ordered a fallback. It was disorderly—"Each man for himself," said one trooper—as frightened men "made for the bushes." Burgoyne eventually regained control, first pulling back to a safer position and later, under cover of darkness and a drenching rain, retreating to Saratoga. Burgoyne had suffered heavy losses. Nearly 900 of his men had been lost, 15 percent of his force. Roughly a quarter of his army had been killed, wounded, or captured in the two engagements at Bemis Heights, and these were atop the staggering losses at Bennington. Gates lost about 150 men at Bemis Heights.[36]

Burgoyne intended to cross the river and retreat to Fort Edward, but that was beyond his means as rebel militia guarded the other side of the Hudson. He was down to two choices: retreat along the west side of the river or stay put and pin his hopes on Clinton bringing a relief force. Retreating was filled with hazards and, possibly, the abandonment of his wounded. He chose to stand fast and hope. Within four days of its second battle the British army was surrounded. Burgoyne's choices now were reduced to attempting to retreat by breaking through the American siege lines, surrendering, or holding out as long as possible in case Clinton was coming. A council of war opted to attempt to retreat, but that option was relinquished when intelligence divulged the strength of the rebel lines. The army would remain in Saratoga, where, in the words of one British soldier, "we had three powerful enemies to contend with—Americans—Winter—and Famine." The trapped soldiers faced several days of utter misery. Gates's artillery ceaselessly bombarded them. It was not yet winter, but the early autumn nights were raw and often wet. Provisions were severely limited. One week after the battle, another council of war voted to open negotiations. Burgoyne hoped to string out the talks as long as possible in the event that Clinton was coming. On the second day of negotiations both Burgoyne and Gates learned of Clinton's action at Forts Clinton and Montgomery. But the news came to Burgoyne from an unreliable source. Another British council of war met. It voted to surrender.[37]

General Phillips said later that it was a question of "capitulate or starve." Gates had better intelligence about Clinton's success and it made him more malleable. "We [were] trembling alive" to the "menacing prospect" that a relief force might save Burgoyne's army, said one of his officers. Gates quickly agreed to a "Convention" under which the Loyalists with Burgoyne were allowed to return to their homes and the prisoners of war were permitted to return to Great Britain and Germany on the condition that they would not serve again in this war. The document was signed on the morning of October 17 and the surrender ceremony took place that afternoon on the blood-tainted field. The downcast and defeated men marched to the surrender site—"Tears (though unmanly, forced their way," admitted one disconsolate British officer—and laid down their arms. The Americans behaved with "delicacy and politeness." The only sound came from an American martial band that played "Yankee Doodle." Some 6,000 men were taken prisoner and the Americans also gained possession of 4,500 muskets, 30 artillery pieces, and a stupendous cache of munitions, clothing, and assorted stores.[38]

It was a tragedy for the British, a turning point that need not have occurred. In lonely introspection, Burgoyne rapidly filed a postmortem with Germain. He respectfully refrained from criticizing the American secretary or Howe, whose campaign for all he knew might culminate in a game-changing triumph. Instead, Burgoyne laid blame on the "defections of the Indians," whom he portrayed as worse than worthless; the "desertion or the timidity of the Canadians"; and the failure of Loyalists to turn out in abundant numbers. A year later Burgoyne said publicly that his campaign would have had a happier outcome had his original plan to "effect a junction" with Howe's army been implemented. Despite pressure by Parliament, Germain refused to release the texts of Burgoyne's and Howe's campaign plans, or to address his role in shaping the final plan.[39]

The Americans, of course, had something to do with the cataclysm that befell Burgoyne's army. Schuyler had risen to the challenge after the surrender of Fort Ticonderoga. In July, August, and September, several states, Congress, and Washington had rushed troops to defend against the invasion. Rebel militiamen, so often disparaged by Washington, performed well at Bennington and on the whole fought credibly in the two Bemis Heights brawls. Arnold's keen judgment at Freeman's Farm may have averted significant complications. Despite Gates's cautionary nature, he eventually gained a huge victory and doubtless saved the lives of a great many American soldiers in the process. But the American victory would have been improbable, nay impossible, without the rich store of French arms and munitions.

The cataclysm that befell the British was due to multiple factors, but Germain and Howe were most deserving of censure. Germain should have ordered Howe to move north to rendezvous with Burgoyne. Howe was blameworthy for having left the invasion army to its own devices despite the readily apparent dangers it faced. He was also indefensibly tardy in launching his campaign to take Philadelphia. Clinton's observation that Howe could not take Philadelphia and head north to aid Burgoyne in the same year was correct. However, had Howe set off for Philadelphia in the spring before Burgoyne moved out on his mission, it is virtually certain that Washington would never have relinquished as many of his troops to defend against the invasion of New York. One can only speculate on whether Gates's army, devoid of those additional resources, would have been able to prevent a breakthrough by Burgoyne in the desperate fighting at Freeman's Farm. As it was, however, the folly of Germain and Howe rendered Burgoyne's campaign a misbegotten venture from the start. Some of the vanquished British officers understood that as they surrendered. One noted in his journal that the calamity of having to surrender was due to a "blundering" American secretary and the "crime" of "stupid inaction" by Howe in "neglecting" Burgoyne's army.[40]

WASHINGTON, IN LATE SPRING, had sought to learn the plans of Burgoyne and Howe. If Burgoyne invaded New York via Ticonderoga, the American commander said, it had to be part of "a preconcerted plan with Genl Howe" who would "co-operate with him by pushing his Whole force up" the Hudson River. It was "almost certain" that Howe would do so, he said, adding there could be "little room to doubt" it. Nothing else made sense. By early July Washington knew that Burgoyne was about to assail Ticonderoga. It was "a certain proof," therefore, that Howe would go north to form a junction with him. However, a week later, intelligence regarding what was being loaded on a British fleet at Staten Island led Washington to think Howe might have other plans, including perhaps an invasion of the southern states. But as the best bet remained that Howe would act in concert with

Burgoyne, Washington moved his army to the Clove, a rugged gorge on the west side of the Hudson above Manhattan, to wait and watch. Washington was more puzzled than ever by the third week in July as Howe's fleet appeared to be sailing out to sea. More days passed. Finally, through an intercepted letter in which Howe had written Burgoyne that he was sailing "Southward," Washington guessed that Howe's target was Philadelphia. The American commander brought his army back across the Delaware River.[41]

In the last days before Howe sailed, General Clinton—now Sir Henry, as he had been knighted while in London—arrived back in New York and in at least three frank conversations sought to dissuade Howe from going after Philadelphia. Clinton's strategic recommendations in 1775 and 1776 had almost always been correct, and they had nearly always been ignored, first by Gage and then by Howe. Once again Clinton's counsel was cogent. Familiar with the mood in London, Clinton "lost no time" emphasizing that authorities at home expected the campaign of 1777 to finish off the rebels. If that did not occur, Clinton predicted that Britain would terminate the war before France could enter it, a step that would bring "an end of British dominion in America." Speaking freely—"too freely," he said later—Clinton advised that the war could be won in Pennsylvania only if Howe destroyed Washington's army, and he believed the rebel commander was too savvy to give Howe the opportunity of doing so. Not only was Burgoyne's failure predicable if Howe did not go northward, but Washington could be brought to battle only through a concerted British threat to establish control of the Hudson River.[42]

Clinton is known to have composed an undated written plan for striking north, and it is possible that he shared this proposal with Howe in hopes of dissuading him from invading Pennsylvania. Clinton's formula called for two forces to move north, one up the Connecticut River Valley, a supposed hotbed of Loyalism, and the other up the Hudson. The latter would destroy rebel installations in the Highlands before moving on West Point. Before attacking that pivotal installation, wings of the British force would sever all avenues of escape for West Point's garrison, after which the rebels would be bombarded into submission.[43] Howe listened to Clinton's assorted arguments, and the two generals argued. But in the end Howe ignored Clinton's advice.

On July 23, not long after Howe's secretary assured the ministry that "this ungrateful rebellion will be crushed" by the end of the year, the fleet bearing the British army weighed anchor and sailed south. The task force need not have sailed any farther than Perth Amboy on the New Jersey coast, and from there the army could have proceeded overland. It was 75 miles from Perth Amboy to Philadelphia, roughly the same distance that Burgoyne had to traverse from Skenesborough to Albany. Howe had good reasons for spurning such an endeavor. He believed that by sailing to Chesapeake Bay he could reach the environs of Philadelphia much faster and without having to strip men from his force to guard a lengthy supply line. It seemed the best option until things went wrong.

The voyage was expected to take a week. It took 32 days, twice the anticipated length of an overland march, and the journey was a nightmare. A lack of favorable winds slowed, and then stopped, the vessels, leaving men and horses below deck to suffer day after day in the scorching summer heat. Fierce thunderstorms now and again erupted, tossing the ships about as if they were toys. On more than one occasion lightning struck ship masts, killing men and horses. The men's water supply turned rancid, food spoiled, and meat and biscuits crawled with worms and maggots. By the time the fleet reached Head of Elk at the top of Chesapeake Bay in late August, 27 soldiers and 170 horses had perished and another 150 equines no longer fit for duty had been thrown overboard. Howe's cavalry arm was thereafter in the depths of the Atlantic Ocean. As men disembarked, walking unsteadily after nearly five weeks at sea, Howe's army was still 57 miles from Philadelphia.[44]

Once the British fleet stood out to sea, Washington lost track of it, reducing him to "a State of constant perplexity and the most anxious conjecture" as to the enemy's intentions. After a couple of weeks, he discovered that the fleet was in the vicinity of Cape May. Believing that indicated Howe intended to approach Philadelphia via the Delaware River, Washington summoned units of the army toward Philadelphia. He personally sped to the vicinity of Wilmington, thinking the British would land nearby and advance on Philadelphia from there. Soon, however, Washington received information that the enemy squadron had turned and was sailing in a southerly direction. Once again Washington was reduced to a "state of conjecture." On August 21, now thinking the enemy must be planning to assail Charleston, Washington and a council of war agreed to march the army up the Hudson River to assist against Burgoyne's invasion. But the next day, before the army moved, word arrived that Howe's flotilla had entered Chesapeake Bay. Beyond a shadow of a doubt Philadelphia was Howe's target. Washington began to search for a desirable site to meet the enemy west of the city.[45]

Members of Congress in Philadelphia had been just as concerned as Washington about Howe's destination. The fleet's departure from New York "has left us in good Earnest," was how one congressman put it. Another spoke of the "vexation" over where Howe would strike. They worried over being in Howe's crosshairs and about the recently received news that the supposedly impregnable Fort Ticonderoga had fallen in a matter of hours. "Our affairs are now in a very critical Situation," said Samuel Adams on August 5, a conclusion with which each congressman would have agreed. When Washington learned that Howe had entered Chesapeake Bay, Congress learned it too. On the one hand, John Adams thought it was good news, as it meant that Gates could "at Leisure . . . kill or catch Burgoine." On the other hand, it meant that the "Moments are critical here." Most congressmen put on a brave face and expressed confidence that things "will turn out Very Chearfully." When Washington's army paraded through Philadelphia on August 24, Richard Henry Lee thought the soldiers "made a fine appearance" and that Howe's "ruin will be sure." John Adams watched the parade and was not so sure. "Our soldiers have not yet, quite the Air of Soldiers," he said, before hurrying to a church to pray.[46]

Clinton had thought Washington would never meet Howe on the battlefield. John Adams, who had never soldiered and knew far less than Clinton about strategic choices, also doubted that Washington would fight, and the thought displeased him. "Washington will maneuvre it with him, a good deal to avoid" a pitched battle, said Adams, who was "sick of Fabian systems" that drew out the war. Adams wanted Washington to fight and he was not disappointed. After having clung steadfastly for the past year to a Fabian strategy, Washington intended to put his entire army at risk. It was a perplexing decision. His adversary would enjoy a slight numerical superiority—15,200 to Washington's 14,000—but all of Howe's troops were regulars and his officers were professionals. Close to half of those in Washington's army were untested militiamen. Unlike at Bunker Hill, White Plains, or Bemis Heights, the rebel army would derive no advantages from the terrain. General Greene, in fact, said the countryside was "favorable to the Enemy, being very flat and leavel."

Washington may have chosen to fight because he now had more confidence in his field grade officers, nearly all of whom were now combat veterans. John Adams felt that an American victory would "ruin" Howe. Washington concurred and concluded the risk was worth taking. Other factors may have led Washington to his risky choice. By now he was aware of Bennington and the flood of troops rushing to Gates's support, and he suspected the rebel army up north would soon score a sensational victory. Aware of the criticism that had been leveled at him following the New York campaign in 1776, Washington may have feared rebuke if Howe took Philadelphia without a fight while Gates fought and prevented Burgoyne from taking Albany. He may have felt pressure from Congress, real or imagined, to make a stand. Washington clearly was anxious that morale on the home front might suffer if Philadelphia fell after an inadequate defense. There can be no doubt that he was also quite concerned about how France—which had furnished the Continental army with the sinews of war so that it could fight—would respond should he not engage the British. Some in the army were perplexed by Washington's decision. One of his officers, who looked askance at the choice his commander had made, thought "our great and good Washington made a sacrifice of his own excellent judgment upon the altar of public opinion."[47]

Howe's army did not take a step toward Philadelphia until 10 days after disembarking, a delay brought on by widespread illness in the ranks and the need to forage. Once Howe moved forward, he faced no man-made obstacles such as Schuyler had fashioned to hinder Burgoyne. But Washington had been busy. He and his officers considered several spots for making a stand and he appealed for additional militiamen. He also sought to inspire his troops. He told them that Howe's goal was to take Philadelphia. "[T]heir all is at stake—they will put the contest on the event of a single battle." If they lose that battle, "they are utterly undone—the war is at an end. . . . One bold stroke will free the land . . . and female innocence from brutal lust and violence." He added that northern militiamen had been valiantly fighting Burgoyne. "Who can forbear to emulate their noble spirit?" Victory would bring "peace and happiness to millions in the present and future generations. . . . The eyes of all America, and of Europe are turned on us. . . . [T]he critical moment, the most important moment is at hand."[48]

As Howe advanced, he sent out scouting parties and daily consulted with Loyalists from the area. Washington neither sufficiently reconnoitered nor adequately attempted to secure good information from local residents, some of whom were militiamen in his army. By the eve of battle the British commander had a better understanding of the topography than did the American commander. On September 9, the British army entered Chester County in Pennsylvania. At last, Washington knew the route that Howe would take. That same day the American army marched nine miles to Chadd's Ford on Brandywine Creek. It was there that Washington would make his stand. For the first time in a year, the quarry was in the sights of the hunter. Here glittered the opportunity for which Howe had yearned.[49]

Washington posted militia on his left, the least likely place where the enemy would seek to cross the creek. Washington was aware of two fords in this region, Chadd's and Buffington's, and given his paltry reconnaissance he thought the next ford beyond Buffington's was 12 miles away. Judging Chadd's Ford as the most likely site of the enemy crossing, Washington assigned some 5,500 men under General Greene to defend that sector. General Sullivan was given some 1,800 men with which to guard the right flank near Buffington's Ford.

Thanks to proficient scouting and intelligence provided by Loyalists and local farmers in the pay of Tories, Howe was aware of three fords a few miles above Buffington's.[50] His plan was to do more or less exactly what he had done on Long Island 13 months earlier. He would begin his assault on the enemy center at Chadd's Ford, a diversionary attack made by 6,800 British and Hessian troops led by General Wilhelm von Knyphausen. Meanwhile, General Cornwallis—accompanied by Howe and Joseph Galloway, a Pennsylvania Loyalist who had served in the Continental Congress before casting his lot with the British—would lead 8,500 men on a 17-mile march to one of the unguarded fords, cross it, and pounce on the surprised and heavily outnumbered Sullivan. Howe ran the risk that Washington, with overwhelming numerical superiority, would strike against Knyphausen. But Howe correctly assumed that while Washington was adept at surprise attacks, he shrank from offensive warfare. On Long Island, Howe had circled around Washington's left wing. This time, his objective was to skirt the enemy's right wing. If all went well, the American right would collapse, and Howe and Knyphausen would combine to crush the rebel center in a devastating pincer assault. The rebels had been deceived by Howe's simple textbook strategy on Long Island. Howe's similar maneuver on the Brandywine would once again catch them off guard.

Cornwallis set off at 5:00 A.M. Knyphausen moved out an hour later. Knyphausen was seven miles from the Brandywine, and throughout the advance his force skirmished with the 1,000 men in a light infantry brigade under General William Maxwell, which Washington had posted west of Chadd's Ford. Maxwell, a New Jersey bachelor who had soldiered in the Seven Years' War, posted his riflemen in the forests and wooded hills and made the enemy pay for every mile they covered. The fighting at times was intense and Maxwell's men performed spectacularly against a vastly superior force of regulars. Knyphausen was not ready to launch his diversionary thrust at Chadd's Ford until 10:30, more than four hours after beginning his march. The fight that ensued consisted primarily of skirmishing and artillery duels. Although what was unfolding was suspiciously similar to what had occurred on Long Island, it raised no red flags at American headquarters.

As early as 8:00 A.M. Washington received a report that a large British force was on the move to flank his right wing. Similar reports arrived over the next several hours. Washington dispatched scouts and sifted through their reports, but he neither sent a sufficient number of lookouts nor directed them to patrol well above Buffington's Ford. Contradictory information poured in, not unusual in the frenzy of battle. Most scouts spotted nothing, largely because their ability to see was obscured by fog and as Cornwallis was traveling a road unknown at American headquarters. Had Washington communicated adequately with local residents, as Howe had done, he might have learned the truth early on. Around noon he did learn from the commander of the First Pennsylvania Regiment that a force of perhaps 5,000 men, with upwards of 18 artillery pieces, had been spotted on the Great Valley Road, but given his shoddy reconnaissance Washington did not think the thoroughfare led to a ford. He concluded that the enemy force did not intend to join this fight and, instead, was on its way to attack a rebel supply depot in Reading.[51]

Sometime that morning Washington rode from his headquarters in the Benjamin Ring house, not far from Chadd's Ford, to observe the fighting in Greene's area, where he presumed the enemy was making its major thrust. He was a safe distance from enemy musket fire, but green-clad British riflemen under Captain Patrick Ferguson were just across the river. Ferguson, a 33-year-old Scotsman who had soldiered for more than 15 years, had made advances in the design of rifles, leading many to label the weapon he and his men sported the "Ferguson rifle." Ferguson spotted a high-ranking rebel officer on a bay mount. He crept closer to get off a good shot; he was easily within range to gun down his target. Ferguson may have had Washington in his sights, as he and others later thought. If so, the American commander was saved because at the last moment Ferguson decided it was "not pleasant to fire at the back on an unoffending individual who was acquitting himself very coolly of his duty."[52] Later that day Ferguson took a musket ball in his right elbow. He would never again be able to productively use that arm.

Probably a bit after Ferguson had drawn a bead on what might have been a very fortunate George Washington, Cornwallis's force made its initial crossing of the Brandywine. At 11:00 A.M. it passed over the south branch at Trimble's Ford. Three hours later it went across the upper branch at Jeffries Ford, not too far above Buffington's Ford and the right wing of Washington's army. The latter crossing occurred as Washington was having dinner at headquarters. (As incongruous as it seems for him to have been dining during the engagement, Gates chowed down on oxen heart in the midst of the Battle of Bemis Heights.) During the meal a report reached Washington that British units were across the Brandywine north of Buffington's. His great biographer, Douglas Southall Freeman, argued that to this point

Washington "had conducted the Brandywine operation as if he had been in a daze."[53] Washington had committed error upon error, but Freeman's judgment was too harsh. Like many another commander in this war and every war, Washington was the victim of conflicting intelligence. Since he was without a clear picture of what was taking place, his propensity for indecisiveness was magnified. But whatever irresolution he manifested disappeared once he learned the enemy was across the Brandywine. Thereafter, he immediately moved some units from the center of his line to bolster the imperiled right wing under Sullivan. His response was fraught with peril, as it opened the door for Knyphausen's troops to surge over the river and attack the suddenly weakened rebel center. Washington had little choice but to run the risk. At 4:00 P.M., when Cornwallis struck near Birmingham Hill, the rebel right wing—even with the newly arrived reinforcements—totaled only about 3,000 and the units were in disarray. The right wing, and indeed the entire rebel army, was in great peril.

In the first minutes of the fray a young major in the Continental army called the action "the grandest sight I ever saw." He served in Sullivan's division and noted that when the enemy appeared "We broke and Rallied and Rallied & broke." His day was soon over, as a "Ball with a Wad" struck his left forearm and "the fuse set [his] coat and shirt on fire."[54] Some of Sullivan's units, exposed and subjected to bayonet charges and a withering fire, hastily fell back, though two brigades of Virginians and some 800 Pennsylvanians fought resolutely from behind walls and fences before they retreated. Sullivan later said that his division was driven from Birmingham Hill five times and five times it regained the hill.[55] During the frenzied battle, Marquis de Lafayette arrived from elsewhere on the field to join the fight. Given his vivid imagination, Lafayette thought his presence inspired the American troops. He had not been in the fight for very long before he took a bullet in the leg. With assistance, Lafayette mounted a horse and rode to safety, likely narrowly avoiding capture.[56] He left behind units that were so scattered that reorganizing the force on the right wing appeared impossible. Cornwallis was close to turning the rebel flank, the object of Howe's grand plan. It appeared that an American calamity was unfolding, an outcome that seemed even more likely when at 5:00 P.M. Knyphausen's troops began crossing the Brandywine to close the trap.

Just then Washington scurried to the battlefield aboard his powerful charger. After riding like the wind—his mount jumped fences along the way as the commander allegedly spurred it on by repeatedly shouting, "Push along, old man— Push along old man"—the American commander reached the imperiled right wing and took charge.[57] The earlier stouthearted fight mounted by the Virginians and Pennsylvanians, among others, had bought valuable time that Washington utilized. He ordered Greene to bring his division from the center to right and the men dog-trotted some four miles into the savage brawl. A British officer noted that the "balls [were] ploughing up the ground. The trees cracking over ones heads. The branches rive by the artillery—the leaves falling as in autumn by the grapeshot." The arrival of Greene's division somewhat shored up the American defenses, and the British advance, which had seemed inexorable, was stopped at least for a time. Meanwhile, the remaining rebel units in the center, including Maxwell's weary light infantrymen, Pennsylvania militia, and the division under Anthony Wayne—made up of men who for the most part had little or no combat experience—fought tenaciously, fell back, and fought hard again, often from behind walls and houses. They slowed Knyphausen's advance to a crawl. It was now late in the day and darkness was on the verge of cloaking these Arcadian fields. It would be dark before Knyphausen and Cornwallis could crush their adversary. The Americans knew it was "fortunate for us that night came on" and stopped the fighting, as one of Washington's staff officers remarked. Another hour of daylight might have been catastrophic for the rebels.

Around 6:30 P.M. Washington ordered a retreat. It was messy. Lafayette, whose exalted reputation among Americans was made on this day, remembered the "horrible confusion, in the gloom of night," and claimed that 12 miles from Chadd's Ford, his gaping wound notwithstanding, he succeeded in reestablishing "a degree of order" in the minutes before Washington arrived.[58] The fight was over. It might not have been had Howe possessed a cavalry arm to strike his disorganized foe as it fell back, but without horses there was nothing more the British could do in the last minutes of feeble light. A British sergeant later remarked that with "an hours more daylight," Howe could have inflicted "a total overthrow" of his adversary. The sergeant may have been correct. But that was not the outcome of this bloody day during which American casualties topped 1,300 and Howe's ran somewhere between 600 and 900. The British were victors of sorts, as at the end of the day they were "masters of the field," though to reach Philadelphia they still faced getting through Washington's army, which remained in existence.[59]

Howe's army was more nearly intact following the engagement than was his retreating foe's, and had he moved aggressively against the disordered rebels he might have inflicted considerable harm. However, Howe did not move for four days. His army was exhausted, the dead had to be buried, and hundreds of wounded were transported to Wilmington for care. Even so, Howe almost got a second shot at the American army. Washington and his officers were ready for more. They felt the army had performed well at Brandywine, and that whatever misfortunes had arisen could be traced to faulty information. Their judgment ignored the reality that historian Stephen Taaffe disclosed. The British had "outmaneuvered and outfought the Americans at every turn" and the rebels' response had been "confused" and "muddled," particularly by officers who failed to "understand their tasks" and "how to fulfill them." But Washington was committed to another fight and he posted his army between the British and the Schuylkill fords that led to Philadelphia. Another grand showdown was imminent on September 15. It was checked when the dull gray skies opened and rain deluged the area for two days. One historian called it "the best storm in American history, for it saved an American army." He was probably correct. Given an opportunity to rethink matters, Washington moved away and kept moving. As he maneuvered, he ordered Maryland militia, Maxwell's light infantry, and Wayne's division of 1,500 men to shadow Howe's movements, harass the adversary, and be on the alert for ambushes. None of the three accomplished anything of importance and, in fact, on September 20 a British force surprised Wayne's Pennsylvanians in a devastating nighttime attack at Paoli. Wayne got away with most of his men, but 13 percent of his force was lost.[60]

Many congressmen expected Washington to mount a stout defense against Howe's further advance toward Philadelphia. "The City is the Stake, for which the Game is playd," said one. Another hoped the British army "will meet with . . . their Deserts" when they attempted to cross the Schuylkill. Should the "murderers" take the city, said another, "the blow must be terrible & the Wound deep." Washington was aware of those expectations, and his reports to Congress gave the impression that he planned to fight again. His intention, he said, was to move his army to the "most probable" ford the enemy would "attempt to pass" in crossing the Schuylkill. He would make another stand at that site. He even spoke of hoping to attack Howe's force rather than taking up a defensive position, and on one occasion he advised Congress that his planned assault was foiled by rain. Always, he said, he maneuvered with the "firm intent of giving the Enemy Battle wherever I should meet them." In the unlikely event that Washington ever intended any of this, his thinking changed over time. His most recent brush with disaster had made him wary of another risky general engagement. Besides, his army had been battered and his men were exhausted and hungry after days of maneuvering. For nine days, said one of his soldiers, "When they marched,—we marched; when they stopped,—we stopped." All the while that soldier never changed clothes or slept indoors, and on many days he "had to beg on the road" for food. Brandywine reminded Washington of just how unpredictable a battle could be, and with time to think through his options, he shrank from again putting his army at risk. He was willing, even eager, to strike the rear of his foe as it slowly crossed the Schuylkill and was at its most vulnerable. Such an assault could cause considerable damage to the enemy army and its invaluable baggage train.

Washington felt either that he could not prevent the fall of Philadelphia or that waging another grand battle to prevent the loss of the city was too hazardous. General Knox had come to consider losing Philadelphia of not "so much consequence," and defending it not worth the destruction of the Continental army. Washington appears to have agreed with him. When the British outmaneuvered Washington and got across the Schuylkill without opposition, he fancifully portrayed it as due to the failure of his "disaffected" intelligence sources. Four days later, and four days after the Battle of Bemis Heights far to the north, the British army paraded through Philadelphia. Cornwallis rode at its head, accompanied by Galloway and other Loyalists. Large and conspicuously happy crowds lined the streets. A martial band played "God Save Great George Our King."[61]

"If Howe comes here I shall run away, I suppose with the rest," Congressman John Adams remarked a month before Brandywine. He and colleagues did just that once Howe's army reached the Schuylkill. The congressmen had already packed or burned their papers and removed all printing presses from the city. Civilians hauled church bells and the Liberty Bell to safety. When alerted in the middle of the night by Washington's young aide, Alexander Hamilton, that Howe's arrival was imminent, the congressmen set off. Their destination was York, about 100 hundred miles west of Philadelphia. It would be Congress's home for the next nine months.[62]

Howe had entered the city with only about 4,000 men, a quarter of his army. The remaining 11,000 or so were scattered. Some were in Chester and Wilmington. The lion's share were posted in Germantown just outside the city, a garrison that was to protect Philadelphia in the event of a rebel attack. Some British troops in Philadelphia were immediately put to work constructing bulwarks. Others went into action against rebel forts that guarded the approach to the city via the Delaware River.[63]

Washington, who had taken his army to Pennypacker's Mill northeast of the city, convened a council of war on September 28 to consider attacking Philadelphia. The generals were no more interested in attacking entrenched British forces in 1777 than they had been when the redcoats in Boston were protected by battlements two years earlier. Like Washington, however, the generals were eager to do something "should we see a proper opening," but they cautioned against acting until the arrival of reinforcements that were anticipated daily. Their focus, and Washington's, soon turned to Germantown. Washington knew the layout of the hamlet, having been there during his maneuvering after Brandywine. He had good intelligence for a change and believed the garrison in Germantown totaled around 8,000, a spy's estimate that was right on target.[64]

During the next two days several militia units arrived, as did regulars who were no longer needed for the defense of Albany. Altogether, 2,500 men reinforced Washington's army, bringing his total to around 11,000. Before September closed, he made the decision to attack Germantown on October 4. He would be risking his army, but it would be a surprise attack, not another set-piece battle akin to Brandy-wine. A grand victory would so dilute the British army in Pennsylvania that Howe would have to abandon Philadelphia. At the very least, Washington hoped for something along the lines of his Christmas-night success at Trenton in 1776, a star-tling triumph that had boosted morale throughout the country. He devised a complex battle plan, as he had done at Trenton. His plan for Germantown called for four columns to approach the hamlet from different directions. Sullivan's division was to strike the British on the northwest side of the village, Greene's on the north side, Maryland and New Jersey militiamen on the east side, and Pennsylvania militia on the west side. All four columns were to strike simultaneously at 5:00 A.M. It was a plan that looked good on paper, but incredibly good fortune would be necessary for four separate divisions to march several miles—the shortest trek was 14 miles, the longest 16 miles—and simultaneously launch an attack.[65]

On the eve of the army's departure, Washington sought to buoy his soldiers. He told them that the men in Gates's army had displayed "the highest spirit and bravery," and had been successful. "[S]urely," he said, this army will "not suffer itself to be out done by their northern Brethren."[66] With that, the men—carrying food for two days and 40 rounds of ammunition—set off for Germantown in the dark, chilly October night. Only Sullivan's division arrived on time. Greene's guide got lost and took the wrong road, putting his division behind schedule. The New Jersey and Maryland militiamen, facing the longest march, also arrived late. Each of the columns was hindered by a thick fog that gathered during the night and blanketed Germantown in the morning, making it difficult for the commanders to get their bearings. Sullivan's men attacked at 5:00 A.M. as planned. Greene's force did not go into action until 30 minutes later. Nevertheless, in the early stages the American attack unfolded successfully. Although not taken by surprise, British units retreated to the town itself, with Sullivan all the while attacking. As more Americans entered the action, a huge rebel victory appeared possible. But a turn in the battle occurred when a knot of 120 redcoats occupied Cliveden, the two-story stone mansion of Pennsylvania's chief justice. The prudent course for the advancing Americans would have been to bypass those soldiers, and many officers urged that choice on Washington. Instead, he listened to Knox, who thought it unwise to leave a worthy opponent in the rear. It was one of Washington's worst mistakes in this war. His men assailed the house for an hour, taking heavy casualties and never succeeding in dislodging the enemy troops. While Washington was glued to the spot, failing to exercise central command over the operation, Howe used the grace period to regroup and counterattack. The British commander threw brigades into the clash that were supposed to have been tied down, but were available given the late arrival of some rebel units and the near uselessness of the militia in making planned flank attacks.

The tide was turning against the Americans. Howe's rapid response was crucial. So, too, were a series of rebel misfortunes. With fog and thick smoke hanging low and reducing visibility, one rebel force mistook their comrades for the enemy and opened fire. The mishap provoked panic and a retreat. Confusion and exhaustion also dogged the American soldiers. Having not eaten in 24 hours and made long marches to reach Germantown, most were "tormented with thirst all the morning, fighting being warm work," as a rebel private explained. Ammunition was running low, which, as always, stoked uncertainty and fear. With some rebel units falling back, brigade commanders began the difficult task of disengaging their troops and undertaking an orderly withdrawal. The fallback was well ordered in some sectors, panicky in others. With the retreat underway, General Cornwallis arrived from Philadelphia with three grenadier battalions and gave chase. With a large cavalry arm, Cornwallis might have inflicted considerable damage on his fleeing adversary, but that was not in the cards. Within three hours of its start, the Battle of Germantown was over. The Americans had lost 1,100 men, the British half that number. Thirty-five percent of the rebel fatalities occurred at Cliveden, where the British lost just four men.[67]

The Americans had come close to scoring a triumph of some consequence, despite the near impossibility of carrying out the labyrinthine synchronized plan of attack that Washington had devised. Washington, in a letter dark with prevarication, told Congress that the failure "was rather unfortunate, than injurious," as

"We sustained no material loss of Men." Confusion and misunderstandings sown by the fog and smoke had robbed his army of victory, he said. He did not mention his egregious blunder at Cliveden, the pivotal moment in the battle, as some of his fuming officers and their happy counterparts on the other side immediately recognized. On this crucial day, as the historian who has most exhaustively studied the Battle of Germantown concluded, "George Washington failed the Continental army; the army did not fail him."[68]

In the weeks that followed, Howe completed the job of opening the Delaware River—his lifeline to indispensable supplies—and made an attempt or two to bring the once again Fabian Washington to battle. But the campaign of 1777 really ended in Germantown and Saratoga. It had been a British disaster, with one entire army lost and its rival, the Continental army, still intact. Seldom in history has a military commander in chief so mismanaged a campaign as did General Howe in 1777. His strategic myopia doomed Burgoyne. Although he had taken Philadelphia, Howe was in a "Snare" and unable to "get away" from his prize, as John Adams and General Clinton had predicted would be the case weeks before Brandywine. His army remained stationary in Philadelphia for the next eight months. Even Joseph Galloway remonstrated that Britain's "misfortunes" in 1777 were due less to "the genius and valor of the rebels" than to "blunders so gross—so contrary to the least degree of military knowledge" that were made by General Howe.[69] Meanwhile, with patches of snow already on the ground in December, Washington took his army into winter quarters at Valley Forge.

Howe's appalling foundering in 1777 was now added to his grievous failures of 1776, and it prompted a wag in London to write in a popular magazine: "Any other General in the world than General Howe would have beaten General Washington, and any other General in the world than General Washington would have beaten General Howe."[70] The imp was only half right. Given the size and condition of the America army at Brandywine, neither Washington nor any other rebel general could have beaten Howe.

CHAPTER 7

BUILDING CASTLES
IN THE AIR

LONDON WAS ACCUSTOMED TO receiving unwelcome news from America. Disturbing tidings of colonial defiance had crossed the Atlantic since the 1760s. Disheartening accounts of the war's first day along Battle Road had reached London early in the summer of 1775. A few weeks later word arrived of Bunker Hill. Later still Londoners watched as 170 soldiers wounded at Bunker Hill came home "some without legs, and others without arms; and their cloaths hanging on them like a loose mourning gown." They were followed ashore by 60 of the deceased soldiers' widows and children. A newspaper described it as "a most shocking spectacle."[1] Now, at the tag end of 1777, the year that many in Great Britain had thought had to be the last year of an increasingly unpopular war, came the most disconcerting news of all. An entire army had been lost at Saratoga and General Howe had failed to destroy the rebel army in Pennsylvania. Victory was no closer than it had been a year earlier. What is more, the Americans were stronger and Britain weaker, and the danger of French belligerency had increased.

In the enveloping gloom that swaddled England's halls of power, speculation was rampant that the ministry would not survive the crisis. London was a blizzard of rumors, including that Lord Chatham would form a coalition government. Chatham soon responded that it was too late to the save the country and, besides, he would not accept the challenge unless the king granted him full power to seek peace. That was not going to happen. Perhaps the real test of the ministry's survivability came on December 5, three days after word arrived of General Burgoyne's surrender, when David Hartley—asserting that "your armies are baffled and disgraced; one entire army is swallowed up"—proposed an end to the war and the formation of a "federal alliance" with America, something akin to a common-wealth system. Parliament voted down his proposition. North's majority held sway.[2]

Nonetheless, dismay in Parliament was widespread. Even some previously stal-wart supporters of hostilities looked with scorn on continuing the war, proclaiming that it was hopeless and America was lost. It was said that to persevere was to court "national suicide." One summed up the anguish with the comment that the "whole force of the kingdom, and all we can hire" could not crush the colonial rebellion. In their consternation, some sought to bring down Lord Germain, the American secretary. Charles James Fox charged that Germain had offered no solution to the American problem but the use of force. "[M]ore blood! more blood! still more blood!" had been his cry, said Fox, and now an entire army had been lost "through the ignorance, the obstinate, willful ignorance, and incapacity of the noble lord." For a time in December it appeared that Germain could not survive. He weathered the storm because most in Parliament felt that Howe, not the American secretary, was responsible for the debacle at Saratoga. One MP asserted, "No man with common sense would have placed . . . two armies in such a position . . . that made it absolutely impossible that the one should receive any assistance from the other." But that was what Howe had done. Another railed that the general deserved "to be brought home in chains." But George III refused to believe that the war was lost. The "present misfortune" was "very serious but not without remedy," he argued. Britain, he appeared to say, might not be able to crush the rebellion, but it might possess the resources and staying power to compel the rebels to accept a negotiated peace short of American independence. Lord North meanwhile managed the crisis, pledging to offer a peace proposal following Parliament's holiday adjournment.[3]

The king and North did not by themselves keep Britain in the war. North's majority included a great many who felt that America's economic infirmities and war weariness would ultimately force the insurgents to accept a negotiated peace. The ministry's backers also included hard-core nationalists who yearned to avenge Burgoyne's defeat and powerful interests that had grown wealthy from America's subordinate colonial status and were loath to sever ties with the colonies. Glasgow's merchants, for instance, had steadfastly decried the "unprovoked and unnatural" colonial rebellion, and after Saratoga the city council not only advocated continuing the struggle but also raised a battalion with public funds and private subscriptions to help replace those that had been lost through Burgoyne's surrender. Manchester and other towns similarly funded regiments.[4]

Burgoyne, Germain, and Howe were subjected to invective in the press throughout the holidays and when Parliament reconvened, many of its members savaged all three. Behind the scenes the king advised North that he must choose between Germain and Howe. One had to go. Howe drew the short straw as North concluded that removing Germain would be politically risky. Besides, in late October, in what was tantamount to a letter of resignation, Howe had asked to be recalled. Howe was gone. Germain survived the crisis.[5]

Lurking all the while was the palpable fear that Saratoga would bring France and Spain into the war. London's relations with France since the Seven Years' War, and before hostilities erupted with America in 1775, had been generally friendly. France's naval weaknesses and economic woes, as well as Louis XV's known aversion to war, had kept tensions at a relatively low level. Comte de Vergennes's coming to power in 1774, after Louis XVI assumed the throne, had even caused a sigh of relief in Britain. London thought Vergennes was less bellicose than several other possible foreign ministers, and he was certainly preferable to the Anglophobic Duc de Choiseul, whom many feared would be returned to power by the new king. Not even the outbreak of the American war provoked much alarm regarding an imminent slide to war with France. Belief that the war across the sea would be short and end with the defeat of the rebels, and the knowledge that Spain was ambivalent about the American rebellion, tamped down concerns about war with the Bourbons. Even London's initial response to the supposedly secret French assistance to the rebels was muted by the belief that it, and the war, would soon be ancient history. However, concern in London increased in 1776 to such a degree that for the first time an entire Cabinet meeting was devoted to the French problem. London's worries had only increased by early 1777, brought on by a belief that the three American envoys in Paris were seeking an alliance, awareness of French assistance to the rebels, and intelligence reports that France had blatantly stepped up its naval preparations. These worrisome matters were exacerbated by the British military's failure to crush the American insurgency in the campaign of 1776 and irrefutable evidence that American privateers were making increased use of French ports. The prevailing belief within Lord North's ministry at the outset of 1777 was that French intervention was inevitable in the event that Britain's armed forces failed to crush the American rebellion during that year's campaign.

As safeguards, however, the British in 1776 and 1777 had bent over backward to mollify the Spanish. At one point even Lord North, who seldom meddled in diplomacy, conducted discussions with Spain's ambassador in London, hoping to reassure Madrid of Britain's peaceful intentions. London remained tight-lipped when American privateers, denied use of French ports, sold their prizes in Bilbao and El Ferrol.[6]

Any lingering doubts about French intentions were shattered by the news of Saratoga. Is Britain now to fight both the American rebels and the "whole force of Bourbon," one member of the Commons asked? Is there "any chance of recovering" the American colonists "from the power of France," asked another?[7] When North, in December, told Parliament that he would soon propose peace terms, he acted not just to save his ministry but to terminate the war prior to Spanish and French belligerency. Working so hard that he pushed himself to the brink of a serious health crisis, North pursued two tracks. He sent secret agents across the English Channel to conduct exploratory discussions with the American commissioners in Paris and patiently crafted his peace proposal.

One of North's agents, who of course stipulated that his was an unauthorized undertaking, met with Silas Deane two weeks after London learned of Burgoyne's surrender. Not long thereafter the agent called on Franklin. "America is ready to make peace," Franklin told him, but if North's peace offering was no better than his 1775 proffer, "it will not avail any thing." America, Franklin went on, sought unqualified independence and would accept nothing short of that. The following day Franklin met with a second agent, Paul Wentworth, a New Hampshire native and committed Loyalist who also had been sent by North. Wentworth was received "very kindly." However, when he asked if America would accept anything "short of Independence," Franklin replied that in light of the "devastation and Cruelty" that Britain's military had wrought since 1775, Americans desired independence more than ever. Wentworth tried an enticement. If the colonies remained within the empire, Britain would loan them one million pounds at 7½ percent interest for the purpose of eradicating their war debts. Franklin did not nibble. Throughout the discussions with North's agents, Deane and Franklin could not have been more explicit. Toward the end of his conversation with Wentworth, Franklin advised that the United States would fight for another 10 years if necessary to secure its independence. The commissioners immediately notified the French foreign ministry of their conversations with British agents. They hoped to hasten France's entrance into the war by stoking Comte de Vergennes's gnawing fear of an Anglo-American reconciliation.[8]

On Christmas Day, David Hartley, who was an old friend of Franklin's and who had earlier unsuccessfully proposed a federal union with America, got into the act. In a communiqué to Franklin, Hartley opened with the argument that since 1776 the Americans had never proposed any way to end the war other than through Britain's recognition of American independence. Could Franklin not propose terms short of independence? Hartley suggested an armistice during which negotiations could begin. When Franklin did not respond, Hartley, in February, wrote again: "Let nothing ever persuade America to throw themselves into the Arms of France. . . . An American must allways be a Stranger in france. Great Britain may for ages to come be their home." Franklin replied that he could say nothing concerning "healing [the] Breach" until he learned the terms of Lord North's anticipated conciliatory proposals. Hartley answered immediately. North, he said, would not offer independence, but in a cryptic passage he held out hope that Britain might offer independence if America agreed to a "compact of trade." Remember, Hartley added, "France has no affection for America." Hartley wrote again on the day after North revealed his peace plan, divulging that he had been authorized to come to Paris to conduct negotiations with the American commissioners. He closed by saying that the crowning touch to Franklin's extraordinary life would be to leave "behind him peace to his Country and to Mankind." Two days later Hartley wrote again that he personally wished to "arrest the conclusion of any fatal [American] treaty with the house of Bourbon."[9]

Franklin did not respond until he had seen the prime minister's peace plan. Long before revealing its contents, on February 17, North glumly anticipated that Britain's "approaching rupture" with France would lead the Americans to spurn his terms. But he went forward with a plan of conciliation. His peace plan in 1775 had been fraudulent. This one was genuine. He sincerely wanted peace and he offered all that was politically feasible in early 1778. If North foresaw its failure that year, he acted in the hope that as the war dragged on, the day might arrive when a peace faction in the American Congress might embrace his peace proffer.[10]

North, in mid-February, unveiled his peace plan in a lengthy speech to a crowded House of Commons. He humbly confessed that his Coercive Acts in 1774 had been ill-advised and, once again self-effacingly, acknowledged that the conflict "in America had turned out differently" than he had expected. However, he emphasized that "we are in a condition to carry on war much longer," adding that he was not now offering peace terms from necessity. North then sprang a surprise. He announced that he would send peace commissioners to America to conduct talks with "Congress as if it were a legal body," or with the provincial assemblies, General Washington, "or any other officer." Then came his terms. Many were virtually identical to the demands made by the First Continental Congress:

Parliament would never attempt "to tax them again";

the colonists might make "some reasonable and moderate contribution to the common defence";

all American legislation enacted by Parliament since 1763 would be repealed;

the American Congress was permissible so long as it did not breach Parliamentary sovereignty;

Britain would not station a standing army in the colonies in peacetime;

the Crown would never again change a colonial charter without the colonists' consent;

Americans would be given preference when colonial offices were filled;

the customs service would be staffed solely with Americans; and

aid would be extended to help the colonists reduce their war debts.

But North would not recognize American independence and insisted that Parliament must regulate commerce within the British Empire.[11]

Parliament approved North's peace plan and the dispatch of what came to be known as the Carlisle Commission to conduct negotiations with the Americans. The opposition in Parliament endorsed North's initiative, though few foresaw success. As Fox put it, the Americans not only would accept nothing less than independence; they would not "receive the olive branch when held out to them by hands so stained with the blood of their countrymen." Saliently, Edmund Burke pointed out the incongruity of the British government's position. In 1775, Britain had made war on the colonists in order to preserve Parliament's authority to tax the Americans. Now the ministry was proposing "a surrender of the right of taxation," though Britain would continue to wage war against America if it rejected the North peace plan.[12]

THROUGHOUT 1776 AND 1777 Vergennes had watched and waited, and at times saw that French newspapers published inflated accounts of American troop strength and successes in battle. He also subsidized a propaganda rag, *Affaires de l'Angleterre et de l'Amérique,* that was edited by a clerk in the Foreign Ministry. The publication, which postured as a Dutch newspaper and ran from 1776 until late 1779, put out cheery news about the war and affairs in America, some of which was true, and it tirelessly sought to reshape the French citizenry's view of Americans. During the Seven Years' War, the American colonists—who called that conflict the French and Indian War—had fought against France. Indeed, the first shots of that war had been ordered by a colonist, Colonel George Washington, commander of the Virginia Regiment, in a surprise assault on an unsuspecting French party in a dark forest near the Ohio River. Ten French soldiers died in the attack. Thereafter, the Americans, like the British, had been portrayed in the French press as barbarians and Washington as a "butcher." But to smooth the way for French assistance to the Americans after 1776, and possibly for someday entering the war as their ally, Vergennes sought to refashion the image of Americans. Americans were depicted in the pages of *Affaires* as enlightened and virtuous, and their armies were portrayed as fighting in the manner of European armies, not "a la Sauvage." The paper acknowledged that the American rebels were republicans, but maintained that they were not foes of monarchy in general. Washington was represented as kind and virtuous, even pro-monarchical.

Franklin contributed occasional pieces to *Affaires,* including reprints of earlier tracts assailing Great Britain and new essays designed to show the soundness of American credit. He also inserted copies of the first constitutions adopted by several American states. Beginning in 1778 John Adams posted what he called "many little speculations" in the paper, saw to the reprinting of essays in Thomas Paine's *American Crisis,* and included letters he received from Americans that offered positive news about the war or lauded Washington's "Bravery." Other letters revealed that "Our finances want the support a Loan," denied that Congress ever ordered the burning of Loyalist houses, and urged the establishment of French naval superiority.[13]

Throughout 1777 Vergennes closely watched the war in America, managed thorny issues with the American commissioners, and oversaw French ties with Spain. However, nothing was more important than France's relationship with Great Britain. French shipments of arms to the American rebels, and the departure of French volunteers to help their fight, had transformed relations between the two nations into a cold war marked by a mutual arms race. With the rehabilitation of the French navy not expected to be completed until early the next year, Vergennes remained anxious to avoid war. While on the one hand he daringly sanctioned aid to the American insurgents, he simultaneously acted cautiously, even pliantly at times, toward Britain. Early in 1777 he spurned the American commissioners' entreaties for a commercial accord. It would be too provocative. For similar reasons he refused Spain's request that France augment its fleet in the West Indies. Vergennes felt that his hands were tied until the rebuilding of the French navy was completed. Once it was, Vergennes anticipated achieving near parity with the Royal Navy and overwhelming naval superiority if France and Spain acted in concert. All along he appeared to think war with Britain was likely in 1778, though not a certainty.[14]

Aside from arms shipments, the actions of American privateers posed the greatest danger that France would stumble into war with Britain in 1777. As a neutral nation, France traded with the United States, but it could not tolerate American privateers selling their prizes—cargoes seized from captured British merchant ships—in French ports. In February, France took the first steps to prevent the practice, and in May it arrested and imprisoned Gustavus Conyngham, an American captain who had ignored the injunctions against selling his prizes to French businessmen. Conyngham's incarceration followed a protest by Britain's ambassador, Viscount Stormont. In July, when the British envoy yet again protested French collusion with rebel privateers, Vergennes was vexed and alarmed. Later in the summer, after a squadron of American privateers captured 18 British vessels in St. George's Channel and Lord North dispatched a special envoy to Versailles, Vergennes panicked. He feared war was imminent. Britain demanded that the privateers' prizes be returned and threatened hostilities if France did not take concrete steps forbidding the sale of prizes in French ports. Vergennes walked a thin line. He was not ready for war, but hardly wished to drive the Americans back into the arms of Great Britain. In the midst of the privateering crisis, the first news of the campaign of 1777 reached Versailles. It was not good news. Fort Ticonderoga had fallen in a matter of hours. Vergennes rapidly complied with Britain's demands.[15]

Vergennes had planned for war with Britain since the day he became foreign minister. He envisaged war as the means to enhance French security and restore the king's realm to its once exalted place. Vergennes was certain that Britain had risen to great-power status largely as a result of its colonial possessions in America. Trade with the colonies had expanded Britain's economy and created bevies of experienced merchant seamen that the Royal Navy could utilize in wartime. If Britain lost America, Vergennes surmised, its wealth and trade would diminish, and Britain's economic, naval, and military might would be acutely weakened. Furthermore, if America won its independence, France might secure the preponderance of the new nation's commerce. Vergennes had done what he could to sustain the American insurgency, though he had always suspected that even with secret French assistance, America could not win a protracted war against a great power. The best chance for America to gain independence, he believed, would come through France joining the war. Yet while Vergennes was a risk-taker, he was not about to embark on an inescapably losing cause. He restlessly awaited word of the outcome of campaign 1777.[16]

Work on readying the French navy went forward concurrently. France's naval budget was now five times greater than at the outset of the American war. As work intensified in French shipyards, Vergennes studied war plans. The best bet, he believed, would be to open with an attack on the Royal Navy in New York. He also sounded out Conde de Floridablanca, who had recently succeeded Grimaldi as Spain's minister of state. Now 49, Floridablanca had risen from middle-class origins and years of practicing law. By and large, he continued Grimaldi's policies, though he was more cautious. Vergennes pressed him, arguing that the "time has come to decide" whether to "abandon America to its own devices or . . . effectively come to its side." Floridablanca replied that Spain would not be ready for war in 1778 and, though it went unsaid, he wanted no part of the war until Spain's annual treasure fleet—groaning with its customary haul of around $50 billion worth of New World silver—arrived home safely late in the year. Floridablanca also doubted that Britain would end the war in America even if it suffered major setbacks in 1777. He played a canny waiting game, thinking that in time either France or Britain would make concessions to Spain—the one to bring it into war, the other to keep it out of the war.

Throughout the summer and fall Vergennes beseeched his ambassador in London for news about the military situation in America. What he received was a bundle of contrasting information: Burgoyne was succeeding. No, he was in trouble. Often there was no word at all from America. As December dawned, Vergennes did not know whether Burgoyne had reached Albany or if Washington's army still existed.[17]

Early that month the American commissioners learned of Burgoyne's fate. The son of Franklin's nephew, a resident of Boston, arrived in Passy with word that "God be prased . . . General Burgoyne and his Whol Armey [are] Prisoners of War." The news allegedly made Franklin weep with joy. He and his colleagues wasted no time in sending a courier to notify Vergennes. The foreign minister beamed with "the most perfect Satisfaction" at the tidings. That evening, during dinner with an influential banker who had ties to the Americans, Vergennes subtly shifted from referring to the insurgents as "your friends" and instead spoke of them as "our friends." Soon, official word arrived from Congress. Burgoyne's army had surrendered and, although Philadelphia had fallen, Washington still commanded "a good army."[18]

The war had dictated the timing of the Declaration of Independence, and the outcome of the campaign of 1777 made it easier for Vergennes to take the step he had long planned on taking. To this point, Vergennes had thought that if France someday opted to enter the war, it would be because the Americans were too weak to any longer fend for themselves. But suddenly in December the Americans had never seemed stronger. An entire British army had been vanquished at Saratoga, the Continental army was intact, and Washington's attack at Germantown—though a failure—had convinced Vergennes that the Americans were resilient, strong, and capable of waging offensive war and that Washington remained vigorous and bold. John Adams, who had been appointed as Deane's successor and arrived in Paris early in 1778, thought Washington's daring attack was pivotal in convincing the French that "America would finally succeed." In December, Vergennes initiated the steps toward recognition of the United States. He directed his secretary, Conrad Alexandre Gérard, to notify the American envoys that as "there now appeared no doubt of the ability and resolution of the states to maintain their independency," the diplomats should renew "their former proposition of an alliance." Within 48 hours the three Americans advised Vergennes that a commercial treaty would have "the most happy Effect" on American morale and credit, and in "discouraging and diminishing their internal Enemies," the Loyalists. While at it, they requested a gift of French warships. They did not mention a formal alliance.[19]

Vergennes had work to do before he signed any accord. Louis XVI, who, like his father, had expressed reservations about getting into any war, had to be persuaded that the moment had arrived for France to enter hostilities and dispatch a large squadron to America to destroy the Royal Navy's American fleet. In July, around the time that Burgoyne's British army approached Fort Ticonderoga, the monarch and his Conseil de Roi had conducted renewed discussions concerning war with Britain, talks that led to a preliminary decision to commit to hostilities, though to watch and wait as the campaign of 1777 unfolded. The king's qualms about going to war lingered, however, an aversion that to some degree was based on the earlier counsel of Controller General Turgot, who had steadfastly warned of economic catastrophe should France yet again find itself at war.[20]

By December, Vergennes was able to counter with several arguments. While Saratoga demonstrated the Americans would be a dependable ally and the war would not be prolonged, Washington's failure to defeat the British in the Philadelphia campaign indicated that French belligerence was essential if the Americans were to win their independence. Furthermore, if Britain was faced with a two-front war against both France and the American rebels, it would be vulnerable as never before. The moment to act had arrived. If France did not enter into hostilities now, Britain and its colonies would reconcile, a step that would restore British power and possibly result in a joint Anglo-American attack on France's West Indian possessions. While working on his monarch, Vergennes made one last stab at bringing Spain into the fray. He felt that he had to move rapidly, as following Parliament's Christmas recess it was virtually certain that Britain would offer the Americans enticing peace terms.[21]

Vergennes told Floridablanca what he had told Louis XVI. The time for war had arrived. Nothing "can justify . . . letting slip through our fingers the only opportunity in many centuries to put England in its place." Louis XVI came around, and ever after Vergennes insisted—perhaps as salve for his conscience or for self-protection—that he had merely acted "as a consequence of [the king's] orders." Spain, however, balked at making the leap. It would remain neutral, though it would continue to provide secret aid to the American insurgents. Vergennes learned of Madrid's decision on New Year's Eve. He was disappointed, but ready to go it alone. One week later Gérard opened negotiations with the three American envoys. The discussions took place in Deane's apartment in Paris.[22]

France had been moving steadily in this direction for months and it is possible that only an American catastrophe, such as the destruction of the Continental army, would have forestalled French intervention. Such a calamity had not occurred. Instead, word of the outcome of the campaign of 1777 coincided with the realization of France's long-sought effort to achieve naval parity with England. At the outset of 1778 France had 53 ships of the line, all of which could be manned. The Royal Navy could man 66 of its great warships, but not all would be in North American waters. The French navy, at least for a time, would enjoy superiority in the American theater.[23]

Gérard's meeting with the American commissioners came two years almost to the day since the appearance of *Common Sense*, the pamphlet in which Thomas Paine had urged a declaration of independence in order to secure French military assistance. Negotiations proceeded rapidly. On the first day of discussions the

Americans vowed to "reject firmly all propositions made to them of Peace from England." Gérard then proposed a military alliance. On February 6, a month after the talks began, Gérard and the American commissioners signed two treaties: the Treaty of Amity and Commerce and the Treaty of Alliance. There was no ceremony and the signing, which consumed only a few moments, occurred in private in ministerial offices across the Seine from the Louvre. The commercial treaty specified reciprocity. France did not ask for a monopoly of American trade, and the Americans made it clear that they must be free to choose their trading partners. The Treaty of Alliance stipulated that France would enter the war at a time of its choosing, a bitter pill for the Americans, who hoped for an immediate French declaration of war. The two countries pledged not to make a separate peace with Britain and to remain at war until Britain recognized American independence. France forswore "forever the possession" of Bermuda and all parts of North America that had belonged to it before 1763, which of course meant Canada, but it would have the right to attack and gain any British island in or near the Gulf of Mexico. The United States was to retain whatever additional possessions "or conquests that their Confederation may obtain during the War."

A few days after the treaties were signed, the American envoys were introduced to Louis XVI as the "ambassadors of the Thirteen United Provinces." Vergennes lauded their "wisest, most reserved conduct" throughout their 14-month mission in France. American diplomacy had been crowned with success, but the alliance with France was largely the result of French and Spanish assistance, victory at Saratoga, the survival of the Continental army through three desperate years of war, and the completion of France's naval rearmament at just the right time.[24]

LORD NORTH PRESENTED HIS peace plan to Parliament 11 days after the treaties were signed, though weeks passed before France publicly announced the accords. The treaties hardly surprised London. Early in January, North told the king that war with France was a virtual certainty, and later that month he informed a friend of the "approaching rupture." Rumors of war had swirled in Paris during and after the January negotiations, scuttlebutt that London newspapers reported. As Paris was a warren of spies and Hôtel de Valentinois in Passy was Grand Central Station for British secret agents, North had a good idea of what was brewing. Finally, on March 13, the French ambassador in London notified the British government of the commercial treaty, though he did not mention the alliance. War with France was

now unavoidable unless Britain recognized American independence, and early in
April several members of Parliament urged that course. The ensuing debate was
sharp and it brought the feeble Earl of Chatham to the chamber for the last time.
Supported by two friends so that he could stand, and admitting that he had "more
than one foot in the grave," Chatham for the final time advocated peace through an
offer of a commonwealth arrangement in which the Americans would have virtual
autonomy within the British Empire. But the ministry never had an appetite for
such a plan. It had long since made the decision to continue this war, even if a
French alliance with the Americans assured a wider war.[25]

In the first days after learning of Saratoga, North's ministry had concluded that
the war would continue unless the colonists accepted the prime minister's peace
proposal. Their resolve was strengthened by George III's unwavering support. The
monarch admitted that the war had "impoverished" the country, but he clutched
unyieldingly to the belief that this was "the most serious" challenge that Britain had
ever faced. American independence, he insisted, would result in the systematic
unraveling of the British Empire until, little by little, every part of it was lost.[26] The
choice of the king and his ministers to continue the American war was made with
the realization—and by late January, the virtual certainty—that France would
enter hostilities. For the first time in the series of four wars with France that had
begun nearly 90 years earlier, Britain would face the prospect of engaging the French
without a European ally. There would be nothing to dilute what France might
throw at them.

Great Britain had been the spectacular victor in the Seven Years' War, but a
mid-century shuffle of alliances among the European powers left Britain diplomati-
cally isolated. Beginning early in the 18th century, France, under Louis XIV,
had cobbled together alliances with the Ottoman Turks, Sweden, and the Polish-
Lithuanian Commonwealth as a means of checking Austria, the great power to its
east. Austria, in turn, sought security against France through an alliance with Great
Britain. Russia at that time was "an army rather than a state," in the words of one
historian, but as the century progressed, both it and Prussia grew in power, Prussia
through the modernization of its military and Russia as it was conspicuously large
and increasingly capable and energetic. The power of both Prussia and Russia was
enhanced by the War of the Austrian Succession, which ended in 1748, raising
concerns in Vienna that its interests in eastern Europe were imperiled by the inexorably growing strength of those two nations. The looming menace to its east
drove Austria into the arms of France, its traditional rival. Austria severed ties with

Britain, its traditional ally. The Austro-French entente and alliance was most famously formalized in 1770 through the marriage of 14-year-old Maria Antonia, daughter of the Austrian empress Maria Theresa, to the dauphine of France, who eventually became Louis XVI. On arriving in France, Maria Antonia changed her name to Marie Antoinette.

During the Seven Years' War, France fought in Europe against Britain and Prussia, and in the American theater against the British and its American colonists. The two-front war was disastrous for France, something not lost on Vergennes or his predecessors in the foreign ministry. They feared a repeat cataclysm should the nation find itself at war not only with Britain but also with Prussia as a result of its troubles with France's new ally, Austria.

That threat, however, abated in 1772 when Austria, Prussia, and Russia resolved their differences, at least for the time being, by agreeing to the partition of Poland. The step temporarily ameliorated the security concerns of each power through the resolution of their territorial differences. It meant something else entirely for Vergennes. The partition of Poland assured European stability for the next few years, freeing France from the likelihood of a European land war—and of yet again dividing its military resources on two fronts—while it was at war with Britain. While Vergennes grasped the reality of the new situation, Britain's statesmen gave every appearance of not understanding that the accommodation reached by the eastern powers stripped London of the possibility of acting on the differences between those nations in order to achieve an alliance.[27]

Britain was without a European ally, and with the possible exception of Russia, no European power saw any benefit from allying with Britain. Russia and Britain had been on opposite sides in the Seven Years' War, though they were never formally at war, and economic interests—Britain secured vital naval stores from Russia, and the Russians derived precious manufactured goods from Britain—caused the ostensible enemies to continue trading with each other throughout the conflict. In the aftermath of the Seven Years' War, Russia remained important to Britain's economy and power, and the two signed a commercial accord in 1766, updating a pact they had agreed to more than 30 years earlier. However, Russia and Britain never allied. London's failure to secure an alliance with Russia, a dereliction that led to what has been called Britain's "Splendid Isolation," has been attributed to numerous factors: a stubborn, uncompromising monarch; "bankrupt statesmanship" by several woebegone secretaries of state; unbending xenophobia; an unshakable reluctance to increase taxes, which would have been necessary to meet Russia's demand that London subsidize the tsar's client states; and Britain's inward turn after 1765 due in part to the American insurgency. While some officials in London were troubled by Britain's isolation—Chatham preached the need for security against the Bourbons through the restoration of the earlier partnership with Prussia and an alliance with Russia, the "great cloud[s] of power" in eastern Europe, in his lexicon—most of the many ministries after 1763 shrugged it off. After all, Britain was superior at sea, France was incapable of successfully waging war, and it was believed that Spain would never dare risk destabilizing its vast New World empire by helping the American colonies achieve independence.

It was not that Britain did not want an ally. Their leaders through these years were not isolationists. However, neither Austria nor Prussia, with whom Britain had once had close ties, any longer had compelling reasons for allying with Great Britain. Furthermore, Britain's leaders had no wish to pay a vexatious price for obtaining an ally. They told themselves that in the event of another European crisis, one of the continental powers would find it in their interest to seek a British alliance.

The British did send an envoy to Russia as early as 1762 to explore the prospect of an alliance. The likelihood of allying seemed promising. Russia and Britain were economically interdependent and shared a mutual hatred of France, and the two countries were not cleaved by rival aspirations or clashing interests. But Britain's interest in a Russian alliance in time fell victim to the reality that not only did Catherine II, the empress, have a secure ally in Prussia, but that Britain and Russia did not share substantive interests. In the 1760s and 1770s the only danger that Britain might someday face would come from France and Spain, and there was little incentive for Russia—whose interests were shifting to the southeast—to make enemies of them. Likewise, southeastern Europe—the Russian sphere—was not a region of paramount interest for Britain. Furthermore, a Russian alliance might drag London into unwanted hostilities with the Ottoman Turks, which could lead to serious commercial damage to British trade. Indeed, officials in London who explored coming to terms with Russia spoke of what they called the "Turkish clause" as the insurmountable stumbling block to an accord. They were alluding to Catherine's insistence on British support in the event that Russia was attacked by the Ottoman Turks. It turned out, of course, that Britain might have benefited from a Russian alliance during the Revolutionary War, but no one foresaw such a need until two or more years into hostilities. During the approach of the American war, the prevailing view in London was that extended war against the rebellious colonies was unimaginable. Peace would come before France and Spain could enter the conflict.

Britain remained isolated, a situation that, in the words of historian Michael Roberts, was "unsought, unwanted, but accepted with a stolid confidence born of England's insular situation." During the initial 30 months of the American war, London looked on its diplomatic isolation as vexing but not fatal. But in 1778 Britain found itself at war with France without a European ally.[28]

AFTER SARATOGA THE NORTH ministry understood that Britain stood alone and its former military strategy had failed. In the murk of winter following word of Saratoga, the cabinet undertook a strategic reappraisal. Some advocated holding what Britain possessed in North America, but henceforth primarily focusing on defending the valuable sugar colonies in the West Indies against the impending French threat. These ministers argued that the war against the colonial insurgents should now be carried on by the Royal Navy through its blockade and punishing raids on coastal towns. For them, waging offensive war in America would be a thing of the past. But George III urged that the war to suppress the rebellion in the 13 colonies be continued, though he also pointed out that if the sugar islands were lost, there would be no money to continue the war in North America. Germain called for focusing on crushing the insurgency in the southern colonies. He believed the South had ingrained economic ties with Great Britain through its tobacco, rice, and indigo trades. He insisted that anti-republicanism, fear of losing slave properties, and deeply rooted ties to the Anglican Church caused a majority of southerners to remain loyal to the mother country. The American secretary also pointed to deep divisions between residents of the backcountry and the coastal elite that might be exploited. Now that Burgoyne's force had been lost and what remained of the British army in America was almost certain to be reduced by having some divisions redeployed to protect the Caribbean, Germain added that the South would offer fertile ground for recruiting additional soldiery.[29]

Following lengthy battles over the numerous strategic choices, the ministry essentially adopted all of them. A portion of the army in America would be detached to the Caribbean, and the navy was to be augmented in order to safeguard the colonies in the tropics and wage war at sea. The shrunken army in America, together with its naval arm, would strike civilian enclaves, sowing misery and terror, which the king labeled "distressing America." It was an approach conceived in the belief that Britain could outlast the insurgents and that, in time, rebel attrition, America's internal weaknesses, collapsing morale, and French weariness would compel the rebellious colonists to accept a peace short of independence. Finally, Britain was to turn to a "southern strategy." It would seek to crush the rebellion in Georgia and South Carolina, and the belief was widespread that if South Carolina was reclaimed, North Carolina would inevitably return to the fold. Some officials in London had always looked on the South as what has been called "the soft underbelly of the rebellion." If the southern strategy succeeded, at war's end Britain would at the very least possess a vast empire in America that stretched from Canada to the wealth-generating Caribbean islands, and included not only boundless stretches of trans-Appalachia but four valuable cash-crop-producing southern colonies (the two Carolinas and Georgia, as well as Florida, which Britain had acquired from Spain in the Seven Years' War). If the United States somehow survived years of war, it would be a weak nation surrounded on every side by powerful Great Britain. The United States of 10 or so states might be independent, but it would face a bleak and uncertain future.[30]

In the first days after his victory at Saratoga, General Gates remarked that Great Britain now needed a "Great State Physician" to save it by granting American independence. However, Gates added, if the loss of Burgoyne's army did not teach "Old England" what it must do, then its obstinacy would be its ruination.[31] Gates's view encapsulated the outlook of a great many Americans: Saratoga had changed the war, guaranteeing British defeat if it unwisely chose to continue to fight.

IN DECEMBER, WHILE DIPLOMATS in Europe were busy and North's cabinet chartered Britain's future course, Washington took his army into winter quarters at Valley Forge. He had not wanted to go there. He thought it would be easier to supply men in numerous encampments throughout eastern Pennsylvania, but congressmen from states near occupied Philadelphia wanted the army posted on Howe's doorstep to curtail British foraging and destructive raids. Congress, in late November, even directed Washington to wage "a winter's campaign with vigour and success." Washington relented with regard to Valley Forge, but he was furious at the intrusion on his strategic choices. Just before Christmas, his rage boiled over and he wrote intemperately to Congress. No army can protect every person or every square foot of territory, he said. In every war, some regions will inevitably be ravaged and plundered. It "is time to speak plain," he told the congressmen. It "is a much easier and less distressing thing, to draw Remonstrances in a comfortable room by a good fire side" than to face a soldier's life on "a cold, bleak hill" or to "sleep under frost & snow without Cloaths or Blankets."[32]

Washington may soon have regretted speaking so rashly. Predators prowled at his heels. Some inside Congress and within the army thought Washington should be replaced. Some were mesmerized by Gates, others disenchanted with Washington. Confidence in the commander's abilities had been eroded by his blunders and indecisiveness during the New York campaign in 1776 and further damaged by his failure to win at Brandywine and the missteps he made at Germantown. Some army officers said that Washington was "only fit to command a regiment" or "to be the head clerk of a London countinghouse." He was "a weak man," even "ignorant," some thought. Frustration over Washington's conduct swelled in Congress and other circles when he failed to fight Howe a second time after Brandywine to prevent the fall of Philadelphia, refused to attack after the British occupied the city, and took only minimal steps to impede the enemy's destruction of the Delaware River forts. Not a few believed that Washington was surrounded with sycophants who peddled bad advice. Benjamin Rush, physician general in the army's medical department, characterized the four generals on whom Washington allegedly had come to rely the most as "timid, speculative, without enterprise" (Greene), "in the field a madman" (Sullivan), "proud, vain, lazy, ignorant" (Stirling), and "a sordid, boasting, cowardly sot" (Adam Stephen). Some questioned the wisdom of his Fabian strategy. Others deplored what they saw as an undisciplined soldiery and the shoddy administrative structure of the army. John Adams, who never advocated Washington's removal, was among those who thought changes were necessary to "bring order out of this Confusion."[33]

Washington was aware that one general, Thomas Conway, a French volunteer, had declared that the war could never be won so long as the army was commanded by such an inept leader. Meanwhile, Virginia's delegates tipped Washington to the criticism within Congress.[34] Washington was thin-skinned, angry at Congress's intrusiveness, and weighed down by enormous pressures. In these circumstances, he imagined that a widespread conspiracy hatched by a "malignant faction" inside and outside Congress had formed to relieve him of command—plotters that historians once labeled the "Conway Cabal." Washington, who concluded that Gates was part of the conspiracy, greatly exaggerated the scope of disaffection, though to be sure there was what one delegate called a "buz" in Congress. The president of Congress, Henry Laurens, a steadfast supporter of Washington, acknowledged concerns among his colleagues over blunders at Germantown, and privately noted that Washington's opinions were "treated with . . . much indecent freedom & Levity" by many congressmen.[35]

Despite Washington's concerns, Congress never came close to replacing him. Most congressmen continued to believe in his virtue and ability, and the majority recognized that he had faced a more formidable adversary than Gates's army had confronted. Congress knew, too, that ousting Washington would be terribly divisive, perhaps fatally so. Furthermore, every delegate had to know that changing the army's leadership might have a harmful impact in Versailles. But Congress did wish to establish greater control over the army's strategy, organization, and supply system. Some thought the commander's gargantuan task of managing the war prevented him from dealing with the army's problems. Others felt Washington lacked the necessary administrative skills for coping with the ills that plagued the army. In time, Washington understood that he was in no danger of being removed, but his control of the army was threatened, and he fought back. Washington had honed his political skills while commanding the Virginia Regiment in the 1750s and sitting in his colony's assembly for more than 15 years. When Congress sent committees that posed threats to his authority, he handled them with aplomb. Furthermore, many high-ranking Continental army officers were devoted to Washington or feared that his dismissal would damage the war effort and their standing. Several went to bat for him, lobbying and, in the case of fearsome Daniel Morgan, intimidating some who were thought to pose a threat to the commander. Thomas Paine pitched in as well, defending Washington in his ongoing *American Crisis* essays, much as he had done in his initial entry following the calamitous New York campaign. (The commander, he now wrote, was a man of "unabated fortitude" who in 1776 had "saved the spark" of the American Revolution that has since "blazed . . . with unrivalled lustre.") By winter's end, Congress understood that provoking the army would be dangerous. The reform movement collapsed.[36]

That Washington remained in command was crucial, but equally pivotal was the campaign that followed to make him an iconic figure. According to John Adams, Congress from the outset had hidden Washington's flaws and mistakes from the public—and the enemy—and had represented his "every defeat as a victory and every retreat as an advance." Aware that monarchs in Europe were the symbols around which the citizenry could unite, Congress now sought to provide republican America with a figure around which its people could rally. Washington was to be made into that person. As Adams put it, Congress "agreed to blow the trumpet of panegyric" in order to make Washington "the central stone in [America's] geometrical arch." Dr. Rush thought it a "state necessity" for Congress to transform Washington into a heroic figure and suppress open attacks on him that could fatally endanger the war effort. Congress sought to convince the citizenry of what many congressmen deeply believed: Washington was "a great & virtuous man" and no other commander could have done a better job.[37]

Congress was the architect of iconography, but its campaign could succeed only if the public willingly accepted the notion of Washington's magnanimity, honesty, rectitude, and talent. Many Americans already esteemed Washington, seeing him as the very symbol of virtue and sacrifice. He had left Mount Vernon to serve his country and had never returned home or been away from the army, save for once in 1776 when Congress summoned him to Philadelphia. He served without pay, bore heavy burdens, often risked life and limb, and had never abused his power. Newspaper essays—correctly, it turned out—characterized Washington as a modern Cincinnatus who, like the Roman of antiquity, would relinquish power and return home once victory was won. Seen as the embodiment of the dreams and spirit of the American Revolution, Washington was praised in the press as "an honour to the human race" who had been "raised by Heaven to . . . guide the chariot of War." He was also seen as the glue that held together the Continental army through 30 months of warfare against a great power. The time was right in 1778 for the nation to honor and celebrate Washington. He, with his army, endured the brutal first months of 1778 at Valley Forge, and there were many who believed he had brought the army through that test. Toward the end of those tribulations, word at last arrived of the alliance with France. It was as if the sun burst through dark, threatening clouds and shined its rays on America. To many Americans, no one was more responsible for this breathtaking achievement than General Washington.

With a touch of the sacramental, Washington's birthday was widely celebrated during the winter of 1778, he was venerated in almanacs, books were dedicated to him, and toasts raised to him were commonplace at banquets. As never before, Washington was seen as a heroic figure. For many, he was the indispensable man. He had also become the untouchable man, an official who was neither to be questioned nor whose authority was to be disputed. No American had ever been seen in such a manner, nor would any thereafter be looked on in this fashion.[38]

SOMEWHERE BETWEEN 11,000 AND 14,000 Continentals set off for Valley Forge on December 11, a couple of days after Conrad Gérard opened a dialogue with the three American envoys in Paris. Eight days later, with snow swirling in gusty winds, the soldiers entered their most famous encampment during the Revolutionary War, a rustic site 18 miles northwest of Philadelphia. While militiamen patrolled the nearby Schuylkill River and some Continentals were detached to outlying areas to guard the several roads that led in and out of Philadelphia, most of Washington's soldiers were posted within the camp. Even before laying eyes on Valley Forge, months of campaigning and the army's deplorable supply system had already reduced the soldiery to what one trooper called "a truly forlorn condition—no clothing, no provisions, and . . . disheartened." The initial state of affairs at Valley Forge did nothing to improve their situation. Some soldiers had nothing to eat during their first two days in the cantonment. Before December ended, 5,000 men were hospitalized. Those who were still healthy were "now absolutely in danger of perishing," thought a private, whose diet during his initial 48 hours in camp consisted of half a pumpkin. Those who could work were immediately assigned duties. Some felled and sawed trees, others—divided into teams of 12 men— constructed 14-by-16-foot log huts, and still others built fortifications, including five redoubts. Thomas Paine, who visited the site early on and watched as trees right and left came down, said the soldiers resembled "a family of Beavers." Washington had anticipated problems in coming to Valley Forge as it was in an area that had been picked over for months by the rival armies, but from the outset conditions were likely worse than he had envisaged. He had hardly gotten off his horse before he wrote Congress that his army was without meat, soap, and vinegar and had insufficient quantities of flour, clothing, shoes, and blankets. He also advised that he did not see how he could hold the army together. Inevitably, he warned, the men must "Starve—dissolve—or disperse."[39]

If no one starved to death, 2,000 men perished that winter and spring as a result of diseases brought on by malnutrition and inadequate clothing, blankets, and shelter. Nor did the army dissolve or disperse, as Washington had feared. However, some 1,000 men deserted during the first three months, and hundreds of officers, mostly lieutenants and captains, resigned their commissions and returned home.[40] Valley Forge is rightly remembered as a place of incredible anguish and misery, but—at least as far as food was concerned—the army was not afflicted with an unabated crisis. Food shortages occurred episodically. The first two weeks witnessed the worst scarcity, a second came 30 days later, and a third and final food shortage materialized late in February. Much of the time ample food was available, due in part to a gutsy move by Washington who in February sent off upwards of

2,000 men under several commanders into parts of New Jersey, Pennsylvania, Maryland, and Delaware in a six-week foraging campaign. The absence of so many troops exposed the remainder of the army at Valley Forge to attack, but the British neither struck Valley Forge nor made a concerted effort to assail the foragers.[41]

In a sense it was odd that the soldiery experienced food shortages, as Valley Forge was in a rich farming area. Garden and dairy farms dotted the landscape all around, and 75,000 farmers lived within a 75-mile radius of the camp. However, many yeomen preferred to sell their goods to the British army, which paid in specie, and some pacifist Quaker farmers refused to sell their wares to soldiers. But the chief culprit was the army's faulty supply system, whose inherent problems were exacerbated by the weather. Contrary to mythology, 1778 was an unseasonably mild winter at Valley Forge, but it rained plentifully, rendering unpaved roads impassable. There were also shortages of teamsters, wagons, and horses, and corruption was rampant within the Wagonmaster Department.[42]

If food shortages were sporadic, the men's woefully inadequate living conditions never improved. The Continentals lacked adequate winter clothing and bedding and lived in drafty and improperly heated dwellings. They may have been spared the region's customary quantity of snow, but this was still Pennsylvania in wintertime, and it was cold and damp. As the men faced deprivation and lived in close proximity, transmissible diseases rapidly appeared and just as quickly spread. Soon the death rate mounted. "[W]e have lost a good many men," Washington reported late in March. By the end of April approximately 10 percent of the Continentals who had entered Valley Forge in December were dead. In fact, more men died at Valley Forge than in the combined battles of Freeman's Farm, Bemis Heights, Brandywine, and Germantown.[43] Congress, which had insisted on a lone winter encampment, bore considerable responsibility for the calamity.

Washington worked diligently to alleviate the suffering. He mandated steps to rid the camp of "Filth and nastiness," saw that every soldier was inoculated against smallpox, rapidly got the men into housing, did his best to make them keep their quarters clean, and repeatedly inveighed state officials to act to halt the "sufferings and loss of Men." He also worried about the loss of the army's horses, which perished at an even greater rate than the men. "[C]ould the poor Horses tell their tale," he said, it would be as "lamentable" as that of the soldiers.[44]

No field grade officers died at Valley Forge. They found accommodations in snug homes in the area and enjoyed an abundance of food, wine, and liquor, and many were joined by their wives and families. On numerous weekends, while the

needy soldiery shivered a few hundred yards away in their primitive huts, the officers enjoyed plays, recitals, and dances, all held in a comfortable hall that had been
constructed by soldiers on Washington's orders. The Revolutionary ideal of human
equality was not in evidence at Valley Forge.

Joseph Galloway, the Tory who had guided Howe to a ford across the Brandywine, sent strikingly accurate reports to the British commander describing the
plight of the Continentals during the earliest weeks at Valley Forge and urging a
British attack. Washington expected and feared a strike, and even one of his
soldiers, Private Joseph Plumb Martin, thought an attack would have left "our poor
emaciated carcasses . . .'strewed [on] the plain."[45] But Howe closed his career in
America by failing to act.

Valley Forge is largely remembered for the unsparing agony that the soldiers
endured, but in two respects it was a pivotal moment in this war. The gruesome
shared experiences forged a bond among the soldiers, many of whom thereafter
saw themselves as a "band of brothers" who made noble sacrifices for reasons of
patriotism. Indeed, while praise was heaped on Washington for getting his army
through the ordeal, two of his greatest defenders celebrated the soldiery, not their
commander in chief. General Greene lauded the "patience" of the common soldiers
who had borne the greatest hardships with "chearfulness." Similarly, Gouverneur
Morris, a congressman from New York, marveled at the "Poor Dogs" loyalty to the
cause despite their being "without Cloaths to wear, Victuals to eat, Wood to burn
or straw to lie on."[46]

That winter at Valley Forge was also a time of training. Washington emphasized drilling the soldiers in order "to bring them into the Field in a more regular
manner" when the campaign of 1778 opened. French volunteers made Washington
aware of accelerated training methods and at Valley Forge he in turn gave instruction responsibilities to Friedrich Steuben, a former Prussian officer who had
fought in the Seven Years' War. The tab for Steuben's crossing to America had
been paid by Achard Bonvouloir, but he arrived without a commission in the fall
of 1777. However, he brought letters of introduction from Silas Deane and
Benjamin Franklin, and Congress appointed him inspector general of the army
while the Board of War gave him money to cover his travel expenses to Valley
Forge. Steuben hailed from the Prussian aristocracy, as recent research has established, but he had inherited neither wealth nor property, and at this juncture he
was essentially penniless. Inventing the title "baron" for himself and bedecked
with the Star of Fidelity, a German medal of merit, the 47-year-old veteran soldier

was rapidly embraced by Washington, who put him to work training the troops despite his inability to speak and understand English. Steuben, speaking in French and German, with a sprinkling of English profanities, began by teaching the drill to a "model company" of around 100 men who, in turn, went on to train others in what the soldiers soon called the "Prussian drill."[47] Steuben stressed order and strictness, but he also counseled the company officers to know their men by name, visit them, and look in on those who were sick. Washington praised Steuben's "indefatigable industry" and the results he produced. By spring, Washington was convinced that his soldiers were instilled with a new "spirit of discipline." Washington also saw to the printing of the training standards that Steuben taught. The publication came to known at the "Blue Book," a manual used thereafter in this war by the army.

Washington also felt that the army had been improved through reforms that he sought, including a revamped means of promotion, pensions for the officers—a step taken in part to stop so many from leaving the army—and the creation of a military police. After months at Valley Forge, a Virginia officer, remarking on the remade army, thought the Continentals "were 50 times in better order this spring than we were last [spring] to receive the Enemy." Washington never went that far, but he doubtless thought the army that would leave Valley Forge was better than the one that had arrived five months earlier, and a far better military force than the one he had commanded at the outset of 1777. He also had Charles Lee, whom he had leaned on early in the war, back at his side, as the general—who was captured in 1776—had recently been liberated in prisoner swap.[48]

Philadelphia newspapers in April ran stories claiming that France and Spain had recognized American independence. Washington was properly skeptical of wartime newspaper accounts, and he so doubted the veracity of these stories that he suggested Congress might want to dispatch a plenipotentiary to Versailles to help the commissioners, or to supersede them. Washington's sense of urgency had been quickened by other news, which he knew was all too accurate. He had just learned of Lord North's mid-February peace proposal, a step that he regarded as "more dangerous than their efforts by arms." He warned that it "threatens a fatal blow" to independence, as it could "poison the minds of the people & detach the wavering" citizens, especially those who had been die-hard reconciliationists in 1776. Loyalist newspapers, which Washington called "Engine[s] of Ministry," printed numerous copies of North's peace offering, which they circulated in occupied areas and even rebel strongholds.[49]

North's peace offering was a short-lived crisis. At the end of April, Washington at last learned of the treaties of alliance and commerce. The disheartened atmosphere among the officers at Valley Forge vanished. "[N]o event was ever received with a more heart felt joy," he exclaimed.[50] Washington felt that the contours of the war would change, though in unfathomable ways, and he instinctively believed that America's chances of realizing independence would be improved. Furthermore, he had the standing army he had long sought, and it was an army of battle-hardened veterans who had just completed months of intensive training. Washington was not given to radiating optimism, but he allowed that his "utmost wish" had come true.[51]

In May, 12 days apart, the British and American armies held celebratory events, each in a way to bid farewell to the past and look to the new war that was coming. The British army honored the looming departure of General Howe with a carnivalesque gala to commemorate his supposed accomplishments. They called the affair a "Mischianza," a daylong and nightlong festivity of dining, drinking, dancing, fireworks, and even a medieval jousting contest, all conducted in the shadow of a newly erected "triumphal arch." One week after learning of the treaties with France, Washington ordered "a day of General Joy" to honor the alliance and celebrate the army's survival at Valley Forge. The soldiers gathered on the lush, green parade ground and listened to an hourlong sermon, a summary of the contents of the treaties with France, and remarks that extolled "the greatness of mind and policy of Louis XVI." Thereafter, they paraded past the reviewing stand. Following the review, 13 rounds of artillery boomed. After each the men cheered: "Long Live the King of France," "God Save the Friendly Powers of Europe," and "To the United American States."[52]

CHAPTER 8

STALEMATE

WASHINGTON KNEW THAT AMERICA'S treaties with France would leave Britain with "no choice but War," though he had no idea when hostilities would begin and no knowledge of his new ally's military plans. Nor did he know that France was sending a large naval squadron across the Atlantic. Nevertheless, he was convinced that events were "verging fast to one of the most important periods that America ever saw," as French belligerency would give "a most happy tone to all our affairs." The "dark and tempestuous Clouds which at times appeared ready to overwhelm us" were gone, he said, exuberantly adding that the alliance with France would "chalk out a plain and easy road to independence" and put "the Independency of America out of all manner of dispute." Washington likely foresaw one of two scenarios: Britain would realize the futility of continuing the war and make peace; or American forces, perhaps with French help, would score victories over their now more vulnerable enemy that would bring the war to a close.[1]

Congress ratified the two treaties with France within five days of receiving them. It had acted weeks before the members of the Carlisle Commission, the peace envoys that Lord North had dispatched, arrived in Philadelphia. When they finally alighted in June and Congress learned that they had no authority to recognize American independence, discussions ended. But the war was still going on and Congress advised the citizenry that "if we have courage to persevere, we shall establish our liberties and independence."[2]

In April, and again in May, Washington convened councils of war to contemplate how the army should respond to the changing situation. The advice he received included attacking the British in Philadelphia and assailing the smaller enemy force garrisoned in New York, but most generals recommended awaiting a British move or "put[ting] nothing to the hazard" until French plans were known.[3] The army remained at Valley Forge and waited.

In mid-May, Washington learned that General Howe had resigned and Sir Henry Clinton had been named his successor. Clinton, at 48, was two years older than Washington, but his background and appearance could hardly have been more different. Washington hailed from a second-tier gentry family that lacked the means to provide him with much of a formal education. Clinton, a British aristocrat, had received an excellent pre-university education commonplace in elite circles, and he had grown up in New York City, where his father was the colony's royal governor. As a young man, Washington had soldiered for Virginia, though he had spent the bulk of his adult years as a farmer-businessman at Mount Vernon. Clinton was a professional soldier. He had entered the British army at age 15 and had fought in two earlier wars, suffering a serious wound in combat in Germany in the Seven Years' War, an injury that continued to nag him so that on some days he got around with difficulty.

Washington looked like a leader. He stood close to six foot four inches tall and in middle age weighed a trim 210 pounds. Washington exhibited massive upper-body strength and moved with grace and elegance. He was widely thought to be without equal as an equestrian, the hallmark of athleticism in that age. Clinton was of average height for a full-grown male—around five foot seven inches—and, though handsome, in middle age he had grown a bit paunchy and was balding. Many were immediately captivated by Washington. Abigail Adams spoke of his "majestic fabric"; James Monroe, a young Continental army officer in 1776, thought Washington manifested an unrivaled charisma; Jedidiah Morse, a Connecticut preacher who had graduated from Yale, exclaimed that Washington was "born to command his fellow men"; even an aide to General Howe, who was briefly in Washington's presence, was "awestruck." Washington's leadership qualities extended beyond his appearance. He had an uncanny and nearly unmatched knack for swiftly judging other men's talents and character.

Hardly any who encountered Clinton were awed. Yet he possessed important qualities. He was an experienced, skilled, and thoughtful officer, and his service in this war had been exemplary. He had offered sound advice to Generals Gage and Howe—much of which, to their detriment, had been ignored—and his leadership in capturing Newport in 1776 and American installations in the Hudson

Highlands the next year had been textbook examples of how to conduct campaigns. Both the king and Lord Germain discerned Clinton's talents, especially his deftness as a strategist.

Clinton had been Germain's first choice to lead the invasion of New York from Canada. Later, the American secretary lauded Clinton's "gallant behavior" and masterful planning in attempting to rescue Burgoyne. Virtually every observer was struck by Clinton's fearlessness, even recklessness, under fire, a quality that Washington matched. Clinton was prudent and temperate, as was Washington. Of the two, Clinton was the more intellectually curious. He was a voracious reader with widespread interests, including the study of nature. He displayed an abiding attachment to the violin and grew to be a worthy amateur musician. He could not match Washington's athletic attributes, though he, too, was a skilled horseman. While introverted, Clinton left his door open to other officers, young and old, for conversations about military history, strategy, and tactics. He was shy and had few close friends, though he had more than Washington, who may never have enjoyed a true friendship. After years of studying Washington, historian Peter Henriques concluded that the American commander knew that he was a remarkable man. Clinton wanted to be an extraordinary general, believed that he was a better commander than most recognized, and felt that he was held back by his diffidence and other forces beyond his control.[4]

Clinton's moment at last arrived in 1778. The decision to name him the commander in chief of Britain's armies in North America had been made in March, and he received the gratifying news in May through a communiqué from Germain. The American secretary had been the chief proponent of a southern strategy and he outlined his plans, such as they were, for carrying out the new scheme for conducting the war. After exhorting Clinton to wage war with the "utmost vigour," Germain instructed him to try to bring Washington to battle, conduct coastal raids from New York northward to Nova Scotia that might destroy rebel shipping and shipbuilding facilities, and to launch diversionary forays in Virginia and Maryland. Much of this replicated directives issued to General Howe during the previous two years, though the plan now was to contain the Continental army in the north and prevent it from funneling troops to the South. Clinton was additionally to retain possession of Newport and New York and attack "the southern colonies with a view to the conquest and possession of Georgia and South Carolina." It was a colossal list of undertakings and it was followed by an order for Clinton to redeploy about one-third of his army to Canada; St. Augustine, the capital of East Florida;

Pensacola, the capital of West Florida; and the Caribbean. As he would also not have the men lost at Saratoga, Clinton would be left with about 15,000 fewer troops than had made up the British armies in North America in 1776 and 1777. To compensate, Germain told Clinton to abandon Philadelphia—"an object of small importance"—and raise provincial regiments in the South, where "the generality of people desire nothing more than a full security of all their rights and liberties under the British constitution."[5]

Germain's directives were a mixture of reality and fantasy, which Clinton readily discerned, and his joy at learning of his appointment as commander in chief immediately turned to despair. An army the size that Howe had possessed when he attacked New York would have been hard pressed to carry out all the objectives outlined by Germain. Clinton not only would have a smaller army, but he also would have to cope with American forces that now were allied with France. Furthermore, as Germain's communiqués revealed word of the Carlisle Commission and London's hopes of opening negotiations with Congress, it appeared that Lord North and Parliament no longer believed the insurrection could be suppressed in all 13 colonies. Indeed, Germain acknowledged that if the southern strategy succeeded, "we may reasonably hope . . . that all America to the south of the Susquehanna would return to their allegiance" while "the northern provinces might be left to their own feelings." Clinton was disgusted. He told a friend that Germain's letter "ruined all my hopes" of crushing the American rebellion, and if Britain lost the war, he likely would be shackled with blame for his country's failure. "My fate is hard," he exclaimed.[6]

Meanwhile, Washington in his last days at Valley Forge radiated optimism. He was eager to test what he thought was his vastly improved army. In May, he commanded 15,000 men, close to the same number of enemy troops in Philadelphia. Recruiting had lagged, but the Continental army had grown over the winter in part because Rhode Island and Massachusetts defied Congress's 1775 stipulation that Black men were unwelcome in the army. The Rhode Island state government purchased slaves who were willing to serve and promised to emancipate them at the end of the war. By midsummer some 250 Black soldiers were in Rhode Island's First Regiment, the only exclusively African American regiment during the war. Massachusetts also recruited Black men, free and enslaved, and other states permitted white men faced with military service to hire Black men as substitutes.[7]

Clinton had been ordered to bring Washington to battle and he was all too willing to do so. Following orders to abandon Philadelphia, Clinton, in June, eschewed a return voyage to New York, preferring instead to march across New Jersey in the hope that Washington would make a stand along the way. Washington's army did depart Valley Forge and stayed on Clinton's heels, daily slogging through a horrendous early summer heat wave that saw temperatures and the humidity climb to deadly levels. Some British troops died during the march. Washington met twice with his generals while shadowing the enemy. Neither council of war agreed to risk a pitched battle. The first recommended avoiding any sort of clash. The second authorized a strike against Clinton's rear. It seemed a safe bet, given that the British army, accompanied by thousands of anxious Pennsylvania Loyalists and an immense baggage train, was strung out over a dozen miles.[8]

While Washington was keen for action, there were troubling issues. There would be no opportunity to reconnoiter prior to a battle, he was unaware of the exact size of his enemy, and several of his generals counseled that it would be best to do nothing before potential French help arrived. In the end, however, Washington took General Greene's advice that if the army did not act, many congressmen would think "our courage faild us."[9]

On June 28, Clinton's army shuddered to a stop near Monmouth, a pause to rest the men and induce Washington to attack. Washington was ready and sent a force of 4,500 under Charles Lee to strike the rear of the British army. Once again turning Fabian, Washington anticipated a small-scale action designed to surprise his adversary, produce significant British casualties, and perhaps result in the capture of much of Clinton's valuable baggage. He hoped to accomplish all this and withdraw to safety before Clinton could respond in strength. Washington's decision was unavoidably made in haste. As a result, Lee did not know the exact location of the enemy's rear, the precise position of the bulk of Clinton's army, or anything about the terrain where he was about to fight. Moreover, intelligence had badly underestimated the size of the British army; Clinton had 17,600 men, not 10,000, as Washington had been led to believe. Things went well for Lee in the early stages of the engagement. But Clinton rushed in reinforcements more rapidly than had been foreseen. Within an hour the British enjoyed numerical superiority. Not long thereafter Lee's right and left wings began to withdraw, signaling that what had been thought to be a safe undertaking was suddenly turning alarmingly dangerous. Lee opted to pull his entire force back behind a ravine and make a defensive stand while awaiting reinforcements.

Three hours into the engagement, Washington arrived on the scene. He was astonished to learn of Lee's retreat. Deprived of reliable information, Washington jumped to the conclusion that Lee, one of the generals who had recommended against an attack, was sabotaging the operation. Washington had a volcanic temper and on this day, at this moment, it erupted. He cursed Lee in a spray of venom, removed him from command, and took the reins himself. Then he did exactly what Lee was attempting to do: He withdrew behind a ravine and made a defense stand.

Clinton rushed in reinforcements, but his army was too widely scattered to bring in the numbers that might have proved decisive. Utilizing what he had, Clinton time and again attacked first one rebel flank and then the other. Washington competently directed his army's response and his men fought well, vindicating the move to a standing army, the Valley Forge training, and the experience garnered by the officers and many of the soldiers over the past couple of years. The fighting raged throughout the heat-blistered afternoon, ending only as the day's last glint of pink sunlight was overtaken by darkness. It had been a brutal fight. The Americans suffered about 375 casualties (37 of whom died of heatstroke); Clinton lost slightly more men. Washington anticipated a second round the next day, but Clinton, aware that he could not commit a sufficient force to another battle, slipped off toward New York in the colorless light of dawn. The Battle of Monmouth, the last major engagement fought in the North, was over. Recalling the winter campaign to remove Washington, Alexander Hamilton and others who had hitched their wagons to the commander's star broadcast the fiction that the draw at Monmouth was a great American victory and that Washington had saved the day, preventing the "dismay and disgrace" that would have ensued had Lee been left in command. In the aftermath of the battle, the irascible and humiliated Lee recklessly demanded a court-martial. Pitted against Washington in a trial judged by Washington's loyal officers, Lee lost and was suspended for a year. He never returned.[10]

HAD WASHINGTON BEEN AWARE that a French fleet was crossing the Atlantic, he unquestionably would have trailed Clinton's army to the coast. But secrecy was paramount and the authorities in Versailles, aware that Paris was an oasis of spies, had disclosed nothing to America's envoys or Congress. The French decision to dispatch a fleet had begun to take shape in January, when the treaties with the Americans that would make war inevitable were coming to fruition. France had an Atlantic squadron in Brest and a fleet in Toulon on the Mediterranean. It might combine the two and attack England—which it had attempted with catastrophic consequences in 1759—or it might send the Toulon fleet to America. The final decision rested with Louis XVI. His chief advisors on the matter were Vergennes, naval minister Sartine, and Jean-Frédéric Phélypeaux, Comte de Maurepas, once the naval minister and now the nominal prime minister. Inch by inch during the past two years the naive and unexceptional monarch—he was only 20 years old and had worn the crown for merely a year when the American war erupted—had been moved toward this moment by those who dreamed of restoring French grandeur and security. As so often had been the case, Vergennes played the crucial role. He urged sending the Toulon fleet to America. The foreign secretary envisaged the possibility of a joint allied attack or, with naval superiority, that the French fleet with the assistance of the Continental army might blockade the British navy and army (maybe in Philadelphia, maybe in New York) and starve its foe into capitulation. Vergennes anticipated that for a time in 1778 France would rule the waves, as the 92 British warships in North American waters were scattered from Canso, Nova Scotia, to St. Augustine West Florida, and the lion's share were engaged in blockade duty, escorting convoys, and carrying dispatches. The greater warships were also widely dispersed, posted here and there for the defense of Halifax, Quebec, Newport, Philadelphia, and New York. When the monarch consented to sending a naval force, Charles-Hector Théodat, Vice Admiral Comte d'Estaing, at age 49 the senior active officer in the navy, was given command of a Toulon squadron of 12 ships of the line and five frigates.[11]

D'Estaing hailed from a military family that enjoyed close ties to the king. He became a soldier in the French army in adolescence and fought in two wars before the Revolutionary War. During the Seven Years' War, d'Estaing switched from the army to La Royale, France's navy, and was made a rear admiral, a step that angered junior officers who, looking on him as an outsider, questioned his competence.[12]

D'Estaing sailed from Toulon in mid-April, 10 days before Washington was even aware of the Treaty of Alliance. The admiral carried sealed orders to open hostilities when he reached the United States, though Vergennes regretted that this meant the French would fire the first shot in the coming war with Great Britain, an outcome the foreign minister had hoped to avoid, principally because he believed there was a better chance of Spanish belligerency if Britain started the war. Vergennes's wish came true when, in mid-June, a Royal Navy frigate fired on French warships off the English coast, causing considerable damage and casualties.

In addition to 4,000 marines packed into transports, d'Estaing brought Conrad Gérard, who had negotiated the treaties with the American commissioners and whom Vergennes had appointed minister plenipotentiary to the United States. The

French fleet made the crossing without having been spotted by the Royal Navy, thanks to a roundabout voyage that consumed three months. The squadron finally arrived at the mouth of the Delaware River about two weeks after Clinton's army had departed Pennsylvania. D'Estaing sent Gérard upriver to Philadelphia, where he was greeted by a large, friendly crowd as he rode into town in John Hancock's fancy coach escorted by a party of soldiers and a handful of congressmen. Benedict Arnold, whom Washington had appointed as military commander of the city while he recovered from the wound suffered at Bemis Heights, welcomed Gérard and made him a guest in his house, a mansion that General Howe had inhabited during the occupation of Philadelphia.

Meanwhile, d'Estaing hurried up the coast only to discover that Clinton's army had reached Manhattan a few days earlier. By the narrowest of margins, the new allies had missed an opportunity to trap Clinton's army between Washington's and the French fleet. Charles James Fox, with a sigh of relief and a degree of truth, told Parliament that had d'Estaing arrived six days earlier, the "glory of Great Britain" would have been destroyed.[13]

Two weeks after Monmouth, Washington at last learned that d'Estaing was off the Jersey coast. Washington immediately contacted him. In their initial exchange of letters, the admiral referred to Washington as the "deliverer of America," and the American commander spoke of d'Estaing as "a Gentleman of . . . distinguished talents" in the service of "our Great Ally." Through his French-speaking aides Alexander Hamilton and John Laurens, Washington pledged his "most strenuous efforts" and shared his ideas for a campaign to retake New York that he believed would lead to "probable" success. He strongly opposed a blockade. It would be lengthy and of "uncertain issue." He hoped instead that d'Estaing would seize Sandy Hook, which commanded New York Harbor, destroy the British vessels on Staten Island, and secure the Upper Bay and the Narrows. Meanwhile, in a three-pronged strike, Washington would land troops on Long Island, northern Manhattan, and just above New York City, isolating the widely dispersed elements of Clinton's army.[14]

D'Estaing's hopes and Washington's dreams vanished rapidly. The vice admiral learned not only that New York's channel was so shallow that his huge warships could not enter the harbor and assail the nine British warships anchored there, but also that Clinton had hurriedly posted artillery on Sandy Hook. The New York enterprise fizzled before it began. Washington attributed the disappointment to bad luck. The second in command of the Royal Navy credited Clinton with having saved the day, as his prompt reaction condemned the French to "lose their ships if they should attempt the harbor."[15]

Thereafter, Washington and d'Estaing wasted no time concurring on a campaign to take Newport, on Rhode Island's Aquidneck Island, and the 4,700 British troops garrisoned there under Sir Robert Pigot. There was no time to waste. D'Estaing was aware that once London learned he had sailed from Toulon, it ordered a squadron of 13 ships of the line under Vice Admiral John Byron to sail for New York and join Admiral Richard Howe's fleet. What d'Estaing did not know was that Byron's fleet had been slow to get away and was further delayed by bad weather. It would not be a factor in the course of the Allies' campaign to reclaim Rhode Island.

The Allies envisioned a joint operation in Rhode Island. D'Estaing's heavy ships would block up Narragansett Bay and bombard Pigot's entrenched troops in Newport. Simultaneously, armies of around 14,000 men—including French marines, 2,500 Continentals, and at a minimum 7,500 vaunted Yankee militiamen— would make amphibious landings. The American force was to be commanded by General Sullivan. At first glance, it was odd that Washington would entrust Sullivan with such a crucial assignment. Sullivan's many failures had aroused antipathy in Congress, including among North Carolina delegates who vowed that never again would any men from their state serve under him. Horatio Gates was the obvious choice to command the American army. He was a proven winner and a leader around whom droves of New England militiamen had rallied in New York. But Nathanael Greene knew the truth. Washington would not give "a doubtful friend" the opportunity to win additional laurels. Washington, all too aware of Sullivan's spotty record, provided the sort of counsel he seldom felt the need to proffer: "weigh every desperate matter well before it is carried into execution." When Sullivan told the commander that he contemplated an assault on Pigot's fortified lines, Washington counseled against such an attack unless there was "a moral certainty of success." Washington was keenly aware of how much was riding on gaining a major victory in Rhode Island. Allied success, he said, would almost certainly "operate powerfully . . . upon the minds of the British Nation, and bring matters to a speedy conclusion."[16]

Clinton had also been busy. Eleven days before the Allied commanders agreed on the Newport campaign, he had already bolstered Pigot's force with another 1,800 men, additional artillery, and sufficient provisions to see the garrison through a prolonged siege. They were in place two weeks before d'Estaing arrived and a month prior to the arrival of the last of the New England militiamen, who responded slowly to the summons to duty.[17]

D'Estaing and Sullivan could not act until a sufficient number of militiamen had arrived. Days, then weeks, passed. All the while, Pigot set his 6,500 men to work strengthening Newport's fortifications. The Allied commanders eventually agreed to launch their attack on August 7, about a week after the arrival of the last of the Continentals under the Marquis de Lafayette that Washington had dispatched. Their plan was for the Americans to land on the east side of the island, the French on the west. Once they linked up, the British in outlying posts to the north would be isolated and heavily outnumbered. Thereafter, the Allies were to attack or besiege Pigot's main force. The August 7 date passed when Sullivan requested a two-day postponement. Amphibious landings were slated for August 9, but through that morning's summer haze d'Estaing spotted an enemy fleet coming after him. The Royal Navy in New York had cobbled together an armada under Admiral Howe during the interminable delays brought on by the sluggish response of New England's militias. Howe had been augmented by two ships of the line from Halifax, one from the West Indies, and one of Byron's that had succeeded in reaching New York. Howe had eight heavy warships, but possessed massive fire-power and was ardent for a fight. So, too, was d'Estaing, who spent the day departing Narragansett Bay, where the shallows teemed with the wreckages of unfortunate vessels from earlier days. Both sides spent another day maneuvering. The showdown was to get underway on August 11, but as the hour of battle approached, heavy squalls at sea turned into a tempestuous storm. Either a hurricane or violent nor'easter had struck. It was impossible to fight.

Both fleets were impaired and scattered by the gale-force winds, dissolving any hope of taking up battle-ready formations. Isolated encounters occurred in the bedlam that followed, resulting in further damage to both sides. D'Estaing soon concluded that his mangled fleet was in no shape for battle. Turning a deaf ear to Sullivan's entreaties to remain, d'Estaing sailed for Boston Harbor, where his pummeled vessels could be refitted.[18]

Sullivan was livid and drafted an intemperate letter to d'Estaing that was signed by John Hancock, commander of the Massachusetts militia, and all rebel generals in Rhode Island. Only Lafayette refused to sign. The operation against Pigot had remained salvageable, the feverish communiqué asserted, and it went on to savage d'Estaing for having abandoned the enterprise, a desertion that stained the honor of France and threatened to turn Americans against "their *hitherto Esteemed Allies*."

Now it was d'Estaing and his officers who were incensed. Washington, too, was outraged by the letter and fearful of harmful diplomatic consequences that might result. Understanding how indispensable the French were to American success, he sought to mollify them. He wrote to d'Estaing praising his "bravest exertions" and explaining that the "thinking part of Mankind" recognized the necessity for the French fleet's departure. Washington also endeavored to placate Lafayette, who had spoken of the letter's impact on his "afflicted, injur'd heart . . . injur'd by the very people I came from so far to love and support." Calling himself Lafayette's "friend," Washington urged him not to take exception at words uttered in the "first transport of disappointed hope." He spread treacle by telling Lafayette that all Americans admired his virtue, service, and principles. With time to rethink his actions, Hancock also sought to appease d'Estaing by presenting him with a portrait of Washington. Lafayette, whose vivid imagination was operating in over-drive, told Washington of d'Estaing's joy at receiving the gift and exclaimed, "I never Saw a man so glad of possessing his sweet heart's picture, as the admiral was to Receive yours."[19]

Immediately after the storm, Sullivan launched a siege operation. He knew it would be futile if he acted alone, but he clutched to the vain hope that d'Estaing would return. It was risky for Sullivan to maintain his army on Aquidneck Island, and Clinton, in New York, in an instant understood the hazard that Sullivan was running. Demonstrating yet again how different his generalship was from that of the torpid Howe, Clinton acted expeditiously. Hopeful of "reducing General Sullivan to something like the Saratoga business," Clinton personally led a fleet of 77 vessels and an army of 4,300 toward Rhode Island. His plan was to land his men at the north tip of Aquidneck Island while Pigot's men, at the southern end, came out of their emplacements and advanced on the rebels. Caught between the two British forces, Sullivan's army would be trapped on the island and destroyed. American intelligence foundered, leaving Washington unaware that Clinton's force had sailed. But given the ever-present lag in communications, Pigot was also ignorant of Clinton's plans. He emerged for a fight before Clinton's relief force arrived and, on August 29, took on Sullivan. The rebel army, severely reduced by desertions in the wake of the great storm, survived the fray, but barely. It was driven to the northern end of the island. Luck was with Sullivan. The next day he learned that Clinton was coming and d'Estaing would not be returning. Sullivan evacuated Aquidneck Island only hours before Clinton's force, whose progress at sea had been slowed by contrary winds, came ashore. Sullivan had escaped being "very critically circumstanced," as

Clinton put it. By the narrowest of margins Clinton was denied not just a victory but also the likely capture of an American army close in size to that which Burgoyne had surrendered at Saratoga a year earlier.[20]

Washington thought d'Estaing might return to Manhattan once his fleet was refitted, giving the Allies another shot at British-held New York. Almost bemusedly, Washington noted that after "two years of Maneuvering and undergoing the strangest vicissitudes," the British and American armies would soon be back where they had been in August 1776, one on Manhattan and the other on the periphery. This time, however, it would be the British who were "reduced to the use of spade and pick axe for defense."[21]

But an Allied push to take New York in 1778 was not to be. Once his ships were repaired, d'Estaing sailed for the West Indies to see to French interests in that theater. The brief campaign of 1778 in North America was over. When Clinton learned of d'Estaing's departure, he finally complied with the orders that Germain had sent him seven months earlier. He took the "heart breaking" step of redeploying about one-third of his army, sending most of the men to the Caribbean. His army had "dissolved," Clinton bitterly remarked. Left with fewer than 14,000 men, Clinton thought his army was too small to properly defend New York. Undertaking a major offensive was out of the question.[22]

The optimism that Washington had radiated earlier was nowhere to be seen in the last weeks of the year. Despite French belligerency, the campaign of 1778 had resolved nothing. Now the French fleet was gone and would not return for another eight or nine months, if it ever came back. Furthermore, by year's end, the American insurgency faced a new and potentially fatal problem: The American economy had utterly collapsed.

Economic problems had first appeared late in 1776 after Congress and the states responded to wartime exigencies with unchecked emissions of paper money. Inflation soared to alarming levels. Congress took remedial steps in 1777 that arrested the free fall in the value of money. But once d'Estaing arrived, Congress needed money, and quickly, in order to act in concert with its new ally. Congress gambled that the presence of the French fleet meant the war was nearly over. The uncontrolled spending that ensued precipitated the most rapid rate of depreciation in American history, prompting Washington to soon declare that the value of money was "melt[ing] like Snow before a hot Sun." The cost of the endless list of supplies needed by the army skyrocketed and the price of civilian necessities spiraled out of control. Rampant inflation made recruiting more difficult and, according to Washington, "conspired to Sour the temper of the Army." Cash-strapped and fearful of losing home and hearth, not a few disgruntled officers quit the service. Many that remained in the army acridly concluded that the nation was indifferent to their deprivations. Ominously, Washington observed that "the people and the Army appear to grow dayly more tired of the War."[23]

Washington understood that he had a new war on his hands, one that was perhaps even more dangerous. He wondered yet again, "Can *we* carry on the War much longer?" He answered that his country could remain at war indefinitely only if it found some means of rehabilitating America's economy. The war's outcome, he now thought, would be determined by "whose Finances (their's or ours) is most likely to fail." He knew that economic tribulations created misery and eroded the will to persist. A year earlier he had thought that Britain, seeing that victory was impossible, might quit the war. He now sensed that Britain would do what it could to prolong the war, hopeful that America's ailing economy would undermine morale and compel the rebels to accept "terms short of *Independence.*" Given America's troubles, Washington expected the enemy to "act with vigor" in 1779. Not since the last days in 1776 had Washington been so apprehensive about his country-men's willingness to fight on. That "we [will] ruin & defeat ourselves . . . is infinitely more to be dreaded than the whole force of G. Britain," he said.[24]

At Christmas, Washington, accompanied by his wife, Martha, who had joined him for the winter, journeyed to Philadelphia for consultation with Congress about the economy and next year's campaign. Nearly every evening the couple dined at the homes of wealthy Philadelphians whose tables groaned with delicacies and an incredible abundance of food. The war and the suffering of the men in the Conti-nental army appeared to be a matter of indifference to the elite in the city, whose chief interest—in Washington's estimation—was how to use hostilities to further enrich themselves. The American commander departed Philadelphia convinced that the "rapacity" of the city's most affluent residents was evidence of "declining zeal" for the cause and, possibly, a harbinger of a widespread "extinction of public spirit."[25]

SIR HENRY CLINTON WAS aware of his enemy's cascading economic distress. It could not be hidden. He, too, had concluded that the rebel populace was "tired of the war," frustrated by their growing troubles and the failure to score a decisive victory in 1778. Clinton had thought the Americans were vulnerable in 1776 and

again in 1777, and in vain he had counseled Howe about how to exploit their suscep-
tibility. Now Clinton commanded the British army and he yet again believed the
Americans were imperiled, more so than at any moment since 1776. Where Washington's optimism withered late in 1778, Clinton now had bright hopes for the
coming year. "One more vigourous [British] campaign," he believed, could compel
the Americans to accept peace terms short of independence. But he needed reinforcements in order to wage that campaign. Clinton pleaded with London for more
men, preferably natives of Great Britain as the Hessians, though "faithful," were
not "equally zealous."[26]

"You may depend upon every possible attention being given to the augmenting
your army," Germain promised, though the number of available men would depend
on whether Spain remained neutral or England was threatened with invasion. He
also praised Clinton's performance, which had "banishe[d] every apprehension of
failure" that had cloaked England after Saratoga. But whereas Germain had given
Howe a free hand, he was not about to make that mistake again. He exhorted
Clinton to be active through the winter. Many Americans "were disposed to peace,"
he contended, and their numbers would grow in the wake of British successes. He
reminded Clinton that the new southern strategy awaited implementation and
urged him to act before the miasmic southern summer set in. Begin by crushing the
insurgency in South Carolina, Germain advised, but if that was not feasible, go
after Georgia. It was crucial that he act soon, as war in the Caribbean was about to
commence and "our islands in the West Indies might draw supplies" from the
southern mainland colonies that would sustain them. Aware of Clinton's manpower
problems, Germain gave him permission to recall some or all of Pigot's troops from
Rhode Island to make up the deficit, and he goaded his commander to step up the
recruitment of Loyalists.[27]

Clinton responded by setting the southern strategy in motion. He put together a
3,000-man force under Lieutenant Colonel Archibald Campbell to capture
Savannah. Campbell, a veteran of more than 20 years in Britain's army, had been
captured in 1776 and spent two years in captivity, but a prisoner swap had enabled
him to rejoin his comrades the previous spring. Late in November, after Washington
had scattered his army in winter quarters from the Highlands to New Jersey, Campbell and his men sailed for Georgia, where he expected to be joined by a force under
Brigadier General Augustine Prevost, commander of Britain's army in Florida.[28]

Campbell's force arrived on the windswept Georgia coast a bit before Christmas.
Following nearly a week with no sign of Prevost, Campbell opted to act alone. He

had used the wait for additional troops wisely, gathering information about the defense of Savannah from enslaved persons who appeared to be more than willing to provide guidance. The small Georgia capital was some 18 miles up the Savannah River. Campbell's plan was to put his men ashore about two miles below Savannah at a viable landing site, guarded by a small rebel army of some 600 Continentals and 100 militiamen. The American force was commanded by Brigadier General Robert Howe, a wealthy North Carolina planter who had served in the Seven Years' War, fought at Charleston in 1776, and led an aborted invasion of Florida earlier in 1778.[29]

Campbell's men made an unopposed landing at sunrise on December 29. Before nightfall, the British had reclaimed Savannah. Informed by a slave of a secret route, Campbell's men circled behind the rebel lines, much as Howe had done against Washington on Long Island. When the British opened fire, the startled Americans broke and ran for the presumed greater safety of Savannah. But they found no refuge in the capital. Campbell's men pursued their prey and toward day's end what little resistance the Americans offered had ended. More than 530 of Howe's men had been killed, wounded, or captured. Campbell lost only 24. The southern strategy had gotten off to an electrifying start. Campbell boasted that he had "ripped one star and one stripe from the rebel flag of America." Within days the royal governor of Georgia and the province's pre-revolutionary legislature were reinstated and every rebel law passed since 1776 had been repealed, steps that had "an astonishing effect" in London, where people were "elated beyond measure knowing the consequence of the Conquest" of Savannah.[30]

"The province of Georgia is ours," Clinton boasted. Its retrieval was of the "utmost importance to us," he rejoiced, as it secured Florida and would not be furnishing men and provisions for Washington's army. Washington was less impressed than Clinton by the enemy's achievement. His initial reaction was to dismiss the South as a sideshow of little importance. For a spell, he looked on Britain's interest in the South largely as a means of obtaining supplies for the defense of its Caribbean sugar islands.[31]

IF CLINTON WAS COMING to believe that the war might—just might—be turned around, Washington at the outset of 1779 was deeply anxious. Yet while he worried that attaining independence had never been "in such eminent danger," he refused to undertake any major action without French support. He agreed with Nathanael Greene that if the Continental army was destroyed, "the Country is conquer'd," for the army was "the Stamina of American liberty." Washington had every intention of safeguarding the army until he could act in concert with his ally.[32]

Month after month in 1779 Washington remained largely idle. Clinton, however, was active. With a chunk of his emasculated army in faraway Georgia, Clinton felt hamstrung until reinforcements arrived. But he was under pressure from London to act. Germain even provided a fanciful wish list of measures to take. If it was impossible to bring Washington to battle, Clinton was to force the rebel army into the Hudson Highlands and confine it there. With Washington tied down, Clinton was to launch devastating coastal raids and forays up the rivers and inlets that splayed out from the Chesapeake in Virginia and Maryland. There was more. Clinton was to assist Indians in instigating "alarming and harassing" raids in the New York and New England backcountries, onslaughts that would prevent those provinces from providing men and supplies to Washington. Taking all of these steps was unrealistic, though Germain expected Clinton to do some-thing and promised to send him an additional 6,600 men before the summer.[33]

Clinton exploded when he read the American secretary's catalog of initiatives, much as Washington had when Congress pressured him to go into winter quarters near Philadelphia late in 1777. Not only would compliance leave too few men to adequately defend New York, but Clinton felt that he should be given "every latitude" to formulate and implement his strategy. "I am upon the spot," he said, meaning that he was in America and better understood the current state of affairs than officials in distant London. "[L]eave me to my self," he implored. Clinton was frustrated and angry, and his blistering reply to Germain was the most unrestrained communiqué that he dashed off to his superior during the war. But Clinton was a soldier and he did his best to follow orders.[34]

In May, Clinton sent Commodore George Collier with a flotilla of 28 ships and 1,800 men to ravage the Virginia coast near Norfolk. Over two weeks the raiders destroyed forts, shipyards, 137 merchant and privateering vessels, acre after acre of crop-rich fields, and one town (Suffolk) and liberated 518 slaves. The expedition returned to New York with 17 ships crammed with items that a few days earlier had been the property of Virginians. The pillaging had been undertaken to erode rebel morale, the chilling danger that Washington most feared.[35] Not long passed before Clinton sent a force of raiders into Connecticut. He selected William Tryon, a general and New York's royal governor, a man not known for restraint when dealing with insurgents. Clinton was old-fashioned enough to detest making war against civilians, but he cast aside his scruples in this instance in the hope that Tryon's depredations would force Washington into the field to defend the Yankee hamlets that were to be coldheartedly assailed. The raiders struck New Haven, Norwalk, and Fairfield in July. Barns, mills, even churches went up in flames; orchards were decimated, houses and farms were plundered, one entire town (Fairfield) was razed. The terrorized citizens were robbed, humiliated, and abused in countless ways. Although the raiding stretched over nine days, Washington did not come to the victims' assistance, and his inaction left Clinton to conclude that there was "no chance" of bringing his adversary to battle.[36]

Between the two devastating coastal raids, Clinton, in May, sent Commodore Collier on another mission. This time he was to sail up the Hudson River and decimate the rebel forts at Stony Point and Verplanck's Point. He was spectacularly successful. By gaining control of King's Ferry, Clinton closed a vital area of transit to the rebels and impeded communication between the two sides of the Hudson. Clinton was convinced that his step would compel Washington to fight to regain what he had lost. He was wrong again. Washington acknowledged that he had suffered a painful loss—he said this was "one of the wisest measures" Clinton had taken—but he would not be drawn into battle. "[A]ll we can do is lament what we cannot remedy," he said.[37]

Clinton contemplated one further step that summer: a strike against the fortress at West Point, the northernmost fortification in a string of rebel strongholds in the Hudson Highlands. He believed that its capture would open the door to control of the Hudson River, assuring Britain's victory in this war. While historians are not of one mind regarding whether the loss of the Hudson River would have doomed the American insurgency, Washington had no doubts, and he believed that the post at West Point was the key to possessing the river. Clinton wanted to strike, but he had inherited a third-rate intelligence system and possessed no knowledge of West Point's defenses or the number of men posted there. He knew that the rebels had been given five years to fortify West Point; Washington would muster every possible Continental and militiaman to defend the installation; it could not be taken by surprise, as every other fort in the Highlands would first have to be seized; and the mountains and rugged country from Peekskill to West Point would immeasurably increase the odds against success. In the end, Clinton judged that the risks of assailing West Point were too great. Clinton was subsequently deprecated for not taking the risk, but he made a prudent call. General Knox, who was quite familiar with the citadel, remarked that it could withstand a siege, "much less a storm."[38]

Clinton, like Washington, was loath to take on an excessively risky operation. Britain's commander had come to believe that time might be on his side. He would have fought Washington had the opportunity presented itself. Otherwise, his strategy in 1779 was to await reinforcements and to do what he could short of having his army face unbridled peril in order to break the enemy's will to endure protracted war.

Washington had not responded to the raids in Connecticut. He correctly saw that as the job of state militias. His army could not march time and again from one state to another in response to coastal raids. Given that enemy raiders were swiftly transported by what he referred to as the Royal Navy's "canvass wings," the Continental army could not even respond to nearby raids. But Washington knew that he could not remain entirely inactive. Thinking it would be "very disagreeable" for the "reputation of the army" should he do nothing while the enemy marauded, Washington conceived a surprise attack against the British garrison that Clinton had installed at recently captured Stony Point. In putting Anthony Wayne in command of the operation, Washington chose not only an intrepid leader but one who lusted to avenge the mortifying losses he had suffered in the surprise attack on Paoli two years earlier. Wayne, with 1,300 men, conducted a daring midnight raid on July 15. Armed with bayonets, swords, and axes—it was too dangerous to fire muskets in the inky darkness—the American volunteers took the British by surprise and overwhelmed them. The British lost 676 men, more than at Monmouth, while American losses ran upwards of 100. The American troops, said Wayne, had fought like "men who are determined to be free."[39]

A month later, Washington sought to replicate that victory through a surprise nighttime assault against British-held Paulus Hook, directly across from New York City. To command the attack, he chose a fellow Virginian, stonehearted Colonel Henry Lee, a man whose zeal and bravery he admired. Through no fault of his own, Lee failed to achieve the element of surprise and the Americans did not take possession of their objective. The British lost another 200 men in the fray, against the loss of about 20 rebels. Clinton had effusively praised the valor of the rebels at Stony Point, but he thought an attack under his nose at Paulus Hook was mortifying.[40]

Washington had one other operation in mind as he awaited d'Estaing's return. Hostilities between Indians and settlers on the far northern frontier had increased dramatically during the past two years. The tribes that made up the Iroquois (Haudenosaunee) Confederacy of Six Nations, which exercised hegemony between the Adirondacks and Lake Erie, were bitterly divided over what role, if any, to play in the Revolutionary War. The Mohawk tribe, the easternmost Indigenous people

within the Confederacy and the ones most impacted by the colonists' encroach-
ments since the Seven Years' War, saw siding with Britain as the means of driving
out the settlers who had taken their lands and of keeping others from coming in.
But some tribes favored neutrality while waiting to see how things played out.

At the outset of the war, the Oneida, one of the six tribes in the Confederacy,
had asked to meet with American officials. Congress consented and in August 1775
sent emissaries to a council fire in Albany with representatives from three Iroquois
tribes. The Americans explained that the British king, led by iniquitous advisors,
had broken its covenant with the colonists. The war that had just begun, they
added, was "a family quarrel between us and Old England." They did not ask for
help and, in fact, both Congress and Washington hoped the Indians would remain
neutral. "We don't wish you to take up the hatchet. . . . We desire you to remain at
home, and not join on either side," they told the Native American representatives.
After two days of deliberation, the Indians consented, saying they bore as much
affection for the English in England as for the English living "on this island."[41]

Many Iroquois were unhappy with the agreement reached at Albany. The royal
superintendent of Indian Affairs had been mobilizing the Iroquois along the
St. Lawrence and urging Governor Carleton in Quebec to unleash the Indigenous
warriors, a step he was unwilling to sanction. Carleton would use the tribes for
defensive purposes, but he feared that turning them loose would result in wanton
massacres and retaliation by New York and the New England colonies. A leading
Mohawk leader, Joseph Brant, known to his people as Thayendanegea, chafed at
Carleton's restraint. Late in the year, the 33-year-old Brant, who had learned to read,
write, and speak English, accompanied several British officials who favored a more
aggressive policy on a voyage to London. In the Seven Years' War, he had fought
with the British and in 1775 he was among the warriors who had taken up arms to
resist the rebel foray against Quebec. Brant was convinced that the colonial insurgents had "in great measure begun this Rebellion to be sole Masters of the Continent."[42] If they succeeded, all tribes in the Six Nations Confederacy, and eventually
all Indigenous people in North America, would face a bleak future. Brant was
convinced that siding with the British to suppress the insurgency offered his people
their best chance of retaining their lands and enjoying a peaceful future.

While in London, Brant met with numerous officials and influential citizens,
sat for a portrait painter, was received by George III—of whom he said "a finer
man" could not be found—and had an audience with Lord Germain, whom he
addressed as "Brother" and "Great One." After emphasizing that the Mohawk had

always been loyal to the Crown, Brant stressed that the English colonists had made "an unjust claim" to the lands of the Six Nations and, unless impeded by the King, would "cheat us" and take the Natives' lands. The American secretary, who unlike Carleton longed for the Indians to take the warpath against the rebels, concluded a bargain with Brant. Germain pledged at war's end to redress every Iroquois grievance over the settlers' inroads on their lands. Brant, in return, vowed to mobilize the Iroquois to assist the English against the American rebels.[43]

On returning home in 1776, Brant worked tirelessly to carry out his end of the bargain. Presciently understanding that Britain alone stood between his people and the incessant advance of land-hungry American settlers bent on taking what had long been the home and dominion of the Indians, Brant visited one village after another in his quest to have each of the six tribes in the confederacy take up arms. He did not act alone. John Butler, the Crown's deputy Indian agent in the region, also sought to mobilize the tribes. Brant and Butler were only partially successful. Four Iroquois tribes—the Mohawk, Cayuga, Seneca, and Onondaga— sided with the British, while the Oneida and Tuscarora stayed with the Americans. During the crucial campaign of 1777 the Seneca and Mohawk joined with General Burgoyne and Colonel St. Leger. Following Burgoyne's surrender at Saratoga, General Schuyler sent a wampum belt to the Six Nations urging their neutrality and threatening retribution if they returned to the warpath, a position echoed by General Lafayette when in March 1778 he met with 700 representatives of the tribes at Johnstown. Some tribes pledged their friendship. The Seneca and Mohawk did not. By late spring they were conducting raids on the Pennsylvania frontier and in New York's verdant Mohawk Valley. The Indians often acted in concert with Butler's Rangers, a corps of combatants raised in Canada with the consent of Governor Carleton. Sometimes they were joined by bands of Loyalist armed vigilantes who occasionally dressed as Indian warriors.

Raiding parties struck again and again, assailing isolated farms and remote hamlets. They burned houses and fields lush with crops, confiscated cattle and stores of grain, killed and maimed residents and militiamen sent to protect the settlers, and sent prisoners into a terrifying captivity. War is brutal and warriors are often heartless, and that was never more true than in this cruel war against civilians. Before long, Butler reported that over "many hundred miles [there] is now nothing but an heap of ashes" along the Pennsylvania frontier, adding that all the "miserable people" among the survivors had "taken refuge in small forts." That was not entirely true, as in July, in what soon was known as the Wyoming Massacre, more than

300 settlers were killed. One of Butler's Rangers ghoulishly remarked that he "had worked so hard with my tomahawk and scalping knife that my arms were bloody above the elbows." In November, some 800 Rangers, Indians, and Loyalists assailed Cherry Valley, a Mohawk Valley settlement to which a regiment of 300 Massachusetts Continentals had been sent. The soldiers saved those who escaped to a fort, but the village was destroyed, 16 Continentals and 32 residents—mostly women and children—perished, and more than 70 settlers were taken captive. Even royal officials who subsequently viewed the devastation were shocked by what they saw. They spoke of the "wanton cruelty" of the "bloodthirsty savages" and described the "bloody scene" as "almost past description."[44]

At Christmas 1778, Washington arrived in Philadelphia for his meeting with Congress to plan for 1779 and discuss an assortment of issues. He and Martha reached the city just days after word of the bloody events in Cherry Valley trickled in. It was the seventh New York village to have been demolished, and hundreds of frontier residents had been killed in the year since Saratoga. A congressional panel made clear that it wanted Washington to act against "the savages" that "infested our frontier." Washington required no arm-twisting. Not only did his army draw provisions from that agriculturally rich region, but if the plundering of the New York and Pennsylvania frontiers continued, those states would commit ever larger numbers of militiamen—a resource that Washington needed—to defend the back-country inhabitants. Furthermore, Washington was already looking ahead to America's postwar boundaries. He believed his country's claim to the region would be enhanced by driving out the Indians. His objective was precisely what Brant had told London was the goal of the insurgents.[45]

The Declaration of Independence had denounced the British for inciting the Indians to make war against the colonists, and Washington and other insurgents had decried destructive British raids on American villages. The rhetoric had not prevented Americans from pursuing similar tactics. In 1776, in reprisal for Cherokee warriors having set upon southern frontier hamlets, Continental and militia units conducted four bloody expeditions against the Indians, attacking and burning their towns and homes and killing some 2,000 Natives. Washington defended the brutal counterattacks, asserting that the Cherokees "were foolish enough . . . to take up the Hatchet Against Us" and in revenge "our Warriours went into their Country, burnt their Houses [and] destroyed their Corn."[46]

It now was the turn of the Iroquois. While in Philadelphia for his meetings with Congress, Washington set about planning a campaign of terrorism against them in the Ohio Country, or "Ohio Territory," as he referred to the region that he believed was part of the United States. He chose General Sullivan to lead the expedition. Washington likely gambled that Sullivan, eager for redemption following his earlier missteps, would carry out this assignment with utter ruthlessness. Washington wanted the campaign to be conducted as soon as possible so that Sullivan's force could rejoin the main army before d'Estaing's expected return in late summer. Few campaigns on either side came together swiftly in this war, and it was August before Sullivan's force of 5,000 men moved out. They faced no opposition as they marched across the frontier. British forces in Canada, fearing that Sullivan's army was bent on crossing the border, did not move to assist the Indians. The Iroquois warriors, limited in numbers and clearly unable to mount an effective resistance, retreated in the face of their overpowering adversary. Sullivan had been ordered to "lay waste" to every Indian village. Their country was to be "destroyed," said Washington, not "merely overrun."

The terrorism that Sullivan practiced matched that which Tryon, on a smaller scale, had earlier inflicted on the coastal Connecticut villages. Sullivan's army stormed into one after another empty and ghostly silent settlement, where it proceeded to kill or take away every head of livestock, burn homes and crops, and torch corn cribs bulging with provisions for the coming winter. Forty-one towns and an estimated 160,000 bushels of corn were destroyed. Congress lauded Sullivan for the thorough job he had done in assailing Indians who "had perfidiously waged an unprovoked & cruel war against these United States." Washington praised him for having applied the "rod of correction" that would be "productive of great good." Probably most of the soldiers who rode with Sullivan showed no remorse for the terror they sowed. But some did. One lamented that "a civilized people" would recoil in horror at the savagery of the troops and another acknowledged feelings of guilt for having "applied the torch to huts that were Homes of Content until we ravagers came spreading the desolation everywhere." Despite the misery that was produced, the Sullivan expedition pacified the frontier for only one year. In 1780 the Indians fought back—and with a passion fueled by revenge. In that year alone more than 300 American backcountry residents in this region perished in Indian attacks, over 1,000 homes were burned, and hundreds of thousands of acres of grain went up in smoke.[47]

FRENCH OFFICIALS HAD REJOICED when Admiral d'Estaing safely crossed the Atlantic in the spring of 1778, but otherwise little sunny news arrived from

America during the year. Washington had undertaken no major campaigns, and d'Estaing had failed to capture or destroy a single great British warship, much less lay waste to the British fleet in New York Harbor or liberate the city. Meanwhile, the clock was ticking against France. When seeking the king's authorization for the American alliance late in 1777, Vergennes had advised that the war could soon be brought to an end. His counsel seemed sound. France could enter the war assured of virtual naval superiority in North American waters, but only for a spell, unless d'Estaing succeeded decisively against the overmatched British fleet. That had not occurred, and at the approach of 1779, the French were aware that the Royal Navy would reestablish supremacy when Admiral Byron's fleet finally arrived in North America. As never before, Vergennes was persuaded of the urgency of convincing Spain to enter the war.

Long before the dawn of 1779, Conde de Floridablanca, Spain's minister of state, had the whip hand and he knew it. The war's outcome could well be determined by Madrid's choice of war or peace. When word arrived of d'Estaing's misadventures, the Spanish could not have been more aware of the leverage they possessed.

The booty that Spain foresaw gaining through this raging war included the recovery of Gibraltar and Minorca, lost years before to Great Britain, and the reacquisition of Florida, taken by Britain in 1763. Throughout 1778 the Spanish conducted talks with both France and Britain, probing to learn what the one was willing to offer for Madrid's neutrality and what the other would tender for its belligerency. Spain also offered to mediate, a gambit to see what it might acquire short of war. London knew early on that it was not about to meet the terms floated by Madrid as its price for neutrality, which included the return of Gibraltar, withdrawal of British troops from America, and the recognition of American independence. However, Britain dragged out the negotiations, playing for time in order to reinforce Minorca and Jamaica, and to strengthen its fleet in the English Channel.[48]

Just as Germain and other British ministers had recognized the need for new approaches in the aftermath of Saratoga, Vergennes now believed that France could gain its long-sought ends only if Spain became a belligerent. Unless he admitted defeat, a step Vergennes was unwilling to take, his only option was to surrender to Spain's extortionate demands. In December 1778, Vergennes told Louis XVI that victory in the near future was out of the question without Spanish belligerency and that "a prolonged war . . . could entertain the ruin of his navy" and cripple France economically. Spain's price for entering hostilities would be "gigantic," Vergennes acknowledged, but it would have to be met, for victory could not be attained short of "combined operations" by the two Bourbon powers. Louis XVI assented and on Christmas Eve 1778 Vergennes opened serious negotiations.

The terms pressed by Floridablanca were indeed colossal and went beyond his earlier demands, as he now insisted on a joint invasion of England. After weeks of tortuous discussions, marked at times by acrimony, France and Spain in April 1779 concluded the Treaty of Aranjuez. The secret pact committed Spain to make war against Great Britain for the purpose of reacquiring Gibraltar, Minorca, and Florida, and to drive the British from the coast of Campeche (modern Belize, Honduras, and Guatemala). In addition to French objectives contained in its pact with the United States, France listed its goals as the recovery of trading posts in Senegal and India, and its maintenance of Dominica. France agreed to continue fighting until Britain returned Gibraltar to Spain, a secret proviso that could leave the United States at war for a much longer time than it wished. The Bourbons also agreed that neither would make peace with Britain without the other's consent. Spain did not commit to an alliance with the United States, although it recognized France's commitment to remain at war until American independence was recognized. Floridablanca had gotten all that he wanted except an agreement stipulating Spain's recovery of Minorca and Florida as a prerequisite for peace with Britain. Spain immediately sent an ultimatum to London demanding that it agree to an armistice with France and disarmament on the high seas. Floridablanca did not anticipate Britain's assent, and he was not surprised when, in June, London rejected the ultimatum. Spain followed with a declaration of war.[49]

Vergennes had consented to Spain's demands to invade England, though like much in the accord it was not a choice that he savored. He feared that an invasion would spook nations that had no wish to see Europe's existing balance of power come unglued, a turn of events that could trigger diplomatic reshuffling on the continent that might not be in France's best interests. Vergennes also believed that the best means of bringing London to the peace table was through victories in the Western Hemisphere. But he was tethered to Spain's leash, and Madrid was convinced that an invasion offered the best hope of prying Gibraltar from Britain. The military plan the Bourbons agreed on appeared to be built on shifting sand. Change after change was made throughout the spring and deep into the summer, most at Madrid's behest, prompting the seldom-flustered Vergennes to privately complain of Spanish "windbags" who couldn't resist tinkering. It was finally agreed that France was to furnish an army of 20,000 men and 32 ships of the line. Spain was to commit 20 heavy warships and keep another 20 in reserve off the Canary Islands for intercepting British shipping and instituting a blockade of Gibraltar. At the last minute Spain insisted that France expand its army to 30,000. France complied. Portsmouth was the agreed-on invasion site, although months later Spain and France settled on landing at Falmouth in the southwest corner of England. The change was made because it was believed that taking Falmouth would not necessitate a lengthy siege and its capture would facilitate taking nearby Plymouth, a major port. The navies were to be at sea by early June and rendezvous before the end of the month. Once the Allied armada gained control of the English Channel, the French army would be transported to the landing site.[50]

Early on, British intelligence learned of the enemy's plans and that either Portsmouth or Plymouth, or both, would bear the brunt of the invasion. Lord Jeffery Amherst, the British army's commander in chief, distrusted the intelligence and made his primary defensive preparations for a landing nearer to London in southeast England. British army forces on the home front totaled about 20,000 able-bodied regulars. There were also 67 militia battalions totaling about 30,000 men. Throughout the summer Britain sought to augment its army by volunteerism and impressment, in essence the conscription of those described as "incorrigible rogues" who had deserted their families. The age and physical requirements for entering the army were lowered, cash bounties were offered, and convicts were promised freedom in return for enlisting, though only about half thought the army was preferable to prison. By late summer, 3,200 men had been added to the ranks. Meanwhile, seaports and coastal areas peppered authorities with appeals for protection against both the coming invasion and the soldiers garrisoned in their midst who sometimes threatened and assaulted civilians.[51]

The Bourbons were confronted with numerous problems that slowed preparations for the invasion, including bad weather; shortages of sailors, dockyard workers, and provisions; and an epidemic of mysterious origins that broke out in both the French army and navy. The two navies rendezvoused nearly six weeks later than originally planned, and by then not only were supplies running low, but also the English fleet had increased its strength to 37 ships of the line. In August, the epidemic in the French ranks spread to the Spanish navy. Within three weeks, 2,400 men were ill and 140 had died. Other woes beset the sailors. The fleets were hampered by impenetrable fog, contrary winds, and a severe storm that at one point blew the armada out of the Channel. Atop these difficulties, the Allied squadron spent three weeks in August searching in vain for the English fleet. That was the last straw. France and Spain called off the projected invasion.[52]

A season of recriminations ensued among the Bourbons, throughout which Madrid pushed for again attempting to invade England. Vergennes rapidly called a halt to such talk. He wanted nothing more to do with what he was certain would be another misbegotten venture. He was no longer convinced that the Allied fleet could win a naval battle. Even if successful at sea, an invasion force would face a numerically superior foe on land. The focal point of his gaze, as always, was across the ocean. It was there where the war would be won or lost.[53]

Spain's focus was centered on Gibraltar. While the attempt to invade England unfolded, Madrid could commit only seven ships of the line to a blockade of Gibraltar, but in the autumn it increased its fleet to 11 and sent an army of 10,000 to the Mediterranean for a siege operation. The British garrison, which never exceeded 7,000 men, had been caught by surprise. Toward year's end its provisions were dangerously low. London responded by readying a relief convoy under Admiral Sir George Rodney. It consisted of 22 ships of the line and 14 frigates, and in January 1780 it caught the Spanish squadron by surprise despite ample warnings furnished by French intelligence. Rodney's much larger fleet captured or destroyed six of Spain's great warships, after which he replenished the famished British troops on Gibraltar and delivered needed supplies to Minorca.[54]

The Spanish enjoyed greater success in America. Madrid, in 1776, had sent Don Bernardo de Gálvez to New Orleans as governor of Louisiana. The huge region sprawled from the Mississippi River to the Rocky Mountains but boasted only 30,000 inhabitants, about the same number as occupied Georgia, the smallest of Britain's 13 insurgent colonies. Most of Spain's colonists dwelled in or near New Orleans, though there was an additional knot of settlements well up the Mississippi River in and around St. Louis. Spain saw Louisiana as crucial for the defense of Mexico and reclamation of the Spanish Gulf Coast, lost to Britain in the Seven Years' War. Possession of the coast from New Orleans through the southern tip of Florida was indispensable for controlling shipping in the Gulf of Mexico. Spain additionally feared America's westward expansion, whether by British colonies or an independent United States, as it would ultimately threaten Louisiana.

Long before Spain entered the war, Gálvez, an ambitious, aggressive, and incredibly experienced 30-year-old military officer (he had already seen combat in both the French and Spanish armies, fought Apache in North America, and studied at Spain's military academy), set about restoring Spanish prestige through a multitude of economic and administrative reforms. At the same time, he strengthened his network of defenses, gathered intelligence, and prepared for the possibility of hostilities with Great Britain. He sought alliances with Native American tribes, built a strong militia of some 1,500 men in 17 companies that included free Black men, and fashioned an elite cavalry, the Carabineros de la Luisisana. In the event of war, Gálvez's orders were to "expel [the English] from the Mexican Basin and from the banks of the Mississippi, where their settlements are harmful to our trade and to the security of our richest possessions." When war came in 1779, four years after he took office, Gálvez was ready. His immediate objective was to secure Spanish hegemony on the lower Mississippi River. Gálvez succeeded through a lightning campaign that commenced at the same moment the Bourbon allies terminated their projected invasion of England. He commanded a multinational and ethnically diverse army of some 650 men. His troops included native Spaniards, Irish, French-speaking Acadians, American-born volunteers, men from the Canary Islands, subjects from every corner of Spain's American empire, numerous Black men, and roughly 160 Indians from four or more tribes. Within six weeks, Gálvez's little army took every British installation from New Orleans to Natchez.[55]

Although Spain did not have diplomatic relations with the United States, it sent Juan de Miralles to Philadelphia as an observer. In the spring of 1779, before Gálvez took the field, Miralles visited Washington. The Spanish envoy urged the American commander to send a detachment to take St. Augustine, a diversionary step that would aid Gálvez in his campaigns. To sweeten the pot, Miralles sent Washington a 100-pound sea turtle and 800 lemons. He later forwarded bottles of lemon juice, 26 chocolate cakes, raisins, and a jar of almonds to the American commander. It was to no avail. Congress thought sending a force into Florida would be "highly imprudent."[56]

If Britain's commander in West Florida had been resolute, Gálvez might have been denied the opportunity to achieve more. Brigadier General John Campbell, who now was in command at Pensacola, was an experienced veteran who had served valorously in the Seven Years' War, but he was cautious and indecisive. Lord Germain had directed that should Spanish belligerency materialize, Campbell was to strengthen his naval arm with reinforcements from the Caribbean and assail New Orleans. Typically, the American secretary portrayed the mission as posing little challenge given that the Spanish force there was "greatly inferior" and lacked popular support. But Campbell had not attacked New Orleans and he additionally failed to rapidly reinforce the garrison in sturdy, brick-faced Fort Charlotte in Mobile. While Campbell was idle, the audacious Gálvez was on the move. In January 1780, with about 700 men, including a score or so of Choctaw, and 11 ships—the largest of which was a brigantine—he sailed for Mobile. A raging Gulf storm caused delays, as three ships and several men were lost in the tempest. But in March Gálvez was ready to attack the British installation. Once aware of the threat posed by Gálvez, Campbell at last acted "to rectify sinister circumstances" that could result in Fort Charlotte's fall to "His Catholic Majesty's arms." Campbell personally led a relief expedition composed of two divisions and about 100 Choctaw. The men tramped 72 miles, wading through swamps thick with ankle-deep mud and slick and slimy submerged logs, and rambling across overgrown terrain where the sometimes razor-sharp grass was taller than the warriors' heads. They had closed to within 30 miles of Mobile when Gálvez launched his attack with a relentless and deafening fusillade that blew breaches in the fort's wall. The doomed British commander surrendered. Within nine months of Spain's entrance into the war, Britain had lost more than a thousand men, a huge complement of weaponry, and its toehold in the Mississippi Valley and along the Gulf Coast. All that remained in West Florida was Pensacola, and Campbell told Germain that in all likelihood it "will soon be invested and besieged."[57]

These were not the sole setbacks that Britain experienced in the American West. With Spanish belligerency a certainty, Germain in 1779 had envisaged British forces from Pensacola sweeping up the Mississippi River while General Frederick Haldimand, Burgoyne's successor as commander of Britain's forces in Canada, sent troops from Detroit to assist in regaining control of the river from St. Louis southward. Haldimand responded with alacrity, sending off a force made up of regulars, traders, and braves from four Indigenous tribes. Aware of the looming threat, Fernando de Leyba, the lieutenant governor of Louisiana and commander at St. Louis, strengthened his stockade and obtained reinforcements—about 150 men characterized as "all good shots"—bringing his garrison to some 300 men, half the number of the enemy advancing on him. A British siege likely would have succeeded. Instead, in May 1780, two months after Mobile fell, the British force rashly charged the entrenched defenders. They ran into a deadly artillery and rifle fire. The campaign ended that same day. The British army, riddled with casualties and deser-tions, threw in the towel. From the confluence of the Ohio and Mississippi to New Orleans, Spain remained in control.

The British were challenged in the Illinois Country as well. Virginia, on the basis of its 1609 charter, claimed a vast area that stretched west from the Appala-chians to the Mississippi, relishing it for the bonanza it would be for land speculators and the land-hungry citizenry, and the prospect of lucrative trade with the Spanish in the bordering western territory. Settlers breached the mountain barrier just as the Revolutionary War erupted, seeking cheap land offered by land companies and speculators. Virginia, under Governor Patrick Henry, established a government and militia units in Kentucky. In 1778, it authorized its military commander in trans-Appalachia, brave and cold-blooded George Rogers Clark, to raise seven companies totaling 500 men and lead them against British-affiliated settlements in Illinois. He garnered only about 180 men, but that summer—around the time of the Battle of Monmouth—Clark took Kaskaskia and won to his side some Indians and even more of the French who inhabited the region. Although Clark lacked the resources to make the most of his success, Virginians poured into Kentucky. Its population swelled to 8,000 by 1782 and would climb to 73,000 just 10 years after the war. Whatever Clark hoped to achieve, his campaign helped keep open the flow of Spanish supplies from New Orleans to American forces on the trans-Appalachian frontier.[58] The West was a blood-soaked ground, with people of every background and persuasion victimized, including upwards of 1,000 American settlers who died in Kentucky. But it was in this war's backwater. No belligerent could spare the resources from what were deemed more vital theaters. However, each understood that military successes and failures in the West might shape territorial settlements and postwar interests in the eventual peace treaty, and all understood that they ignored the region at their peril.[59]

The British had waged a defensive war in America's southwest, but from the Yucatán Peninsula and Campeche to the Gulf of Honduras, they were more entrenched, having established numerous settlements and plantations to facilitate their timber and agricultural enterprises. The British struck first in the fall of 1779, mounting an offensive in that region and in Nicaragua, a step toward the establishment of a British port on the Pacific Ocean. Not long elapsed before the Spanish were on the move, led by Matías de Gálvez, the 62-year-old father of Bernardo and the captain general of Guatemala. He counterattacked in Honduras in November and in 1780, with reinforcements from Cuba, Gálvez succeeded in taking the offensive in Nicaragua. The Central American theater "was not a sideshow," as historian Thomas E. Chávez observed. Both sides poured in large numbers of men and ships. Armies that at times approached 2,000 men marched, attacked, besieged, and defended outposts. Spain succeeded early on in checking Britain's initial advances, and thereafter for the next several years, the fighting settled into a war of attrition along several fronts.[60]

FRANCE'S SOLE ACHIEVEMENTS IN its initial 18 months of belligerency resulted from Admiral d'Estaing's success in the Caribbean. Before his arrival the French had taken Dominica, but lost St. Lucia, their principal base in the eastern Caribbean. At virtually the same moment that the British captured Savannah late in 1778, d'Estaing made a perfunctory, and unsuccessful, attempt to regain St. Lucia in the Windward Islands. A different story unfolded in 1779. Bolstered by the arrival of a large fleet early in the year under François Joseph Paul, Comte de Grasse—and benefiting from Britain's inability to reinforce the West Indies due to the threatened Bourbon invasion of the English homeland—d'Estaing seized St. Vincent, which France had lost to Britain in the Seven Years' War. The handful of British troops on the island, almost devoid of ammunition and food, surrendered to their prodigious adversary without firing a shot. Nine days later, d'Estaing took Grenada, the second-largest sugar-producing island in the Caribbean. In July, with superior numbers, d'Estaing scored a sensational victory over a Royal Navy fleet under Admiral Byron. D'Estaing had earlier proclaimed that when he completed his work in the Caribbean, George III would not have enough sugar "to sweeten his tea for breakfast." His boast might have come true had he pursued Byron's crippled and outnumbered fleet, but d'Estaing was impatient to hurry back to North America. He was so eager to get back, in fact, that he ignored the recent orders of Antoine Sartine, France's naval minister, to return to France before the tropical hurricane season commenced in late summer. D'Estaing appears to have been a man driven to gain redemption. Not only had his mission in 1778 been a dismal failure, but the stinging rebuke by Sullivan and other rebel generals may have continued to haunt him.[61]

Both Washington and Clinton expected to see the French fleet in late summer, and throughout 1779 both commanders watched and prepared for its arrival. In February, a gloomy Washington, fearing that d'Estaing would be bottled up in the Caribbean by a more powerful British fleet, despaired, "I Cannot bear the thoughts of the War Continueing another year." He knew that would be the case if d'Estaing did not return. In early May, Minister Gérard called on Washington at his head-quarters in Middlebrook on the Raritan River in New Jersey. Following the army's parade—described by one officer as a "great and splendid cavalcade ... in martial pomp and style" replete with "field manoeuvres and evolutions" and the "firing of cannon and musketry"—Gérard and Washington huddled. The minister brought word that d'Estaing would be coming in late summer and he might seek to either liberate Savannah or join with Washington in a campaign to take New York. Where Washington had once dismissed the war in the South as inconsequential, he now spoke of retaking Savannah as an "object of the greatest magnitude," as it would alleviate the "disaffection" and "general languor that has seized the people" in the South and throughout the country. Washington was persuaded that d'Estaing could rapidly capture Savannah and still have time to come to New York. He brimmed with a newfound optimism, convinced that the Allies would have an excellent shot at reclaiming New York before the end of the year. Washington pledged to "collect our whole force in this quarter" for what he was certain would be the "decisive" action of the war.[62]

In the last days of summer Washington and Clinton learned that d'Estaing's fleet had arrived off the Georgia coast. Still convinced that d'Estaing would not be detained long in Georgia, Washington apprised him of the size of the Royal Navy in New York and the number and location of British troops in and around Manhattan. Simultaneously, Washington and his generals devoted several days to preparing elaborate plans for the anticipated campaign of New York. Washington also asked the governors of five states to call to duty 12,000 militiamen. Clinton at the same moment was feeling "alarming apprehensions for New York." He responded by consolidating his army for the coming showdown, recalling all his troops at King's Ferry and Newport.[63]

The French fleet reached Tybee Island off the Georgia coast at the beginning of September. The prodigious armada consisted of 22 ships of the line, nine frigates, and 4,450 troops, including 750 free men of color who had been recruited in St. Domingo—the first Black men to serve in the French armed forces. The British troops in Savannah were commanded by Augustine Prevost. In April, Prevost had slipped across the Savannah River with 1,000 men and marched to Charleston, where he demanded that the city surrender or face destruction. It was a bluff. He did not have the troops or artillery to take Charleston, but Governor John Rutledge fell for the deception and offered terms: South Carolina would drop out of the war in return for Prevost's pledge not to occupy the city. Feeling that he lacked the authority to agree to such terms, Prevost rejected Rutledge's terms and demanded the city's surrender and all the rebel troops defending it. When the governor refused, Prevost—to the astonishment of South Carolina's authorities—marched back to Georgia. That close call spurred South Carolina to beseech help from d'Estaing.[64]

On arriving in Georgia, d'Estaing discovered that the American forces in the southern theater were now commanded by General Benjamin Lincoln, a Massachusetts farmer and activist who had served since the siege of Boston and had been seriously wounded in the Saratoga campaign. The French admiral also learned that Lincoln had a tiny army, though militiamen had been summoned that would bring the rebel force up to 2,500 men. As the Allies possessed only a slight numerical superiority against a foe that had been given a year to work on Savannah's fortifications, d'Estaing opted to besiege the city. The siege operation came together sluggishly as day after day the French soldiers and marines muscled heavy artillery into place and the leaders awaited the arrival of Lincoln's militiamen. Prevost used the time wisely. He put upwards of 500 slaves to work building fortifications and summoned 800 reinforcements from coastal South Carolina. He also successfully deceived d'Estaing by offering to negotiate, spinning out the talks to give the supplemental troops the time they needed to make the 40-mile trek. Those British soldiers hurried through the persistently hot and humid early-fall coastal weather, at times thrashing through swamps teeming with alligators and poisonous snakes. Arriving in the course of the siege, they slipped through the Allied lines and linked up with Prevost's troops.

The big French siege guns finally opened up October 4, 18 days after d'Estaing's troops had landed. They bombarded Prevost's lines around the clock for five days. With no sign of a white flag, d'Estaing on October 8 decided that if he was to have any chance that year of campaigning with Washington, he must abandon the siege operation and attack the entrenched British defenders. Lincoln was cool to the idea, and the highest-ranking French officers sharply objected, doubtful that a frontal attack could succeed. Besides, they argued, Prevost must be low on provisions and could not hold out much longer. D'Estaing did not listen. His obstinacy would be a crucial mistake.

The attack that d'Estaing ordered was launched at dawn on October 9. It was an Allied bloodbath. They did not have the numbers to prevail against a capable British army protected by strong fortifications artfully designed by a professional engineer, an officer who "understood his business," as Clinton later remarked. Hordes of men were mowed down attacking Prevost's impenetrable lines. The engagement at Savannah was the closest that Americans came in this war to experiencing their own Bunker Hill. The Allies lost around 850 men, 20 percent of those who stormed the British emplacements; another 125 men had already been casualties during the six weeks preceding the attack. Prevost lost only 63 men. D'Estaing, who along with Lincoln led the charge, was among the Allied wounded, having taken shrapnel in the arm and a bullet in the leg.[65]

Lincoln and Governor Rutledge, and some of the senior French officers, urged d'Estaing to remain, fearing that Charleston would soon be lost if he departed. But he would not stay. He had attempted a "vigorous blow," he said, and that was all he could do.[66] He also ruled against sailing for New York. He could not depart Georgia before late October and it would be deep into November before he and Washington could begin a campaign for New York. That was no time of year for instituting a crucial, and possibly protracted, operation in the northern theater. Besides, he was under orders issued long before to return to France.

Washington spoke sadly of the "Disaster at Savannah," while Clinton rejoiced that this was "the greatest event that has happened the whole war."[67] The gloom that had weighed heavily on Clinton when he took command 18 months earlier had lessened. His emasculated army had survived two campaign seasons. The grinding fear aroused by France's commitment of a naval force in 1778 and d'Estaing's antici-pated return in 1779 had, for the time being, diminished. Of the two commanders, Washington was the more despondent as he took his army into winter quarters at Morristown at the close of the campaign season in 1779. Two years earlier he had thought the French alliance meant that the war was nearly over and the attainment of American independence was at hand. After meeting with Gérard in the spring, Washington had hoped that Savannah and New York would be retaken and the war would be brought to a glorious conclusion. Instead, the war had become a stale-mate. The French navy had not turned the tide. France had gained next to nothing from two years at war. The implications were not lost on Washington, who could only hope that French staying power would persist. For two long years Washing-ton's army had remained largely idle. Perhaps he had followed a prudent course, but now he understood with crystal clarity that the longer the war continued, the greater the likelihood of a lethal erosion of the will to continue, both in America and in Versailles. At the dawn of 1780, Clinton saw time as his ally. Washington saw time as his enemy. Washington had to pin his hopes on the American people's perseverance and French resilience and durability. At the close of 1779 Washington grimly acknowledged that American "virtue & patriotism are almost kicked out . . . whilst a virtuous few struggle—lament—& suffer."[68]

CHAPTER 9

ARMIES AND NAVIES, SOLDIERS AND SAILORS

IN THE FRAUGHT DAYS of early 1775 there had been talk in the colonies of waging a guerrilla war.[1] Neither General Washington nor Congress embraced the idea. Both were wedded to establishing a conventional army under civil control. Fears existed that the extreme violence—"inhumanity" might be a better term— endemic to irregular war would turn large chunks of the population against hostilities. Congress and Washington also thought that officers should be "Men of Character," the gentlemen in society who hailed from prominent families, an end that could hardly be guaranteed in bands of guerrilla warriors. The two also believed that logistical problems, recruiting soldiers, and the looming task of training engineers and artillerymen could best be met through a regular army. Congress wanted the fight against Great Britain to be a national effort, a struggle "in the *common cause* of defending our rights and liberties," and a national army was seen as most likely to realize that goal. Finally, those in 1775 who already leaned toward American independence thought a national army would have a nationalizing impact crucial for the war effort and the formation of the new nation. The name given to the army that Congress created, the Continental army, did not come about by happenstance.[2]

Congress had created the army and appointed the original batch of general officers, but much remained undecided, including the organization of the new army. During the fall of 1775, Washington and his officers in the siege army outside

Boston drew up an organizational plan that Congress quickly adopted. The army would consist of 20,000 men grouped into 26 infantry regiments and detached units of rifleman and artillery, a plan modeled on the structure of Britain's army. Many modifications would be made as the war progressed and the size of the army and the number of regiments and battalions fluctuated.[3]

One later consequential change was the creation of a cavalry arm. Washington had little prior experience with cavalry, which may have led him to initially under-estimate its value. He also appeared to regard the cavalry as a burden that could not be borne, as it would mean more men—and horses—to feed. Washington's eyes were opened by events in 1776. In October, at White Plains, British light dragoons routed militia units that anchored the rebels' right flank. Six weeks later a British cavalry patrol captured General Charles Lee, the second-in-command in the Continental army, who only days before had complained to Washington of being "destitute of L[ight] Horse." At least two other general officers had also advised Washington that "without the assistance of horse," their hands were tied. Wash-ington hurriedly responded, telling Congress in December that he had come to understand "the utility of Horse," adding that he was "now convinced there is no carrying on the War without them." Congress swiftly authorized the creation of four cavalry regiments composed of 3,000 troopers. In the northern theater during 1777 and 1778, the new cavalry wing served primarily as scouts, messengers, and reconnoiterers, though rebel horse soldiers played minor roles in the engagements at Brandywine and Germantown. After 1778, when the war shifted to the South, mounted units on both sides played critical, even decisive, roles in several important engagements.[4]

The process of transforming the New England army that besieged Boston in 1775 into a truly national army brought on the question of the appointment of its officers. Congress had named the general officers but stipulated that the "appoint-ment of all Officers as high as a Colonel" was to be left to the Government in which the Regiments originated." As the new army was initially the Grand American army in different clothes, the result, as Washington pointed out, was that in the summer of 1775 the officer corps was "monopolized" by the four New England colo-nies, an outcome that he called "improper" and "impolitick." Others agreed that something had to be done. Late in the summer, when New Jersey and Pennsylvania formed regiments for the new army, Congress looked into the matter. The congres-sional debate over who would make the appointments was heated and revealed a division that has never disappeared from American politics: the degree of state sovereignty versus central authority. Those who opposed vesting Congress with the appointment power warned that fashioning a too powerful national government was "big with mischief." Those on the other side contended that the well-being of the new "Union . . . depends much upon breaking down provincial conventions."

Washington quietly confided to an acquaintance in the Virginia delegation that it might be best to give him the appointment power. Few agreed. The congressional debate concerned whether Congress or the provinces possessed the appointment power. Ultimately, it was decided that Congress would possess the authority to appoint officers above the rank of captain while the provinces would select ensigns, lieutenants, and captains. Throughout the war, however, Congress almost always abided by the wishes of the provinces with regard to the regimental field grade officers, and it deferred to the wishes of the provinces when elevating their field grade officers to the Main Army. Early in 1776, for instance, Congress affirmed the provincial appointments of Colonels Anthony Wayne (Pennsylvania) and Adam Stephen (Virginia) when it named them brigadier generals in the Continental army. The following year it even raised Brigadier General Benjamin Lincoln of the Massachusetts militia to the rank of major general in the Continental army.

Within weeks of taking command, Washington concluded that some of his general officers were unfit. Some from Massachusetts were not from the cream of society, he remarked, scorning them as "of the same Kidney with the Privates." He would have liked a role in the promotion of field grade officers, but that, too, was controlled by Congress. In 1776, Washington sought authorization to promote officers at the company level, but Congress denied his request and the authority remained at the provincial level. Early on, Congress sought to establish criteria for promotion to the general officer ranks, but after days of what one delegate characterized as "perplexed, inconclusive and irksome" debates, it cobbled together an oblique formula that allowed the promotion of whomever it wished after taking into consideration seniority, merit, and the quota of troops raised by the candidates' states.[5]

The selections and promotions made by Congress were not always salutary. The first batch of general officers included some who had clearly been political choices. Not much was made of it until the setbacks in the New York campaign in 1776. Thereafter, John Adams privately complained that at least four generals were "[in]capable of the great Commands they hold. . . . I wish they would all resign." It was a view doubtless shared by many congressmen. Adams grumbled that selecting and promoting officers had caused him more distress than any of his other responsibilities. Congress's choices bred "Jealousies, Envys, and Distrusts," he lamented. He added that he was also "wearied to Death with the Wrangles between military officers. . . . They Quarrell like Cats and Dogs. They worry one another like Mastiffs. Scrambling for Rank and Pay like Apes for Nutts."[6]

From the outset Washington sought what he thought was the proper type of officer: men of merit and personal honor. He wanted officers who manifested courage, dedication, selflessness, republican virtue, and public spirit. He believed the soldiery would trust and follow such officers.[7] In countless general orders, and through the example he set, Washington sought to mold his officers. Each day he also invited two young officers to attend the afternoon mess so that they could observe the behavior of senior officers. He likely also frequently passed along the same instructions that he had given at the outset of the war to a colonel who asked for guidance:

> be strict in your discipline; that is, to require nothing unreasonable of your officers and men, but see that whatever is required be punctually complied with. Reward and punish every man according to his merit, without partiality or prejudice; hear his complaints; if well founded, redress them; if otherwise, discourage them, in order to prevent frivolous ones. Discourage vice in every shape, and impress upon the mind of every man, from the first to the lowest, the importance of the cause. . . . For ever keep in view the necessity of guarding against surprises. . . . Be plain and precise in your orders, and keep copies of them to refer to that no mistakes may happen. Be easy and condescending in your deportment to your officers, but not too familiar, lest you subject yourself to a want of that respect, which is necessary to support a proper command.[8]

In the meantime, given the unavailability of uniforms, he designed "badges of distinction" for his officers, ribbons and cockades emblematic of authority and the barrier that separated them from those of a lower rank.[9]

A study of the social origins of New Jersey's officers during the war revealed that an overwhelming percentage were drawn from the wealthiest one-third of the population, with 32 percent from the state's most affluent 10 percent; none came from the poorest one-third. Many officers, including some from middling social backgrounds, came to believe that their service elevated them to an even more exalted rank. Class consciousness prevailed to an extraordinary degree in early America, as people kept to their social class and deferred to those at a loftier level, doffing their hats, bowing obsequiously, and not daring to assume the prerogatives of their social superiors. The cleavage between officers and enlisted men in the army existed to an even greater degree than the social divides in civil society. Officers were immune from the horrendous punishments inflicted on enlisted men and lived more comfortably than their troops. While in winter quarters, field grade officers found housing in snug dwellings and were blessed with bountiful meals, and many were joined by their wives and families. Military service introduced some officers to holding power, acquiring and relishing entitlements, and gaining status. Many came in contact with genteel French officers, some of whom were part of the Old World's titled nobility, and their social habits and practices rubbed off on some in the Continental officer corps, who thereafter scorned their prewar lives. Not a few officers came to look down on ordinary people, and many disparaged both the ideal of equality promulgated in the Declaration of Independence and the democratic fervor that emerged and accelerated during American Revolution. Jefferson worried that "military habits" were corrupting, as did two fellow signers of the Declaration of Independence, Samuel Adams and Benjamin Rush, who early on warned of the tendency for officers to "claim superiority over the rest of their countrymen" and to transition from defenders of liberty to exponents of authoritarianism.[10]

One of the more troubling matters confronting Washington and other officers was the annual slog to recruit an army, a chore that grew increasingly difficult after the gusto for serving during the war's first couple of years waned. At the outset of hostilities the army strikingly mirrored society. Not untypically, in 1775 two-thirds of those in the Third Regiment of Foot, New York Line, were farmers, laborers, and tradesmen; the regiment included a blacksmith, cobbler, cooper, carpenter, weaver, and teacher. Most of these men were between the ages of 20 and 25, but there were six teenagers and a 10-year-old boy. The ranks of the army in 1775 and 1776 teemed with property-owning citizens infused with patriotism who dreamed of winning glory, were eager for adventure, and not infrequently had been encouraged to serve by authoritative local figures, especially clergy and veterans of earlier wars.

It did not take long for the reality of war to set in. A soldier's life was harsh and could be dangerous. It also involved lengthy separations from loved ones and lost income. Soon enough, word spread that the Continental soldiery often lacked adequate food and clothing, and that army camps were breeding grounds for disease. After the Continental army suffered severe setbacks in the New York campaign in 1776, the early ardor for soldiering vanished. One-third of the men of military age in the frontier town of Peterborough, New Hampshire, served in the army in 1775, but by 1777 only 14 percent were in the army and the following year just 4 percent. Peterborough was hardly unique, a fact of life that prompted Washington to despair that those who agreed to soldier "upon Principles of disinterestedness are . . . no more than a drop in the Ocean."

Only about 7 percent of those under Washington in 1776 reenlisted at year's end, and had it not been for cash bounties, pledges of postwar land grants, and rosy promises of pay, blankets, ample food, and abundant clothing—typically two pairs of shoes, two hunting shirts, two pairs of overalls, a wool or leather coat, and a hat—the Continental army probably would have lacked the manpower to take the field in 1777. The army survived, but its demographics underwent a sea change. Thereafter the soldiery was drawn largely from among the poor and landless, those whom contemporaries often labeled the "lower sort" or the "idle," and which one Continental general described as "riff raff—dirty" men. Most were from the poorest two-thirds of society. One study showed that nearly half owned no taxable property. Maryland conscripted vagabonds and offered freedom to convicted felons and Loyalists charged with treason if they would enlist in the army. Now and then, captured British deserters chose the Continental army over a rebel prison camp. Some citizens were so down-and-out that for a price they agreed to serve as another's substitute. Many impoverished recent immigrants enlisted, seeing military service as the quickest route toward gaining land. Most of the foreign-born were from Ireland and Germany, but Canadians, Swiss, French, and even an occasional Scandinavian drifted into the army. Nearly all the foreign-born who soldiered were residents of Pennsylvania, New Jersey, Delaware, and Maryland, and by 1778 they made up roughly 15 percent of the soldiery. Close to half of the men in several Pennsylvania regiments were foreign-born, and both Pennsylvania and Virginia created a "German Regiment." During the first two years of hostilities, New England contributed the largest number of soldiers, but by 1778 roughly half of those in the Continental army had been raised in the four mid-Atlantic states. In one respect the army never changed: The overwhelming number of enlistees remained young men. In 1777, the median age of new recruits was 20, and that changed little during the war's remaining years.[11]

In the first years of the war nearly every soldier was white. When Washington assumed command in July 1775 he found some Black men in the Continental army, New Englanders who had transitioned from militiamen to soldiers in the new army. Some had fought along Battle Road and on Bunker Hill. Washington, a Virginia slave owner, had never experienced anything of the sort, and he did not want Black men in the army. His response sprang from racism, fear that Black soldiers would pass along their weapons to slaves, and worries that their presence would hinder recruiting. He quickly secured a vote from a council of war banishing them from the army. Two months later Washington had a change of heart, telling Congress that he wished to permit his Black soldiers to remain in the army, lest they "Seek employ" in the British army. Congress responded that Black soldiers already in the army "may be re-enlisted," but "no others" were to be recruited. The Continental army remained almost entirely white through the war's first three years.[12]

During the anxious weeks of the New York campaign in 1776, a New Jersey congressman approached John Adams about the wisdom of his state recruiting a battalion composed of Black men. Adams replied, "Your Negro Battalion will never do. S. Carolina would run out of their Wits at the least Hint of such a Measure." Notwithstanding Adams's reservations, and the congressional edict against permitting Black men to enter the Continental army, New Jersey took them into its Continental line in 1777. Ongoing recruiting difficulties soon led other provinces to think along those lines. In 1778, when Rhode Island found it impossible to fill its ranks, several of its Continental officers, led by Brigadier General James Varnum, asked Washington if he would accept Black soldiers should the state assembly sanction their recruitment. Desperate for men, Washington consented. In February, while the army suffered at Valley Forge, the Rhode Island legislature—a majority of whose members were slave owners—agreed to permit free and enslaved Black men to enter their Continental line, and it decreed that all chattel who soldiered would henceforth be "absolutely FREE." These recruits entered the all-Black First Rhode Island Regiment (all Black, that is, with the exception of its white commander). The regiment's first great test came in late August when General Pigot's British force nearly drove General Sullivan's army off Aquidneck Island. The First Rhode Island repulsed two bayonet charges by Hessian troops, a crucial action that prevented the enemy from breaking through Sullivan's right flank. Eleven Black soldiers perished in the fighting, prompting Washington to write that the men in the First Rhode Island were "well entitled to a proper share of the honor of the Day."[13]

Rhode Island's innovative example, and the fighting qualities exhibited by the First Regiment in Rhode Island, led other states to recruit Black soldiers. In 1779, Black soldiers were part of Anthony Wayne's force that took Stony Point and the Sullivan Expedition that marauded through Iroquoia. No precise record of the number of Black soldiers who served in the Continental army exists, and estimates have ranged from 3,000 to more than 8,000, although historians have generally settled on 5,000 as the likely total. If so, roughly 5 percent of all who soldiered as Continentals between 1775 and 1783 were Black.[14]

Beginning in 1777 the Continental army became a standing army, even though a fear of standing armies had a long history in Britain and the American colonies. Standing armies had been shunned as dangers to liberty and the tools of tyrants, and the common soldiers that filled the ranks—usually drawn from the "lower sort"—had a distasteful reputation as profligate and menacing sorts. When armed and banded together, such men were often viewed as little better than dangerous gangs given to plundering. The notion that armies and pillaging went hand in hand was not entirely mistaken. General Greene once remarked that it was "impossible to carry on a war without oppressing the inhabitants." Jedediah Huntington, a Connecticut brigadier general, acknowledged that even a "friendly" army could be "a dreadful Scourge to any People. . . . Devastation and Distress mark their Steps." Such a frame of mind could not be hidden from the soldiers, and not a few of the army's rank and file blamed their many privations on what they saw as an uncaring populace. In time, the civilians' fear of soldiers was matched by the soldiers' brooding resentment of civilians, indignation shared by numerous officers who came to think that public virtue had evaporated and that many on the home front were living comfortably—too comfortably—and had renounced the "spirit of '76."[15]

The transition to a standing army hardly solved recruiting problems, and in the fall of 1777, following his close call at Brandywine and while facing yet another year of fighting, Washington renewed his call for conscription. He told Congress that "every idea of voluntary enlistments seems to be at an end," and he complained that the rarely deployed "mode of drafting" heretofore utilized "has been carried out with such want of energy" that it resulted in "but a small accession of force." Bounties and other inducements no longer worked, for "the country have been pretty well drained, of that class of men whose tempers, attachments and circumstances, disposed them to enter . . . into the army." He urged conscription for one year of service, contending that a longer period would be "disgusting and dangerous, perhaps impracticable." Congress did not order universal conscription. It continued to set manpower quotas for the states, determined the number of battalions to be raised by each state, and stipulated that those who were recruited were to be healthy and free males between the ages of 17 and 50. It additionally mandated that if the assigned quota of men could not be attained by voluntarism, the states were to either draft militiamen or employ any other method that worked. The new law did not apply to South Carolina and Georgia.[16]

The New England states set quotas for towns, Pennsylvania for counties, and Virginia for newly created military districts, and some states levied hefty fines on districts that failed to meet their quota. Most states appointed recruiting officers, and in the winter and spring the Continental army sent out sergeants and junior officers to secure enlistees. It was tough sledding, as it always had been. Indeed, throughout the war the means of getting men into the army and the length of service seemed to always be flux. Congress, beginning late in 1776, wanted men to enlist for the war's duration. However, the states found few takers, and after a couple of months Congress rolled out a new policy. Only men who enlisted for three years or the duration would receive a land bounty following the war. The less restrictive states frequently enlisted men for one year and proffered the usual inducements to get them. Year after year the yield was disappointing. Reluctance to serve forced the states to turn to additional lures, and to coercion. Some states permitted volunteers to select which regiment they would serve in, offered lifetime exemptions from taxation, tendered full-pay pensions for life in the event of a disabling wound, and promised perpetual care for widows of the mortally wounded. In 1780, Virginia offered volunteers a healthy young slave. If none of the allurements worked, most states resorted to conscription, a practice that netted what historian John Shy described as those who were "poorer, marginal, less well anchored in the society." Every state permitted those faced with the draft to hire a substitute or pay a fine in lieu of soldiering, escape hatches for the more affluent. One-sixth of all recruits in Virginia after 1777 were substitutes and one-third adolescents. A 17-year-old who in 1777 agreed to go "into the scrape" as a substitute was fatalistic. Facing conscription, he decided "to get as much for my skin as I could."[17]

Some whose service was coming to an end chose to reenlist. The prospect of another bounty led some to stay on. Others cherished the comradeship among soldiers. Private Joseph Plumb Martin, who enlisted in 1776 and subsequently reenlisted, described the bonding experience among the soldiers:

> We had lived together as a family of brothers for several years . . . had shared
> with each other the hardships, dangers, and sufferings incident to a soldier's
> life; had sympathized with each other in trouble and sickness; had assisted
> in bearing each other's burdens and strove to make them lighter by council
> and advice; had endeavored to conceal each other's faults or make them

appear in as good a light as they would bear. In short, the soldiers, each in his particular circle of acquaintance, were as strict a band of brotherhood as Masons.[18]

For all the struggles of recruiting, it is generally agreed that about 100,000 men served in the Continental army. This amounted to an incredible portion of the free population, which stood at about two million at the time of the Revolutionary War. As half of the free population would have been females and somewhere around half of all males would have been too young or too old for service, a conservative estimate is that roughly one in five free males of military age served in the Continental army, a vastly larger percentage than soldiered in any European army during the 18th century or who served in the American military in World War II.[19]

Getting men into the army was difficult. Keeping them in the army was also a problem. Roughly a quarter of Continental army soldiers, some 25,000, deserted. Some ran away in order to enlist again and receive another cash bounty. A handful joined the enemy. Most sought to go home or escape to a supposedly safe spot. Within a month of taking command, Washington lamented the "great Number of Soldiers . . . who absent themselves." It was a headache that never went away. At the end of 1780 Washington was still ordering his officers to "use your utmost endeavor to keep your men from deserting." One year into the army's existence, the judge advocate general urged Congress to take steps to curb "infamous Desertions." Congress responded in September 1776 with a revised Articles of War that permitted capital punishment for deserters. Had Washington strictly enforced the law, his already small army would have been inoperable. Washington's prudent response was to order his officers to report "the Inst[ant] a Soldier is missing" so that "an immediate pursuit" could begin. Pursuits did not always lead to the capture of the deserter. It was a big country, and civilians, both Loyalists and patriots, sometimes aided the escapees. On rare occasions civilians even liberated fugitives following their capture by a search party. Washington, in 1777, was driven to ask Congress to urge the states to "inflict a severe and heavy penalty upon those who harbour deserters," as "Our Army is shamefully reduced by desertion." Desertion continued until nearly the last day of the army's existence.[20]

It is not difficult to understand most men's reluctance to go into the army or to remain in its clutches. Life for enlisted men in the Continental army included gluts of boredom, excessive regulation, harsh discipline, and episodic periods of extreme peril. There were instances of intolerable deprivation and unremitting assignments of duties—gathering wood, tending to one's weapon, foraging, patrolling, and lonely and uneasy nights staring into the spectral distance while standing sentry. When the army moved, the highest-ranking officers rode horseback. The lower-grade officers and enlisted men traveled on foot. When the newly formed Third Virginia Regiment marched from Williamsburg to Manhattan in 1776, the soldiers trekked an average of 15 miles each day for 26 days. When they finally crossed the Hudson into New York, one-third of the men were pronounced unfit for duty. Armies in the field sometimes traveled hundreds of miles during the campaign season and on occasion tramped long distances in one fell swoop. One soldier noted that he had covered 45 miles within a 24-hour period. A private in the Delaware Regiment recorded journeys that totaled 4,513 miles on foot during a 24-month period. It is hardly surprising that one weary soldier bemoaned his "pained and lacerated" feet, and another mentioned having been "obliged to march . . . night and day without rest or sleep. . . . I have often been so beat out with long and tedious marching that I have fallen asleep while walking," he said.[21]

Destitution was the common lot of the Continental soldiers. Men often lacked decent shoes and some had no shoes. In winter, the men not infrequently were without sufficient blankets or an adequate coat. One soldier remembered that "many times [he] had to lie down like a dumb animal in the field [and] bear the pelting of the pitiless storm, cruel enough in warm weather, but how much more so in the heart of winter."[22] In winter quarters, men sometimes went days with little or no food, and there were times when the soldiers were given musty or spoiled meat that they declared they would not feed to their livestock back home. General Greene spoke of times when the lack of firewood compelled his troops to "Eat their Provision Raw."[23]

The army's seemingly irresolvable supply problems accounted for much of the misery. Procuring food and provisions for the army was the job of the quartermaster, and dispensing victuals fell to the army's commissary. Both faced stupendous challenges. Supplies frequently had to be transported over vast distances, and the soldiery consumed an incredible amount of food. On average, 10,000 Continentals devoured 2.225 million pounds of beef, 2.297 million pounds of flour, and 500,000 gills (2 million ounces, or 78,000 fifths) of rum and whiskey every three months. The army's indispensable horses ate 2.5 million tons of hay and 253,000 bushels of grain annually. No single factor accounted for the army's logistical woes. Few in Congress were sufficiently experienced in administrative and military matters to develop meaningful solutions to the army's supply problems. What is more, the supply services were hindered by poor leadership, corruption, and shortages of wagons, horses, and laborers. Six years into the war, Washington said that despite what France and Spain had shipped to America, and the cornucopia of goods within the states, his men were hungry and malnourished. He raged that they "never see" much that had been acquired because it lay "wasting and rotting" somewhere in a storage facility. The supply system was additionally victimized by America's decentralized political system. The states secured the supplies, and Congress and the army were at the mercy of the states. Most provinces had primitive administrative systems, and not a few were more zealously devoted to protecting the private property of potential suppliers than to meeting the needs of the army. State officials were also known to shrink from expropriating horses, tools, crops, and other items the army wanted.[24]

Soldiers lived highly regimented lives. Camp police actively inspected barracks, saw that tents were properly erected and spaced, enforced sanitation measures, and watched to see that the soldiers—who had to cook their own meals—properly prepared their food. Soldiers faced days that were customarily filled with work details or training exercises, and if one pulled sentry duty after nightfall, the long day grew even longer. Enlisted men were in an army that used harsh disciplinary measures to maintain order and compel compliance with orders. Washington said that discipline was the soul of an army, and from the outset in 1775 his orders dwelled on the need for a "well disciplin'd Soldiery" and the necessity that a "due Subordination ... prevail thro' the whole Army." Six weeks after taking command, he told the troops that "the Army and Salvation of the Country ... essentially depend upon a strictness of discipline." He vowed to "give no Countenance ... to delinquents," a pledge he carried out.

Under the Articles of War adopted by Congress in 1776, violators of army policy were tried by court-martial—not by a jury of one's peers but by a panel composed solely of officers—and those who were convicted could be mercilessly flogged or subjected to other appalling punishments, many of which appear to have been conceived by sadists. They included tying by neck and heels, riding the wooden horse (which could lead to hernias), prolonged suspension by one arm (a ghastly measure called the "piquet," which could result in a dislocated shoulder), and running the gauntlet, which sometimes was fatal. Some were sentenced to incarceration for days or weeks and subsisted on bread and water throughout all or a goodly portion of their confinement. The articles, as revised in 1776, stipulated nearly a score of capital crimes, and more than 40 Continental soldiers were executed, mostly for repeatedly deserting. Approximately 80 percent of those sentenced to die were pardoned, but even so, some 100 times more men served in the United States army in World War II and only one GI was executed. After 1778, the Maréchaussée Corps, a mounted police force, was the army's enforcement arm. It was composed almost entirely of men of German extraction who were recruited in eastern Pennsylvania. The corps usually consisted of 45 to 50 men, including four hard-bitten individuals who served as the army's executioners.[25]

Soldiering was dangerous. Approximately 25,000 men serving in America's armies perished in the war's first three years. During the eight years of war, more than a third of those who entered the Continental army died, compared with the roughly 1 percent of GIs who died in World War II. Of those who died in the Revolutionary War, about 20 percent were victims of battlefield wounds. Disease claimed far and away the largest percentage of victims. Despite Washington's endlessly repeated orders to maintain proper sanitary conditions and his required vaccinations for smallpox, maladies such as scurvy, dysentery, typhus, typhoid, and assorted pulmonary and respiratory diseases made unwanted visits to army encampments. Diseases that were especially transmissible had a field day amid men living in close quarters who, all too often, had compromised immune systems due to subpar diets and insufficient apparel and accommodations. One officer spoke of seeing ill soldiers covered with vermin and sick men with inch-long maggots "Crawl[ing] out of their ears." Another observed men so afflicted with rheumatism and arthritis that they could not care for themselves. One officer was so troubled by the hideous scenes he had witnessed that he got "handsomely Drunk" to blot out the awful sights. There were doctors and surgeons in the army, but medical knowledge and practices were primitive, and effective drugs were on a very distant horizon. Bleeding and purgatives were conventional therapies, and at times men were given medications that included gunpowder or mercury mixed with assorted other items. Soldiers regarded army hospitals as death traps, and one Continental army physician waggishly suggested that the way to defeat the British army was to lure it "through any of the villages . . . where we have a hospital and . . . in 6 weeks there shall not be a man of them alive or fit for duty."[26]

One place more deadly than an army hospital was a British prison. Thousands of American prisoners of war were confined in warehouses, jails, barns, stables, churches, sugar refineries, and—worst of all—British prison ships. Some were jailed in Independence Hall during Britain's occupation of Philadelphia. Conditions everywhere were deplorable. The captives subsisted on meager diets and, now and then, tainted water. Most lived in unsanitary and overcrowded facilities that were poorly heated throughout winter, a problem often compounded by an inadequate allocation of blankets. Many were denied fresh air or sunshine. A young officer, captured in the Battle of Germantown on his very first day of combat, was transported to a jail in Philadelphia, where he was squeezed into a small room with 15 other officers, quarters that were so tight that the men "covered the whole floor" while sleeping. The enlisted men sent to that jail experienced worse conditions, as more than 30 men shared similarly sized rooms. They were given such meager provisions that the prisoners trapped and ate rats to supplement their diet. Not surprisingly, conditions in that lockup took an appalling toll. More than half the enlisted men, about 400 of 700, perished during the first 90 days of confinement. Upwards of 19,000 American soldiers died in captivity during the war, close to half of all rebel soldiers who lost their lives during the conflict.[27]

Some men found themselves through soldiering. Some gloried in the newfound respect they attained or believed they achieved through their service. Others discovered a fondness for a regimented lifestyle. Living and working shoulder to shoulder with other men was foreign to those who until now had lived on isolated farms, and thereafter some did not wish to return to the lonely seclusion they had previously known. Some reveled in the anticipation of danger and, at times, the all-too-real omnipresence of peril, which was unlike anything they had experienced in their humdrum civilian lives. A few found meaning in the violence and pain they were given license to inflict.

War is often romanticized by those who know no better or who for ulterior motives crassly weave a web of deception. But those who know the reality of war see things differently, and many who face combat never escape the stabbing memories of their experiences. That was true for veterans of this war. Etched deeply in their minds were haunting recollections of disquietingly anxious times, none more so than the dark loneliness of awaiting battle and the ghastly terrors of the battlefield, where they saw comrades maimed and killed and heard the cries of the wounded. Many survivors suffered lasting nightmares contoured by their experiences. For some veterans it was the unrelenting remembrance of shrunken courage at the moment of truth and the irremediable shame revived each time that came to mind. For others it was the dismaying recollection of killing, perhaps even of having grown too fond of slaying men deemed the enemy. Some who had seen combat experienced firsthand the twin sides of human nature. Humans, as Martin Luther King Jr. taught, are creatures of wisdom and decency, but face "the ever present possibility of swift relapse not merely to animalism but into such calculated cruelty as no other animal can practice." The destiny of many was to repeatedly relive the legion of evils that are part of war, including iniquities they saw or inflicted, and, above all, the haunting, crippling realization of what they themselves became, if only momentarily, in their transformation from a humane soul into an unblinking monster.[28]

An assortment of civilians hovered in and around the Continental army. Teamsters delivered supplies, and sutlers, contractors, and merchants who peddled goods routinely accompanied the army. The army welcomed and legitimized the sutlers, placing them under orders and occasionally even punishing them as it punished the soldiers. At times, the army recognized a specific sutler for each brigade and stipulated that he could vend food and other items, but for much of the war these merchants were forbidden to sell liquor to the troops. Their business hours were tightly regulated, and the army sometimes fixed prices on the commodities they vended. On the whole, army commanders felt that the presence of sutlers buoyed the troops. The contractors, who accompanied the army and negotiated deals for the acquisition of goods and services, were also embraced by the military. Prostitutes were the one element that tagged along that Washington sought to make unwelcome. The earliest orders prohibiting the presence of these "nuisances" antedated Washington's arrival, but he, too, sought to keep them away, though he never entirely succeeded. Despite Washington's outlook, some officers thought the presence of prostitutes boosted morale.

Prostitutes were far from the only women with the army. Martha Washington and the wives and families of many field grade officers arrived annually when the army went into winter quarters, and most stayed on for four or five months until the eve of the next year's campaign. Nathanael Greene said, "Mrs. Washington is excessive fond of the General and he of her," which partially explains the risks she ran in coming each year to the army's encampment. She faced some danger of capture during her journeys and considerably greater peril from the ever-present camp diseases. She came to be with "the pore General," whom she referred to as "her Old Man." While she sometimes acted as a secretary, making copies of her husband's correspondence, she mostly helped with assorted social functions. More than anything, however, her presence was an antidote for the stress that her husband faced.[29]

The girlfriends and spouses of a small percentage of enlisted soldiers stayed with the army year-round. The British army had long permitted the presence of up to six women per company of 100 men, a practice that Washington had seen firsthand when he served alongside redcoats in the Seven Years' War. Because of episodic food shortages, Washington was concerned about the number of females with his army, but he made no attempt to banish all women. He recognized that they performed useful services—cooking, washing, sewing, and nursing the ill and wounded—and he saw their presence as a deterrent to desertion. As with sutlers, the women were subject to army regulations, and the army provided them with quarters, medical attention, and an allotment of provisions. Some of these women brought their children, and some gave birth in the army's camps. The number of women varied from camp to camp and year to year, but on the whole, camp women likely totaled about 3 percent of the camp occupants. Numerous officers, including Washington, hired camp women to serve their households' needs, including tending to their clothing and securing forage for their horses. The commander in chief and some other officers also brought slaves from home to attend to their needs.[30]

Not every American who soldiered did so in the Continental army. More than twice the number of men who served in the army did stints as militiamen. (Some militiamen had served or later would also soldier in the army.) Early in the 17th century the first English immigrants re-created the English militia system in their colonies, and by the time of the Revolutionary War, it had long existed in each of the 13 colonies. All able-bodied males between the ages of 16 and 60 were customarily obligated to serve in the militia, though during the Revolutionary War some provinces exempted congressmen, certain state officials, ministers, college students, Indians, Black people, and mulattoes. On the eve of hostilities, militia units in most colonies began to drill frequently. Militiamen did all the fighting on the war's first day, but in the crucial first weeks and months of hostilities militia activities were not limited to battlefields. Militias, carrying out the orders of local and state committees of safety and sometimes of Congress, played decisive roles in enforcing the boycott of British trade and in preemptive actions to control the home front, such as disarming and cowing Loyalists. Their vigilance and activism were hugely important, especially in crippling whatever opportunity the Loyalists might have had for organizing and fighting back. As historian Don Higginbotham pointed out, it "guaranteed that the patriots would maintain control of the political and law-enforcing machinery in every colony." As the war progressed, militia units also served as internal security forces, at times taking on roles tantamount to that of a police force or responding to Britain's coastal raids. Scores of clashes occurred between militia units and Loyalist bands on the frontier and in the no-man's land in the New York and New Jersey borderlands, grim encounters in which the summary execution of captive warriors was all too commonplace. The most important checkmate of Tory objectives through 1779 was the utter destruction of the Loyalist force at Moore's Creek Bridge in North Carolina in 1776, a militia victory crucial to the preservation of rebel control in three southern provinces.[31]

As Congress never imagined that provincial militias could effectively wage a protracted war against British forces, it created the Continental army in the first weeks of hostilities. However, Congress saw the militia as a necessary supplemental arm, and militiamen routinely served with regular soldiers in the Continental army's major engagements. Neither Congress nor Washington could summon the militia to duty. That was the prerogative of state governors. When campaigns beckoned or emergencies threatened, Washington and the commanders in the Northern and Southern departments appealed to the governors of nearby states to activate their militias. On occasion, Washington directed the Continental officer in command in a region—Sullivan in Rhode Island in 1778, for instance—to request that militiamen be called to duty. In September 1776, during the crisis-laden New York campaign, Massachusetts summoned to active duty 20 percent of its militia units. There were instances when states could not meet their manpower quota assigned by Congress and entire militia units were conscripted for the duration of the campaign. Militiamen played especially substantive roles in gaining the crucial American victory at Saratoga. A militia force inflicted the debilitating defeat on the Hessian force at Bennington, and militiamen composed much of Gates's army in its clashes with Burgoyne. Militiamen impeded British foraging parties in occupied New Jersey in 1777 and around Philadelphia early the next year. Militia conducted sapping hit-and-run attacks against British patrols throughout the war. Burgoyne summed up his situation when he remarked, "Wherever the King's forces point, militia . . . assemble" to counter them.[32] Unlike regulars, militiamen were on active duty for only brief periods, and most states limited their out-of-state service to three months. In fact, Washington and other commanders did not want them around for long stretches, as their presence depleted the Continental army's already scant food supply.

Many historians have denigrated the militiamen's fighting qualities, and to be sure they were seldom the equal of the better disciplined, battle-hardened Continentals after 1777. Much of the jaded view of militiamen stemmed from an abundance of derogatory comments by Washington and other officers. During the New York campaign in 1776, Washington deplored the militiamen's lack of "brave & manly" conduct under fire, adding that "Dependance . . . upon the Militia . . . will totally ruin, our Cause." General Greene summarized the feelings of many

Continental officers in declaring that militiamen, having just departed their "home with all the tender feelings of domestic life," were "not sufficiently fortified with natural courage to stand the shocking scenes of war." Colonel Alexander Hamilton labeled militiamen "the *mimicry of soldiers.*" While there was considerable truth to the disparaging remarks, militias were an indispensable part of America's war effort. State militias never failed to answer Washington's summons for reinforcements and at times functioned as a draft board. When locales failed to meet their troop quotas for the army through voluntarism, men could be plucked out of the militia and forced into service. Those taken were nearly always young, unmarried men. Despite Washington's critical remarks, there were instances when militiamen performed well in combat, including along Battle Road, atop Bunker Hill, and at Bennington, Freeman's Farm, Bemis Heights, Brandywine, and some engagements later in the South. British officers, who understood the trouble that rebel militia could cause smaller British units, were often less deprecating than Washington. General Cornwallis, for instance, spoke of the troubles caused by "the clouds of militia which sometimes pour down on us," adding that "the list of British officers and soldiers killed and wounded by them . . . proves but too fatally that they are not wholly contemptible."[33]

AS BRITISH LAW FORBADE conscription, the king's army was a volunteer force overseen by a professional officer corps. Officers' commissions and promotions in the British army could still be purchased, and in the 1770s roughly 30 percent of officers had paid for their position. In 1777, a lieutenant colonelcy in the infantry sold for about £4,500, this at a time when a skilled artisan was fortunate to earn that much from a lifetime of toil. While an occasional noncommissioned officer of great merit rose into the ranks of officers, nearly all who secured the king's commission were from society's upper strata. As Britain did not have a military academy, the officer corps consisted of wealthy amateurs who hopefully acquired the knack of leading men and making wise decisions through experience. William Howe's circumstances were not untypical. He grew up in Langer Hall, a three-centuries-old mansion that locals in rural Nottinghamshire referred to as a castle. Gardens, moats, meadows, and pastures splayed out from the home. The family owned a racehorse, and its male members indulged in the country passion of fox hunting. William and his brothers, George and Richard, began boarding school at age six and went on to a brief stay at Eton. William, at 15, was a page of honor to the king.

He entered the army as a cornet at age 17, and before he turned 30, he was a lieutenant colonel.

Prior to the Revolutionary War, men enlisted in the British army for the prime years of their lives, entering as teenage boys or young adults and remaining until they were no longer capable of meeting the physical demands of soldiering, usually around the age of 50. But the American war necessitated a larger British army—and one in which the ranks had to be rapidly filled. When the war began, Britain's army numbered 48,647 men, a quarter the size of the peacetime armies in France and Austria. More than 60,000 entered the army during the next six years, and by war's end one in eight adult British males had soldiered. The urgent and unremitting need for manpower brought about a significant change. Those who enlisted after December 16, 1775, were to be released at war's end, so long as they had served for three years. The reasons men enlisted hardly differed from what led Americans in this war to soldier. As was true of many colonists who rushed to the colors in 1775 and 1776, William Crawford, an Irishman who enlisted while in his mid-20s, was drawn in by the "splendid uniform and glittering epaulettes, the beauty of the horses and grandeur of the parade." Also like the Americans who entered the Continental army in 1777 or later, Crawford and most of his fellow British soldiers were attracted "above all [by] the king's gold guineas in form o' a bounty." The incentive that Crawford alluded to was customarily one pound one shilling, roughly a month's income for a member of the working class. Many joined to escape disagreeable economic circumstances or unpleasant family situations, and not a few were enticed by the proffer of land in a British colony, a small lifetime pension—a perquisite that otherwise was nonexistent in 18th-century England—and the promise of postwar exemptions from highway duty or service in the army, navy, or militia.

It was once thought that only those from the very bottom of society enlisted, but it is now known that many unemployed craftsmen and other hard-pressed workers thought the army was preferable to a life of penury at home. Upwards of 20 percent of Britain's soldiery in this war consisted of former textile workers driven to desperation by the conflict's adverse impact on their industry. Nevertheless, most enlistees hailed from the lower social and economic orders. Faced with setbacks in gaining recruits, Britain not only permitted royal pardons for prisoners in exchange for military service but, four years into the war, allowed the impressment of "able-bodied and disorderly Persons." However, not more than 2 percent of Britain's soldiers in the Revolutionary War were obtained by these methods. Nor were all enlistees from Great Britain. Beginning about 30 months into the war, large numbers of Americans joined the British army. Just as the Continental army consisted of men from diverse ethnic and racial backgrounds, the British army included Black soldiers and small numbers of volunteers from Germany, Sweden, France, Switzerland, Denmark, Poland, and Hungary. Most who enlisted were in their late teens and early 20s, and because of the length of the war and the long stretch of their service, many by 1779 were older that the average Continental. By late in the war the average British soldier was about 30 years of age.

As the war dragged on, numerous modifications were made in recruiting standards. The proscription against recruiting Roman Catholics fell almost immediately. Initially, recruits were to be between the ages of 17 and 45, but later men between the ages of 16 and 50 were accepted. The requirement that men must be five feet four inches in height was soon winked at, and by 1779 perhaps as many as 20 percent of the soldiery were no longer that tall. (Some officers complained that they were getting men who were so short and weak that they could not cope with the long, heavy musket.) However, the average British soldier stood five feet seven, the same height as the average rebel soldier. The law bound recruiters to reject men with hernias, broken bones, running sores, and obvious infirmities. The law was never changed, though it was adhered to less scrupulously in the war's latter years.

Recruiting was carried out by regiments, and for the most part each sought men in the area where it was posted in Britain. A noncommissioned officer, drummer, and perhaps two or three trusted and credible veteran soldiers usually made up the recruiting party, which often started by visiting fairs and markets in economically depressed areas. While some chicanery cannot be ruled out, recruits did not actually enter the army until a few days later, when they swore before a magistrate that they indeed wished to soldier. Training began immediately. The men were taught proper hygiene and military habits and behavior, learned to march, and began the physical conditioning necessary for the demanding life of a soldier. At some point the new recruits were sent to one of the two training depots in England or the facility in Cork, Ireland. There they received arms and equipment, including the Brown Bess, a flintlock smoothbore musket, which weighed 14 pounds. The new soldier was also introduced to his bayonet, which was 14 inches long and weighed a pound, and was to be affixed to his musket. That was just the beginning. The soldier would also carry a short knife, spade, cartouch box (for his ammunition), knapsack, additional clothing (including a greatcoat), blanket, hatchet, and canteen. Altogether, a British soldier toted about 60 pounds, and even more in the field when his knapsack was loaded with a three-day supply of food. It has been equated to carrying an adult deer on one's back. A very few were given a spontoon (a five- or six-feet-long pike) and possibly a halbert (a weapon of the same length that was topped with an axe blade). Trainees were taught the multistep process of loading and firing their musket while maintaining formation. They also learned how to maintain their weapon. The ultimate goal was for soldiers in combat to be able get off three shots in a minute. The men's stay in a depot was for an indefinite period, as Britain usually shipped recruits to America only once or twice a year when a convoy was cobbled together.[34]

Transporting the recruits to America ordinarily consumed five to eight weeks. It often was a grim ordeal. Many men were seasick for long stretches, and poor packing or grievous conditions at sea often rendered the food unsavory long before America was glimpsed. Disease frequently erupted, and some men—and vast numbers of horses—perished during the Atlantic crossing. The morbidity rate among those who sailed to the Caribbean theater in one three-year period reached 11 percent; two regiments that crossed in 1780 experienced upwards of a 25 percent mortality rate. Britain's generals repeatedly told London, as did Sir Henry Clinton when his long-awaited reinforcements arrived in September 1779, that a large number of the arriving troops were "very Sickly."[35] The woeful condition of the newcomers often delayed plans. For instance, General Howe was forced to launch the New York campaign weeks later than he had originally planned, a delay that perhaps had enormous consequences. One can only guess whether he might have sought to capture Philadelphia had he chased Washington across the Delaware River in October rather than in early December 1776.

Once the soldiers reached America, their lives may not have been much different from their counterparts' in the Continental army. British soldiers also faced ongoing training, camp and guard duties, foraging details, long marches, and now and then the terrors of combat. They, too, were subjected to fearsome punishments and were also ravaged by the same diseases that preyed on the rebels and accounted for the lion's share of fatalities within Britain's army. Not smallpox, however, as British generals, like Washington, saw to the inoculation of their men.[36]

Logistical issues caused problems for the armies on both sides and added another rung to the hard lot experienced by all soldiers. The British escaped the severe food crises that the Continentals episodically faced, but there were times when they, too, experienced shortages. Supplying the Continentals was a colossal task, but the British faced even greater challenges. Most of their provisions were gathered and loaded in Britain before being transported across the ocean. The Treasury was responsible for providing the army, the Board of Ordnance supplied arms and ammunition, and the Navy Board sent food and equipment to the Royal Navy. Meeting the demands of military forces thousands of miles away—demands that were at times outdated due to the communications lag—would have challenged the most resourceful officials, and those in England who superintended logistical operations were not cut from that cloth. They were mostly amateurs drawn from the privileged elite and given responsibility for departments that lacked an experienced bureaucracy.

By 1779 thousands of British and Hessian soldiers who had to be fed were posted from Canada to Florida, in the Caribbean and Mediterranean, and in Africa. Armies consumed staggering amounts of food. The ostensible daily ration for Britain's soldiers was one pound of meat and one pound of bread, supplemented with such items as butter, cheese, peas, rice, oatmeal, and cabbage. An army of 35,000—roughly the number of troops under Howe in New York in 1776—devoured 37 tons of food daily. Supplying an army on the move was even more difficult. General Cornwallis's army needed approximately 150 tons of food during the couple of weeks that it pursued Washington's force through New Jersey. Not every scrap of food arrived from abroad. The army established gardens in America, purchased comestibles from American farmers, and at times plundered, though official policy prohibited such behavior. Food was not all the army needed. Britain sent over weaponry, horses and their provender, coal, tents, equipment for cooking and eating, replacements for worn-out uniforms (especially shoes), and the other multiple items carried by the soldiers.[37]

If Britain's soldiers never starved, the army at times came close to running short of meat and flour. During several months in 1778, Clinton's first year as commander, the army in New York was within two or three weeks of facing an empty pantry; in September 1780 it had only six days' of provisions in reserve when a supply fleet at last arrived. Those crises, and others, stemmed in part from procurement delays. For instance, the supply fleet scheduled to reach the army in New York in April 1778 did not sail until late June. There were instances when anticipated vessels never reached America, having fallen victim to enemy navies and privateers, and the hazards of the sea. When provisions arrived late, or never arrived, Britain's soldiers for a spell suffered privations. At times they endured leaky tents, and in 1779 the troops in occupied Savannah could not cook rice because of a dearth of kettles. A severe shortage of gunpowder was one factor in Clinton's relative inactivity throughout the summer of 1779. Furthermore, the appearance of a supply fleet did not always guarantee that all stores were intact. Horses for the cavalry and land transport did not fare well during a long ocean crossing. Fifty percent of the horses sent in June 1776 for Howe's first major campaign perished before the fleet dropped anchor in New York. Shoddy packing, porous containers, leaky ships, and tempestuous weather often resulted in damaged cargoes. Sometimes protracted voyages led to spoilage. Roughly two-thirds of the flour shipped to the army in Boston in 1775 and in the initial shipment to New York in 1776 was condemned as unusable.[38]

As with the rebels, not all those with the British army were men. The British had a long-established system of civilians providing services to the soldiery, and many were women who accompanied the army and were paid wages as laundresses, seamstresses, nurses, and laborers who gathered hay and cut turf for fuel. The British government provided shipping for 60 wives per regiment, but as redcoats often married women they met in America, the actual number of females per regiment was sometimes 25 percent greater. The number permitted to come along on campaigns was determined by the commander. Women in the field with the army at times joined in the plundering undertaken by soldiers, and some, like the men, were on occasion made prisoners of war. Thirty-four women and children were taken prisoner in the 1775 rebel attack on Fort Ticonderoga; later that year General Montgomery's army captured over 70 women during the invasion of Canada, sending them into captivity in Lancaster, Pennsylvania. Over 200 women who accompanied Burgoyne's army were taken prisoner at Saratoga, and many spent years in captivity.[39]

Nearly 19,000 Hessian soldiers served Britain's king during the Revolutionary War and more than one-fourth perished in this conflict. The initial batch arrived in the summer of 1776 after long marches to embarkation ports in Germany or Holland, followed by a voyage of a week or 10 days to an English port from which they eventually sailed for America. By the time they completed the Atlantic crossing, many, like their British comrades, suffered from scurvy—a disease caused by a lack of vitamin C that resulted in bleeding gums, the reopening of old skin wounds, and weakness in the arms and legs—and scabies, a parasitic skin disorder that brought on a rash and intense itching. The mercenaries first saw action in the New York campaign. They played an especially crucial role in taking Fort Washington and were part of nearly every major battle thereafter. They were subordinate to the British and, though invited to attend councils of war, Britain's officers were responsible for deciding strategy and other crucial matters, such as those that Burgoyne made during his descent through New York's backcountry. While bonds sometimes developed between officers in the two armies, for the most part relations were cordial at best. Language and cultural differences, the distaste for mercenaries among British officers, and their belief that the Germans were "outrageously cruel" posed barriers to close ties. For their part, many Germans were convinced that the British saddled them with the most dangerous assignments. Nor were relations any better between the rank-and-file soldiery. There were instances of fistfights between the supposed companions.

Many Hessian soldiers were so impressed by the standard of living in America that they were puzzled by the colonists' wish to break away from Great Britain. The Americans rapidly discovered the Germans' envy of their prosperity, and thereafter rebel leaders often played on it to encourage them to desert. In August 1776 Congress went further. It offered 50 acres to any German who deserted. Few took the bait, as at that juncture America's defeat seemed likely and Hessian officers warned of reprisals against the families of deserters. Only 66 Hessians deserted that year. The desertion rate increased in subsequent years as the odds favoring British victory declined and Americans made a more concerted effort to encourage the Hessians to desert. Broadsides printed in German promised full rights of citizenship, payment for the arms they brought along, gifts of land and livestock, and a pledge that, following the war, Congress would lay out townships that would be restricted to German deserters. Nearly half the Hessians in a prisoner swap in 1778 choose taking land in Pennsylvania to returning to the army. More than 200 German soldiers deserted during Clinton's march from Philadelphia to New York in June of that year. Roughly 15 percent of the Hessians deserted during the war, a larger rate than the British army experienced.[40]

Loyalists also served with the British army. Some were incorporated into existing units, but many enlisted in provincial regiments, where they received the same pay and provisions as British regulars and were subject to the same disciplinary code. Wealthy Loyalists sometimes raised a provincial regiment and were awarded a colonel's commission, but for the most part a regular British officer was in command. Many regular junior officers and sergeants eagerly volunteered to serve in the corps, seeing it as a means of hastening their promotion. The British army sought to enlist Loyalists as early as 1775 and dispatched recruiters to New York, North Carolina, Halifax, and Quebec who found more than 1,000 willing to join. Thereafter, little headway was made until late 1776. But when New York and a portion of New Jersey were occupied, and Philadelphia was taken late the following year, recruiters reaped a bountiful harvest of Loyalist volunteers. At the same moment, the East Florida

Rangers was formed. Two years later, nearly 400 Loyalists fled South Carolina and made a 350-mile trek to East Florida, where many joined the newly established South Carolina Royalists. By the end of 1777 some 4,400 Loyalists were soldiering for the king. Even larger numbers of Loyalists enlisted once Britain's southern strategy began in earnest, and by 1781 roughly 10,000 Loyalists were under arms in some 300 companies.

Approximately 15,000 American colonists served in provincial regiments during the war. By late 1780 more Americans were serving in the British army than in the Continental army. A substantial number of Loyalists additionally joined volunteer companies, serving without pay or uniforms, and some were members of county units that existed only briefly. Loyalists took up arms for the same reasons that led men to join the rebel army, including patriotic motives and the lure of bounties. Ads placed in newspapers in occupied New York dangled cash bounties of 40 shillings, new clothes like shirts, shoes, and stockings, and the promise of 50 acres of farmland following Britain's victory. The average soldier in the British Legion in 1778, a Loyalist unit formed that year in occupied Philadelphia, was 25 years old and a farmer, and 88 percent were natives of Britain's American colonies. In addition to those who bore arms, countless Loyalists provided passive support for the British army by acting as guides, teamsters, spies, and, most of all, as sources of intelligence.[41]

Both Black freemen and enslaved persons in quest of freedom joined Britain's efforts to suppress the American insurgency. Generals Gage and Howe had considered enlisting Black men before Lord Dunmore formed the Ethiopian Regiment in Virginia in 1775, but in the end neither actively sought Black recruits. However, General Clinton made a concerted effort to recruit auxiliaries during his unsuccessful foray in South Carolina in 1776. Thinking "they might be very useful to us for many purposes in these [southern] climates," Clinton formed a company of Pioneers, a manual labor unit that among other duties gathered food and fuel for the army. They were given clothing, provisions, and pay, and Clinton ordered that the men be treated with "tenderness & affection." He also went on record expressing his hope that they would be "intitled . . . to their freedom" following the war. Seventy-one Black men joined the company. Clinton was so devoted to his Pioneers that over the years he took them into his subsequent campaigns in Rhode Island and South Carolina. By 1778 Black men were serving in the army in a variety of capacities. Some joined provincial units and the regular army; others were part of Loyalist militia contingents. Some were armed and fought, and some raided plantations, driving away livestock and liberating slaves. Perhaps most served as order-lies, musicians, officers' servants, laborers, boatmen, pilots on royal vessels, scouts, guides, teamsters, and skilled craftsmen, including as blacksmiths, carpenters, wheel-wrights, and sawyers. In addition, escaped slaves who fled behind British lines were utilized as farmers, cattlemen, foragers, and laborers who cleared roads, built and repaired bridges, procured firewood, and constructed fortifications. When Georgia once again became a royal province in 1779, the assembly passed legislation that required slave owners to make available their male bondsmen between the ages of 16 and 60 when needed for service in a labor corps. Over 400 enslaved men were put to work constructing Savannah's fortifications prior to the Allied siege that autumn. During the siege, two companies of Black volunteers totaling more than 200 men were armed and fought against the Allied attackers. Late in the war the British created the Black Dragoons, a cavalry unit of onetime slaves that for a time was led by a former slave. It consisted of at least 50 Black troopers.[42]

The British army, like its adversary, was plagued by desertion. That the homes of most redcoats were across the ocean likely acted as a brake on a dash for freedom, although the desertion rate in the British army hovered around 10 percent in many regiments.[43] The same factors that induced Americans to abscond also led British soldiers to desert. They, too, found that soldiering was rife with hardships and dangers. The brutal wintertime sufferings of rebel soldiers is deeply embedded in Americans' remembrance of the war, but less well known are the travails of British soldiers in America's climate. Most had never experienced the oppressive summer-time heat and humidity they encountered in North America, especially in the South. (The French, similarly dismayed by the South's climate, equated October in Virginia to summer in North Africa.) Burgoyne's troops thought northern New York in July was stiflingly hot. Worse was to come. Scores of British soldiers suffered heatstroke in Clinton's 1778 march across New Jersey, and two months later nine died and 63 others were stricken by the heat while on duty near Manhattan. The driver of Clinton's carriage perished from heatstroke during an August 1780 journey across Long Island.[44]

British soldiers did not minimize the severity of combat in the American theater. Many veterans of previous wars spoke in sepulchral tones of Revolutionary War engagements, calling them the equal of the worst European battles in which they had fought. One thought the enemy fire at Freeman's Farm was greater than anything he had previously encountered, while another described the battle as a "scene truly distressing." A redcoat at Brandywine spoke of the "most infernal fire" on that battlefield; another was shocked by the "horrors of battle . . . in all their hideousness," a gruesomeness that "defies all power of language to describe." One soldier never forgot his first battle. In his first moments under fire, the man to his right was shot through the heart and the man to his left "received a ball in his forehead, which took off the roof of his skull! he reeled round, turned up his eyes, muttered some words, and fell dead at my feet!" Such an initiation convinced him that "war . . . is a picture of desolation." Some thought the day after a battle was worse than the fighting. That was when they tended to the wounded who had lain between the two armies throughout the night. One old hand at Freeman's Farm spoke of men who "were insensible, benumbed with the night dews, and weakened with loss of blood, while others seemed to have arrived at the extreme point of suffering, when a desirable separation of partnership between the soul and the body was about to deliver them from a troublesome state." Another soldier spoke of finding wounded comrades, some "past all pain," others in "the most excruciating torments," and most "upon the point of expiring with faintness."[45]

A FRENCH ARMY ARRIVED in America in 1780, disembarking in Rhode Island in their resplendent white uniforms. France's army, like its navy, had not shined in the Seven Years' War. It was a match for Britain's army, but not that of much smaller Prussia, and its failings led a later French minister of war to declare that his "King has the worst infantry under the sun." The army had been deeply conservative and resisted change, and its hidebound ways caught up with it during that war. Its staff organization had been archaic; a formal intelligence organization remained nonexistent; the fiscal organization of the ministry of war had been chaotic; the supply system was obsolete; the infantry had not been significantly reformed since the era of Louis XIV; the artillery was a muddle of disorganization; and the officer corps was the preserve of the aristocracy and glutted with too many general officers, roughly one for every 160 soldiers. If many French officers had been amateurs, the soldiers were not. As in England, those who enlisted served for years. France had fielded huge armies, raising about 40,000 recruits annually and year after year maintaining a force of nearly 300,000. French society was not militaristic, as was Prussia's, but French failings in the Seven Years' War were due less to the soldiery than to the rot in the army's DNA.[46]

France's military disaster spurred reforms designed to professionalize and modernize the army. While serving as secretary of state for war, Duc de Choiseul sought to reorganize the army. Even before the end of the Seven Years' War he set about restructuring the infantry by altering the number of companies in a battalion and assuring that each battalion contained at least one grenadier company. The cavalry was similarly refashioned. Choiseul was disgusted by the performance of the French army in both the War of the Austrian Succession in the 1740s and the Seven Years' War, conflicts in which he said that a "single cannon shot ... was enough to scatter the royal army beyond hope of recall." He urged greater discipline, emphasized the Prussian drill, sought to substantively improve the army's offensive capability by redesigning the column of attack, and attempted to refashion the conduct of the field grade officers, insisting that while in the field they live among their troops rather than in luxurious housing. He also sought to improve morale among enlisted men through better housing and richly publicizing their heroism in combat. His end game was to reduce the desertion levels that had reached epidemic proportions in the last war.

Choiseul's reforms led to the establishment of military academies with notoriously difficult entrance examinations, an overhaul of the supply system, and the streamlining of the army's methods of acquiring war materials. The officers' schooling continued through illuminating sessions at Versailles and in salons, as well as via numerous journals and books, some of which were subsidized by the Crown. The *Encyclopédia militaire* boasted that it was the "school of young warriors," though the most influential military publication was Marshal de Saxes's *Mes rêveries*, which ruminated on strategy, tactics, fortifications, armaments, and even uniforms. Not every reform effort took root, although by the time of the War of Independence French army engineers were widely regarded as being in a class unto themselves, and significant improvements were realized in the artillery corps and among military physicians, who studied new surgical techniques, practiced with improved tools, and introduced mobile hospitals.

Much of the reform zeal focused on the top-heavy officer corps. Not only were there too many officers, but the number of pensioned officers equaled or exceeded those on active duty and added to the nation's economic distress. The cost of paying the 60,000 officers who had served during the Seven Years' War exceeded the total revenue spent on the rest of army. Nearly all had been drawn from the nobility, and a great many came to be seen as incompetent. One of Choiseul's reforms was the state financing of new captaincies, an effort undertaken to facilitate the rise of more competent officers. However, when all was said and done, the officer corps remained the bailiwick of the aristocracy. By the time of the

Revolutionary War, a would-be officer was required to provide proof of noble ancestry for four generations on his father's side, a requirement that actually tightened earlier requirements. Furthermore, the advancement of middling noblemen was all too often blocked by those born into the upper strata of the nobility. It is not difficult to see why military service was alluring to young noblemen from influential court families. It was plausible for them to expect to be a subaltern at age 15, a captain at 18, and a colonel at 23. Furthermore, seniority continued to outrank merit as a cause for promotion. In the final analysis, the attempt to enhance the army's effectiveness was grounded in preserving the nobility's traditional relationship with the military.[47]

REGARDLESS OF THE ARMY, the men who fought shared the commonalities of 18th-century warfare. It would be incorrect to say that the War of Independence was a modern war, but ongoing changes in the technology of war after 1500 altered the manner in which wars and battles were waged. By the late 18th century, warfare was conducted in a more modern fashion than had been true only 75 years earlier. For two centuries after 1500, most soldiers were armed with smoothbore matchlock muskets, an unreliable weapon with an exasperatingly lengthy loading process that generally prevented infantrymen from getting off more than one shot per minute. Early in the 18th century the matchlock was superseded by the smoothbore flintlock musket, which would remain the infantryman's main weapon for the next 150 years. By today's standards, readying a flintlock musket for firing was a cumbersome process, though faster than had been true of the matchlock. The result was that a trained soldier could usually fire three rounds per minute, and on occasions some got off four shots, so that battles featured enormously greater firepower than previous ones.

The muskets carried by all soldiers in this war were about five feet long and weighed 12 or more pounds. Smoothbore muskets were not accurate, but a man who was hit with a musket ball usually suffered a ghastly wound. The ball, made of soft lead and fired from a relatively low-velocity weapon, could pierce armor but seldom passed completely through a body. Instead, the projectile made a huge entry wound, shattering bones and carrying fabric and grime into the body, which might result in a fatal infection. Once inside a body, the ball tumbled about, causing incredible organ damage.

Frederick North by Nathaniel Dance, 1773–1774. © NATIONAL PORTRAIT GALLERY, LONDON

Howard Pyle (American illustrator, 1853–1911), *The Fight on Lexington Common, April 19, 1775,* 1898 for "The Story of the Revolution," by Henry Cabot Lodge, in Scribner's Magazine, January 1898. Oil on canvas 23 1/4 x 35 1/4 in. (59.1 x 89.5 cm), frame: 29 1/4 x 41 1/4 in. (74.3 x 104.8 cm). DELAWARE MUSEUM OF ART, MUSEUM PURCHASE, 1912

The Battle of Bunker Hill by Howard Pyle, 1897. WIKIMEDIA COMMONS

Charles *avieu* Comte de Vergennes
Conseiller d'État Ordinaire, *Ministre et Secrétaire d'État*
et Chef du Conseil *Royal des Finances*

Comte de Vergennes Vincenzo Vangelisiti after Antoine Francios
Callet, 1784. PHILADELPHIA MUSEUM OF ART: THE MURIEL AND
PHILIP BERMAN GIFT, ACQUIRED FROM THE JOHN S. PHILLIPS
BEQUEST OF 1876 TO THE PENNSYLVANIA ACADEMY OF THE
FINE ARTS, WITH FUNDS CONTRIBUTED BY MURIEL AND PHILIP
BERMAN, GIFTS (BY EXCHANGE) OF LISA NORRIS ELKINS, BRYANT
W. LANGSTON, SAMUEL S. WHITE 3RD AND VERA WHITE, WITH
ADDITIONAL FUNDS CONTRIBUTED BY JOHN HOWARD MCFADDEN,
JR., THOMAS SKELTON HARRISON, AND THE PHILIP H. AND A.S.W.
ROSENBACH FOUNDATION, 1985-52-20460

George Washington by James Peale after Charles Willson
Peale, c. 1787–1790. COURTESY OF INDEPENDENCE
NATIONAL HISTORICAL PARK

Sir William Howe, engraving by J. Rogers, date unknown.
FROM THE NEW YORK PUBLIC LIBRARY, THE MIRIAM AND IRA
D. WALLACH DIVISION OF ART, PRINTS AND PHOTOGRAPHS:
PRINT COLLECTION

Thomas Paine, engraving by William Sharpe after George Romney, 1793. LC-DIG-PGA-12728 (DIGITAL FILE FROM ORIGINAL PRINT) LC-USZC4-2542 (COLOR FILM COPY TRANSPARENCY)

Left: John Sullivan by Richard Morrell Staigg after John Trumbull, date unknown.
Right: Thayendanegea, or Joseph Brant, by Charles Willson Peale, 1797.
COURTESY OF INDEPENDENCE NATIONAL HISTORICAL PARK

Lord George Germain by Dororthy Hardy after George Romney, 1928. WILLIAM L. CLEMENTS LIBRARY, UNIVERSITY OF MICHIGAN

John Burgoyne by Sir Joshua Reynolds, 1766. ART IN THE FRICK COLLECTION: PAINTINGS, SCULPTURE, DECORATIVE ARTS, NEW YORK: HARRY N. ABRAMS, 1996.

Horatio Gates by James Peale after Charles Willson Peale, 1782. COURTESY OF INDEPENDENCE NATIONAL HISTORICAL PARK

Sir Henry Clinton by John Smart, 1777.
NATIONAL ARMY MUSEUM, LONDON

The Count of Floridablanca by Francisco
Goya, 1783. WIKIMEDIA COMMONS

Don Bernardo de Galvez
by an unknown engraver,
date unknown. LIBRARY
OF CONGRESS PRINTS AND
PHOTOGRAPHS DIVISION

Left: The Nation Makers by Howard Pyle, ca. 1902. © BRANDYWINE RIVER MUSEUM OF ART/PURCHASED THROUGH A GRANT FROM THE MABEL PEW MYRIN TRUST, 1984/ BRIDGEMAN IMAGES

Below: Sketch of American Uniforms by Baron Ludwig von Closen, 1781. ANNE S. K. BROWN MILITARY COLLECTION, BROWN UNIVERSITY LIBRARY

Marquis de Lafayette by Charles
Willson Peale, 1779–1780.
COURTESY OF INDEPENDENCE
NATIONAL HISTORICAL PARK

Left: Thomas Jefferson by Charles Willson Peale, 1791.
Right: Conrad Gerard by Charles Willson Peale, 1779.
COURTESY OF INDEPENDENCE NATIONAL HISTORICAL PARK

Benjamin Lincoln by Charles Wilson Peale, c. 1781–1783. COURTESY OF INDEPENDENCE NATIONAL HISTORICAL PARK

Left: Banastre Tarleton by Sir Joshua Reynolds, 1782. PHOTO 12/UNIVERSAL IMAGES GROUP VIA GETTY IMAGES

Above: Jean-Baptiste D'Estaing engraving by H.B. Hall's Sons, early nineteenth century. GRANGER

ES EARL CORNWALLIS. 1783.

Charles Cornwallis by Thomas Gainsborough, 1783. DEAGOSTINI/GETTY IMAGES

Nathanael Greene by
Charles Willson Peale, 1783.
COURTESY OF INDEPENDENCE
NATIONAL HISTORICAL PARK

Daniel Morgan by Charles
Willson Peale, c. 1794.
COURTESY OF INDEPENDENCE
NATIONAL HISTORICAL PARK

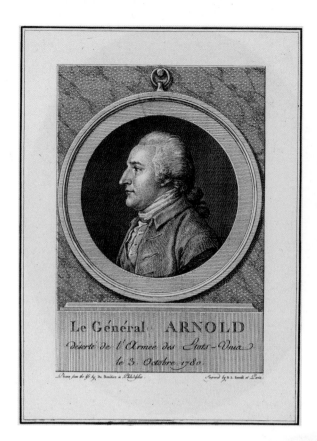

Benedict Arnold by Benoît-Louis Prévost after Pierre Eugène Du Simitière, 1780. NATIONAL PORTRAIT GALLERY, SMITHSONIAN INSTITUTION

Chevalier de La Luzerne by Charles Willson Peale, 1781–1782. COURTESY OF INDEPENDENCE NATIONAL HISTORICAL PARK

Comte de Rochambeau by Charles Willson
Peale, c. 1782. COURTESY OF INDEPENDENCE
NATIONAL HISTORICAL PARK

Admiral de Grass by an unknown artist, date unknown.
© CORBIS/CORBIS VIA GETTY IMAGES

American Commissioners of the Preliminary Peace Negotiations with Great Britain by Benjamin West, begun 1784. GIFT OF HENRY FRANCIS DU PONT. COURTESY WINTERTHUR MUSEUM, GARDEN & LIBRARY

Armies had moved toward the concept of volley fire in the prior century, and it remained a common practice in America's Revolutionary War. Foot soldiers were trained to follow the orders of their officers. The aim was that soldiers would not fire at will but would discharge their weapons simultaneously on the orders of the commanding officer at what was thought to be the ideal moment. The result was the concurrent blast of hundreds or even thousands of weapons, creating a thunderous roar that confounded inexperienced soldiers. Men described the awful noise as "intimidating and terrible," almost "as if heaven and earth had fallen in." The jarring cacophony was made more frightening to callow soldiers by the thick, dark cloud of smoke and dust that suddenly enveloped the battlefield. All armies used linear tactics, and in the course of the 18th century all turned to arranging the men in lines two or three rows deep and in tight formations, thinking it the best means through which a commanding officer could control his men. The soldiers laid down a sheet of fire at the lines of enemy troops, who often were only some 50 yards away. If the volley caused sufficient damage or disorientation, an assault by bayonet-wielding men might be ordered and the enemy's flank might be turned, the crux of the process.

Drilling the men was essential, given the nature of linear warfare, and drill was an endless ingredient in the lives of the soldiers in every army. When it was introduced to the Continentals at Valley Forge, Private Joseph Plumb Martin complained that he "was kept constantly . . . engaged in learning the Baron de Steuben's new Prussian exercise" to the point that his life became "a continual drill." Drilling was thought to be necessary to make the soldier "steady and skillful." As historian Paul Lockhart has written, endless drilling was also part of a process designed to "turn men into unthinking cogs in a larger military machine." The soldier was molded so that in the terror of combat he would obey commands rather than instinctively contemplate the dire situation in which he found himself. Among a person's natural inclinations when confronted with someone pointing a gun at him is to fire his own weapon or to flee. But if one soldier fires in panic, his comrades will likely reflexively fire their weapons and the desired volley fire at the optimum moment will be lost. If trepidation causes even one soldier to take flight, others are likely to make a break for safety, and the entire regiment's usefulness would be mitigated and conceivably the entire army endangered. Hence, drilling and more drilling was the practice in all armies. Drill books, or military manuals, appeared in Europe in the middle of the 18th century. George Washington turned to these books for guidance when he first soldiered in 1755, and during the Revolutionary War he urged his officers to read them. Drill manuals were useful in readying men for battle, but they did not prepare men for the appalling things they encountered in battle or its aftermath. One writer described the sea of horrors met by soldiers as including the "abattoir reek of open bodies, the foxy stench of bloody hair, and the roast-pork smell of gunners who had been blown up by their ammunition wagons."

There were exceptions to this highly stylized manner of waging war. Neither the American colonists nor the Indians they fought had practiced this sort of warfare, and there were occasions in the War of Independence when what many called "bush-fighting" or the "irregular way of war" prevailed. Along Battle Road, on April 19, 1775, many of the colonial militiamen fought as they were accustomed to fighting, squeezing off a round from a hidden spot and then moving down the line to another concealed position from which they fired again at their exposed redcoat adversaries. By and large, however, the European armies fought in America as they had in recent generations in European conflicts, and Congress and General Washington thought it preferable to emulate them.

Prior to the 17th century, artillery had been largely immobile and was employed chiefly in naval warfare, in siege operations, and as fixtures at fortresses. But in time metallurgical innovations reduced the size and weight of artillery pieces, and they came to play a more prominent role on the battlefield. Where oxen had previously pulled artillery, teams of horses now did the job, and they were faster than their predecessors and consumed less fodder, which eased an army's logistical issues. If armies could more easily transport artillery to a battle site, field pieces were difficult to move during an engagement and prone to being captured if things did not go as hoped and a retreat was ordered.

The presence of artillery was standard equipment for the armies in the War of Independence. Weapons that once had customarily been utilized to tear down walls could cause incredible damage to a line of men. Solid shot projectiles could decimate a man. Unlike musket balls, they could tear through him and strike several others deeper in the formation. But as solid shot wasn't terribly efficient—it had to hit something to cause damage and even then it might strike only one or two men—antipersonnel ammunition was more commonly utilized. Cannister was the favorite, as the ball that was fired broke apart and scattered deadly projectiles into the ranks of men and horses not far away. Facing musket fire at close range was daunting, but to be confronted by the sight of cannon pointed in one's direction was even more blood-curdling.[48]

Eighteenth-century warfare was not the equivalent of modern warfare, but fire-power was greater than in previous times. Militarists had found ways to increase the rate of killing, and the battlefields in this war were truly shocking and horri-fying places.

BRITAIN COULD RECRUIT AMPLE numbers of volunteers for its Royal Navy in peacetime. Signing on as a sailor meant better food, more dependable pay, and less work than employment in the merchant marine. Wartime was a different matter. Since the 17th century, Britain's navy had been saved from wartime manpower shortages by enemy embargoes that idled some merchant shipping and freed up mariners, and by resorting to impressment, the navy's method of conscription when enlistees were not to be had. On occasion men on homebound commercial vessels were kidnapped and dragooned into the navy, though raids by press gangs in dock-yards and waterfront grog shops garnered most of the needed sailors. While officers were known to complain that impressment landed too many "shacome-filthies, raga-muffings and scrovies," the practice continued. Gaining seafarers was an acute problem for Great Britain during the Revolutionary War. The need for sailors doubled between the immediate prewar years and full mobilization a couple of years into hostilities, and this at a time when many professional seamen were already serving on supply ships and privateers. What is more, mariners from the rebellious colonies were no longer available. By 1779 the difficulty in gaining sailors had become so acute that laws shielding some from impressment were suspended. More than 230,000 men were inducted into the Royal Navy during the war, almost twice the number that served in Britain's army. About one-third of the sailors were garnered through impressment. Volunteers were attracted by cash bounties and the opportu-nity to choose their ship and captain, and wartime economic dislocations prompted many to choose going to sea rather than facing destitution at home. Whereas magis-trates could offer criminals the choice of jail or the army, the law permitted judicial officers to commit lawbreakers to naval service, though the navy was not obligated to take what the Earl of Sandwich, First Lord of the Admiralty, labeled as "wretches," who were thought likely to instigate desertion and villainy.

British sailors, like their counterparts in the army, faced the danger of disease. Scurvy was rampant among sailors who spent months at sea, and many of the camp diseases that haunted the army also flourished on crowded ships. Typhus, influenza, and dysentery were widespread, although late in the conflict enhanced efforts toward cleanliness, improved ventilation, and healthier diets reduced the death rate to 1 percent.

British sailors faced a heavy workload and crowded living accommodations, as upwards of 600 men served on ships of the line, sleeping in narrow hammocks below deck in congested circumstances. One naval officer compared life on giant warships to confinement in a birdcage. Generally at 8:00 A.M., noon, and around nightfall the men consumed their daily meals. All too often, sailors shared their limited space with vermin, especially rats, a fact of life that led to cats being seen as essential shipmates. Discipline was harsh, though much depended on the character of the captain and how well he controlled the midshipmen who interacted with the sailors. Mutinies, of course, were suppressed with severity, but they were few in number and most occurred in the last months of the war, when the labor market was returning to a peacetime footing and sailors were eager to return to better-paying prewar jobs. Danger was always a sailor's companion, though those in the Royal Navy faced less peril than those on small merchant vessels; in fact, the work-load and the hazards the sailors faced often were no greater than they had encoun-tered in their seafaring days prior to their military service. One benefit that sailors experienced was that when a ship reached port, they enjoyed shore leave and freedom for a spell, often in an exotic locale. Moreover, when the vessel returned to sea it was usually stocked with fresh food and a renewed supply of liquor, bounties far less frequently enjoyed by soldiers. But not every mariner thought a sailor's life was a bed of roses. One in three sailors in the Royal Navy deserted, with the deser-tion rate peaking at 16 percent in 1776.[49]

Some in the Royal Navy were assigned shore duties, and others became part of the 5,700 men who made up units of Marines. The majority of sailors were at sea, and those on warships knew they might someday be involved in a cataclysmic engagement, although such occurrences were rare. Before the late stages of the war the only grand naval confrontation was the Battle of Ushant, a clash of French and British fleets in 1778 at the southwestern end of the English Channel. It resulted in heavy casualties and damage to both flotillas, though neither side captured an enemy vessel. Encounters between fleets in the age of sail were often inconclusive, given the difficulty of maneuvering vessels in changing wind conditions and attempting to hit a pitching target with smoothbore guns fired from a vessel that was also bobbing in the water. Nevertheless, naval battles could be horrific, perhaps worse than what most soldiers experienced on the battlefield.

Many ships of the line sported 74 heavy cannon as well as swivel guns and mortars, called coehorns, that could lob explosives onto the deck of an enemy ship. The shot fired from the big guns included heavy iron balls, chain-and-bar projectiles designed to tear down masts (and anything else in their path), grapeshot and canister shells, and hot shot, iron that had been heated in a furnace prior to its discharge and was designed to produce fires. Though the use of fire ships sent on a collision course with an enemy vessel had diminished by this war, it remained a weapon that could be turned to. The incredible firepower of a battle fleet could take a ghastly toll. The most fortunate victims were those who died outright. Star-crossed casualties often suffered hideous wounds and became part of the ship's detritus, including body parts and buckets of blood sloshing to and fro on the ship's planking. Vessels armed with dozens of guns were packed with tons of gunpowder and shells, making them floating arms depots. Raging fires or a lucky mortar shot that fell below deck into the munitions store could set off a catastrophic detonation. But the object in a naval battle was less to sink crafts than to disable enemy vessels through the destruction of masts and rigging or to compel a rival ship captain to surrender due to the incapacitation of his crew or fear of an imminent explosion.[50]

Every British official agreed with William Pitt on one thing: Britain's "great and acknowledged" source of national security was its "superior naval force." It emerged from the Seven Years' War with the world's greatest navy. When Lord North's ministry debated the use of force in 1774 and 1775, some officials thought naval power alone would be sufficient to crush the colonial insurgency. Due to a slackened pace in the construction of new ships prior to hostilities, the Royal Navy in 1775 was not fully prepared for the task of subduing the American rebellion. The navy's problem was in some measure brought on by an obsessive anxiety over the national debt incurred during the Seven Years' War, indebtedness of some £148 million that required annual payments of £5 million to service it. (That supposed liability was, in part, the reason Parliament for the first time sought to tax the colonists in 1765 and later.) Rumors of France's naval rehabilitation program sprouted in England after the mid-1760s and caused concern, though not enough to persuade one ministry after another to jettison fiscal retrenchment and match the French ship for ship. During the interwar years the construction of new ships of war proceeded, though not at a brisk pace. In addition to fiscal concerns, production was slowed by labor problems, shortages of timber, the destruction of a major shipyard by an accidental fire, and the Admiralty's decision to install copper bottoms on the entire fleet and to build ships slowly with seasoned wood, a process that required long periods of weathering on the stocks. Copper bottoms were added to 313 vessels, a step that made them sturdier and faster and enhanced their worthiness in battle. In the five years after 1766, the construction of new ships in France and Spain was twice that in Britain. By 1770, the tonnage of the combined Bourbon fleets exceeded that of the Royal Navy and the disparity grew over the last five prewar years, even though Britain stepped up naval production during that period.[51]

Britain had 30 widely scattered warships in American waters when the war began. Some defended Nova Scotia, others assisted General Gage's army in Boston, and still others were posted at significant ports from New England to Georgia and West Florida. Over the next year vessels of all kinds were dispatched in every direction in quest of firewood and forage, and to protect vessels at sea loaded with supplies from Britain. The remainder attempted to blockade the coast, though there were simply too few ships to effectively fence off the 3,000-mile-long American coastline.

A naval buildup in North America commenced in 1775, and by year's end there were 51 warships manned by 7,555 sailors in American waters. By the end of 1776 Lord Howe's squadron had increased to about 70 warships, though the augmentation did not result in the boycott's success, as numerous vessels were employed in transporting soldiers and their supplies. Besides, the more territory the army took, the greater the burden on the navy to help secure what was taken. In December 1776 only 20 ships were on blockade duty, each responsible for scouring a stretch of some 50 miles. The vessels laden with Beaumarchais's treasures easily penetrated the permeable blockade.

While Lord Germain, in 1776, doubted that French belligerency was imminent, Lord Sandwich thought it a real danger and urged full wartime mobilization, a step that was not forthcoming until January 1778. When hostilities commenced in 1775 the Royal Navy had only about one-third of its ships, fewer than 100 in all, ready for service. Full mobilization changed things, though it was slowed due to shortages of shipyard space, skilled artisans, and government funding. Even so, by war's end 486 naval vessels—including 174 ships of the line—were on the seas. The numbers were striking, but the navy faced awesome challenges, including blockading the American, French, and Spanish coasts; supporting the British army; coping with rebel privateers; searching for American commerce raiders and rebel merchant vessels; and, after 1778, waging war around the globe. Wartime mobilization put more British ships at sea, but Lord Howe continued to acknowledge that the blockade of the North American coastline remained a persistent failure. Once France entered the war, Admiral Howe declared that the navy's "principal object" must henceforth be "the distressing" of its naval adversary. The blockade of the American coastline was for all practical purposes abandoned after 1778.[52]

TWO MONTHS AFTER TAKING command, Washington, without authorization, channeled army funds to a Marblehead regiment loaded with sailors and fishermen. He ordered them to outfit a ship and search for British supply vessels carrying goods that his army desperately needed. Soon six Yankee craft were on the high seas. Newspapers dubbed the little fleet "Washington's Navy." The vessels were owned by those who had responded to the commander's exhortation to "run all Risques" considering the "Magnitude of the Cause & the [army's] absolute Necessity" of gaining war-making materials. In addition to the so-called navy, some merchants undertook hazardous sallies to the Caribbean and enticing ports in Europe in search of commodities that supported the war effort. These were businessmen driven primarily by the hope of profiting from the war. Especially powerful merchants, with a foot in the door in Congress, increased their wealth by leaps and bounds, thanks to Congress's quest for war materials. Congress, in July 1775, appropriated $50,000 for use by selected merchants to purchase munitions. At year's end it issued $300,000 in contracts to merchants for the purchase of arms and military provisions.[53]

Late in 1775, as more and more British ships arrived, Congress created the Continental navy and two battalions of American marines. Some congressmen thought the step was "the maddest idea in the world," but Congress appropriated $100,000 to acquire and convert four commercial vessels to warships, and over $800,000 for the construction of 13 frigates, three-masted craft that carried between 24 and 36 cannon. Congress ordered the construction of additional frigates in 1776 and 1777, and ultimately 19 of the 23 that were planned sailed in the course of the war. Beginning late in 1776 America's diplomats sought, without success, to persuade neutral France to give America either ships of the line or frigates, although once the alliance was consummated, the French loaned small warships to the United States. The United States also purchased ships abroad and incorporated captured British naval vessels into its navy. If every rebel vessel is counted, including the tiniest lake galley, the Continental navy possessed around 100 craft armed with some 1,300 guns. If the number is limited to warships that Congress authorized or were acquired by other means, 57 vessels ultimately made up the rebel navy, of which 40 percent were built in the United States. Eight percent of congressional military expenditures was earmarked for the naval war.[54]

Congress envisaged several roles for the navy, some of which it performed reasonably well. It was to patrol the coast and the principal bays and sounds in search of smaller enemy craft. The navy formed convoys to shepherd merchant fleets, primarily on their runs to and from the West Indies. Naval ships at times also carried cargo and messages. Congress hoped that naval squadrons might reopen the Newfoundland fisheries, although that quickly proved illusory given the presence of Britain's formidable naval strength. A prime undertaking was to roam the Atlantic in search of wayward British ships loaded with provisions for the king's army. Plundering was consequential, but its primary objective, as Robert Morris explained early in 1777, was to compel the Royal Navy to "divide their Force" by adding an additional chore to the British navy's responsibilities. The step helped diminish the effectiveness of Britain's blockade while affording the Continental navy "elbow room," as Morris put it, through which to achieve greater success. By the fall of 1776, Continental navy vessels were cruising in Britain's home waters and claiming prizes that were mostly taken to French ports, activity that gave Comte de Vergennes a few additional gray hairs prior to France's entrance into the war. In time, Continental navy vessels, usually in small squadrons, sailed from French ports to maraud in the English Channel, the Bay of Biscay, and the open seas before returning to French ports. Some sailed with French pilots and a handful of French crewmen. After a three-vessel American squadron captured 18 British ships in the Irish Sea in June 1777, the British Admiralty posted four warships there to guard against the further danger. It was the sort of "elbow room" of which Morris had spoken. Once France entered the war, the American navy's primary role became one of ferrying men and supplies. However, by 1780 those missions had grown infrequent, for by then most of the fleet had been destroyed or captured, or was bottled up somewhere in port.[55]

Some 3,000 sailors served in America's navy during the war. Congress, seeking a ratio of one officer for every 10 enlisted men, commissioned 340 officers. It appointed Esek Hopkins as the navy's commander in chief, but his skills were a far cry from those that Washington possessed, and after a bit more than a year Congress removed him. Thereafter, it never appointed anyone to flag rank, and Congress, through its Marine Committee, simply dealt with the navy's captains. Seven of those officers were court-martialed in the course of hostilities, and five were dismissed from the navy.[56]

Although there were thousands of unemployed seamen in the colonies in 1775, the navy faced recruiting problems throughout the conflict. Many mariners preferred service on privateers, where the monetary rewards could be considerably better and only a few months' service was required. Enlisting in the navy was a one-year commitment. Congress, which never offered a land bounty to sailors as a recruiting inducement, ultimately resorted to conscription and the use of press gangs, an oppressive British practice that had turned many seamen into supporters of American independence. Sailors lived under articles of war modeled on those of the Royal Navy, though the Continental navy's code was less severe, having been mitigated somewhat by the spirit of the republican revolution and the traditions of the colonial merchant marine. Seamen faced the hazards of the sea and supreme danger if they encountered their powerful British adversaries, including the peril of capture and long years in a British prison, where the death rate stood close to 5 percent. Sailors endured a heavy work regimen, but far fewer sailors than soldiers died of disease, and there is no evidence that any were executed. While an occasional vessel experienced a food or clothing shortage, sailors fared better at the dining table than the soldiery in the Continental army. Sailors were also more likely to get out of this war alive. Roughly one in three soldiers in the Continental army died, but seven of every eight sailors in the Continental navy survived their service. Nevertheless, the desertion rate hovered around 25 percent, approximating that within the Continental army.[57]

American newspapers closely followed the war at sea. Much of the news about the navy was bad. In the course of the war, 13 Continental vessels were captured, 18 were ruined in action, and two others were lost at sea. Now and then there was good news that lifted morale. In the spring of 1776, an eight-vessel squadron under Commodore Hopkins—sporting a red-and-white-striped American flag sewn by Margaret Manny, a Philadelphia milliner—successfully struck the British garrison on New Providence Island in Nassau Harbor. Given that the Continental army was still a year away from benefiting from France's secret aid, the treasure trove that Hopkins brought home sparked celebrations. Among other things, his cargo holds bulged with cannon, mortars, and barrels of much-needed powder. However, it was the exploits of John Paul Jones that aroused the most interest.[58]

A native of Scotland, Jones had gone to sea at age 13 and by his 21st birthday was a ship's captain. Jones immigrated to Virginia just prior to the war and was one of the first to secure an officer's rank in the new Continental navy. He served under Hopkins on the New Providence venture and later in 1775, on his initial command, captured British coal ships and a transport off Nova Scotia. Early in 1778, just weeks after Burgoyne's surrender at Saratoga, Jones first gained notoriety. Sailing from France on *Ranger*, a black and yellow frigate, he raided Whitehaven, a coastal hamlet in England just across from Belfast. It was the first wartime raid on an English town in more than a century. A few days later Jones raided St. Mary's Isle in Kirkcudbright Bay, after which he bested HMS *Drake* in a showdown, the first instance in the three-year-old history of the Continental navy that an American ship had defeated a British warship of similar size and power. Jones's feats spread fear along the English coast. He became something of a household name in France and within the enemy's lair. In 1779, while planning the Franco-Spanish invasion of England, France's marine minister Sartine found a role for Jones in the enterprise. Jones and others were to conduct diversionary operations to distract the Royal Navy. Jones was given a four-ship squadron—two frigates, a corvette, and a cutter—with which to campaign in northern England and Scotland. His flagship was the 40-gun frigate *Bonhomme Richard*, and he put to sea with 1,071 mariners. Fewer than 80 were Americans, garbed in Continental navy uniforms of blue coats with white lapels, flat yellow buttons, and blue waistcoats and trousers.

Departing from France, Jones rounded Ireland and Scotland, entering the North Sea on the east side of Scotland. His objective was to present the astonished authorities in the Scottish port of Leith with an ultimatum: Pay a ransom to the "much injured citizens of America" or face the city's destruction. However, a sudden storm blew up and led to his discovery. He aborted his plan and sailed south, taking seven prizes along the way. Alerted to Jones's whereabouts, the Royal Navy dispatched vessels to find him. HMS *Serapis*, a 50-gun frigate commanded by Richard Pearson, a veteran sailor, tracked down its prey late in September, 20 days after France and Spain aborted their planned invasion of England. The two drew so close that men on both sides could hear the voices of the enemy sailors. In the last reddish light of day, the assorted guns on both vessels opened up. The devastation was as ghastly as it got when two large ships pounded away at each other at short range. An hour or more into the fray, *Serapis* rammed *Bonhomme Richard*, causing a worrisome fire. Cordage, booms, shrapnel, spent shells, and dead and dying men covered the decks of both ships. Crewmen on the snarled vessels, armed with muskets and pistols, fired at their foes, and sometimes fought hand to hand. After two hours, Pearson asked if Jones was ready to capitulate. His response, later re-created to make it more lustrous, was subsequently conveyed to the American public as "I have not yet begun to fight." More fighting indeed followed, but when a member of Jones's crew succeeded in lobbing a grenade through *Serapis's* open hatch and setting off a series of small explosions, Pearson asked for quarter. The four-hour battle was over. *Bonhomme Richard* had gone into battle with 320 men, *Serapis* with about 270. More than half of the sailors on each vessel were casualties. *Bonhomme Richard* was victorious, but so fatally damaged that it had to be abandoned. Jones and his crew returned to France aboard the mangled but navigable *Serapis.* Thereafter London newspapers teemed with stories about Jones's exploits, one saying that he was "the most general topic of conversation" across the land. Ballads were sung in England about the achievements of this "rogue and vagabond." He was acclaimed in America as well, which learned of his heroics at the same moment that disappointing word spread of the failed Allied assault at Savannah.[59]

American privateers also played a considerable role in this war. Upwards of 2,000 American privateering vessels went to sea and in some years as many as 500 sailed. More than 50,000 men served on privateers, several times the number that saw duty in the navy. In the course of the war, rebel privateers captured hundreds of British vessels. John Adams, in 1776, characterized their contribution as "three Quarters of a War," meaning that they disrupted British commerce, interdicted the flow of supplies to Britain's army, and assisted in providing the hard-pressed Continental army with much-needed provisions. In 1777, London merchants claimed to have lost £1.8 million to privateers and the American navy, and by the next year Britain's trade with the West Indies had been reduced by two-thirds.

Privateering might best be described as capitalism gone to war. Privateers were bankrolled by one or more individuals willing to gamble venture capital. The enterprise was legitimate once Congress or a provincial government issued a commission granting "license and authority." The privateers then roamed the sea in search of "prizes," capturing vessels and their cargoes, which were brought to the nearest port, where an Admiralty court would determine the treasure's legitimacy. Privateering crafts were sometimes refitted whaleboats and merchant vessels, and on occasion newly constructed boats. No privateer was as large as the capital ships in the French, Spanish, and British navies, though as the war dragged on and cannon were more readily available, larger privateers grew more abundant. Always, however, the primary requisite of a privateer was speed. Once a vessel was chosen, it was stocked with munitions and provisions. Its crew often included specialized craftsmen—perhaps sailmakers, blacksmiths, coopers, joiners, or carpenters—and now and then a physician. Crews typically ranged from about 25 to 100 men. Articles of agreement specified how the money realized from the sale of captured prizes was to be distributed.

These agreements varied, but generally the entrepreneur received 50 percent of the booty while the remainder was divided among the mariners in descending order according to rank. Although Great Britain also sanctioned privateering—it issued 7,352 privateering commissions during the war, including the licensing of nearly 200 Loyalist privateers—British officials designated American privateers as pirates. Initially, some Americans opposed the practice and Congress did not legalize privateering until the war was nearly a year old. When it did act, Congress justified this as fighting back against the British ministry that had taken "every step that cruelty and revenge can dictate for the destruction of American liberty."

Privateering was dangerous. Simply putting to sea could be hazardous, as vessels went down in squalls, men were struck by lightning, and accidents on shipboard were far from unheard of. Attempting to capture a British ship was filled with peril. Men died in battles and not a few were captured. On the other hand, those who survived unscathed largely escaped the privations that tormented Continental soldiers and militiamen, and if they succeeded in capturing prizes, they reaped material rewards. Moreover, most crewmen had been mariners prior to the war and, combat aside, were accustomed to the virtues, demands, and dangers inherent in living and working at sea.

The outcome of prolonged wars hinges on numerous factors, and the role played by privateers contributed to America's success. Their existence, and achievements, forced Britain to divert critical resources, eroded British morale, and not only brought needed supplies to America's army and its home front, but also was a prop against sinking spirits in what many came to think was a never-ending war.[60]

CHAPTER 10

OFF THE BATTLEFIELD

THE WAR TOUCHED ALL Americans, not just soldiers and sailors. Most wars, and especially those that are protracted, have a habit of reverberating into virtually every corner and shadow of society. Each year that America's drawn-out Revolutionary War continued, ever more people felt its long reach.

Most Americans were farmers, and farming from spring until autumn was a labor-intensive pursuit. Most farm families coped with the demands they faced through a division of labor. The husband and older sons prepared the fields for planting as winter faded, cared for the crops through the growing season, mowed the meadows two or three times annually to gather and store hay, harvested in late summer or early fall, and, after the crop was in, felled trees and split wood for the coming winter, mended fences, made house repairs, slaughtered an animal or two, and dressed and cured the meat. All the while, day in and day out, they fed the chickens, gathered eggs, slopped the hogs, milked the cows, and got the livestock into the pasture in the morning and back into the barn in the evening. The wife and older daughters, meanwhile, may have been putting in even more hours caring for the garden, making candles, spinning, weaving, sewing, preparing meals, preserving food, bearing children and looking after them, and maintaining the house (and pitching in with the harvest and meat-curing activities). The endless array of tasks led parents to put their children to work at an early age, first with light chores, though by early adolescence—if not before—girls were doing much of the same work as their mothers, and boys were toiling alongside their fathers.

The war forced changes on many farmers. Many southern planters, faced with curtailed tobacco exports, shifted to the production of wheat and other grains. Some who once had enjoyed a flourishing market were driven to subsistence farming, though a few flourished by selling their produce to an army, especially the British who paid specie. Wartime scarcities brought on changes. Farm folks wore threadbare garments and more homespun clothing, often had to put up with coffee or herbs instead of their preferred tea, and were confronted with shortages or absences of necessities, such as salt, cloth, and needles for sewing. With so many men off to war, it was often impossible to hire laborers to help with the work. Families unlucky enough to be in the path of an army on the move, or in an occupied zone, faced the possibility that their crops, firewood, livestock, and household possessions might be confiscated by friend or foe. Continentals billeted late in 1777 at a home in Elizabethtown, New Jersey, stole panes of window glass, furniture, wallpaper, and lead from the roof, and cut down trees and used the stairway banisters for firewood. Residents of Morris County reported that rebel troops had stolen their horses, fences, a male slave, punch bowls, and silk gloves. Even when they were not looting, the soldiers were often unwelcome guests. They were strangers who made women "afraid to go to Bed" at night and aroused fear in all that they might spread fatal diseases.

When the man of the household went to war—whether for a year or more as a Continental or for several weeks or months as a militiaman, a tour of duty that might recur two or more times over the years—his farm duties fell to his wife and children. If they did not do the work, there would be no food on the table and no family income. If no money came in, necessities could not be purchased and the tax collector could not be paid, and not paying him meant the loss of the farm. The result was that the already heavy workload faced by women and children increased exponentially when the man was away. Not a few wives agreed with the woman who said that she "had no time for aught but my work." "What was done, was done by myself," declared another. One woman affirmed that her lot had degenerated into a life of "troble & disappointments." A woman whose husband was off to war captured what many felt when she said she "live[d] a widow for the present." Historian Laurel Thatcher Ulrich categorized the woman left at home as the "deputy husband," and indeed women's new responsibilities included more than additional laboring. Managing a farm meant negotiating the sale of crops, buying supplies, and securing hired hands and seeing that they were paid. For some, it meant purchasing slaves. Abigail Adams, who managed the family's farm outside Boston during John's years in Congress and his five years abroad as a diplomat, was forced by the dearth of workers to turn to farm tenants and sharecroppers. Some of the more affluent women invested in bonds, collected rent, took on their husband's business affairs, and harried debtors. Whatever their social class, the tasks and loneliness were wearying and disheartening. Not a few probably felt like Abigail Adams, who in 1777 exclaimed that she was "obliged to summons all my patriotism" given that she had "sacrificed much of my own personal happiness" to "this cause," including having lived "for more than 3 years in a State of widowhood." That same year Lucy Flucker Knox, the wife of the general, wrote to her husband, "Would to heaven I could see you for one half hour." She asked, "Do you wish for your Lucy, do you think of me, do you ever shed a tear for me. Tis very hard thus to be parted." Later in the war she anguished, "Oh horrid war, how hast thou blasted the fairest prospect of happiness . . . depriving me of the Society of my husband, who alone could repair the loss."

Despite being already overburdened with work, some women had additional demands placed on them by revolutionary governments. Just as towns assigned quotas for furnishing soldiers, some communities were given quotas for supplying clothing to the soldiery. Hartford, for instance, was to provide 1,000 coats and 1,600 shirts for the army in 1776, and the burden of making some of the garments fell on the village's female inhabitants. Solitude weighed heavily on many women. Alongside daunting loneliness was the sobering possibility that the husband might not return from the war, or might not come home in one piece. Many men did not return, and some came home physically or emotionally impaired from the horrors they had experienced.[1]

Necessity compelled many women to make crucial decisions that previously had been made by their husbands. In some instances, the new responsibilities appear to have altered attitudes among both wives and husbands. Women learned that they were capable of managing the farm and making difficult decisions about the family's finances and well-being. Some husbands, who at the outset of their absence had taken a condescending tone when advising their wives, changed step as they came to appreciate their spouses' ability to cope, and to do so wisely. The "distinctions between masculine and feminine traits" were dissolved in some marriages, and as historian Mary Beth Norton demonstrated, some women thereafter came to "expect equal treatment." Some thought the travail of war would usher in "a new era of female history," though social constraints on women remained largely intact for generations.[2]

Patriotism was tested by the immeasurably harsh ordeal of war, and some women bent under the strain, somberly pleading with their husbands not to enlist or to refuse to reenlist following the expiration of their commitment. However, most bore up, and many stubbornly pitched in to help the popular cause. Women volunteered to spin and sew, and to collect money for the acquisition of clothing, shoes, and blankets for the soldiers. Some devoted time and energy to caring for wounded soldiers. James Monroe, a 19-year-old Virginia Continental, was severely wounded at Trenton in 1776, but he survived his injury thanks in some measure to the nursing he received from women in their homes. Some women willingly surrendered their silver to be melted down and turned into bullets. A few risked life and limb serving as spies and couriers, and reports circulated that during the engagement at Monmouth one woman on the battlefield took up her husband's musket after he was wounded and fired away at the enemy. The famous story of Molly Pitcher helping her husband's artillery crew at Monmouth may be mythical, but women did indeed at times assist soldiers in the heat of battle. One, Deborah Sampson, a Massachusetts woman, went even further. She posed as a man, enlisted in the Continental army, and soldiered for 17 months.[3]

A small segment of the population consisted of skilled artisans, some of whom lived in small hamlets, some in cities. When a tradesman left to bear arms, his family could be placed in an especially precarious situation. Women and children on farms had access to preserved meat, fruit, and vegetables. Families of artisans, perhaps no longer with an income, had to purchase their food. Furthermore, whereas farm women and their children could do much or all of the work their husbands had been doing, the wives of artisans lacked the skills their spouses had learned through years as apprentices. The stringency of this long war forced many of these women and some of their children to find unskilled work outside the home, including toiling as laborers on farms. Many such women, and their children, were reduced to an austere existence. More than 30 food riots occurred in 1776 and 1777, almost all in urban areas. The rioters included women from laboring families that had been driven to desperation.[4]

Women did not face the terrors of the battlefield that their husbands experienced, but many still experienced the shock and horror of war. Diseases spread into civilian sectors and took the lives of thousands of women during the war. Some women who lost a child at birth wondered if the tragedy was brought on by the anguish and distress occasioned by the war. Women additionally faced the potential danger of molestation by soldiers on both sides. General Howe later claimed that he was aware of only a single instance of one of his soldiers having been accused of rape, but historians have uncovered evidence of numerous such atrocities and are also cognizant that most such dreadful occurrences were never reported. Incidents of rape occurred when an army was garrisoned nearby or passed through while campaigning. Every incident was outrageous, but some were especially hideous. One such case occurred in late in 1776 when British soldiers plundered an isolated farm in New Jersey. Some of these soldiers returned on three consecutive evenings and raped the 13-year-old daughter of the owners, and on the third night they also raped her older sister, aunt, and a young female visitor.[5]

Regardless of their social status, every American on the home front faced some level of economic adversity because of the war. Trade with the mother country had been the heart of prewar colonial commerce, but it immediately collapsed once the war began. The value of British imports plummeted from nearly £2 million to £82,000 in the initial year of hostilities, and exports to British markets similarly crumpled. The exportation of indigo, meat, and cattle vanished, while shipments of tobacco, rice, and grain fell by 85 percent. Britain's naval blockade and the war on the high seas impeded trade in alternate markets. Merchants were idled and dockhands laid off. The war was a calamity for residents of coastal fishing communities because of Royal Navy patrols and the loss of access to the Newfoundland fisheries. Farmers received depreciated paper currency for the crops they sold. They often found that many merchants would neither accept their worthless money as payment for debts nor extend loans, plunging many yeomen further into arrears. Some farmers, in turn, deliberately withheld their produce from market in hopes of provoking an increase in prices, a practice that led to food scarcities in the cities and embittered urban dwellers who knew that nearby farmers had produced and were sitting on the year's "Remarkable great Crop."

While per capita income declined, prices soared, driven into the stratosphere by inflation and the laws of supply and demand. By 1779, the prices of imported goods such as tea, rum, and molasses had risen by 1,000 percent since the onset of hostilities. The overall level of prices in Pennsylvania in 1779 was seven times what it had been two years earlier. Many commodities were priced beyond the reach of ordinary farmers and laborers. Urban residents who yearned for corn on the cob could only dream, as five years into the war the price of corn had skyrocketed by 1,255 percent. One frustrated New Englander hardly exaggerated when he declared that the Continental dollar was "fit for nothing but Bum Fodder"—toilet paper. Lawlessness increased during the war years. Incidents of theft and armed robbery especially rose, due in part to the worthlessness of the currency and the misery it spawned.

Soaring prices and lost income were bad enough, but the war also brought on stupendous tax increases. The colonists had traditionally experienced a relatively light tax bite, only about one-tenth of what was paid by Britons in the home islands. Hostilities had hardly begun before local and state governments raised taxes, and thereafter they only escalated. Many provinces immediately imposed a tax on those who refused to sign a loyalty oath to the revolutionary government. Pennsylvania's first wartime tax, a £3-per-head levy, fell on those who would not take the oath; the tax rapidly raised more than £3,000. Congress, in 1777, formally requisitioned funds from the states, assigning an annual quota for each province based on population estimates. Two years later Congress set monthly requisition quotas for each state. Each requisition led not only to further increases in taxation but to the creation of new taxes. By 1779 Pennsylvania was taxing property, trades, land, mills, horses, and cattle. Late in the war Congress persuaded the states to demand payment in commodities, including horses, flour, beef, pork, rum, and wagons, which could be sent to the army. Massachusetts eventually levied taxes on towns that failed to meet their troop quotas, and it imposed assessments on grain and hay to pay for its militia and Continentals. Before the war, tiny Rhode Island levied taxes totaling about £4,000; by 1779, it sought £433,000. The 13 states collected taxes in the amount of £25 million in 1778. In 1780, the amount rose to £60 million, some 100 times more revenue than was raised in the last years of peace. Some states set discriminatory tax rates for Loyalists. New York's Tories paid double the rate of taxation facing those who took loyalty oaths in support of the war, and some counties in the state compelled Loyalists to pay special taxes to cover the cost of repairing damages done by British raiding parties.[6]

The widespread economic dislocations brought on by revolution and war was at times, and in some places, accompanied by a breakdown in law and order. Economic adversity, the weakened machinery of authority, the unwillingness of both the Continental army and the British army to act as civilian police forces, and the incapability of militias to serve as watchful instruments of law enforcement opened the door for criminal activities. The examples set by armies that plundered and the aura of a revolution, in which long-standing legitimate authority was disputed, perhaps contributed to criminality. Marauding bands formed, especially on Long Island, above Manhattan, in New Jersey, on Virginia's eastern shore, and along the coast of Georgia. In the mid-Atlantic, one band designated as "cowboys" and another known as "skinners" marauded and pillaged, the former preying on rebel settlers and the latter ostensibly victimizing Loyalists, though their villainy was too widespread to have been purely ideological. These malefactors then sold their booty, mostly crops and livestock, with the cowboys often eyeing the British army as its prime market, and the skinners more often turning to whoever had money and a willingness to acquire stolen goods.[7]

THOSE WHO REMAINED LOYAL to Great Britain were a sizable portion of the population. John Adams thought that only a third of Americans supported the rebellion, another third were Loyalists, and the remaining third were indifferent. Historians now believe that about 80 percent of activists were rebels and 20 percent were Loyalists. An assortment of factors contributed to the choice of Loyalism. "Loyalty to the mother country was the colonial norm," as historian Ruma Chopra observed. Substantive economic ties kept some in Britain's camp, while others admired the parent country's stability and freedom, which was virtually unmatched throughout Europe. Many Americans feared that revolutionary republicanism would result in disorder and violence, including class warfare. Ties to the Anglican Church, Britain's state church, contoured the outlooks of many. Nearly every American thought continued prosperity hinged on westward expansion, and not a few believed the goal could be realized more rapidly with Britain's helping hand. Many simply believed that the rebels could never win the war and they wished to be on the winning side. "You have roused the British Lion; you have incensed that power which hath crushed much greater powers than you can boast of," a Massachusetts Tory warned in 1775. Another Loyalist, in a 1776 pamphlet, warned that it was illusory to expect aid from foreign powers and that without that aid the war could not be won. France and Spain, he wrote, would never be so "deluded" as to assist anti-monarchical American rebels who someday soon might possess "power astonishing to imagination" and conquer their New World colonies.[8]

Loyalists almost everywhere were treated as enemies, stripped of their rights, and placed under surveillance by the authorities in the earliest days of the war. In 1777, Congress enacted a war measure that went a step further. It authorized the confiscation of Loyalist properties. Some states turned to this expedient with gusto from an abundance of motives, including revenge against hated foes of the Revolution, the search for scarce revenue, and the hope that sufficient revenue would be collected to permit a reduction in the level of taxation. The motives of some were not war-related. They glimpsed the opportunity to acquire property that they coveted.

New Jersey had been the first to snatch Loyalist property, acting after the British expropriated rebel properties in occupied New York. Massachusetts was the first to act on the step that Congress had authorized, commandeering property owned by "open avowed enemies." Ten New York counties recorded some 850 confiscations, prompting many Loyalists there and elsewhere to sell their property before it was seized. New Hampshire acted to prevent such sales and promptly seized more than two dozen estates valued at £70,000. Rhode Island "sequestered" and rented Loyalist properties early in the war, but later confiscated the homes and farms of Tories. Late in the war Connecticut acted similarly, taking hold of property valued at £250,000. In 1778, Pennsylvania identified 453 "traitors" and clasped over 40,000 acres of their property in the first year of confiscations, raising over £400,000. Maryland grabbed 200,000 acres, which it sold for £450,000. Every state expropriated Loyalist properties, and the sales generated an abundance of revenue, but it was almost entirely in depreciated paper currency that did little to lighten the load of the taxpayers or help the war effort. The commandeered property was put on the market and sold, and in most instances the affluent walked off with it. In Maryland, for example, merchants, lawyers, and state officials acquired the lion's share of the booty and for a pittance. New Jersey governor William Livingston, who watched the fleecing firsthand, charged that the well-to-do "plundered" through an extraordinarily corrupt tactic.[9]

Wars create refugees and America's Revolutionary War was no exception. Many people on both sides who lived on the war-ravaged frontier moved to safer locations, as did others seeking to escape enemy-dominated areas. Some fled abroad while others chose Canada or an older and presumably safer area in one of the 13 rebellious provinces. Many rebels left cities taken by the British army, but by far the greatest number of refugees were Loyalists who left for British-occupied cities or departed America altogether. General Howe's army was accompanied by 1,100 Tories when it evacuated Boston early in 1776. Some settled in Nova Scotia, but most crossed to England. After the British regained Manhattan in 1776, a great many rebels moved out and thousands of New England and mid-Atlantic Loyalists—and other displaced persons, including runaway slaves and craftsmen and laborers drawn by the prospect of finding civilian jobs offered by Britain's army—poured in. The city's population doubled over the next four years. Housing was at a premium and food was rationed by the military government. The inspector of refugees adhered to guidelines laid down by General Clinton stipulating that rations were to be allotted according to each individual's "station in life," a grossly unequal system under which men received the same portion allotted to the soldiers, women were given a half ration, and children a quarter ration. The refugees in New York scrambled for work and many toiled at jobs hardly akin to their prewar employment. Hundreds of men and women found work in a corps of woodcutters commanded by a British officer. Similar situations later existed in other British-occupied areas. In 1782 a New Yorker estimated that some 40,000 Loyalist refugees had taken up residence in New York, Savannah, Charleston, and St. Augustine, a guess that appears to have been uncannily accurate. Almost all were disconsolate, having lost their property, occupation, and social standing, and were living far from their prewar homes. Their lot worsened at war's end as most of the Loyalist refugees moved on yet again. As the war wound down, some 60,000 Loyalists migrated to Canada, British islands in the Caribbean, and the British home islands, an exodus five times greater than that of émigrés in the later French Revolution.[10]

The war brought countless hardships to friends and foes of the Revolution, travail that shaped the thinking of the military commanders on both sides. By 1780 General Washington, confronted with a stalemated war with no favorable end in sight, feared that rebel morale would buckle on the home front if the Allies did not soon score a decisive victory. General Clinton simultaneously saw the plight of American civilians as a source of hope, and he foresaw success not solely through winning victories but also by avoiding defeat and drawing out hostilities.

THE AMERICAN STATES WERE nearly sovereign, and congressional powers were severely limited. Congress lacked the authority to tax—it had to requisition money from the states—and to regulate commerce, which also could have generated revenue. Congress, of course, was not powerless. It created the Continental army, drew up its Articles of War, offered land and cash bounties to aid in recruiting, and appointed its highest-ranking officers. It could and did remove and replace generals. Following the loss of Fort Ticonderoga, for instance, it replaced General Schuyler with Horatio Gates, a step that prompted Schuyler to resign his commission. Congress chose the commanders in the Northern and Southern Departments, sought to resolve intractable logistical difficulties, and created the Board of War which, among other things, was vested with the responsibility to oversee recruitment, prisoners of war, and the production of weaponry. It also possessed authority that it perhaps wisely chose not to exercise. It deferred to Washington on many matters that otherwise might have produced toxic strains. Congress was at the mercy of the states with regard to some key war measures. Provincial chief executives decided whether or not to summon militiamen to service, dispatch them out of state, and act in concert with the Continental army. Most state governors usually sought to comply with the wishes of army commanders and Congress, though there were times when a governor balked at furnishing certain provisions sought by a general.

Congress toiled incessantly to resolve the new nation's economic plight, trying one expedient after another. It repeatedly urged additional taxation by the states, stopped paper money emissions at the state and national levels, devalued the currency, imposed price restraints, opened a loan office, sponsored a lottery, and in 1780 not only issued bills of credit (currency that paid 5 percent interest) but transferred to the states the responsibility of paying military salaries. Congress never attempted to establish wage and price controls, though some states and urban centers sought without much success to set limitations. Congress, in 1777, urged the states to send deputies to regional conferences in hopes of finding viable solutions to runaway inflation. Only the New England conference met, and its recommendations fizzled when several Yankee states refused to comply.[11]

Congress was paramount in one area. It alone managed foreign policy. It appointed the nation's diplomats, approved the treaties its envoys negotiated, and secured loans and subsidies from foreign countries. After learning of the Treaty of Alliance, Congress named Benjamin Franklin the minister plenipotentiary to Versailles. Congress could also remove its diplomats. In November 1777 it recalled Silas Deane, one of the three commissioners sent to France a year earlier, acting in response to the bevy of unauthorized military commissions he had given to French volunteers. A year later it summoned home Arthur Lee, who had been acting as commissioner to Spain.[12]

Before 1779 Congress had largely avoided friction when making American foreign policy. But early that year Conrad Alexandre Gérard, France's first minister plenipotentiary to the United States, told Congress that as Spain's offer of mediation might prompt peace negotiations, it was essential that the congressmen determine America's peace terms. For three years Congress had avoided confronting what it hoped to achieve beyond independence, fearing likely bitter partisan battles that could threaten disunity.

Minister Gérard, who hailed from a middle-class Alsace family, was 49 years old and a veteran diplomat. Austere in his manner, Gérard was talented and won the esteem of numerous congressmen and Philadelphians, one of whom said he was "dear" to all as "the Republican Minister." Another declared that he was "beloved by every Body here (except the Tories)."[13] Optimism reigned in America when Gérard arrived in Philadelphia in July 1778. The defeat of a British army at Saratoga, French belligerency, and the arrival of Admiral d'Estaing's squadron appeared to herald an imminent end to the war. Gérard, in step with the buoyant mood, initially provided Vergennes with glowing reports on America's army and militia. Soon, however, he began to paint a gloomy picture of American capabilities. France's ally was exhausted and militarily ineffectual, he advised. He further reported that Washington was capable, but many Continental army officers left much to be desired, the army's supply system was beyond hope, and the states were riven by provincial ambitions and too often heedless of the national interest.[14] His appraisal of the young nation's military weaknesses was spot-on, but he misunderstood much about Congress. In particular, he mistook wariness toward the alliance among those who feared that France would put its interests above of the United States for a wish to reconcile with Britain.

In February 1779 Gérard received Comte de Vergennes's directive to push Congress not only to define its peace terms but also to align America's objectives with those of France. Chief among the foreign minister's concerns was that Congress must not deter Spain from entering the war.

Congress responded by creating a committee that rapidly reported America's peace ultimata:

The United States would agree to mediation only after Britain recognized its independence;

The British army was to be removed from all United States territory;

The northern border would extend into Canada and include much of present-day Ontario;

The right of navigation on the Mississippi River, which must be the western border;

The United States would cede Florida to Spain if Britain ceded it to the United States, and in that eventuality, the southern border would terminate at the northern border of East and West Florida;

American fishing rights would be acknowledged in the Grand Banks of Newfoundland;

Nova Scotia was to become independent or be ceded to the United States.[15]

The committee's proposed terms clashed with the interests of both France and Spain. Vergennes preferred that Britain retain Canada and Nova Scotia, as that might compel the feeble new American nation to remain dependent on France, and he abhorred the thought of having to compete with the Americans in the Newfoundland fisheries. As Vergennes was tending to both French and Spanish interests, he had directed Gérard to see that the western boundary of the United States was set at the crest of the Appalachians, hundreds of miles east of the Mississippi. Surprised and aghast at the terms laid out by the committee, Gérard responded that France was committed to securing American independence, but it would not wage a protracted war to secure the other conditions in the draft peace ultimata. He also paid several Americans—whom a Yankee congressman labeled Gérard's "Lickspittles"—to write newspaper articles that urged more moderate peace terms. Congress wrangled over the matter for nearly eight months. Sharp sectional divisions were apparent. New England remained adamant on the fishing and Canadian-boundary issues; southern delegates, faced with the shift of the war to their sector, were more eager to placate France. In September, following tempestuous sessions when many "unjust & impolitick" words were uttered and considerable "invective and abuse" flowed, Congress finally agreed to terms. With the exception of two major concessions, Congress's objectives differed little from those in the committee's February draft. Congress conceded that during the eventual peace talks, the United States would seek fishing rights through a commercial treaty with Great Britain and navigation rights on the Mississippi River via an accord with Spain. Despite the intense pressure brought by Gérard, Congress did not categorically abandon any of the objectives set forth in February's ultimata.[16]

With peace talks possibly looming, Congress had to choose an envoy to conduct negotiations and someone to send to Madrid to seek Spanish recognition and to negotiate the treaty concerning navigation rights on the Mississippi. These deliberations were nearly as divisive as the fight over peace terms. The committee charged with recommending an envoy proposed that all American diplomats in Europe be recalled, including Franklin. Now 73 years old, some thought his prime lay in a distant past. Others felt he was too servile. Still others, roiled by recent allegations that Silas Deane had misused public money while in Paris, wondered if Franklin might also be complicit. A majority of delegations voted to recall Franklin, but Gérard saved him, arguing that he was extremely popular in France. The minister refrained from mentioning that Vergennes wished to keep Franklin in place as he thought him pliable. To be sure, many delegates thought Franklin an "upright, firm Friend to America.[17]

The selection of a peace commissioner turned into a battle between the supporters of John Adams and John Jay. New England's delegates backed Adams, hoping to have one of their own at the negotiating table to fight relentlessly for fishing rights and an advantageous northern boundary. Mid-Atlantic delegations backed Jay, a New Yorker who could be expected to fight hard to protect the region's mercantile interests. Gérard was not under orders to prevent Adams's selection, but he was aware that Vergennes had qualms about him, looking on him as intransigently independent. Gérard would have preferred that Congress leave the negotiations to Franklin or choose Jay, though in the end Congress chose Adams and voted to send Jay as a plenipotentiary to Madrid. Henry Laurens, the former president of Congress, assured Adams that he had been selected because of his uncompromising fidelity to independence and as the members of Congress had no "apprehensions [of his] incompetency or negligence"—a guarded reference to the distrust many felt toward Franklin. Elbridge Gerry, a Massachusetts congressman, told Adams that Congress thought his "Character is as high as any Gentleman's in America."[18]

These were not Congress's first acrid clashes. Many battles had been fought over framing a federal union, skirmishes that commenced once the war began and intensified in the summer of 1776 when the delegates formed a committee to prepare a charter of confederation. It reported a plan for a powerful central government armed with substantive authority over the states. After a month of haggling over the committee's draft, Congress suspended its deliberations, convinced that the states would never ratify such a constitution. Nearly a year passed before Congress returned to the matter, and work sputtered until word arrived of the victory at Saratoga. Thereafter Congress acted quickly, hopeful that both the great military victory and a constitution would be sufficient to remove the last obstacles to bringing France into the war as an ally. The Articles of Confederation were approved and submitted to the states for ratification in November 1777, but not ratified for four years. Its approval changed relatively little in what had existed since the First Continental Congress in 1774. A federal union was created in which the states possessed nearly total sovereignty. Article 2 stipulated "Each State retains its sovereignty, freedom and independence," possessing all powers other than those explicitly granted to Congress, which included the sole authority to declare war, make treaties, borrow money, and control the currency. Such a highly decentralized federal union was inevitable, given that the colonists had chosen revolution and war rather than submit to centralized British authority. Deep into hostilities, there still was little desire for a powerful national government.[19]

A great many delegates found serving in Congress to be unpleasant, and the body was troubled by continuous turnover and absenteeism. Congressmen faced long absences from home and for many a distressful loss of income. They endured long, tedious days filled with repetitive discussions of issues that all too often appeared to be inconsequential. Congress generally sat for seven hours each day, Monday through Saturday, and delegates put in additional hours on committee assignments. For most of the war, Congress met in Philadelphia, which had long, cold winters and long, oppressively hot and humid summers. Summers were made more unbearable by Congress's habit of meeting in a shuttered, airless chamber, lest a Tory or British spy eavesdrop on their secret deliberations. Some delegates thought their sedentary daily regimen within the confines of a dirty city might ruin their health, but few went as far as John Adams, who once claimed that serving in Congress was as dangerous as soldiering. His remark was ludicrous, although as a signer of the Declaration of Independence, Adams knew he would likely swing on the gallows if the war was lost.[20]

AFTER THE INCONCLUSIVE CAMPAIGN of 1776, capped by the reversals at Trenton and Princeton, the sense had gathered in many quarters in Great Britain that it must win the war in 1777 or agree to peace terms. When that year ended in the cataclysm of Saratoga and Howe's failure to destroy Washington's army, there was talk of forming a coalition ministry that would withdraw all troops from America and negotiate peace. George III opposed those steps, and in the end Parliament not only remained committed to the war but also grew more bellicose when France entered the conflict. The French war, at least for a time, appeared to move Britain's American troubles to a back burner. In 1778 and 1779 the British press devoted less space to the deadlocked struggle against the rebels, focusing instead on the war at sea and in the Caribbean, and of course on the threat of invasion. The new priority was captured by Charles James Fox, an incorrigible foe of war with the American rebels: "Attack France, for she is your object. The nature of the war with her is quite different. The war against America is against your own countrymen; that against France is against your inveterate enemy and rival." Others contended that every victory scored against France would cause the Americans to grow "detached from her as useless to them," paving the way to a favorable settlement with the colonial insurgents.[21]

Reflecting the new mood, the king opened the 1779 session of Parliament with a speech that did not mention the American war, the first time since well before hostilities that he had said nothing about the colonial rebellion in his annual address. But the American war was still on the minds of many, who in petitions, pamphlets, and the press decried higher taxes, rising national debt, economic hardships, and commercial disruptions brought on by the conflict. Capturing the disenchantment, a pamphleteer lashed out against the accumulating "general distress" resulting from a war in which there was "no hope of peace," a conflict that for no good reason was devouring "the last resources of an exhausted nation." Many contended that America was already "irreparably lost," a conviction that had swelled over the past couple of years. George III may have looked the other way, but in mid-1779 Parliament once again heatedly wrangled over the American war. Some who had long opposed the war argued that the colonial insurgents would never negotiate with Lord North's ministry. They were joined by those who insisted that it was past time to remove all troops from the colonies and focus exclusively on fighting France and Spain. One member pointed out that Britain had poured vast numbers of soldiers into the American sinkhole, yet they had never been "found . . . to be adequate" for suppressing the rebellion. The idea of pulling out all troops was widely attacked, including by some foes of the war. Such a step, they contended, would ensure the loss of Canada, trans-Appalachia, and Florida. Those who argued for continuing the war observed that royal governance had been restored in Georgia and called it a sign that the southern strategy might succeed in regaining other valuable southern colonies. Some who backed the war called on Lord North to offer more generous peace terms, urged that he deal with state authorities and ignore the American congress, and inveighed the ministry to propose an armistice and resumption of commerce with America while negotiations proceeded. Lord Germain, speaking for the ministry and a majority in the Commons, branded as "highly reprehensible" an offer of new terms to the rebels. At the same moment he privately advised General Clinton that due to the serious situation in the Caribbean, no troops from that theater could be redeployed to North America. Clinton would receive some reinforcements, but not as many as he desired.[22]

Clinton was pleased that Britain was not ready to abandon the struggle in America, but he knew that not all was well at home. While Britain's inhabitants were spared the significant fighting that the colonists endured, the nation's economy and society had not escaped unscathed. British trade had been severely damaged. By 1778 the value of overseas trade was one-fourth what it had been in the last year of peace. Additional losses piled up the following year when Spain entered hostilities. By early 1778, before French ships marauded on the high seas, Britain had already lost hundreds of vessels to rebel privateers and the Continental navy. The contraction of Britain's overseas trade had a particularly damaging impact on textile industries. Woolens had constituted 30 percent of prewar exports to the colonies, and that traffic had stopped entirely in the first year of hostilities. Metalworking trades suffered the layoffs of one-half of all workers in some communities. Nor was it solely commerce with the American colonies that was buffeted by the war. Exports to Ireland had fallen by nearly 50 percent by 1777 and trade in Europe, Asia, and the Caribbean suffered as well. Scarcity was the order of the day when it came to some commodities. Just as some urban dwellers in America learned to live without corn, some tobacco addicts in Britain did without a smoke, chew, or snort of snuff, while those who had prospered from vending the weed tightened their belts.

Wars are expensive. Britain's annual expenditures tripled during the war, and the national debt doubled. Taxes spiked, as they did in America, reaching what one historian called "harrowing levels." Levies on customary consumer goods such as soap, salt, and alcohol fell with a crushing impact on the poor. Parish poor rates, collected to provide care for the families of militiamen on duty, climbed steadily. Meanwhile, Parliament raised the land, carriage, stamp, and customs duties, and imposed new excise and house taxes, as well as a levy on servants. By late in the war 23 percent of per capita income was taken in taxation, a greater proportion than befell the citizenry of any other belligerent. Liverpool and other ports, as well as textile centers such as Lancashire that had thrived in the prewar years from the expanding overseas commerce, were ravaged by the twin jolts of excessive taxation and the loss of distant markets. Britain experienced occasional food riots that required summoning the militia to restore order, and by 1780 some 40 county associations had come into existence and were peacefully agitating for an honorable end to a war they condemned as unwinnable. The Dorset Association typically asserted that Britain's "unhappy state" was due to "the rash and imprudent contest so long and so unprosperously pursued with North America." Towns sent resolutions to the monarch. Westminster complained to the king of "the large addition to the national debt, a heavy accumulation of taxes, a rapid decline of the trades," and the staggering amount of money "improvidently squandered" as a result of the war. Some towns urged the dismissal of the ministry, and others called for the removal of Lord Germain.

Britain did not escape an inflationary spiral. Although inflation in Britain was a pittance compared with that in America, it was a fact of life. Wages rose for some due to the demand for labor as more and more men were taken for military service, but inflation crimped the purchasing power of many workers. Newspapers reported that some workers were so hard-hit that they had been driven into military service, and there was an increase in female wage earners. These women, drawn exclusively from poorer families, mostly found employment as agricultural workers. Throughout much of the war, investors in the stock market faced a bumpy ride, and in 1778 it fell precipitously when French belligerency became a reality. The war did not result in significant movement up and down the social ladder, but it widened the gulf between the most affluent and those with the lowest incomes, to some degree because wartime taxation fell disproportionately on those in the lower ranks of society. There were occasional signs of social unrest, but the closest that England came to a consequential demonstration of class warfare occurred in the Gordon Riots in June 1780.[23]

The riots began in an outpouring of anti-Catholicism sparked by a parliamentary religious-reform measure. On a steamy day in June a crowd of 60,000 in St. George's Fields heard inflammatory speeches assailing papacy and Romanism, after which many who were provoked and impassioned by the rhetoric surged across the Thames into the heart of London. Some coursed through the city wreaking damage. Others forced their way into Westminster Hall, where Parliament was meeting. The Lords and Commons continued to meet for hours while the unpredictable crowd milled ominously in the lobby outside their chambers. Finally, around 11:00 P.M., troops escorted the legislators to safety. This had been the first day of what was to be eight days of rioting, the worst rampage in British history. Nearly 500 died in the carnage. The homes of several officials were attacked. Lord North's residence on Downing Street was damaged, but saved by the grenadiers guarding it. Others were not as fortunate. Several officials had close brushes with disaster. Edmund Burke, with his family in tow and clutching whatever valuables they could carry, fled to the home of General Burgoyne, who, with a squad of regulars, successfully defended his dwelling. Lord Sandwich narrowly escaped being murdered. Several Catholic chapels and schools suffered damage. Many prisons were targeted and inmates set free. Some banks—symbols of injustice and the financial woes of the times—were vandalized or destroyed. Shops were looted. Fires blazed. Horace Walpole thought the sixth day of rioting was the worst, saying that "Black Wednesday" was the "most horrible night I ever beheld." He was sure that half the city would soon go up in flames, but the next day troops arrived and restored order within 48 hours.

The press looked for an explanation for the upheaval. Their answers were often tinged with a conspiratorial ring. It was said that France had financed the rioters, French and American spies had directed the mobs, and the culprits had been set in motion by the antiwar rhetoric of some in Parliament. None of this was true. There were myriad causes of the riots, but to a considerable degree the rampage was a revolt against authority, a rising against a ruling class that ignored and insulted a vast swath of the population, and that had taken Britain into a seemingly endless war that had sown disorder and hardship in the lives of countless numbers.[24]

CONCERN OVER THE COURSE of the war was growing in official circles in France as 1780 beckoned. Two campaigns had passed and the French had little to show for having gone to war, including absolutely nothing of consequence in the North American theater. The invasion of England had been aborted and the stinging news of Admiral d'Estaing's mortifying defeat in Savannah had just arrived. Nor was d'Estaing's failure all that was disconcerting with regard to American affairs. Some officers who had volunteered to serve in America equated the health of the insurgency with that of a desperately ill patient. Brigadier General Louis Duportail reported to the minister of war that the Americans acted "without spring or energy," if they acted at all. There "is a hundred times more enthusiasm for this Revolution in any one coffee house at Paris than in the thirteen [American] provinces united," he added. At least one officer, Johann de Kalb, a veteran of more than 20 years of military service, had lost confidence in Washington, characterizing him as "the weakest general" under whom he had ever served, an indecisive leader surrounded by sycophants who fed him bad advice. Minister Gérard thought more highly of Washington, but his reports on America's military troubles tallied with an abundance of other information that reached the foreign ministry. By late in 1779 Vergennes was grumbling that Washington and his army, distinguished by its "spirit and enterprize" prior to the alliance, had over the past two years exhibited nothing but "inactivity." If the Americans did not "put more vigor into their conduct," he said, he would have to conclude that they now had "but a feeble attachment" to securing independence. These concerns stoked the foreign minister's apprehension that if the war dragged on, his American ally might be tempted to reconcile with Great Britain. Vergennes's confidence in Washington was shaken, but he was cognizant of the difficulties the American commander faced. Returning French officers had expressed shock at the deplorable state of the American army. It needed "clothes, arms, money, or, even still more, effective support," one reported. Washington, early in 1780, confessed as much to Gérard, expressing his "uneasiness" over the dearth of men and provisions, concerns that were promptly relayed to Vergennes.[25]

The impact of the war fell less heavily on the French citizenry than on American and British residents. There was never a vibrant antiwar movement, and within Parisian salons—and among those who followed such things—it remained a popular cause. Some sympathy existed for the Americans, but there was a stronger yearning to humble Great Britain and restore French prestige. However, all those in power were aware that the war was not going well, and many were alarmed at the war's deleterious impact on France's debt-ridden financial system. French expenditures were extraordinary even in peacetime, its methods of taxation outdated, and ancient trade and manufacturing regulations hampered the modernization of commerce, further impeding economic growth and the enlargement of the nation's revenue base. Prior to providing assistance to the embattled American rebels, France's national debt was already six times that of its annual income.

The comptroller general, Anne-Robert-Jacques Turgot, had coped with the nation's economic distress since nearly the outset of Louis XVI's reign. Aware of the danger that the ancien régime was drifting inexorably toward the abyss, he not only sought refinements to transition France from its feudal past but also warned unsparingly about the financial dangers inherent in warfare. In 1776 Turgot was dismissed, though not because he cautioned against the lavish outlays necessary for keeping the American insurgency afloat. His economic measures, especially his recommendation that all current taxes be abolished and replaced with a proportional land tax that would have fallen heavily on society's most privileged groups, stirred fury that led to his downfall. The heedless ruling class, on its somnolent stroll toward suicide, wanted no rectifications that would impinge on its privileges. Turgot was soon succeeded by Jacques Necker, a Swiss native and successful banker, who it was hoped would find alternative solutions to the national economic tribulations. Necker, no less than Turgot, understood France's financial dilemma and the dangers it posed, and he, too, sought reforms. Whereas Turgot had focused on restructuring the economy and social system, Necker with virtually no success urged administrative reforms to reduce waste in government and new means of streamlining the collection of taxes. Necker, like Turgot before him, also repeatedly cautioned that aid to the Americans would have a harmful impact on the French economy. In 1777, the first year of massive French aid—a year in which French loans and shipments of military supplies to the Americans exceeded 9.5 million livres—Necker borrowed to cover the steadily growing deficit. Late that year, when Vergennes sought the king's consent to enter the war, Necker counseled that the economic consequences of such a step could be dire. His warnings fell on deaf ears. In the first two years that France was at war, expenditures skyrocketed. The operations of d'Estaing's fleet alone cost in excess of 25 million livres. Soon military expenditures were five times or more greater than in peacetime. Ultimately, the war cost France more than one billion livres.[26]

Two years into the war, Vergennes was awash with problems. He, too, acknowledged that French finances were "truly alarming." No one had to remind him that the longer the war continued, the more steadily voices would be raised about its harmful impact on the French economy. Vergennes also learned that a low-level British intermediary was engaged in talks at San Ildefonso with the goal of persuading the Spanish to make peace, seizing on Spain's unhappiness over the failed invasion of England and even greater displeasure at France's refusal to try again. Vergennes was aware, too, that Parisian bankers, speculators, and war contractors were howling about the losses they were incurring due to the depreciated American currency. That was troubling enough, but Vergennes had also learned that Necker was quietly putting out peace feelers. The growing sentiment to end the war was hardly unexpected, given that for the past two years mostly bad news had come from America. Gérard's somber reports on American military capabilities, as well as Washington's persistent inactivity, convinced many—including Vergennes—that under current conditions there was no hope that the stalemated war might turn in the Allies' favor. But Louis XVI, like Vergennes, continued to think that the war could be won and that the prizes that might come with such a victory were too alluring to be cast aside just yet. Besides, Vergennes and possibly his monarch as well sensed that peace was a moot point, as all signs pointed to Britain's unwillingness to conclude the war.[27]

While France would remain at war, changes were necessary. In 1778, following Saratoga, Britain had reassessed its strategy. In 1780, in the wake of d'Estaing's lack of success, France reappraised its approach to the war. Some who wished to remain at war argued that the nation's ends could best be attained in Europe, not America, and particularly by acting in concert with Spain against British-held Gibraltar. Others asserted the vital importance of the American theater. To this point, the French had assumed that committing a navy to act jointly with the vigorous and daring General Washington would be sufficient to swiftly gain victory. Discussions at Versailles now swirled about sending an army to America, a step that Congress had never requested, though a year earlier Franklin had suggested to Vergennes that a French army of about 5,000 men might be "advantageously employed" in defeating the British.[28]

A decision to send an army to America could not be taken lightly, and not simply because of France's fiscal troubles. General Sullivan's misguided conduct toward d'Estaing in 1778 gave Vergennes pause about how French troops would be received. He also feared that should a tempestuous relationship develop between Washington and the French commander—or if the French army suffered a defeat—the Americans might look with new interest on a rapprochement with Britain. The Marquis de Lafayette, who had returned to France early in 1779 in hopes of playing a prominent role in the invasion of England, was among those Vergennes consulted. Vergennes's principal interest was in learning whether Washington could be trusted to work harmoniously with a French commander. Lafayette provided sound counsel, assuring the foreign minister that Washington could be depended on, but warning that the Continental army was on its last leg and that if a French army was not sent, America could never gain its independence. He urged that France send 15,000 muskets and tons of powder to the Americans, as well as an army of 4,000. Lafayette also met with other officials and to them he advised that the Continental army was "judged with far too great severity in this country." Other advisors recommended dispatching a larger army, even as many as 12,000. Lafayette stressed that it was imperative that the army be "well led." Predictably, he suggested that he was just the man to lead it, contending that he, more so than any other French officer, knew "the sentiments in Congress and the different sentiments in each state." Lafayette added that his "intimate friendship" with Washington and phenomenal *popularity* in America made him the logical choice to command "a corps of gallant French."[29]

Many advisors also recommended that another fleet be sent along with the army. The matter percolated for weeks, until early in 1780 when Louis XVI's court, aware that time was of the essence if a French army was to join with the Continental army in the campaign of 1780, finally reached a decision. A small naval squadron and an army of 4,000 led by Comte de Rochambeau, a veteran who had spent three-fifths of his life in the French army (and who had been a brigadier general before Lafayette was born), would be sent to America. By the time the decision was reached, the French were aware that General Clinton had abandoned Rhode Island and it was to be Rochambeau's destination. Following Rochambeau's entreaties, the army for the so-called Expédition Particulière was increased to 8,000 men, and an additional

1,000 infantrymen were to accompany the sailors and serve under Chevalier de Ternay, a 40-year veteran who was given command of the navy.[30]

WHILE THE WAR RAGED, a revolution was taking place in what had been Britain's colonies in America. Some insurgents had seen independence as the means—the only means—of securing seminal domestic reforms. Like Thomas Jefferson, they believed that transformative change was the "whole object of the present controversy." Six months before independence was declared, Thomas Paine, who shared that outlook, urged a republican revolution characterized by annually elected assemblies composed of assemblymen obedient to the wishes of the voters. The object of government, said Paine, was "the happiness of the governed," and the task of the new revolutionary governments was to secure the "freedom and property" of "*all* men."[31]

Some revolutionaries were shocked by such radical ideas, but most—in a newfound antipathy toward monarchy brought to a head by resistance to Britain's new colonial policies—fervently embraced the notion of republicanism and to varying degrees sought changes in American government and society. The dynamics unleashed by the war were especially crucial in bringing on change. People who were being asked to sacrifice in order to create a new nation wanted a stake in that new country, and many believed, as Paine had told them, that their sacrifices were undertaken "to begin the world over again." The payday for their sacrifices, again as Paine had written, would be the "birthday of a new world." These were extremely radical ideas. The very notion of replacing centuries-old hereditary monarchies with governments chosen by the people was "as radical for the eighteenth century as Marxism was to be for the nineteenth century," as historian Gordon S. Wood observed. Suddenly, subjects became citizens. John Adams put it another way. People were either free or slaves, and if independence was secured, the American Revolution would assure that free white American males were really free men. Not every change in the republican revolution was foreseen by everyone in 1776. One was the propulsive growth of democracy. Within a decade of the end of the war, one of the country's two political parties was avowedly democratic, and its first successful presidential candidate—Jefferson—in his 1801 inaugural address pledged his commitment to "the right of election by the people," "absolute acquiescence in the decisions of the majority," and governance by the "sacred principal" that the "will of the majority is in all cases to prevail."[32]

Prior to 1776 virtually every colony was dominated by an oligarchy. Merchants prevailed in most northern provinces, planter–slave owners in the southern. Societies had grown increasingly stratified, particularly in urban centers, and laws and government services not surprisingly tended to favor the oligarchs and the eastern regions where they mostly lived and had long been dominant. Many saw the Revolution as "one of the fairest opportunities ever offered" to bring about substantive changes, for by necessity the colonial insurgency and war "puts all servants of the public under the power of the people" whose support was indispensable.[33]

Within scant days after July 4, 1776, three states began to write constitutions, and five more soon joined in. Before 1777 ended, every state had a written constitution. The goal everywhere was to protect the people's liberty from overarching government. The main thrust was to curb the authority of the chief executive, diminishing the powers that had been wielded by colonial governors. The new constitutions stripped governors of their sway over assemblies and the judiciary, denied their right to veto legislation, reduced their appointment powers, subjected them to annual elections (by the assemblies), imposed term limits, and provided for their impeachment and removal. Pennsylvania eliminated the office of governor altogether. Real authority in the new republican governments was transferred to the state assemblies. Most were bicameral. Electoral districts were created in which the voters would annually choose an assemblyman who was to be a resident of the district. In the colonial era, members of the upper houses had been put there by royal authority and were drawn overwhelmingly from what passed as the provincial aristocracy. Now, those who sat in the upper chambers were also elected officials. Suffrage rights were enlarged almost everywhere. In every colony before 1776 it was necessary to meet property qualifications in order to vote, and between 20 and 50 percent of free adult males had been disenfranchised. But under nearly every new state constitution, property qualifications were lowered or abolished, and some provinces extended voting rights to all free taxpaying adult males. Many states followed the advice of John Adams "to make the acquisition of land easy to every member of society," a step that enfranchised many living in provinces that maintained property qualifications. Change was almost immediately perceptible. The upper houses of the state assemblies became more representative of the people as the representatives from the backcountry and the percentage of members who were farmers—and small farmers at that—nearly doubled; half as many wealthy members as previously now held seats, and the number of men from elite families shrank by half. Of 231 men from the governing elite who held the highest offices throughout

America on the cusp of the Revolution, only 52 ever held office again after independence.[34]

South Carolina was the outlier with regard to the sweeping constitutional reforms set in motion by the American Revolution. That state "enshrined the old order," as historian Jackson T. Main noted. Ownership of thousands of acres and numerous slaves was required for holding office, and suffrage rights were not expanded. The state assembly remained in the firm grip of the planter-dominated tidewater slaveocracy. It held 10 of 13 seats in the upper house, and Charleston alone was given half as many seats in the lower house as all the western districts combined. Western South Carolina, home to three-fourths of the state's free population, had only one-third of the seats in the lower house.[35]

The Revolution also unleashed a powerful new idea—the idea of equality. Bold and daring activism in the protest against Britain and hazarding one's all by bearing arms were principal sources of radicalization. So, too, was the Declaration of Independence's transfixing natural rights philosophy and its spellbinding pronouncement: "All men are created equal." Historians continue to debate what Jefferson meant when he wrote those words and what Congress thought they meant when it approved the Declaration, but once it was put forth as the national creed, it could not be taken back. In coming years, the more conservative Founders would seek to temper its meaning, but this was a genie that could not be put back in the bottle. Escaping the long suppressing hand of Europe's privileged aristocracies was what one insurgent called the "life and soul" of republican revolution, and all the more so as the means to that end was through a protracted war that imposed hardships on the citizenry. For some, the American Revolution was at its core exactly what Jefferson had proclaimed: All of humankind was equal. For others, it meant there would be no formal aristocracy in America and that one's ability would determine one's place in society. For still others, the idea of equality meant that no person was better than any other person. George Robert Twelves Hewes was an example of those who repudiated their earlier habits of deference toward wealth and authority. Young Hewes, a shoemaker in prewar Boston, had bowed and scraped in the presence of a rich and powerful man such as John Hancock, but after risking his life in the war for American independence he refused to recognize any man as his superior. No longer would he doff his hat or step aside in acknowledgement of his inferior status when he passed on the street one who was wealthier or more powerful.[36]

Soon after writing the Declaration of Independence, Jefferson left Congress to work toward transforming Virginia. He sought to curtail the reach of Virginia's planter aristocracy. He succeeded in abolishing entail, a legal practice that had concentrated property in fewer and fewer hands, and in opening new lands in the west that would become the home of property-owning, voting farmers. Jefferson also joined the fight for religious freedom, seen by some as freedom from religion. Jefferson was slightly ahead of his time on this score, though a decade later his friend James Madison secured what he had been after and a bit later made it the basis of the First Amendment to the U.S. Constitution. Jefferson saw an educated populace as essential in a democratic polity and he pushed for a system of free public education, but again such a reform was too radical for the conservative majority in his state. Jefferson did not achieve all that he hoped for, but as historian Joyce Appleby wrote, he "rallied his countrymen with a vision for the future" that would coalesce throughout America within a few years of the Revolutionary War.[37]

While serving in the Virginia assembly after 1776, Jefferson also sought to end slavery. His cause went nowhere. However, revolutionary rhetoric—the equation of a colonial status with the misery and anguish of slavery and Jefferson's ringing natural rights and egalitarian ideals within the Declaration of Independence—led some to see that slavery could not be reconciled with republicanism or enlightened thought. Wartime necessity, especially the recruitment of Black men, free and slave, to soldier for American independence also led some to reconsider old shibboleths. It prompted Colonel John Laurens, a South Carolinian and Washington's young aide, to propose that his state raise an army of thousands of slaves who would be liberated following the war. His friend Alexander Hamilton, another of Washington's aides, supported the idea, arguing that the "natural abilities" of Black men were "as good as ours" and that they would make "very excellent soldiers." The scheme might have succeeded with Washington's support, but he refused to endorse it. He feared a backlash in planter-dominated South Carolina that might drive it to embrace neutrality. Washington was also apprehensive that such a step would spur the enemy's recruitment of enslaved men for its army.

Although the hopes of Laurens and Hamilton were foiled, a nascent spirit of abolitionism took hold in most northern states, where only a tiny percentage of those in bondage resided. Some Continental soldiers returned home as foes of slavery after seeing the many cruelties faced by chattel in the southern theater, while religious beliefs and Revolutionary idealism turned others against slavery. The Pennsylvania assembly in 1780 became the first legislative body in the western world to abolish slavery, phasing it out through gradual abolition. Connecticut, Rhode Island, Vermont, New York, and New Jersey later took similar steps, Massachusetts ended slavery through a judicial decision, and New Hampshire terminated the institution through its state constitution.[38]

Since early in the war some slaves, at great peril, had sought to flee behind British lines in quest of freedom. More than 1,000 slaves in Virginia acted on Lord Dunmore's promise of freedom in 1775 by taking flight. Numerous slaves in the middle states fled to New York and Philadelphia following the British army's occupation of those two cities; South Carolina's Henry Laurens believed that thousands of enslaved people fled to Georgia following Britain's capture of Savannah at the tag end of 1778. During the following summer, the British commandant of New York ordered that "All Negroes that fly from the Enemy's Country are Free." Three weeks later, General Clinton issued the Phillipsburg Proclamation, a decree ordering that captured Black rebel soldiers be sold into slavery, but promising "full security" to rebel-owned slaves who fled to the British army. Clinton saw his act as a war measure designed to add to the rebels' growing demoralization. He did not achieve all that he had hoped for, but thousands of slaves bolted for the welcoming arms of the British army. So many slaves escaped to New York City that by 1780 local authorities appealed to officials in Britain's New Jersey strongholds to stanch the flow, as the number of freedmen flooding into the city had become a "burden to the town." The same lust for freedom that had impelled Washington to support the insurgency also burned bright among his slaves. Remarking that "Liberty is sweet," Mount Vernon's farm manager informed Washington that every one of his slaves would "make their escape" if only they could. It has been estimated that 5 percent of slaves in the South fled behind British lines and thousands more absconded elsewhere. By war's end, the enslaved population of the Chesapeake colonies had been reduced by some 30 percent.[39]

Before the American Revolution most colonies had made it extremely difficult for slave owners to free their slaves, but revolutionary ideals sparked a revision in those laws, including in parts of the South. Some who owned slaves manumitted their chattel. An additional 500 or so Virginia slaves acquired their freedom in exchange for agreeing to serve as substitutes for slave owners faced with military service. The percentage of free Blacks in Virginia rose from 1 to 7 percent between 1775 and 1800. By 1800 the percentage of free Blacks nationally had increased to nearly 14 percent.[40]

However, throughout the South, where most slaves lived, abolitionism never took hold. "We risked our Lives and Fortunes, and waded through Seas of Blood" to protect property from the British government's intrusion, said one former southern

soldier who was dead set against freeing slaves. In fact, the growth of slavery accelerated in the South following the war. By the middle of the 19th century there were
roughly four times as many slaves in the southern states as in 1776. At the same
moment, the rights of Blacks who had been freed in the revolutionary era were
circumscribed. Throughout the land they were denied the vote and the right to serve
on juries, among other civil rights.[41] That was true, too, for the slaves who soldiered
to win their freedom, notwithstanding their sacrifices in helping the states win their
freedom from British control and despite the new nation's professed commitment to
natural rights and equality. These Black soldiers would succeed in gaining liberation
from slavery, but when it came to equality and civil rights, the states and the new
American nation would turn their backs on these veterans of the Continental army.

Although many of the leading Founders thought slavery was reprehensible, they
feared that any overt attempt to end it would jeopardize the national unity necessary
for winning the war and preserving the fledgling United States. Even so, most hoped
to confine it to where it existed in 1776, believing that slavery would wither and die
if it could not expand. Congress abolished slavery in the territories north of the Ohio
River in 1787. But Jefferson, once again a member of Congress, failed in 1784 by the
margin of a single vote to make slavery illegal in all the western territories, the step
that would have solidified slavery's confinement. Within a few years of the war's end,
hundreds of thousands of slaves were toiling in cotton fields in Tennessee, Alabama,
and Mississippi, states that had not existed in 1776. Foreseeing the scabrous future,
Jefferson immediately understood the magnitude of the defeat of his abolition bill.
That single negative vote condemned "millions unborn" to a lifetime of slavery, he
said, adding that "heaven was silent in that awful moment."[42]

For most white Americans of the revolutionary generation, and for many succes-
sive generations, the resounding ideals and rhetoric of the American Revolution
were meant for whites only.

CHAPTER 11

INTO THE
SOUTHERN VORTEX

EARLY IN 1779 SIR Henry Clinton, frustrated by the inadequacy of British arms and Lord Germain's intrusiveness that impeded his "latitude . . . to act as the moment should require," had asked to be permitted to resign as commander in chief in North America. Clinton's outlook changed as the year progressed. Whereas the two years that he been in command had largely involved "defensive retrenchment" due to a lack of troops and the anticipated Allied campaigns to retake New York, Clinton had at last been somewhat reinforced, and the French fleet was gone in the wake of the failed attack in Savannah. His army had also accumulated a six-month reserve of provisions that British generals thought imperative for beginning offensive operations. Furthermore, Clinton had been joined in August by General Cornwallis, who returned from a trip to London. Friendship between the two had been strained in 1776 when Cornwallis tattled to William Howe that Clinton was critical of his generalship and word of his friend's loose tongue got back to Clinton. Time helped heal the breach, but so did Cornwallis, who from London pledged his loyalty to Clinton and proclaimed his "sincere wish [to be] your faithful servant and friend." Clinton said that he was "happy" to have an officer of Cornwallis's caliber as his second in command. The two were veterans of the severe tribulations of soldiering in Germany in the Seven Years' War, an experience that Clinton and numerous others believed had made them better officers than those who had served in America. An enthused Clinton spoke of Cornwallis's "indefatigable zeal, his knowledge of the country, his professional ability, and the high estimation in which he is held by this army." By year's end Clinton was avid to remain in command and to act.[1]

As 1780 approached, Clinton turned his attention toward taking Charleston. For two years, Germain had nudged him in that direction. The American secretary had urged a campaign to seize Charleston, followed by the pacification of South Carolina's backcountry and a foray into North Carolina. Typically, Germain added, "it is not doubted" that the Carolinas could easily be reclaimed given the vast number of Loyalists who would "flock to the King's standard." Of late, Germain had stepped up his calls for Clinton to act, candidly acknowledging the need to soon bring "the American war to an honourable conclusion" in light of the dire threat Britain faced from the Bourbon powers and unrest at home. Germain went on to say that the "feeble resistance" General Prevost had encountered in May when he advanced on Charleston offered "indubitable proof" that the city and South Carolina could rapidly be brought back into the royal fold. Retaking South Carolina, Germain added, would guarantee the recovery of North Carolina.[2]

Clinton required no prodding. Unlike Germain, he did not minimize the likely difficulties in capturing Charleston, but he was aware of the splendid opportunities to be reaped by taking the city. If his campaign succeeded in the midst of "the universal dejection" that blanketed America in the wake of the Allied failure at Savannah and the collapsed economy, it might drive the rebels to accept an accommodation short of American independence. Clinton had also sought for two years to bring "Mr. Washington" to battle and thought that the threat of losing South Carolina might compel the American commander to fight. The time to act was right, too, as Clinton now had ample troops to defend New York while campaigning in South Carolina.[3]

Washington's army, meanwhile, was in winter quarters at Morristown, beleaguered by conditions every bit as bad as those at Valley Forge two years earlier. Veterans subsequently thought of this as "the hard winter," a time of seemingly incessant snow and unrelenting cold. But it was not just the weather that made their lives difficult. This was yet another winter when provisions were in short supply, if they existed at all. Having meat with their meals was a rarity for the soldiers, and there were occasions when they had no food whatsoever. On a frigid and blustery January day, General Greene exclaimed, "Poor Fellows! they exhibit a picture truly distressing. More than half naked, and above two thirds starved." The next day he said that "hundreds and hundreds" were "without shirts and many other necessary articles of clothing." Seven percent of the soldiers deserted, and many perished that winter, though the mortality rate was not as great as at Valley Forge.[4]

Aside from dealing with the problems that sprang from still another supply crisis, Washington, like Clinton, contemplated the looming campaign. He had no knowledge of French plans in the aftermath of Savannah. In September, he had met at West Point with the new French minister to the United States, Chevalier Anne-César De La Luzerne, who inquired whether Washington would welcome another French navy and a few infantry regiments. That would be "advantageous," Washington replied. But throughout the winter and deep into the spring he did not know if either would materialize. Nor was Washington aware of Clinton's plans, although in December he knew that British troops were boarding transports in New York Harbor. Washington guessed that the enemy was preparing to either strike West Point or invade South Carolina. Given the season, the latter was more likely. Reinforcements had already been sent to General Benjamin Lincoln, the commander in the Southern Department, who had advised Washington that he believed the British were coming. Lincoln had also professed his "insufficiency and want of experience" as a commander and asked Washington's advice on how to prepare for the likely onslaught. Reading between the lines, Lincoln appeared to be seeking Washington's assent to abandon the city in order to save his army, as Washington had done in New York in 1776. Disquietingly, Washington never responded, though he told others that Lincoln would be "putting too much to the hazard" should he attempt to defend the city.[5]

As Clinton's intentions became more apparent, additional reinforcements were dispatched to Lincoln, some by Congress, some by Washington. But Washington never gave the slightest thought to taking his army southward to join in the defense of Charleston. His outlook had not changed since his close call at Brandywine. He would take his army into the field only if he possessed "certain assurances that an adequate [French] naval force will be ready to cooperate with us through all contingencies." When that moment arrived, Washington said, it would be to pursue "an offensive and decisive campaign."[6]

The British armada that sailed for Charleston late in December included 14 warships and 90 transports tightly packed with 8,700 men and hundreds of horses. Clinton believed he was launching what could be the action that would thwart the colonists' bid for independence. "This is the most important hour Britain ever knew. If we lose it, we shall never see such another," he declared in the last days before sailing.[7] He had seized the moment.

Clinton anticipated a voyage of 10 days. Instead, one savage storm after another kept the fleet at sea for more than five weeks. Several ships were lost to the swirling ocean, including those carrying the army's siege guns, much of the baggage, 223 cavalry mounts, and countless draft horses. The British were eventually able to secure replacements for some lost items from their armies in Florida and the Caribbean, and by plundering horses from Carolina residents. During the investment of Charleston, Clinton utilized the heavy artillery from the warships to supplant his missing siege guns. In 1776, Clinton and Admiral Peter Parker had sailed directly to Charleston Harbor. This time, Clinton landed well south of the city and undertook an unsettling overland advance—much of it through marshlands infested with alligators and poisonous snakes—that finally culminated in late March.

By the time the storm-tossed British fleet rendezvoused off the Georgia coast early in February, Lincoln knew that his hunch that the British were coming had been correct. By then, or shortly thereafter, he had decided to defend Charleston, a decision based on numerous calculations, many of which proved to be inaccurate. Militiamen by the thousands had turned out to oppose the threats to Boston, New York City, Albany, and Philadelphia. Lincoln presumed that southern militia would respond similarly. He was wrong. Charleston's units took the field, but residents in the backcountry, long exploited by tidewater planters and urban merchants—and more recently discriminated against in the state's newly drafted constitution—did not rush to arms to save the eastern elite. Lincoln also believed that desperation would drive South Carolina's officials to offer freedom to slaves in return for their military service. Wrong again. Economic interests and racism trumped the military emergency and quest for independence. Lincoln's decision to defend Charleston also stemmed from the counsel of Commodore Abraham Whipple, who commanded six Continental navy frigates sent south by Congress. Whipple assured Lincoln that he could construct a chain of obstructions at the entrance to the harbor that would make any Royal Navy vessel a sitting duck in the face of barrages by his frigates and shore batteries. Whipple misjudged the complexities of his task. The obstructions were not completed when the British warships sailed into Charleston Harbor.[8]

Above all else, Lincoln's decision to defend Charleston issued from his belief, not unlike Clinton's, that the loss of the city would be a crumpling blow to America's cause. He had spelled out the dangers to Congress two months before Clinton sailed. The fall of Charleston would imperil the insurgency throughout the lower South and enable the British to funnel crucial supplies to its forces in the

Caribbean. Such a turn of events would threaten French interests in the West Indies, possibly leading to losses that could erode France's will to remain at war. Lincoln knew, as did everyone else, that the loss of three southern states would be pernicious for an independent United States, as it would be "encircled by land and cooped by sea" by Great Britain. One additional factor weighed heavily on Lincoln. Governor John Rutledge demanded that he defend the city, telling him that "nothing but an invincible and extreme necessity" could justify a withdrawal from Charleston, and "such [a] necessity will never exist." Lincoln had to presume that should he not defend Charleston, South Carolina would drop out of the war, a step Rutledge had threatened a year earlier. Lincoln was encumbered with the realization that jettisoning Charleston was fraught with an unbearably heavy price, including the possibility that it might cost America its independence. Washington had dodged fights and was seen as a hero for having done so. But only Washington, it seemed, could do so and not pay a severe penalty.[9]

Given Washington's inability to successfully defend New York and Philadelphia against powerful British armies, Lincoln had to know that to succeed in repulsing the enemy was the longest of long shots. But he was not without strength. What was left of his Continental army after Savannah had been reinforced, with the last of the additional troops—regulars sent from Virginia—arriving early in April. Militiamen furnished by North Carolina and Virginia had also joined Lincoln, bringing his manpower total to 5,660, roughly two-thirds the number that Clinton possessed. Lincoln also knew how well numerically inferior but entrenched troops had performed at Bunker Hill and more recently in Savannah. His army was ensconced behind fortifications that included stone walls, redans, redoubts, deep ditches secured by abatis, a man-made canal, and numerous concealed deep holes called "wolf traps," a network of barriers that Clinton soon described as "by no means contemptible."[10]

Clinton immediately opted to besiege the city. Sieges were commonplace in Europe's wars, and Clinton proceeded with a by-the-book operation. Bombardment of the city commenced on April 6, and two days later British warships, commanded by Vice Admiral Marriot Arbuthnot, entered Charleston Harbor. The British also quickly sealed all exits from the city, something Clinton without success had urged Howe to do on Manhattan Island in 1776. Not long passed before it was clear that Lincoln's army could not escape.

All the while, the city's residents faced the unsparing British cannonade. The death toll mounted, homes and businesses were damaged and destroyed, the streets were littered with debris, food grew progressively scarce, the quality of drinking water declined, and looting increased. Clinton offered surrender terms five days into the siege and again two weeks later. Lincoln, not easily chastened, rejected both offers, prompting Clinton to label his adversaries "Blockheads." On May 10, Clinton learned from Germain that a French fleet with "a very considerable armament"— which he correctly took to mean a French army—had sailed for America from Brest. Knowing that he must wrap up the operation quickly and return to New York, Clinton took to pounding the city with "hot shot." With fires raging across the town, Lincoln capitulated five weeks after the siege began and a month after Governor Rutledge had fled the city. Some 225 rebel soldiers had been killed and wounded in the siege and 5,000 were taken captive.[11]

Clinton, with an eye on the impending trial of pacifying the backcountry, had offered Lincoln lenient terms. The 2,200 captured Continentals were to remain in captivity until exchanged. Lincoln was set free by promising not to soldier again until he could be swapped for a captive British officer. All militiamen could return home on parole, which barred them from ever again soldiering for the rebels. The British had won an enormous victory, one that nearly made up for the extent of the British defeat at Saratoga three years earlier. In addition to the capture of the large rebel army, the British seized nearly 400 artillery pieces, 6,000 muskets, three Continental frigates, and huge quantities of rum and rice. They also now possessed the two key southern ports, Savannah and Charleston. As it turned out, none of the captive Continentals would soldier again in this war, as all spent the duration of the war, or what was left of their lives, confined in loathsome prison ships that were death traps.[12]

Clinton bubbled with joy, telling a friend that he had "conquered the two Carolinas in Charleston."[13] He had successfully unleashed Germain's southern strategy and in 18 months taken the two cities the American secretary had wanted captured. Even more, Clinton had scored a greater victory than either of his predecessors. England was swept with joy at word of Charleston's fall. A friend at home notified Clinton that he was "the most *popular* man in England." Church bells pealed in London and across the countryside, and newspapers proclaimed the fall of Charleston a triumph of the "utmost importance." Some publications predicted the surrender of the huge rebel army would produce negotiations leading to reconciliation. Rebel hopes for independence had "evaporated," according to one paper, and other journals spoke of "approaching peace." Germain, expecting "the recovery of the southern provinces" in the coming months, advised the House of Commons that the majority of southerners were "ready and desirous to return to their allegiance." Buoyed by Clinton's conquest and disclosures that Washington's army was dwindling, Lord North dissolved Parliament and ordered autumn elections, the first since the eve of hostilities. North's majority held its own. The ministry that had taken Britain into the war would continue to oversee the war. Some went so far as to say that General Clinton had enabled Britain to remain at war.[14]

When George III opened the newly elected Parliament, he spoke with exultation about the war in America, a subject he had ignored in opening the previous year's session. He lauded the "conduct and courage . . . the valour and intrepidity" of the officers and men at Charleston, adding that their victory would be consequential in "bringing the war to a happy conclusion" and lead to "safe and honourable terms of peace." Several members of both houses followed with praise for Clinton's "gallant conduct." Many were confident that as Britain had destroyed the rebel army at Charleston and had not "suffered any signal defeat" in the three years since Saratoga, peace on satisfactory terms was imminent. Foes of the war were not silent. Charles James Fox and others observed that throughout the war all British victories had been depicted as "forerunners of greater ones." Instead, "every gleam of success had been the certain forerunner of misfortune." Fox urged the recall of all British troops in America so that Britain could center its focus on France. In the last war "France was conquered in Germany," he said, adding he was certain that "if ever America was to be conquered, it must be in France." Fox's comrades continued to characterize the American war as built on a "rotten foundation" and "fatal in it consequences to this country." But North's ministry held a two-to-one margin. The American war would go on.[15]

NOW THAT CHARLESTON HAD been taken, Clinton was anxious to get back to New York, but he lingered for a month that was filled with crucial occurrences, some that would have an enduring and consequential legacy for the British. From the first, Clinton had been skeptical of Germain's claim that vast numbers of southern Loyalists would fight for their king. In no time, however, 3,600 back-country residents and nearly 1,900 in Charleston "offered their services to His Britannic Majesty," and several distinguished South Carolinians who had supported the insurgency petitioned for reinstatement of their British citizenship. As never before, Clinton now believed that with a strong Loyalist arm, he could crush the rebellion in three southern provinces.[16]

In the meantime, Clinton tended to some immediate military matters. He dispatched units to secure the periphery of Charleston, assuring that no Continental force could besiege the city as Washington had been able to do in Boston at the outset of hostilities. Aware that some 380 Virginia Continentals had arrived after the city was sealed off and were now on their way home, Clinton also sent cavalry troopers under Colonel Banastre Tarleton to find them. Tarleton hailed from a comfortable and distinguished background in Liverpool—his father had been its mayor—and he had briefly studied at Oxford with an eye on a legal career. But he was addicted to gambling and suffered heavy losses, whereupon he purchased a commission in the Dragoon Guards in 1775 and arrived in America the following year. He rose rapidly. By 1778 he was a lieutenant colonel in command of one of two Loyalist regiments created that year. His was the British Legion, a mixture of cavalry and infantry, and his soldiers were almost entirely Loyalists from the mid-Atlantic provinces. They sported green tunics with black cuffs and collars, and the officers wore red cloaks trimmed with gold lace. Tarleton and his men performed ably at Charleston, though there were reports that some British Legion troops had committed atrocities in an attack on a rebel camp.[17]

In late May, following Clinton's orders, Tarleton with 270 troopers set off on a hell-bent-for-leather pursuit of the Virginia Continentals under Colonel Abraham Buford. He caught up with them on May 29 in the Waxhaws near the North Carolina border. When Buford refused to surrender and formed a defensive line, Tarleton ordered a cavalry charge. Buford's men had no chance of winning. Tarleton's horses covered the 300 yards that separated the two forces before the rebel soldiers could get off more than one shot. The Virginians were overwhelmed. What followed made Tarleton's reputation as a pitiless butcher. The Continentals screamed, "Quarter! Quarter!"—the universal military signal for surrender and mercy. Whether Tarleton lost control of his men or they followed his orders, there was no mercy on this blood-soaked battlefield. In what Tarleton himself subsequently characterized as a "slaughter," 113 rebels were killed and 150 wounded. Abominations are not uncommon in war. Not all are even remembered. But what occurred in the Waxhaws was not forgotten. It was seared into the minds of southern rebels as a "massacre" perpetrated by "Bloody Tarleton." Henceforth, Tarleton was seen in the South as a monster and the events of that day in the Waxhaws tainted the reputation of the British army in the South.[18]

While Tarleton was in the field, Clinton issued an injudicious proclamation that would haunt the British army in South Carolina. Hoping to identify friends and foes, he stipulated that all who did not take an oath of loyalty to the Crown would be seen as rebels. Many pardoned militiamen had hoped to put the war behind them and live peacefully as neutrals, but Clinton had scrapped the neutrality option. Men had to choose sides. Remaining neutral was one thing. Proclaiming loyalty to the king was a step few would take. Many saw his act as a disavowal of the recent surrender terms, and thereafter many were persuaded that the word of British officials was not to be trusted.[19]

Prior to sailing back to New York, Clinton gave Cornwallis responsibility for suppressing the insurgencies in South Carolina and Georgia. His was a reluctant decision, but one that he felt could not be avoided, as Cornwallis was his second-in-command and a man with the backing of powerful political allies in England. Clinton's renewed misgivings about Cornwallis were of recent origin. For months after the earl's return from London the previous summer, the two men's relationship had been good, as Cornwallis had promised it would be. But a potential derailment of their rapport lingered. A year earlier Clinton had asked to be relieved of his command. If it was granted, Cornwallis would be his successor. Cornwallis may have been aware of that before he departed London, and it may have prompted his decision to return to America, as he had gone home insisting that he was finished with the American war. Following his return, Cornwallis served loyally under Clinton, who consulted him on all substantive matters regarding the Charleston campaign. However, after word arrived from Germain that the king refused to recall Clinton, the grievously disappointed Cornwallis declined to any longer give advice to his commanding officer. "I do not think his conduct has been military," Clinton subsequently remarked in a striking understatement, and thereafter he questioned Cornwallis's character, probity, and judgment.[20]

Clinton left Cornwallis with 1,706 men in Georgia and 6,753 in South Carolina. He never imagined those would be all the soldiery available to Cornwallis. Buoyed by the early Loyalist response, Clinton anticipated that thousands more would enlist in provincial regiments or serve in a newly created and robust Loyalist militia. He left Cornwallis with detailed orders. He was to defend Charleston, pacify the interior of Georgia and South Carolina, and seek to recover North Carolina, although the "security" of South Carolina was to be his paramount responsibility.[21]

Despite some bumps along the way, things went well for Cornwallis into early autumn. He rapidly established and occupied a number of interior bases in an arc from about 50 miles above Charleston to Camden in the Waxhaws in the north, on to the town of Ninety-Six on the northwest frontier, and finally to Augusta on the Savannah River, South Carolina's western border. Camden was the anchor, strategically situated to serve as the shield against the flow of enemy supplies or the approach of another rebel force sent as the successor to Lincoln's lost army. Regular infantry, including provincial regiments, and Loyalist militia were posted in these bases. Britain's basic plan was that regulars would clear areas of insurgents, after which Loyalist militia units would police and secure the reclaimed areas, keeping open the lines of communication between the posts.[22]

Before departing, Clinton had put tireless and charismatic Major Patrick Ferguson in charge of recruiting Loyalist militiamen. Ferguson, the officer at Brandywine who had declined to squeeze off an easy shot at a rebel officer that might have been George Washington, set to work with his customary zeal. By mid-August he had filled seven militia battalions with more than 4,000 recruits. His rapid success led Ferguson to conclude that most South Carolinians were "disgusted" with the insurgency, a view more or less echoed by Lieutenant Colonel Nisbet Balfour, who commanded on the northwest frontier and for weeks had encountered no resistance. Other commanders along the frontier also reported that the rebels thought "the game [is] up" and "seem desirous to return their allegiance" to the Crown. Six weeks after Charleston's fall, Cornwallis reached the same conclusion. He wrote to Clinton that there was "an end to all resistance."[23]

The optimism radiated by Britain's officers was premature. Cornwallis's first hint of trouble came from brooding reports filed later in the summer by his field commanders. They grimly divulged that the frontier was no longer "in any sort of settled state." More worrisomely, they advised that partisan bands were forming under the leadership of rebels who were "wonderfully and successfully . . . stirring up the people." These bands had begun to strike British patrols and supply trains. Particularly dire news arrived early in July. A British Legion detachment commanded by Captain Christian Huck, a Philadelphia lawyer before hostilities, had been sent for the second time to scour communities known to be rebel strongholds in the Catawba River Valley. He had wielded a heavy hand on his initial foray, torching property, destroying an iron furnace, and carrying off 90 slaves owned by rebels. He was no less harsh the second time around, sacking residences, leaving farm families with only the clothes they were wearing and "not meal enough to make . . . a hoecake." Residents united and went after Huck. There were about 120 men under Huck, nearly half of whom were Tories from northern states who had signed on to fight for the king; the band of insurgents consisted of around 350 men. Concealed in a peach orchard, they emerged to strike Huck's unsuspecting force on July 11. In a one-hour engagement, the rebels killed Huck and largely wiped out the Loyalist force. Cornwallis responded, "Affairs . . . do not look so peaceable as they did." Two weeks later he expressed concern that the partisan attacks would "shake the confidence of our friends in this province."[24]

Cornwallis had good reason to worry about what he called the "violent rebels" that were surfacing in the field. Many Charlestonians may have welcomed peace at any price, but that was not true of most backcountry residents. Their zeal for American independence was undiminished and they now looked on Great Britain as a foreign country. Some saw the American Revolution as the best hope for realizing substantive social, economic, and political change and breaking the Tidewater's stranglehold on political power, and Baptists and Scotch-Irish Presbyterians longed to escape the reach of the Anglican Church. Some less idealistic insurgents saw hostilities as an opportunity to attain Loyalist properties, including slaves. Some of the "common people hate us in their hearts," concluded the Earl of Carlisle in 1778 on landing in Philadelphia with Lord North's peace plan. Cornwallis and his officers were reaching a similar conclusion about the South Carolinians in 1780. Some residents had been ready to accept South Carolina's return to the royal fold in the wake of Charleston's fall, but their will to resist had been rekindled when the British occupiers confiscated their farm produce, declaring it to be "legitimate prizes of war," seized personal possessions, and committed atrocities, including rapes, murders, and vicious floggings.

The plundering by British regulars had turned many inhabitants of New Jersey from Loyalists to rebels in 1776, and before the summer ended many South Carolinians who had been ready to return to the fold in the spring had transitioned to the rebel cause. Aware of the harm that Britain had suffered in New Jersey a couple of years earlier, Cornwallis worked diligently to prevent its repeat, but controlling every soldier throughout the backcountry was beyond his reach. Cornwallis's regulars were not solely responsible for provoking wrath among civilians. Despite Clinton's orders to his officers to "pay particular attention to restrain the [Loyalist] militia from offering violence to innocent and inoffensive people, and by all means in your power protect the aged, the infirm, the women and children from insult and outrage," Cornwallis and Ferguson were often unable to control their Tory allies. Bent on retribution after years of oppression, Loyalist militiamen wreaked terror through wanton behavior. By July, the counterblast that Cornwallis had feared was gathering momentum. Innumerable civilians were coming to feel like the Georgetown planter who at first had accepted the return of royal rule but was made a convert to resistance by the "horrors" visited on him and his neighbors by those who took up arms for the king.[25]

Partisan bands sprang up, confronting British forces in the field and the government at home with something with which it had little experience—counterinsurgency warfare. The largest guerrilla force was led by Thomas Sumter, known "the Carolina Gamecock" and referred to by Cornwallis as "an active and daring man." A 46-year-old wealthy planter and former soldier, Sumter had not served in the defense of Charleston and may have been ready to put the war behind him when the British Legion visited his plantation. They humiliated his wife, looted at will, and burned his house, foolhardy acts that "roused the spirit of the lion," as some put it. Sumter rode to Salisbury, North Carolina, where the remnants of the Continental army in the southern theater were headquartered, and volunteered to wage guerrilla war. He was given $19,000 to get started. His original band of warriors consisted of a few veterans who had served under him previously and 200 Catawba Indians, but given his personal magnetism and the swelling fury aroused by the provocative conduct of the British, his force grew rapidly. Within six weeks he commanded 1,000 men eager to serve and fight to prevent the reestablishment of British control. Colonel Francis Marion, a wealthy planter and former Continental army officer who had fought in earlier engagements in this war, also turned to guerrilla warfare. Dubbed the "Swamp Fox," Marion was a "hard visaged" man, lean and with boundless energy, though his knees and ankles were so badly deformed he walked with a limp that at first glance shrouded his soldierly qualities. Marion's first action came about a month after Sumter's, and then and later his primary focus was on the low country around the Santee and Pee Dee Rivers. Andrew Pickens was another major partisan leader. Born to Scotch-Irish parents, he had moved to South Carolina from Pennsylvania when he was a child. He had soldiered in Indian wars, served as a justice of the peace, and fought as a militiaman in numerous actions in Georgia and South Carolina in this war. He accepted parole after the fall of Charleston, but joined the rebels following a Loyalist raid on his property.[26]

The partisans had no intention of fighting their enemies in formal set-piece battles. They were mostly mounted warriors given to hit-and-run tactics, emerging from sanctuaries to launch surprise strikes followed by hurried retreats to their havens. Sometimes they took up positions in the deep shadows of thickly wooded areas and awaited the opportunity to ambush an approaching British unit. Before the summer ended, the attrition rate in Cornwallis's army had begun to approach serious levels, but that was not the partisans' sole impact on the enemy force. Their unrelenting threat forced the British to commit troops to a steadily wider area in order to safeguard their supply lines, dispersions that only enhanced the vulnerability of larger numbers of their soldiery. Guerrilla warfare is calculated on gaining victory through attrition and terror, and before long the partisans terrorized the isolated farmsteads of those who had volunteered for Loyalist militia duty. Partisans looted, torched, scourged, and sometimes killed those who had consented to fight for their king. The Tory zest for militia service began to shrink.[27]

Cornwallis continued his efforts at restraining the malicious behavior of his troops, but he also felt that Clinton had been too lenient toward those who had defended Charleston, and he vowed not to make the same mistake. He ordered retribution, including "exemplary punishment" imposed with the "greatest rigour" against known insurrectionaries. He put his mounted troops into the field and did not look too closely when they sowed terror matching that of the partisans. Like Cornwallis, Tarleton and other cavalry leaders turned their heads when Loyalist militia accompanying them exacted pitiless retributive justice on suspected supporters of the Revolution. By midsummer a ghastly civil war was raging in the South. South Carolinians fought South Carolinians, perpetrating "horrid outrages" and displaying "more Savage [behavior] than the Indians," in the estimation of a British officer, and fighting "with as much relentless fury as beasts of prey," according to a rebel officer.[28]

As midsummer approached, Cornwallis appeared unflappable. Despite undeniable evidence of hostility to British rule in the backcountry, he insisted, "We have not . . . lost ground" since Charleston's fall. As he wrestled with how to cope with the irregular war all about him, he learned that a new rebel army was forming in North Carolina. Dealing with it was Cornwallis's first order of business.[29]

Congress had wasted little time after the fall of Charleston before forming another army in the southern theater. What had passed as a rebel army since May had been commanded by General Johann Kalb, the Bavarian who had joined the French army, risen rapidly, and in 1767 had been sent to America by Duc de Choiseul to discover whether there was a chance that the colonial unrest might lead to revolution. Ten years later, Kalb volunteered to serve in America and accompanied Lafayette in crossing the Atlantic. Styling himself Baron de Kalb, he had fought at Brandywine and elsewhere, and during the Charleston crisis he was given 1,400 Maryland and Delaware Continentals and ordered south to reinforce Lincoln. Kalb had reached Petersburg, Virginia, when Lincoln surrendered, but he continued on and in May took command of the 2,600 Virginia and North Carolina militiamen camped near Charlotte. A few days thereafter Congress named Horatio Gates, the victor at Saratoga, as Lincoln's successor. It was an easy choice. Gates had gained something of an iconic status after defeating Burgoyne. Besides, since militiamen had flocked to serve under him in New York, many presumed that his presence would similarly rouse southerners to take up arms.[30]

Gates reached his army in North Carolina in July and dubbed it the "Grand Army." There were only 1,500 Continentals and a tiny cavalry force, but there were some militiamen and more were on the way. Gates quickly discovered that his men were on short rations and that he had "a Military Chest, without money" to purchase provisions. He beseeched Abner Nash and Thomas Jefferson, the governors of North Carolina and Virginia, respectively, to send him "Droves of Bullocks" and an assortment of other provisions. By early August axes, tomahawks, and horses had trickled in, as had more militiamen. By then, too, Gates thought he had 7,000 men. It was more likely that he had around 4,000. Gates's focus was centered on the British installation in Camden, commanded by Lord Francis Rawdon. Capturing the outpost and its garrison of British troops would deal the enemy a crumpling blow, offsetting some of the gains made by the enemy during the past 90 days. Gates knew that his army outnumbered Rawdon's, though he was also aware that his counterpart had summoned reinforcements and his numerical superiority might not last forever.

Whereas Gates had responded cautiously when confronted by Burgoyne, his behavior in 1780 was more impulsive. He took the field rapidly after assuming command. He wished to act before Rawdon's reinforcements arrived and, following advice offered by Sumter and the commander of North Carolina's militia, he believed there was no time to waste. However, some of his decisions were questionable. He set off with only 60 dragoons to act as his intelligence arm. Moreover, although a lengthy route through Salisbury and Charlotte that teemed with abundant provisions was available, Gates chose the shortest way, a 15-day, 175-mile trek under the searing August sun through a parched and barren landscape. His already ill-nourished men were dog-tired and famished long before they neared Camden. With a battle on the horizon, some officers feared a mutiny. However, an even greater problem loomed for the Grand Army. Cornwallis, in Charleston, had been alerted that the rebel army was advancing on Camden and he knew that he had to respond. He had planned a late-summer incursion into North Carolina, an undertaking that would be foiled if Camden was lost. Cornwallis set off on August 10 to join with Rawdon and arrived four days later, and four days after Gates reached Rugeley's Mill, less than 20 miles from Camden.

Some rebel officers advised that Gates should fall back to a secure position, reconnoiter the area, and await provisions and reinforcements. Doing so, according to one officer, would give Gates "such a superiority" that he would have "no difficulty in recovering the country as far as Charleston."[31] Gates was not persuaded. Even after discovering on the cusp of the engagement that his superiority in numbers was far from as great as he had thought, Gates brushed aside recommendations to delay an action. Whether it was hubris or a passion to outshine Washington, who had not scored a major victory in four years and never equaled Gates's achievement at Saratoga, he was passionate about fighting.

In the hours before the battle, Gates thought it best to dip into his pantry and give his men a large meal, including a heaping serving of molasses for dessert. Providing a sumptuous dinner was a mistake. It triggered gastrointestinal disorders throughout the ranks. Instead of "enlivening our spirits," it "served to purge us as well as if we had taken jallop."[32] The already debilitated men were further weakened. Nevertheless, the sick and enervated men were on the move that night, shuffling in the inky darkness across the flat terrain to get into position for a set-piece battle on an open plain. Gates had slightly over 3,000 men, Cornwallis about 2,300. Roughly half of the Americans were militia. Cornwallis had some of the best regular units in his army, well-trained provincial troops, and Loyalist militiamen.

Gates had made some mistakes during the past two weeks, and on August 16 he erred again in assembling his Grand Army for the impending battle. He positioned his force so that his militiamen would face British regulars and his Continentals, under Kalb, would take on a mixture of provincial troops and militiamen.[33]

Few in the rebel army had ever experienced combat, and in short order the Virginia militiamen buckled in the face of the fierce-looking, bayonet-wielding British regulars and the appearance of Tarleton's cavalry. The panic-stricken "broken Troops . . . ran like a Torrent and bore all before them," Gates said later. The North Carolinian militiamen next "broke & dispers'd." As the militiamen "left the field helter-skelter," Gates's left wing vanished, enabling Cornwallis's collective force to focus on Kalb's Continentals. The American regulars fought valiantly, but they now were outnumbered and soon were routed. Kalb was killed. His aide said the general "was pierced with eight wounds of bayonets and three musket balls" mostly inflicted, the aide hinted, as Kalb sought to surrender following his initial wounding. The survivors fell back, a withdrawal that turned into a rout. Gates courageously rode about the battlefield in a forlorn attempt to restore order, but eventually he, too, fled, unpardonably leaving behind the remnants of his army. More than 40 percent of the American army was lost, either in the battle or when hunted down by Tarleton and his Legionnaires. Along with the manpower losses, Gates's artillery, 130 baggage wagons, and vast numbers of muskets fell into British hands. "Never was there a more compleat victory," crowed one of the Loyalists with Cornwallis, though Gates allowed that he did "not think Ld Cornwallis will be able to reap any advantage of consequence from his Victory."[34]

Cornwallis was not finished. Receiving intelligence about the whereabouts of Sumter's partisans, he sent Tarleton's weary men off to find them. Seventy-two hours after Camden, Tarleton found his quarry at Fishing Creek. The rebels were preparing their evening meal and Sumter was shaving when Tarleton struck. Losing only 16 men, Tarleton killed, wounded, or captured 450 partisans. He liberated the prisoners Sumter had taken and captured the rebels' entire supply train and artillery, as well as 800 horses and 1,000 firearms. Some in the guerrilla band, including Sumter, escaped.[35]

These were just the latest catastrophes to befall the rebels in the South. In the 20 months of Britain's southern strategy, the Americans had lost four armies—two at Savannah, Lincoln's at Charleston, and now Gates's at Camden—some 8,500 men, and an incredible amount of weaponry and provisions.

The news of the rebels' back-to-back disasters at Charleston and Camden was received with jubilation in England. The press howled with delight at word of Gates's contemptible flight all the way back to Charlotte, and many writers observed that Camden yet again demonstrated the superiority of British forces, leaving dangling the implication that had General Howe made greater use of his forces in 1776 in New York and New Jersey, he might have crushed the rebellion. The House of Commons adopted a motion of thanks to Cornwallis and Tarleton, and formally expressed its gratitude to General Clinton. Foes of the war in Parliament supported the motion, thought they continued to label the war "a public calamity."[36]

Britain's summertime victories in South Carolina were not all that was on the minds of officials in London. Troubling problems in Europe also captured their attention. Britain's relationship with the Dutch Republic, long dark and unsettled, reached crisis proportions in 1780. The Dutch Republic was the leading commercial nation in Europe and its most important neutral one. The British and Dutch had been nominal allies since 1678, when the two had agreed to come to the aid of the other if attacked. Although the Dutch were not obligated to assist their ally in its civil war with the colonial rebels, American hostilities strained relations between Britain and the Netherlands. For one thing, London for generations had kept the Scots Brigade, a force of about 2,000 men, in the Netherlands as a deterrent against French aggression, and during Britain's wars in 1715 and 1745 the Dutch, despite their neutrality, had complied with London's requests that the troops be sent to

England. But when Britain in 1775 again asked for these garrison troops, the Dutch agreed on the condition that the troops were to be used only in Europe. After a spell, the British simply dropped the matter. Despite abundant protests and threats, Britain had also endured the readily apparent clandestine trade that the Dutch conducted with American rebels through St. Eustatius. On average, around 120 American vessels had annually filled their cargo holds with war materials sent from Europe (often in Dutch ships) to the Caribbean island. British officials labeled the port a "nest of Spys and Rogues," a cradle "of outlaws" that sustained the colonial insurgency. A British admiral went so far as to declare that St. Eustatius had caused Britain "more harm than all the arms of her most potent enemies."

Tensions between Britain and the Dutch Republic grew to alarming levels once France entered the war. The Dutch insisted on their neutral status, a stance that had served them well during England's wars over the past half century, as it begot a lucrative trade with all belligerents. But Britain, faced now with what it saw as a life-and-death struggle, moved in August 1778 to stamp out all neutral commerce in contraband materials with France and Spain. The rub, of course, lay in the meaning of what constituted a war material. Britain's definition was expansive; the Dutch and other neutral countries saw the issue in far more narrow terms. Britain, for the first time in 1780, conducted armed searches of Dutch vessels on the high seas and dragged some to prize courts, though it stopped short of declaring war when it found evidence that the Dutch were trading in contraband items with the Bourbons. London preferred Dutch neutrality, such as it was, to Dutch belligerency, as the Hollanders not only had a long naval tradition but also possessed Europe's fourth-largest navy, a fleet that included 15 ships of the line. Dutch provocations only grew. They continued to refuse to assist the British war effort, provided refuge to a squadron commanded by John Paul Jones, formed armed convoys to protect its merchant fleet, and carried crucial naval stores, including timber and masts, to France and Spain. The latter particularly vexed the British, who feared that Bourbon naval strength might be their undoing.

The tipping point in Britain's troubled relationship with the Dutch Republic came that spring when Empress Catherine II of Russia issued the Declaration of Neutral Rights and invited commercial states to make "common cause" in the League of Armed Neutrality under Russian leadership. Fashioned to protect the "legitimate commerce" of what they regarded as non-contraband cargoes of neutral countries from interference by belligerents, the members of the League embraced the doctrine that "free ships make free goods." European maritime nations had long acquired masts, yards (a spar on a mast from which sails are set), planking, cordage, and pitch from the Baltic. Much of the traffic in these naval stores was conducted by Baltic countries, especially Denmark and Sweden, but merchants from the Dutch Republic were also heavily involved in transporting these commodities from Russian waters. Many cargoes wound up in French ports and eventually became parts of French warships. Once France entered the war, Britain declared that Baltic naval stores were contraband, announced a blockade of French ports, and ordered the Royal Navy to capture or destroy all French ships it came across. As all vessels bound for France with "Naval or Warlike Stores" in their cargo holds were liable for seizure, Russia and the Baltic countries faced egregious commercial losses. These provocations first led Catherine to close the White Sea to all commerce raiders and contemplate establishing an armed convoy system. She eventually glimpsed a solution through the League of Armed Neutrality.

Denmark and Sweden quickly joined the League and ultimately Prussia, Austria, Portugal, and Naples joined as well. The Dutch Republic sent an envoy to St. Petersburg for discussions. Foreign minister Vergennes, whose need for naval supplies was considerable, looked favorably on the League and encouraged the Dutch to join, as their inclusion could only help the French and harm the British. The League indeed posed a huge risk to British security and its wartime strategy. London responded by seeking to keep the Dutch Republic, Europe's most important neutral shipper, from gaining the protection of the League. Britain stepped up its harrying of Dutch trade. Later, following the capture of an American vessel carrying documents that revealed an extraordinary level of Dutch intrigue with American rebels, Britain proclaimed Dutch actions the "equivalent to actual aggression," but stopped short of declaring war. Its threat fell on deaf ears. The Dutch feared a British attack and were especially anxious about the safety of their colonial possessions, but their gainful wartime commerce eclipsed all else. In December, the Dutch joined the League of Armed Neutrality. Britain declared war, citing the republic's trade with France and America through St. Eustatius. Lord North characterized the war as unavoidable given that the republic's actions would "assist the House of Bourbon in an unjust war against Great Britain," possibly tipping the balance in this to Britain's enemies. War soon proved to be disastrous for the Dutch, who immediately lost St. Eustatius and much more. Had Britain taken this step five years earlier, it might also have spelled disaster for the American insurgency, but it now would have little impact on the rebels unless this stalemated conflict continued indefinitely.

It soon was evident that London had exaggerated the threat posed by the League. Many captains of Russia's Baltic fleet were British citizens, and they informed the empress that they would no longer continue to serve should Russia and Britain go to war. Furthermore, Denmark and Sweden opted for peace by negotiating pacts with Russia and Britain that renounced foreign trade in contraband. London had dodged what the First Lord of the Admiralty branded as a threat replete with "fatal consequences."[37]

WELL BEFORE CAMDEN, CORNWALLIS'S thinking about the problem on his hands had crystallized. Aware by midsummer that he faced serious troubles, he gradually concluded that a new approach was necessary. After some eight weeks in the field in South Carolina's backcountry he decided that he must take the war into North Carolina. Clinton had authorized such a step if necessary to pacify South Carolina, Cornwallis's "principal and indispensable" task. Cornwallis had come to think that going into North Carolina was unavoidable. "[I]f we do not attack that province, we must give up both South Carolina and Georgia," he told Clinton 10 days before Camden. Cornwallis, like Germain, thought North Carolina teemed with a "very considerable amount" of Loyalists who would fight for their king. After Camden, Cornwallis was even more confident that the Tories would take up arms. Crucially, too, he believed the partisans were sustained by arms and munitions that mostly entered the country through New England ports and thereafter flowed southward to Virginia, from there to Charlotte, and eventually into Georgia and South Carolina. Cornwallis in large measure saw a foray into North Carolina as necessary to interdict and shut down rebel supply routes. Before departing, he asked Clinton to send a diversionary force into Virginia. It would keep Virginia's militia at home and out of his hair.[38]

The British army in Camden could not move immediately. Men and horses were frayed by their exertions in the implacable southern heat and humidity, the 800 prisoners taken at Camden had to be transported elsewhere, and Cornwallis awaited supplies and reinforcements. Illness was rampant in his army. Tarleton, among others, was "dangerously ill" with yellow fever. Unavoidably, 30 days passed after Camden before the British moved out for North Carolina, a march that would take Cornwallis deeper into the forbidding American backcountry.[39]

Cornwallis, with some 1,800 men, was headed for Charlotte, a town that was intersected by the main road from Virginia to South Carolina. After closing the supply artery to rebel traffic and securing the area, Cornwallis planned to seek out and destroy the remnants of Gates's forlorn army. Meanwhile, Major Ferguson, the exemplary recruiter, was dispatched with 350 men into western North Carolina to recruit the Loyalists thought to be waiting for the British with open arms. Cornwallis knew the dangers that lurked in the backcountry and the risk of dividing his force. But he felt that Ferguson would make fast work of his assignment. Once he was reunited with Ferguson and had accomplished all that needed tending in central North Carolina, Cornwallis, with a force that had grown to formidable proportions, would march to eastern North Carolina. There he would link up with both the diversionary force that he had asked Clinton to dispatch and vast numbers of Scottish Highlander Loyalists thought to be living near the Cape Fear River. In a few weeks, North Carolina would be in British hands and the insurgency in Georgia and South Carolina would be doomed.

The British reached Charlotte late in September and were astonished by what they found. The region abounded with rebels. A veteran of campaigns in four provinces, Cornwallis thought the area was "the most rebellious" he had encountered, more so even than South Carolina. Tarleton, now recovered from his illness, concurred. The Charlotte area, he said, was "more hostile to England" than anyplace in America where he had soldiered. The country was "so disaffected" that the army's communications with units back in South Carolina were jeopardized. It was enough to make Cornwallis worry that Ferguson might get "into a scrape."[40]

Cornwallis's apprehension was not misplaced, although Ferguson's mission got off on the right foot. As usual wearing a bright plaid hunting shirt over his red British uniform, Ferguson again demonstrated his ability as a recruiter. He issued flamboyant proclamations that called on Loyalists to demonstrate that they were "real men" who would no longer tolerate being "pissed" on by rebel "mongrels" drawn from the very "dregs of mankind. . . . [G]rasp your arms in a moment and run to camp," he appealed. Loyalists poured into his camp, rugged frontiersmen whom Ferguson thought were perfect candidates for engaging rebel militiamen. Within a few days, he had rounded up more than 900 battle-hungry Loyalists.[41]

Some British officers had expressed misgivings about Ferguson's command capabilities, doubts that Cornwallis did not share. He would have been wise to listen more closely. Ferguson, an unquenchable egotist enraptured with his renewed success in procuring recruits, soon committed a string of egregious errors. He disregarded intelligence about the size of the rebel force that was gathering against him and fatally delayed his march to rejoin the main army. He did not start eastward until ordered to do so by Cornwallis in early October. By that time, patriot bands totaling around 900 men had coalesced in his neighborhood. The rebel soldiery included militiamen, known as "over mountain men" from what would become Tennessee, and tough-as-nails southerners who grabbed their weapons—often more accurate long rifles rather than muskets—and set off to repel the British invaders before they committed "cool and deliberate murder and other enormities alike atrocious." Discovering that there were too many rebels to muscle his way through, Ferguson opted to assume a defensive posture atop King's Mountain until relief arrived from Cornwallis. The so-called mountain was in reality a hill about as tall as a six-story building and some 20 miles west of Cornwallis's army. Ferguson thought he could hold out until the arrival of reinforcements. It was one more fatal mistake, for he misjudged the speed with which his adversary could climb the steep hill and the proficiency of his untrained men. Furthermore, in his over-the-top starry-eyed manner, Ferguson threw up no fortifications during the couple of days while he awaited the rebel attack. For the next-to-last time he had made the wrong decision.[42]

Ferguson appears to have anticipated another Bunker Hill, only this time the rebels ascending the hill would be the ones who were decimated. It did not play out that way. The two forces were nearly equal in size, and with the exception of Ferguson, all who saw combat at King's Mountain were Americans. It rained throughout the morning of October 8, but when it cleared the rebels began their ascent up the craggy hill flush with trees and boulders, nudged forward by a leader's injunction to "shout like hell and fight like devils." Ferguson's pickets opened fire, the start of a 65-minute battle, and moments later Ferguson ordered a bayonet charge, a tactic that forced a brief retreat in some sections. Soon the rebel advance resumed. Men fired, took momentary refuge while reloading, fired and reloaded again, then resumed climbing and darting upward toward "another place where we could stoop & be safe until we reloaded." One recalled that he had "stood behind one tree, and fired until the bark was nearly all knocked off." Some men coming up the slope were hit. Nearly all were "shaved . . . pretty close" by Tory fire, as one put it.

Ferguson's men may have gotten off three shots a minute, but they were firing downhill, which bollixed their accuracy. They could not stop their adversary's inexorable advance. The dust-caked rebels kept coming from every side and reached the summit of King's Mountain at different times, where they discovered that Ferguson had dug no entrenchments. His men were behind rocks or wagons that had been assembled as bulwarks. But with an enemy pouring fire at them from every angle, the

Loyalists were in a hopeless predicament. They soon threw down their weapons, begged for quarter, and waved white flags, which one attacker later unconvincingly claimed was a signal the rebels did not understand. A bloodbath ensued. A great many Loyalists were killed in cold blood by embittered rebels bent on exacting revenge for what had befallen Buford's force in the Waxhaws five months earlier. They went about their grim retribution shouting, "Tarleton's Quarter." Ferguson could have surrendered and might someday have been exchanged. Instead, he mounted his horse and sought to escape. It was his final mistake. He was gunned down, riddled with nine bullets. Thereafter, several rebels urinated on his lifeless body.[43]

Ninety rebels were casualties, while 1,019 men in Ferguson's army were killed, wounded, or captured.[44] King's Mountain was a greater blow to the British than Camden had been to the rebels, as thereafter a great many Loyalists—most, in fact—were no longer willing to take up arms. King's Mountain pulled the rug from the very undergirding of the southern strategy.

The incursion into North Carolina a shambles, the disconsolate Cornwallis retreated to South Carolina. He knew the Loyalists were "so dispirited" that they could no longer be relied on. Clinton, who learned of King's Mountain in November, understood at once that the debacle was as great as or greater than the British setbacks at Bunker Hill and Trenton. In private, he raged at Cornwallis's capital mistakes of first having divided his army and later having abandoned the Loyalists he had drawn to his side in Charlotte, twin blunders that likely "threw away forever" the Loyalists' trust in the British army. Gates had been correct after all. Cornwallis had not gained much by his victory at Camden. Clinton knew that, too, and he also recognized that a new master plan was necessary if the southern strategy was to have any chance of success.[45]

CHAPTER 12

THE WAR'S OUTCOME HANGS IN THE BALANCE

GEORGE WASHINGTON RADIATED AUTHORITY and such Olympian detachment that he struck some as unapproachable. A young French officer, who was more than slightly accustomed to haughty aristocrats, described Washington as "noble and majestic," and "very cold," adding that he exuded "the air of a hero" while remaining "polite and civil." What surprised him most about Washington was that an "air of sadness pervades his countenance."[1] Most of the Continental officers who were regularly in his presence looked on him as worthy of the highest respect, and some were beguiled by his personal magnetism, but none thought they were his friend, which was exactly the way Washington wanted it. His officers strived to be seen as trustworthy, loyal, and subservient. That was not the scene at headquarters in Morristown on May 10, 1780, when Marquis de Lafayette, back from France after a two-year absence, was shown into Washington's presence. Lafayette hugged the commander in chief and likely kissed him as well. If so, Washington was more embarrassed than angered. He was delighted that Lafayette was back and anxious to learn what news he brought from France.

Washington had known since the previous autumn that France might send another fleet and, for the first time, an army to North America. Lafayette reported that six ships of the line and an army of 10,000 under Comte de Rochambeau were on their way and should arrive in June. In fact, seven ships of the line and 10 smaller vessels of war were at that moment crossing the Atlantic, but they were carrying only 5,500 troops. The French had committed to sending an army of 8,000, but numerous problems had arisen at Brest, necessitating the decision to send the remaining soldiers at a later date. Nor had the Expédition Particulière gotten away on time. It was weeks late in sailing, having weighed anchor only eight days before Lafayette met with Washington. Lafayette also divulged that General Rochambeau had been directed to "take orders from" Washington, who was "to decide which operations will be most useful." Chevalier de Ternay, the naval commander, was to "support with all his power" whatever plan of action was chosen. Washington could not have been more delighted. France was providing the resources he had repeatedly said he needed for taking the field in quest of the long-sought decisive victory.[2]

While still in Charleston, Sir Henry Clinton had learned that a French army was coming. In fact, he received the news from Lord Germain on the same day that Washington learned of it from Lafayette. Clinton was back in New York in June before the enemy fleet arrived, and he hoped the Royal Navy—recently augmented when the Admiralty dispatched Rear Admiral Thomas Graves with six ships of the line to join Vice Admiral Arbuthnot—could find Ternay's fleet before it reached the American coast. If the navy succeeded, its considerable numerical superiority would give it the means of shattering the enemy navy and army before it landed. Inflicting such a momentous blow would probably force France to abandon the war. Clinton's hopes died after two cruisers caught sight of the French fleet off the Delaware Capes, then lost it. Ternay's squadron reached Newport safely on July 10.[3]

Clinton had a plan ready in the event that the enemy succeeded in landing at Newport. While the Royal Navy destroyed its adversary, the British army would decimate Rochambeau's force. But his plan hinged on acting before the French could construct adequate defenses and a week passed after the allied army came ashore before the news of Rochambeau's landfall reached New York. What is more, the British had no idea how many troops Rochambeau commanded. Nevertheless, Clinton and Arbuthnot pushed ahead, though their operations proceeded exasperatingly slowly. The navy had to reconnoiter to learn the size of the enemy fleet and the disposition of the French army. Contrary winds brought on further delays, as did the navy's need to take on fresh water for crewmen before it sailed. Meanwhile, Washington did what he could to throw Clinton off stride. He posted a furtive notice in newspapers that the Continental army was preparing to attack New York City while much of the British army was tied down by going after the French. Washington was not bluffing. He brought his army northward from New Jersey and ordered his forces in the Hudson Highlands, including West Point, to prepare to march south to Manhattan. Ultimately, Clinton scrapped the proposed attack on Newport, less from fear of Washington's possible assault than because once the French landed, 17 days elapsed before Arbuthnot's squadron could sail and still more time would have passed before the British could launch an attack.[4]

Sometimes taking a great risk pays dividends, as Washington demonstrated at Trenton. Sometimes, as Admiral d'Estaing discovered in attacking Savannah, taking a great risk is to court an unforgiving failure. In July 1780 Clinton shunned a chancy onslaught against the French at Newport. It will never be known how an attack would have played out, though Clinton likely made the proper choice, as Rochambeau and one of his aides-de-camp said his fortifications were adequate within 12 days of landing. Another of Rochambeau's aides said that the French army was safe six days after landing, which was before Clinton learned that the enemy had arrived.[5]

Rochambeau was a veteran French officer. Now 55 and seven years older than Washington, Rochambeau hailed from an aristocratic background and had embarked on a military career in adolescence, seeing action in two wars before America's Revolutionary War. Following the Seven Years' War, he had been appointed inspector general of infantry, a post that brought him close to Duc de Choiseul, at the time the minister of war, and facilitated his rise within France's army. He was to have played a key role in the invasion of England in 1779. That fizzled, but in 1780, his 37th year of soldiering, Rochambeau—stocky, ruddy-faced, tight-lipped, a bit aloof, a stern disciplinarian who habitually radiated an air of self-assurance—was commander of the French army in America.[6]

Following the arrival of the French forces in Newport, Washington, through Lafayette, whom Rochambeau had designated as a go-between, presented the French commander with his plan for operations in 1780. Washington urged a joint attack on British-held New York once Ternay established "a decisive Naval superiority" in the harbor and rivers around Manhattan Island. Thereafter, Washington's forces would invade Manhattan from Morrisania to the north and Staten Island on the southwest side while the French captured the enemy posts on Long Island. The campaign would conclude with a joint operation to take New York City. Rochambeau was to receive his orders from Washington, but he was not ready to act that summer. His army was at work on the fortifications in Newport, and a great many of his men were ill following their Atlantic crossing. Besides, he saw flaws in Washington's plan that would easily result in disaster, though he only told the American commander that he wished to delay acting until the remainder of his troops, additional weaponry, and more ships of war arrived. He left some other things unsaid, including that he had not been impressed with the American troops he had seen on Rhode Island and was skeptical of Washington's claim that he could field an army of 35,000 Continentals and militiamen. Furthermore, Rochambeau knew that Lafayette was eager to open the New York campaign, leading him to suspect that the young officer had embellished his reports concerning the size and efficacy of Washington's army. Before any decision was made, Rochambeau wanted to meet with Washington. When he learned in August that the remainder of his army was bottled up in Brest by the Royal Navy, a turn of events that made any campaigning on his part unlikely in 1780, Rochambeau thought it imperative that the two commanders confer. A meeting was scheduled for Hartford in September.[7]

While Washington awaited the meeting, his spirits sank. Weary and disheartened, he told Congress that conditions in the South were "exceedingly disordered and their resources so much exhausted" that he wondered if those states were capable of continuing the struggle. Britain also had problems, he acknowledged, but it was still able to muster "resources as extra ordinary as unexpected." Conditions in Europe were favorable, but the "caprice of a single Minister" could in a flash change everything to the detriment of the American cause. He wondered how much longer America could continue to fight and how much longer France could remain at war. His hopes for a decisive stroke in 1780 had been dashed. The only thing that was clear was that there would not be "a speedy end to the War," and that reality caused him "extreme disquietude."[8]

THINKING THE ALLIES MIGHT strike New York during the summer, Clinton prepared for the attack that never came, while he and Arbuthnot planned the foray against the French in Rhode Island that never happened. While readying to act, Clinton was absorbed with another matter. More than a year before he had learned that an undisclosed high-ranking rebel official wished to repudiate the Revolutionary cause and defect to the British. Months passed before Clinton learned that General Benedict Arnold was the Judas. Clinton and Arnold communicated through intermediaries for several more months. Clinton had to be sure that this was not some deceitful rebel enterprise, the terms of Arnold's payoff had to be worked out, and Arnold had to be in a position to offer the British something of consequence. All the ingredients came together that summer.

Wounded at Bemis Heights in October 1777, Arnold faced a long, slow recovery. When his leg wound would not heal, he underwent surgery in March 1778. Still hobbling three months later, Arnold was named by Washington as the military commander of Philadelphia when the British abandoned the city. In the words of historian Stephen Brumwell, Washington had given Arnold "a poisoned chalice." Some thought Arnold's governance was heavy-handed, others were angered by his lavish lifestyle, and some suspected that not all of his speculative moneymaking schemes were on the up-and-up. Arnold's warm relationship with the wealthiest Philadelphians also aroused resentment, as did what some saw as his indulgence of suspected Loyalists. His April 1779 marriage to Peggy Shippen, a young woman whose parents were thought by many to be Tories, was bitterly resented. It was in this combustible environment that Pennsylvania's Supreme Executive Council brought eight charges of malfeasance against Arnold, essentially for profiteering and using public property for private purposes. Congress and the civil authorities agreed that Arnold should be court-martialed on four of the charges, and in December 1779 he was convicted on two minor counts. Washington reprimanded Arnold, but in a tempered manner, thinking it would have an emollient effect. Washington may or may not have believed that Arnold's conviction was justified, but above all he thought him an extraordinary officer and wanted him in the army. Arnold, however, remained a stew of anger and resentment over his prosecution. With greater justification, Arnold felt that Congress had not properly rewarded his meritorious military service. During 1779, acting anonymously, he made contact with British officials to learn what they might put on the table.

While Arnold's clandestine talks with the British spun out, Washington on more than one occasion offered him a field command. Arnold always responded that his gimpy leg prevented him from accepting such an assignment, and much of the time that was true. By the summer of 1780 he was likely capable of once again serving in the field, but instead he angled to become the commander in the Hudson Highlands. In July, he got what he wanted. His jurisdiction encompassed all the rebel posts in that region, including West Point. With this momentous prize under his thumb, Arnold's talks with the British—conducted through Colonel John André, Clinton's trusted aide—grew more serious. The terms were worked out over a period of weeks. Arnold would turn over plans of West Point, weaken its defenses, and surrender the installation when a British force sailed up the Hudson. In return, he was to receive £10,000, a £500 annuity, and a command position in the British army. Arnold's gnawing bitterness was a crucial factor in his decision to turn coat, but the tipping point may have been opportunism. His fateful final decision came in the immediate aftermath of Britain's crucial victories at Charleston and Camden. Arnold appears to have been betting on what he saw as the war's likely winner.[9]

Arnold and Rhode Island converged on Clinton in September. As Clinton prepared for the assault on West Point, Admiral Sir George Rodney arrived without notice in New York with a squadron of 10 ships of the line. Suddenly, the Royal Navy had a huge numerical superiority over the French fleet in Newport; the Continental army was scattered, with its main force in New Jersey, far from Rhode Island, and it was unlikely that a significant rebel militia force could be raised in time to aid Rochambeau's army.[10] All the advantages that a commander could wish for were in place for an attack on the French garrison, though going into battle with the upper hand does not guarantee success, as a veteran soldier like Clinton knew full well. He had to choose between a strike against the French and the wager negotiated with Arnold. Each would mesh with Germain's orders in 1778 to actively seek to confine Washington's troops in the northern theater so that pacification could proceed in the South. Each would also be a supreme gamble. Success in either case would be so colossal that America's bid for independence would be foiled. A huge victory in Rhode Island might knock France out of the war and, devoid of an ally, the Americans could not continue to fight. The capture of West Point would give Britain its long-sought control of the Hudson River, a turn of events that could knock New England out of the war, crippling America's ability to continue the fight. There was no assurance of success with either option, but if Arnold did his part, taking control of the Hudson might be the most likely of the two choices to succeed. Clinton chose the seemingly glittering opportunities offered by going for West Point and the Hudson.

The timing for an operation to take West Point could not have been better. Washington was away from his army—in Hartford for the meeting with Rochambeau that had been arranged weeks earlier. The two commanders met six days after Rodney's fleet reached New York. They had no more than sat down when Rochambeau told Washington that a joint campaign in 1780 was off the table. With that out of the way, the two agreed to do nothing until French naval superiority was guaranteed, but once that occurred, retaking New York through a siege operation would be their focal point. The French were impressed with Washington, finding him stately and prudent. All in all, both sides were satisfied with the meeting's outcome.[11]

Washington set off from Hartford for West Point, which he had not inspected in 10 months. Unbeknownst to him, British troops were already on transports for their voyage up the Hudson. All that remained before they weighed anchor was a final meeting between André and Arnold to wrap up details of the pending operation. The two met on September 21. Thirty-six hours later, Washington began his ride for West Point. Washington did not find Arnold at the installation when he arrived. André had been captured by rebel militiamen shortly after meeting with Arnold. When Arnold received the news, he bolted for the safety of a British sloop on the Hudson, making his getaway just prior to Washington's arrival. When Washington perused the papers that had been in André's possession, he knew instantly what Arnold had planned. Washington was shaken to the core and filled with murderous rage. He wanted to capture Arnold. When that failed, he wanted him killed. He did have André and offered Clinton a swap—André for Arnold. Clinton refused. After a brief trial the Americans executed André.[12] Clinton grieved for his young aide and likely lamented having chosen the gamble for West Point over assailing the French in Rhode Island.

DAYS AFTER LEARNING OF Ferguson's fate at King's Mountain—which had occurred just days after Arnold's betrayal was discovered—Cornwallis ordered a withdrawal from North Carolina to Winnsboro, west of Camden, a relatively secure area of South Carolina where food was plentiful. His plan was to rest his men, many of whom had been struck by the petulant fevers that stalked the South, as well as to reinforce his army, lay in provisions, and dispatch Tarleton to search for partisan bands. Aside from Cornwallis's loathing of fighting "a defensive war on this frontier," his future campaign plans remain unclear, as during the retreat he, too, was laid low by "a severe fever" that sent him to bed for nearly a month. His most significant step during that period was to order Major General Alexander Leslie, who commanded the diversionary force of 2,200 men that Cornwallis had asked Clinton to send to Virginia, to bring his army southward and join him. Even in early December, when he at last wrote to Clinton about King's Mountain, Cornwallis remained unsure "whether my campaign was [to be] offensive or defensive."[13]

Meanwhile, Clinton, who had often demonstrated his ability as a strategist, had been jostled by King's Mountain to rethink how to cope with the challenges facing Britain's southern strategy. He ultimately decided to commit an army to Virginia and task it with stanching the flow of supplies to the Carolinas, destroying rebel storage depots, obstructing the Old Dominion's trade with the outside world, conducting morale-shattering raids against enticing targets, and establishing a base on the Chesapeake that would do double duty by serving as a sanctuary for Loyalists who assisted the British and through which the army could be provisioned. Meanwhile, Cornwallis's role remained unchanged. He was to crush the insurgency in South Carolina. Clinton felt that Cornwallis's mission would be made immeasurably easier if the passage of arms and munitions to the lower South could be terminated. Putting an army in Virginia would also assist Cornwallis if the step compelled Governor Jefferson to keep his militia at home to guard against the internal threat. Clinton put his plan into operation in December, selecting his new brigadier general, Benedict Arnold, to command a force of 1,800 men. Arnold was to establish a base at Portsmouth on the Elizabeth River, construct craft for the forthcoming raids, and recruit Loyalists. Every operation was attended with risks, but the mission that Arnold was given was singularly filled with dark menace. Should the French establish even a temporary command of the Chesapeake while a rebel army gathered to press him, Arnold and his diminutive force would be in a world of trouble.[14]

Congress was also busy making changes. In the wake of the disaster at Camden, Congress, in October, replaced General Gates with Nathanael Greene, who would command yet another army that was to be put together in the Southern Department. Before acting, Congress asked Washington to name Gates's successor. Washington had previously refrained from such matters, looking on it as a political hornet's nest. Not this time. The stakes were too high. A new year was approaching and nearly everyone on both sides thought that 1781 would be the last year of fighting in North America. Not only was it unlikely that the rebellion could be sustained beyond another 12 months, but also discomfiting rumors swirled that French staying power was waning. Washington was among those who felt that this was the last year during which the Allies would have a shot at achieving the elusive decisive victory. If such a victory was not secured, the war likely would end in a negotiated settlement in which American independence might or might not be recognized. Those who negotiated the settlement would additionally determine whether Britain or the United States—if there was a United States—possessed Georgia and the Carolinas. Washington wanted a dependable commander in the South and felt that Greene was his best general.

Greene, now 38 years old, huddled with Washington for five days. Thereafter, he met with Congress and several state officials, and there can be no question that he requested help of every conceivable kind. As Greene rode south in November 1780, he was aware of some troubling realities: He would be taking command of an army that "exists more in name than substance"; virtually all of his logistical support would have to come from the northern states; he would have little money at his disposal; and aside from the shattered remnants of Gates's army, his soldiery would consist of whatever militiamen the southern states provided. However, while begging for help in Philadelphia, he had wrangled additional cavalry under Colonel Henry Lee and he knew that Daniel Morgan—who had been sidelined for some time with health issues and caustic anger over having been passed over for promotion— was coming out of retirement and would be joining him. He also brought along Colonel Thaddeus Kosciuszko, the French-trained military engineer who had served in America since 1776 and whose expertise would prove invaluable. Nevertheless, Greene was hardly optimistic. He was certain that he faced "a dull prospect" and that "the American cause is at deaths door."[15]

Cornwallis learned of Greene's appointment early in December. He knew at once that the existence of a rebel army would bolster southern insurgents and undermine Loyalist spirits, and he quickly resolved to make another incursion into North Carolina to "drive back the enemy's army." Meanwhile, Greene slowly prepared for what was coming, gathering information, locating boats for river crossings and transporting necessities, procuring supplies, building and filling magazines, sizing up his officers, and meeting with partisan leaders, including Francis Marion and Thomas Sumter. Throughout December thousands of muskets and bayonets poured in, as did much-needed wagons and horses. All the while, Greene wrestled with his strategic choices. He could withdraw northward with his 2,000 men when Cornwallis came after him, lengthening his enemy's supply line and luring him ever deeper into the hinterland. He could enter South Carolina and fight time and again, hoping to wear down his adversary, though such an option was fraught with grave risks and logistical nightmares. At length, Greene chose neither option. He opted for an unconventional strategy, one that Clinton, the superb strategist, viewed as remarkably unwise. Greene would divide his army, taking half of it into southeastern South Carolina. He would place the remaining 940 men under Morgan and send them into western North Carolina. If Cornwallis with his entire army came after Greene, Morgan would attack Britain's vulnerable frontier outposts in South Carolina. If Cornwallis's army went after Morgan, Greene would assail the enemy's exposed posts above Charleston.

Greene did not appear to foresee what Cornwallis chose to do. Despite the disaster he had recently suffered at King's Mountain after dividing his army,

Cornwallis yet again divided his forces, a risk he need not have taken. Choosing to focus on Morgan, who posed the greatest threat to key British posts, Cornwallis sent Colonel Tarleton ahead with 1,200 men and orders to "push [Morgan] to the utmost" and bring him to battle if possible. Cornwallis doubted that Morgan would fight. It was more likely, he thought, that the rebel general would retreat eastward in hopes of rendezvousing with Greene. Shortly after Tarleton took the field, moving west in search of his prey, Cornwallis with the remainder of his army advanced northward from Winnsboro in the general direction of King's Mountain. When Morgan came east, as the British commander anticipated, Cornwallis would trap him between the many rivers that flowed through the region and the two British forces, which together would total roughly 3,200 troops.[16]

Things did not go as Cornwallis had planned. Morgan retreated northward, though he wished to fight, and as he withdrew he searched for a good site to square off against Tarleton. He found it at a place called Cowpens, a mostly flat meadow, though the terrain rose and formed a low ridge in the north. Unlike at Camden, there were no woods on its peripheries to provide a refuge for panicked soldiers. Morgan's men would have to stand and fight.

Nearly every general officer in the Continental army hailed from either a privileged or somewhat affluent background. Not Daniel Morgan. The son of ordinary farmers who had crossed to America from Wales, Morgan moved to the frontier when he came of age and worked as a teamster and manual laborer. While a wagoner for the British army during the Seven Years' War, he struck a redcoat officer in a fit of rage. Morgan was subjected to a brutal flogging that left him with an unrelenting hatred of the British army and its officers. After the war, he farmed and married—a common-law marriage—and sometimes fought Indians. When the Revolutionary War erupted, he signed on in a light infantry company and earned laurels for his service in the invasion of Canada in 1775 and in the two battles against Burgoyne in 1777. Morgan was large and rugged, and so alike most militiamen and Continental soldiers that they willingly followed him. Fear of Tarleton had grown to epidemic proportions among rebel soldiers following the Waxhaws massacre, but many of the men at Cowpens so believed in Morgan that they were willing to take on the British Legion.

Tarleton was a brave and daring soldier, but he lacked command experience in contesting a formidable and well-led enemy in a set-piece encounter. At Cowpens, he faced a foe that conceived an ideal, if unorthodox, battle plan. Morgan placed militia riflemen in his forward units, militia infantrymen in the next line, and

Continental infantry in his third line. Behind them, hidden by the ridge at the north end of the field, was the cavalry. Morgan instructed his men to "squinney well" when taking aim and, if possible, to first gun down the British officers. On the raw morning of January 17, Tarleton's men advanced on their foe in the day's bright early sunlight. They suffered losses at the hands of Morgan's forward riflemen. Next, they ran into three rounds of deadly fire laid down by militiamen. But the British kept coming. After several minutes of engagement, the battle could have gone either way. When the Continentals fell back to protect their flank, the British thought it portended a panicky flight, as at Camden, so they rushed forward and darted into hell. The Continentals resumed firing, and the militiamen got off a deadly enfiladed salvo into the ranks of Tarleton's men. It was at this moment that Morgan unleashed his hidden cavalry, which quickly gained the upper hand against their stunned adversary. Derisively shouting "Tarleton's Quarter," the Americans showed little mercy. The bloody showdown was over in 40 minutes. Tarleton and a few of his men escaped, but 900 of his troops had been killed, wounded, or captured, and he lost a treasure trove of arms, specie, and horses. It was, as Morgan later said, "a devil of a whipping."[17]

Cornwallis had lost 2,000 men in 90 days, but he still possessed a force that was nearly twice the size of Morgan's, which he hoped to catch before it could cross the Catawba River and eventually reunite with Greene. Cornwallis might have succeeded had he possessed decent intelligence. As it was, he did not know Morgan's whereabouts until it was too late. Morgan crossed the Catawba on January 25, when Cornwallis was miles away. But Cornwallis, a fighter through and through, spurned another retreat. He thought he still might catch Morgan, who yet faced a long march to link up with Greene. Furthermore, given that Morgan was encumbered with hundreds of prisoners and every river was swollen and possibly could not be crossed due to a deluge of recent rains, Cornwallis thought he might yet overtake his adversary. He was aware that he would face "infinite danger" in pursuing his foe through the unwelcoming backcountry. But Cornwallis, still hopeful that Loyalists remained committed to the cause, was convinced that the British mission in the South would face "certain ruin" if he did not give chase. He stripped his army of every superfluous item, including his own baggage, so that it could move speedily.

If Morgan had rivers to cross, so did Cornwallis. He could not even try to cross the swollen Catawba until February 1, a week after Morgan had traversed the river in the boats that Greene had earlier collected. Morgan was well on his way to rendezvousing with Greene's army while Cornwallis waited day after day to cross the swiftly flowing river. When the opportunity arrived, his crossing was slow and hazardous. The river was bitterly cold and swirling, and North Carolina militiamen on the other side laid down a heavy fire against the British. Some men were lost to drowning and gunfire. Cornwallis was fortunate to survive. His horse was shot in midstream, though it somehow managed to reach the other shore.[18]

For the next two weeks Cornwallis tracked the rebels. Greene, who had linked up with Morgan and taken command of the rebel force, stayed a few miles ahead of his pursuer. Meanwhile, Cornwallis's men experienced a grueling ordeal that their commander characterized as "every species of hardship and fatigue." They subsisted mostly on turnips and corn, and had no tents for shelter on cold winter nights. Day after wearying day they trekked eight to 10 miles. Some possessed threadbare shoes. Some men plowed on in their bare feet, though February's daytime high temperatures in this part of North Carolina were lucky to top 50 degrees. Much of the time every man was wet and shivering. Twenty-eight days after the brawl at Cowpens, Greene's weary, ragged men reached Virginia, and safety, a few hours ahead of their pursuers.[19]

Cornwallis rested his debilitated army at Hillsborough and awaited much-needed Loyalist volunteers. The field army he had possessed in January had shrunk as a result of Cowpens and the hardships endured while pursuing Greene. Barely more than 2,000 of the regulars with him were now fit for duty. Cornwallis's wait for Loyalists was futile. King's Mountain had been transformative, as Clinton had foreseen, and so too was Cowpens. What little fervor remained among the Tories vanished entirely in the wake of a late-February surprise attack by Colonel Henry Lee's cavalry against a 400-man Loyalist troop of horse soldiers under Colonel John Pyle, a physician who in peacetime had practiced nearby. The result was a massacre every bit as gruesome as anything Tarleton was thought to have perpetrated. One hundred Tories were killed and nearly every survivor was wounded.[20]

Cornwallis might have retreated to South Carolina, but he wanted a shot at Greene, who he thought would retake the field when reinforced. Whether or not Cornwallis realized it, he was experiencing a situation eerily akin to that which had confronted General Burgoyne four years earlier in the New York backcountry. Burgoyne had lost 15 percent of his army at Bennington, while Cowpens had cost Cornwallis an even greater portion of his; neither general garnered the expected assistance from the Loyalists; and both generals suffered substantial attrition due the rigors of long, arduous campaigns, while their adversary relentlessly gathered more and more militiamen. Nevertheless, Cornwallis stayed on, awaiting Greene's return. His hunch that Greene would take the field again was correct. As the rebel force gradually swelled, Greene dropped back into North Carolina, though, unlike hasty Horatio Gates, he patiently avoided battle until more reinforcements arrived. When his army reached about 4,200, Greene was ready to fight. So, too, was Cornwallis. Although outnumbered by a two-to-one margin, Cornwallis was confident that his regulars could best a larger rebel army composed mostly of militia, and he hoped that Greene, who had little command experience under fire, might err egregiously. For days the two forces circled warily, looking for an opening and a good place to fight. Greene found his spot at Guilford Courthouse, a much larger tract than Cowpens. Some of it was farmland; much of it was heavily wooded, which Greene liked, as it would reduce the enemy's chances of unleashing one of its feared bayonet charges. On March 15, Cornwallis came after the rebel army that he had first begun chasing some seven weeks earlier.

Greene deployed his force somewhat as Morgan had done at Cowpens. He placed raw North Carolina militiamen behind a flimsy split-rail fence in the front line. Virginia militiamen were posted 300 yards farther back in the woods. Greene's regulars were 500 yards behind them. Early on that mild afternoon, Cornwallis's regulars set off after them. What Colonel Lee called the "day of blood" was at hand, and the men on both sides who knew what was coming were touched by frissons of fear. Greene hoped his militiamen would perform as well as those at Cowpens, but when the British returned the fire of the North Carolinians and prepared for a bayonet charge, the terror-stricken militiamen broke for the rear. The Virginians were more resolute. They did not buckle, and neither did the Continentals, who remained in place and fought. Greene's flanks also held firm. Once the fighting moved into the dark and thick forest, linear tactics gave way to a contest between small units commanded by junior officers. At one point, the British left wing crumpled, opening the door to the encirclement of Cornwallis's army. Greene failed to take advantage of it. Later, when faced with a rebel cavalry action that might have been a fatal blow for his army, Cornwallis ordered his artillery to break it up by firing grapeshot into a knot of soldiers that included some of his own men. Such is war. Cornwallis's steely act killed some of his own men, but may have saved the day for his army. Two hours into the engagement, pressed by an enemy counterattack, Greene withdrew and the Battle of Guilford Courthouse sputtered to a close.[21]

The British owned the battlefield following the fighting, the sort of thing that leads generals to claim victory, which Cornwallis did. But his supposed triumph came at heavy price. Although Greene lost 300 men and all of his artillery, Cornwallis's losses stood at 532, fully 25 percent of those who fought that day. Greene's strategy of dividing his army in January, an unconventional move thought by many to have been ill conceived, had paid off. It was Cornwallis's response of also dividing his army that turned out to have been ill judged.

Cornwallis was suffering an unsustainable rate of attrition. He had lost more than 300 men at Camden in August, 1,000 at King's Mountain in October, and in excess of 1,500 between January and March. It is estimated that another 1,000 regulars had been lost in small skirmishes and partisan attacks, as well as through desertion and illness. Only an army that is close to total victory can cope with losses of that magnitude. Cornwallis was not close to victory, he could expect no reinforcements from Clinton, and he knew that it was now nearly impossible to find any Loyalists who were willing to serve their king.[22]

A few days after the Battle of Guilford Courthouse, Cornwallis with his remaining 1,723 men set off on a 180-mile trek to Wilmington, North Carolina, where he planned to refit his army and think through his next move. The march was one of the more grim episodes that a British army faced in this war. Many men were sick or wounded, some died along the way, and virtually all were ill clad and undernourished. But they were not harassed by Greene, who had watched helplessly as many of his militiamen departed for home soon after the battle.[23]

GENERAL CLINTON, WHO WAS aware of Cowpens but for weeks knew nothing else of Cornwallis's ventures, at least received welcoming news from Benedict Arnold. His expeditionary force landed under scudding wintry clouds at Portsmouth in the first hours of 1781. The new British general wasted no time before taking the field. Within 48 hours he led 900 infantry and cavalry up the James River with plans to raid Richmond, the state capital. At nearly the same moment in early January that Cornwallis sent Tarleton after Morgan, Arnold and his men entered Richmond unopposed. While Governor Jefferson watched helplessly from a hillock across the river, Arnold's American Legion took seven cannon and spiked 52 others, seized several river craft, pillaged homes, destroyed warehouses and manufacturing facilities, and torched public buildings, while carting away huge stores of grain, powder, rum, and assorted other goods. Some wind-driven fires spread to several residences and a church.[24]

Anticipating more of these "predatory expeditions," Jefferson did what he could to see that Arnold had conducted his last one. He offered a handsome reward for Arnold's capture or murder, a threat that led the new British general to carry two pistols at all times and, according to rumor, sleep with another beneath his pillow. Arnold was perhaps more apprehensive that a French squadron from Rhode Island would enter the Chesapeake and trap him. That was precisely what was on Washington's mind, and in December he approached Rochambeau about sending men and a fleet to Portsmouth. The French commander refused. His orders, he said, were not to divide his army. However, when a February nor'easter severely damaged the Royal Navy's fleet in New York, the French navy acted. Thinking that "a naval operation alone will probably be ineffectual," Washington urged Jefferson to summon more militia to duty and dispatched Lafayette with 1,200 Continentals to Virginia. Lafayette was to join with Steuben's Continentals and Virginia's militiamen and act in concert with the French fleet in destroying Arnold. Should Lafayette capture Arnold, Washington instructed him to "execute [him] in the most summary way," a hanging that would be "as pleasing as it will be useful."[25]

Washington was giddy with hope until he learned that Chevalier Charles Sochet Destouches, the new commander of the French navy in America—Ternay had died of a "putrid fever" in mid-December—had sent only one ship of the line and three frigates under Captain Armand Le Gardeur de Tilly. Predictably, Arnold was left unscathed, though Tilly captured several British vessels, including a frigate, and some 500 marines. Tilly's success convinced Destouches to gather a squadron of 10 warships and 1,120 marines, prompting Rochambeau to suddenly decide to send some of his men as well. Rochambeau may have been moved by a further plea from Washington, who stressed that the destruction of Arnold's army was of "immense importance" to American fortunes in the South. But the undertaking unraveled due to Destouches's decision to take a long, indirect route in hopes that the armada would not be discovered by the British. His plan did not work. Arbuthnot, who learned that the enemy had sailed, was waiting at the entrance to the Chesapeake with 14 Royal Navy warships when Destouches arrived. The British had numbers on their side; the French had the most firepower. On March 16—the day after Guilford Courthouse—the two fleets fought the Battle of Cape Henry. Both sides suffered heavy damage, but both were sufficiently intact for another round on another day. The second engagement never occurred. Destouches, the more cautious of the two naval commanders, returned empty-handed to Newport. In the six months between September and March, Clinton, through the wrong choice, had conceivably missed the chance to inflict a crippling defeat on the French fleet and army in Rhode Island, while the French, in turn, had muffed the possibility of inflicting a crushing blow to the British army in Virginia.[26]

ALTHOUGH WASHINGTON HAD ENDURED many low points, the six months or so from midsummer 1780 to year's end was one of his most despondent periods since the dark days of the New York campaign four years earlier. Charleston was lost, an American army had been annihilated at Camden, and America's new ally would not take the field. That was not all that troubled Washington. Whether Georgia and South Carolina, and possibly North Carolina, could be saved was open to question. The American economy was a shambles. Morale was sagging to the point that Washington privately complained that a potentially fatal "lethargy" had begun to creep into the corners of the country. A South Carolina congressman felt that after Camden the "Spirit to oppose the Enemy" had vanished within his province. Even in lionhearted Massachusetts some officials were heard to say that a peace settlement short of American independence was inevitable.

As Washington looked toward the crucial year of 1781, he saw mostly black clouds. Mutinies had flared in Virginia's militia, uprisings that Jefferson characterized as a "dangerous fire." Intelligence accurately reported that British reinforcements were on the way. They "are probably preparing to push us in our enfeebled state," Washington sighed. The ebullience that Washington had radiated two years earlier on learning of the French alliance was long gone. It had "vanished as the morning dew," he lamented. He and Rochambeau had agreed at Hartford on a joint campaign in 1781, but Washington now feared that America would be unable to continue waging war unless it received "a large and immediate foreign aid of money." He told an acquaintance that "every Idea you can form of our distress will fall short of reality," and to another he confessed that he saw "nothing before us but accumulating distress." Before, Washington had always seemed to think that something—perhaps luck, maybe Providence—would see America through its tribulations. But for the first time in years he acknowledged that he had "almost ceased to hope" that independence could be achieved.[27]

In somewhat similarly menacing circumstances in 1776, Washington had gambled on a risky attack on the Hessians in Trenton. He contemplated something akin to that as 1780 wound down; a surprise attack on the British fortifications on northern Manhattan. If successful, it would jolt the British and likely dissuade

Clinton from committing reinforcements to the southern theater. It would be a risky, even rash, operation for his underequipped army, and in many ways more dangerous than the attack at Trenton. Washington may have contemplated the undertaking from frustration or to prove to Congress and his French ally that he remained the activist general of the war's early years. His official explanation for the proposed action was that he thought it essential to close the "Campaign with some degree of éclat." But another Trenton was not in the cards. This was too big an operation to hide, and the British discovered their adversary's plans. Furthermore, a series of storms caused one delay after another, and the repeated postponements gave Washington time to reconsider. He was not the type to admit a mistake, although in this instance he privately confessed that his "wishes had . . . got the better of my judgment." He scrapped the attack and took his army into winter quarters.[28]

Washington may have thought things could not get much worse, but his problems were alarmingly compounded on January 1, 1781, when soldiers in the Pennsylvania Line mutinied. This was the gravest of grave threats, the peril that Washington feared above all else.

There were plentiful reasons for the soldiers' disaffection. Atop the privations that were their daily lot, the soldiers had not been paid in a year, and some never received the cash bounty that had spurred their enlistment. However, the immediate spark for the rebellion was that men who had enlisted for three years, and whose service was now complete, were told that the terms of their enlistment was for "three years or the duration." General Wayne, who commanded these men, tried to negotiate a settlement. Instead, the soldiers bargained with Pennsylvania's civil authorities, who had money. The terms of settlement were generous. No one would be punished, those who had served three years were given 20 dollars and back pay, and they were permitted the choice of reenlisting or going home. About half reenlisted, either because they thought the army was their home or they were unflinchingly committed to American independence.[29]

Washington feared that the concession to Pennsylvania's mutineers would trigger other insurrections, and another was not long in coming. New Jersey Continentals mutinied before the month ended. This one, Washington decided, must be ruthlessly suppressed, and he dispatched a force of 500 men under General Robert Howe to deal with it. Howe's orders were stark: "you will instantly execute a few of the most active and incendiary leaders." Howe's men, who were not told of the fate that awaited their fellow soldiers, marched for days through heavy snow and brutally cold weather to reach New Jersey. The insurrection was over before they arrived, but Howe intended to follow his orders. Deep in the night, after tattoo and while the unsuspecting soldiers slept, Howe met with their commanders. He ordered them to prepare a list of 15 principal ringleaders and to designate the three most responsible for the uprising. What followed was drumhead justice. There was no court-martial, no hearing, no interrogation. The three doomed men went before a firing squad composed of the other 12 men on the list of culprits. Two men were shot. The third was spared. There were no more mutinies that winter.[30]

But problems facing Washington and the American war effort remained. On January 2, James Lovell, a Massachusetts congressman, notified his friend John Adams, "We are Bankrupt with a mutinous army." Lovell added, "Our Distress for money is extreme. We can pay neither our civil officers, nor our Army, nor our Loan Interest, nor [find the money to] send a Brigade of Waggons" loaded with supplies to the army. A Delaware congressman said that "clothing is our greatest want," but the needed specie to obtain shirts, trousers, and shoes could not be found. The acute crises that ushered in 1781 appeared to be a wake-up call. John Sullivan, now a member of Congress, thought that many who "have for years past been Employed in amassing wealth" were "now Alarmed for the Publick Safety." Thomas Paine campaigned to induce wealthy Philadelphians to create an army relief fund, and his efforts led Esther Reed, the wife of Joseph Reed, Pennsylvania's chief executive, to organize female volunteers in several states to conduct drives to raise money and garner needed items for the soldiers. Her efforts seemed to activate many churches, which joined the crusade. Congress also took action. It appealed to France for a loan of 25 million livres and, rather than entrusting Franklin, voted to send Washington's young aide, Colonel John Laurens, who spoke French, on the mission to beg for money.[31]

Laurens carried with him an appeal from Washington warning that the "patience of the army" was "nearly exhausted" by the "most calamitous distress" brought on by America's inability to supply the soldiery. Furthermore, morale on the home front was waning due to the "heavy burthens" borne by the citizenry. A loan was essential, he went on, so that "allied arms on this Continent" can at last "effectuate . . . the great objects of the alliance; the liberty and independence of these states."[32] Five years almost to the day since Paine's *Common Sense* had hit the streets with its appeal for foreign aid that would enable the insurgents to continue their fight, the American rebels were calling on the French for assistance in order to remain at war.

WASHINGTON HOPED THAT FRANCE would steadfastly stand by the 13 American states in their struggle for independence. America's ally remained committed, though French support was anchored on shakier ground than Washington may have realized. In recent months both France and Spain had explored the means of extricating themselves from a terribly costly war in which they had gained little or nothing. Spain had come to understand that its chances of regaining Gibraltar, the grand prize that once had made its belligerency attractive, might exceed its grasp. Early that year the Royal Navy had cobbled together a squadron of 24 ships of the line under Admiral George Rodney to relieve and reinforce its blockaded 5,000-man garrison on Gibraltar. Although forewarned by France, the Spanish were surprised by Rodney, who not only captured or destroyed seven of Spain's great warships but also succeeded in getting a huge relief convoy to Gibraltar. In a war with few decisive actions, this was one of the most consequential.[33]

The disaster spurred Conde de Floridablanca, Spain's secretary of state, to engage in secret exploratory conversations with Britain, unilateral talks that violated the terms of his Treaty of Aranjuez with France. The discussions were arranged by an Irish priest, Thomas Hussey, the chaplain at Spain's embassy in London, and conducted with Richard Cumberland, a British agent who traveled to Madrid. Floridablanca proposed that should London return Gibraltar to Spain and make peace with France, Madrid would support a truce in the American war on the basis of uti possidetis, a formula under which Britain and America each would retain what it possessed at the moment the truce took effect. Floridablanca made no mention of American independence, and under his proposal, Britain would have kept possession of Canada, a large chunk of Maine, Manhattan, Long Island, and the southern ports of Wilmington, Charleston, and Savannah. Britain might well have also held on to Georgia and South Carolina, while North Carolina likely would have been up for grabs. The negotiations sputtered along throughout 1780 until London, unwilling to hand over Gibraltar, recalled Cumberland.[34]

Floridablanca was not alone in sounding out the British. During 1779 France's director general of finance, Jacques Necker—who was deeply troubled by the American war that was costing 150 million livres annually while each year France ran budget deficits of nearly 50 million livres—appears to have used a friend in Geneva to act as a go-between in pursuit of peace. Necker, through his friend, approached Lord Mountstuart, the well-connected son of a former British prime minister. London, in 1779, was not ready to pursue talks. In 1780 Necker personally established contact with the London banker Thomas Walpole, who was visiting Paris.

Necker probed to see if the influential Briton was a promising channel for opening negotiations, a secret inquiry that ran aground when George III was unwilling to permit Walpole to conduct diplomatic discussions. In the fall Necker turned to Britain's envoy to the court of Savoy, as well as to Nathaniel Parker Forth, formerly the secretary to Britain's ambassador to France and now an agent of sorts that Lord North kept in Paris. North thought the initiative was promising. However, George III, more confident than ever in the wake of Clinton's recent capture of Charleston, once again turned thumbs down on pursuing talks, even though Necker was willing to concede more than Vergennes was believed to be willing to yield. In December, Necker made one final attempt to jump-start talks. He wrote directly to North, a move that went nowhere as Britain's monarch concluded that Necker's diplomatic flailing must be a sign of French desperation, probably brought on by apprehension that Spain was soon going to drop out of the war.[35]

Comte de Vergennes eventually learned of the diplomatic forays by Floridablanca and Necker and found them acutely troubling. The worried foreign minister was cognizant of his ally's myriad problems, as he had been informed by his ambassador to Madrid that Spain, in the grip of a prolonged drought and wartime economic woes, could not remain at war beyond 1781. But when Floridablanca failed to reach an accommodation with London, Vergennes knew that his ally was on board for one final campaign. Vergennes took Necker's warnings of French financial troubles seriously but sought to undermine the finance minister by telling others that in matters of foreign policy he was "shortsighted" and incompetent. London's intransigence spared Vergennes further difficulties with Necker, but in September 1780, about the time of Cornwallis's initial incursion into North Carolina, several members of Louis XVI's Conseil du Roi urged an immediate peace. Vergennes was confronted with a fresh crisis.

The king's counselors, alerted by the warnings of Necker and Anne-Robert-Jacques Turgot, had grown steadily more disheartened by the war's serious impact on French finances, all the more so as the end of hostilities appeared to be nowhere in sight. By the autumn of 1780 they knew that France was shackled with a chronically inactive American commander in chief and a war that many presumed to be hopelessly stalemated. However, the immediate cause of their pleas for peace was a Spanish proposal for a huge joint campaign to capture British-held Jamaica. Concluding that the stalemate could be broken only through taking Jamaica, Madrid tendered the notion of the Bourbon allies sending upwards of 25,000 troops and 50 ships of the line for the operation. It would be a stupendously expensive endeavor, roughly akin to the previous year's attempted invasion of England, and it raised fears in Versailles of plunging France ever deeper toward economic catastrophe. Vergennes was compelled to acknowledge that France's economic situation was "genuinely alarming" and that "peace at the earliest opportunity" was essential, but he was unwilling just yet to admit that the time had come to end hostilities. As Rochambeau's army and the small French fleet had just arrived in Rhode Island, Vergennes hoped that in the autumn, or in 1781, the Franco-American forces could achieve military successes that would lead to satisfactory peace terms, including American independence. Vergennes carried the day. There would be a campaign of 1781. Moreover, he secured Louis XVI's consent to approach Madrid with a compromise proposal: By year's end France would commit 20 ships of the line to the Caribbean and conduct diversionary strikes against Saint Lucia and Saint Christopher while Spain struck Jamaica. Although disgruntled, Floridablanca accepted the French plan.[36]

In December 1780, with it abundantly clear that France had failed to achieve its war aims in the nearly three years since entering hostilities, neutral Russia offered its services as a mediator. London was interested in the Russian proffer, although it insisted that mediation proceed only after the cessation of foreign assistance to the American rebels. For the time being, that rendered mediation dead on arrival. Nevertheless, behind the scenes many British officials were coming to see that mediation leading to peace based on uti possidetis was preferable to continued hostilities and might result in the best possible settlement that Britain could achieve. Lord North's ministry discussed ceding Minorca to Russia as the payoff for the czarina's mediation, but the step was never taken, as George III categorically refused to yield the island.

Austria, which joined the League of Armed Neutrality early in 1781, also offered to serve with Russia as a mediator. The Habsburgs wished to be part of an endeavor that would have international implications. Austrian leadership additionally sought peace in order to further the nation's economic interests. The war had dislocated maritime trade in Tuscany, but more importantly in the Austrian Netherlands (now Belgium). During the war numerous Austrian merchants had become deeply involved in exporting arms and other goods through Ostend, on the North Sea, to the markets in the Caribbean. The war played havoc with the trade of neutral nations, prompting the Austrian emperor to rage at British "despotism at sea." Furthermore, Austrian commercial interests, which had gotten a foot in the door though hostilities, glimpsed the possibilities of lucrative Atlantic trade once peace

was established. Austrian leadership envisaged the belligerents negotiating mediation terms at an international conclave in Vienna, which would be held while the
belligerents observed a one-year armistice. The Austrian solution for the question of
American independence—the thorniest issue of all given the intransigence of France
and Britain—was the partition of America. France would regain Canada, and
Britain would retrieve the Carolinas and Georgia. The sovereign American republic
would lie east of the mountains and stretch from New England through Virginia.

Spain welcomed Russia's offer, but stressed its desire to first regain Gibraltar and
Florida and to secure its Central American interests. Vergennes, too, saw promise in
mediation. He was hopeful that it might either lead London to agree to what in the
view of Versailles would be agreeable peace terms or, in a worst-case scenario,
provide the face-saving means for France to extricate itself from the war. Vergennes
remained committed to gaining American independence and seeking a decisive
victory in 1781, but he was not inflexible. In January 1781, the very month that
Colonel Laurens sailed for France in hope of securing a loan through which the
United States could wage one final campaign, Vergennes privately acknowledged
his willingness to settle the war in America on terms of uti possidetis. Vergennes
thought Britain must relinquish New York, but otherwise it would be left in possession of much of the western territory above the Ohio River, the northern reaches of
Maine and Vermont, Georgia and much or all of South Carolina, and possibly
North Carolina as well. An independent United States would possess the scraps
that were left east of the Appalachians. In a confidential memorandum dated
February 1781, Vergennes granted that the Americans would have "just cause for
complaint." At the same moment, he understood that France could not propose
such a settlement. It could be realized only through the initiative of Europe's would-
be mediators. In May, the Bourbons and London received a formal Austro-Russian
proposal. Vergennes responded that he welcomed their interest in securing peace,
but he first must consult his American ally. In June, he summoned John Adams, the
envoy that Congress in 1779 had designated to conduct peace negotiations should
they someday occur.[37]

Adams had sailed for France 15 months earlier, but in the absence of peace talks
he spent nearly half a year in Paris with little to do. He had gone to the Netherlands
in mid-1780 to seek a loan from the United Provinces, and he was in Amsterdam
when he heard from Vergennes. Adams hurried to Versailles, arriving in July 1781.
Vergennes provided him with the Austro-Russian proposal for an armistice in the
American war during which Britain and "the American Colonies" would negotiate

the "Re-establishment of Peace." Vergennes did not reveal that the Austrian chancellor favored the partition of America, a step that would diminish the size of the independent United States and leave it encircled by major European powers. Adams read the proposal that he had been given and wrote to Congress that same day that he would neither consent to mediation without a prior recognition of American independence nor agree to an armistice under any circumstances. Given America's war weariness, Adams knew that it was unlikely his country could ever resume fighting following a pause in hostilities.[38]

Despite the clarity in his message to Congress, Adams's response to Vergennes was muddled. He first rejected an armistice and demanded British recognition of American independence and the removal of its troops from "every Part of the United States" as a precondition to peace talks. Two days later, in a second answer, Adams dropped his demand for prior recognition of independence, but stuck to his refusal to countenance an armistice and added that he could never accept a peace based on uti possidetis. On "further Reflection," Adams sent a third communiqué to Vergennes. He once again stipulated that Britain's recognition of American independence must precede any peace negotiations. Despite his disordered response, Adams was consistent on two matters. He would not consider an armistice or a territorial settlement based on "the Statu quo."[39]

Adams waited anxiously for word of the next step, but none came from Vergennes. "All was total silence and impenetrable mystery," Adams said of what he called Vergennes's "midnight silence." Adams was certain of one thing: Mediation was more dangerous than the war itself. He had long feared that Vergennes would break faith with the United States if it was in France's interest to do so, and he believed that the moment for "chicaning the United States out of their independence" had arrived. Vergennes did put the interests of France above all else, but what Adams did not know in mid-1781 was that the foreign minister—aware by now of Britain's growing military problems in the South and hopeful of Allied success in the approaching military campaign—was not yet ready to welcome mediation. In August, Vergennes advised Russia and Austria that mediation could go no further due to American objections, which he laid out, incorporating what Adams had said in his final response.[40]

Vergennes felt that mediation at that juncture would foil the aspirations that all along had driven his American policy—the weakening of Great Britain and the gains that France could derive from commerce with an independent United States. That spring, weeks before Adams arrived in Versailles, France had given the United

States £500,000—some as a loan, some as a gift—and huge quantities of arms and munitions. Benjamin Franklin, who together with Colonel Laurens had played a part in obtaining the funds, exulted that French largesse would "put the Army into comfortable & respectable Circumstances. God grant!" Adams, putting aside his mistrust of France, gushed that Louis XVI's assistance "will be a most essential Service to the Common Cause, and will lay a Foundation of Confidence and affection between France and the United States, which may last forever and be worth ten times the Sum of Money."[41]

Nor was Spain ready for mediation. It hoped against hope that Gibraltar and Jamaica might yet be taken, and plans were on the drawing board for a campaign to seize Minorca. Pensacola and East Florida—the prizes that would assure Spanish control of the Gulf—remained in British hands, and Madrid was readying a campaign to reclaim those prizes. Vast numbers of Spanish troops, supported by numerous naval craft, were making headway in Central America in the ongoing struggle to remove the British from Campeche, but more fighting was required if Spain was to retain a region rich in timber and sugar plantations. The Spanish were continuing to fight to deny Britain control of Lakes Nicaragua and Managua, lest the British emerge from the war as an even more powerful rival in the Pacific. Floridablanca, like his counterpart in Versailles, wished to continue the war through 1781. Thereafter, Madrid might be ready to entertain mediation or to sit across the negotiating table from Britain's envoys.[42]

There would be no Congress of Vienna in 1781. Hope of a favorable outcome yet existed in every camp. Washington pinned his dreams on the long-anticipated joint Allied campaign in quest of a decisive victory. Vergennes and Floridablanca wanted the campaign of 1781 to play out before mediation could be considered. Lord North told the Commons that Britain, through its arms, still possessed the means to obtain "a just and honorable peace." General Clinton, convinced that the American rebels could not continue to wage war beyond 1781, thought the outlook for Britain was good so long as it avoided a catastrophic loss in 1781.[43]

CHAPTER 13

ON THE KNIFE'S EDGE

IT WAS 1781, THE seventh year of hostilities. The Franco-American forces urgently needed a decisive victory if they were to secure their war aims, which included American independence, and it likely would be Spain's last chance to vindicate having gone to war. It was a year when Britain had to avoid a humiliating defeat and solidify its hold on South Carolina and Georgia. All was uncertain. The war's outcome hung in the balance deep into the crucial year.

It had been a very long war, dragging on interminably as John Dickinson in July 1776 had warned would be the case should Congress declare American independence. But nearly everyone thought this would be the conflict's final year. It seemed inconceivable that the war-weary, bankrupt American rebels could continue much longer. Pressure was building in France and Spain to achieve victory or make peace. Britain's leaders had been badly shaken by the Gordon Riots, which threatened the survival of the warring faction's majority in Parliament and, with it, the nation's ability to remain at war. Additional riots might occur if the war continued beyond 1781. Many neutral countries in Europe wanted peace, the only true balm for the disruption of their trade by the faraway war. Their recent offer to mediate had failed, but if the war remained stalemated, their next mediation proposal was more likely to be embraced by Europe's belligerents. This war had come to its defining moment.

On the brink of 1781 Sir Henry Clinton had sent Benedict Arnold with an army into Virginia. However, Captain Tilly's abortive attempt to enter the Chesapeake with four French warships and Washington's dispatch of an army to the Old Dominion under Marquis de Lafayette opened Clinton's eyes to the unmistakable danger that Arnold and his small army faced. Holding to his plan to stanch the flow of rebel supplies through Virginia to the Carolinas, Clinton in early March ordered General William Phillips with 2,000 men to reinforce Arnold and take command. Days later, learning that reinforcements were crossing the Atlantic, Clinton rushed more troops to Phillips. By April, a British army of 5,500 regulars was in Virginia. Clinton was confident that it was adequate for interdicting enemy supply lines, destroying rebel supply depots, tying down Virginia's militiamen, and inducing more southern Loyalists to take up arms.

Clinton never imagined that Phillips's entire army would remain in Virginia beyond midsummer. Given Virginia's "universally hostile" attitude toward Great Britain, Clinton knew that he would never possess a sufficient army to establish and "retain a respectable hold" on the extensive and populous province. Phillips's mission had the short-term objective of clearing the way for Cornwallis to succeed in the Carolinas in 1781. Clinton was primarily concerned—"obsessed" might be a better term—with the challenge of meeting what he foresaw as an inevitable Allied attempt to retake New York. He was convinced that the Allies would seek a decisive victory that year through attacking or besieging New York. He felt that Washington was consumed with reclaiming New York, undeniably the greatest prize the Allies could win. Furthermore, Clinton was informed in the spring that a French fleet of 26 sail and perhaps 12,000 troops had departed for the Caribbean. The squadron could be expected to come to North America in late summer or early autumn, and he anticipated that its most likely destination would be New York. Clinton, in April, advised Phillips that he and most of his troops would be summoned to Manhattan sometime that summer. Only a small force would remain in Virginia, just sufficient to defend Britain's Chesapeake toehold and enhance General Cornwallis's efforts to complete the pacification of South Carolina.[1]

Clinton, of course, was beholden to Lord Germain, but at the outset of 1781 the two appeared to be on the same page. Three days into the new year the American secretary made it clear that London was eager to bring the war in America to an end, as Britain could no longer "support a protracted war." He urged Clinton to act aggressively. Germain supported the "expedition into the Chesapeake," adding that every "advantage must therefore be seized, every occasion profited of." Foreseeing a negotiated settlement to this war in the near future, Germain pushed to strengthen Britain's claim to as much territory as possible before diplomats shaped the peace settlement. The British army's presence in Virginia would be helpful on that score. Germain stressed the importance of maintaining the base in Portsmouth, contending that the station would nourish the "flame of loyalty" among Britain's "secret friends." He encapsulated his perspective on strategy at the outset of 1781 with the comment that possession of Portsmouth would also "deter the French from sending any troops there *to make a diversion in favour of Washington.*" The revealing comment disclosed that at this juncture, Germain, like Clinton, anticipated that the Allies were most likely to seek a pivotal victory through a campaign to retake New York.[2]

Germain had much to say during that winter and spring about America's problems. The American secretary's understanding of the capabilities of his American foe was unrealistic, as it was founded primarily on the exaggeratedly rosy appraisals peddled by Loyalists. Germain contended that America's economic woes had left the rebels "so weak" that they could offer "little opposition." In March, he told Clinton that "so very contemptible is the rebel force now *in all parts* and so vast is our superiority *everywhere* that no resistance on their part is to be apprehended that can materially obstruct the progress of the King's arms in the speedy suppression of the rebellion." Germain was 3,000 miles away and out of touch. Portions of his letters during the first 90 days of 1781 were chimerical, which is likely how Clinton construed them in the bitter aftermath of King's Mountain, Cowpens, and Guilford Courthouse.[3]

VERGENNES HAD KNOWN AT least since the late summer of 1780 that the war in America was running on borrowed time. Support for the protracted war had waned among Louis XVI's counselors, and grew more tenuous after Jacques Necker, in one of his final acts as director general of finances, made public the Statement of Accounts to the King that revealed for all to see the troubling details of French revenue and expenditures. French citizens, and those in Britain as well, were now aware of the disconcerting economic troubles that had unsettled many of the king's advisors. Vergennes, and the American cause, weathered the peace storm and, in fact, crucial decisions by the Conseil du Roi soon followed that gave the foreign minister hope for the coming campaign. Although it was decided not to send the promised second division to General Rochambeau, the king had agreed to make the United States a gift of 6 million livres (£500,000) and to send a squadron of 20 ships of the line across the Atlantic. The armada would include more than 3,000 marines, and it was assumed the fleet commander might pick up perhaps 10 or more additional ships in the Caribbean to go with the eight in Newport. Yet Vergennes was nagged with worries. Spain's quest to retake Gibraltar remained unfulfilled, and in April 1781 the Royal Navy for a second time succeeded in getting a relief convoy through the porous Spanish blockade and to Britain's beleaguered garrison. It was especially bad news for Vergennes, who was left with anxious nights, lest his Bourbon ally might now make a separate peace with Britain and leave France and the Americans to fight on alone. Vergennes also anguished that Russian ambitions and the recent death of Austrian empress Maria Theresa might destabilize Europe. Both powers looked covetously on the decaying Ottoman Empire, which France for ages had seen as essential for containing Russia, and Vergennes could not have been more aware of the weak hand he wielded in eastern Europe so long as the American war continued.[4]

At the dawn of 1781 Vergennes was certain that peace negotiations were at most a year away whether or not the Allies won a decisive victory in that year's campaign. Mediation accompanied by negotiations would ensue if the Allies came up short yet again, but if victorious on the battlefield that year, the Allied diplomats would negotiate peace terms with a vanquished foe. Either way, Vergennes longed for Congress to remove the fiercely independent John Adams as America's peace commissioner and replace him with someone more tractable. Vergennes looked on Adams as a nuisance, an uncompromising sort who would balk at any attempt by the French foreign ministry to manage him. For his part, Adams understood that France supported the United States because it was in its interest to do so and, just as assuredly, that the French would pursue their long sought war aims at the peace table, whatever the cost to the United States. Adams intransigently believed the United States must look after its interests in the war and the eventual peace settlement. Vergennes feared that if Adams drew out the eventual peace talks in quest of America's ends, French goals might suffer in the final treaty. The foreign minister would be happy if Congress recalled Adams, placed him under the control of the French diplomat who conducted peace negotiations, or named additional peace commissioners who might be "capable of containing" the New Englander. Vergennes tasked Chevalier La Luzerne—Minister Gérard's successor, who had arrived in Philadelphia the previous September—with the task of handling the problem. Vergennes never specifically ordered his emissary to seek Adams's removal, and La Luzerne—wisely thinking it imprudent to request anything of the sort—never sought Adams's removal.[5]

Following an army career, La Luzerne transferred to the foreign ministry in the 1760s and was appointed ambassador to the Bavarian Court, where he served until the year before he was named minister plenipotentiary to the United States. La Luzerne was corpulent, ruddy-faced, jovial, outgoing, and so ingratiating that one congressman's wife called him "one of the most amiable, politest, easiest behav'd Man I ever knew." He received Vergennes's instructions in May 1781. The foreign minister directed La Luzerne to assure Congress that the issue of American independence was not negotiable and that France would not agree to peace terms that diminished the prewar territory of any of the 13 states. This tallied with the terms of the Treaty of Alliance, though it unquestionably meant that France was not committed to the territorial goals that Congress had outlined in its 1779 peace ultimata, objectives that included extending the boundaries of the United States deep into Canada and to the Mississippi River. Vergennes additionally directed La Luzerne to have Congress instruct its peace envoy or envoys to be subservient to French wishes. While La Luzerne did not ask Congress to recall Adams, he rapidly let Congress know that Vergennes was unhappy with America's peace commissioner, information that Franklin had already provided. The previous summer Franklin had written to Congress that Adams had "much offended" Vergennes by his "improper and unbecoming" tone.[6]

La Luzerne's first task was to reshape Congress's thinking about what it might have to accept during peace negotiations. He secretly hired writers to publish newspaper essays urging that America temper its objectives, extended under-the-table bribes to some congressmen to make them willing accomplices, and in the end cobbled together an obliging bloc of seven states. The two Carolinas, as well as Georgia, Pennsylvania, New Jersey, New Hampshire, and Maryland, either badly needed French military assistance or their war weariness led them to cave in to the demands of their ally. La Luzerne was skilled and aided by the bleak military situation facing the United States. Most congressmen would have concurred with the New Hampshire delegation's description of wartime realities: The United States with a "most feeble" army was faced with an enemy that was "possessed of two States" in the South while "carrying their conquests into others." The United States had not gained a seminal victory in the three years since Saratoga, and during that period it had suffered painful losses at Savannah, Charleston, and Camden. Washington had recently advised Congress that the war effort faced dire challenges. He conceded that continuing the fight rested entirely on French assistance. Carrying on without further "indispensable" French aid was beyond "the natural abilities of this country," the commander advised. By late spring many congressmen believed the country had been "reduced to a weak and Abject State" and had "lost all . . .

Spirit and dignity." They knew that many Americans were "ready to Accept of peace on Any Terms." La Luzerne found some congressmen more than willing to help, either by passing along inside information or by taking positions that the minister recommended. John Sullivan, the former general who now represented New Hampshire, was his chief toady, and La Luzerne privately referred to him as his agent. Working surreptitiously, and in numerous meetings at his home with select congressmen, La Luzerne carried out Vergennes's instructions.

La Luzerne had gotten things moving when Congress, at his entreaty, appointed a committee of five chaired by John Witherspoon—a native of Scotland who became the president of what now is Princeton and later as a congressman signed the Declaration of Independence—to consider alterations to the instructions that had been given to Adams two years earlier. At times, La Luzerne even rewrote committee drafts. While the committee worked on the instructions, Congress took up the matter of Adams as the lone American peace commissioner. To "discharge" him would be "an act of too great obsequiousness" toward France, Witherspoon told Congress, and it responded by creating a five-member commission that included Adams, Franklin, John Jay, Henry Laurens, and Thomas Jefferson (who subsequently declined to serve given his wife's serious illness).

The peace ultimata had consumed Congress for eight months, but writing the new instructions and naming the team of commissioners was completed in about three weeks. With only Massachusetts and Connecticut in opposition, Congress' instructed its envoys "to accede to no Treaty of Peace" which did not secure independence and the "Sovereignty of the thirteen United States." They were to be guided by military "circumstances" and, if necessary, "to accept in due form the Mediation" of Russia and Austria. The envoys were also "at liberty to agree to a truce." These were the very things that Adams at nearly that same moment was telling Vergennes the United States would never consider. In a best-case scenario the commissioners were directed to seek a northern boundary that included much of British Quebec and extended west well above the Great Lakes, a western boundary in the middle of the Mississippi River, and a southern boundary deep into present-day Alabama and Mississippi. However, the new instructions included a virtual suspension of American sovereignty. As Vergennes wished, Congress commanded its diplomats to "undertake nothing in the negotiations for peace or truce without their [France's] knowledge and concurrence; and ultimately to govern yourself by their advice and opinion." The compliant Congress had authorized Vergennes to shape the peace settlement with which the United States must abide. La Luzerne summed up what he had achieved by immediately telling Vergennes that negotiations would be "in the hands of His Majesty except for independence" and the terms of the Treaty of Alliance. Congress meanwhile informed the states that the United States might face the "hard necessity of acceding" to a peace based on uti possidetis. It did not have to mention that such an outcome would leave some of the 13 American provinces, or certain parts of them, within the British Empire. Without mentioning his role in the proceedings, John Sullivan notified Washington that the looming peace settlement might "deprive us of very important parts of the united States."[7]

The instructions had jettisoned neither the goal of independence nor the territorial ambitions that Congress had adopted in 1779. La Luzerne had not resisted Congress's territorial objectives. There was no reason for him to have done so. Vergennes had been given authority to control America's peace commissioners, and besides, if the peace treaty stipulated that each state's territory coincided only with what it possessed when hostilities commenced, that would be in accord with the Treaty of Alliance that Congress had ratified three years earlier.

Not everyone was happy with what Congress had done. John Jay, one of the new peace commissioners, told the legislators that it was "difficult for me to reconcile myself to the idea of sovereign independent States of America submitting" to the dictates of a foreign power. Gouverneur Morris, the former New York congressman, bristled at the "servility" imposed on America's diplomats. Similarly, Joseph Reed, Pennsylvania's chief executive, fumed over Congress having imposed "a State of Dependency" on its diplomats that was "not very compatible with the dignity of a Sovereign Power." Massachusetts's James Lovell said that permitting "our allies to rule the roost" was "ill judged" and a "disgrace." He also revealed to Adams's wife, Abigail, that "old Fkln" had seen to the "stabbing" of her husband. She responded with incandescent rage, calling Franklin "a selfish avaritious designing deceitful Villan." Outwardly, Adams himself remained calm, even telling Franklin that he was "very well" with the addition of others to the peace commission. In reality, it was a crushing blow for Adams, who had hoped through diplomacy to emerge from the war with a reputation as great as Washington's. Adams, disappointed and overwrought, fell ill. An American physician who resided with him spoke of Adams's "inexpressible" anxiety, sudden penchant for isolating himself from others, and tendency to rant and rage against his enemies.[8]

MONTHS BEFORE LA LUZERNE worked his magic in Philadelphia, France and Spain had contemplated their campaign plans for 1781. Spain wanted to attempt another invasion of England. Vergennes wished no part of that. He remained convinced that France's best chance of gaining its ends in this war lay in the North American theater. France did agree to send a formidable naval squadron to the Caribbean and to consult with the Spanish. Should the Spanish remain bent on retaking Jamaica, France would leave roughly 40 percent of its fleet with them when the remainder sailed northward to campaign in concert with the armies of Rochambeau and Washington. The French appeared to be a most benevolent ally, although early in the year Vergennes had learned from his ambassador in Madrid that the Spanish in the Caribbean had been handsomely reinforced from Mexico and Cuba. It was unlikely that Madrid would ask its ally for much help in the West Indies.[9]

The French, in January, were discussing sending the naval squadron when the commander of its West Indian fleet suddenly retired due to health concerns. The naval department quickly chose François Joseph Paul, Comte de Grasse, as his successor and promoted him to rear admiral. De Grasse, who had been a sailor since he was 11, was now 60 and a veteran of three wars. Like Washington, he was exceedingly tall and had little formal education but was cultivated and socially adept. He differed from the American general in that he was a professional military man with an abundance of leadership experience. In February, de Grasse visited Versailles and met with Louis XVI and the queen, Marie Antoinette, who accompanied him on a walk through the palace galleries. Some thought de Grasse intrigued to gain command of the squadron, but others, aware that he was recuperating from a recent illness, believed he did not want the post. Whatever de Grasse's aspirations, the king wanted him. De Grasse was named commander of the fleet that would be an integral part of France's pursuit of a decisive victory in 1781.

De Grasse's instructions were to sail to the Caribbean, but with Spanish approval he was to proceed to North America late in the summer. The instructions said nothing about his destination in North America. Before departing, de Grasse met with Marquis de Castries, the naval secretary, who likely passed along the information La Luzerne had sent regarding the woeful condition of the Continental army. But as he would not sail for North America for another seven or eight months, de Grasse at this juncture had no idea where he might wind up, although he wrote to Rochambeau asking for pilots to guide him to wherever in North America he might go.

He sailed from Brest on the first day of spring with 20 ships of the line, three frigates, and 3,200 marines. His orders were to see to the defense of French interests in the Caribbean and thereafter to sail north and cooperate with Washington and Rochambeau. Before departing, de Grasse wrote to Rochambeau that it "will not be till the 15th of July, at the soonest, that I shall be on the coast of North America." De Grasse's fleet arrived in Martinique in April, taking the British under Admiral Samuel Hood by surprise. A brief clash was sufficient to persuade the outnumbered Hood to sail away to safety. For the first time in the war, France had command of the sea in the West Indies. With numerical superiority, de Grasse quickly sought to take St. Lucia—the colony to which Clinton three years earlier had reluctantly deployed nearly a third of his army—but it was too well defended to be attacked and time did not permit a siege. Instead, de Grasse struck at Tobago, which he took in June. Thereafter, as instructed, he sailed to Cap François in St. Domingo (on the north coast of what now is Haiti) to make contact with his Bourbon ally. In mid-July he met with Francisco de Saavedra, a bright young member of the Council of the Indies who had been sent to work with de Grasse. When the French admiral explained that his squadron was crucial to the looming Allied campaign in North America, Saavedra in essence authorized de Grasse, whose fleet had swelled to 29 ships of the line, to go where he was most needed. However, Saavedra asked de Grasse to return to the West Indies when his business up north was completed. The admiral promised to do so.[10]

ROCHAMBEAU'S ARMY AND CHEVALIER de Ternay's small fleet had arrived in Rhode Island in July 1780 and both were still there a year later. Throughout that time, the French had faced problems, perhaps the greatest of which was that their sailors deserted in such numbers for better-paying jobs in America's merchant marine that the navy was badly undermanned. The army fared better on that score, though Rochambeau faced some disgruntlement within his corps of officers at the army's inactivity. One concern that had tormented Rochambeau before he departed France turned out not to be a problem. Relations between the Yankees and d'Estaing had soured after the abortive Rhode Island campaign in 1778, but Rochambeau faced no major concerns along those lines. The French troops, in fact, appeared to like the Americans, though they were startled at the "happiness of their marriage[s]" and surprised to find that the average Yankee ate cornbread—not bread made from wheat—and instead of wine, drank rum mixed with water. All in all, Rochambeau's greatest worry stemmed from what he learned and saw of America's military capabilities. During his first six months in Rhode Island, news arrived of the fall of Charleston, the debacle at Camden, Arnold's treason, and mutinies in the Continental army. Rochambeau was left with misgivings at America's "untenable military" abilities.[11]

Weeks passed, then months. The cold and wet New England winter of 1781 gradually faded and a less anemic sun signaled that spring had arrived. Yet, aside from the two unsuccessful naval forays in the Chesapeake, the French forces remained inactive throughout their first year in America. During the spring Washington, Rochambeau, and Chevalier Destouches contemplated simultaneous actions involving an American strike against the British at Penobscot in northern Massachusetts (now Maine) and a French raid on bases from which Tory privateers operated at Lloyd's Neck on Long Island Sound. Nothing came of these notions. In May the French considered moving all their forces to the Chesapeake—a notion that La Luzerne was championing—but ultimately scrapped the idea for lack of troop transports. At Hartford, during the past September, the Allied commanders had agreed to a 1781 campaign to retake New York, and early in the spring Rochambeau indicated that at Washington's pleasure he would link up with the Continental army outside Manhattan. But Washington was not yet ready. Recruiting for that year was incomplete, it was too early to summon militiamen, and Washington first wished to keep an eye on the southern theater in case he had to send "large detachments" to reinforce General Greene or Lafayette. More than anything, however, Washington wished to leave nothing to chance. The coming campaign was so critical, he told Rochambeau, that it "warrant[s] every necessary preparation."[12]

French idleness in the summer and fall of 1780 had been matched by Spanish inactivity in the Gulf Coast theater, though it was not by choice that Bernardo de Gálvez was immobilized. He wanted to move against Pensacola, Britain's last stronghold on the Gulf Coast, before the scorching coastal summer commenced, but he had neither ships of the line nor frigates, and many of the vessels he possessed had been badly damaged by the Gulf storm preceding his attack on Mobile. When his pleas for heavy warships were denied by the chief of the Spanish navy in the West Indies, Gálvez sailed for Havana to see what he could get. Arriving in Cuba about a month after Rochambeau landed in Newport, Gálvez beseeched the authorities for additional troops, provisions, and above all large warships. He succeeded. Recent Spanish successes in Central America had freed troops and ships. Gálvez was also helped by the arrival of word that he had been promoted to field marshal and commander of all military operations in North America. Nor could the fact that Carlos III obviously looked favorably on Gálvez be ignored. In October, Gálvez was given an armada of 12 warships and 3,800 men. The squadron sailed for Pensacola, but at nearly the same moment as the battle at King's Mountain, it was overtaken by an autumn hurricane and devastated. Gálvez and his pummeled soldiers and sailors limped back to Havana.

Gálvez languished in Cuba until deep into the winter of 1781, his renewed entreaties for men and ships falling on deaf ears until the arrival of Francisco de Saavedra. Fresh from Madrid, Saavedra knew that his country and France favored a campaign to take Pensacola. The French wanted to tie down General Campbell's British forces; Madrid coveted Pensacola because it was crucial to Spain's control of shipping in the Gulf of Mexico and the defense of Florida westward to the Mississippi River. Saavedra immediately convened councils of war that approved the campaign for Pensacola. On March 1, nearly 11 months after Mobile fell to Spain, Gálvez's squadron put to sea. It was not as powerful as the armada that had sailed in the autumn. He had only one ship of the line, though several brigantines and frigates were in the fleet, along with 1,300 troops. He was about to go up against the most formidable target he had yet faced. Campbell, with 1,700 troops, had numerical superiority and most of his troops were in Fort George, a double stockade installation protected by supporting batteries, redoubts, and mounted artillery. After Gálvez landed his troops, he called for reinforcements from New Orleans. Late in March, 16 vessels arrived with 1,600 regulars and militiamen and a three-month supply of provisions.

The Spanish settled in for a long siege that included an ongoing bombardment. Campbell kept his army within the fortifications, but used Choctaw, Creek, and Chickasaw allies as snipers and raiders, hoping they could cause sufficient attrition to force the enemy to lift the siege. Their attacks, always a surprise and often costly, frayed the nerves of the Spanish. The men in the siege army also battled frequent storms, oppressive heat and humidity, swarms of mosquitoes, and trenches that seemed to always be thick with mud or knee-deep with brackish water. Nevertheless, the Spanish gradually advanced on Fort George, each step increasing the accuracy of Gálvez's powerful siege guns. On April 18 two Spanish vessels arrived with supplies. The next day a huge Spanish squadron appeared over the horizon: 15 warships, four of which were French, three frigates, and more than 100 transports with 1,600 Spanish regulars from Cuba, 700 French soldiers, and 1,400 sailors.

By month's end the Spanish were on the doorstep of Fort George, where Campbell's troops had remained for seven weeks while their pantry steadily emptied. Campbell confessed to Germain on May 7 that unless relief arrived, "our fate appears inevitable." He added that Pensacola was "besieged both by land and sea" and week after week "the enemy proceeded more daringly and openly in forwarding their works." Later on that same day a Spanish shell hit the fort's powder magazine, setting off a huge explosion that killed 71 and wounded 24, the majority of whom were Loyalists from Pennsylvania and Maryland serving in Britain's provincial corps. Campbell knew immediately that it was folly to continue to hold out. On May 10, he surrendered Pensacola and yielded all of West Florida to Spain. Spanish losses were three times those of their adversary, but the prize they won—which included 1,113 prisoners and 153 artillery pieces—had been one of the primary objectives that Madrid had sought on entering this war. For Spain, the Pensacola enterprise, and the earlier Gulf Coast and lower Mississippi ventures, had been waged to secure vital interests, some of which had been lost 20 years earlier in the Seven Years' War. French support had been given to help an ally, but also to encumber the British, who might otherwise have funneled men and weaponry from the Gulf Coast to Cornwallis in the Carolinas.[13]

Spain had realized heady successes in North America, but its blockade of Gibraltar, now two years old, had been futile. Nor had Minorca been recovered, a Spanish goal agreed to by Vergennes in the Treaty of Aranjuez. In the spring of 1781 Floridablanca proposed a joint campaign against the British-held island. Madrid coveted Minorca and also understood that taking it would deny its resources to the blockaded British troops on Gibraltar. Spanish intelligence had accurately reported that the Minorcans considered themselves Spanish. Indeed, they resisted British attempts to recruit them for militia service, and their skilled artisans refused job offers to repair military installations. Bourbon planning culminated in an August launch of an invasion force of numerous warships and 85 transports packed tight with 7,500 troops. The Royal Navy, scattered through several theaters, could not challenge such an armada. Nor did the British defenders, taken by surprise, offer much resistance. The Spanish rapidly captured half the island and nearly half its defenders, and a colossal amount of war materials. The remainder of Minorca was defended by 2,500 British troops, who held out through a five-month siege in which hundreds of George III's soldiers perished of diseases brought on in part by their insubstantial diet. The end came early in 1782 in an attack by a Franco-Spanish force that produced another British capitulation and Allied victory, a triumph that would provide the Bourbon allies with massive amounts of manpower and naval craft for a final attempt to take Gibraltar.[14]

AT HARTFORD, IN SEPTEMBER 1780, Rochambeau and Washington had agreed on the need for additional troops and naval superiority before launching any campaign to recover New York. They also agreed to send an emissary to France to seek needed assistance, and Vicomte de Rochambeau, a colonel in the Bourbonnais Regiment and the 24-year-old son of the French commander, agreed to undertake the mission. He carried with him a summary of the Hartford conference, prepared by Alexander Hamilton and Lafayette. In the event that young Rochambeau did not reach Versailles, Lafayette—who was better connected at the king's court—also wrote to Vergennes.

"The situation of America demands your most serious attention," Lafayette began his communiqué. The Allies could have fielded an army of 24,000 men, "and even more had it been necessary," for a campaign to take New York in 1780, but they had they been stymied by the lack of naval supremacy. A larger naval commitment and reinforcements for the army "would relieve us of three-fourths of our difficulties," Lafayette continued, and it would enable the Allies to undertake the campaign in 1781. Whether a campaign would occur in 1781—as well as what could be attempted—depended entirely on additional French aid, as "Congress has no money and little power." The "lack of money stops us at every point," he added. But with adequate assistance, success would loom, for the Continental soldiers were "as good as the enemy in every respect, and they have a fortitude in their misery that is unknown to European armies." Lafayette concluded that it was possible "the British would, through wrong moves, happen to defeat themselves." While that was speculative, what was "not uncertain" was "our present inability" to conduct the war in such a manner as to score a decisive victory.[15]

The appeals for help carried by young Rochambeau and addressed by Lafayette may have been unnecessary. Gambling that victory was still possible, the Conseil du Roi had agreed during winter to send de Grasse's fleet and money to its hard-pressed ally. Colonel Rochambeau, aboard *Concorde*, landed in Boston in May and hurried to Newport with the news and one million livres, one-sixth of France's generous gift to the United States. The rest would arrive in two additional shipments that summer. It was earmarked for the Allied armies, not Congress. Vergennes and the king's court wanted it spent on military essentials, and indeed John Laurens had already gone on a shopping spree in Paris, purchasing 16,000 muskets, munitions, and military uniforms, which had been shipped to Philadelphia.[16]

Immediately following his son's return, General Rochambeau notified Washington that he had important news and suggested that they meet. The two quickly scheduled a conclave for May 21 in Wethersfield, Connecticut, about five miles south of Hartford. It took place over two days at the resplendent home of Joseph

Webb, the next-door neighbor of Silas Deane. The French once again sized up the American commander and were pleased. A young French officer who saw Washington for the first time described him as "very tall," adding that he "has a noble air, a fine face. His temperament is cool but mild and affable. His demeanor is easy and inspires confidence. He often has the impression of thought depicted on his face." Later in the war, the same officer spoke of Washington's "aura," which "bears the imprint of the manners and the character of a leader."[17]

At Wethersfield, Washington was delighted to learn of his ally's generosity, but disappointed that France was sending only 600 additional troops. Next to French aid, the best news that Washington received was that a French fleet was coming late in the summer and, when joined with the eight vessels already in Newport, the Allies should at long last enjoy naval superiority in American waters.

Most of the conference concerned the coming campaign. Discussions grew heated at times, and some observers thought Rochambeau now and again was uncivil. The sticking point was Washington's insistence on campaigning to retake New York. There could be little doubt that Britain's war was over if it lost New York. However, Rochambeau argued that it "could not be taken with the available forces" by storm. Britain had held Manhattan, Staten Island, and Long Island for five years, time enough to have constructed formidable defenses. Only a siege operation might succeed, and it would be dicey. Over the past five years the British presumably had stockpiled huge stores of supplies, which would necessitate a lengthy siege. But American militiamen, who would compose upwards of one-half of the Allied army, customarily served for no more than 90 days, and de Grasse's fleet could not stay indefinitely. Rochambeau pressed for turning south. Unaware of Clinton's plans, Rochambeau presumed that Virginia was threatened and that if it fell, the three provinces to its south would also fall to the British. But Washington was adamant and insisted that the Allies, assured of a two-to-one numerical majority, could retake New York. In the end, Rochambeau relented.[18]

Soon after Washington departed on his ride back to New Windsor, New York, Rochambeau wrote to de Grasse. Given that the Americans were "at the end of their resources," the coming campaign would be the last in America in this war. It was now or never if victory was to be won, and he appealed to de Grasse to sail for the Chesapeake before continuing on to New York. The southern states faced "a very grave crisis" and the fleet could "render the greater service" in the southern theater, he advised. Rochambeau's message was confusing. He appeared to suggest that New York would be the focal point of the year's campaign, though he also seemed to say that more of greater value could be achieved in the Chesapeake. Two weeks later Rochambeau wrote again to de Grasse, though that communiqué hardly clarified matters. He spoke of New York as "a *diversion* in favor of Virginia," though he urged de Grasse to sail for New York after tending to business in Virginia, which included the destruction of the British base in Portsmouth. A week later, Minister La Luzerne also wrote to de Grasse and appealed to him to sail for Virginia. Throughout the spring the British suspected the French might make a diversion in Virginia to help with their attack in New York, but by early summer Rochambeau saw the threat of a campaign for New York as a diversion to assist the Allies in destroying British forces in the Chesapeake.[19]

On June 10, three weeks following the Wethersfield conference, Rochambeau confessed to Washington that he had asked de Grasse to sail first to the Chesapeake, though he attached a copy of the letter showing that the admiral was made aware that Washington preferred to campaign for New York. Washington was not terribly upset at having been kept in the dark. He had grown more flexible. Although he and Rochambeau had agreed in Wethersfield that New York was "the only practicable object," he now thought it best to "leave him [de Grasse] to judge" where to sail based on what he learned concerning "the situation of the enemy's Fleet upon this Coast." Taking out the Royal Navy would be a crucial accompaniment to wherever the joint armies eventually campaigned.[20]

Meanwhile, the French army had begun its long-anticipated march from Rhode Island to New York to link up with its ally, a move that could no longer be delayed, as de Grasse might arrive soon. Rochambeau left behind 400 men to safeguard Newport and guard supplies in Providence, as well as those soldiers who were too ill to march. He also furnished the shorthanded navy with 700 men. Finally, during the second week in June he and his men, and more than 100 horse-drawn wagons, set off to join with the Continental army. To beat the heat, they moved out every third morning at 4:00 A.M. and covered roughly 15 miles before calling a halt. On July 8, 26 days after the tramp began, the first units reached Philipsburg above Manhattan and approximately five miles north of Washington's 6,300 men at Dobb's Ferry on the Hudson River. The Allied armies were at last united. They would "commence an operation against New York," Washington noted in his diary, unless de Grasse established "a Naval superiority" to the "southward."[21]

GENERAL CLINTON KNEW LITTLE or nothing about the fate of his army in the Carolinas during the initial four months of 1781. Cornwallis had sent him a misleading account of Cowpens on the day after the battle. He minimized Tarleton's losses and wildly exaggerated the damage inflicted on the rebel cavalry. Although Cornwallis kept Germain informed, he did not write to Clinton again for nearly 100 days after Cowpens. On the last day of April, Clinton finally heard from him, a letter penned while Cornwallis's army was refitting in Wilmington. It contained the first hard news of Guilford Courthouse, though Clinton thought Cornwallis's claims of a "very complete" victory were questionable. It hardly squared with what Clinton had already gleaned from rebel newspapers. Besides, Nathanael Greene's army remained in the field, not what one would expect from a thoroughly vanquished force.[22]

Embroidered reports were troubling, but Clinton was more concerned by something else Cornwallis had written. He had proposed making Virginia "the seat of war, even (if necessary) at the expense of abandoning New York." Until Virginia was "in a manner subdued, our hold of the Carolinas must be difficult if not precarious," Cornwallis added. Clinton had no intention of abandoning New York. To do so would be to abandon thousands of Loyalists and open the door for an Allied conquest of Quebec. Clinton also knew all too well that he lacked a sufficient army for the conquest of Virginia. Clinton had long expected the climactic showdown in this war to take place in New York and, like Rochambeau, he was reasonably confident that an Allied attack or siege would fail. Going into Virginia would risk courting substantial losses and possibly ruination, the very thing Britain had to avoid in 1781. Clinton subsequently remarked that by late spring all signs led him to conclude that "if we could only persevere in escaping affront, time alone would soon bring about every success we could wish."[23]

Clinton hoped against hope that Cornwallis was not thinking of taking his army to Virginia. Given Germain's observation that Britain could no longer wage a protracted war, Clinton, like almost everyone else, believed that 1781 was to be the last year of the war and that the war's outcome was far from decided. He conceived his strategy for the coming year with an eye on the peace conference that likely would follow the year's campaign. Clinton anticipated that Cornwallis in the lower South, with General Phillips's helping hand in blocking the flow of supplies through Virginia to both partisans and Greene's army, could suppress the rebellion in Georgia and the Carolinas at least to the degree that Britain could lay claim to those provinces at the peace table. Clinton also believed that his army in and around Manhattan—enhanced in midsummer by the recall of most of Phillips's army—could check the Allied threat to New York. If foiled in the lower South and unsuccessful in their bid to retake New York, the enemy would be left with "little to induce them to [continue to] support the war."[24] In the peace conference that followed these culminating events, Great Britain was likely to retain two, possibly three, southern colonies, and perhaps a great deal more elsewhere. Whatever was decided at the peace conference would be the work of diplomats, but Clinton would have successfully completed the job he had been given in 1778.

But Cornwallis's proposal to make Virginia the focal point of Britain's 1781 campaign was starkly at odds with the strategic plan that Clinton had formulated in the aftermath of King's Mountain. Clinton immediately wrote to him that his "presence in Carolina cannot be so soon dispensed with."[25] He thought of sailing to Wilmington to speak with Cornwallis, though had he done so, Cornwallis would have been long gone by the time he arrived. Cornwallis's army marched for the Old Dominion on April 26, four days before Clinton received the letter in which his subordinate recommended the conquest of Virginia.[26]

"It is very disagreeable to me" to step off to Virginia and not return to South Carolina without his "directions or approbation," Cornwallis dissembled in a letter to Clinton, adding that his decision to violate his orders "sits heavy on my mind." However, waging a "defensive war" in South Carolina was futile. It was better to "push the war" in Virginia. Besides, he contended unconvincingly, his "little corps" might be trapped and defeated by Greene and the partisans while on the move from Wilmington to Camden.[27]

The disposition of Cornwallis's army was Clinton's decision to make. The British commander had recognized the difficulty Cornwallis faced in pacifying South Carolina, and that prompted him to commit a large force to Virginia. Yet, while Clinton hoped the insurgency in South Carolina could be extinguished, his principal objective in the South was to maintain what Britain possessed until the anticipated peace conference took place. Following the conquest of Charleston, British forces had established numerous outposts throughout South Carolina's backcountry, ranging from the coast to the Georgia border. While Cornwallis had been unable to quash the rebellion, the presence of his force had prevented the loss of those bases. If the British still possessed those installations at year's end, London would have a strong claim to the retention of South Carolina and Georgia at the peace table.

As Cornwallis prepared to abandon South Carolina, he was in the dark as to what Greene might do. Greene's army had shrunk considerably after Guilford Courthouse, but it still existed and had trailed after Cornwallis on his retreat to Wilmington. At times, Cornwallis said that if he marched to Virginia, Greene would also march there, though on other occasions he said that he expected his adversary to plunge into South Carolina. Should Greene choose the latter option, he told Clinton that "we shall meet with no serious misfortune in that province." However, Cornwallis admitted to Colonel Balfour, whom he left in command in South Carolina, that should Greene enter the province, the British likely would "lose some of the outposts and the [back]country of South Carolina."[28]

It is impossible to know precisely what ran through Cornwallis's mind in April as he contemplated disobeying his orders and leaving South Carolina. He did say that it was his "mature" judgment to abandon South Carolina because time was of the essence. He clearly thought that Britain's best hope for scoring a decisive victory in 1781 was in Virginia. He also believed he could achieve that feat by taking command of Phillips's force and thrashing the rebel armies under Lafayette and Greene when they combined against him. He might have thought that his presence in Virginia would pull Washington and Rochambeau to the Old Dominion, moves that would force Clinton to bring his army southward. In that eventuality, the great showdown battle of this war would be fought in Virginia.[29] But there were other strands to his thinking. Throughout his seven years in America, Cornwallis had been restive with defensive warfare. He was geared for offensive action and convinced that Britain could win this war only by waging offensive operations that would lead to the destruction of the enemies' armies. In New York, Britain would be on the defensive, but in Virginia it would have to wage offensive warfare. Furthermore, Cornwallis, like every officer, hungered for glory, though, aside from Camden, laurels had eluded him in the American war. Failure, or at least a lack of success, had been his lot. Washington had eluded him in New Jersey and slipped out of his grasp on the Assunpink Creek early in 1777. During the past eight months Cornwallis's armies had suffered anguishing misfortunes at King's Mountain and Cowpens, and had failed to score a decisive victory thereafter, including at Guilford Courthouse. Cornwallis's violation of his orders in April 1781 appears to have been the act of a man who sought atonement that could be achieved only by winning this war's pivotal victory.[30]

No one can know if a 1781 campaign to win control of Virginia would have succeeded. Taking the offensive had led to British success on Long Island and at Brandywine, Savannah, Charleston, and Camden. On the other hand, Burgoyne's offensive had ended in disaster and Cornwallis had little but misery to show for his two offensive forays into North Carolina. The conquest of Virginia might have involved attempts to overcome entrenched enemy forces, and in this war, assailing well-fortified adversaries—as the British learned at Bunker Hill, Pell's Point, and White Plains, and as d'Estaing discovered at Savannah in 1779—had nearly always failed. To this point, each British success had come against a rebel force. But in Virginia the British might have faced Allied armies composed of French regulars, American Continentals, and large numbers of rebel militia. Clinton expected the war's climactic event to be an Allied attempt to retake New York, and he thought his army—in fortifications that had been years in the making—stood the best chance of repulsing the enemy onslaught. How a battle for New York would have turned out is unfathomable, but the outcome of previous engagements suggests that Britain was more likely to win a colossal victory—or avoid a shattering defeat—through defending New York than through campaigning to take Virginia.

Cornwallis's secret admission to Balfour that in his absence Britain would lose much that it had held in South Carolina was soon borne out. When Greene took his army into South Carolina," he said that the step would "draw the war out of North Carolina." He took risk after risk, and waged the most active sustained campaign conducted by an American commander in this war. He did not succeed in every endeavor, but he kept at it, prompting his famous remark that spring: "We fight get beat rise and fight again." In the Second Battle of Camden, fought in April, he suffered what he variously termed a "little repulse" and a "defeat." In the summer, he besieged, and ultimately attacked, Ninety-Six, Britain's strong outpost in far western South Carolina. He failed to take it as well. Nevertheless, Balfour concluded that as a result of Greene's appearance in South Carolina—and Cornwallis's disappearance—the "whole interior country had revolted." One British post after another fell to partisans and Continental cavalry; others were relinquished— including Camden and Ninety-Six—as Balfour understood that they could not be held forever and he needed their troops to hold Charleston. By late summer, 100 days after Cornwallis had marched into Virginia—and at roughly the moment that Rochambeau's army linked up with Washington's—nine former British outposts in a stretch from the coast to the Savannah River were in rebel hands or were besieged, and nearly 900 British troops had been killed, wounded, or captured in the spring and summer fighting. The "revolt is universal," said Balfour, who added that "the minds of the people are bent on their [revolutionary] principles."[31]

CLINTON FIRST SAID HE had been "exceedingly hurt" by Cornwallis's aban-donment of South Carolina, but as the magnitude of the disaster sown by his subordinate became clear, the commander was profoundly shaken and his outrage was boundless, much like that of Washington toward General Charles Lee at Monmouth. Washington, with the help of obsequious and ambitious officers, was able to rid himself of Lee, but Clinton's hands were tied. Cornwallis was a favorite of Germain's. Indeed, the American secretary's letters to Clinton were often filled with cant about Cornwallis's "rapid and decisive" conduct and "vigorous exertions," communiqués intended to be read as the American secretary's hardly subtle disapproval of Clinton's supposed lack of vigor. Although Cornwallis had laid waste to Clinton's grand plan for retaining two or more southern provinces, the commander in chief quietly endured what he rightly perceived as yet another act of bad faith by his subordinate. His glowering silence was made all the more difficult as news reached him that British posts in South Carolina "were daily dropping into the enemy's hands," calamities brought on by what Clinton rightly saw as Cornwallis's "opposition to every principle of policy as well as duty." Clinton, with justification, also raged in private that Cornwallis's poor generalship during the past six months had been deeply injurious to Britain's cause in the South. Cornwallis, he contended, had botched two incursions into North Carolina, and his imprudent pursuit of Greene and Morgan—which left his bedraggled army in poor shape for battle—had contributed to his inability to decisively defeat the rebels at Guilford Courthouse. Now his inexcusable decision to march to Virginia had not merely resulted in ongoing "heavy misfortunes" in South Carolina; it placed Cornwallis's army where it was not needed and could do little good.[32]

Although his strategic plan for retaining hold of the Carolinas and Georgia seemingly had been dealt a mortal blow, Clinton continued to believe that the war's outcome hinged on the approaching campaign. As there had seemingly been more British spies than Allied officers in Wethersfield in May, Clinton was aware that Washington and Rochambeau had agreed on an operation to take New York "with all the force they can collect." In July the Allied armies had rendezvoused above Manhattan, leaving Clinton with little doubt that "the enemy will *certainly* attack" New York that summer or fall.[33]

CHAPTER 14

THE DECISIVE ALLIED VICTORY IN THE AMERICAN THEATER

WASHINGTON HAD SEEMED AMENABLE to a Chesapeake campaign in June, but by July the gravitational pull of New York weighed heavily on him. Nonetheless, both Washington and Rochambeau understood that it was Admiral de Grasse who would ultimately decide where the campaign would play out, and neither general knew when he would come, his intended destination, or what he would find and do once he got there. They waited in suspense for six long weeks, spending some of their time reconnoitering in northern Manhattan and making battle plans for a campaign in New York in case that was to be their target. All the while Washington prepared for a march to the Chesapeake, in the event that was where the armies would campaign. He sent out orders to stock magazines along the route the armies would travel to Virginia, took steps to collect large numbers of vessels at the top of the Chesapeake for transporting the troops farther south, alerted authorities in the Old Dominion to prepare for funneling provisions to the armies, and called on the northern states for men and supplies. In the event that the coming operation was in the South, he also had to decide how many men would go to Virginia and how many would remain to protect America's possessions near Manhattan. By August, he had decided that 6,300 of his men would march for the Chesapeake, if that was de Grasse's destination, and about 2,000 would remain in the Hudson Highlands.[1]

General Clinton also knew that de Grasse was coming, but he, too, was in the dark regarding the admiral's destination. If New York was to be the site of the showdown, Clinton had about 13,000 regulars to face an anticipated enemy force of around 20,000. Although he presumed that about 40 percent of the Allied troops would be militiamen, Clinton needed a larger army and planned to recall most of the 7,250 British soldiers presently in Virginia. Cornwallis with over 1,400 men had arrived there in May to find that General Phillips was deceased, the victim of a virulent fever. Cornwallis had taken command. After reading the orders that Phillips had been given, Cornwallis advised Clinton that he would carry out those orders: Destroy rebel magazines and supply depots; drive Lafayette from Richmond and, if possible, annihilate the rebel army; and ultimately take his army to Yorktown, a tiny hamlet on the York River well down the long peninsula that extends below Richmond between the York and James Rivers. Phillips had deemed Yorktown a "proper" site for a "station," as large warships could find anchorage there, it "stands high" above the river, and the terrain was suitable for quickly and easily digging entrenchments.[2]

Three weeks after entering Virginia, Cornwallis made his lone stab at destroying a supply depot, a largely ineffectual raid at Point of Fork west of Richmond. He also marched to Richmond only to find that Lafayette was long gone. While retreating, Lafayette acknowledged that he was "Guarding Against My Own Warmth," a lust for glory that at times had led him to act imprudently. With "few Militia and less arms," he confided to Washington that if he was to fight a battle his army would be "Cut to pieces, the Militia dispersed, and the Arms lost." Lafayette fell back into the welcoming arms of the backcountry. Cornwallis set off after him, allegedly boasting, "the boy cannot escape me." Lafayette escaped. When Cornwallis had contemplated remaining in South Carolina and contesting Greene, he had frankly acknowledged that he was "quite tired of marching about the country in quest of adventures." His wearying chase of Morgan and Greene had been sufficient for one lifetime, and his pursuit of Lafayette was perfunctory. Cornwallis's only wholehearted initiative was to send Colonel Tarleton on a surprise night visit to Charlottesville, where Virginia's assembly was meeting and Monticello, the home of Governor Jefferson, was located. Forewarned, Jefferson eluded his would-be captors, as did all but seven laggard assemblymen. By June 25, six weeks after entering Virginia, Cornwallis's army was in Williamsburg, a stone's throw from Yorktown. He had nothing to show for having abandoned South Carolina, and he knew that better than anyone. Likely divining the dark stain that could blemish his reputation for having abandoned his mission in the lower South, Cornwallis asked Clinton's permission to return to South Carolina with the 1,435 men he had brought to Virginia. In a moment of astonishing candor, he confessed that the "measure which I adopted" in coming to Virginia was "Perhaps . . . not the best."[3]

While in Williamsburg, Cornwallis received a bevy of communiqués from Clinton. He learned of his commander's displeasure that he had forsaken South Carolina, a move that was transparently "dangerous to our interests in the southern colonies." But with Germain's shadow hanging over him, Clinton did not sanction Cornwallis's request to return to South Carolina. Two essential points stood out in Clinton's orders. He wanted Cornwallis to establish "a naval station for large ships of war as well as small" at Yorktown and adjacent Gloucester. Clinton also told Cornwallis that as a large army was unnecessary in Virginia, most of the troops were soon to be redeployed to New York. Benedict Arnold had reported that 2,000 troops could defend Yorktown, and as Lafayette's force—even though recently augmented by Continentals under Anthony Wayne—did not exceed that number, Clinton wanted more than 5,000 of Cornwallis's men as he prepared for what he believed would be the certain Allied attack on New York. Ominously, however, Clinton added that any army in the Chesapeake would be secure only so long as Britain was "superior at sea." Between the lines he appeared to be saying that it was too risky to maintain a large army in Virginia, as its presence would be an inviting target.[4]

Cornwallis in July learned that Clinton wanted 3,000 of his men as well as "a proportion of artillery as can be spared." Another 2,000 troops would be summoned once Yorktown's fortifications were completed. Cornwallis, of course, was unhappy with the diminution of his force, and all of a sudden he expressed concern for South Carolina, cheekily questioning "the utility of a defensive post in this country which cannot have the smallest influence on the war in Carolina." But he complied with Clinton's order. Fearful of leaving too few men at Yorktown, Cornwallis had his entire army make the 50-mile tramp to Portsmouth, the embarkation site.[5]

The transports were loaded and on the verge of sailing for New York when Cornwallis received orders from Clinton to cancel the redeployment. Clinton's turnabout was due to his receipt of a communiqué from Germain that was to have profound consequences. Given the "vast importance of the possession of Virginia," said the American secretary, it was to his and the king's "great mortification" to learn of Clinton's plan to withdraw any troops from the province. If anything, Germain wanted Clinton to pour more troops into Virginia and to push "the war in that quarter," given that the "prospect we have of recovering the whole of the southern provinces this campaign is so fair." In a subsequent communiqué, Germain said that "the opposition to be expected" in Virginia would be "very inconsiderable" as the "rebel cause [is] sunk and declining." Germain's appraisal was unsound, as Clinton knew full well. Clinton also understood that Germain's order would eviscerate his carefully planned strategy for restoring order in the deep South and preparing for the Allied strike against New York. But Clinton felt that he had no choice but to follow his superiors' wishes. By August 2, Cornwallis's entire army was back in Yorktown.[6]

When Cornwallis, in June, had plodded from Richmond to Williamsburg, his army had been trailed by Lafayette's, and thereafter the marquis's force had taken up positions on the peninsula. Lafayette understood, and hoped, that his tracking of Cornwallis would give "the appearance of a [British] retreat." If there was a peace conference in 1782, Lafayette believed that Cornwallis's "retreat" would conclusively demonstrate to the peacemakers that Virginia was not in Britain's possession. Lafayette had already concluded that the rebel gains in South Carolina in the wake of Cornwallis's disappearance had suddenly given the war "a tolerable face" for the United States. It led him to hope that America's independence would be recognized at the peace conference and that all 13 states would be part of the United States. Otherwise, said Lafayette, there was "no bond that holds together" the fledgling nation.[7]

CLINTON'S KNOWLEDGE OF THE Allies' decisions reached at Wethersfield, as well as captured enemy correspondence and the reports of his intelligence network, convinced him that de Grasse and the Allied armies intended to campaign to take New York. Even so, on three occasions that summer Clinton cautioned Cornwallis to be prepared for a possible enemy strike in the Chesapeake. Everything that Clinton knew about de Grasse's fleet came from Germain's upbeat messages. The American secretary allowed that he was "not apprehensive." The Royal Navy would be a match for de Grasse. Furthermore, the enemy fleet would not linger long enough "to do you any material injury." Germain added a further positive note, and an accurate one. The French were not sending Rochambeau substantial reinforcements.[8]

Throughout the summer, Clinton set his troops to strengthening New York's fortifications, and late in the summer he summoned Loyalist militiamen to duty. There were times when he considered defying Germain and recalling most of

Cornwallis's army to New York. Clinton needed more troops, and throughout the summer he anguished that it might be impossible "to defend this extensive post" against "so powerful an armament" as the Allies might muster. A seasoned commander, Clinton understood what Germain and the king in remote London did not see. Even 23-year-old Lafayette realized it, surmising: The "Ennemy [must] either . . . throw a Reinforcement into Newyork or Come with all their force in this State [Virginia]." Clinton, like young Lafayette, fully grasped the peril presented by his divided army. There result might well be too few troops in both New York and Virginia. But in the end he adhered to Germain's orders and did not consolidate his army.

Clinton not only felt that he needed most of the troops at Yorktown, but he also may have reckoned that if only 2,000 British troops remained in Virginia, the Allies—desperate to score a truly decisive victory—would not trifle with such a minuscule force. Indeed, removing most of the troops from Yorktown might assure that the Allied blow would come in New York, which the Royal Navy guarded and where the British for years had prepared for an enemy attack. But Clinton was a soldier and he would not disobey orders. Besides, he feared the fallout that would ensue if disaster struck even a small army in Yorktown, especially as Cornwallis had insisted that he needed all 7,500 men to adequately defend it. Clinton was not in Yorktown and had never been there to judge for himself. He left Cornwallis's army intact, telling himself that if he had ample warning that de Grasse's destination was New York, there might time to recall Cornwallis's army. Getting the troops out of Virginia would hinge on the Royal Navy maintaining supremacy, and Clinton found it difficult to imagine that the British navy would lose its mastery. His belief was based in part on the assumption that de Grasse would not bring his entire fleet and leave France's valuable sugar islands unprotected, a notion that Germain had broached weeks before. That Germain must have been correct appeared confirmed in August when the brigantine *Swallow* arrived in New York from the Caribbean with word that the greatest part of de Grasse's heavy warships would go to Europe with the annual French convoy that transported booty back home. Clinton had also been advised that when de Grasse sailed, Admiral Sir George Rodney, Britain's foremost naval officer, would bring his large West Indian squadron to North America to join the fleet in New York. "They cannot move but I will be on them," Rodney had declared.[9]

In July, when the armies of Rochambeau and Washington linked up, some officers sought to persuade Clinton to assail the Allied forces above Manhattan. He ruled against that option. For years the British had intended, and planned, to wage a defensive campaign to defend New York, and Clinton adhered to that policy, preferring the security offered by fortifications. Clinton did push for one offensive action, though nothing came of it. Once Rochambeau's army marched to New York, intelligence reported that the French fleet in Newport was "totally unprotected." Clinton urged a strike by the Royal Navy, now under Rear Admiral Thomas Graves, Arbuthnot's successor. However, Graves refused to act until four of his heavy warships were out of dry dock. By the time they were repaired, conditions had changed and it was too late to act.[10]

WHEN ADMIRAL DE GRASSE reached Cap François in mid-July, he found the letters from Rochambeau written soon after the Wethersfield conference. Rochambeau had reported that Cornwallis had arrived in Virginia and there were now at least 6,000 British troops in the province. He additionally indicated that Washington wished to threaten or attack Manhattan "to ease the pressure" on Virginia. America, Rochambeau added, was in a "very grave crisis," especially in the South, but de Grasse's arrival with "sea superiority" would "save this situation." The "southwesterly winds" in the Chesapeake and "the state of distress in Virginia" might make it the preferred destination of the fleet, Rochambeau advised. He concluded by saying that if the great confrontation occurred in New York, the combined Allied armies would "hardly be more than a third more" than Clinton's. In his letter of June 11 Rochambeau emphasized that the Americans "are at the end of their resources" and implored de Grasse to come with troops. If he could bring 5,000 men, that "will not be too many."[11]

Rochambeau had all but asked de Grasse to come to the Chesapeake. To help along his preference for Virginia, Rochambeau included a letter he had recently received from Minister La Luzerne in Philadelphia. The envoy had emphasized the dire situation in the Old Dominion. La Luzerne had been in regular communication with Lafayette, who repeatedly stressed his predicament and hopes. His army lacked provisions and men, Lafayette reported, but he would fight if he must. Lafayette added that if he was "not annihilated" and Virginia was "not conquered"—and if Greene was successful in South Carolina—"the French and Americans arm in arm" could persuade a peace conference to award independence to a United States of 13 states. In the communiqué that Rochambeau passed along to de Grasse, La Luzerne advised that it was "imperative" that the coming French campaign should focus on the Chesapeake.[12]

On July 28, de Grasse sent to Newport a letter to Rochambeau announcing his plan to sail on August 3 for the Chesapeake. It seemed to be "the surest [place] to operate best," he said. But de Grasse emphasized that could not stay long. The "common cause" required that he soon return to the West Indies to assist with Spain's military plans.[13] Weeks passed before Rochambeau, who was in New York, saw that crucial letter.

THROUGHOUT THAT TORRID AUGUST, Cornwallis's men labored to fortify Yorktown. Clinton, since April, had emphasized that a post be established at Yorktown; yet before August, not a spade of dirt had been turned at the site. Phillips had been in the field in the spring seeking to destroy enemy forces and magazines, activities that Cornwallis desultorily continued in May and June. In August, Cornwallis was at last ready to commence work on Yorktown's defenses, but he was unable to start for days because he had neglected to bring entrenching tools from Portsmouth. When work finally began, Cornwallis sent to Portsmouth for "laboring Negroes," pleading that the merciless "heat is too great to admit of the soldiers doing" such labor. However, he was informed that the Blacks who had escaped behind British lines in Portsmouth were "dying by scores every day" from "some fatal distemper," probably smallpox. In mid-August all the British troops and civilians in Portsmouth arrived at Yorktown, and thereafter whites and Blacks, often side by side, worked hour after hour in the bone-deep heat. Despite the delays, work had at last begun and de Grasse had not yet arrived, convincing Clinton that in a worst-case scenario, Cornwallis's army was safe. Cornwallis would have sufficient time to ready Yorktown's defenses. Furthermore, Clinton understood that Cornwallis had ample provisions to sustain 10,000 men until mid-November, which was later than de Grasse would probably linger.[14]

While the arduous toil continued at Yorktown, Washington and Rochambeau waited impatiently to learn of de Grasse's plans. In the meantime, they continued to reconnoiter and make plans for a New York campaign; "our untiring general spent every day on horseback to study and know the area perfectly," said one of Rochambeau's aides. But in the event that the French fleet was sailing for Virginia, Washington established a "Chain of Expresses" to speed communications with Lafayette. Throughout July and August, Washington was so swamped with the "load of business" that he was required "to husband time." The anxious weeks of idleness afforded the French an opportunity to scrutinize the soldiery in Washington's army. All were struck by their "destitution," as "three quarters of them have no shoes," as well as by the large number of Blacks, oldsters, and extremely young men in the ranks. The abundance of graybeards and youngsters was worrisome. The French were less concerned about the presence of so many Black soldiers, seeing that they were "the most precise in . . . maneuvers" of the American soldiers.[15]

On August 14, 39 days after the French and American armies united, the word the generals awaited finally arrived. A courier from Newport delivered the July 28 letter that de Grasse had written in Cap François. The French fleet was sailing for the Chesapeake. Rochambeau brought the news to Washington, who, according to one of the French commander's aides, "did not seem very satisfied" as he was fixated on the "capture of New York." Whether or not the account of that witness was accurate, Washington notified Lafayette and ordered him to round up every horse and wagon he could get his hands on. The marquis was also to take every necessary step to assure that Cornwallis "may not be able to escape you." Within five days the Allied armies moved out on what was to be a 450-mile journey to Yorktown. They crossed the Hudson and, in two columns a few miles apart, headed south across New Jersey. Steps had long since been taken to fool Clinton into believing that a New York campaign was in the offing and that one division of the Allied armies would strike at Staten Island while the remainder rendezvoused with the French fleet at Sandy Hook. Field ovens, a customary accompaniment of sieges, had been built, and a "dummy camp" that included batteries, ovens, and boats had been assembled across from Staten Island. Clinton was fooled to a degree, but given his inflexible belief that New York would be the enemy's target, he may have mostly fooled himself.[16]

However, to a greater degree Clinton's undoing was the result of chance and the information he received—and failed to obtain—during that critical month of August. Admiral Rodney had learned in late July that de Grasse was about to sail and that he was accompanied by Virginia pilots. Rodney possessed the key to the puzzle, but inscrutably two weeks passed before he communicated the indispensable information to the fleet in New York. Had Rodney acted expeditiously the Royal Navy would have had a shot at rescuing Cornwallis and most of his army from their imminent snare. Or it might have blocked the entrance to Chesapeake Bay, a step that could have given the British the advantage in a showdown between the rival fleets.

Clinton had been promised that a British squadron would tail de Grasse on his voyage northward, and that did occur, but matters went awry for the British as a consequence of quirks, the sort of thing on which history sometimes hangs. For one thing, de Grasse took an improbable course to the Chesapeake. Rather than hewing to the most direct route far out in the Atlantic, the French fleet first sailed toward Cuba and Florida, and then northward off North America's Atlantic coast. De Grasse likely chose that course to take advantage of the natural elements after consulting the pilots that Rochambeau had sent him and sounding out experienced Spanish mariners in Cap François. It made for a longer journey and one that became even more protracted when unanticipated currents pushed the fleet away from its intended destination. The French were compelled to track westward, but the squadron arrived safely on August 30 after 26 days at sea. It had avoided detection by the Royal Navy.

As Rodney had returned to England, the job of pursuing de Grasse fell to Admiral Samuel Hood, who scraped together a fleet of 14 ships of the line, though others were denied him by assorted British officials in the Caribbean. Aware that the French had sailed days earlier, Hood departed Antiqua on August 10. He took the direct route and arrived at the entrance to Chesapeake Bay on August 25, five days prior to de Grasse's arrival. Given de Grasse's head start, Hood reckoned that the French fleet should have been there if that had been its destination. But glimpsing no sign of the enemy, Hood logically assumed it had sailed to New York or Newport. He hurried to New York, arriving on August 28 with his critically important information. No one understood that Hood had beaten the French to the Chesapeake, the result of de Grasse having taken the longer route and drifted off course, which extended the voyage, or that Hood's copper-bottomed vessels were faster than de Grasse's less modernized ships.[17]

All the while, Clinton had watched every step taken by the enemy armies since they had begun crossing the Hudson on August 19. Crucially, however, he made no attempt to intercept his adversaries and thwart or delay their advance. Here at last was Clinton's chance to fight Washington. Although it would have been a confrontation with the rebel army and French regulars, the two sides likely would have been roughly the same size and the British might have possessed far more artillery, given that the French siege guns were being shipped by sea from Rhode Island to the Chesapeake. In retrospect, Clinton's failure to act was an egregious blunder. But he was acting in real time and he persisted in thinking his enemies were readying a New York campaign. As late as August 28, the day that Hood arrived in New York, the Allied armies were about 20 miles west of Staten Island and farther still from Sandy Hook, the site where Clinton all along had expected them to rendezvous with de Grasse's fleet. Clinton had not acted during those critical 10 days, not even by attacking the enemy baggage trains as Washington had done at Monmouth. Throughout this anxious period, Clinton knew that if the enemy armies crossed the Raritan River, they were heading for Virginia. They crossed unmolested on August 30—the same day that de Grasse reached the Chesapeake—and only then did Clinton know for certain that Cornwallis was in the Allies' crosshairs.

Clinton has been castigated by historians for his inaction, which one labeled "one of the foremost blunders of the war." Some have portrayed him as habitually overly cautious, and one, utilizing the questionable approach of psychohistory, argued that Clinton craved power but subconsciously felt "he ought not to have it," a dilemma that led to a "paralysis of will" and an inability to act.[18] No one can know what would have occurred had Clinton contested the enemy's advance. He might have suffered egregious losses or he might have fatally weakened the enemy force. He might also have so delayed the arrival of the Allied armies in Virginia that Cornwallis could have escaped or the pending siege operation would not have been completed before de Grasse sailed away.

Like all commanders, Clinton had to make his decision to act or not to act based on the information he possessed. As de Grasse was not expected to bring his entire fleet, Clinton assumed that the Royal Navy would retain its mastery of the seas and shield Cornwallis's army from mortal danger. Based on Hood's report, he believed until August 30 that de Grasse and the Allies planned a campaign to regain New York. Given the British system of defenses in and around Manhattan, Clinton was more confident of gaining victory in that encounter than in scoring something consequential in a set-piece battle in New Jersey. With hindsight, we know that Clinton made the wrong decision. Given what he knew at time, Clinton acted prudently.

On the day the Allies crossed the Raritan and de Grasse arrived at Chesapeake Bay, Admiral Graves—who outranked Hood—sailed for the Chesapeake with 19 ships of the line. Like Clinton, Graves guessed that the French flotilla contained no more than 20 great warships. With virtual parity, the Royal Navy would have been in good shape and Cornwallis might not have been in dire straits. But de Grasse had sailed with 28 ships of the line and five frigates. On the day after Graves sailed, August 31, Cornwallis learned that perhaps as many as 40 French vessels, most of them ships of the line, were in Chesapeake Bay. By sunset that same day he knew that de Grasse had blocked his exit via the York River and taken out of play the Royal Navy vessels already in the Chesapeake. Within another five days, Cornwallis knew that more than 3,000 French marines had landed on the James River and were joining with Lafayette's Continentals and militiamen.[19]

Clinton advised Germain that the situation was "very alarming" and Britain's wartime hopes were "coming fast to a crisis."[20] Clinton was an old soldier who understood the realities of war, and he knew that Britain's fate in this conflict hinged on the looming clash in the Chesapeake between Graves and de Grasse. Only six of 15 great naval battles waged between 1692 and 1782 ended in a decisive victory. The Battle of the Virginia Capes fought on September 5 was one of them. Graves was outnumbered 24 to 19, but he had the faster warships, two of which carried 90 guns, compared with only one such vessel in de Grasse's fleet. The encounter lasted two hours and was fought principally by the lead vessels, as strong gales and wind shifts kept numerous vessels out of the fray or reduced their effectiveness. Nevertheless, naval clashes often resulted in horrific damage and this was no exception. Five British ships were severely damaged and 336 men were killed or wounded. The French suffered heavy damage to two ships and lost 330 men. When the last gun was fired, de Grasse was still in a position of supremacy in the Chesapeake. Graves hoped to give it another go once hasty repairs were made to his most impaired vessels. But over the next few days, eight French ships of the line arrived from Newport, giving de Grasse an overarching superiority. Seeing the hopelessness of his situation, Graves sailed for New York.[21]

Six councils of war met in New York to consider a mission to rescue Cornwallis. "[W]e give up the game" if no attempt was made to extricate Cornwallis, New York's royal governor maintained, but the first several parleys spurned a risky venture. After three ships of the line arrived from London, together with a message from Cornwallis stating, "If you cannot relieve me very soon, you must be prepared to hear the worst," the generals and admirals voted late in September to send a fleet and 5,000 men in a last-ditch effort to save the trapped army. It would depart when Graves's damaged vessels were repaired. At the earliest, the task force would sail on October 5. Given the provisions in Cornwallis's pantry, there appeared to be time to make a stab at rescuing his trapped army.[22]

For his part, Cornwallis contemplated seeking to escape by fighting his way through Lafayette's defenses, but he knew that his adversary had spent a month fortifying his lines and his troop strength had recently increased. Furthermore, Cornwallis was aware that in venturing to break out, he would have to abandon numerous incapacitated men and great quantities of precious weaponry and powder. In all likelihood, Cornwallis quickly saw the futility of daring to fight his way out of the trap, though he later claimed that he abandoned making the attempt only when word arrived from Clinton that a rescue mission would be attempted.[23] He remained in Yorktown cleaving to three hopes: A hurricane might blow up and decimate the French squadron; he might outlast the stay of the enemy fleet; he might be rescued by Clinton and the Royal Navy.

FOUR DAYS AFTER CROSSING the Raritan, the Continental army paraded through Philadelphia, stirring up a choking cloud of dust. Residents lined the streets and cheered the soldiers, hopeful the war's numbing stasis of the past four years would soon end. The French, immaculate in their white uniforms, marched through the city's streets two days later. A large throng gathered to see their ally and "shouted loud praise from the windows along the route." Members of Congress stood on the steps of Independence Hall and saluted. The congressmen were delighted by the prowess exhibited by the Allied forces, heartened by their numbers, and thrilled by the determined appearance of the Continentals and the professional military air displayed by the French. They had another reason to be happy. John Laurens arrived in Philadelphia that very day with the remainder of the money that France had long ago agreed to give to the United States. It could not have come at a better time. Washington's men had not been paid in ages and they were grumbling. Washington soon quieted them with one month's pay in specie.[24]

A couple of days later, on September 6, a courier caught up with Washington as he was passing through Wilmington, Delaware. The messenger possessed an important dispatch. De Grasse was in the Chesapeake and had landed his troops. In what might have been his only uninhibited display of joyous emotion in the entire war, Washington hugged Rochambeau as he shared the news. Betraying little sign of passion, Rochambeau responded, "If M. de Grasse is or makes himself master of the Bay, we hope to do some good work." Washington notified Congress, which disseminated the tidings, prompting a large crowd to gather before Minister La Luzerne's residence and shout, "Long live Louis the Sixteenth."[25] Later that same day, the armies reached Head of Elk, where they encountered the only real hitch in the operation. Boats ordered by Washington were there, but too few of them. Provisions, artillery, and some men were loaded on the vessels. The remaining soldiers had to complete their journey on foot. Most who boarded crafts and those who walked wound up reaching the James River at about the same time, and those on foot—who could forage or plunder—enjoyed a more ample diet.[26]

While the soldiery headed for Yorktown, Washington and his staff, accompanied by Rochambeau and his staff, rode to Mount Vernon. It was Washington's first trip home since he had departed for the Second Continental Congress more than six years earlier. He and his guests arrived four days after the Battle of the Virginia Capes, of which they had no knowledge, and spent four days at the sprawling estate. The French were impressed with Washington's plantation, though one young officer was put off by Martha Washington, who, he thought, did not "respond to the grandeur of her husband." While at home Washington wrote to Lafayette, "We are . . . on our way to you. . . . I hope you will keep Lord Cornwallis safe, without Provisions or Forage untill we arrive. Adieu." On September 14, the day after Graves weighed anchor for his return voyage to New York, Washington and Rochambeau rode into Williamsburg. When Washington alighted from his horse, Lafayette kissed him from "ear to ear," according to one astonished American soldier.[27]

While the Allied soldiery trickled in, Washington, Rochambeau, Lafayette, Henry Knox, and others visited de Grasse on *Ville de Paris*, his flagship. De Grasse was ebullient. He had recently been joined by Jacques-Melchior, Comte de Barras, Destouches's successor as commander of the Newport squadron, who had brought eight ships of the line, four frigates, and numerous vessels loaded with siege guns and ammunition. De Grasse greeted Washington with a hug and kiss on both cheeks and, to the merriment of all but the American commander, exclaimed, "My dear little general." According to one observer, corpulent Henry Knox laughed "till his fat sides shook." Once the "interview," as Washington called it, got down to business, de Grasse said that he might be able to stay through October and that he could furnish 2,000 men if the Allies were compelled to end the siege with an assault. As the Allied commanders estimated they would have their siege guns in place and firing by October 5, they would have 26 days to secure Cornwallis's capitulation.[28]

Forty days after departing Dobbs Ferry, the Allied armies marched from Williamsburg to Yorktown under an unforgiving early autumn sun. In the tilting light of late day the commanders got their first look at the enemy's defenses. Rochambeau, who had taken part in numerous siege operations, was impressed, though he did not think Cornwallis's fortifications were insuperable. The Allied armies rapidly sealed off every road from Yorktown, and 2,000 French and American troops were posted across the York River to prevent the enemy from escaping to Gloucester. Meanwhile, the bulk of the French army took up positions on the left and the Americans on the right. There were 8,600 French troops, 8,280 Continentals, and 5,535 American militiamen, providing the Allies with roughly a three-to-one numerical superiority. For one of the first times in this war, Washington exuded optimism. "I think in all probabililty Lord Cornwallis must fall into our hands," he said, a sentiment echoed by Knox, who thought that "if the respective parts harmonize, we hope to do something handsome."[29]

Digging on the first parallels began on October 6. Washington was given the honor of turning the first spade full of earth. Strangely, Joseph Plumb Martin, who had soldiered in the Continental army for six years, had no idea who the "stranger" was that made that initial ceremonial dig. The men then took over and dug through the long, dark night until the trench extended hundreds of yards and was four feet deep and about eight feet wide. It was 600 yards from the British lines. While some soldiers spent the next two days constructing redoubts and batteries, other sweating, grunting troops wrestled the huge siege guns into place. At last on October 9, four days later than the commanders had advised de Grasse that the bombardment of Yorktown would commence, the Allied guns opened fire. Again there was a ceremony on the American side and Washington fired the "first salutation," as an American soldier remarked. No one was more relieved to hear the artillery's thunderous rumbling than de Grasse, who had churned with apprehension throughout the extended delay in opening fire. This was war and operations were always laced with unpredictability. The uncertainty had moved him to confide his fear: "I have launched myself into an affair that can turn out to my own disadvantage and to the humiliation of the nation."[30]

The bombardment was relentless. Shelling continued day and night. Up to 90 field and siege guns, and mortars, bombarded the besieged British troops with some 3,600 rounds every 24 hours. Perhaps the only person inside the British lines who was safe was Cornwallis, as he had his men dig him an underground bunker beneath the gardens that wreathed the house he used as his headquarters. "We continue to lose men very fast," Cornwallis advised New York within 48 hours of the beginning of the pounding, and added, "we cannot hope to make a very long resistance." Men suffered ghastly shrapnel wounds, falling houses and debris injured others, and now and then a soldier was blown to bits by a direct hit. Bodies and body parts of men and horses littered the landscape. By the time work began on the second parallel, on October 11, the British were responding with only about 120 rounds each day. One ball nearly took out Rochambeau. He was on foot during a reconnaissance and standing on a hill when a round "buried itself more than 2 feet in the ground between his legs."[31]

Completion of the second parallel brought the Allies to within 300 yards of the British lines, but two enemy redoubts yet guarded the region. The Allied commanders concluded that if the redoubts were not taken, Cornwallis might hold out for another 10 days. That was unacceptable and it was decided that the redoubts would have to be taken by assaults. The French would attack Redoubt 9; the Americans, Redoubt 10, the so-called Rock Redoubt. It was in Lafayette's quarter and he selected a French colonel to command the strike. Alexander Hamilton immediately appealed the decision to Washington. Hamilton wanted a shot at glory and he likely also sought to persuade Washington that this should be an American action, lest the public conclude that the victory at Yorktown was due entirely to the French. Washington consented, and as an inky darkness tightened over the terrain on October 14, Hamilton led three infantry battalions in storming the redoubt. The attackers possessed a 10-to-1 numerical superiority, but it was still dangerous business. They had to overcome professional soldiers armed with bayonets and fighting for their lives. The rebel force prevailed in hand-to-hand combat. Forty-four of Hamilton's men were killed or wounded in the attack, and more than half of the British defenders were casualties. The French suffered heavier losses at Redoubt 9, but their attack also succeeded. In the orange glaze of the next morning's dawn, Cornwallis discovered what had transpired. Weary and disheartened, he advised New York: Our "situation now becomes very critical."[32]

The Allied bombardment that morning was the most intense of the siege. After four hours, Cornwallis dolefully ordered one soldier to wave a white flag while a drummer beat the chamade, the age-old signal that a besieged army wished to negotiate. The guns were silenced while the Allied commanders studied—and rejected—the terms that Cornwallis proposed, but formal negotiations between representatives of the two armies soon began at the nearby home of a local landowner. Cornwallis hoped to drag out the talks as long as possible, thinking that Clinton's relief force might miraculously appear. Rochambeau and Washington were not about to permit the talks to go on indefinitely, and they gave Cornwallis until 11:00 A.M. on October 19, 48 hours after the chamade was beaten, to accept their terms or face a resumption of the firing. He accepted. Disease and the constant shelling had taken their toll. He could not go on. To do so, he said, would have been "wanton and inhuman to the last degree." He had only 3,800 men fit for duty, almost exactly half the number he had possessed when the siege commenced. He later reported that his losses included 133 killed, 285 wounded, and 63 missing.[33]

The surrender document signed by Cornwallis was delivered to Washington, who signed it and asked an aide to inscribe at the bottom of the document "Done in the trenches before York Town in Virginia, Oct 19, 1781." It was six and a half years to the day since the first shots of the war—the shots heard round the world—had been fired at Lexington and Concord. Cornwallis had agreed to surrender his entire army, all of his arms and stores, and every British vessel at York-town. While the soldiery that surrendered would become prisoners of war, Cornwallis and his staff were "permitted to go on parole." (One month later he was in New York.) Washington had consented to two concessions. Loyalists serving in provincial units went into captivity but otherwise were not to be punished. Cornwallis was also permitted to send one vessel to New York that carried "dispatches to Sir Henry Clinton." Washington knew full well that, along with the communiqués, Cornwallis would send off Loyalist civilians who had accompanied the British army. Looking the other way was preferable to risking a delay in the surrender.[34]

That same afternoon, two surrender ceremonies were conducted. Washington and Rochambeau attended the formalities at Yorktown, together with Comte de Barras standing in for de Grasse, who had been laid low by a "rather serious indisposition." The other surrender took place at Gloucester, where Banastre Tarleton was the British commander. At Yorktown, under a mild autumn sun, the grim-faced British marched from what had been their malodorous cage to the shaggy surrender field, trudging past quiet Allied soldiers and scores of civilians who had come to see the long-dreamed-of capitulation of the king's troops and, if possible, to reclaim runaway slaves that had fled to the British in recent months. One-third of the British soldiers who were shortly to become prisoners were too ill or too badly wounded to attend. Cornwallis was absent as well, pleading illness. He left it to General Charles O'Hara to surrender, a duty he performed with tears streaming down his face. As O'Hara was Cornwallis's second-in-command, Washington instructed him to surrender to his second-in-command, General Benjamin Lincoln, who had surrendered to the British at Charleston 17 months earlier. Some Americans said many of the British troops were "disorderly and unsoldierly," and some were intoxicated. At Gloucester, the anxious Tarleton confessed to a French officer that he feared for his safety. His counterpart took steps to assure that Tarleton would not be harmed. In the two ceremonies, 5,950 British troops and 1,100 seamen surrendered. Benedict Arnold had been ordered back to New York in June. Washington did not get his hands on him.[35]

Five days after the surrender ceremonies, the relief expedition organized by Clinton and Graves arrived at Cape Charles, Virginia. Graves's promised departure date of October 5 had not been met, as repairs to the ships damaged in the Battle of the Virginia Capes dragged on interminably. Two weeks passed following the original projected time for sailing before the fleet weighed anchor. It sailed from

New York on October 17, the day that Cornwallis waved the white flag. Clinton, anticipating a savage battle to liberate Cornwallis, had prepared his will before leaving Manhattan. But Clinton's force would face no battle. On reaching Cape Charles he learned what had transpired at Yorktown, getting the news from crewmen of a British ship that somehow had escaped de Grasse's net. Clinton, in a classic understatement, immediately informed Germain, "This is a blow." He shrank from telling the American secretary what he really thought about why the catastrophe had occurred, but with piercing anger he told a friend that Yorktown and the unfolding disaster in South Carolina were due to Cornwallis's "ill judged, ill timed" abandonment of the Carolinas.[36]

While Clinton lamented a disaster that he believed should never have befallen British arms, Americans celebrated. Joyous crowds "nearly approached madness" in the streets of Philadelphia, according to a witness. Across the land candles were burned in windows, fireworks lit the night sky, cannon boomed, Benedict Arnold was hanged in effigy, and Washington was hailed as the victor. Washington, who had exulted following his victories at Trenton and Princeton, displayed no emotion in his correspondence and in his diary said merely that Cornwallis had agreed to surrender and it was "accordingly done." Others were overjoyed and displayed it. Comte de Maurpas, Louis XVI's minister of state, hearing the news of Yorktown on his deathbed, proclaimed: "I die content." John Adams called it "glorious News!" Now that Cornwallis, like General Burgoyne, had surrendered an army, Benjamin Franklin exclaimed, "Infant Hercules in his Cradle has now strangled his second Serpent." The American people saw it in a similar light. Most were certain that the surrender of yet another large British army meant that the end of the war was near. They sensed what James Madison, a young congressman, put into words: The "severe doses of ill fortune" inflicted on the enemy at Yorktown and in South Carolina would compel Britain to abandon "her folly" and make peace.[37]

CHAPTER 15

WAR AND PEACE

CORNWALLIS'S ARMY HAD SURRENDERED at Yorktown, but the war was not over. Admiral de Grasse had promised to return to the Caribbean after finishing his business up north and cooperate with Spain in a spring campaign to take Jamaica. Furthermore, plans were under consideration in Madrid and Versailles for an attack on Gibraltar, hostilities raged on the high seas, and rival ambitions on the subcontinent and in Africa spurred continued fighting. But Yorktown was colossal and its implications reverberated throughout Britain and Europe.

Word of Cornwallis's surrender arrived in London late in November. Fittingly, it fell to Lord Germain to bring word of the disaster to Lord North. The prime minister reacted as if he had "taken a ball in the breast," according to Germain. North paced his office muttering again and again, "Oh God, it is all over!"[1] He understood that the disaster across the sea doomed his ministry and Britain's war in America.

Long-established foes of the war in Parliament, vindicated by what some called the "Burgoynishing" of Cornwallis, denounced further fighting, although George III publicly called for continuing the war, and Germain insisted that it was still possible to prevent American independence. Opposition spokesmen responded as they had for years. The war, "conceived in folly, tyranny, servility, and corruption," had resulted "in national ruin and disgrace," they proclaimed. Charles James Fox reminded his colleagues that seven years earlier the Earl of Chatham had told Parliament that the war could not be won, but "blind and incapable men" had taken the nation to war. Through their "iniquitous measures," Fox added, "We have lost

13 provinces of America, we have lost several of our islands . . . we have lost the empire of the sea, we have lost our respect abroad."[2]

North's government did not fall at once. The prime minister played for time, less from a hope of saving his ministry than from a desire to tamp down the cries for an immediate end to the war, lest those unbridled whoops weaken Britain's negotiating position in the almost-certain pending peace talks. The king tried to help North by easing Germain out of the cabinet and recalling General Clinton, both publicly saddled with blame for the lost war. Hanging by the slimmest thread, North spent much of his remaining time—about 90 days—in diplomatic maneuvers aimed at dividing the Allies. He hoped to entice either America or France to make peace, leaving England to continue the war against the other. North once again turned to David Hartley, having him write to Benjamin Franklin that Yorktown provided "a very fair opening" for peace "under liberal constructions." But it hinged on America agreeing to separate peace. Hartley warned that if the Americans would not come to terms, Britain would continue to fight on "to the last man, and the last shilling." North also dispatched an agent to Versailles who offered France a separate peace treaty based on uti possidetis in all theaters, the termination of British rights in Dunkirk, concessions in India, and possibly the return of Canada to France. Neither the Americans nor the French took the bait. Franklin told Comte de Vergennes what North was doing and informed Hartley that the United States would not desert "a noble and generous Friend for the sake of [peace] with an unjust and cruel Enemy."[3]

If the press was an accurate indicator, the prevailing mood throughout England by mid-January was for peace with the Americans. They "have fought nobly" for independence "and have gained it," one London newspaper proclaimed, and another advised the government that after seven years of war, "Your enemies are triumphant." When Parliament returned from its holiday break in January 1782, the opposition determinedly introduced motion after motion—six in all over 60 days—censuring North's government. Each failed, but North's majority shrank throughout the challenges. In February a motion asserting that the war with America "may no longer be pursued" failed by one vote. The next week the opposition moved to brand as "enemies to his Majesty and this country" all who supported "the farther prosecution of the offensive war" in America. It passed by 19 votes on February 28. The prime minister hung on for three additional weeks, but on March 20, with the king sighing, "At last the fatal day has come," North resigned the office he had held for a dozen years. Many thought him happy to be released from the burdens of his office.[4]

ON ALMOST THE SAME day that word of Cornwallis's surrender reached London, Admiral de Grasse was back in the Caribbean, having been trailed by the heavily outnumbered Admiral Hood, who had sailed from New York with 17 ships of the line and three smaller warships. Both France and Spain had approved de Grasse's agreement with Francisco de Saavedra for a joint campaign in the spring in quest of Jamaica, and over the winter both sent convoys loaded with weaponry and materials for the operation. While de Grasse awaited the provisions, he was busy with other activities. Weather frustrated his sortie against Barbados, but in February he took St. Kitts and Nevis. He came within a hair of trapping Hood at one point, but the British fleet escaped and soon thereafter was augmented by the arrival of 17 additional ships of the line under Admiral Rodney. Britain suddenly had naval superiority, although should de Grasse's fleet combine with Spain's, the Allied navies would once again be superior.[5]

De Grasse sheltered at Martinique for weeks, but early in April he sailed for Cap François to rendezvous with the Spanish fleet and 9,000 Spanish soldiers under General Bernardo de Gálvez. Three of de Grasse's great warships were elsewhere—one was in dry docks and two were tending to other duties—and three other ships of the line had sustained damage through accidents. De Grasse was aware that Rodney's now vastly superior force was nearby at St. Lucia and awaiting his move, but he thought he could outrun his adversary to Cap François. He could not. Rodney quickly pounced, and on April 12 the two fleets squared off just south of Guadeloupe in the Battle of the Saintes. A sudden shift in the wind allowed Rodney's ships to sail through a gap in de Grasse's formation and into position to lace the French squadron with a blistering and deadly fire. The French were overwhelmed. Most of their vessels escaped, but seven were captured, including *Ville de Paris* with de Grasse on board. The rigging on de Grasse's flagship had been destroyed, the masts were teetering, the hull was a mass of holes, and dead and wounded covered the deck. The surviving ships limped into Cap François, but 502 French officers and sailors had been killed and 1,611 wounded, and many vessels faced weeks or months of repair. The crippling of the French fleet left the Allies with no choice but to scrap the foray against Jamaica. On the very day that the projected campaign was scuttled, a Spanish fleet sailed from Havana for the Bahamas. The squadron included the *South Carolina*, a 40-gun frigate with a crew of hundreds from South Carolina's navy, a ship ordered by America's original team of diplomats and constructed in Amsterdam in 1778. The Spanish operation, the final significant action in the Caribbean, succeeded. Britain lost the Bahamas.[6]

In the last moments of twilight on the day of the Battle of the Saintes, de Grasse surrendered to Hood. One British seaman who boarded *Ville de Paris* said he was "over his buckles in blood" from the carnage. De Grasse, unhurt, watched as the French flag was lowered by the victors, after which he went aboard Rodney's flagship as a prisoner of war. He was first taken to Jamaica and, in late May, transported by his captors to London. His treatment in captivity could not have been more different from that of ordinary seamen taken prisoner. He lived comfortably, was introduced to the king and queen, sat for his portrait, and was permitted to keep his money—about £5,000—which he invested in British bills of exchange.[7]

GIBRALTAR REMAINED IN BRITISH hands despite a Spanish siege that had lasted for more than three years. It was Britain's last garrison in the Mediterranean and taking it had been a primary allure for Spanish belligerence, although in 1781 the Allies had put Gibraltar on the back burner while they focused on North America. Following Yorktown and the taking of Minorca, France and Spain began planning an assault on the bastion, preparations that consumed months and dragged through the summer of 1782. Vergennes looked on with mixed emotions. Success might render the British more accommodating in the peace talks, yet taking Gibraltar could tempt the Spanish to conclude a separate peace with London. Despite his reservations, France honored its alliance with Spain, and by September the Bourbon powers had committed 35,000 troops, one-third of which were French, and 39 ships of the line to the operation. Planning on how to take the seemingly impregnable fortress hinged on an innovative idea conceived by a French military engineer. His brainstorm was to use heavily armored floating batteries bristling with firepower to shell British fortifications on the western side of Gibraltar. It was hoped that the concentrated bombardment would breach Britain's lines and, following an amphibious landing, Allied soldiers would pour through the openings. Grandstands were constructed for the nobility who traveled from France and Spain to watch the show and the Allied triumph.

The attack began at daybreak on September 13, just over a year after the Allied armies had gathered at Yorktown. It did not go well for the Allies. The floating batteries took up positions 1,000 yards beyond the beach, too far to be effective, and the troops that landed found no openings that could be penetrated. Toward the afternoon, both the floating batteries and the land batteries ran out of ammunition. The big guns on the ships of the line were no more effective. Over a stretch of 36 hours, 40,000 rounds of artillery shells were fired at the thick rock walls of Gibraltar, a pounding that did little more than joggle Britain's defenders. By then, the beach was littered with the bodies of over 700 Allied soldiers, not quite the sight the spectators had hoped for. The attack was suspended, although the drawn-out siege continued without success until the end of the war. A month after the assault, the British for the third time in two years succeeded in getting a relief convoy through the Spanish investment.[8]

Among the penalties France had suffered for losing the Seven Years' War was its forfeiture of territorial holdings in India. After 1763, it retained only five commercial outposts. Thereafter, its policy in the East Indies was to reduce Britain's supremacy through the restoration of rajahs and sultans who had been displaced by British ascendancy and who might lead revolts that would banish the British from their homeland. In a convoluted sense, French strategy in India mirrored Britain's in utilizing Loyalists in America.

Much of the fighting was at sea, and from the perspective of the French was inconclusive, given that their navy was stretched thin by this war's multiple theaters. French soldiers and sailors died in droves, and in vain, as at war's end the balance of power on the subcontinent remained largely what it had been at the inception of hostilities. One who perished while soldiering for France was Achard de Bonvouloir, who had visited Philadelphia in 1775 on the mission that ultimately led to the creation of Caron de Beaumarchais's fictitious Roderigue Hortalez et Compagnie. Bonvouloir perished in Manjakuppam in an epidemic. He was 33 years old.[9]

When Lord North stepped down, the king reluctantly turned to the Marquis of Rockingham to form a new ministry. Rockingham's faction in Parliament had steadfastly opposed the war and there was no question that he welcomed peace talks. The looming negotiations led to administrative adjustments. The old framework of three secretaries of state gave way to the new office of home and colonial secretary and the post of foreign secretary. Rockingham selected Charles James Fox as foreign secretary. The Earl of Shelburne got the colonial post. Shelburne was a veteran diplomat who had questioned the wisdom of the war but, unlike Fox, all along unblinkingly opposed American independence. Shelburne claimed a role in the imminent diplomacy on the grounds that the American colonies were within his jurisdiction. Both Fox and Shelburne approved peacemaking, though Shelburne hoped negotiations would terminate in a formal connection between Britain and its American colonies; Fox was prepared to rapidly recognize American independence, a step that might divide the Allies and leave Britain to fight France and Spain. Fox's naiveté in the world of diplomacy and his unbridled commitment to American independence immediately aroused concerns over whether he was the right choice to represent Britain at the peace table.[10]

Shelburne spotted his opportunity to act when, on April 5, he received a letter from Franklin sent before he was aware that North's ministry had ended. Ostensibly, Franklin had written to thank Shelburne for sending some gooseberry bushes to a mutual friend. Franklin's timing might have been a fortunate happenstance, but the American envoy was artful and his good fortune was more likely the residue of design. Franklin applauded Parliament's recent resolutions "in favour of America" and expressed his hope that they would lead to "a general Peace" that "I am persuaded your Lordship, with all good Men, desires." Shelburne quickly responded with a flattering missive and word that he was sending Richard Oswald to Paris, a man he described as "fittest for the purpose" of conducting discussions that might lead to peace. In all, six British diplomats would eventually cross to France for negotiations during the next seven months. By and large, they were a credible contingent. Oswald was the least experienced of the envoys in politics and public affairs, but while an amateur in his new role, he was neither an innocent nor a simple soul.[11]

In mid-April, Oswald called on Franklin at his residence in the Hôtel de Valentinois in Passy, and the two were immediately comfortable with each other. Both were septuagenarians, each was thoroughly a man of the Enlightenment, and each had a background as a businessman. Before the war, Oswald, a Scot, had commercial dealings with the colonies and owned American real estate, and some in his family resided in America. He was amiable, but as one historian remarked, "a tough and wily old bird." The same could be said of Franklin. The two understood each other, and it helped them to get along well. Oswald found Franklin to be "Sparing of his words," but cordial and hopeful that the British and Americans could once again "be good friends" and trading partners. Oswald, with striking candor, promptly told Franklin that the English people wanted a separate peace with America, but wished to continue the war with France and Spain. The government, he said, desired a "General Peace ... providing that France does not insist upon Conditions too humiliating for England." Franklin said that a separate peace was "impracticable," as the Americans were "much obliged to France." Franklin added that he could do nothing without consulting Vergennes, and in fact he immediately informed France's foreign minister of this initial discussion. The next morning he took Oswald to Versailles to meet Vergennes.[12]

Oswald had hardly crossed the channel before Fox rushed an envoy to France, choosing Thomas Grenville, who for the most part carried on discussions solely with Vergennes. For more than three months Franklin was the only available American diplomat. During the previous summer Congress had created the five-member team of peace negotiators. Jefferson had declined the appointment, and Henry Laurens was captured while crossing to England in 1780; although recently released from a lengthy confinement in the Tower in London after Oswald posted his bail, Laurens refused to serve. Otherwise, John Adams remained in Holland to close the deal on a critical Dutch loan to the United States, and John Jay continued his diplomatic mission in Madrid.[13]

Grenville's talks went nowhere with Vergennes, whose hands were tied given that Spain would not consider serious negotiations prior to the assault on Gibraltar, still months away. It was a difficult period for Vergennes, who wished to speedily conclude peace. Given France's economic problems, he knew that if negotiations dragged on, those in the Conseil de Roi who longed to end hostilities would only grow stronger, perhaps compelling him to accept an unfavorable peace settlement. Furthermore, after a revolt erupted in June 1782 against the khan of Crimea, leading Prussia to intrude in the suddenly chaotic situation, Vergennes anguished that France's position in eastern Europe was growing more perilous. But Vergennes's greatest uneasiness stemmed from worry that one of his allies might conclude a separate peace, leaving France alone and at war with Britain. He had few worries about America's negotiations so long as the trustworthy Franklin was conducting the talks, but someday Jay and Adams would arrive and the tenor of the American delegation could drastically change.[14]

Early in the spring Franklin spoke with both Grenville and Oswald. Grenville, true to Fox's designs, probed for the means of persuading the Americans to make a separate peace. Franklin responded that the Franco-American bond was shatter-proof. Oswald, whom Franklin found to be "Wise & honest," stuck more to learning America's objectives, and soon Franklin told Shelburne, "I desire no other Channel of Communication between us than that of Mr Oswald." By May,

Rockingham's ministry understood that it was implausible to any longer believe that America would remain part of the British Empire. From that point onward, the issue in the cabinet was not whether to recognize American independence, but the terms on which it would be recognized.[15]

That did not mean a settlement was imminent. Throughout the spring the talks remained stalemated. Late in June, however, significant changes occurred. Rockingham died of influenza, which had reached pandemic proportions in Britain and elsewhere in Europe. The king elevated Shelburne to head the ministry. As it soon was evident that he would take a hands-on approach in the peace negotiations, Fox resigned as foreign secretary and Grenville bowed out as an envoy. Shelburne dispatched Alleyne Fitzherbert to conduct talks with Vergennes, left Oswald in place to treat with the "colonies"—that is, to continue discussions with Franklin— and sent Benjamin Vaughn, a leading English radical and foe of the American war, to see what he might tease out of Franklin.

Franklin responded by taking the initiative. He told Vaughn of having heard "from several Quarters" that "Shelburne's Plan" was that America would remain dependent on Britain and recognize the sovereignty of the king, though like Ireland, it would have its own parliament. Franklin called the notion a "preposterous chimera" and advised Vaughn that if that was really Shelburne's intention, "our negotiations for peace will not go very far; the thing is impracticable and impossible." Franklin chose this same moment to play his hand. He ticked off to Oswald what he labeled "hints" for a peace settlement. He presented two sets of terms, one that was "necessary" and one that was "advisable." The "necessary" articles were recognition of American independence; satisfactory American boundaries; and "freedom of fishing on the Banks of Newfoundland and elsewhere." The "advisable" terms—an ill-advised revelation of what the Americans would not fight doggedly to attain—included British compensation for the destruction it had wrought in American towns; London's admission of its "error" in waging war against America; the cession of "every part" of Canada to the United States; and the waiving of British custom duties on American "ships and trade." In passing along these ideas, Oswald told Shelburne that Franklin had "expressed himself in a friendly way towards England," hoped for bountiful postwar commercial ties between the two countries, and looked forward to the day when the United States and England would unite in a "foederal union."[16]

Shelburne badly wanted peace, as did most Britons and a majority in the House of Commons. But he was not about to accept everything that Franklin proposed, though the prime minister understood that complete American independence was inescapable and his dream of retaining the American provinces in something akin to a commonwealth system could not be realized. He now hoped that through making generous concessions to the Americans, France and Spain would realize that they must either agree to suitable peace terms or watch as America concluded a separate peace.[17]

Serendipitously, it was near this moment that Admiral de Grasse, on parole in London, paid a courtesy call on British officials, which led to his receipt of a purported offer from Shelburne of extremely generous peace terms for France and Spain. De Grasse was released to journey to Versailles and present Shelburne's terms, which, said the admiral, included American independence, the return of St. Lucia to France, restoration of French fishing rights on the Grand Bank and commercial rights in India, recognition of all Spanish conquests on the Gulf Coast, and the return of either Minorca or Gibraltar to Madrid. The message that de Grasse brought so intrigued Vergennes that he at once dispatched Joseph-Mathias Gérard de Rayneval, his private secretary, to London to confer with Shelburne. It was the first of numerous trips that Rayneval would make to England, visits that usually caused the financial markets to spike in London's stock exchange. Just as Franklin's hints had ushered in something of a thaw in his talks with Oswald, the terms that Shelburne conveyed through de Grasse—which the prime minister soon denied having made, though he discussed them with Rayneval anyway—defrosted the chill that had characterized the Anglo-French discussions. An immediate settlement was not in the offing, but more meaningful talks followed.[18]

While de Grasse was carrying out his assignment as a courier, an important change occurred in the American delegation. Jay arrived late in June, though he almost immediately fell ill with influenza. Claiming to be more "severely attacked" than any other patient treated by his doctor, Jay was unable to take up his duties until the first week in August. Deep into autumn he complained of having "little Strength," though he also said he was "neither very well nor very sick." Once he was able to return to work, it took Jay little time to understand that he saw Shelburne in a different light than his colleague. Franklin no longer doubted Shelburne's sincerity, if he ever had, whereas Jay saw him as wily and duplicitous. "Ld. Shelburne . . . says that our Independence shall be acknowledged—but it is not done, and therefore his Sincerity remains questionable," Jay quickly concluded. His outlook was the legacy of two decades of dealing with what nearly all American insurgents looked on as British deceit, but Jay was also aware that Shelburne had recently told Parliament that "nothing short of necessity" would compel him to recognize American independence. Shelburne had doubtless spoken from temporary political expediency, but the wary Jay took his remark at face value. Jay wrote to John Adams at The Hague of his distrust of Shelburne and found that his soon-to-be fellow commissioner shared his viewpoint. Adams shot back that the British were given to "insidious Intrigue and wicked Falshood." We will be "undone" if "we entertain an Idea of their Generosity . . . towards us." Adams added that he and Jay were not the representatives of a client state or the "American Colonies. . . . I think we ought not to treat at all, until we see a [British] minister authorized to treat with 'The United States of America.'"[19]

Adams also harbored a distrustful view of Vergennes and positively pulsated with bitterness toward Franklin. Adams did not doubt for a minute that French wartime assistance had been given so that France would benefit, and he was just as certain that Vergennes would seek peace terms that were in France's interest and possibly harmful to the United States. Adams was intent on breaking free of Vergennes's talons and striving at the peace table to make the postwar United States independent in fact as well as in name. His dislike of Franklin grew from his awareness that his fellow envoy had sought his ouster as America's peace negotiator. Adams looked on Franklin as Vergennes's toady, even telling America's secretary of foreign affairs, "Dr. F." is "an Index" of the French foreign minister's "Sentiments." Jay did not come to Paris with such malevolent views, but in short order he, too, brimmed with cynicism toward Vergennes and Franklin.[20]

Jay spent his first week back at work in discussions with Conde de Aranda, Spain's minister to France, about the boundaries the United States wished to achieve in the eventual peace treaty. Aranda proposed that the western boundary of the United States be set more or less at the crest of the Appalachians, hundreds of miles east of the Mississippi River. Such a settlement would deny the United States a massive region from which 11 states would eventually be carved, and in all likelihood, it would mean that the new American nation was surrounded by territories belonging to powerful European nations. Britain would possess Canada and trans-Appalachia, while East and West Florida were in the custody of Spain. Confined between the mountains and the sea, with British Canada to the north, Spanish Florida to the south, and Spanish America to the west, the United States would be unable to expand, and the preservation of its independence would be doubtful.

Both Franklin and Jay were appalled by the position taken by Aranda, and the two hurried together to Versailles hoping for help from Vergennes. His assistance was not forthcoming. Vergennes resolutely supported American independence, but the Treaty of Alliance did not compel France to guarantee the boundaries or territories of the new American nation. France, in 1778, had committed to assuring the "liberty, sovereignty and independence" of what the United States possessed at that moment and whatever "possessions . . . additions or conquests" it "may obtain during the War." Whether the United States had actually obtained any territory beyond the Appalachians was far from readily apparent. Other factors were also in play. Vergennes, as Adams had long suspected, wished to keep the United States a weak client state dependent on French assistance, a goal that would be realized through the western boundary that Aranda sought. Furthermore, Vergennes sought to aid his Bourbon ally, which not only had designs on some of trans-Appalachia but also looked on the region as a buffer zone to protect its interests against the rising new American nation. Vergennes said little during his meeting with Jay and Franklin, but Rayneval, who had collaborated with Aranda on the western boundary question, insisted that the Americans were asking for too much. Jay correctly assumed that Rayneval's outlook coincided with that of Vergennes.

Marquis de Lafayette, who seemed to be everywhere during this war, did not play a significant role in the peace negotiations in Paris, though on a couple of occasions he interceded on behalf of the Americans. Congress, in November, had directed Franklin to "confer" with Lafayette on "the situation of public affairs in the United States," though it said nothing about utilizing him when it came to diplomacy, which was how Franklin more or less played the directive. Lafayette, whom John Adams characterized as a man of "unlimited Ambition" who thought himself essential "in every Thing," whether politics, war, or diplomacy, interpreted Congress's wishes more broadly. Soon after the two American commissioners met with Vergennes and Rayneval, Lafayette sought out Aranda and encouraged him to recognize American independence. According to Jay, Lafayette's intrusion angered Aranda, who served a Spanish government fearful that American independence would inspire revolutionary movements for independence within Spain's American colonies. Six months later, Lafayette, with the blessing of the peace commissioners, traveled to Spain and was instrumental in persuading Floridablanca to promise American recognition, though many months would pass before Madrid formally recognized the United States.[21]

During the fateful August meeting with Vergennes, Jay had spoken of the necessity for Britain to recognize American independence before further talks ensued. Vergennes brushed that aside as a mere technicality. Britain's acceptance of

Franklin's and Jay's plenipotentiary powers was tantamount to acknowledging American independence, he argued. So long as American independence was recognized in the final peace treaty, Vergennes explained, the issue was of no consequence. Franklin remarked that Vergennes's position was fine with him. Jay snapped that he did "not like it." From this point onward Jay shared Adams's mistrust of the foreign minister and some of his colleague's misgivings regarding Franklin.[22]

For Jay and Adams, and many others, the American insurgency had been about more than breaking away from Britain. The two envoys were among those who saw the Revolution and war as the means to create an expansive new nation that was capable of standing alone, prospering, and possessing the resources to grow ever more powerful, all of which were essential for sustaining American independence. Jay understood that France was committed to American independence, as that would weaken Great Britain. But he now understood, if he had not previously, that it was not in France's interest that "we should become a great and formidable people" and that the French "will not help us to become so." It was imperative, Jay insisted, that the peace commissioners not abide by the instructions that Minister La Luzerne had earlier induced Congress to accept, including the directive that the envoys act in accordance with French wishes.

Franklin was mortified by Jay's perspective. Five years in France had left him with no "reason to doubt the good faith of the King of France," he told Jay, adding that Vergennes had always "treated us very fairly" and advising Jay to entertain no "suspicions" of his integrity. "Let us be mindful of the generosity of France to us in the past," Franklin said. Jay would not violate the Treaty of Alliance, but he thought it essential that the envoys vigilantly protect American interests, which he feared would be in peril if the peace commissioners blindly trusted matters to Vergennes.[23] Franklin knew that Adams would share Jay's point of view and the two would ultimately outvote him. Franklin, mostly alone, had been the American envoy who dealt with France throughout this long war, and on his own he had conducted his country's early negotiations with Britain in the aftermath of Yorktown. By and large he had excelled as a diplomat. But Franklin's reluctance to confront Vergennes, which struck many as intractable subservience, had outlived its usefulness. Franklin had always found Vergennes to be trustworthy, more often than not accommodating, and steadfast in his support of his beleaguered American ally. More than most, Franklin understand that France, at considerable sacrifice, had saved the American insurgency, and he suspected that his country might in the future need France's help. However, at this critical moment for the future of the United States,

Franklin's gratitude, faithfulness, and fidelity toward Vergennes potentially threatened his obligation as an American diplomat to protect the interests of his country above all else.

In the wake of his meeting with Vergennes, Jay took two important steps. He suspended further talks with Oswald, insisting that their resumption hinged on Britain's prior recognition of American independence. Grudgingly, Franklin agreed. For the next seven weeks the Americans and British did not negotiate. Soon after Jay broke off talks with Oswald, Franklin fell ill with kidney stones—a malady that now and again left him in misery for the remainder of his life, and prompted Shelburne to send him medicine to ease the pain—and for some time Jay acted alone. He continued discussions with Aranda on America's western boundary. The Spanish envoy grew more flexible, though not sufficiently so from Jay's perspective. In September, Jay unilaterally took his second audacious and terribly risky step. During the second week of that month he learned of Rayneval's first trip to London—the mission occasioned by the message that de Grasse had brought from Shelburne—and jumped to the mistaken conclusion that Vergennes, at America's expense, was about to conclude an "underhanded bargain" with Britain leading to an immediate peace. Jay responded by asking Benjamin Vaughn, the negotiator that Shelburne had earlier sent to Paris, to travel to London and inform the British prime minister that the United States was willing to abandon its alliance with France. He did not bother to inform Franklin of what he had done and he refrained from notifying Congress, as he knew all too well that "No Letter sent to the Congress is ever kept secret."[24]

Jay had taken a huge gamble. That it did not backfire on him was due to factors that he could not have foreseen. For some time Shelburne had been ready to conclude an honorable peace that recognized American independence, and he was more ready than ever by September. Already politically vulnerable, he was eager to wrap up negotiations before Parliament reconvened late in November. What is more, the failure of the Allied attack on Gibraltar occurred while Rayneval was conferring with Shelburne. The prime minister saw it as an opening for reaching an accord with his European enemies. Late in August, a couple of weeks before Jay spoke with Vaughn, Shelburne secured his cabinet's authorization for accepting the "necessary" peace terms that Franklin had long ago conveyed to Oswald. While Vaughn was en route to London, Shelburne sent an intermediary to inform Franklin that the king had agreed to recognize America's "full, complete, and unconditional Independence" in the first article of the eventual treaty. In September, days after Vaughn's arrival in London, Shelburne gave Oswald a new commission charging him to engage in talks with representatives of the United States. The sticking point that had dictated much of Jay's recent behavior was resolved. Oswald handed his new commission to an "entirely satisfied" Jay on October 2. Franklin immediately notified Congress that the "Negotiations for Peace have hitherto amounted to little more than mutual Professions of sincere Desires," and while "there are many Interests" yet to be resolved, serious talks with Britain were about to begin.[25]

With the impasse over American independence settled, Jay summoned Adams, who had secured the Dutch Republic's recognition of the United States, a 5-million-guilder loan for his country from several Amsterdam bankers, and a commercial treaty. Adams quickly departed for Paris, but his journey was frustratingly slow. Heavy rains caused delays, and a broken carriage axle stopped his journey altogether until repairs could be made. Night had fallen on October 26 when Adams finally reached Paris. The next morning he bathed at a public bathhouse on the Seine; visited the shops of a tailor, wigmaker, and shoemaker; and met with Matthew Ridley, a Maryland merchant who had been retained by his state to seek a loan. Ridley provided Adams with some idea of the activities of Jay and Franklin. The following day Adams met with Jay, but his hatred of Franklin was such that he had no intention of calling on him. "I have no Friendship for Franklin I avow," said Adams, whose feelings were a stew of jealousy toward his better known and widely admired colleague and acidic animosity owing to Franklin's betrayal in telling Congress that Adams would be a hindrance to peace negotiations. Adams characterized Franklin's treachery as "an assassination upon my Character." Franklin, he believed not entirely without justification, wants to "sweep Europe clear of every Minister but himself, that he might have a clear unrivalled Stage."[26]

Ridley persuaded Adams that it was advisable to pay a social call on Franklin. If the British learned that the American delegation was riven with friction and incivility, he explained, they might exploit it. After three days in town, Adams rode to Passy and managed to be cordial. He thought Franklin was "merry and pleasant." Adams did not bother to notify Vergennes that he had arrived, something the foreign minister only discovered two weeks later in the "returns of the Police." When the three American envoys finally met together, Adams was pleased at much that he learned. However, he was dismayed to discover that Jay had reached agreements touching on the northern boundary and fishing rights that were disadvantageous to New England, issues that Adams vowed to pursue.[27]

From early October onward, diplomacy proceeded at an accelerated pace. Much remained to be settled, as Franklin had said, but agreements were gradually reached on an array of issues. All three American envoys were active in the negotiations: Jay, with considerable help from Franklin, focused on boundary questions; Franklin bore much of the weight in the talks on Britain's demand that the United States compensate the Loyalists for their losses; Adams concentrated on the fisheries and the northern boundary. On the whole, the discussions were cordial and on some evenings the British and American emissaries dined together.[28] Throughout the final weeks of discussions, carried out as fall's foliage faded and eventually disappeared altogether, the diplomats alternated between long and intense daily negotiations and intermittent lulls while the British representatives awaited instructions from London.

Boundary questions consumed session after session, prompting Henry Strachey, one of the British envoys, to exclaim in frustration that "the Americans are the greatest quibblers that I have ever seen."[29] The area between the Ohio River and the 31st parallel (today's Kentucky, Tennessee, and much of Alabama and Mississippi) was not an issue, but the Ohio Country's borders—the region above the Ohio River that the Americans saw as stretching to the Mississippi River in the west and to who knew where in the north—was hotly contested.

In the end, the American commissioners got nearly everything they were after west of the Appalachians, largely because it was not a matter of vital concern to the British. The region was important for Spain. However, the final peace accords resulted from a "complex . . . set of interlocking negotiations," as historian Jonathan Dull observed, and the Spanish, aware that they could not attain all of their objectives, had to make choices. They eventually found that gaining other ends was more alluring than securing a large chunk of territory between the mountains and the Mississippi that they likely knew they could not retain indefinitely.[30]

For the most part, Britain's possession of Canada was not an issue. The Americans had little claim to it, having failed to take it in the 1775 invasion, and the British were as inflexible on this issue as the Americans were on the matter of their western boundary. If America's acquisition of Canada was off the table, setting the boundary between British Canada and the United States resulted in considerable haggling. The Americans, adhering to Congress's 1779 instructions, sought a border running from New York to the Mississippi River at what came to be known as the Nipissing Line, essentially today's southern Ontario as well as considerable territory north of present-day Michigan and Wisconsin, and above the Great

Lakes. The British were unyielding on that issue too, and the Americans eventually relented, a concession that gave the British access to the Great Lakes and possibly opened the door for reciprocal compromises on other issues. The boundary in the New England region sparked even more disputation. The British coveted today's Maine, a region from which it acquired timbers for its shipbuilding industry and which it foresaw for as a tract for the resettlement of American Loyalists. But the Yankee John Adams, a renowned lawyer in prewar Boston, had lugged maps and records across the Atlantic in preparation for these negotiations, and he attacked the matter like an attorney building a case for judge and jury. He produced documents that revealed land grants in the disputed region that King James I had made to the Massachusetts Bay Colony more than 150 years earlier. Both sides ultimately made concessions on New England's border, leading Adams to later remark that the final agreement was the result of "the greatest moderation" by both parties. As far as the Americans were concerned, the outcome was quite close to what they had sought.[31]

Boundary issues were resolved before the matter of American access to the Newfoundland fisheries, also a substantive matter for New England that was handled almost solely by Adams. He swam upstream on this matter, as the fisheries were all-important for Britain and France. "We had a constant Scuffle Morning noon and night about Cod and Haddock," Adams later said. He gallantly told the British that when God made the Newfoundland Banks only 300 leagues from America and 600 from France and England, the deity had as much as given the Americans "a right" to the fisheries. Furthermore, American colonists had fought and died alongside British troops in earlier wars to secure Anglo-American rights to the fisheries. One of the British envoys conceded that the "Argument is in your Favour," but he would not fully yield, and in the end the Americans accepted the "right" to fish and the "liberty" to dry their catch in Nova Scotia, the Magdalen Islands, and Labrador, though not in Newfoundland. Although the settlement resulted in Anglo-American contention for generations, Adams had not done too badly for New England's fishing industry and the collateral interests tied to it. He expressed "tolerable Satisfaction" with the final resolution of both the boundary and fishery issues. As for the latter, he boasted that "our Tom Cod are Safe, in Spight of the Malice of Ennemies [and] the Finesse of Allies." When asked at dinner on the final evening of negotiations if he wished fish, Adams declined, adding, "I have had a pretty good meal of them today."[32]

The questions of prewar American debts and compensation for the Loyalists likewise sparked sharp clashes and were among the last matters to be resolved. Shelburne was intractable on the debt issue. His position was that "*honest* debts may be *honestly* paid in *honest* money," and as late as mid-October the cabinet wrote new instructions for Oswald directing him to fight "strongly" for the payment of the debts. The Americans ultimately consented to Britain's recovery of debts incurred before the war at full value in sterling money. But the Americans held firmly to their refusal to indemnify the Loyalists. Shelburne saw the matter as a political life-and-death issue and his envoys fought hard. Neither Jay nor Adams was moved by the dire plight of the Loyalists or by Shelburne's touching earnestness. Both were aware that most of their countrymen sought vengeance against those who had helped the enemy. Furthermore, Jay thought the Tories were "dishonorable" people who had "outstripped Savages in perfidy and Cruelty" on New York's frontier. Adams railed that the Loyalists' "Misrepresentations" had "deceived" Britain's leaders, prolonging hostilities. He reminded his counterparts that Britain had confiscated Irish property and never compensated the victims, adding that it would cost Britain less to compensate the Tories than they were spending each month that the war continued. Nonetheless, Adams and Jay were somewhat willing to make amends, and Adams later urged officials in Massachusetts to show "as much moderation . . . towards the Tories as possible." However, Franklin, whose son was a Loyalist, was immovable. The best the British could do was agree that Congress would "earnestly recommend" that the states make restitution to the Loyalists, a treaty clause that all parties understood was meaningless.[33]

The weary British and American diplomats brought the talks to a close on November 29, the day that Henry Laurens, who had finally decided to participate, arrived in Paris. As snow showers swept across the city on the following day, Saturday, November 30, the four American commissioners met their counterparts at Oswald's apartment in the Grand Hôtel Muscovite to sign a "preliminary" treaty, given that it was conditional on the agreement that the other belligerents eventually reached. Laurens, who had participated in none of the meticulous and stressful negotiations, proposed the inclusion of a sentence that prohibited the British from seizing property following the treaty's ratification. Laurens, a slaveowner, knew that the word "property" meant enslaved peoples and he wished to protect his interests and those of all American slave owners. "We all agreed" there should be no further "Plunders . . . of Negroes," Adams said. Their casual and indifferent acquiescence consigned countless human beings to bondage in subsequent generations. Neither press nor spectators were present at the ceremony, if it can be called that. There was no pomp and the affair was brief and simple. Thereafter, all the diplomats traveled under a heavy sky to Passy for a relaxing farewell dinner at Franklin's residence.[34]

The negotiations that Lord North had sought to generate 11 months earlier, and that Shelburne and Fox had gotten off the ground in April, were over. The accord was a signal achievement for the American commissioners, who had wrestled with the thorniest of issues and made difficult, even intrepid, decisions. In October and November the American envoys had made an excellent team, and as Jay remarked, possibly truthfully, there had not been "the least difference in sentiment" among them on the questions of boundaries and access to the fisheries.[35] Two years earlier General Washington had said that he had almost ceased to hope for a good outcome to the war, and 18 months earlier Congress, under the thumb of Minister La Luzerne, had in essence instructed its commissioners to seek far less than they finally obtained. Independence was secured, as were generous boundaries and some fishing rights, and Britain's promise to remove its troops from the United States. In exchange, the Americans agreed to honor prewar debts and what all knew was a worthless stipulation concerning compensation for the Loyalists. All in all, the British had not fared too badly considering that they had lost two large armies and two crucial naval battles in the course of the war. However, had George III agreed to the earlier opportunities to settle the war on the basis of uti possidetis, Britain would have retained a vast expanse of territory that now was to be left to the United States. The recognition of American independence was not seen as a capitulation by British diplomats. American independence was virtually guaranteed once Parliament, in March, prohibited further offensive war. Furthermore, Britain's boundary and fishing concessions were hardly crippling.

It fell to Franklin to ride to Versailles to inform Vergennes that his American ally had signed a separate peace. With considerable chutzpah, he then asked for another French loan, which the French agreed to three weeks later in what Franklin errantly characterized as a "friendly and good humoured" manner. Vergennes, in fact, told Franklin that it had been "indecent" of the American commissioners to make a separate peace. Franklin penitently responded, "we hope it may be excused" as "we all love and honour" Louis XVI.[36]

With the job finished, Jay praised Adams's "useful" contributions and extolled Franklin's eventual "firmness and exertions." Similarly, Adams confided to his diary that Jay, with whom he had once crossed swords in Congress, had been the most capable of the American commissioners. "I love him," Adams said later, calling him "my Comforter." He even acknowledged that Franklin had been "very able" in the last weeks of discussions. Indeed, whereas a couple of years earlier some in Congress had sought Franklin's recall, in part because they thought him too old for the rigors of diplomacy, he had borne up with remarkable vigor throughout the strain and grinding toil of negotiations. Adams's magnanimity toward his colleagues stemmed from more than having gotten a good treaty. In mid-November during the final stages of the talks, Vergennes invited him to dinner at Versailles and, in a gambit at manipulation, praised Adams as the "Washington of Negotiation." Adams was swept off his feet. "This is the finishing Stroke. It is impossible to exceed this," he gushed. A month later, when a Dutch envoy told him that the treaty was a "noble Tryumph" that Franklin alone could never have achieved, Adams beamed again. Adams may have generously appraised the roles played by Jay and Franklin, but his thinking about Vergennes never softened, not even after the foreign minister lauded his talents. But Adams was not a historian, and the dispassionate assessment of Vergennes by historians has been more munificent. The French foreign minister did not seek to prevent the separate talks that the Americans conducted with the British, and he never attempted to force the American peace commissioners to adhere to the instructions that La Luzerne had conjured Congress to write.[37]

The American diplomats had every reason to rejoice, aware, as Jay remarked, that the "affairs" of the United States "have a very promising aspect."[38] But there were losers. The British lost 13 of their North American colonies, which the Earl of Chatham and Edmund Burke in 1775 had warned would be the outcome of going to war to quell the colonial insurgency. The Loyalists got nothing from the peace treaty and lost everything as a result of their support of Britain's war against the American rebels. America's Indigenous peoples were in the long run the greatest losers of all. Germain, in 1776, had pledged to Joseph Brant that Great Britain would stand behind the Iroquois who fought the American rebels and, at war's end, would redress their grievances. The Iroquois did fight, tying down Continentals and rebel militia, but in Paris in 1782 Britain's diplomats forsook them and other tribes. They gave ownership of Britain's land east of the Mississippi River to the United States, a shameful sellout that Shelburne later defended with the lame argument that "the Indian nations were not abandoned to their enemies; they were remitted to the care of their neighbours, whose interest it was as much as ours to cultivate friendship with them."[39]

While the Americans and British haggled throughout October and November, French, Spanish, and British diplomats were simultaneously at work, in talks that stretched into the first days of 1783. Although most discussions occurred in France, the key talks took place in England, as Rayneval continued to shuttle across the channel to negotiate with Shelburne at Bowood Park, the prime minister's country estate, and at his London residence in Berkeley Square. Vergennes and his predecessor, Duc de Choiseul, had for years sought retaliation against Great Britain and the weakening of their nemesis by helping the American colonies to break away. Ultimately, Vergennes had been willing to go to war to gain those ends, including regaining the Newfoundland fisheries lost in the Seven Years' War. By late summer it was clear that Britain, through the loss of its colonies, would be weaker, but resolution of the fisheries question dragged into autumn. Reclaiming the right to the fisheries was crucial not only because of their economic value but also because they were vital to France's naval strength, as they stimulated ship construction and promoted the training of mariners. As the British had similar interests with regard to the fisheries, negotiations were arduous, but in the end France won a restoration of the "exclusive rights" it had obtained in the Treaty of Utrecht in 1713. France also secured Britain's removal from Dunkirk, but after four years of costly warfare it had not achieved appreciable gains in the West Indies or on the subcontinent, although it regained Senegal, a former colony in Africa. France came away with Tobago and St. Lucia in the West Indies, but relinquished its claims to all other Caribbean conquests.[40]

In addition to Spain's ambitions regarding trans-Appalachia, Floridablanca had been obsessed with regaining Gibraltar and Minorca. He had also taken Spain to war to secure his country's control of the Gulf of Mexico—vital for the protection of the shipments of vast quantities of riches shipped from Mexico—and to secure and advance its interests in the West Indies and Central America. From the outset of negotiations, Madrid doubted it could attain all that it wished unless it was willing to continue the war. That was not in the cards. The Spanish, too, understood what Vergennes perceived. The English "have to some degree regenerated their navy while ours [the Bourbon's] has been used up," Vergennes confided to his ambassador in Madrid. Moreover, like every other belligerent by the fall of 1782, Spain faced severe economic problems that made it anxious for peace. Nevertheless, Floridablanca clung tenaciously to his demands until mid-December when, at last, Vergennes persuaded Minister Aranda, who was conducting the talks in France, to drop the demand for Gibraltar.[41]

Negotiations between the European belligerents continued for a month and a half following the conclusion of the Anglo-American preliminary treaty. Shelburne's hand was strengthened once the Americans consented to a separate peace, a settlement that was more to the disadvantage of the Spanish than the French. Had it not been for the preliminary treaty, Spain might have gotten Gibraltar. In November, Shelburne told the Spanish they could have Gibraltar, but they could not have it and Minorca, West Florida, and Puerto Rico as well. But in the aftermath of the preliminary treaty, Shelburne was altogether unwilling to yield Gibraltar. To have done so atop what the Americans had won would have been political suicide. In the end, Spain kept Minorca, obtained East Florida—giving it all of the Floridas from the Atlantic to the Mississippi and ensuring Spanish dominion in the Gulf of Mexico—held its own in Central America, though it ceded logging rights in the region to Britain, and returned the Bahamas to Britain.

Of all the European belligerents, the war had been the most disastrous for the Dutch. Vergennes negotiated for them and secured only the return of Trincomalee, an important Dutch naval base in Ceylon, though the Dutch had to relinquish a minor port to get it. The envoy the Netherlands sent to Versailles raged that the "diabolical" Vergennes had played all the other belligerents against one another "and all of you against us and us against all of you, according to [his] own interests."[42]

The exhausting negotiations had stretched over many months and were handled by several envoys. Some were superior to others, and some made mistakes, but no diplomat was an egregious failure. There were four instances of notable courage displayed by diplomats that were crucial in the negotiating process. The decision by Jay, with Adams's support, to ignore Congress's instruction to "undertake nothing" during the negotiations without France's "knowledge and concurrence," and "to govern yourself by their advice and opinion," undoubtedly led to more bountiful peace terms for the Americans. Despite his slim majority in Parliament, Shelburne bravely made concessions, each of which threatened the life of his ministry, which in fact fell following the negotiations. When Rayneval was first sent to London to sound out Shelburne on the validity of de Grasse's claim that Britain was offering generous peace terms, his instructions were to return home immediately if the British prime minister denied his supposed proffer. Shelburne did disavow de Grasse's story, but Rayneval disregarded Vergennes's orders and stayed on in England, a pivotal decision that kept the peace talks alive and moving. Finally, Aranda disobeyed orders from Floridablanca in turning his back on Gibraltar. He did so to gain for Spain what he saw as the bigger—and more readily available—prizes of Minorca and West Florida.

The American commissioners had been kept in the dark about the progress of the negotiations between the British, French, and Spanish, and were surprised when they were suddenly summoned to Versailles for the signing of that peace accord. It, too, was a preliminary peace, as it instituted an armistice while the belligerent nations scrutinized and, hopefully, approved the accords. As Jay and Laurens were out of town, Adams and Franklin hurried to Versailles and, on January 20, signed for the United States. It was done with "little Ceremony, and in as short a Time as a Marriage Settlement," said Adams. He added: "Thus drops the Curtain on this mighty Trajedy. It has unraveled itself happily for Us. And Heaven be praised."[43]

Throughout the months that followed, no substantive changes were made to the preliminary treaties—"We could obtain no Improvement Amendment or Alteration" in discussions with the British over the past nine months, said Adams—and, on September 3, 1783, the Definitive Treaty of Peace, known more generally as the Treaty of Paris of 1783, was signed by representatives of each warring nation.[44] The occasion was so anticlimactic that Adams did not even mention it in his diary.

The preliminary and final treaties provoked joy in the United States. Members of Congress exclaimed, "Hostilities to Cease in America," and rejoiced that "America is now free and Independent." One congressman happily predicted, "The day is now Come when the Sun will Raise on Amirrica never to set." Alexander Hamilton thought something like that was possible, but only if "solid establishments" were made to strengthen the national government, a vital step needed to "perpetuate our union [and] prevent our being a ball in the hands of the European powers." If that can be, Hamilton told Washington, "our independence [is] truly a blessing."[45]

In time there was some nitpicking at the treaties, but Benjamin Franklin may have come closest to capturing the popular spirit at learning of peace. "I hope it will be lasting, & that Mankind will at length, as they call themselves reasonable Creatures, have Reason and Sense enough to settle their Differences without cutting Throats. For in my Opinion *there never was a good War, or a bad Peace.*"[46]

CHAPTER 16

REFLECTIONS ON AMERICA'S REVOLUTIONARY WAR

FOLLOWING CORNWALLIS'S SURRENDER, THE armies in America remained intact waiting to learn if Yorktown would end the war. Rochambeau's army wintered in Virginia. Washington's Continentals returned to the vicinity of Manhattan, where 14,000 British troops were garrisoned. Roughly 10,000 additional British troops remained in Charleston, Savannah, and Wilmington, North Carolina. In July 1782, about the time that Benjamin Franklin presented his "hints" to Richard Oswald, the French army leisurely marched to Peekskill, where it briefly rendezvoused with a portion of the Continental army before tramping to Boston. On Christmas Eve, a couple of months before word of the Anglo-American Preliminary Treaty reached Philadelphia, the French army sailed away.[1]

No major campaigns were undertaken in America after Yorktown, though in a meeting with Rochambeau in Philadelphia in July, Washington proposed a siege of New York or a joint invasion of Canada. Rochambeau turned him down. Throughout 1782 the Americans and British discussed prisoner swaps, talks that were unavailing. But change was in the air once word arrived in the spring of 1783 of the preliminary accord signed by the four belligerents in Versailles. The treaty called for an armistice, news that Washington kept secret until he had taken steps to prevent mass desertions. Finally, on April 19, 1783, the eighth anniversary of Lexington and Concord, America's commander in chief, in camp at Newburgh on the Hudson River, announced the armistice in a celebration of the "Cessation of Hostilities."[2]

The armistice led to fruitful talks concerning prisoners, and within 100 days the last of the captives held in America by both sides had been liberated. Demobilization of the Continental army occurred as well. Washington commanded a restive army of unpaid soldiers who were eager to return home. Discipline was breaking down and the fear of bloody mutinies was palpable. To prevent a catastrophe, Congress in May authorized Washington to furlough most of the men, and by July about 80 percent of the soldiers had departed. They were given certificates that supposedly could be redeemed for cash in six months. That was fiction. Congress knew it and so did the dispirited troops. One enraged young officer called it the final betrayal of men who had sacrificed "to make [the] Country Happy." He added, if "this Continent and its inhabitants were worth fighting for," the government should not have sent "the brave deliverers of [the] Country" home "without one farthing of reward for their services." In time, nearly all the former soldiers sold the certificates to affluent speculators, mostly moneyed men who a decade later realized windfall profits thanks to economic reforms undertaken in Washington's presidency. Not for the last time in American history a redistribution of wealth from those at the bottom to those at the top had occurred. Many soldiers were bitter when they left for home, and presumably not a few remained angry over how they had been treated while on active duty. On enlisting they had been assured of receiving adequate food, clothing, and a monthly paycheck; most had never received what had been promised. At the end, they were handed certificates of no immediate value and sent away. A soldier who had spent eight years in the army, and now faced a long trek home with empty pockets, pithily captured his blazing rancor and that of his comrades, "It was, soldiers, look to yourselves; we want no more of you."[3]

The British army evacuated all of its southern posts in the course of 1782, bringing most of the troops to New York, where General Guy Carleton, Sir Henry Clinton's successor, awaited orders regarding the evacuation of New York. London would not issue those orders until the Definitive Treaty of Peace was signed. The deep chill of autumn 1783 had settled in before word of the Treaty of Paris and the orders to depart New York at last arrived. As Carleton made preparations for his army's departure, Washington, in November, delivered a farewell address to his army, now posted at West Point. He said the soldiery that had been a "patriotic band of brothers" united in quest of winning "such a wonderful revolution," and he allowed that America's victory was "little short" of a "miracle."[4]

When Carleton at last set November 22 as the date for abandoning New York, Congress discharged all but 800 of the troops at West Point. Washington led these few remaining men down to Manhattan and to the edge of New York City to await Carleton's departure. The British were slow getting away, as more than 20,000 troops—including nearly 6,000 Americans who had served in provincial units—as well as hundreds of horses and tons of supplies and ordnance had to be loaded on transports. Finally, in the late morning on November 25, the evacuation was completed. The minute the last British soldier was off the island, the Continental army began its victory parade down Broadway.[5]

Washington remained in the city for several days attending one ceremonial event after another, the last of which was a tearful farewell luncheon with several officers. Thereafter, he hurried to Philadelphia for a shopping spree and finally to Annapolis, where Congress was meeting. He submitted his wartime expense account, as in 1775 he had agreed to serve without pay and asked only that he be compensated for expenses incurred. Congress accepted what he presented without question, though it said he had shortchanged himself by one dollar. On December 23, in one last ceremony, Washington surrendered his commission and delivered one final farewell address. America's victory, he said on this occasion, was due to his officers, the dogged commitment of the people, and the hand of God. He did not mention the enlisted men in the Continental army, militiamen, or partisans. Nor did he mention the help the United States had received from France and Spain.[6]

Once he completed his speech, Washington was out the door in a flash and on his way to Mount Vernon, which he reached at twilight on Christmas Eve. The war was truly over. The diplomats and governments had officially brought it to an end, and the soldiers had gone home or been redeployed elsewhere. Those who had survived this long, bloody war were the fortunate ones, if they had gotten through the ordeal with body and soul intact. A great many warriors had not come through. Some 36,000 American soldiers are believed to have died, somewhere in the vicinity of one in 14 free American males of military age, and perhaps as many as one in 10 of those in the 18-to-23-year-old age cohort from which most of the troops were drawn.[7]

No one knows the number of civilians that died as a result of the war. But many perished from diseases that spread from armies into the civilian sector, some residents of coastal hamlets were victims of naval bombardments or British raiding parties, numerous frontier inhabitants were killed in Loyalist and Indian attacks, and countless enslaved people who risked all in flights for freedom died in the course of their attempted escape from bondage or after reaching the British army.

One quarter of the British and Hessian troops—roughly 10,000 redcoats and 7,500 Germans—who served in America perished. Another 40,000 British soldiers and sailors died in other theaters or on the high seas. Some 20,000 French soldiers and sailors perished, as did thousands of Spaniards at sea and on land and in far-flung theaters. Somewhere in the vicinity of 100,000 of America's enemies and allies did not make it home.[8]

One can only guess at the number of Native Americans who died either fighting or from disease, or who perished from deprivation brought on by the destruction of their homes and verdant fields by enemy troops and marauding parties.

The War of Independence comes down to subsequent generations in the form of preserved battlefields that are lush and green, and betray little or no sign of the terror, atrocities, and miseries that occurred there. We remember the war through paintings of officers in resplendent uniforms and clean-shaven soldiers who customarily display little evidence of privation and hardship. In reality, this war, like all wars, was filled with pain and suffering, paralyzing fear, destitution, loneliness, and death—often agonizing deaths far from home and the care and compassion of loved ones. This war spread to many corners of the globe, and before it ended people who had never heard of Lexington and Concord, Massachusetts, where the war's first shots were fired, were touched by hostilities.

GOING TO WAR IS akin to crossing the threshold into unknown territory. What awaits those who enter the dark, mysterious region cannot be known.[9] Britain went to war in 1775 expecting ineffectual resistance from disunited and poorly led colonists thought to be utterly incapable of contending against a professional army. The ministers in Lord North's cabinet who chose to use force were not entirely incorrect. The Americans, faced with a dearth of weaponry and powder, were woefully unprepared for war. As it turned out, so was Britain. It had too few troops in America to crush the rebellion in the first year of hostilities. The British were better prepared in 1776; the Americans only marginally so. A year into the conflict the Continental army lacked sufficient manpower and its supply system remained dreadfully inefficient. The army was led by an amateur commander who made grievous mistakes and by callow officers at the field grade level and below. Its troops were unseasoned. Britain could have, and should have, closed out the war in 1776. But General Howe, in the New York campaign, threw away several chances to crush the Continental army. He failed to act aggressively in Brooklyn Heights, languidly invaded Manhattan, twice permitted his trapped adversary to escape what should have been ironclad snares, and blundered egregiously in permitting Washington's forlorn army to cross the Delaware River in December. If Howe's generalship was faulty that year, it was untenable in 1777. Britain still might have won the war, but by dividing his forces that summer Howe orchestrated the cataclysm that befell the British army at Saratoga and brought France into the conflict. During the war's initial 30 months the British at times were surprised, but they were mostly undone by miscalculations made before going to war, Howe's repeatedly mistaken choices, and in 1777 by Lord Germain's failure to compel his commander in America to adhere to a realistic campaign plan.

From 1778 onward, Britain possessed only a slim chance of destroying the insurgency, though the possibility remained that it might yet retain some colonies and all of trans-Appalachia, and it might even prevent American independence. Following Saratoga, Britain sought to retake control of two or more southern colonies while exhausting its enemies through prolonged hostilities. It was a tall order, but not an impossible one, and as late as April 1781 General Clinton—Britain's best commander in this war and a far better one than most historians have recognized—had a shot at achieving what Britain had laid down as its goals in the aftermath of Saratoga. But the strategy that he had carefully conceived was ruined when General Cornwallis abandoned South Carolina, and Germain and George III—neither of whom had a cogent understanding of the war in America—ordered Clinton to maintain a large British army in Virginia.

When Lord North's ministry considered the use of force, it understood that having to campaign in the backcountry could present formidable hazards. However, the ministers dismissed that possibility as unlikely, a misjudgment of spectacular proportions as early as the first day of the war. North's government additionally comprehended the danger of French belligerence, but thought the war could be won before France intervened. The ministry was partially correct. Three years passed before France entered the war. But the ministry had failed to foresee the extent of covert assistance that France would provide, aid that sustained American resistance in the wake of the crippling disasters of 1776 and without which the capture of the British army at Saratoga could not have been achieved.

One thing that was not hidden from the ministers was that for the first time in a century Britain would be going to war without a European ally, and that could be an invitation for the unfettered Bourbon allies to intervene. But anticipating a short war, the ministers dismissed the possible peril. They were wrong.

Going to war is always filled with calculations and gambles. Britain wagered that most of the colonists remained loyal to the Crown, a supposition based largely on misinformation provided by Loyalists and royal officials in some colonies. There were plenty of Loyalists, though not as many as London imagined. Furthermore, a substantial percentage of the Tories had been cowed prior to hostilities and disarmed soon after Lexington and Concord. Britain also banked on ending the war quickly, a bet that did not pan out, leaving London with a wider war for which both its army and navy were ill equipped.

Britain's unmistakable errors are crystal clear with 20-20 hindsight. So, too, are problems the British war effort faced that were not adequately appreciated prior to hostilities. There was much talk before the war of severing the head of the snake—crushing the insurgency in New England, whereupon the rebellion would wither away in the remainder of North America. Instead, the British faced putting down a revolt in a huge country that stretched thousands of miles from northern New England to deep into the South. Accustomed to campaigning primarily in the spatially limited Low Countries and western Germany, Britain's commanders were confronted with a prodigious American theater in which communication and coordination between separate commands was slow and difficult. Furthermore, the commanders did not always have maps, and if they did, they were often of poor quality. Their armies had to campaign in environments for which the officers and soldiers were largely untrained—forested areas, primitive roads, terrain intersected by rivers and swamps, and persistently torrid conditions in the South that were unlike anything Britain's armed forces had endured in Europe.

London's armies were also hampered by a precarious supply system that originated in Britain and culminated 3,000 miles away in America after the supply ships had run a treacherous gauntlet of privateers and enemy navies. Their armies were frequently dogged by shortages, especially a dearth of horses, a scarcity that restricted mobility and at times robbed British commanders of a crucial cavalry arm. Years passed before the British, faced with a hostile population, succeeded in establishing a superb intelligence system. The British had sent an army to America in the Seven Years' War that received considerable assistance from the colonists. But the Americans were their enemy in this war, an enemy that grew in size as warfare and the sometimes wanton behavior of the British hardened attitudes.

From before hostilities to the last decisive campaign, the British discounted the effectiveness of American militia. Sometimes their suppositions were correct. But given its own long militia tradition, Britain curiously underestimated the difficulties that colonial militiamen would pose. The officials who took Britain to war did not foresee the role militia units would play in checkmating Loyalists, disrupting foraging parties and patrols, and harrying the army's supply lines. Those same officials never imagined the combat effectiveness that militiamen would display along Battle Road, atop Bunker Hill, in the Saratoga campaign, and at Cowpens and Guilford Courthouse.

Britain also faced an unaccommodating enemy. Britain's officers and men were principally trained for waging war as it was traditionally conducted in Europe, set-piece engagements fought in open terrain. Generals Howe and Clinton, and Germain in London, recognized the need to bring the Continental army to battle, for if it was utterly destroyed the rebellion would collapse. At times the Americans unwisely obliged them. They did so on Long Island in August 1776 and later at Brandywine and Charleston, paying a heavy price in each encounter. However, after his close call in 1777, Washington stuck to his Fabian strategy, no longer accommodating the British high command's hope of facing off against the Continental army in a general action.

Perhaps Britain's most profound problem should not have come as a surprise. The British army in 1775 and in the years after 1777 was often not large enough to effectively wage war in America. Long before hostilities erupted, General Gage, Britain's prewar commander in chief in America, had advised that the rebellion was widespread and an immense army would be needed to put it down. The British army grew by leaps and bounds after 1775, eventually peaking at around 100,000, of which less than half that number could be spared for the North American theater. Britain hired some 19,000 German mercenaries, recruited Loyalists, sought assistance from runaway slaves, and beseeched friendly Indians to take up their weapons. But in the war's first year Britain lacked the manpower to adequately cope with the Americans. Following France's entry into hostilities in 1778, the British were stretched to the limit and often beyond their limits.[10]

In the face of all of this, Piers Mackesy, a distinguished British historian, specu-lated that Yorktown was not necessarily "a portent of doom." Had Britain continued to wage war, he wrote, it might yet have prevented American independence. His intriguing argument centered in part on America's exhaustion and bankruptcy and France's insolvency, which would have left the former incapable of continuing hostilities beyond 1781 and the latter unwilling to do so. Furthermore, the damage suffered by the French navy in the Battle of the Saints early in 1782 and Spain's likely willingness to quit the war following its failure to take Gibraltar later in the year might well have forced Vergennes to abandon the Americans in 1783. There is no way to test Mackesy's scenario. What is known is that long before the British cabinet finally agreed to American independence—months after learning of York-town and the defeat of Admiral de Grasse's fleet in the Caribbean—Parliament and British public opinion had concluded that the pain and expense of continuing the war was too great to bear.[11]

The French, seeking to gain from Britain's miseries, were better able to appre-hend the dangers they would face in going to war. While providing secret aid to the American insurgents, Versailles warily watched for three years, assessing the rebels' strength and Britain's weakness before entering into hostilities. But the French also encountered the unexpected. The navy it committed in 1778, though superior in numbers to the Royal Navy in America, utterly failed in two campaigns. Foreign Minister Vergennes had imagined that Washington, the bold and active risk-taker at Trenton and Germantown, would remain a daring ally. Instead, after 1777 the American commander cautiously husbanded his army until it could act in concert with the French. Vergennes, like Lord North and his ministers, had also expected a short war. He, too, was wrong. By 1779 the war in America had stalemated and Vergennes had to make choices he had not anticipated. He was compelled to make drastic concessions to Spain to get it into the war, and eventually he had to commit a French army to America. By 1781, the beginning of France's fourth year at war, Vergennes faced mounting pressure to make peace short of victory. He, too, had discovered ample surprises lurking in the puzzling unpredictability of war.

The Americans had the most realistic view of what to expect in going to war. They recognized that they would face a professional army and the world's greatest navy. At the outset, the colonists were fully aware that they could not wage a protracted war, but as they were not seeking independence, they did not anticipate a lengthy conflict. Their aim down to July 1776 was to make Britain understand that this was a war it could not win and that it must reach an accommodation with the American insurgents on America's terms. Congress bet that a victory or two in the first year or so of hostilities would wring satisfactory concessions from London. The rebels inflicted major setbacks on the British in Massachusetts in the first two months of hostilities, but those were insufficient to force London to back down. By early 1776, after suffering myriad disasters in Canada and alarming shortages of every wartime necessity, the Americans found themselves in the position of the proverbial man riding the back of a tiger. They declared independence, praying the step would induce Britain's major European enemies, France and Spain, to provide help in sufficient quantities to see them through what unavoidably was going to be a long war.

Assistance poured in, but unexpected troubles arose. America's economy utterly collapsed and by 1779 morale was tottering. During the 18 months after December 1778, when Savannah fell, the British scored several important victories. By the summer of 1780, ragged murmurings were surfacing that America might of necessity have to make peace short of independence. Washington did not share that outlook, though he confessed that year to having nearly lost hope of winning independence. Halfway through 1781 no one on either side knew who would win this war, or if anyone could win it. By then General Clinton appears to have been more optimistic of securing Britain's primary objective than Washington was about winning American independence. When the war ended in an American victory, Washington spoke of his "astonishment" at what he called the miraculous outcome. Thomas Paine, who in 1776 had argued in *Common Sense* that the Americans could win the war, looked back with amazement in 1783 on what he called "the long and raging hurricane." After all the "uncertainties of fate" and the "numerous and complicated dangers we have suffered or escaped," he wrote, the American victory was a "wonder." [12]

Few lengthy wars have a single turning point. That was true of the two world wars and America's Civil War, and it was no less the case in the War of Independence. Long wars turn on numerous choices made over several years of fighting. In each instance a different choice here and there might have caused all that followed to have been substantially different. The War of Independence might have progressed along a profoundly dissimilar course had

Britain sent General Gage substantial reinforcements before ordering him to use force;

Gage heeded General Clinton's advice on how to take Bunker Hill;

General Howe opted to attack, not besiege, the rebel fortifications in Brooklyn;

Howe ordered the troops landing at Kip's Bay to rapidly close all roads leading from New York City;

Howe attacked or besieged Washington's trapped army on Manhattan Island in September 1776;

General Cornwallis continued to pursue Washington in November 1776, pinioning him at the Delaware;

Howe opted to seek to link his army with General Burgoyne's in the summer of 1777;

Burgoyne, after Bennington, seen the futility of advancing and pulled back to
Fort George for the winter;

Howe attacked the Continental army at Valley Forge in 1778;

Clinton chosen to attack the French in Newport rather than gambling on Benedict Arnold and West Point;

The Conseil du Roi and Louis XVI in 1780 spurned pleas to fight one more year;

George III agreed to peace on terms of uti possidetis in 1780 or 1781;

Cornwallis not divided his army in North Carolina in 1780 and again in 1781;

Cornwallis not abandoned South Carolina and marched to Virginia in 1781;

Lord Germain and George III not ordered Clinton to leave a large army in
Virginia in 1781;

Washington not consented to a Chesapeake campaign in 1781; or

Clinton resisted the Allied armies' march to Virginia in August 1781.

But this book is a work of history, and historians know they are better served by
seeking to understand what actually took place. Historians know that the Allies
won a decisive victory at Yorktown in Virginia, although none of the principal
actors foresaw that pivotal triumph a few months earlier. Both Washington and
Clinton anticipated a New York campaign and Rochambeau would have reluctantly consented to that undertaking had his ally remained intransigent. In a sense,
however, the road to the Allies' decisive victory at Yorktown was paved long before
1781. Much that occurred from 1776 onward could be traced to Britain's having
gone to war without a European partner and to France's commitment to aid the
American insurgents, a choice Vergennes might never have made had there been an
acrid rival and British ally at his back. Without French assistance, the American
insurgency likely could not have continued beyond 1776. Neither secret French aid
nor the belligerency of the Bourbon allies assured Britain's defeat, but once France
and Spain entered the war, Britain was confronted with a global conflict that
rendered crushing the American insurgency beyond the reach of its military forces.
During much of the period after Saratoga, General Clinton had so few troops that
he was akin to a man fighting with one arm tied behind his back.

Similarly, the Royal Navy faced what has been called a fatal "dispersal of
effort."[13] It found itself tasked with defending British possessions in North America,
South and Central America, the Caribbean, Mediterranean, India, and Africa,
blockading the American coast, and protecting British shipping on the high seas.
Moreover, prior to this war one-third of the British fleet had been constructed in
the American colonies and a considerable number of its sailors had come from the

13 colonies. The war brought a screeching halt to the acquisition of those invaluable resources. Britain's great victory in the Seven Years' War had stemmed in large measure from the navy's ability to blockade French fleets in Brest and Toulon. But d'Estaing in 1778, Ternay's squadron bearing the Expédition Particulière in 1780, and de Grasse in 1781 all got to sea. Furthermore, nearly every bit of French secret aid in 1777 and its subsequent shipments made it safely across the Atlantic. Throughout these years the Royal Navy was stretched beyond its capabilities, though the British war effort survived. Fate caught up with the Royal Navy in 1781 in the Chesapeake. It did not have an adequate fleet to cope with de Grasse's task force.

This is not to suggest that Yorktown was inevitable. Important events occurred and crucial decisions were made in the six months before Yorktown that led to the decisive Allied victory in Virginia. General Cornwallis's fruitless and debilitating chase of Morgan and Greene that winter, and his dismay in the aftermath of the unsuccessful showdowns at Cowpens and Guilford Courthouse, prodded him to bring his army to Virginia. Rather than concurring with Washington's entreaties to attack New York, General Rochambeau and Minister La Luzerne appealed to Admiral de Grasse to bring his fleet to the Chesapeake. De Grasse listened to and acted on their entreaties. At the behest of London, Clinton left a large British army in Virginia after the summer of 1781, a previously unintended turn of events that perhaps led to the decisive engagement being fought in Virginia and not in New York. Incredibly good fortune also smiled on the Allies. In a war in which few military plans panned out as imagined, it was something of a miracle that in an age before telegraphs, telephones, steamships, aircraft, and computers, the Allied armies marching south from New York and de Grasse's fleet sailing north from the West Indies were able to come together within days of one another in the Chesapeake and have sufficient time to conduct a joint siege operation.

In a war of this magnitude and complexity, no one person or event was responsible for its outcome, but five individuals were especially important. General Howe's star-crossed leadership in 1776 and 1777 doomed Britain's best chances of quashing the rebellion. General Cornwallis's ill-judged decisions at the Assunpink in New Jersey in 1777 and in the interior of the Carolinas in 1780 and 1781, as well as his abandonment of South Carolina in 1781, were fatefully disastrous choices. Vergennes glimpsed opportunities for France and made perilous choices that ultimately brought about the possibility of victory in 1781. Rochambeau foresaw the likelihood of success in the Chesapeake and the perils of campaigning to retake New York, and more than any other he deserves credit for getting the Allied armies and de Grasse's squadron to Yorktown. Washington learned from his early mistakes, grew steadily more capable as the war progressed, possessed a superb understanding of logistical complexities, molded an army that gradually earned greater respect from Britain's commanders, was an unsullied figure around whom the American people could rally, won the trust of Congress and the French, and from 1778 onward pursued a circumspect course of avoiding risky actions until he could at last act in concert with his ally. He was the right man for leading the American people and American army, something that Congress saw when it chose him in 1775 and when it stuck with him following his early failures.

The war almost certainly would have played out differently had any of these five not been part of the cast of characters, but it was Comte de Vergennes who did the most to contour hostilities and make possible the decisive events in 1781. Vergennes at great risk in 1776 secured approval for secret aid to be funneled to the American rebels. Without those French resources it is unlikely the war could have continued into 1777 and a virtual certainty that the American victory at Saratoga would not have been achieved. In 1778 Vergennes understood that the time had come to ally with the Americans and enter the war, and he dauntlessly seized the moment. In 1779, and again the following year, Vergennes faced intense opposition to the American war from those at Versailles who shrank from any longer risking national security and France's beleaguered economic fabric. But Vergennes played a pivotal role in overcoming the dissenters. He won the battle to maintain France's commitment to its hobbled ally and in time—and at just the right time—was instrumental in securing the king's consent to send the Expédition Particulière and later Admiral de Grasse's squadron to the North American theater. Had Vergennes been foiled at any of these crucial turns, or had he declined to take any of these decisive steps, the war would have come to a different end.

History is filled with astounding twists and turns, and few things in this long war were more astonishing than that American independence in all likelihood would never have been gained had it not been for Vergennes. After all, Vergennes, a privileged nobleman who faithfully served an absolutist monarch, played an outsize role in enabling republican revolutionaries to realize their dream of achieving American independence and establishing a new republican nation. History's odd twists don't end there. Vergennes sought an independent United States, but a weak nation that would remain dependent on France for maintaining its independence. Yet as peace negotiations unfolded in 1782 and it became clear that the American commissioners were seeking conditions that would enable the United States to be a truly independent nation, Vergennes did not utilize his considerable authority to inhibit them. Between 1776 and 1783 Comte de Vergennes was instrumental in the creation of the United States, a new republican nation that just might have the means of standing alone. Although John Adams never overcame his rancor toward Vergennes, in the aftermath of the peace talks he confessed to looking back "with Wonder . . . and with Gratitude" at France's instrumental role in saving "Some of our dearest Interests." He added, "We have a Thousand Reasons, to be thankfull." Believing the United States was now truly independent, Adams in the spring of 1783 triumphantly proclaimed, "The United States of America are not a Power to be trifled with." Adams being Adams, he also noted, "There has been too much trifling" in recent years.[14]

IT WAS THOMAS PAINE'S reverie, and aspiration, that winning independence and establishing an American republic would be the "birthday of a new world." Its example, he believed, would usher in sweeping, liberating change, and not only in America.[15] In the War of Independence, like nearly all wars, not every belligerent achieved the chimeric expectations they sought and that sustained them through years of hostilities. Of all the combatants, the United States came closest to meeting the hopes of its leaders and peoples. Within a decade of peace, the enfeebled national government had been strengthened, the ruined economy was on the road to recovery, the population was growing by leaps and bounds, most freemen enjoyed a bountiful prosperity, and people were flowing into regions beyond the mountains that the tough-minded peace commissioners had secured. Given that "Europe is too thickly planted with Kingdoms to be long at peace," Paine had also prophesied in 1776 that independence would spare America from involvement in European wars, and for over 130 years, until World War I, what he foresaw was borne out. Thomas Jefferson, in his inaugural address as president in 1801, cataloged the rewards of independence won by the "blood of our heroes":

A rising nation, spread over a wide and fruitful land, traversing all the seas with the rich productions of their industry, engaged in commerce with nations who feel power and forget right, advancing rapidly to destinies beyond the reach of mortal eye.

Jefferson echoed Paine's lofty dream of a quarter century earlier. The American republic was "the world's best hope" and the wide Atlantic—as well as a commitment to avoid "entangling alliances"—would shelter the new American nation from Europe's chronic "exterminating havoc."[16]

The American Revolution was not the dawning of a new world for all who lived within the bounds of the new United States. Little changed for women or most Black people. Those Black men who soldiered to escape slavery—about 1 percent of the Black population within the United States—gained their freedom, but the promise of natural rights held forth in the Declaration of Independence was denied to them and other free Black people. Nearly all the Black population remained enslaved, and the number of enslaved persons grew propulsively, from roughly 500,000 in 1776 to nearly 4 million at the time of the Civil War. In 1858, 80 years after Black men were first actively sought for the Continental army during the Valley Forge winter, John Brown, in one of his final utterances prior to his execution at Harpers Ferry, warned that the "crimes of this guilty land . . . will never be purged away; but with blood." He was prescient. Another bloody war had to be fought to finally end slavery, though that war also failed to bestow the long-since-pledged natural rights to Black Americans. A century after Brown was hanged, President John F. Kennedy lamented, "One hundred years have passed since President Lincoln freed the slaves, yet their heirs, their grandsons, are not fully free." He introduced legislation to ensure that "all Americans are to be afforded equal rights and equal opportunities." It was enacted and provoked visceral resistance, including in states where British armies in 1781 had suffered defeats at Cowpens, Guilford Courthouse, and Yorktown at the hands of American armies fighting for the "Glorious Cause" of liberating humankind.[17]

Despite having lost the war, Great Britain was not mortally wounded by the loss of the American colonies. It still held Canada, which rapidly swelled in population as some 60,000 Loyalists settled there, and it possessed lucrative colonies in the Caribbean. A propulsive growth soon took place in new areas under British control in Asia and the Pacific. Within a few years Britain was supreme in numerous territories in the West Indies, Mediterranean, and Africa, and on the subcontinent, a domain termed the "second British Empire" by some historians. By early in the 19th century nearly a quarter of the world's population were subject peoples of Great Britain. British exports to its former American colonies also experienced only a slight setback. During the five years prior to the war, exports to the colonies annually averaged more than three million pounds. Within five years of the end of the war, exports to the United States again topped three million pounds. National indebtedness had grown by 91 percent as a result of the war, provoking fears that Britain faced bankruptcy and social upheaval. But Britain not only had long been a fiscal-military state capable of sustained warfare; its immediate postwar economic policies reduced the debt. Within four years of the peace settlement, government income exceeded expenditures. Furthermore, Britain's economy boomed. Exports increased by 90 percent in the decade after the war, mostly due to the American market's inexhaustible appetite for British manufactured goods and the growing number of Americans who were capable of purchasing some of the commodities they wanted. The industrial revolution was in full swing within a few years of peace. Factories and mills dotted the landscape, work habits changed, and England urbanized to the point that by 1800 a quarter of the population lived in cities. England looked different in 1800, but the ruling class, which had taken the nation to war, lost the American colonies, and was responsible for the deaths of thousands of British soldiers, remained Britain's ruling class and continued to enjoy its caste privileges.[18]

France was a victor, though not every high official was a celebrant. Marie Antoinette early on questioned the wisdom of the support given to the Americans, and some in the Conseil du Roi all along worried that Vergennes's policies were burdening France with onerous and menacing problems. Even as the Allied victory was rapturously celebrated in Parisian theaters and cafés, and in lavish dinners at Versailles, Vergennes felt sufficient pressure to justify the war in a memoir to Louis XVI in the spring of 1784. French intervention, he wrote, had not only prevented the American insurgency from becoming detrimental to the interests of France; it had seriously weakened Great Britain. To others, he expressed his hope that in the long term the war might lead to a rapprochement with Britain.

What was clear to many, and to Vergennes as well, was that the war had added drastically to France's economic troubles. France had provided loans, subsidies, and gifts to the United States, spent lavishly to rebuild its navy, and disbursed enormous sums in sending fleets and soldiers to America and other theaters. French intervention in America's Revolutionary War had cost more than one billion livres. By 1783 the French debt stood at three billion livres, leading to staggering annual interest costs. Before the decade was out, the debt had climbed to over four billion livres and more than half the annual budget was devoted to coping with it.[19] French indebtedness contributed to the onset of a fatal crisis for the old order that uncoiled when Louis XVI summoned the Estates General in 1789 in search of a solution to the nation's economic maladies.

If the debt crisis was the immediate cause of the French Revolution, ingrained causes were also crucial, particularly the spirit of reform set in motion in the Age of Enlightenment. Jefferson, who spent five years in France on a diplomatic mission that began in 1784, early on discerned the presence of an entrenched "pitch of discontent" in some sectors. He thought it could be traced to the longstanding "monstrous abuses" of monarchy and aristocracy, including France's steep and unfair system of taxation. With a good grasp of history, Jefferson recognized that deep transitional changes during the previous couple of centuries helped shape the thinking of the generation of the 1780s.

However, like a great many of his countrymen, Jefferson was caught up in the largely blissful illusion that the American Revolution had inspired the French to act to remedy their discontentment, unleashing a mighty burst of reform. The "flames kindled on the 4th of July 1776" had "awakened the thinking part of the French nation . . . from the sleep of despotism," he said. The changes that swept over America during its revolution had reacquainted the French with their "sacred rights that have too long been forgotten." Jefferson also believed that many French officers who served in America had been inspired by America's revolutionary republicanism and returned home seeking a somewhat similar transformation in France. Jefferson was not alone in thinking the American Revolution had triggered waves of reform in France. As early as 1777 Benjamin Franklin proclaimed that America's "Cause is the cause of all Mankind," and indeed the notion circulated in books, newspapers, pamphlets, salons, and French cafés during and after the war. Paine developed that idea at length in *Common Sense*, and in 1792 he came back to it in *Rights of Man*, writing that the American Revolution had been about more than American independence. The Americans had "made a stand . . . for the world" in bringing on "a revolution in the principles and practice of governments."

Jefferson ultimately argued that the American Revolution had spawned a "revolution in public opinion" in France that aimed at "a change in constitution." When the Estates General in 1789 initiated the first reforms of the French Revolution, Jefferson, in high spirits, wrote Washington that France "has been awaked by our revolution." Throughout the remainder of his life, Jefferson remained convinced that people everywhere were uplifted by the American Revolution. In his final letter, written in 1826, he asserted that the American Revolution had continued to be "the signal of arousing men to burst the chains under which monkish ignorance and superstition had persuaded them to bind themselves, and to assure the blessings and security of self-government."[20]

Jefferson mistakenly thought France could carry out its reforms bloodlessly, but the French Revolution and its experiment with republicanism soon grew brutal and filled with terror. Vergennes was spared witnessing what French ties to the American war had helped to bring about. He died two years before the Estates General met. But others who had lent a hand to the American insurgents were not so fortunate. Lafayette was jailed for five years, and Louis XVI, Marie Antoinette, and Admiral d'Estaing were put to death along with thousands of others during the Reign of Terror. Paine, who had gone to France early in the Revolution and was elected to the French legislature—and later was imprisoned and narrowly escaped execution—had voted against the death penalty imposed on Louis XVI. America, he said, could not have won its freedom from the "tyrannical yoke of Britain" without the help provided by the king, and he urged that Louis be exiled to America, where he would learn that "the true system of government consists not in kings, but in fair, equal and honorable representation."[21] Washington, who was president of the United States at the time, and whose skin likely was saved by the assistance provided by Louis XVI after 1776, said and did nothing.

Instead of the rapprochement with Britain that Vergennes had hoped for, the two countries were at war again within 10 years of the Treaty of Paris. It was a war that Paine said was necessary given that the monarchical "tyrants of the earth are leagued" against revolutionary France. The war ultimately led to Napoleon's rise to power and lasted with hardly a break for more than 20 years.

It would be fanciful to say that the American Revolution alone caused the French Revolution and its wars. Going to war can bring unintended, and unwelcome, consequences not just for contemporaries but for future generations as well.

Spain escaped the war's ravaging economic jolt. Aided by the largely unimpeded flow of wealth from its American colonies, and through a disciplined management of its economy, Spain avoided a fiscal crisis akin to that in France. Furthermore, as Madrid never allied with the United States, the revolutionary fervor that eddied from America to France after 1776 never took hold within Spain. Madrid in fact ferociously sought to prevent news of America's revolt from penetrating its New World colonies, and to an amazing degree it succeeded. In time, the old regime's good fortune skidded to an end, though the Spaniards went so far as to shred the time-honored Bourbon alliance in hopes of keeping the corrosive ideas of the

French Revolution at bay. However, before the wars of the French Revolution ended, Napoleon occupied Spain and installed his brother in place of the Spanish monarch, and revolutions for independence rocked one Spanish colony after another. In some, declarations of independence were promulgated that rang with the very words of Jefferson's masterpiece. Within 40 years of having entered America's revolutionary war, Spain had lost many of its American colonies, including East and West Florida. Spain also ceded New Orleans and all of Louisiana to Napoleon in 1800 and he, in turn, sold it to the United States three years later. Whereas in 1776 there had not been an independent country in the Western Hemisphere, 24 independent nations existed in 1825. By then, too, Spain was no longer a truly major power.[22]

In the summer of 1782, while peace negotiations were underway, John Adams in a wistful moment reflected that America's insurgents had "set the World in a blaze." But fearing that the global war and revolutionary radicalism would sow unsavory events, Adams added, "Glorious however as the flame is, I wish I could put it out." Adams succeeded in making peace for America, but he could not extinguish the blazes that spread after 1789. The world that had existed when the American militiamen at Lexington and Concord fired the shots heard round the world was gone, or going, as the 18th century came to a close. The new world featured new ways of thinking, for, as Jefferson put it, "All eyes are opened, or opening, to the rights of man."[23] The genie of liberation was out of the bottle and could not be put back. Thomas Paine had been right. His rapturous vision that the American Revolution would give birth to a new world had come to pass, though not exactly as he had foreseen.

But what kind of world would it be? No one watched more closely than John Adams and Thomas Jefferson, American revolutionaries who had been instrumental in moving Congress from a limited war to a quest for independence and a longer war that eventually crept into the far corners of the globe. Adams foresaw disaster from the first days of the French Revolution. In the wake of the Reign of Terror he came to believe that the new world was "anything but the Age of Reason." It had become "the Age of Folly, Vice, Frenzy, Brutality, Daemons. . . . Call it then the Age of Paine." In 1816 Jefferson admitted that Adams had been correct about the French Revolution—"Your prophecies . . . proved truer than mine," he said—though he still believed that a "better final result" for humankind was possible. The "light from our West seems to have spread and illuminated," giving people "a glimmering of their rights" so that the "idea of representative government has taken root and growth among them."[24]

The future was opaque. It would be for those who inhabited the 19th, 20th, and 21 centuries to determine whether the world in the aftermath of America's Revolutionary War would be an age of folly and demons or one of human progress characterized by reason and wisdom.

ACKNOWLEDGMENTS

Debts accumulate in the course of writing of a book, and it is with gratitude that I acknowledge the support, help, and guidance provided by many people. I am particularly grateful to my close friends and fellow historians Jim Sefcik and Keith Pacholl. In the course of numerous chats, both offered encouragement and advice and helped with questions that arose during my research. I am also thankful that Jonathan Dull, Larrie Ferreiro, Don Hagist, and Stephen Taaffe took the time to answer queries that I posed. Lindsey Winchester in the Irvine Sullivan Ingram Library at the University of West Georgia kindly secured books for me when the stacks were closed due to the COVID-19 pandemic during the first weeks that I worked on the book. Billy Willey and Charlie Sicignano bent over backward to acquire books that were indispensable for my research. Angela Mehaffey and Margot Davis in the interlibrary loan office time and again complied with my frequent requests for books and articles. Julie Dobbs, Chris Harris, and Caroline McWhorter helped me out of numerous scrapes with my computer. I want to especially thank Brendan Kelly, the former president of the University of West Georgia, for his support in providing an office that I have used almost every weekday during the more than three years that I worked on the book.

John Schline, my literary agent, supported my hope of writing this book and provided encouragement—and much more—in seeing to its inception and completion.

A special thanks to Maureen Klier, long my copy editor and simply the very best at her calling.

Anton Mueller, my editor, was supportive and understanding, and a storehouse of ideas. Sometimes I think that Morgan Jones, the associate editor, worked as hard as I did on this book, and she was unflaggingly cordial and helpful.

Simon, Sammy Grace, and Clementine will never read this book, but they were at my side as I worked on it, and all three enriched my life and made the often trying work of writing a bit easier.

Carol, my wife, has always supported my writing, and her understanding and patience have been crucial to my literary and scholarly activities.

BIBLIOGRAPHY

PRIMARY SOURCES

Abbot, W. W., et al., eds. *The Papers of George Washington: Confederation Series.* Charlottesville, VA, 1992–1997.

Adams, Charles Francis, ed., Correspondence Between John Adams and Mercy Warren, reprinted in *Collections of Massachusetts Historical Society*, 5th Series, 1878, 317–491.

Anderson, Enoch. *Personal Recollections of Enoch Anderson.* New York, 1971.

Baurmeister, Baron Karl Leopold. *Revolution in America: Confidential Letters and Journals, 1776–1784.* Westport, CT, 1973.

Blanchard, Claude. *The Journal of Claude Blanchard.* Edited by Thomas Balch. Albany, NY, 1876.

Bloomfield, Joseph. *Citizen Soldier: The Revolutionary War Journal of Joseph Bloomfield.* Edited by Mark E. Lender and James Kirby Martin. Newark, NJ, 1982.

Boyd, Julian P., et al., eds. *The Papers of Thomas Jefferson.* Princeton, NJ, 1950–.

Burgoyne, Bruce E., ed. *Enemy Views: The American Revolutionary War as Recorded by the Hessian Participants.* Bowie, MD, 1996.

Butterfield, L. H., et al., eds. *Adams Family Correspondence.* Cambridge, MA, 1963–.

———. *Diary and Autobiography of John Adams.* Cambridge, MA, 1961.

———. *Letters of Benjamin Rush.* Princeton, NJ, 1951.

Campbell, Archibald. *Journal of an Expedition Against the Rebels of Georgia in North America.* Edited by Colin Campbell. Darien, GA, 1981.

Cappon, Lester J., ed. *The Adams-Jefferson Letters: The Complete Correspondence Between Thomas Jefferson and Abigail and John Adams.* Chapel Hill, NC, 1959.

Chase, Philander, et al., eds. *The Papers of George Washington: Revolutionary War Series.* Charlottesville, VA, 1985–.

Chastellux, Marquis de. *Travels in America in the Years 1780, 1781, and 1782.* Edited by Howard C. Rice. Chapel Hill, NC, 1963.

Clinton, Sir Henry. Papers, William L. Clements Library, University of Michigan, Ann Arbor.

———. *The American Rebellion: Sir Henry Clinton's Narrative of His Campaigns, 1775–1782, with an Appendix of Original Documents.* Edited by William B. Willcox. New Haven, CT, 1954.

Closen, Ludwig von. *The Revolutionary Journal of Baron Ludwig von Closen, 1780–1783.* Edited by Evelyn Acomb. Reprint, Chapel Hill, NC, 1958.

Commager, Henry Steele, and Richard B. Morris, eds. *The Spirit of Seventy-Six: The Story of the American Revolution as Told by Participants.* Indianapolis, IN, 1958.

Cubbison, Douglas R., ed. *Burgoyne and the Saratoga Campaign: His Papers.* Norman, OK, 2012.

Dann, John C., ed. *The Revolution Remembered: Eyewitness Accounts of the War for Independence.* Chicago, 1980.

Davis, K. G., ed. *Documents of the American Revolution.* Dublin, Ireland, 1972–1981.

Deux-Ponts, William de. *My Campaigns in America: A Journal Kept by Count William de Deux-Ponts.* Edited by Samuel Abbot Greene. Boston, 1868.

Dunkerly, Robert M., ed. *The Battle of Kings Mountain: Eyewitness Accounts.* Charleston, SC, 2007.

Dunne, W. Bodham, ed. *The Correspondence of King George the Third with Lord North, 1763 to 1783.* Reprint, New York, 1971.

Elmer, Ebenezer, ed. "Journal of Surgeon Ebenezer Elmer." *Pennsylvania Magazine of History and Biography* 35 (1911): 103–7.

Ewald, Johann. *Diary of the American War: A Hessian Journal.* Edited by Joseph P. Tustin. New Haven, CT, 1979.

Feltman, William. *The Journal of Lieut. William Feltman, of the First Pennsylvania Regiment, 1781–82.* Philadelphia, 1853.

Fitzpatrick, John C., ed. *The Writings of Washington.* Washington, DC, 1931–1944.

Foner, Philip S., ed. *The Complete Writings of Thomas Paine.* New York, 1945.

Force, Peter, ed. *American Archives*, 4th ser. Washington, DC, 1837–1846.

Ford, Paul Leicester, ed. *The Writings of Thomas Jefferson*. New York, 1892–1899.

Ford, Worthington C., ed. *Journals of the Continental Congress, 1774–1789*. Washington, DC, 1904–1937.

———. *Statesman and Friend: Correspondence of John Adams and Benjamin Waterhouse, 1784–1822*. Boston, 1927.

Gage, Thomas. *The Correspondence of General Thomas Gage with the Secretaries of State, and the War Office and the Treasury*. Edited by Clarence E. Carter. Reprint, New York, 1969.

Gilbert, Benjamin. *Winding Down: The Revolutionary War Letters of Benjamin Gilbert of Massachusetts, 1780–1783*. Edited by John Shy. Ann Arbor, MI, 1989.

Gordon, William. *The History of the Rise, Progress, and Establishment of the Independence of the United States of America*. London, 1788.

Greene, S. A., ed. "Three Military Diaries." Proceedings of the Massachusetts Historical Society, 2nd series, 12 (1897–1899): 78–102.

Gregory, James, and Thomas Dunnings, eds. *Horatio Gates Papers, 1726–1828*. Microfilm. Sanford, NC, n.d.

Guttridge, George H., ed. *The Correspondence of Edmund Burke*. Chicago, 1958–1978.

Hagist, Don N., ed. *British Soldiers, American War*. Yardley, PA, 2014.

Hamer, Philip, et al., eds. *The Papers of Henry Laurens*. Columbia, SC, 1968–2003.

Hamilton, Phillip, ed. *The Revolutionary War Lives and Letters of Lucy and Henry Knox*. Baltimore, 2017.

Historical Manuscripts Commission. *Report on American Manuscripts in the Royal Institution of Great Britain*. London, 1904–1909.

Idzerda, Stanley, et al., eds. *Lafayette in the Age of the American Revolution: Selected Letters and Papers, 1776–1790*. Ithaca, NY, 1976–1983.

Jackson, Donald, et al., eds. *The Diaries of George Washington*. Charlottesville, VA, 1978.

Jensen, Merrill, ed. *English Historical Documents: American Colonial Documents to 1776*. London, 1964.

Johnson, Henry P., ed. *The Correspondence and Public Papers of John Jay, 1763–1826*. Reprint, New York, 1971.

Klingelhofer, Herbert E., ed. "Matthew Ridley's Diary During the Peace Negotiations of 1782." *William and Mary Quarterly* 20 (1963): 95–133.

Labaree, Leonard W., et al., eds. *The Papers of Benjamin Franklin*. New Haven, CT, 1959–.

Lamb, Roger. *An Original and Authentic Journal of Occurrences During the Late American War from Its Commencement to the Year 1783*. Dublin, Ireland, 1809.

Lauberdière, Comte de [Louis-François-Bertrand du Pont d'Aubevoye]. *The Road to Yorktown: The French Campaigns in the American Revolution, 1780–1783*. Edited by Norman Desmarais. El Dorado Hills, CA, 2021.

Lee, Henry. *Memoirs of the War in the Southern Department of the United States*. Philadelphia, 1812.

Lesser, Charles, ed. *The Sinews of Independence: Monthly Strength Reports of the Continental Army*. Chicago, 1976.

Lipscomb, Albert A., and Albert Ellery Bergh, eds. *The Writings of Thomas Jefferson*. Washington, DC, 1900–1904.

Mackenzie, Frederick. *Diary of Frederick Mackenzie, Giving a Daily Narrative of His Military Service as an Officer of the Regiment of Royal Welsh Fusiliers During the Years 1775–1781 in Massachusetts, Rhode Island and New York*. Reprint, New York, 1968.

Meng, John J., ed. *Dispatches and Instructions of Conrad Alexandre Gérard, 1778–1780*. Washington, DC, 1939.

Monroe. James. *The Autobiography of James Monroe*. Edited by Gerry Stuart Brown. Syracuse, NY, 1959.

Moore, Frank, comp. *The Diary of the American Revolution, 1775–1781*. New York, 1967.

Morris, Richard B., ed. *John Jay: The Winning of the Peace: Unpublished Papers, 1780–1784*. New York, 1980.

Morris, Robert Clark, ed. *Memoirs of James Morris of South Farms in Litchfield*. New Haven, CT, 1933.

Mundy, Godfrey B., ed. *The Life and Correspondence of the Late Admiral Lord Rodney*. London, 1830.

Murdoch, David H., ed. *Rebellion in America: A Contemporary British Viewpoint, 1765–1783*. Santa Barbara, CA, 1979.

Peckham, Howard H., ed. *The Toll of Independence: Engagements and Battle Casualties of the American Revolution*. Chicago, 1974.

Piecuch, Jim, ed. *The Battle of Camden: A Documentary History*. Charleston, SC, 2006.

Rice, Howard C., Jr., and Anne S. K. Brown, eds. *The American Campaigns of Rochambeau's Army, 1780, 1781, 1782, 1783*. Princeton, NJ, 1972.

Roberts, Kenneth, ed. *March to Quebec: Journals of the Members of Arnold's Expedition*. New York, 1948.

Rochambeau, Jean-Baptiste-Donatien de Vimeur, Comte de. *Memoirs of the Marshal Count de Rochambeau*. Reprint, New York, 1971.

Rogers, George C., ed. "Letters of Charles O'Hara to the Duke of Grafton." *South Carolina Historical Magazine* 65 (1964): 158–80.

Ross, Charles, ed. *Correspondence of Charles, First Marquis Cornwallis*. London, 1859.

Saberton, Ian, ed. *The Cornwallis Papers: The Campaigns of 1780 and 1781 in the Southern Theater of the American Revolutionary War*. Uckfield, UK, 2010.

Scheer, George F., ed. *Private Yankee Doodle: A Narrative of Some of the Adventures, Dangers and Sufferings of a Revolutionary Soldier*. Boston, 1962.

Scheer, George F., and Hugh F. Rankin, eds. *Rebels and Redcoats*. Cleveland, 1957.

Schutz, John A., and Douglas Adair, eds. *The Spur of Fame: Dialogues of John Adams and Benjamin Rush, 1805–1813*. San Marino, CA, 1966.

Scull, G. D., ed. *Memoir and Letters of Captain W. Glanville Evelyn, of the 4th Regiment ("King's Own") from North America, 1774–1776*. Oxford, UK, 1879.

Showman, Richard K., et al., eds. *The Papers of Nathanael Greene*. Chapel Hill, NC, 1976–2005.

Simcoe, John. *Simcoe's Military Journal. A History of the Operations of a Partisan Corps Called the Queen's Rangers*. Reprint, New York, 1968.

Simms, William Gilmore, ed. *The Army Correspondence of Colonel John Laurens in the Years 1777–1778*. Reprint, New York, 1969.

Smith, Paul H., ed. *Letters of Delegates to Congress, 1774–1789*. Washington, DC, 1976–2000.

Smith, William. *Historical Memoirs from 26 August 1778 to 12 November 1783.* Edited by William H. W. Sabine. Reprint, New York, 1971.

Stedman, Charles. *The History of the Origin, Progress, and Termination of the American War.* Reprint, New York, 1969.

Stevens, Benjamin F., ed. *The Campaign in Virginia, 1781. An Exact Reprint of Six Rare Pamphlets on the Clinton-Cornwallis Controversy.* London, 1888.

———. *Facsimiles of Manuscripts in European Archives Relating to America, 1773–1783.* Reprint, New York, 1970.

Sullivan, Thomas. "Before and After the Battle of Brandywine. Extracts from the Journal of Sergeant Thomas Sullivan of H. M. Forty-Ninth Regiment of Foot." *Pennsylvania Magazine of History and Biography* 31 (1907): 406–18.

Syrett, Harold C., and Jacob E. Cooke, eds. *The Papers of Alexander Hamilton.* New York, 1961–1987.

Tallmadge, Benjamin. *Memoir of Colonel Benjamin Tallmadge.* New York, 1968.

Tarleton, Benjamin. *A History of the Campaigns of 1780 and 1781 in the Southern Provinces of North America.* Reprint, Cranbury, NJ, 2005.

Tatum, Edward H., Jr., ed. *The American Journal of Ambrose Serle.* Reprint, New York, 1969.

Taylor, Robert J., et al., eds. *The Papers of John Adams.* Cambridge, MA, 1977–.

Thacher, James. *Military Journal of the American Revolution.* Edited by Thomas Bulch. Reprint, New York, 1969.

Uhlendorf, Bernhard, ed. *The Siege of Charleston.* Reprint, New York, 1968.

Wade, Herbert T., and Robert A. Lively, eds. *This Glorious Cause: The Adventures of Two Company Officers in Army.* Princeton, NJ, 1958.

Wharton, Francis, ed. *The Revolutionary Diplomatic Correspondence of the United States.* Washington, DC, 1899.

Wortley, Mrs. E. Stuart, ed. *A Prime Minister and His Son: From the Correspondence of the 3d Earl of Bute and of Lt.-General the Hon. Sir Charles Stuart.* London, 1925.

SECONDARY BOOKS

Alden, John. *Charles Lee, Traitor or Patriot?* Baton Rouge, LA, 1951.

——. *General Gage in America: Being Principally a History of His Role in the American Revolution*. Baton Rouge, LA, 1948.

Allen, Gardner W. *A Naval History of the American Revolution*. Reprint, New York, 1962.

Allen, Thomas B., and Todd W. Braisted. *The Loyalist Corps: Americans in the Service of the King*. Tacoma Park, MD, 2011.

Allison, David K., and Larrie D. Ferreiro, eds. *The American Revolution: A World War*. Washington, DC, 2018.

Anderson, Troyer Steele. *The Command of the Howe Brothers During the American Revolution*. New York, 1936.

Armitage, David. *The Declaration of Independence: A Global History*. Cambridge, MA, 2007.

Atkinson, Rick. *The British Are Coming: The War for America, Lexington to Princeton, 1775–1777*. New York, 2019.

Atwood, Rodney. *The Hessians: Mercenaries from Hessen-Kassel in the American Revolution*. Cambridge, UK, 1980.

Ayling, Stanley. *The Elder Pitt: The Earl of Chatham*. New York, 1976.

Babits, Lawrence E. *A Devil of a Whipping: The Battle of Cowpens*. Chapel Hill, NC, 1998.

Babits, Lawrence E., and Joshua B. Howard. *Long, Obstinate, and Bloody: The Battle of Guilford Courthouse*. Chapel Hill, NC, 2009.

Baer, Friederike. *Hessians: German Soldiers in the American Revolutionary War*. New York, 2022.

Bailyn, Bernard. *The Ideological Origins of the American Revolution*. Cambridge, MA, 1967.

Bass, Robert D. *Gamecock: The Life and Campaigns of General Thomas Sumter*. New York, 1961.

——. *The Green Dragoon: The Lives of Banastre Tarleton and Mary Robinson*. Orangeburg, SC, 1973.

Becker, Ann M. *Smallpox in Washington's Army: Disease, War, and Society During the Revolutionary War*. Lanham, MD, 2023.

Bemis, Samuel Flagg. *The Diplomacy of the American Revolution*. New York, 1935.

Bennett, Charles E., and Donald R. Lennon. *A Quest for Glory: Major General Robert Howe and the American Revolution*. Chapel Hill, NC, 1991.

Berkin, Carol. *Revolutionary Mothers: Women in the Struggle for America's Independence*. New York, 2003.

Bernier, Olivier. *Lafayette: Hero of Two Worlds*. New York, 1983.

Bezanson, Anne. *Prices and Inflation During the American Revolution: Pennsylvania, 1770–1790*. Philadelphia, 1951.

Bickham, Troy. *Making Headlines: The American Revolution as Seen Through the British Press*. DeKalb, IL, 2009.

Billias, George A., ed. *George Washington's Generals*. New York, 1964.

———. ed. *George Washington's Opponents*. New York, 1969.

Black, Jeremy. *War for America: The Fight for Independence, 1775–1783*. Stroud, UK, 1991.

Blaufarb, Rafe. *The French Army, 1750–1820: Careers, Talent, Merit*. Manchester, UK, 2002.

Bodle, Wayne K. *The Valley Forge Winter: Civilians and Soldiers in War*. University Park, PA, 2002.

Bonwick, Colin. *English Radicals and the American Revolution*. Chapel Hill, NC, 1977.

Borick, Carl P. *A Gallant Defense: The Siege of Charleston, 1780*. Columbia, SC, 2003.

Bouton, Terry. *Taming Democracy: "The People," the Founders, and the Troubled Ending of the American Revolution*. New York, 2007.

Bowler, R. Arthur. *Logistics and the Failure of the British Army in America, 1775–1783*. Princeton, NJ, 1975.

Braisted, Todd. W. *Grand Forage 1778: The Battleground around New York City*. Yardley, PA, 2016.

Brewer, John. *The Sinews of Power: War, Money and the English State, 1688–1783*. London, 1989.

Brown, Gerald Saxon. *The American Secretary: The Colonial Policy of Lord George Germain, 1775–1778*. Ann Arbor, MI, 1963.

Brown, Weldon. *Empire or Independence: A Study in the Failure of Reconciliation, 1774–1783*. Reprint, Port Washington, NY, 1966.

Brumwell, Stephen. *George Washington: Gentleman Warrior*. New York, 2012.

———. *Redcoats: The British Soldier and War in the Americas, 1755–1763*. Cambridge, UK, 2002.

———. *Turncoat: Benedict Arnold and the Crisis of American Liberty*. New Haven, CT, 2018.

Buchanan, John. *The Road to Charleston: Nathanael Greene and the American Revolution*. Charlottesville, VA, 2019.

———. *The Road to Guilford Courthouse: The American Revolution in the Carolinas*. New York, 1997.

———. *The Road to Valley Forge: How Washington Built the Army That Won the Revolution*. New York, 2004.

Buel, Richard, Jr. *Dear Liberty: Connecticut's Mobilization for the Revolutionary War*. Middletown, CT, 1980.

———. *In Irons: Britain's Naval Supremacy and the American Revolutionary Economy*. New Haven, CT, 1998.

Burrows, Edwin G. *Forgotten Patriots: The Untold Story of American Prisoners During the Revolutionary War*. New York, 2008.

Bush, Martin H. *Revolutionary Enigma: A Re-Appraisal of General Philip Schuyler of New York*. Port Washington, NY, 1969.

Calhoun, Robert McCluer. *The Loyalists in Revolutionary America, 1780–1781*. New York, 1965.

Callahan, North. *Henry Knox: George Washington's General*. New York, 1958.

Calloway, Colin G. *The American Revolution in Indian Country: Crisis and Diversity in Native American Communities*. Cambridge, UK, 1995.

———. *The Indian World of George Washington: The First President, the First Americans, and Birth of the Nation*. New York, 2018.

Cantlie, Neil. *A History of the Army Medical Department*. Edinburgh, UK, 1974.

Carp, Benjamin L. *The Great New York Fire of 1776: A Lost Story of the American Revolution*. New Haven, CT, 2023.

Carp, E. Wayne. *To Starve the Army at Pleasure: Continental Army Administration and American Political Culture, 1775–1783*. Chapel Hill, NC, 1984.

Carpenter, Stanley D. M. *Southern Gambit: Cornwallis and the British March to Yorktown*. Norman, OK, 2019.

Cecere, Michael. *The Invasion of Virginia, 1781*. Yardley, PA, 2017.

———. *They Behaved like Soldiers: Captain John Chilton and the Third Virginia Regiment, 1775–1778*. Bowie, MD, 2004.

Chávez, Thomas F. *Spain and the Independence of the United States: An Intrinsic Gift*. Albuquerque, NM, 2002.

Chernow, Ron. *George Washington: A Life*. New York, 2010.

Chopra, Ruma. *Choosing Sides: Loyalists in Revolutionary America*. Lanham, MD, 2013.

———. *Unnatural Rebellion: Loyalists in New York City During the Revolution*. Charlottesville, VA, 2011.

Clark, Dora Mae. *British Opinion and the American Revolution*. Reprint, New York, 1966.

Coggins, Jack. *Ships and Seamen of the American Revolution: Vessels, Crews, Weapons, Gear, Naval Tactics, and Actions of the War of Independence*. Harrisburg, PA, 1969.

Conway, Stephen. *The British Isles and the War of American Independence*. New York, 2000.

Corwin, Edward S. *French Policy and the American Alliance of 1778*. Reprint, New York, 1970.

———. *The War of American Independence, 1776–1783*. London, 1995.

Countryman, Edward. *Enjoy the Same Liberty: Black Americans and the Revolutionary Era*. Lanham, MD, 2012.

Crow, Jeffrey J., and Larry E. Tise, eds. *The Southern Experience in the American Revolution*. Chapel Hill, NC, 1978.

Curtis, Edward E. *The Organization of the British Army in the American Revolution.* New Haven, CT, 1926.

Davies, Huw J. *The Wandering Army: The Campaigns That Transformed the British Way of War, 1750–1850.* New Haven, CT, 2022.

Desjardin, Thomas A. *Through a Howling Wilderness: Benedict Arnold's March to Quebec, 1775.* New York, 2006.

Dolin, Eric Jay. *Rebels at Sea: Privateering in the American Revolution.* New York, 2022.

Drury, Bob, and Tom Clavin. *Valley Forge.* New York, 2018.

Duffy, Christopher. *The Military Experience in the Age of Reason.* London, 1987.

Dull, Jonathan. *Benjamin Franklin and the American Revolution.* Lincoln, NE, 2010.

——. *A Diplomatic History of the American Revolution.* New Haven, CT, 1985.

——. *The French Navy and American Independence: A Study of Arms and Diplomacy, 1774–1787.* Princeton, NJ, 1975.

——. *The Miracle of American Independence: Twenty Ways Things Could Have Turned Out Differently.* Lincoln, NE, 2015.

Duncan, Mike. *Hero of Two Worlds: The Marquis de Lafayette in the Age of Revolution.* New York, 2021.

Dunkerly, Robert M., and Irene B. Boland. *Eutaw Springs: The Final Battle of the American Revolution's Southern Campaign.* Columbia, SC, 2017.

DuVal, Kathleen. *Independence Lost: Lives on the Edge of the American Revolution.* New York, 2015.

Dwyer, William M. *The Day Is Ours! An Inside View of the Battles of Trenton and Princeton.* New York, 1983.

Dykeman, Wilma. *With Fire and Sword: The Battle of Kings Mountain, 1780.* Washington, DC, 1978.

Edgar, Walter. *Partisans and Redcoats: The Southern Conflict That Turned the Tide of the American Revolution.* New York, 2001.

Egerton, Douglas R. *Death of Liberty: African Americans and Revolutionary America.* New York, 2009.

Elliott, Steven. *Surviving the Winters: Housing Washington's Army During the American Revolution*. Norman, OK, 2021.

Ellis, Joseph J. *The Cause: The American Revolution and Its Discontents*. New York, 2021.

———. *His Excellency: George Washington*. New York, 2004.

Evans, Eric J. *The Shaping of Modern Britain: Identity, Industry and Empire, 1780–1914*. Edinburgh, UK, 2011.

Fenn, Elizabeth A. *Pox Americana: The Great Smallpox Epidemic of 1775–1782*. New York, 2001.

Ferguson, E. James. *The Power of the Purse: A History of American Public Finance, 1776–1790*. Chapel Hill, NC, 1961.

Ferling, John. *Almost a Miracle: The American Victory in the War of Independence*. New York, 2007.

———. *The Ascent of George Washington: The Hidden Political Genius of an American Icon*. New York, 2009.

———. *Winning Independence: The Decisive Years of the Revolutionary War, 1778–1781*. New York, 2021.

Ferreiro, Larrie D. *Brothers at Arms: American Independence and the Men of France and Spain Who Saved It*. New York, 2016.

Fischer, David Hackett. *Paul Revere's Ride*. New York, 1994.

———. *Washington's Crossing*. New York, 2004.

Fischer, Joseph R. *A Well-Executed Failure: The Sullivan Campaign Against the Iroquois, July–September 1779*. Columbia, SC, 1997.

Flavell, Julie. *The Howe Dynasty: The Untold Story of a Military Family and the Women Behind Britain's Wars for America*. New York, 2021.

Flavell, Julie, and Stephen Conway, eds. *Britain and America Go to War: The Impact of War and Warfare in Anglo-America, 1754–1815*. Gainesville, FL, 2004.

Fleming, Thomas. *Beat the Last Drum: The Siege of Yorktown, 1781*. New York, 1963.

———. *The Perils of Peace: America's Struggle for Survival After Yorktown*. New York, 2007.

———. *Washington's Secret War: The Hidden History of Valley Forge*. New York, 2005.

Flexner, James Thomas. *George Washington in the American Revolution*. Boston, 1967.

Foner, Eric. *Tom Paine and Revolutionary America*. New York, 2005.

Fowler, William M., Jr. *American Crisis: George Washington and the Dangerous Two Years After Yorktown, 1781–1783*. New York, 2011.

———. *Rebels Under Sail: The American Navy During the American Revolution*. New York, 1976.

Fowler, William M., Jr., and Wallace Coyle, eds. *The American Revolution: Changing Perspectives*. Boston, 1979.

Franklin, John Hope. *From Slavery to Freedom: A History of Negro Americans*. New York, 1956.

Freeman, Douglas Southall. *George Washington: A Biography*. New York, 1948–1957.

French, Allen. *The First Year of the American Revolution*. Reprint, New York, 1968.

Frey, Sylvia. *The British Soldier in America: A Social History of Military Life in the Revolutionary Period*. Austin, TX, 1981.

———. *Water from the Rock: Black Resistance in the Revolutionary Age*. Princeton, NJ, 1991.

Frothingham, Richard. *History of the Siege of Boston*. Boston, 1849.

Gallagher, John J. *The Battle of Brooklyn, 1776*. New York, 1995.

Gelles, Edith B. *Abigail and John: Portrait of a Marriage*. New York, 2009.

———. *Portia: The World of Abigail Adams*. Bloomington, IN, 1992.

Gerlach, Don R. *Proud Patriot: Philip Schuyler and the War of Independence, 1775–1783*. Syracuse, NY, 1987.

Gilbert, Alan. *Black Patriots and Loyalists: Fighting for Emancipation in the War of Independence*. Chicago, 2012.

Golway, Terry. *Washington's General: Nathanael Greene and the Triumph of the American Revolution*. New York, 2005.

Goodwin, A., ed. *The New Cambridge Modern History: The American and French Revolutions, 1763–1793*. Cambridge, UK, 1965.

Gordon, John. *South Carolina and the American Revolution: A Battlefield History.* Columbia, SC, 2003.

Gottschalk, Louis. *Lafayette and the Close of the American Revolution.* Chicago, 1942.

Gould, Eliga H. *The Persistence of Empire: British Political Culture in the Age of the American Revolution.* Chapel Hill, NC, 2000.

Gray, Edward G., and Jane Kamensky, eds. *The Oxford Handbook of the American Revolution.* New York, 2013.

Graymont, Barbara. *The Iroquois in the American Revolution.* Syracuse, NY, 1972.

Greene, Jerome A. *The Guns of Independence: The Siege of Yorktown.* New York, 2005.

Gruber, Ira. *The Howe Brothers and the American Revolution.* New York, 1972.

Hagist, Don N., ed. *Noble Volunteers: The British Soldiers Who Fought in the American Revolution.* Yardley, PA, 2020.

———. *These Distinguished Corps: British Grenadier and Light Infantry Battalions in the American Revolution.* Warwick, UK, 2021.

———. *Waging War in America 1775–1783: Operational Challenges of Five Armies During the American Revolution.* Warwick, UK, 2023.

Hargrove, Richard J. *General John Burgoyne.* Newark, DE, 1983.

Harlow, Vincent T. *The Founding of the Second British Empire, 1763–1793.* London, 1952.

Harris, Michael C. *Brandywine: A Military History of the Battle That Lost Philadelphia but Saved America, September 11, 1777.* El Dorado Hills, CA, 2014.

———. *Germantown: A Military History of the Battle for Philadelphia, October 4, 1777.* El Dorado Hills, CA, 2020.

Hawke, David Freeman. *Everyday Life in Early America.* New York, 1988.

———. *Paine.* New York, 1964.

Hazleton, John. *The Declaration of Independence: Its History.* New York, 1906.

Henderson, H. James. *Party Politics in the Continental Congress.* New York, 1974.

Henriques, Peter R. *First and Always: A New Portrait of George Washington.* Charlottesville, VA, 2020.

Herrera, Ricardo A. *Feeding Washington's Army: Surviving the Valley Forge Winter of 1778*. Chapel Hill, NC, 2022.

Hibbert, Christopher. *King Mob: The Story of Lord George Gordon and the London Riots of 1780*. New York, 1958.

Higginbotham, Don. *Daniel Morgan: Revolutionary Rifleman*. Chapel Hill, NC, 1961.

———, ed. *Reconsiderations on the Revolutionary War: Selected Essays*. Westport, CT, 1978.

———. *War and Society in Revolutionary America: The Wider Dimensions of Conflict*. Columbia, SC, 1989.

———. *The War of American Independence: Military Attitude, Policies, and Practice, 1763–1789*. New York, 1971.

Higgins, W. Robert, ed. *The Revolutionary War in the South: Power, Conflict, and Leadership*. Durham, NC, 1979.

Hobhouse, Christopher. *Fox*. London, 1964.

Hoffman, Ronald, and Peter J. Albert, eds. *Diplomacy and Revolution: The Franco-American Alliance of 1778*. Charlottesville, VA, 1981.

———. *Peace and the Peacemakers: The Treaty of 1783*. Charlottesville, VA, 1986.

———. *The Transforming Hand of Revolution: Reconsidering the American Revolution as a Social Movement*. Charlottesville, VA, 1995.

Hoffman, Ronald, Thad W. Tate, and Peter J. Albert, eds. *An Uncivil War: The Southern Backcountry During the American Revolution*. Charlottesville, VA, 1985.

Holton, Woody. *Abigail Adams*. New York, 2009.

———. *Liberty Is Sweet: The Hidden History of the American Revolution*. New York, 2021.

Hoock, Holger. *Scars of Independence: America's Violent Birth*. New York, 2017.

Hubbard, Robert Ernest. *Major General Israel Putnam*. Jefferson, NC, 2017.

Huggins, Benjamin L. *Washington's War, 1779*. Yardley, PA, 2018.

Hulbert, Kylie A. *The Untold War at Sea: America's Revolutionary Privateers*. Athens, GA, 2022.

Huston, James A. *Logistics of Liberty: American Services of Supply in the Revolutionary War and After.* Newark, DE, 1991.

Hutson, James H. *John Adams and the Diplomacy of the American Revolution.* Lexington, KY, 1980.

Jasanoff, Maya. *Liberty's Exiles: American Loyalists in the Revolutionary World.* New York, 2011.

Jensen, Merrill. *The American Revolution Within America.* New York, 1974.

Jones, Colin. *The Great Nation: France from Louis XV to Napoleon, 1715–1799.* New York, 2002.

Jones, T. Cole. *Captives of Liberty: Prisoners of War and the Politics of Vengeance in the American Revolution.* Philadelphia, 2020.

Kaplan, Lawrence S., ed. *The American Revolution and "A Candid World."* Kent, OH, 1977.

Keane, John. *Tom Paine: A Political Life.* Boston, 1995.

Kelly, Jack. *God Save Benedict Arnold: The True Story of America's Most Hated Man.* New York, 2023.

Kelsay, Isabel T. *Joseph Brant, 1743–1807: Man of Two Worlds.* Syracuse, NY, 1984.

Kennett, Lee. *The French Armies in the Seven Years' War: A Study in Military Organization and Administration.* Durham, NC, 1967.

———. *The French Forces in America, 1780–1783.* Westport, CT, 1977.

Kerber, Linda K. *Women of the Republic: Intellect and Ideology in Revolutionary America.* New York, 1980.

Ketchum, Richard M. *Decisive Day: The Battle for Bunker Hill.* New York, 1974.

———. *Saratoga: Turning Point of America's Revolutionary War.* New York, 1997.

———. *Victory at Yorktown: The Campaign That Won the Revolution.* New York, 2004.

———. *The Winter Soldiers: The Battles for Trenton and Princeton.* Garden City, NY, 1973.

Keyssar, Alexander. *The Right to Vote: The Contested History of Democracy in the United States.* New York, 2000.

Knight, John. *War at Saber Point: Banastre Tarleton and the British Legion.* Yardley, PA, 2020.

Knouff, Gregory T. *The Soldiers' Revolution: Pennsylvanians in Arms and the Forging of Early American Identity.* University Park, PA, 2004.

Kolchin, Peter. *American Slavery, 1619–1877.* New York, 1993.

Kranish, Michael. *Flight from Monticello.* New York, 2010.

Lambert, Robert Stansbury. *South Carolina Loyalists in the American Revolution.* Columbia, SC, 1987.

Lawrence, Alexander A. *Storm over Savannah: The Story of Count d'Estaing and the Siege of the Town in 1779.* Athens, GA, 1951.

Lefkowitz, Arthur. *Benedict Arnold's Army: The 1775 American Invasion of Canada During the Revolutionary War.* New York, 2008.

———. *The Long Retreat: The Calamitous American Defense of New Jersey, 1776.* Metuchen, NJ, 1998.

Lender, Mark Edward. *Cabal: The Plot Against General Washington.* Yardley, PA, 2019.

———. *Fort Ticonderoga, the Last Campaigns: The War in the North, 1777–1783.* Yardley, PA, 2022.

Lender, Mark Edward, and Gary Wheeler Stone. *Fatal Sunday: George Washington, the Monmouth Campaign, and the Politics of Battle.* Norman, OK, 2017.

Lengel, Edward. *General George Washington: A Military Life.* New York, 2005.

Lennox, Jeffers. *North of America: Loyalists, Indigenous Nations, and the Borders of the Long American Revolution.* New Haven, CT, 2022.

Lewis, Charles Lee. *Admiral de Grasse and American Independence.* Annapolis, MD, 1945.

Lockhart, Paul. *The Drillmaster of Valley Forge: The Baron de Steuben and the Making of the American Army.* New York, 2010.

———. *Firepower: How Weapons Shaped Warfare.* New York, 2021.

Longmore, Paul K. *The Invention of George Washington.* Berkeley, CA, 1988.

Lumpkin, Henry. *From Savannah to Yorktown: The American Revolution in the South.* Columbia, SC, 1981.

Lutnick, Solomon. *The American Revolution and the British Press, 1775–1783*. Columbia, MO, 1967.

Luzader, John. *Saratoga: A Military History of the Decisive Campaign of the American Revolution*. New York, 2008.

Mackesy, Piers. *Could the British Have Won the War of Independence?* Worcester, MA, 1976.

———. *The War for America, 1775–1783*. Cambridge, MA, 1965.

Madariaga, Isabel de. *Britain, Russia, and the Armed Neutrality of 1780: Sir James Harris's Mission to St. Petersburg During the American Revolution*. New Haven, CT, 1962.

Main, Jackson Turner. *The Sovereign States, 1775–1783*. New York, 1973.

———. *The Upper Houses in Revolutionary America, 1763–1783*. Madison, WI, 1967.

Malone, Dumas. *Jefferson and His Time*. Boston, 1948–1981.

Marshall, P. J. *The Making and Unmaking of Empires: Britain, India, and America c. 1750–1783*. New York, 2005.

Martin, James Kirby. *Benedict Arnold, Revolutionary Hero: An American Warrior Reconsidered*. New York, 1997.

Martin, James Kirby, and Mark Edward Lender. *A Respectable Army: The Military Origins of the Republic, 1763–1789*. Arlington Heights, IL, 1982.

Mattern, David. *Benjamin Lincoln and the American Revolution*. Columbia, SC, 1995.

Mayer, Holly A. *Belonging to the Army: Camp Followers and Community During the American Revolution*. Columbia, SC, 1996.

———. *Congress's Own: A Canadian Regiment, the Continental Army, and the American Union*. Norman, OK, 2021.

———, ed. *Women Waging War in the American Revolution*. Charlottesville, VA, 2022.

Mayers, Robert A. *The War Man: The True Story of a Citizen-Soldier Who Fought from Quebec to Yorktown*. Yardley, PA, 2009.

Mazzagetti, Dominick. *Charles Lee: Self Before Country*. New Brunswick, NJ, 2013.

McBurney, Christian. *The Rhode Island Campaign: The First French and American Operation in the Revolutionary War*. Yardley, PA, 2011.

McCullough, David. *1776*. New York, 2005.

McDonnell, Michael A. *The Politics of War: Race, Class, and Conflict in Revolutionary Virginia*. Chapel Hill, NC, 2007.

Meng, John J. *The Comte de Vergennes: European Phases of His American Diplomacy, 1774–1780*. Washington, DC, 1932.

Messick, Hank. *King's Mountain: The Epic of the Blue Ridge "Mountain Men" in the American Revolution*. Boston, 1976.

Middlekauff, Robert. *The Glorious Cause: The American Revolution, 1763–1789*. New York, 2007.

——. *Washington's Revolution: The Making of America's First Leader*. New York, 2015.

Middleton, Richard. *Cornwallis: Soldier and Statesman in a Revolutionary World*. New Haven, CT, 2022.

Miller, Nathan. *Sea of Glory: The Continental Navy Fights for Independence, 1775–1783*. New York, 1974.

Mintz, Max M. *The Generals of Saratoga: John Burgoyne and Horatio Gates*. New Haven, CT, 1990.

——. *Seeds of Empire: The American Revolutionary Conquest of the Iroquois*. New York, 1999.

Morgan, Edmund S. *Benjamin Franklin*. New Haven, CT, 1992.

Morison, Samuel Eliot. *John Paul Jones: A Sailor's Biography*. Boston, 1959.

Morris, Richard B. *The Peacemakers: The Great Powers and American Independence*. New York, 1965.

Murphy, Orville T. *Charles Gravier, Comte de Vergennes: French Diplomacy in the American Revolution*. Albany, NY, 1982.

Nash, Gary B. *The Forgotten Fifth: African Americans in the Age of Revolution*. Cambridge, MA, 2006.

——. *Race and Revolution*. Madison, WI, 1990.

Nelson, Paul David. *Anthony Wayne: Soldier of the Early Republic*. Bloomington, IN, 1985.

——. *General Horatio Gates: A Biography*. Baton Rouge, LA, 1976.

Nelson, William H. *The American Tory*. Oxford, UK, 1961.

Niemeyer, Charles. *America Goes to War: A Social History of the Continental Army*. New York, 1996.

Nordholt, Jan Willem Schulte. *The Dutch Republic and American Independence*. Chapel Hill, NC, 1982.

Norman, Jesse. *Edmund Burke: The First Conservative*. New York, 2013.

Norton, Mary Beth. *The British-Americans: The Loyalist Exiles in England, 1774–1789*. New York, 1972.

———. *Liberty's Daughters: The Revolutionary Experience of American Women, 1750–1800*. Boston, 1980.

Oberg, Barbara B., ed. *Women in the American Revolution: Gender, Politics, and the Domestic World*. Charlottesville, VA, 2019.

O'Connell, Robert L. *Revolutionary: George Washington at War*. New York, 2019.

O'Donnell, Patrick K. *The Indispensables: The Diverse Soldier-Mariners Who Shaped the Country, Formed the Navy, and Rowed Washington Across the Delaware*. New York, 2021.

———. *Washington's Immortals: The Untold Story of an Elite Regiment Who Changed the Course of the Revolution*. New York, 2016.

O'Donnell, William Emmett. *The Chevalier de la Luzerne: French Minister to the United States, 1779–1784*. Bruges, Belgium, 1938.

Oller, John. *The Swamp Fox: How Francis Marion Saved the American Revolution*. Boston, 2016.

Orrison, Robert, and Mark Wilcox. *All That Can Be Expected: The Battle of Camden and the British High Tide in the South, August 16, 1780*. El Dorado Hills, CA, 2023.

O'Shaughnessy, Andrew Jackson. *An Empire Divided: The American Revolution and the British Caribbean*. Philadelphia, 2000.

———. *The Men Who Lost America: British Leadership, the American Revolution and the Fate of the Empire*. New Haven, CT, 2013.

O'Shaughnessy, Andrew Jackson, John A. Ragosta, and Marie-Jeanne Rossignol, eds. *European Friends of the American Revolution*. Charlottesville, VA, 2023.

Palmer, R. R. *The Age of the Democratic Revolution: A Political History of Europe and America, 1760–1800*. Princeton, NJ, 1959.

Pancake, John S. *The Destructive War: The British Campaign in the Carolinas, 1780–1782*. Tuscaloosa, AL, 1985.

Paquette, Gabriel, and Gonzalo M. Quintero Saravia, eds. *Spain and the American Revolution: New Approaches and Perspectives*. Charlottesville, VA, 2020.

Parkinson, Robert G. *The Common Cause: Creating Race and Nation in the American Revolution*. New York, 2016.

Patterson, A. Temple. *The Other Armada: The Franco-Spanish Attempt to Invade Britain in 1779*. Manchester, UK, 1960.

Philbrick, Nathaniel. *Bunker Hill: A City, a Siege, a Revolution*. New York, 2013.

———. *In the Hurricane's Eye: The Genius of George Washington and the Victory at Yorktown*. New York, 2018.

———. *Valiant Ambition: George Washington, Benedict Arnold, and the Fate of the American Revolution*. New York, 2016.

Phillips, Kevin. *1775: A Good Year for Revolution*. New York, 2012.

Pichichero, Christy. *The Military Enlightenment: War and Culture in the French Empire from Louis XIV to Napoleon*. Ithaca, NY, 2017.

Piecuch, Jim, ed. *The Blood Be upon Your Head: Tarleton and the Myth of Buford's Massacre*. Charleston, SC, 2010.

———. *Cavalry of the American Revolution*. Yardley, PA, 2012.

———. *South Carolina Provincials: Loyalists in British Service during the American Revolution*. Yardley, PA, 2023.

———. *Three Peoples, One King: Loyalists, Indians, and Slaves in the Revolutionary South, 1775–1782*. Columbia, SC, 2008.

Polasky, Janet. *Revolutions Without Borders: The Call to Liberty in the Atlantic World*. New Haven, CT, 2015.

Popkin, Jeremy D. *A New World Begins: The History of the French Revolution*. New York, 2019.

Price, Munro. *Preserving the Monarchy: The Comte de Vergennes, 1774–1787*. Cambridge, UK, 1995.

Pulis, John W., ed. *Moving On: Black Loyalists in the Afro-American World*. New York, 1999.

Puls, Mark. *Henry Knox: Visionary General of the American Revolution*. New York, 2008.

Pybus, Cassandra. *Epic Journeys of Freedom: Runaway Slaves of the American Revolution and Their Global Quest for Liberty*. Boston, 2006.

Quarles, Benjamin. *The Negro in the American Revolution*. Chapel Hill, NC, 1961.

Quimby, Robert S. *The Background of Napoleonic Warfare: The Theory of Military Tactics in Eighteenth-Century France*. New York, 1957.

Rakove, Jack. *The Beginnings of National Politics: An Interpretive History of the Continental Congress*. Baltimore, 1982.

Randall, Willard Sterne. *The Founders' Fortunes: How Money Shaped the Birth of America*. New York, 2022.

Rankin, Hugh. *Francis Marion: The Swamp Fox*. New York, 1973.

———. *The North Carolina Continentals*. Chapel Hill, NC, 1971.

Ranlet, Philip. *The New York Loyalists*. Knoxville, TN, 1986.

Raphael, Ray. *A People's History of the American Revolution: How Common People Shaped the Fight for Independence*. New York, 2001.

Resch, John. *Suffering Soldiers: Revolutionary War Veterans, Moral Sentiment, and Political Culture in the Early Republic*. Amherst, MA, 1999.

Resch, John, and Walter Sargent, eds. *War and Society in the American Revolution*. DeKalb, IL, 2007.

Riley, James C. *The Seven Years War and the Old Regime in France: The Economic and Financial Toll*. Princeton, NJ, 1986.

Risch, Erna. *Supplying Washington's Army*. Washington, DC, 1981.

Ritcheson, Charles R. *British Politics and the American Revolution*. Norman, OK, 1964.

Roberts, Michael. *Splendid Isolation, 1763–1780*. Reading, UK, 1970.

Robson, Eric. *The American Revolution: In Its Political and Military Aspects, 1763–1783*. Hamden, CT, 1965.

Rodger, N. A. M. *The Command of the Ocean: A Naval History of Britain, 1649–1815*. New York, 2004.

———. *The Insatiable Earl: A Life of John Montagu, Fourth Earl of Sandwich, 1718–1792*. New York, 1993.

Rossie, Jonathan Gregory. *The Politics of Command in the American Revolution*. Syracuse, NY, 1975.

Royster, Charles. *A Revolutionary People at War: The Continental Army and American Character, 1775–1783*. Chapel Hill, NC, 1979.

Schecter, Barnet. *The Battle for New York: The City at the Heart of the American Revolution*. New York, 2002.

Schiff, Stacy. *A Great Improvisation: Franklin, France, and the Birth of America*. New York, 2005.

Scott, H. M. *British Foreign Policy in the Age of the American Revolution*. Oxford, UK, 1990.

Sculley, Seanegan P. *Contest for Liberty: Military Leadership in the Continental Army, 1775–1783*. Yardley, PA, 2019.

Selby, John. *The Revolution in Virginia, 1775–1783*. Williamsburg, VA, 1988.

Shelton, Hal T. *General Richard Montgomery and the American Revolution*. New York, 1994.

Shy, John. *A People Numerous and Armed: Reflections on the Military Struggle for American Independence*. New York, 1976.

Simms, Brendan. *Three Victories and a Defeat: The Rise and Defeat of the First British Empire, 1714–1783*. New York, 2007.

Singerton, Jonathan. *The American Revolution and the Habsburg Monarchy*. Charlottesville, VA, 2022.

Smith, David. *William Howe and the American War of Independence*. London, 2015.

Smith, Page. *A New Age Now Begins: A People's History of the American Revolution*. New York, 1976.

Smith, Paul H. *Loyalists and Redcoats: A Study in British Revolutionary Policy*. Chapel Hill, NC, 1964.

Snow, Dean. *1777: Tipping Point at Saratoga*. New York, 2016.

Sosin, Jack M. *The Revolutionary Frontier, 1763–1783*. Alburquerque, NM, 1967.

Spring, Matthew H. *With Zeal and with Bayonets Only: The British Army on Campaign in North America, 1775–1783*. Norman, OK, 2008.

Stephenson, Michael. *Patriot Battles: How the War of Independence Was Fought*. New York, 2007.

Stinchcombe, William. *The American Revolution and the French Alliance*. Syracuse, NY, 1969.

Syrett, David. *The Royal Navy in American Waters, 1775–1783*. Aldershot, UK, 1989.

Taaffe, Stephen R. *The Philadelphia Campaign, 1777–1778*. Lawrence, KS, 2003.

———. *Washington's Revolutionary War Generals*. Norman, OK, 2019.

Taylor, Alan. *American Revolutions: A Continental History, 1750–1804*. New York, 2016.

———. *The Divided Ground: Indians, Settlers, and the Northern Borderland of the American Revolution*. New York, 2006.

———. *The Internal Enemy: Slavery and War in Virginia, 1772–1832*. New York, 2013.

Thayer, Theodore. *Nathanael Greene: Strategist of the American Revolution*. New York, 1960.

———. *Washington and Lee: The Making of a Scapegoat*. Port Washington, NY, 1976.

Thomas, Evan. *John Paul Jones: Sailor, Hero, Father of the American Navy*. New York, 2003.

Thomas, Peter D. G. *Lord North*. London, 1976.

Thompson, C. Bradley. *America's Revolutionary Mind: A Moral History of the American Revolution and the Declaration That Defined It*. New York, 2019.

Tilley, John. *The British Navy and the American Revolution*. Columbia, SC, 1987.

Tonsetic, Robert L. *1781: The Decisive Year of the Revolutionary War*. Philadelphia, 2011.

Tuchman, Barbara W. *The First Salute*. New York, 1988.

Unger, Harlow Giles. *Improbable Patriot: The Secret History of Monsieur de Beaumarchais, the French Playwright Who Saved the American Revolution.* Hanover, NH, 2011.

———. *Lafayette.* New York, 2002.

Urban, Mark. *Fusiliers: The Saga of a British Redcoat Regiment in the American Revolution.* New York, 2007.

Valentine, Alan. *Lord George Germain.* Oxford, UK, 1962.

———. *Lord North.* Norman, OK, 1967.

Van Buskirk, Judith L. *Generous Enemies: Patriots and Loyalists in Revolutionary New York.* Philadelphia, 2002.

———. *Standing in Their Own Light: African American Patriots in the American Revolution.* Norman, OK, 2017.

Van Doren, Carl. *Mutiny in January.* New York, 1947.

Vlack, Milton C. Van. *Silas Deane: Revolutionary War Diplomat and Politician.* Jefferson, NC, 2013.

Ward, Christopher. *The War of the Revolution.* New York, 1952.

Ward, Harry. *George Washington's Enforcers: Policing the Continental Army.* Carbondale, IL, 2006. ·

———. *Major General Adam Stephen and the Cause of American Liberty.* Charlottesville, VA, 1989.

Watt, Gavin. *Rebellion in the Mohawk Valley: The St. Leger Expedition of 1777.* Toronto, 2002.

Weddle, Kevin J. *The Compleat Victory: Saratoga and the American Revolution.* New York, 2021.

Weigley, Russell F. *The Partisan War: The South Carolina Campaign of 1780–1782.* Columbia, SC, 1970.

Wenger, William V. *The Key to American Independence: Quantifying Foreign Assistance to the American Revolution.* El Segundo, CA, 2021.

White, David O. *Connecticut's Black Soldiers, 1775–1783.* Chester, CT, 1973.

Whitely, Peter. *Lord North: The Prime Minister Who Lost America.* London, 1996.

Whitridge, Arnold. *Rochambeau*. New York, 1965.

Whittemore, Charles P. *General of the Revolution: John Sullivan of New Hampshire*. New York, 1961.

Wickwire, Franklin, and Mary Wickwire. *Cornwallis and the War of Independence*. London, 1971.

Wiencek, Henry. *An Imperfect God: George Washington, His Slaves, and the Creation of America*. New York, 2003.

Willcox, William B. *Portrait of a General: Sir Henry Clinton in the War of Independence*. New York, 1964.

Williams, Glenn F. *Year of the Hangman: George Washington's Campaign Against the Iroquois*. Yardley, PA, 2005.

Wilson, David K. *The Southern Strategy: Britain's Conquest of South Carolina and Georgia, 1775–1780*. Columbia, SC, 2005.

Wood, Gordon S. *The American Revolution: A History*. New York, 2002.

———. *The Radicalism of the American Revolution*. New York, 1992.

———. *Revolutionary Characters: What Made the Founders Different*. New York, 2006.

Wood, W. J. *Battles of the Revolutionary War, 1775–1781*. Chapel Hill, NC, 1990.

Wright, Esmond, ed. *Causes and Consequences of the American Revolution*. Chicago, 1966.

———. *Franklin of Philadelphia*. Cambridge, MA, 1968.

Wright, Robert K. *The Continental Army*. Washington, DC, 1983.

Young, Alfred F. *The Shoemaker and the Tea Party: Memory and the American Revolution*. Boston, 1999.

Young, Alfred F., and Ray Raphael, eds. *Revolutionary Founders: Rebels, Radicals, and Reformers in the Making of the Nation*. New York, 2011.

A SELECT LIST OF ARTICLES

Armitage, David. "George III and the Law of Nations." *William and Mary Quarterly* 79 (2022): 3–30.

Berg, Richard. "The Southern Campaigns: The British Effort to Retake the South, 1778–1781." *Strategy and Tactics* 104 (1985): 14–23.

Bowler, R. Arthur. "Sir Henry Clinton and Army Profiteering: A Neglected Aspect of the Clinton-Cornwallis Controversy." *William and Mary Quarterly* 31 (1974): 111–23.

Conway, Stephen. "The British Army, 'Military Europe,' and the American War of Independence." *William and Mary Quarterly* 67 (January 2010): 69–100.

———. "British Army Officers and the American War for Independence." *William and Mary Quarterly* 41 (April 1984): 265–76.

———. "The Politics of British Military and Naval Mobilization, 1775–1783." *English Historical Review* 112 (November 1997): 1179–201.

———. "To Subdue America: British Army Officers and the Conduct of the Revolutionary War." *William and Mary Quarterly* 43 (July 1986): 381–407.

Ellison, Amy Noel. "Montgomery's Misfortune: The American Defeat at Quebec and the March Toward Independence." *Early American Studies* 15 (2017): 591–616.

Ferling, John. "John Adams: Diplomat." *William and Mary Quarterly* 51 (1994): 227–52.

———. "Joseph Galloway's Military Advice: A Loyalist's View of the Revolution." *Pennsylvania Magazine of History and Biography* 68 (1974): 174–76.

———. "Sir Henry Clinton: A Reappraisal of His Generalship in the War of Independence." *Journal of the American Revolution*, April 27, 2021.

———. "The Troubled Relationship Between Clinton and Cornwallis and Their 'War' After the War." *Journal of the American Revolution*, July 15, 2021.

Gallo, Marcus. "Property Rights, Citizenship, Corruption, and Inequality: Confiscating Loyalist Estates During the American Revolution." *Pennysylvania History: A Journal of Mid-Atlantic Studies* 86 (2019): 474–510.

Gibbs, Ronald. "Terrain and Tactics: Detailed Perspectives from William Howe's War Plan of 1776." *Journal of the American Revolution*, October 12, 2021.

Grindon, Blake. "Hilliard d'Auberteuil's *Mis Mac Rea*: A Story of the American Revolution in the French Atlantic." *William and Mary Quarterly* 79 (October 2022): 563–94.

Hutson, James H. "The Partition Treaty and the Declaration of Independence." *Journal of American History* 58 (1972): 877–96.

Kaplan, Roger. "The Hidden View: British Intelligence Operations During the American Revolution." *William and Mary Quarterly* 47 (January 1990): 115–38.

Kyte, George W. "A Projected British Attack upon Philadelphia in 1781." *Pennsylvania Magazine of History and Biography* 76 (1952): 379–93.

Lawrence, Alexander A. "General Robert Howe and the British Capture of Savannah in 1778." *Georgia Historical Quarterly* 36 (1952): 303–27.

Lender, Mark Edward, and James Kirby Martin. "A Traitor's Epiphany: Benedict Arnold in Virginia and His Quest for Reconciliation." *Virginia Magazine of History and Biography* 125 (2017): 315–57.

Lutnick, Solomon M. "The Defeat at Yorktown: A View from the British Press." *Virginia Magazine of History and Biography* 72 (1964): 471–78.

Mackesy, Piers. "British Strategy in the War of American Independence." *Yale Review* 52 (1963): 539–57.

Price, David. "Thomas Knowlton's Revolution." *Journal of the American Revolution*, September 2, 2021.

Procknow, Gene. "Henry Clinton's Plan to End the War." *Journal of the American Revolution*, March 5, 2024.

Ruddiman, John A. "'Is This the Land of Liberty?': Continental Soldiers and Slavery in the Revolutionary South." *William and Mary Quarterly* 79 (2022): 283–314.

Saberton, Ian. "The Decision That Lost Britain the War: An Enigma Now Resolved." *Journal of the American Revolution*, January 8, 2019.

———. "George Hanger—His Adventures in the American Revolutionary War." *Journal of the American Revolution*, February 17, 2017.

———. "Midsummer 1780 in the Carolinas and Georgia—Events Predating the Battle of Camden." *Journal of the American Revolution*, July 15, 2019.

———. "Reflections on the Siege and Capitulation of Yorktown and Gloucester." *Journal of the American Revolution*, April 21, 2021.

Solis-Mullern, Joseph. "From the First Partition of Poland to Yorktown." *Journal of the American Revolution*, March 1, 2022.

Sterner, Eric. "Britain, Russia, and the Armed Neutrality of 1780." *Journal of the American Revolution*, October 20, 2022.

Willcox, William B. "The British Road to Yorktown: A Study in Divided Command." *American Historical Review* 52 (October 1946): 1–35.

———. "British Strategy in America, 1778." *Journal of Modern History* 19 (June 1947): 97–121.

———. "Rhode Island in British Strategy, 1780–1781." *Journal of Modern History* 17 (December 1945):304–331.

Wyatt, Frederick, and William B. Willcox, "Sir Henry Clinton: A Psychological Exploration in History." *William and Mary Quarterly* 16 (1959): 3–26.

NOTES

ABBREVIATIONS

ADA   L. H. Butterfield et al., eds. *The Diary and Autobiography of John Adams.* 4 vols. Cambridge, MA, 1961.

AFC   L. H. Butterfield et al., eds. *Adams Family Correspondence.* Cambridge, MA, 1963–.

AR   William B. Willcox, ed. *The American Rebellion: Sir Henry Clinton's Narrative of His Campaigns, 1775–1782, with an Appendix of Original Documents.* New Haven, CT, 1954.

BF   Benjamin Franklin

CP   Ian Saberton, ed. *The Cornwallis Papers: The Campaigns of 1780 and 1781 in the Southern Theatre of the American Revolutionary War,* 6 vols. Uckfield, England, 2010.

CWTP Philip Foner, ed. *The Complete Writings of Thomas Paine.* 2 vols. New York, 1945.

DAR   K. G. Davies, ed. *Documents of the American Revolution.* 21 vols. Dublin, 1972–1981.

DGW Donald Jackson et al., eds. *The Diaries of George Washington.* 6 vols. Charlottesville, VA, 1978.

Facsimiles Benjamin F. Stevens, ed. *Facsimiles of Manuscripts in European Archives Relating to America, 1773–1783.* 25 vols. Reprint, New York, 1970.

GW   George Washington

JA   John Adams

JCC   Worthington C. Ford, ed. *Journals of the Continental Congress, 1774–1789*. 34 vols. Washington, DC, 1904–1937.

LDC   Paul H. Smith, ed. *Letters of Delegates to Congress, 1774–1789*. 25 vols. Washington, DC, 1976–2000.

LSLP   Stanley Idzerda et al., eds. *Lafayette in the Age of the American Revolution: Selected Letters and Papers, 1776–1790*. 5 vols. Ithaca, NY, 1976–1983.

NG   Nathanael Greene

PAH   Harold C. Syrett and Jacob E. Cooke, eds. *The Papers of Alexander Hamilton*. 27 vols. New York, 1961–1987.

PBF   Leonard W. Labaree et al., eds. *The Papers of Benjamin Franklin*. New Haven, CT, 1959–.

PGWC   W. W. Abbot et al., eds. *The Papers of George Washington Colonial Series*. 10 vols. Charlottesville, VA, 1983–95.

PGWR   Philander Chase et al., eds. *The Papers of George Washington: Revolutionary War Series*. Charlottesville, VA, 1985–.

PH   *The Parliamentary History of England, from the Earliest Period to the Year 1803*. 32 vols. Reprint, New York, 1966.

PHL   Philip M. Hamer et al., eds. *The Papers of Henry Laurens*. Columbia, SC, 1968–.

PJA   Robert J. Taylor et al., eds. *Papers of John Adams*. Cambridge, MA, 1977–.

PNG   Richard K. Showman et al., eds., *The Papers of Nathanael Greene*. 13 vols. Chapel Hill, NC, 1976–2005.

PTJ   Julian P. Boyd et al., eds., *The Papers of Thomas Jefferson*. Princeton, NJ, 1950–.

SHCP   Sir Henry Clinton Papers

SOS   Henry Steele Commager and Richard B. Morris, eds. *The Spirit of '76: The Story of the American Revolution As Told by Participants.* 2 vols. Indianapolis, 1958.

TJ   Thomas Jefferson

WW   John C. Fitzpatrick, ed. *The Writings of Washington.* 39 vols. Washington, DC, 1931–44.

CHAPTER I: DECISIONS FOR WAR

1. GW to Robert McKenzie, October 9, 1774, *PGWC* 10:171.

2. Quoted in David Hackett Fischer, *Paul Revere's Ride* (New York, 1994), 164.

3. Alan Valentine, *Lord North* (Norman, OK, 1967), 1:158, 189; Peter Whiteley, *Lord North: The Prime Minister Who Lost America* (London, 1996), 94.

4. Valentine, *Lord North*, 1:320.

5. JA to Joseph Palmer, September 26, 1774, *LDC* 1:106; JA to William Tudor, October 7, 1774, ibid., 1:157; JA Diary, ibid., 1:110; GW to Robert Mackenzie, October 9, 1774, ibid., 1:166–67.

6. Joseph Galloway, Statement of His Plan of Union, ibid., 1:121; Samuel Adams to Thomas Young, October 17 [?], 1774, ibid., 1:205; JA to James Burgh [?], December 28, 1774, ibid., 1:276; GW to Robert Mackenzie, October 9, 1774, ibid., 1:167.

7. Silvia Marzagalli, "The French Atlantic World in the Seventeenth and Eighteenth Centuries," in *The Atlantic World, 1450–1850*, ed. Nicholas Canny and Philip Morgan (New York, 2011), 236; Orville T. Murphy, *Charles Gravier, Comte de Vergennes: French Diplomacy in the Age of Revolution, 1719–1787* (Albany, NY, 1982), 211–12.

8. For these two paragraphs, see Thomas F. Chávez, *Spain and the Independence of the United States: An Intrinsic Gift* (Albuquerque, NM, 2002), 6–7; Gabriel Paquette and Gonzalo M. Quintero Saravia, "Introduction: Spain and the American Revolution," in *Spain and the American Revolution: New Approaches and Perspectives*, ed. Gabriel Paquette and Gonzalo M. Quintero Saravia (Charlottesville, VA, 2020), 9; Kathleen DuVal, "The International War of the Gulf Coast," in *The American Revolution: A World War*, ed. Daniel K. Allison and Larrie D. Ferreiro (Washington, DC, 2018), 129.

9. Jonathan R. Dull, *The French Navy and American Independence: A Study of Arms and Diplomacy, 1774–1787* (Princeton, NJ, 1975), 8–12, 16–19; Dull, *A Diplomatic History of the American Revolution* (New Haven, CT, 1985), 33–36; H. M. Scott, *British Foreign Policy in the Age of the American Revolution* (Oxford, UK, 1990), 153; Murphy, *Charles Gravier, Comte de Vergennes*, 119; Larrie D. Ferreiro, *Brothers at Arms: American Independence and the Men of France and Spain Who Saved It* (New York, 2016), 5–20; C. B. A. Behrens, *The Ancien Régime* (New York, 1967), 30, 156; James Breck Perkins, *France Under Louis XV* (London, 1897), 2:178–83.

10. Edward S. Corwin, *French Policy and the American Alliance of 1778* (reprint, New York, 1970), 34–44; Samuel Flagg Bemis, *The Diplomacy of the American Revolution* (New York, 1935), 17; Ferreiro, *Brothers at Arms*, 21–26; Orville T. Murphy, "The View from Versailles: Charles Gravier Comte de Vergennes's Perceptions of the American Revolution," in *Diplomacy and Revolution: The Franco-American Alliance of 1778*, ed. Ronald Hoffman and Peter J. Albert (Charlottesville, VA, 1981), 128.

11. George III to Frederick Lord North, September 11, November 17, 1774, in W. Bodham Dunne, ed., *The Correspondence of King George III with Lord North, 1763–1783* (reprint, New York, 1971), 1:202, 215; Ferreiro, *Brothers at Arms*, 34; Dora Mae Clark, *British Opinion and the American Revolution* (reprint, New York, 1966), 76–92; Solomon Lutnick, *The American Revolution and the British Press, 1775–1783* (Columbia, MO, 1967), 42–45.

12. Valentine, *Lord North*, 1:310, 319; Julie Flavell, "British Perceptions of New England and the Decision for a Coercive Colonial Policy, 1774–1775," in *Britain and America Go to War: The Impact of War and Warfare in Anglo-America, 1754–1815*, eds. Julie Flavell and Stephen Conway (Gainesville, FL, 2004), 95–115; Piers Mackesy, *Could the British Have Won the War of Independence?* (Worcester, MA, 1976), 3–4.

13. Thomas Gage to Lord Dartmouth, August 27, September 12, October 3, 17, 30, 1774, in, Thomas Gage, *The Correspondence of General Thomas Gage with the Secretaries of State, and the War Office and Treasury, 1763–1775*, ed. Clarence E. Carter (reprint, New York, 1969), 1:366, 317, 373–75, 378–79, 380, 383; Gage to Lord Barrington, September 25, October 3, November 2, 1774, ibid., 2:654, 656, 659; Gage to Dartmouth, May 31, June 26, August 27, September 2, 20, 25, December 15, 1774, January 18, 1775, *DAR* 8:117, 136, 166, 181–82, 198, 201, 242; 9:30. On General Gage, see John R. Alden, *General Gage in America* (Baton Rouge, LA, 1948); and

Sylvia R. Frey, *The British Soldier in America: A Social History of Military Life in the Revolutionary Period* (Austin, TX, 1981), 9.

14. Dartmouth to Gage, January 27, 1774, *DAR* 9:37–41.

15. Dartmouth to Gage, February 22, 1775, ibid., 9:53–54.

16. Richard Henry Lee to Arthur Lee, February 24, 1775, *LDC* 1:313.

CHAPTER 2: WAR

1. *PH* 18:149–60; Alan Valentine, *Lord North* (Norman, OK, 1967), 1:350; Stanley Ayling, *The Elder Pitt: Earl of Chatham* (New York, 1976), 414, 416.

2. Valentine, *Lord North*, 1:346–47.

3. *PH* 18:198–215, 298–300, 320; Valentine, *Lord North*, 1:355; Andrew Jackson O'Shaughnessy, *The Men Who Lost America: British Leadership, the American Revolution and the Fate of Empire* (New Haven, CT, 2013), 328.

4. *PH* 18:478–538; Jesse Norman, *Edmund Burke: The First Conservative* (New York, 2013), 10–69, 96–97.

5. Gage to Dartmouth, September 2, October 17, 30, 1774, *DAR* 8:181, 213, 221; Don N. Hagist, *Noble Volunteers: The British Soldiers Who Fought in the American Revolution* (Yardley, PA, 2020), 4; David Smith, *William Howe and the American War of Independence* (London, 2015), 31, 35, 38.

6. Gage to Dartmouth, September 2, 1774, *DAR* 8:181–82; Gage to Dartmouth, March 4, 1775, in Thomas Gage, *The Correspondence of General Thomas Gage with the Secretaries of State, and the War Office and Treasury, 1763–1775*, ed. Clarence E. Carter (reprint, New York, 1969), 1:393–94.

7. On Lexington and Concord, see David Hackett Fischer, *Paul Revere's Ride* (New York, 1994), 188–217.

8. Gage to Dartmouth, April 22, 1775, *DAR* 9:102.

9. William Glanville Evelyn to William Evelyn, April 23, 1775, in G. D. Scull, ed., *Memoir and Letters of Captain W. Glanville Evelyn, of the 4th Regiment ("King's Own") from North America, 1774–1776* (Oxford, UK, 1879), 54.

10. See Diary of Amos Farnsworth in S. A. Greene, ed., "Three Military Diaries," *Proceedings of the Massachusetts Historical Society*, 2nd series, 12 (1897–1899): 78.

11. Gage to Dartmouth, April 22, 1775, *DAR* 9:103. On the events in Concord and along Battle Road, see Fischer, *Paul Revere's Ride*, 202–60.

12. Richard Frothingham, *History of the Siege of Boston* (Boston, 1849), 101; Allen French, *The Siege of Boston* (New York, 1911), 117; Mark Puls, *Henry Knox: Visionary General of the American Revolution* (New York, 2008), 27; John Shy, *A People Numerous and Armed: Reflections on the Military Struggle for American Independence* (New York, 1976), 168; Don Higginbotham, *The War of American Independence: Military Attitudes, Policies, and Practices, 1763–1789* (New York, 1971), 65–66.

13. Gage to Dartmouth, May 13, 25, June 12, 1775, *DAR* 9:130–32, 143, 170–71; Earl of Dunmore to Dartmouth, May 1, 1775, ibid., 9:107; William Franklin to Dartmouth, May 6, 1775, ibid., 9:125–28.

14. Huw J. Davies, *The Wandering Army: The Campaigns that Transformed the British Way of War, 1750–1850* (New Haven, CT, 2022), 94, 96, 118, 126; William B. Willcox, *Portrait of a General: Sir Henry Clinton in the War of Independence* (New York, 1962), 48. On Putnam's prior war experience, see Robert Ernest Hubbard, *Major General Israel Putnam* (Jefferson, NC, 2017), 7–68.

15. Howe's papers were destroyed in a fire early in the 19th century, a loss that has hampered hostorians. However, useful information on his early years can be found in Julie Flavell, *The Howe Dynasty: The Untold Story of a Military Family and the Women Behind Britain's Wars for America* (New York, 2021), 39–108.

16. Diary of Amos Farnsworth, *SOS* 1:122; John Burgoyne to Lord Stanley, June 25, 1775, ibid., 1:134; Lord Rawdon to Earl of Huntingdon, June 20, 1775, ibid., 1:130.

17. Peter Brown to his mother, June 28, 1775, ibid., 1:124.

18. For an account of men on the eve of battle, see E. B. Sledge, *With the Old Breed on Peleliu and Okinawa* (New York, 1990), 55–56.

19. Quoted in Hubbard, *Major General Israel Putnam*, 88.

20. Rawdon to Huntingdon, June 20, 1775, *SOS* 1:130; William Prescott to JA, ibid., 1:127; Eyewitness Narrative [undated], ibid., 1:128.

21. Richard M. Ketchum, *Decisive Day: The Battle for Bunker Hill* (New York, 1974), 163; Burgoyne to Stanley, June 25, 1775, *SOS* 1:133, 134.

22. Burgoyne to Stanley, June 25, 1775, *SOS* 1:133; William Howe to British Adjutant General, June 22, 24, 1775, ibid., 1:131.

23. David Price, "Thomas Knowlton's Revolution," *Journal of the American Revolution*, September 2, 2021. For excellent accounts of the Battle of Bunker Hill, see Ketchum, *Decisive Day*, 137–83; Nathaniel Philbrick, *Bunker Hill: A City, a Siege, a Revolution* (New York, 2013); and Rick Atkinson, *The British Are Coming: The War for America, Lexington to Princeton, 1775–1777* (New York, 2019), 103–10. For the carnage in the redoubt, see Katie Turner Getty, "Top 10 Battle of Bunker Hill Quotes," *Journal of the American Revolution*, January 16, 2024.

24. Howe to British Adjutant General, June 28, 1775, *SOS* 1:132; Ketchum, *Decisive Day*, 183; Gage to Dartmouth, June 25, 1775, *DAR* 9:198–99; Gage to Lord Barrington, June 26, 1775, Carter, *Correspondence of General Thomas Gage*, 2:686.

25. Letter of a British Officer, July 5, 1775, *SOS* 1:135–36.

26. Willcox, *Portrait of a General*, 50. The "horror" quote can be found in Davies, *The Wandering Army*, 120.

27. GW to George William Fairfax, May 31, 1775, *PGWC* 10:368; JA to Abigail Adams, May 8, 29, 1775, *AFC* 1:195–96, 207.

28. John Dickinson to Samuel Ward, January 29, 1775, *LDC* 1:303; JA to James Warren, July 6, 24, 1775, ibid., 1:589, 658; Jack N. Rakove, *The Beginnings of National Politics: An Interpretive History of the Continental Congress* (Baltimore, 1979), 62–79; Declaration on the Causes and Necessity of Taking Up Arms (July 1775), *JCC* 2:128–57.

29. Silas Deane's Diary (May 16, 1775), *LDC* 1:351.

30. *JCC* 2:91. The literature on GW is enormous, but good starting places include Ron Chernow, *Washington: A Life* (New York, 2010); Joseph J. Ellis, *His Excellency: George Washington* (New York, 2004); John Ferling, *The Ascent of George Washington: The Hidden Political Genius of an American Icon* (New York, 2009); and James Thomas Flexner, *George Washington: The Forge of Experience, 1732–1775* (Boston, 1967).

31. GW, Address to Congress, June 16, 1775, *PGWR* 1:1, 3n.

32. *JCC* 2:111–23.

33. Roger Sherman to Joseph Trumbull, July 6, 1775, *LDC* 1:599.

34. GW to John Augustine Washington, June 20, 1775, *PGWR* 1:19; GW to Martha Washington, June 18, 1775, ibid., 1:3; GW to Burwell Bassett, June 19, 1775, ibid., 1:12.

35. John Richard Alden, *General Gage in America: Being Principally a History of His Role in the American Revolution* (Baton Rouge, LA, 1948), 280; Peter Whiteley, *Lord North: The Prime Minister Who Lost America* (London, 1996), 157; Valentine, *Lord North*, 1:382, 383, 385; Piers Mackesy, *The War for America, 1775–1783* (Cambridge, MA, 1965), 32–36; Gage to Dartmouth, October 1, 1775, *DAR* 11:135.

36. "The King's Speech to Parliament," in *English Historical Documents: American Colonial Documents to 1776*, ed. Merrill Jensen (London, 1964), 9:851–52.

37. These two paragraphs draw on Gage to Dartmouth, June 12, 1775, *DAR* 9:170–71; Howe to Dartmouth, October 9, 1775, *DAR* 11:140; Dartmouth to Howe, September 5, 1775, ibid., 11:100; Lord George Germain to Howe, January 5, March 28, 1776, ibid., 12:34, 94; Valentine, *Lord North*, 1:374, 382; John Fortescue, *A History of the British Army* (reprint, New York, 1976), 3:175; Higginbotham, *War of American Independence*, 130; Friederike Baer, *Hessians: German Soldiers in the American Revolutionary War* (New York, 2022), 8–31.

38. Alan Valentine, *Lord George Germain* (Oxford, UK, 1961), 17–18, 21, 398, 411–13; Andrew Jackson O'Shaughnessy, *The Men Who Lost America: British Leadership, the American Revolution and the Fate of the Empire* (New Haven, CT, 2013), 169–74; Mackesy, *War for America*, 50–54; Ira D. Gruber, *The Howe Brothers and the American Revolution* (New York, 1972), 23–27, 36–37, 59–63.

39. Howe to Dartmouth, October 9, November 26, 1775, *DAR* 11:138–41, 191–92.

40. See Orville T. Murphy, *Charles Gravier, Comte de Vergennes: French Diplomacy in the Age of Revolution, 1719–1787* (Albany, NY, 1982), 14–207; Orville T. Murphy, "The View from Versailles: Charles Gravier Comte de Vergennes's Perceptions of the American Revolution," in *Diplomacy and Revolution: The Franco-American Alliance of 1778*, ed. Ronald Hoffman and Peter J. Albert (Charlottesville, VA, 1981), 107–9; Munro Price, *Preserving the Monarchy: The Comte de Vergennes, 1774–1787* (Cambridge, UK, 1995), 5–15; Jonathan R. Dull, *A Diplomatic History of the American Revolution* (New Haven, CT, 1985), 48; Richard B. Morris, *The Peacemakers: The Great Powers and American Independence* (New York, 1965), 112–13; Dumas Malone, *Jefferson and the Rights of Man* (Boston, 1951), 36.

41. Price, *Preserving the Monarchy*, 7; Murphy, *Charles Gravier, Comte de Vergennes*, 14–15, 211.

42. Jonathan R. Dull, *The French Navy and American Independence: A Study of Arms and Diplomacy, 1774–1787* (Princeton, NJ, 1975), 11–12, 14, 20–24.

43. These two paragraphs draw on Murphy, *Charles Gravier, Comte de Vergennes*, 211–33; Murphy, "The View from Versailles," 107–30; Edward S. Corwin, *French Policy and the American Alliance of 1778* (reprint, New York, 1970), 63; Dull, *The French Navy and American Independence*, 30; Larrie D. Ferreiro, *Brothers at Arms: American Independence and the Men of France and Spain Who Saved It* (New York, 2016), 49–50.

44. Robert K. Wright, *The Continental Army* (Washington, DC, 1983), 45–50; GW to Charles Lee, July 10, August 29, 1775, *PGWR* 1:99, 371–73; GW to Lund Washington, August 20, 1775, ibid., 1:335; GW to John Augustine Washington, October 13, 1775, ibid., 2:161; GW to Samuel Washington, September 30, 1775, ibid., 2:73; GW to John Hancock, July 10 [–11], September 21, 1775, ibid., 1:90, 2:28; GW to Lewis Morris, August 4, 1775, ibid., 1:241; GW, General Orders, July 4, 7, 14, 23, 24, August 1, 7, 8, 9, 10, 22, October 7, 9, 1775, ibid., 1:71, 73, 115, 119, 128, 158, 163, 207, 260–61, 268, 277–78, 281, 347, 437; 2:121, 255, 357.

45. Erna Risch, *Supplying Washington's Army* (Washington, DC, 1981), 340; GW to Hancock, August 4 [–5], 1775, *PGWR* 1:227.

46. Ferreiro, *Brothers at Arms*, 37–39; Kevin Phillips, *1775: A Good Year for Revolution* (New York, 2012), 297–99, 310; Andrew Jackson O'Shaughnessy, *An Empire Divided: The American Revolution and the British Caribbean* (Philadelphia, 2000), 213–17; Jan Willem Schulte Nordholt, *The Dutch Republic and American Independence* (Chapel Hill, NC, 1982), 14–15; Barbara W. Tuchman, *The First Salute* (New York, 1988), 5–42; Rakove, *The Beginnings of National Politics*, 195.

47. GW to Joseph Reed, November 18, 1775, January 14, 1776, *PGWR* 1:449, 3:89; GW to Hancock, December 4, 18, 25, 31, 1775, ibid., 2:484–85, 574, 602, 615; GW to Massachusetts Council, January 10, 1776, ibid., 3:61, 63n; *JCC* 4:410–13; Douglas Southall Freeman, *George Washington* (New York, 1948–1957), 3:579; Richard Buel Jr., *Dear Liberty: Connecticut's Mobilization for the Revolutionary War* (Middletown, CT, 1980), 55, 69; Seanegan P. Sculley, *Contest for Liberty: Military Leadership in the Continental Army, 1775–1783* (Yardley, PA, 2019), 48.

48. Steven Elliott, *Surviving the Winters: Housing Washington's Army During the American Revolution* (Norman, OK, 2021), 25–36; Loammi Baldwin to GW, September 1, 1775, *PGWR* 1:396; GW to Hancock, January 30 [–31], 1776, ibid., 3:216.

49. Abigail Adams to JA, September 8, 10, 16, 25, 29, October 1, 9, 1775, *AFC* 1:276–79, 284, 287–89, 296.

50. Higginbotham, *War of American Independence*, 390.

51. Council of War, October 18, 1775, *PGWR* 1:450–51; Minutes of the Conference [October 18–24, 1775], ibid., 2:190–203; Hancock to GW, December 22, 1775, ibid., 2:589–90, 590n.

52. Jeffers Lennox, *North of America: Loyalists, Indigenous Nations, and the Borders of the Long American Revolution* (New Haven, CT, 2022), 21–22; Amy Noel Ellison, "Montgomery's Misfortune: The American Defeat at Quebec and the March Toward Independence," *Early American Studies* 15 (2017): 597–98.

53. GW to Philip Schuyler, August 20, 1775, ibid., 1:332. On Benedict Arnold's background and character, see James Kirby Martin, *Benedict Arnold, Revolutionary Hero: An American Warrior Reconsidered* (New York, 1997). On Philip Schuyler, see Don R. Gerlach, *Proud Patriot: Philip Schuyler and the War of Independence, 1775–1783* (Syracuse, NY, 1987); and Martin H. Bush, *Revolutionary Enigma: A Re-Appraisal of General Philip Schuyler of New York* (Port Washington, NY, 1969).

54. Hal T. Shelton, *General Richard Montgomery and the American Revolution* (New York, 1994), 68, 87.

55. Christopher Ward, *The War of the Revolution* (New York, 1951), 1:150–61; Shelton, *General Richard Montgomery*, 79–115; GW to Schuyler, November 6 [–7], 1775, *PGWR* 2:315.

56. Ward, *War of the Revolution*, 1:161–62; Shelton, *General Richard Montgomery*, 117–23, 126.

57. Benedict Arnold to GW, September 25 [–27], 1775, *PGWR*, 2:40–41. On the travail of Arnold's force, see Joseph Hewes to Robert Smith, January 8 [?], 1776, *LDC* 3:58; Thomas A. Desjardin, *Through a Howling Wilderness: Benedict Arnold's March to Quebec, 1775* (New York, 2006); Arthur Lefkowitz, *Benedict Arnold's Army: The 1775 American Invasion of Canada During the Revolutionary War* (New York, 2008); Journal of Dr. Isaac Senter, in Kenneth Roberts, ed., *March to Quebec: Journals of the Members of Arnold's Expedition* (New York, 1946), 216–17.

58. Ward, *War of the Revolution*, 1:190–95; Martin, *Benedict Arnold*, 167–74; Shelton, *General Richard Montgomery*, 138–50; Journal of Abner Stocking, *SOS* 1:204; Account of John Henry, ibid., 1:207; Journal of Thomas Ainslie, ibid., 1:211.

59. Howe to Dartmouth, November 27, December 19, 1775, *DAR* 11:195, 213–14; Smith, *William Howe and the American Revolutionary War*, 43.

60. North Callahan, *Henry Knox: George Washington's General* (New York, 1958), 16–31; Puls, *Henry Knox*, 34; Henry Knox to Lucy Flucker Knox, November 16, 1775, in Phillip Hamilton, ed., *The Revolutionary War Lives and Letters of Lucy and Henry Knox* (Baltimore, 2017), 22; Proceedings of the Committee of Congress, October 18–24, 1775, *PGWR* 2:187, 189n; GW to Hancock, November 8, 1775, ibid., 2:331; GW, Instructions to Colonel Henry Knox, November 16, 1775, ibid., 2:384–85.

61. Knox to GW, December 17, 1775, *PGWR* 2:563; Knox, Inventory of Artillery, December 17, 1775, ibid., 2:565–66.

62. GW to Hancock, January 4, 1776, ibid., 3:19.

CHAPTER 3: SUCCESS AND FAILURE

1. Committee of Secret Correspondence to Bonvouloir, December [?], 1775, *LDC* 2:541; Richard Smith's Diary, December 30, 1775, ibid., 2:538; Secret Committee Minutes of Proceedings, February 14, 1776, ibid., 3:256; Larrie D. Ferreiro, *Brothers at Arms: American Independence and the Men of France and Spain Who Saved It* (New York, 2016), 52.

2. Committee of Secret Correspondence Minutes of Proceedings, March 2, 1776, *LDC* 3:320–22; Robert Morris to Silas Deane, April 4, 1776, ibid., 3:489. Deane's instructions can be found in Milton C. Van Vlack, *Silas Deane: Revolutionary War Diplomat and Politician* (Jefferson, NC, 2013), 195–96.

3. *JCC* 4:40, 71, 186; Hancock to Schuyler, January 24, February 6, 20, 1776, *LDC* 3:146, 205, 288; Hancock to John Thomas, March 6, 1776, ibid., 3:341; Instructions to the Commissioners to Canada, March 20, 1776, ibid., 4:6–9; Hancock to the Massachusetts Assembly, January 29, 1776, ibid., 3:162–63.

4. Thomas to GW, April 7, 22, 1776, *PGWR* 4:49, 151–52; Thomas to Congress, April 8, 1776, in *American Archives*, 4th ser., ed. Peter Force (Washington, DC, 1837–1846), 5:822; Commissioners to Canada to Hancock, May 1, 8, 10, 17, 1776, *LDC* 3:611–12, 639, 645–46; 4:22; Commissioners to Canada to BF, May 11, 1776, ibid., 3:649, 650n.

5. Journal of Thomas Ainslie, May 6, 1776, *SOS* 1:211. On America's disaster in Canada in May and June 1776, see Charles P. Whittemore, *A General of the Revolution: John Sullivan of New Hampshire* (New York, 1961); Paul H. Smith, "Sir Guy Carleton: Soldier-Statesman," in *George Washington's Opponents: British Generals*

and Admirals in the American Revolution, ed. George A. Billias (New York, 1969), 120–23; Burgoyne to Henry Clinton, July 7, 1776, in Douglas R. Cubbison, ed., *Burgoyne and the Saratoga Campaign: His Papers* (Norman, OK, 2012), 151; Christopher Ward, *The War of the Revolution* (New York, 1951), 1:196–201; Rick Atkinson, *The British Are Coming: The War for America, Lexington to Princeton, 1775–1777* (New York, 2019), 273–94.

6. For these paragraphs, see Pierre-Augustin Caron de Beaumarchais to Louis XVI, September 21, 1775, *SOS* 1:245–46; Ferreiro, *Brothers at Arms*, 47–49, 52; Harlow Giles Unger, *Improbable Patriot: The Secret History of Monsieur de Beaumarchais, the French Playwright Who Saved the American Revolution* (Hanover, NH, 2011), 19–56, 95–99.

7. For the foregoing paragraphs see Jonathan R. Dull, *A Diplomatic History of the American Revolution* (New Haven, CT, 1985), 57–61; Dull, *The French Navy and American Independence: A Study of Arms and Diplomacy, 1774–1787* (Princeton, NJ, 1975), 30–66; Ferreiro, *Brothers at Arms*, 54, 89; Unger, *Improbable Patriot*, 112; Orville T. Murphy, *Charles Gravier, Comte de Vergennes: French Diplomacy in the Age of Revolution, 1719–1787* (Albany, NY, 1982), 236–39; Christy Pichichero, *The Military Enlightenment: War and Culture in the French Empire from Louis XIV to Napoleon* (Ithaca, NY, 2017), 13–16; James C. Riley, *The Seven Years War and the Old Regime in France: The Economic and Financial Toll* (Princeton, NJ, 1986), xv, xvi, 41, 50, 53, 59, 70, 109, 115, 132, 143–60; Jeremy Popkin, *A New World Begins: The History of the French Revolution* (New York, 2019), 64–67; Jacques Godechot, *France and the Atlantic Revolution of the Eighteenth Century, 1770–1799* (New York, 1965), 69–70; C. B. A. Behrens, *The Ancien Régime* (London, 1967), 138–42. The quote regarding France's inefficient taxation system is in Godechot, page 69; the Dutch ambassador's assessment is in Riley, page 68; Turgot's comment about the "first gunshot" can be found in James R. Gaines, *For Liberty and Glory: Washington, Lafayette, and Their Revolutions* (New York, 2007), 49. Louis XVI's argument and Vergennes's response can be found in Robert A. Selig, "L'expédition Particulière and the American War of Independence, 1780–1783," *Waging War in America 1775–1783: Operational Challenges of Five Armies During the American Revolution*, ed. Don N. Hagist (Warwick, UK, 2023), 171.

8. These two paragraphs draw on Ferreiro, *Brothers at Arms*, 54–61; Atkinson, *The British Are Coming*, 476; Dull, *A Diplomatic History of the American Revolution*, 62; Dull, *The French Navy and American Independence*, 65; Unger, *Improbable Patriot*, 132–48.

9. Ferreiro, *Brothers at Arms*, 69; Knox to GW, November 27, December 5, 17, 1775, January 5, 1776, *PGWR* 2:434, 495–96, 563–66; 3:29; North Callahan, *Henry Knox: George Washington's General* (New York, 1958), 38–56; Mark Puls, *Henry Knox: Visionary General of the American Revolution* (New York, 2008), 38–39; Journal of Henry Knox, *SOS* 1:175.

10. GW to Joseph Reed, February 10, 1776, *PGWR* 3:289; Council of War, February 18, 1776, ibid., 3:320–22, 323–24n; David Smith, *William Howe and the American War of Independence* (London, 2015), 27, 42; Journal of Samuel Webb, *SOS* 1:176.

11. *PGWR* 3:411n; William Gordon to Samuel Wilson, April 6, 1776, *SOS* 1:178.

12. Gordon to Wilson, *SOS* 1:177–79.

13. Charles Stuart to Lord Bute, April 28, 1776, *SOS* 1:182; Atkinson, *The British Are Coming*, 259–62.

14. *PGWR* 3:377–78n; GW to Reed, February 26 [–March 9], March 19, 1776, ibid., 3:376, 493; Journal of Timothy Newell, *SOS* 1:183.

15. Gage to Dartmouth, October 1, 1775, *DAR* 11:135; Howe to Dartmouth, October 9, November 26, 1775, ibid., 11:139–40, 193; Dartmouth to Howe, October 22, 1775, ibid., 11:159; Josiah Martin to Dartmouth, June 30, 1775, ibid., 9:213.

16. Howe to Germain, June 7, 1776, ibid., 12:145–46; Smith, *William Howe and the American War of Independence*, 50–56.

17. Germain to Howe, March 28, 1776, *DAR* 12:94; Howe to Germain, June 7, 1776, ibid., 12:145.

18. Germain to Henry Clinton, December 6, 1775, *DAR* 11:203–5; Martin to Dartmouth, August 28, 1775, ibid., 11:89; Dartmouth to Martin, September 15, November 7, 1775, ibid., 11:107, 173–75; Dartmouth to Howe, October 22, 1775, ibid., 11:158; William B. Willcox, *Portrait of a General: Sir Henry Clinton in the War of Independence* (New York, 1962), 66–69.

19. *AR*, 26–27.

20. Ibid., 28–29; Peter Parker to Philip Stephens, May 15, 1776, *DAR* 12:138; Clinton to Germain, July 8, 1776, ibid., 12:162.

21. Clinton to Germain, July 8, 1776, *DAR* 12:163; Charles Lee to GW, July 1, 1776, *PGWR* 5:170; *AR*, 31, 35; Dominick Mazzagetti, *Charles Lee: Self Before Country*

(New Brunswick, NJ, 2013), 14–19; Atkinson, *The British Are Coming*, 323–44. The "most heavily fortified city" quotation can be found in Atkinson, 327.

22. *AR*, 37; Clinton to Germain, July 8, 1776, *DAR* 12:164.

CHAPTER 4: PIVOTAL ACTIONS AND INACTIONS

1. GW, General Orders, June 28, 1776, *PGWR* 5:129; GW to William Livingston, June 28, 1776, ibid., 5:136, 137n; Douglas Southall Freeman, *George Washington: A Biography* (New York, 1948–1957), 4:119, 127.

2. For this and the preceding paragraph, see Andrew Jackson O'Shaughnessy, *The Men Who Lost America: British Leadership, the American Revolution and the Fate of Empire* (New Haven, CT, 2013), 57–61. See also Solomon Lutnick, *The American Revolution and the British Press, 1775–1783* (Columbia, MO, 1967), 52, 59, 65, 71, 78.

3. Stephen Conway, *The British Isles and the War of American Independence* (Oxford, UK, 2000), 132–65; Eliga H. Gould, *The Persistence of Empire: British Political Culture in the Age of the American Revolution* (Chapel Hill, NC, 2000), 151, 153; *PH* 23:730, 734, 739, 740, 742.

4. James H. Hutson, "The Partition Treaty and the Declaration of Independence," *Journal of American History* 58 (1972): 877–96. Inglis's pamphlet, *The True Interest of America Impartially Stated* (1776), was designed to refute *Common Sense*. Quotes from the pamphlet are in Hutson's journal article on pages 882–83.

5. Alan Valentine, *Lord North* (Norman, OK, 1967), 407–12; Weldon A. Brown, *Empire or Independence: A Study in the Failure of Reconciliation, 1774–1783* (reprint, Port Washington, NY, 1966), 76.

6. John Dickinson's Notes for a Speech in Congress, [June 8–10?, 1776], *LDC* 4:167; Robert Morris to Reed, July 21, 1776, ibid., 4:511.

7. O'Shaughnessy, *The Men Who Lost America*, 176.

8. David McCullough, *1776* (New York, 2005), 3–4, 10; *PH* 23:695–97.

9. Peter Whiteley, *Lord North: The Prime Minister Who Lost America* (London, 1996), 22; *PH* 23:702, 758, 761, 768, 770, 799.

10. *PH* 23:770–71.

11. Julie Flavel, *The Howe Dynasty: The Untold Story of a Military Family and the Women Behind Britain's Wars for America* (New York, 2021), 124–25; Gerald Saxon Brown,

The American Secretary: The Colonial Policy of Lord George Germain, 1775–1778 (Ann Arbor, MI, 1963), 64; Brown, *Empire or Independence*, 82; O'Shaughnessy, *The Men Who Lost America*, 57–61; Valentine, *Lord North*, 403, 407–12; Whiteley, *Lord North*, 161; Charles R. Ritcheson, *British Politics and the American Revolution* (Norman, OK, 1954), 197–202; Ira D. Gruber, *The Howe Brothers and the American Revolution* (New York, 1972), 72–79.

12. Robert Morris to Charles Lee, February 17, 1776, *LDC* 3:269; ibid., 3:64n; JA to James Warren, May 18, 1776, ibid., 4:32.

13. TJ, Notes of Proceedings in the Continental Congress, June 7–August 1, 1776, *PTJ* 1:313–14.

14. *JCC* 5:428–29.

15. Merrill Jensen, ed., *English Historical Documents: American Colonial Documents to 1776* (London, 1964), 9:867–68.

16. John Dickinson, Notes for a Speech in Congress, [June 8–10?], 1776, *LDC* 4:165–69; Edward Rutledge to John Jay, June 8, 1776, ibid., 4:175; TJ, "Notes of Proceedings," [June 7–28], 1776, *PTJ* 1:309–11.

17. TJ, "Notes of Proceedings," [June 7–28], 1776, *PTJ* 1:311–13.

18. *JCC* 5:428–29.

19. David Syrett, *The Royal Navy in American Waters, 1775–1783* (Aldershot, UK, 1980), 7–8; Edward Rutledge to Ralph Izard, December 8, 1775, *LDC* 2:462; Alan Taylor, *American Revolutions: A Continental History, 1750–1804* (New York, 2016), 148.

20. On Thomas Paine's life in England and his decision to migrate to America, see John Keane, *Tom Paine: A Political Life* (Boston, 1995); and David Freeman Hawke, *Paine* (New York, 1974).

21. Joseph J. Ellis, *The Cause: The American Revolution and Its Discontents, 1773–1783* (New York, 2021), 67.

22. Thomas Paine, *Common Sense* (1776), *CWTP* 1:30–31, 45.

23. Hancock to the Massachusetts Assembly, May 16, 1776, *LDC* 4:7; Hancock to Certain Colonies, June 4, 1776, ibid., 4:136; William Whipple to Joshua Brackett, June 2, 1776, ibid., 4:119; Oliver Wolcott to Laura Wolcott, May 25, 1776, ibid., 4:72; James Duane to Robert Livingston, January 5, 1776, ibid., 3:33; Josiah Bartlett

to John Langdon, May 19, 1776, ibid., 4:39; Morris to James Duane, June 5, 1776, ibid., 4:147; Lee to Henry, April 20 1776, ibid., 3:564; Ward Chipman to Montfort Browne, December [?] 1777, *PJA* 5:375.

24. Elbridge Gerry to James Warren, March 26, 1776, *LDC* 3:442; Joseph Hewes to Samuel Johnston, March 20, 1776, ibid., 3:416; William Whipple to Joshua Brackett, April 11, 1776, ibid., 3:509.

25. JA to Benjamin Hichborn, May 29, 1776, ibid., 4:96; JA to Knox, June 2, 1776, ibid., 4:115; Lee to Landon Carter, June 2, 1776, ibid., 4:117.

26. Hancock to GW, June 11, 1776, ibid., 4:191; Hancock to Certain Colonies, June 14, 1776, ibid., 4:211; JA to James Lowell, June 12, 1776, ibid., 4:197; JA to Horatio Gates, June 18, 1776, ibid., 4:261; Gerry to Warren, June 15, 1776, ibid., 4:220; Josiah Bartlett to John Langdon, June 17, 1776, ibid., 4:255–56; Board of War to GW, June 21, 1776, ibid., 4:279–80; Robert Morris's Memorandum, June 20, 1776, ibid., 4:277, 278n; *JCC* 5:434–35, 438.

27. TJ to Roger Weightman, June 24, 1826, Albert A. Lipscomb and Albert Ellery Bergh, eds., *The Writings of Thomas Jefferson* (Washington, DC, 1900–1904), 16:117–19.

28. C. Bradley Thompson, *America's Revolutionary Mind: A Moral History of the American Revolution and the Declaration That Defined It* (New York, 2019), 11–45.

29. For TJ's draft of the Declaration of Independence, see "Jefferson's 'original Rough draught,'" *PTJ* 1:423–27.

30. JA to Archibald Bulloch, July 1, 1776, *PJA* 4:352.

31. John Dickinson, Notes for a Speech in Congress, [July 1, 1776], *LDC* 4:351–56, 356n; JA to Henry, June 3, 1776, *PJA* 4:235; John Hazleton, *The Declaration of Independence: Its History* (New York, 1906), 161–62.

32. For these two paragraphs, see JA to Samuel Chase, July 1, 1776, *PJA* 4:353; David Armitage, *The Declaration of Independence: A Global History* (Cambridge, MA, 2007), 44. For the frenetic activity leading to Congress's vote, see John Ferling, *Independence: The Struggle to Set America Free* (New York, 2011), 326–35.

33. TJ, "original Rough Draught" of the Declaration of Independence, *PTJ* 1:423–28.

34. JA to Abigail Adams, July 3, 1776, *AFC* 2:28, 31.

35. Friederike Baer, *Hessians: German Soldiers in the American Revolutionary War* (New York, 2022), 62–86; Johann Ewald, *Diary of the American War: A Hessian Journal*, ed. Joseph P. Tustin (New Haven, CT, 1979), 7.

36. Piers Mackesy, *The War for America, 1775–1783* (Cambridge, MA, 1965), 86; Eric Robson, *The American Revolution: In Its Political and Military Aspects, 1763–1783* (New York, 1966), 93–109; Gruber, *The Howe Brothers and the American Revolution*, 101; Ronald Gibbs, "Terrain and Tactics: Detailed Perspectives from William Howe's War Plan of 1776," *Journal of the American Revolution*, October 12, 2021; Roger Kaplan, "The Hidden View: British Intelligence Operations During the American Revolution," *William and Mary Quarterly* 47 (January 1990): 115–38.

37. GW to John Augustine Washington, March 31, 1776, *PGWR* 3:566, 569.

38. GW to Lord Stirling, March 14, 1776, ibid., 3:470; JA to GW, January 6, 1776, ibid., 37; GW to John Augustine Washington, April 29, July 22, 1776, ibid., 4:172, 5:429; GW to Hancock, July 17, 1776, ibid., 5:356; William B. Willcox, *Portrait of a General: Sir Henry Clinton in the War of Independence* (New York, 1962), 102.

39. Lee to GW, February 5 [–6], 9, 29, 1776, *PGWR* 3:350–51, 291, 390–91; Dominick Mazzagetti, *Charles Lee: Self Before Country* (New Brunswick, NJ, 2013), 104–8; John Richard Alden, *General Charles Lee: Traitor or Patriot?* (Baton Rouge, LA, 1951), 95–101.

40. Barnet Schecter, *The Battle for New York: The City at the Heart of the American Revolution* (New York, 2002), 118; John J. Gallagher, *The Battle of Brooklyn, 1776* (New York, 1995), 74, 78–80, 140; GW to John Augustine Washington, May 31 [–June 4], 1776, *PGWR* 4:413.

41. Howe to Germain, June 7, *DAR* 12:145; Howe to Germain, April 26, 1776, in Troyer Steele Anderson, *The Command of the Howe Brothers During the American Revolution* (New York, 1936), 120; David Hackett Fischer, *Washington's Crossing* (New York, 2004), 74–77.

42. Howe to Germain, July 7, 1776, *DAR* 12:157; David Smith, *William Howe and the American War of Independence* (London, 2015), 64–65; Piers Mackesy, *Could the British Have Won the War of Independence?* (Worcester, MA, 1976), 7; Ruma Chopra, *Unnatural Rebellion: Loyalists in New York City During the Revolution* (Charlottesville, VA, 2011), 52.

43. Howe to Germain, July 7, 1776, *DAR* 12:156.

44. Edward H. Tatum Jr., ed., *The American Journal of Ambrose Serle* (reprint, New York, 1969), 71; William Douglas to his Wife, August 23, 1776, *SOS*, 1:431; Fischer, *Washington's Crossing*, 91–92.

45. Howe to Germain, September 3, 1776, *DAR* 12:216–17; Tatum, *The American Journal of Ambrose Serle*, 78–79; Willcox, *Portrait of a General*, 105–6; Christopher Ward, *The War of the Revolution* (New York, 1952), 1:211–37; Gallagher, *The Battle of Brooklyn, 1776*, 101–34; Gruber, *The Howe Brothers and the American Revolution*, 109–13; GW to John Augustine Washington, September 22, 1776, *PGWR* 6:373.

46. *AR*, 44.

47. Smith, *William Howe and the American War of Independence*, 66; Jeremy Black, *War for America: The Fight for Independence, 1775–1783* (Stroud, UK, 1991), 104–5; Gallagher, *Battle of Brooklyn*, 78–79, 156; Howe to Germain, September 3, 1776, *DAR* 12:217.

48. Smith, *William Howe and the American War of Independence*, 66–76; Gruber, *The Howe Brothers and the American Revolution*, 114; Willcox, *Portrait of a General*, 106–7; *AR*, 44.

49. Quoted in Robert Ernest Hubbard, *Major General Israel Putnam: Hero of the American Revolution* (Jefferson, NC, 2017), 121.

50. Council of War, August 29, 1776, *PGWR* 6:153; GW to Hancock, August 31, 1776, ibid., 6:177; Schecter, *The Battle for New York*, 155–67; Patrick K. O'Donnell, *The Indispensables: The Diverse Soldier-Mariners Who Shaped the Country, Formed the Navy, and Rowed Washington Across the Delaware* (New York, 2021), 234–45.

51. GW to Hancock, September 8, 1776, *PGWR*, 6:249.

52. *ADA* 3:419–20; Tatum, *The American Journal of Ambrose Serle* (New York, 1969), 101.

53. GW to Hancock, September 8, 14, 1776, *PGWR* 6:248, 250–51, 308; Council of War, September 12, 1776, ibid., 6:288, 289n.

54. *AR*, 45.

55. Ibid., 46–47.

56. Joseph Plumb Martin, *Private Yankee Doodle: Being a Narrative of Some of the Adventures, Dangers and Sufferings of a Revolutionary Soldier*, ed. George F. Scheer

(Boston, 1962), 34; *AR*, 46–47; Howe to Germain, September 21, 1776, *DAR* 12:228.

57. GW to Hancock, September 2, 6, 8, 16, 1776, *PGWR* 6:199, 231, 248, 313; Knox to his brother, September 23, 1776, *SOS*, 1:479.

58. NG to GW, September 5, 1776, ibid., 6:222–23.

59. *JCC* 5:749; GW to Lund Washington, September 30, 1776, *PGWR* 6:441–42; GW to Hancock, September 16, 18, 24, 25, 1776, ibid., 6:314, 333, 389, 396–97; GW to John Augustine Washington, September 22, 1776, ibid., 6:371–74; GW to Samuel Washington, October 5, 1776, ibid., 6:486–87.

60. William Henry Shelton, "What Was the Mission of Nathan Hale?" *Journal of American History* (1915), 269–89.

61. GW to Hancock, September 2, 22, 1776, *PGWR* 6:200, 369; GW to Lund Washington, October 6, 1776, ibid., 6:494; Diary of Captain Frederick Mackenzie, *SOS*, 1:472; William Tryon to Germain, September 24, 1776, *DAR* 12:231; Schecter, *The Battle for New York*, 205–10. See Benjamin L. Carp, *The Great New York Fire of 1776: A Lost Story of the American Revolution* (New Haven, CT, 2023), an exhaustively researched account of the episode. Carp considers New York radicals among the possible culprits behind the conflagration, but he also acknowledged that a compelling circumstantial case could be made for GW's involvement. Also see Daniel Immerwahr, "Did George Washington Burn New York?" *The Atlantic* (March 2023), 74–77.

62. *AR*, 48; Smith, *William Howe and the American War of Independence*, 84; Howe to Germain, September 28, 1776, *DAR* 12:232; Germain to Howe, March 28, 1776, ibid., 12:94; GW to Hancock, September 8, 1776, *PGWR* 6:250.

63. *AR*, 49; Schecter, *The Battle for New York*, 221; Howe to Germain, November 30, 1776, *DAR* 12:258; Commissioners for Restoring Peace in America to Germain, November 30, 1776, ibid., 12:257.

64. *AR*, 49; *PGWR* 6:536n; GW to William Heath, October 11, 1776, ibid., 6:538; Heath to GW, October 11, 13, 1776, ibid., 6:538, 557–58, 558n; Fischer, *Washington's Crossing*, 100; Huw J. Davies, *The Wandering Army: The Campaigns That Transformed the British Way of War, 1750–1850* (New Haven, CT, 2022), 130; Ward, *War of the Revolution*, 1:255–56; Freeman, *George Washington*, 4:215; Schecter, *The Battle for New York*, 221–24.

65. James Smith to Eleanor Smith, October 7, 1776, *LDC* 5:315; William Ellery to Nicholas Cooke, October 11, 1776, ibid., 5:335; Council of War, October 16, 1776, *PGWR* 6:576.

66. GW to Samuel Washington, October 18, 1776, *PGWR* 6:589–90.

67. Fischer, *Washington's Crossing*, 110; Rick Atkinson, *The British Are Coming: The War for America, Lexington to Princeton, 1775–1777* (New York, 2019), 440–42; O'Donnell, *The Indispensables*, 264–69.

68. *AR*, 44–45; Ward, *War of the Revolution*, 1:262–66; Smith, *William Howe and the American War of Independence*, 85–95; *PGWR* 7:53–54n.

69. GW to Hancock, November 6, 11, 1776, *PGWR* 7:97, 142; Council of War, November 6, 1776, ibid., 7:92; Paul David Nelson, *General Horatio Gates: A Biography* (Baton Rouge, LA, 1976), 72.

70. Smith, *William Howe and the American War of Independence*, 98.

71. GW to NG, November 8, 1776, *PGWR* 7:115; NG to GW, November 9, 1776, ibid., 7:120; *PNG*, 1:354–55n.

72. GW to Hancock, November 16, 1776, *PGWR* 7:165; ibid., 7:166–69n; *PNG* 1:358–59n; Ward, *War of the Revolution*, 1:267–74; Fischer, *Washington's Crossing*, 111–14; Atkinson, *The British Are Coming*, 453–60; Baer, *Hessians*, 110–11.

73. GW to Hancock, November 19 [–21], 1776, *PGWR* 7:181–83; Lord Rawdon to Robert Auchmuty, November 25, 1776, *SOS*, 1:496; Fischer, *Washington's Crossing*, 121–22; Gruber, *The Howe Brothers and the American Revolution*, 135.

74. Richard Middleton, *Cornwallis: Soldier and Statesman in a Revolutionary World* (New Haven, CT, 2022), 3–25; Franklin Wickwire and Mary Wickwire, *Cornwallis and the War of Independence* (London, 1971), 7–91.

75. George F. Scheer and Hugh F. Rankin, eds., *Rebels and Redcoats: The American Revolution Through the Eyes of Those Who Fought and Lived It* (New York, 1987), 204; GW to Heath, November 26, 1776, *PGWR* 7:214; Fischer, *Washington's Crossing*, 126–28; Arthur F. Lefkowitz, *The Long Retreat: The Calamitous American Defense of New Jersey, 1776* (Metuchen, NJ, 1998), 23–28, 99–103.

76. GW to Lee, November 21, 27, 1776, *PGWR* 7:194, 225; GW to Hancock, November 23, 27, 30, December 1, 1776, ibid., 7:196, 223, 232–33, 245; GW to Gates, December 14, 1776, ibid., 7:333; Fischer, *Washington's Crossing*, 132.

77. Howe to Germain, November 30, December 20, 1776, *DAR* 12:264–65, 266.

78. Wickwire and Wickwire, *Cornwallis and the War of Independence*, 92.

79. Howe to Germain, November 30, December 20, 1776, *DAR* 12:264–65, 266.

80. GW to Hancock, November 30, 1776, *PGWR* 7:233; Maldwyn Jones, "Sir William Howe: Conventional Strategist," in *George Washington's Opponents*, ed. George A. Billias (New York, 1969), 56; *AR*, 56–57, 56n; Gruber, *The Howe Brothers and the American Revolution*, 143–44.

81. Commissioners for Restoring Peace in America to Germain, November 30, 1776, *DAR* 10:414; ibid., 12:257; Richard Howe to Sir Peter Parker, December 22, 1776, ibid., 12:271; Tatum, *The American Journal of Ambrose Serle*, 151.

82. JA to Abigail Adams, April 28, 1776, *AFC* 1:399–400; JA to Samuel Parsons, August 19, 1776, *ADA* 3:449; Samuel Adams to Warren, November 29, December 25, 1776, *LDC* 5:552, 661; *JCC* 6:1032; Chopra, *Unnatural Rebellion*, 83.

83. Committee of Secret Correspondence to the Commissioners in Paris, December 21, 1776, *LDC* 5:633; Robert Morris to Silas Deane, December 20, 1776, ibid., 5:624.

84. George F. Scheer and Hugh F. Rankin, eds., *Rebels and Redcoats: The American Revolution Through the Eyes of Those Who Fought and Lived It* (New York, 1987), 175.

85. Thomas Paine, *The American Crisis* 1 (1776), *CWTP* 1:50–57. The quotes are on pages 50 and 53.

86. GW to Lee, November 21, 29, 1776, *PGWR* 7:194, 208; Lee to GW, November 30, December 8, 1776, ibid., 7:235, 276; Lee to Heath, November 21, 23, 1776, ibid., 7:206–7n; GW to Hancock, 2, 5, 1776, ibid., 7:251, 262; Alden, *General Charles Lee*, 147–55.

87. GW to John Augustine Washington, November 6 [–19], 1776, *PGWR* 7:105; GW to Lund Washington, December 10 [–17], 1776, ibid., 7:370–71; William Gordon, *The History of the Rise, Progress, and Establishment of the Independence of the United States of America* (London, 1788), 2:354; *The Journal of Nicholas Cresswell, 1774–1777* (reprint, Port Washington, NY, n.d.), 163–64. Peale is quote in William M. Dwyer, *The Day Is Ours! An Inside View of the Battles of Trenton and Princeton* (New York, 1983), 105.

88. GW to William Livingston, November 30, 1776, *PGWR* 7:236; GW to Samuel Washington, December 18, 1776, ibid., 7:371; GW to Hancock, December 5, 1776, ibid., 7:262.

89. Larrie D. Ferreiro, *Brothers at Arms: American Independence and the Men of France and Spain Who Saved It* (New York, 2016), 69.

90. GW to Reed, December 23, 1776, *PGWR*, 7:423. The "extended too much" quotation can be found in Davies, *The Wandering Army*, 132.

91. Fischer, *Washington's Crossing*, 221–28; Mark Puls, *Henry Knox: Visionary General of the American Revolution* (New York, 2008), 74.

92. Baer, *Hessians*, 123.

93. General Orders, December 25, 27, 1776, *PGWR*, 7:434–36, 448–49; GW to John Cadwalader, December 25, 27, 1776, ibid., 7:439, 449–50; GW to Hancock, December 27, 1776, ibid., 7:454–56; ibid., 7:456–61n; Scheer and Rankin, *Rebels and Redcoats*, 212, 213; Elisha Bostwick Memoirs, *SOS*, 1:512; Knox to Lucy Knox, December 28, 1776, ibid., 1:513; Ferreiro, *Brothers at Arms*, 69; Ward, *War of the Revolution*, 1:292–302; Fischer, *Washington's Crossing*, 206–62; Atkinson, *The British Are Coming*, 511–29; Rodney Atwood, *The Hessians: Mercenaries from Hessen-Kassel in the American Revolution* (Cambridge, UK, 1980), 84–96.

94. Scheer and Rankin, *Rebels and Redcoats*, 217; Richard M. Ketchum, *The Winter Soldiers: The Battles for Trenton and Princeton* (Garden City, NY, 1973), 291; *AR*, 60; Middleton, *Cornwallis*, 28–29.

95. GW to Hancock, January 5, 1777, *PGWR* 7:519–23; ibid., 7:524–30; Fischer, *Washington's Crossing*, 323–406, 413–15; Ward, *War of the Revolution*, 310–18; Patrick F. O'Donnell, *Washington's Immortals: The Untold Story of an Elite Regiment Who Changed the Course of the Revolution* (New York, 2016), 128.

96. Tatum, *The American Journal of Ambrose Serle*, 35, 78–79, 162, 163.

97. Paine, *The American Crisis* 2, in *CWTP*, 2:66.

CHAPTER 5: EUROPEAN AID AND PLANNING FOR CAMPAIGN 1777

1. Reed to GW, February 13, 1777, *PGWR* 8:328; NG to GW, March 24, 1777, ibid., 8:628, 628n; William Whipple to John Langdon, January 3, 1777, *LDC* 6:29; James Morgan, "American Privateering in America's War of Independence," *American Neptune* 36 (April 1976): 80–85. For more on privateering, see chapter 9.

2. Larrie D. Ferreiro, *Brothers at Arms: American Independence and the Men of France and Spain Who Saved It* (New York, 2016), 61–63; Thomas F. Chávez, *Spain and the Independence of the United States: An Intrinsic Gift* (Albuquerque, NM, 2002), 49.

3. American Commissioners to the Committee of Secret Correspondence, March 12 [–April 9], 1777, *PBF* 23:467.

4. "Plan of Treaties," *PJA* 4:260–302; James H. Hutson, "Early American Diplomacy: A Reappraisal," in *The American Revolution and "A Candid World,"* ed. Lawrence S. Kaplan (Kent, OH, 1977), 40–68; William C. Stinchcombe, *The American Revolution and the French Alliance* (Syracuse, NY, 1969), 8.

5. Congress's Instructions to the Commissioners, [September 24–October 22, 1776], *PBF* 22:624–30.

6. Stacy Schiff, *A Great Improvisation: Franklin, France, and the Birth of America* (New York, 2005), 52–53; BF to Arthur Lee, April 3, 1778, *PBF* 26:223.

7. Commissioners to Vergennes, December 23, 1776, *PBF* 23:82; BF to the Committee of Secret Correspondence, January 4, 1777, ibid., 23:114; Commissioners to the Committee of Secret Correspondence, March 12 [–April 9], 1777, ibid., 23:467, 472; Lee to BF and Deane, March 16, 1777, ibid., 23:499–50, 430n; Orville T. Murphy, *Charles Gravier, Comte de Vergennes: French Diplomacy in the Age of Revolution, 1719–1787* (Albany, NY, 1982), 243–44; Jonathan R. Dull, *A Diplomatic History of the American Revolution* (New Haven, CT, 1985), 78.

8. Ferreiro, *Brothers at Arms*, 67–68.

9. Commissioners Memorandum to Vergennes, February 1, March 1, 18, 1777, *PBF* 23:260–63, 410–12, 503–5, 260n, 410n, 502n.

10. For these two paragraphs, see Edmund S. Morgan, *Benjamin Franklin* (New Haven, CT, 2002), 243; Schiff, *A Great Improvisation*, 39, 252; Jonathan R. Dull, *Benjamin Franklin and the American Revolution* (Lincoln, NE, 2010), 67; Dull, *A Diplomatic History of the American Revolution*, 76–78; Esmond Wright, *Franklin of Philadelphia* (Cambridge, MA, 1968), 265–66; BF to Lee, April 3, 1778, *PBF* 26:223. On BF's fur hat, see Jeffers Lennox, *North of America: Loyalists, Indigenous Nations, and the Borders of the Long American Revolution* (New Haven, CT, 2022), 19, 93.

11. Solomon Lutnick, *The American Revolution and the British Press, 1775–1783* (Columbia, MO, 1967), 100–102.

12. Germain to Guy Carleton, August 22, 1776, *DAR* 12:187–88; Alan Valentine, *Lord George Germain* (London, 1962), 151n.

13. Carleton to Germain, September 28, 1776, *DAR* 12:234; William Phillips to Burgoyne, October 23, 1776, in Douglas R. Cubbison, ed., *Burgoyne and the Saratoga Campaign: His Papers* (Norman, OK, 2012), 155–56; Burgoyne to Clinton, November 7, 1776, ibid., 158–59; Mark Edward Lender, *Fort Ticonderoga, The Last Campaigns: The War in the North, 1777–1783* (Yardley, PA, 2022), 12–14; Kevin J. Weddle, *The Compleat Victory: Saratoga and the American Revolution* (New York, 2021), 25–50; John Luzader, *Saratoga: A Military History of the Decisive Campaign of the American Revolution* (New York, 2008), xvii–xviii.

14. *PH* 19:353; Alan Valentine, *Lord North* (Norman, OK, 1967), 1:433–35.

15. *The Annual Register, 1777,* in *Rebellion in America: A Contemporary British Viewpoint, 1765–1783,* ed. David H. Murdoch (Santa Barbara, CA, 1979), 434–35; Stephen Conway, *The British Isles and the War of American Independence* (New York, 2000), 129; Edmund Burke to Richard Shackleton, August 11, 1776, in George H. Guttridge, ed., *The Correspondence of Edmund Burke* (Chicago, 1958–1978), 3:286–87.

16. Burke to the Marquess of Rockingham, January 6, 1777, Guttridge, *Correspondence of Edmund Burke,* 3:309–11.

17. Dora Mae Clark, *British Opinion and the American Revolution* (reprint, New York, 1966), 96–98, 123–25, 135, 141.

18. Howe to Germain, November 30, 1776, *DAR* 12:264–66.

19. Ibid., 12:264–65.

20. Howe to Germain, December 20, 1776, ibid., 12:268–69; Huw J. Davies, *The Wandering Army: The Campaigns That Transformed the British Way of War, 1750–1850* (New Haven, CT, 2022), 133–34.

21. Howe to Germain, January 20, 1777, *DAR* 14:33.

22. Germain to Howe, January 14, 1777, ibid., 14:31–32.

23. Howe to Germain, April 2, 1777, ibid., 14:64–65; Howe to Sir Guy Carleton, April 5, 1777, ibid., 14:66.

24. *PH* 18:990.

25. Germain to Carleton, July 25, 1777, *DAR* 14:151; Germain to Howe, January 14, March 3, 1777, ibid., 14:31, 46–47.

26. John Burgoyne, *Thoughts for Conducting the War from the Side of Canada*, February 28, 1777, ibid., 14:41–46; William B. Willcox, *Portrait of a General: Sir Henry Clinton in the War of Independence* (New York, 1962), 135–36.

27. *AR*, 60–61; Willcox, *Portrait of a General*, 139–41.

28. Germain to Howe, May 18, 1777, *DAR* 14:84; Germain to Carleton, March 26, 1777, ibid., 14:53–56.

29. Germain to Howe, March 3, 1777, ibid., 14:47.

30. Germain to Howe, May 18, 1777, ibid., 14:84.

31. GW to Hancock, November 16, 1776, January 5, 1777, *PGWR* 7:162–65, 521.

32. GW to Hancock, January 7, 1777, ibid., 8:9; GW to Jonathan Trumbull Sr., January 10, 1777, ibid., 8:37; GW to Heath, February 3, 1777, ibid., 8:229; GW to John Parke Custis, January 22, 1777, ibid., 8:123.

33. Charles Royster, *A Revolutionary People at War: The Continental Army and American Character, 1775–1783* (Chapel Hill, NC, 1979), 111, 131–32; Morris to Silas Deane, December 20, 1776, *LDC* 5:62; JA to Knox, August 25, 1776, ibid., 5:62–63; Francis Lightfoot Lee to Walter Jones, December 11, 1776, ibid., 5:598; Richard Henry Lee to Patrick Henry, December 18, 1776, ibid., 5:615; William Ellery to Nicholas Cooke, September 21, 1776, ibid., 5:215; *JCC* 5:762–63; Robert K. Wright, *The Continental Army* (Washington, DC, 1983), 92.

34. GW to Hancock, September 25, 1776, *PGWR*, 6:397; JA to William Tudor, September 26, 1776, *LDC* 5:240; *JCC* 5:788–807.

35. GW to Nicholas Cooke, January 20, 1777, *PGWR* 8:114; GW to Lund Washington, December 10 [–17], 1776, ibid., 7:291; GW to Hancock, January 19, April 12 [–13], May 13, June 2, 1777, ibid., 8:102; 9:128, 411, 593; GW to Samuel Washington, April 5, 1777, ibid., 9:72; GW to Trumbull, April 12, 1777, ibid., 9:143; GW to William Livingston, April 1, 1777, ibid., 9:41; GW to Richard Henry Lee, June 1, 1777, ibid., 9:581.

36. Royster, *A Revolutionary People at War*, 132; Douglas Southall Freeman, *George Washington* (New York, 1948–1957), 4:288–89; Wright, *The Continental Army*, 91–107.

37. GW to William Shippen Jr., February 6, 1777, *PGWR* 8:264; GW to Henry, April 13, 1777, ibid., 9:147; Elizabeth A. Fenn, *Pox Americana: The Great Smallpox Epidemic of 1775–1782* (New York, 2001), 3–95; Ann M. Becker, *Smallpox in*

Washington's Army: Disease, War, and Society During the Revolutionary War (Lanham, MD, 2023), 173–90.

38. Reed to GW, February 13, 1777, *PGWR* 8:328; The Massachusetts Council to GW, March 20, 1777, ibid., 8:604; NG to GW, March 24, 1777, ibid., 8:628; Hancock to GW, March 26, 1777, ibid., 8:637; GW to George Weedon, March 27, 1777, ibid., 8:643.

39. GW to Hancock, February 20, April 10, 1777, ibid., 8:381, 9:113; Don Higginbotham, *The War of American Independence: Military Attitudes, Policies, and Practices, 1763–1789* (New York, 1971), 214–15; Wright, *The Continental Army*, 129–30.

40. Mike Duncan, *Hero of Two Worlds: The Marquis de Lafayette in the Age of Revolution* (New York, 2021), 3–55. The characterization of Lafayette can be found in R. R. Palmer, *The Age of the Democratic Revolution: A Political History of Europe and America, 1760–1800* (Princeton, NJ, 1959), 246.

41. GW to Morris, January 19, February 22, March 2, 1777, *PGWR* 8:107, 416, 487; GW to Gates, February 20, 1777, ibid., 8:377; GW to John Augustine Washington, February 24, 1777, ibid., 8:439; GW to the Continental Congress Executive Committee, February 27, 1777, ibid., 8:452–53; GW to Trumbull, March 6, 1777, ibid., 8:531; GW to James Warren, March 15, 1777, ibid., 8:583; GW to Edward Pendleton, April 12, 1777, ibid., 9:140; GW to Henry, May 31, 1777, ibid., 9:572–73.

42. GW to Samuel Holden Parsons, April 3, 1777, ibid., 9:55; Germain to Howe, March 3, 1777, *DAR* 14:47; David Smith, *William Howe and the American War of Independence* (London, 2015), 121; Ira D. Gruber, *The Howe Brothers and the American Revolution* (New York, 1972), 226–27.

43. Council of War, June 12, 1777, *PGWR* 10:9–10; GW to Hancock, June 13 [–15], 20, 22, 25, 28, 1777, ibid., 10:26, 84, 104–5, 123–25, 137; GW to John Augustine Washington, June 29, 1777, ibid., 10:149–50; Christopher Ward, *The War of the Revolution* (New York, 1952), 1:325–28.

44. GW to John Augustine Washington, June 29, 1777, *PGWR* 10:150.

CHAPTER 6: THE CRITICAL MOMENT IS AT HAND: THE 1777 CAMPAIGN

1. Richard J. Hargrove, *General John Burgoyne* (Newark, DE, 1983), 17–68, 103.

2. Ibid., 120–25; Burgoyne to Germain, May 15, 1777, *DAR* 14:78–79; Howe to Carleton, April 5, 1777, ibid., 14:66.

3. Hargrove, *General John Burgoyne*, 121, 125; Richard M. Ketchum, *Saratoga: Turning Point of America's Revolutionary War* (New York, 1997), 107–9.

4. Ketchum, *Saratoga*, 128–37; Don N. Hagist, *These Distinguished Corps: British Grenadier and Light Infantry Battalions in the American Revolution* (Warwick, UK, 2021), 97.

5. Letter of Thomas Anburey, *SOS* 1:545–48, 553; John Burgoyne, Proclamation, ibid., 1:547–48.

6. Mark Edward Lender, *Fort Ticonderoga, the Last Campaigns: The War in the North, 1777–1783* (Yardley, PA, 2022), 15–16, 28; Kevin J. Weddle, *The Compleat Victory: Saratoga and the American Revolution* (New York, 2021), 40–41, 102–7.

7. Lender, *Fort Ticonderoga*, 22, 23, 26, 28, 31, 34, 35.

8. Ibid., x, 52, 59–64; Burgoyne to Carleton, July 7, 1777, Douglas R. Cubbison, ed., *Burgoyne and the Saratoga Campaign: His Papers* (Norman, OK, 2012), 269; GW to Schuyler, February 19, 23, 1777, *PGWR* 8:373, 434; John Luzader, *Saratoga: A Military History of the Decisive Campaign of the American Revolution* (New York, 2008), xvii–xviii, 47–50; Weddle, *The Compleat Victory*, 108.

9. Schuyler to GW, June 14, 16, 25, 28, 30, 1777, *PGWR* 10:39, 55, 127, 141, 160.

10. Schuyler to GW, June 28, 1777, ibid., 10:140–41; Arthur St. Clair to Schuyler, June 25, 1777, ibid., 10:141–42n; Lender, *Fort Ticonderoga*, 63–66; Luzader, *Saratoga*, 50–51.

11. For these two paragraphs, see GW to Schuyler, July 2, 1777, *PGWR* 10:171; Schuyler to GW, July 7, 9, 10, 14, 1777, ibid., 10:219–20, 234, 244, 279–81; Journal of Lieutenant William Digby, *SOS*, 1:554; Lender, *Fort Ticonderoga*, 87–102, 128; Hargrove, *General John Burgoyne*, 139; Weddle, *The Compleat Victory*, 114–27.

12. Hagist, *These Distinguished Corps*, 100.

13. James Thacher, *Military Journal of the American Revolution* (reprint, New York, 1969), 84; Weddle, *The Compleat Victory*, 128–37; Burgoyne to Germain, July 11, 1777, *DAR* 14:133–40; Ketchum, *Saratoga*, 226–28.

14. Hargrove, *General John Burgoyne*, 141; Don N. Hagist, ed., *Roger Lamb's American Revolution: A British Soldier's Story* (Westholme, PA, 2022), 46.

15. Burgoyne to Germain, July 11, 1777, *DAR* 14:139, 141; Ketchum, *Saratoga*, 239–40; Weddle, *The Compleat Victory*, 139–43, 151.

16. Don R. Gerlach, *Proud Patriot: Philip Schuyler and the War of Independence, 1775–1783* (Syracuse, NY, 1987), 258.

17. Hargrove, *General John Burgoyne*, 147–49; Ketchum, *Saratoga*, 239.

18. GW to Schuyler, July 2, 1777, *PGWR* 10:170–71; GW to Hancock, July 10, 1777, ibid., 10:240; Larrie D. Ferreiro, *Brothers at Arms: American Independence and the Men of France and Spain Who Saved It* (New York, 2016), 71.

19. Schuyler to GW, July 9, 10, 1777, *PGWR* 10:234, 244; GW to Putnam, July 22, 1777, ibid., 10:362; Gerlach, *Proud Patriot*, 257–66.

20. Weddle, *The Compleat Victory*, 141.

21. For these two paragraphs, see Burgoyne to Germain, July 11, 30, 1777, *DAR* 14:142, 153; Hagist, *Roger Lamb's American Revolution*, 42, 51; Hagist, *These Distinguished Corps*, 103; Luzader, *Saratoga*, 77–84; Weddle, *The Compleat Victory*, 141–42.

22. Burgoyne to Germain, July 11, 30, 1777, *DAR* 14:140, 154; Arnold to GW, July 27, 1777, *PGWR* 10:434; Journal of Digby, *SOS* 1:559; Gates to Burgoyne, September 2, 1777, ibid., 1:560; Ketchum, *Saratoga*, 274–78; Paul David Nelson, *General Horatio Gates: A Biography* (Baton Rouge, LA, 1976), 111; Blake Grindon, "Hilliard d'Auberteuil's *Mis Mac Rea*: A Story of the American Revolution in the French Atlantic," *William and Mary Quarterly* 79 (October 2022): 563–94.

23. Arnold to GW, July 27, 1777, *PGWR* 10:434.

24. Burgoyne to Germain, August 20, 1777, *DAR* 14:166; Weddle, *The Compleat Victory*, 179–218.

25. Burgoyne to Germain, August 20, 1777, *DAR* 14:166–67.

26. Ibid.

27. Burgoyne to Howe, August 6, 1777, *DAR* 14:156–57; Burgoyne to Germain, August 20, 1777, ibid., 14:163; Baron de Riedesel to Germain, August 28, 1777, Cubbison, *Burgoyne and the Saratoga Campaign*, 302; Account by [?] Glich, August 16, 1777, *SOS* 1:571; Weddle, *The Compleat Victory*, 231.

28. Weddle, *The Compleat Victory*, 236–50; Ketchum, *Saratoga*, 285–328; Luzader, *Saratoga*, 93–113; Burgoyne to Germain, August 20, 1777, *DAR* 14:165–66; Ferreiro, *Brothers at Arms*, 72.

29. George A. Billias, "Horatio Gates: Professional Soldier," in *George Washington's Generals*, ed. George A. Billias (New York, 1964), 79–84; Nelson, *General Horatio Gates*, 1–39; John Ferling, *Winning Independence: The Decisive Years of the Revolutionary War, 1778–1781* (New York, 2021), 87.

30. GW to Jonathan Trumbull Sr., July 31, 1777, *PGWR* 10:472; GW to Putnam, August 16, 1777, ibid., 10:642; Max M. Mintz, *The Generals of Saratoga: John Burgoyne and Horatio Gates* (New Haven, CT, 1990), 180, 182, 189; Dean Snow, *1777: Tipping Point at Saratoga* (New York, 2016), 35.

31. Weddle, *The Compleat Victory*, 272–73; Mintz, *The Generals of Saratoga*, 189–90.

32. Hagist, *These Distinguished Corps*, 107; Hagist, *Roger Lamb's American Revolution*, 56–57.

33. For this paragraph, see Burgoyne to Germain, October 20, 1777, *DAR* 14:230; Hagist, *Roger Lamb's American Revolution*, 57; Hagist, *These Distinguished Corps*, 107; Recollection of Captain E. Wakefield, *SOS* 1:581; Colonel Henry Brockholst Livingston to Schuyler, September 23, 1777, ibid., 1:583; Christopher Ward, *The War of the Revolution* (New York, 1952), 2:504–12; Mintz, *The Generals of Saratoga*, 187–99; Weddle, *The Compleat Victory*, 272–93; Snow, *1777*, 81–137; Luzader, *Saratoga*, 228–46; Ketchum, *Saratoga*, 359–72; Hargrove, *General John Burgoyne*, 176–86; Nelson, *General Horatio Gates*, 115–21; Ferreiro, *Brothers at Arms*, 73.

34. Howe to Germain, July 7, 1777, *DAR* 14:130; *AR*, 70; Ward, *War of the Revolution*, 2:513; Hargrove, *General John Burgoyne*, 185.

35. Marquis de Chastellux, *Travels in North America in the Years 1780, 1781, and 1782*, ed. Howard C. Rice (Chapel Hill, NC, 1963), 1:96; Clinton to Burgoyne, October 6, 1777, *AR*, 379–80.

36. Burgoyne to Germain, October 20, 1777, *DAR* 14:231–33; Hagist, *Roger Lamb's American Revolution*, 61; Memoirs of Colonel James Wilkinson, *SOS* 1:592; Journal of Digby, ibid., 1:597; Journal of Captain Georg Pausch, ibid., 1: 595, 597; Weddle, *The Compleat Victory*, 307–28; Snow, *1777*, 234–80; Hargrove, *General John Burgoyne*, 191–94; Luzader, *Saratoga*, 275–96; Ketchum, *Saratoga*, 386–407; Ward, *War of the Revolution*, 2:521–31.

37. Hagist, *Roger Lamb's American Revolution*, 64; Minutes of a Council of War, October 12, 13, 14, 15, 1777, Cubberson, *Burgoyne and the Saratoga Campaign*, 342–45.

38. Thacher, *Military Journal of the American Revolution*, 105–7; Journal of Digby, *SOS* 1:605; Weddle, *The Compleat Victory*, 329–50.

39. Burgoyne to Germain, October 20, 1777, *DAR* 14:228–29; *PH* 19:1178–95; Hargrove, *General John Burgoyne*, 221–25.

40. Journal of Digby, *SOS* 1:605.

41. GW to Hancock, July 2, 7, 12, 16, 22, 1777, *PGWR* 10:168, 216, 252, 294, 356; GW to Trumbull Sr., July 2 [–4], 1777, ibid., 10:174; GW to James Bowdoin, Cooke, and the New Hampshire Convention, July 7, 1777, ibid., 10:214; GW to John Augustine Washington, June 29, 1777, ibid., 10:150; Putnam to GW, July 24, 1777, ibid., 10:393–94; editor's note, ibid., 10:394n.

42. William B. Willcox, *Portrait of a General: Sir Henry Clinton in the War of Independence* (New York, 1962), 137, 153–57; *AR*, 61–65.

43. Gene Procknow, "Henry Clinton's Plan to End the War," *Journal of the American Revolution*, March 5, 2024.

44. Ambrose Serle, May 20, 1777, *SOS* 1:609; Bruce E. Burgoyne, ed., *Enemy Views: The American Revolutionary War as Recorded by the Hessian Participants* (Bowie, MD, 1996), 164–65; Baron Karl Leopold Baurmeister, *Revolution in America: Confidential Letters and Journals, 1776–1784* (Westport, CT, 1973), 93–98; Stephen R. Taaffe, *The Philadelphia Campaign, 1777–1778* (Lawrence, KS, 2003), 53; "Before and After the Battle of Brandywine. Extracts from the Journal of Sergeant Thomas Sullivan of H. M. Forty-Ninth Regiment of Foot," *Pennsylvania Magazine of History and Biography* 31 (1907): 408. For an extended account of Howe's voyage, see Michael C. Harris, *Brandywine: A Military History of the Battle That Lost Philadelphia but Saved America, September 11, 1777* (El Dorado Hills, CA, 2014), 70–116.

45. GW to Hancock, July 25, 1777, *PGWR* 10:410; GW to William Sever, August 10, 1777, ibid., 10:578; Council of War, August 21, 1777, ibid., 11:19–20; GW to Sullivan, August 22, 1777, ibid., 10:48; Douglas Southall Freeman, *George Washington* (New York, 1948–1957), 4:443–59.

46. William Williams to Trumbull Sr., August 2, 1777, *LDC* 7:407; James Duane to John Jay, August 3, 1777, ibid., 7:409; Samuel Adams to Samuel Freeman, August 5, 1777, ibid., 7:413; JA to Abigail Adams, August 23, 24, September 8, 1777, ibid., 7:534, 538–39, 627; Duane to George Clinton, August 25, 1777, ibid., 7:548; Lee to Jefferson, August 25, 1777, ibid., 7:551.

47. For these two paragraphs, see JA to Abigail Adams, September 1, 2, 1777, ibid., 7:579, 589; Harris, *Brandywine*, 213; NG to Jacob Greene, August 31, 1777, *PNG* 2:149; Enoch Anderson, *Personal Recollections of Enoch Anderson* (New York, 1971), 38.

48. GW, General Orders, September 5, 1777, *PGWR* 11:147–48.

49. Harris, *Brandywine*, 133–55.

50. Gregory T. Knouff, *The Soldiers' Revolution: Pennsylvanians in Arms and the Forging of Early American Identity* (University Park, PA, 2004), 59.

51. Taaffe, *The Philadelphia Campaign*, 62–66; Harris, *Brandywine*, 239–42, 246–55; Holly A. Mayer, *Congress's Own: A Canadian Regiment, the Continental Army, and American Union* (Norman, OK, 2021), 143.

52. George F. Scheer and Hugh F. Rankin, eds., *Rebels and Redcoats* (New York, 1957), 414.

53. Taaffe, *The Philadelphia Campaign,* 67; Freeman, *George Washington*, 4:488.

54. Mark E. Lender and James K. Martin, eds., *Citizen Soldier: The Revolutionary War Journal of Joseph Bloomfield* (Newark, NJ, 1982), 127.

55. Mayer, *Congress's Own*, 144–45.

56. Taaffe, *The Philadelphia Campaign*, 73–74; Marquis de Lafayette, Memoir of 1779, *LSLP* 1:95.

57. William Darlington to Thomas Wharton Jr., November 29, 1845, *SOS* 1:616.

58. Marquis de Lafayette, Memoir of 1779, *LSLP* 1:95.

59. These paragraphs draw on Hagist, *These Distinguished Corps*, 118; Journal of Timothy Pickering, *SOS* 1:614; Howe to Germain, October 10, 1777, *DAR* 14:204; GW to Hancock, September 11, 1777, *PGWR* 11:200; Harris, *Brandywine*, 275–369; Taaffe, *The Philadelphia Campaign*, 75–76.

60. Taaffe, *The Philadelphia Campaign*, 79–84; GW to Anthony Wayne, September 18, 1777, *PGWR* 11:265, 266n; Paul David Nelson, *Anthony Wayne: Soldier of the Early Republic* (Bloomington, IN, 1985), 52–57; Michael C. Harris, *Germantown: A Military History of the Battle for Philadelphia, October 4, 1777* (El Dorado Hills, CA, 2020), 29–108. The "best storm" quotation can be found in Harris, page 52.

61. For these two paragraphs, see JA, Diary, *LDC* 7:664; Cornelius Harnett to William Wilkinson, September 13, 1777, ibid., 7:655; William Williams to Trumbull Sr., September 13, 1777, ibid., 7:657–58; GW to Hancock, September 19, 23, 1777, *PGWR* 11:268–69, 301; Knox to Lucy Flucker Knox, September 24, 1777, in Phillip Hamilton, ed., *The Revolutionary War Lives and Letters of Lucy and Henry Knox* (Baltimore, 2017), 125–26; Anderson, *Personal Recollections of Enoch Anderson*, 39–40; Harris, *Germantown*, 37–62; Taaffe, *The Philadelphia Campaign*, 90; Ira D. Gruber, *The Howe Brothers and the American Revolution* (New York, 1972), 241.

62. JA to Abigail Adams, August 19, 1777, *LDC* 7:504; James Lovell to Robert Treat Paine, September 24, 1777, ibid., 8:14; Hancock to Dorothy Hancock, October 1, 1777, ibid., 8:38; Harris, *Germantown*, 115; *JCC* 8:754.

63. Harris, *Germantown*, 222–27.

64. Council of War, September 28, 1777, *PGWR* 11:338–39; GW to Hancock, September 29, 1777, ibid., 11:346.

65. GW, General Orders, October 1, 1777, ibid., 11:356; GW, General Orders for Attacking Germantown, October 3, 1777, ibid., 11:375–76, 376–80n; Harris, *Germantown*, 247.

66. GW, General Orders, October 3, 1777, *PGWR* 11:373.

67. Harris, *Germantown*, 268–371, 392–98; Taaffe, *The Philadelphia Campaign*, 96–107; Joseph Plumb Martin, *Private Yankee Doodle: Being a Narrative of Some of the Adventures, Dangers and Sufferings of a Revolutionary Soldier*, ed. George F. Scheer (New York, 1962), 73–74.

68. GW to Hancock, October 5, 1777, *PGWR* 11:394; Benjamin Tallmadge, *Memoir of Colonel Benjamin Tallmadge* (New York, 1968), 23; John Armstrong to Gates, October 9, 1777, *SOS* 1:628; Johann Ewald, *Diary of the American War: A Hessian Journal*, ed. Joseph P. Tustin (New Haven, CT, 1979), 11:393–95; Harris, *Germantown*, 433.

69. JA to Abigail Adams, August 29, 1777, *LDC* 7:567. Galloway's comments can be found in Ruma Chopra, *Unnatural Rebellion: Loyalists in New York City During the Revolution* (Charlottesville, VA, 2011), 89; and T. H. Breen, "Commanders and Courtiers," *New York Review of Books*, February 23, 2023, 38.

70. Maldwyn A. Jones, "Sir William Howe: Conventional Strategist," in Billias, *George Washington's Generals*, 61.

CHAPTER 7: BUILDING CASTLES IN THE AIR

1. Allen French, *The First Year of the American Revolution* (reprint, New York, 1968), 323–24.

2. Charles Ritcheson, *British Politics and the American Revolution* (Norman, OK, 1954), 241–44; *PH* 19:549–60.

3. Solomon Lutnick, *The American Revolution and the British Press, 1775–1783* (Columbia, MO, 1967), 108–9; *PH* 19:471, 488, 524–25, 538, 540, 611, 1200; Alan Valentine, *Lord North* (Norman, OK, 1967), 1:473, 476; Alan Valentine, *Lord George Germain* (Oxford, UK, 1962), 261; Peter Whiteley, *Lord North: The Prime Minister Who Lost America* (London, 1996), 172.

4. Lutnick, *The American Revolution and the British Press*, 108; Stephen Conway, *The British Isles and the War of American Independence* (Oxford, UK, 2000), 272–73; *PH* 19:771.

5. Julie Flavell, *The Howe Dynasty: The Untold Story of a Military Family and the Women Behind Britain's Wars for America* (New York, 2021), 279; Ira D. Gruber, *The Howe Brothers and the American Revolution* (New York, 1972), 275; Howe to Germain, October 22, 1777, *DAR* 14:242–43.

6. H. M. Scott, *British Foreign Policy in the Age of the American Revolution* (Oxford, UK, 1990), 207–51, 257.

7. *PH* 19:742, 772.

8. Sir Philip Gibbes: Minutes of a Conversation with Franklin, January 5, 1778, *PBF* 25:419–23; Paul Wentworth to William Eden, January 7, 1778, ibid., 25:436–40; editor's notes, ibid., 25:420n, 435n; Ritcheson, *British Politics and the American Revolution*, 126, 234–39.

9. David Hartley to BF, December 25, 1777, February 3, 13, 18, 20, 1778, *PBF* 25:349–52, 578, 662–64, 690–92, 699–700; BF to Hartley, February 5, 1778, ibid., 25:581–82.

10. Valentine, *Lord North*, 1:498–506.

11. *PH* 19:762–67.

12. Ibid., 19:768, 772, 777, 778–79.

13. Julia Osman, "American Nationality: A French Invention," in *European Friends of the American Revolution*, ed. Andrew J. O'Shaughnessy, John A. Ragosta, and

Marie-Jeanne Rossignol (Charlottesville, VA, 2023), 17–41; Orville T. Murphy, "The French Professional Soldier's Opinion of the American Militia in the War of the Revolution," *Military Analysis of the Revolutionary War: An Anthology by the Editors of "Military Affairs"* (Millwood, NY, 1977), 226–33; *PBF* 23:480n; 24:508–14; 26:52; *ADA* 2:354–55n; *PJA* 6:192n; 7:xix, 148, 158, 175, 337, 339; JA to Rush, December 6, 1778, ibid., 7:253. For a collation of the contents of *Affaires de l'Angleterre et de l'Amérique*, see *Pennsylvania Magazine of History and Biography* 13 (1889): 222–26. The two quotations can be found in Osman, pages 19 and 22.

14. Jonathan R. Dull, *The French Navy and American Independence: A Study of Arms and Diplomacy, 1774–1787* (Princeton, NJ, 1975), 66–67.

15. Jonathan R. Dull, "France and the American Revolution Seen as Tragedy," in *Diplomacy and Revolution: The Franco-American Alliance of 1778*, ed. Ronald Hoffman and Peter J. Albert (Charlottesville, VA, 1981), 87–88; Dull, *The French Navy and American Independence*, 82–86; Jonathan R. Dull, *A Diplomatic History of the American Revolution* (New Haven, CT, 1985), 82–86.

16. Dull, "France and the American Revolution Seen as Tragedy," *Diplomacy and Revolution*, 87–88.

17. These two paragraphs draw on Orville T. Murphy, *Charles Gravier, Comte de Vergennes: French Diplomacy in the Age of Revolution, 1719–1787* (Albany, NY, 1982), 244–47; Larrie D. Ferreiro, *Brothers at Arms: American Independence and the Men of France and Spain Who Saved It* (New York, 2016), 94–95; Dull, *The French Navy and American Independence*, 89–92; Dull, *A Diplomatic History of the American Revolution*, 91–96; Thomas F. Chávez, *Spain and the Independence of the United States: An Intrinsic Gift* (Albuquerque, NM, 2002), 63–64, 70–82; Larrie D. Ferreiro, "The Rise and Fall of the Spanish-French Bourbon Armada, from Toulon to Pensacola to Trafalgar," in *Spain and the American Revolution: New Approaches and Perspectives*, ed. Gabriel Paquette and Gonzalo M. Quintero Saravia (Charlottesville, VA, 2020), 67.

18. Jonathan Williams Sr. to BF, October 25, 1777, *PBF* 25:113; Massachusetts Council to the American Commissioners, October 24, 1777, ibid., 25:97–98; Massachusetts Board of War to BF, October 24, 1777, ibid., 25:99; Committee for Foreign Affairs to the American Commissioners, October 6 [–9], 31, 1777, ibid., 25:37, 134–35; BF to Massachusetts Board of War, February 17, 1778, ibid., 25:684; Stacy Schiff, *A Great Improvisation: Franklin, France, and the Birth of America* (New York, 2005), 111–12.

19. Conrad-Alexandre Gérard to the American Commissioners, December 5, 1777, *PBF* 25:246; editor's note, ibid., 15:246; American Commissioners to Vergennes, December 8, 1777, ibid., 25:260–61; Orville T. Murphy, "The Battle of Germantown and the Franco-American Alliance of 1778," *Pennsylvania Magazine of History and Biography* 82 (1958), 55–64; JA to James Lovell, July 26, 1778, *PJA* 6:318–19.

20. Munro Price, *Preserving the Monarchy: The Comte de Vergennes, 1774–1787* (Cambridge, UK, 1995), 49–50.

21. Dull, *A Diplomatic History of the American Revolution*, 91; Dull, *The French Navy and American Independence*, 84, 89–90.

22. Ferreiro, *Brothers at Arms*, 96–97; Murphy, *Charles Gravier, Comte de Vergennes*, 252.

23. Dull, *A Diplomatic History of the American Revolution*, 89–91; Dull, *The French Navy and American Independence*, 90, 97–98.

24. Gérard's Report of the Interview, January 9, 1778, *PBF* 25:441–50; American Commissioner's Answers to Questions, January 8, 1778, ibid., 25:450–52; BF and Deane to the President of Congress, February 8, 1778, ibid., 25:634–35; BF to Samuel Cooper, February 27, 1778, ibid., 25:72; Dull, *A Diplomatic History of the American Revolution*, 89–95; Ferreiro, *Brothers at Arms*, 99; Schiff, *A Great Improvisation*, 132. The two treaties are printed in *PBF* 25:585–626.

25. Valentine, *Lord North*, 1:481, 498; *PH* 19:871, 1030–31.

26. George III to North, June 11, 1779, W. Bodham Donne, ed., *The Correspondence of King George the Third with Lord North, 1768 to 1783* (reprint, New York, 1971), 2:253–54.

27. Dull, *A Diplomatic History of the American Revolution*, 13–25; Joseph Solis-Mullern, "From the First Partition of Poland to Yorktown," *Journal of the American Revolution*, March 1, 2022; Brendan Simms, *Three Victories and a Defeat: The Rise and Fall of the First British Empire, 1714–1783* (New York, 2007), 567.

28. These paragraphs draw on Scott, *British Foreign Policy in the Age of the American Revolution*, 55–56, 97–98, 111, 131, 136, 157, 192–206; Dull, *A Diplomatic History of the American Revolution*, 26–32; Ian R. Christie, *Wars and Revolutions: Britain, 1760–1815* (Cambridge, MA, 1982), 47–51; M. S. Anderson, "European Diplomatic Relations, 1763–1790," in *The New Cambridge Modern History: The American and French Revolutions, 1763–1793*, ed. A. Goodwin (Cambridge, UK, 1965), 254–55;

Michael Roberts, *Splendid Isolation, 1763–1780* (Reading, UK, 1970), 39; Simms, *Three Victories and a Defeat*, 528–29. The comment that Russia was "an army rather than a state" can be found in Scott, page 55; Chatham's "great cloud of power" comment is also in Scott, page 97.

29. For this paragraph, see George III to North, January 31, 1778, Donne, *The Correspondence of King George III with Lord North 1763 to 1783*, 2:125–26; Piers Mackesy, *The War for America, 1775–1783* (Cambridge, MA, 1965), 147–61, 180–86; N. A. M. Rodger, *The Insatiable Earl: A Life of John Montagu, Fourth Earl of Sandwich, 1718–1792* (New York, 1993), 137, 146, 154, 266–74; P. J. Marshall, *The Making and Unmaking of Empires: Britain, India, and America c. 1750–1783* (New York, 2005), 363; Gerald Saxon Brown, *The American Secretary: The Colonial Policy of Lord George Germain, 1775–1778* (Ann Arbor, MI, 1963), 139–73; Valentine, *Lord George Germain*, 327–42; Andrew Jackson O'Shaughnessy, *The Men Who Lost America: British Leadership, the American Revolution and the Fate of the Empire* (New Haven, CT, 2013), 294, 334, 343; Rachel N. Klein, "Frontier Planters and the American Revolution: The South Carolina Backcountry, 1775–1782," in *An Uncivil War: The South Carolina Backcountry During the American Revolution*, ed. Ronald Hoffman, Thad W. Tate, and Peter J. Albert (Charlottesville, VA, 1985), 38, 40.

30. Germain to Clinton, March 8, August 5, 1778, *DAR* 15:60–62, 178; John Shy, *A People Numerous and Armed: Reflections on the Military Struggle for American Independence* (New York, 1976), 209; Christopher Hobhouse, *Fox* (London, 1964), 111.

31. Paul David Nelson, *General Horatio Gates: A Biography* (Baton Rouge, LA, 1976), 153; Kevin J. Weddle, *The Compleat Victory: Saratoga and the American Revolution* (New York, 2021), 343.

32. GW to Henry Laurens, December 22, 23, 1777, *PGWR* 12:669–70, 685; ibid., 12:470n; Elbridge Gerry to JA, December 3, 1777, *LDC* 8:373.

33. *ADA* 2:265; Lovell to Samuel Adams, December 20, 1777, *LDC* 8:451; Lovell to Gates, November 5, 27, 1777, ibid., 8:237, 329; Thomas Mifflin to Gates, November 17, 1777, ibid., 8:314–15n; Harry M. Ward, *Major General Adam Stephen and the Cause of American Liberty* (Charlottesville, VA, 1989), 129, 192; Benjamin Rush to JA, February 12, April 22, 1812, in John A. Schutz and Douglass Adair, eds., *The Spur of Fame: Dialogues of John Adams and Benjamin Rush, 1805–1813* (San Marino, CA, 1966), 207, 213; Jonathan G. Rossie, *The Politics of Command in the American Revolution* (Syracuse, NY, 1975), 183.

34. GW to Thomas Conway, November 5, 1777, *PGWR* 12:129; Lund Washington to GW, February 18, 1778, ibid., 13:587.

35. GW to Henry Laurens, January 2, 1778, ibid., 13:119; Henry Laurens to John Laurens, October 16, 1777, January 8, 1778, *LDC* 8:125, 546–47. There were detractors within the officer corps of which GW was unaware. See John Ferling, *The Ascent of George Washington: The Hidden Political Genius of an American Icon* (New York, 2009), 148–49.

36. Mark Edward Lender, *Cabal: The Plot Against General Washington* (Yardley, PA, 2019), 108–236; Thomas Paine, *The American Crisis* 5 (1778), *CWTP* 1:114.

37. JA to Rush, March 19, 1812, in Schutz and Adair, *The Spur of Fame*, 212; JA to Lovell, July 26, 1778, *PJA* 6:318–19; Rush to William Gordon, December 10, 1778, in *Letters of Benjamin Rush*, ed. Lyman H. Butterfield (Princeton, NJ, 1951), 1:221; Henry Laurens to John Laurens, January 8, 1778, *LDC* 8:546–47; Laurens to Isaac Motte, January 26, 1778, ibid., 8:654–55; Laurens to William Smith, September 12, 1778, *PHL* 14:302.

38. Thomas Fleming, *Washington's Secret War: The Hidden History of Valley Forge* (New York, 2005), 191–92; Paul K. Longmore, *The Invention of George Washington* (Berkeley, CA, 1988), 204–8; Don Higginbotham, *The War of American Independence: Military Attitudes, Policies, and Practice, 1763–1789* (New York, 1971), 264.

39. Paine to BF, May 16, 1778, *PBF* 26:487; GW to Laurens, December 23, 1777, *PGWR* 12:683–87; Rush to GW, December 26, 1777, ibid., 13:7; Bob Drury and Tom Clavin, *Valley Forge* (New York, 2018), 107, 123; Joseph Plumb Martin, *Private Yankee Doodle: Being a Narrative of Some of the Adventures, Dangers and Sufferings of a Revolutionary Soldier*, ed. George F. Scheer (Boston, 1962), 102.

40. *PGWR* 14:235n; Alan Taylor, *American Revolutions: A Continental History, 1750–1804* (New York, 2016), 185.

41. On GW's foraging campaign, see Ricardo A. Herrera, *Feeding Washington's Army: Surviving the Valley Forge Winter of 1778* (Chapel Hill, NC, 2022).

42. Wayne Bodle, *The Valley Forge Winter: Civilians and Soldiers in War* (University Park, PA, 2002), 121–88; Drury and Clavin, *Valley Forge*, 212–24, 241–42. On the army's supply problems, see James A. Huston, *Logistics of Liberty: American Services of Supply in the Revolutionary War and After* (Newark, DE, 1991); and E. Wayne

Carp, *To Starve the Army at Pleasure: Continental Army Administration and American Political Culture, 1775–1783* (Chapel Hill, NC, 1984).

43. GW to Cadwalader, March 20, 1778, *PGWR* 14:234, 235n; Charles H. Lesser, ed., *The Sinews of Independence: Monthly Strength Reports of the Continental Army* (Chicago, 1976), 58–59.

44. GW, General Orders, March 13, 18, April 10, 1778, *PGWR* 14:166, 215, 447; GW to Robert Livingston, January 20, 1778, ibid., 13:296; GW to Cadwalader, March 20, 1778, ibid., 14:234.

45. John Ferling, "Joseph Galloway's Military Advice: A Loyalist's View of the Revolution," *Pennsylvania Magazine of History and Biography* 68 (1974): 174–76; Martin, *Private Yankee Doodle*, 102–3.

46. Philip Mead, "'Adventures, Dangers, and Sufferings': The Betrayals of Private Joseph Plumb Martin, Continental Soldier," in *Revolutionary Founders: Rebels, Radicals, and Reformers in the Making of the Nation*, ed. Alfred F. Young, Gary B. Nash, and Ray Raphael (New York, 2011), 117–34; NG to Nicholas Cooke, [before January 13, 1778], *PNG* 2:255; Gouverneur Morris to George Clinton, February 17, 1778, *LDC* 9:117.

47. Paul Lockhart, *The Drillmaster of Valley Forge: The Baron de Steuben and the Making of the American Army* (New York, 2010), 6, 18, 23, 30–46, 87–90, 95–116.

48. For these paragraphs, see GW to Glover and Ebenezer Learned, January 8, 1778, *PGWR* 13:172; Thomas Conway to GW, December 29, 31, 1777, ibid., 13:40–41, 77–78; GW to Livingston, December 27, 1777, ibid., 13:19; GW to Laurens, March 24, April 30, 1778, ibid., 14:292–93, 682; Fleming, *Washington's Secret War*, 207, 210; James Thomas Flexner, *George Washington in the American Revolution* (Boston, 1967), 288–89; Seanegan P. Sculley, *Contest for Liberty: Military Leadership in the Continental Army, 1775–1783* (Yardley, PA, 2019), 119–21; Robert K. Wright, *The Continental Army* (Washington, DC, 1983), 141; Charles Royster, *A Revolutionary People at War: The Continental Army and American Character, 1775–1783* (Chapel Hill, NC, 1979), 231–32, 245–46; Drury and Clavin, *Valley Forge*, 279.

49. GW to John Banister, April 21, 1778, *PGWR* 14:575; ibid., 14:579n; GW to Laurens, April 18, 23, 1778, ibid., 14:547, 600.

50. GW to Laurens, May 1, 1778, ibid., 15:5.

51. GW to John Augustine Washington, May [?], 1778, ibid., 15:286.

52. Gruber, *The Howe Brothers and the American Revolution*, 299; O'Shaughnessy, *The Men Who Lost America*, 207–11; GW, General Orders, May 5, 7, 1778, *PGWR* 15:38–40, 68–70; Royster, *A Revolutionary People at War*, 250–54; John Laurens to Henry Laurens, May 7, 1778, in *The Army Correspondence of Colonel John Laurens in the Years 1777–1778*, ed. William Gilmore Simms (reprint, New York, 1969), 169–70.

CHAPTER 8: STALEMATE

1. GW to Richard Henry Lee, May 25, 1778, *PGWR* 15:216–17; GW to Cooke, May 26, 1778, ibid., 15:223; GW to John Augustine Washington, May [?], 1778, ibid., 15:285–86; GW to Robert Morris, May 25, 1778, ibid., 15:221. Hereafter, Robert Morris is cited as R. Morris and Gouverneur Morris as G. Morris.

2. Thomas McKean to Sarah McKean, May 11, 1778, *LDC* 9:650; William C. Stinchcombe, *The American Revolution and the French Alliance* (Syracuse, NY, 1969), 15–19; *JCC* 11:474.

3. GW to the General Officers, April 20, 1778, *PGWR* 14:567; From a Council of War, May 9, 1778, ibid., 15:83–87.

4. These paragraphs draw on *PH* 19:520; Germain to Howe, December 11, 1777, *DAR* 14:271; William B. Willcox, *Portrait of a General: Sir Henry Clinton in the War of Independence* (New York, 1962), 3–39, 134–37, 206–8; William B. Willcox, "Sir Henry Clinton: Paralysis of Command," in *George Washington's Opponents*, ed. George Athan Billias (New York, 1969), 73–102; Andrew Jackson O'Shaughnessy, *The Men Who Lost America: British Leadership, the American Revolution and the Fate of the Empire* (New Haven, CT, 2013), 207–20. On GW's leadership, see Peter R. Henriques, *First and Always: A New Portrait of George Washington* (Charlottesville, VA, 2020), 1–18.

5. Germain to Clinton, February 4, March 8, 21, 1778, *DAR* 13:247; 15:57–62, 74–76.

6. Germain to Clinton, March 8, 1778, ibid., 15:62; Sir Henry Clinton to the Duke of Gloucester, October 10, 1778, Series 3: Letterbooks, vol. 254, in SHCP (WLCL); *AR*, 85–86; Clinton's "My fate is hard" comment can be found in William B. Willcox, "British Strategy in America, 1778," *Journal of Modern History* 19 (1947): 109. See also Huw J. Davies, *The Wandering Army: The*

Campaigns That Transformed the British Way of War, 1750–1850 (New Haven, CT, 2022), 149.

7. Robert K. Wright, *The Continental Army* (Washington, DC, 1983), 149; David O. White, *Connecticut's Black Soldiers, 1775–1783* (Chester, CT, 1973), 17–31; John Hope Franklin, *From Slavery to Freedom: A History of Negro Americans* (New York, 1956), 135; Woody Holton, *Liberty Is Sweet: The Hidden History of the American Revolution* (New York, 2021), 364; Judith L. Van Buskirk, *Standing in Their Own Light: African American Patriots in the American Revolution* (Norman OK, 2017), 95–141.

8. Councils of War, June 17, 24, 1778, *PGWR* 15:414–17:520–21. The written responses of Generals Philemon Dickinson, NG, Lafayette, William Maxwell, and Anthony Wayne following the second council of war are scattered between pages 522–35. For the length of Clinton's baggage train, see Franklin Wickwire and Mary Wickwire, *Cornwallis and the War of Independence* (London, 1971), 63.

9. NG to GW, June 24, 1778, ibid., 15:525–26.

10. Editor's note, ibid., 15:576n; Alexander Hamilton to Elias Boudinot, July 5, 1778, *PAH* 1:512. On the march through New Jersey and the Battle of Monmouth, see Mark Edward Lender and Garry Wheeler Stone, *Fatal Sunday: George Washington, the Monmouth Campaign, and the Politics of Battle* (Norman, OK, 2017).

11. Jonathan R. Dull, *The French Navy and American Independence: A Study of Arms and Diplomacy, 1774–1787* (Princeton, NJ, 1975), 6, 105–12; David Syrett, *The Royal Navy in American Waters, 1775–1783* (Altershot, UK, 1989), 93.

12. Larrie D. Ferreiro, *Brothers at Arms: American Independence and the Men of France and Spain Who Saved It* (New York, 2016), 172.

13. These three paragraphs draw on Ferreiro, *Brothers at Arms*, 103–4; Dull, *The French Navy and American Independence*, 118–19; *PH* 20:212–14.

14. Vice Admiral d'Estaing to GW, July 8, 1778, *PGWR* 16:38; GW to d'Estaing, July 14, 17, 1778, ibid., 16:67–68, 88–89. On GW's planned campaign, see ibid., 16:70–71n.

15. GW to d'Estaing, July 22, 1778, ibid., 16:125; GW to Laurens, July 22, 1778, ibid., 16:128–29; Willcox, *Portrait of a General*, 238.

16. GW to Sullivan, July 22, 28, 31, August 4, 10, 1778, *PGWR* 16:133, 193, 214–15, 253, 287–89; GW to Richard Henry Lee, August 10, 1778, ibid., 16:286.

17. Clinton to Germain, July 27, 1778, *DAR* 15:173; Willcox, *Portrait of a General*, 247; Christian M. McBurney, *The Rhode Island Campaign: The First French and American Operation in the Revolutionary War* (Yardley, PA, 2011), 76–77, 82–83, 97, 101.

18. McBurney, *The Rhode Island Campaign*, 81–132; John A. Tilley, *The British Navy and the American Revolution* (Columbia, SC, 1987), 147–52.

19. A Protest of the General Officers on Rhode Island to Count d'Estaing, August 22, 1778, *PNG* 2:487–89; Sullivan to GW, August 13, 1778, *PGWR* 16:307; GW to Sullivan, September 1, 1778, ibid., 16:464; GW to d'Estaing, September 11, 1778, ibid., 16:570; Lafayette to GW, August 25[–]26, September 1, 1778, ibid., 16:370, 463; GW to NG, September 1, 1778, ibid., 16:459; GW to Lafayette, September 1, 1778, ibid., 16:461; Sir Robert Pigot to Clinton, August 31, 1778, *DAR* 15:190; Christopher Ward, *The War of the Revolution* (New York, 1952), 2:587–95; Lee Kennett, *The French Forces in America, 1780–1783* (Westport, CT, 1977), 7; Ferreiro, *Brothers at Arms*, 178; McBurney, *The Rhode Island*, 124–32, 152–53.

20. Willcox, *Portrait of a General*, 250; GW to Laurens, August 25, 1778, *PGWR* 16:376; McBurney, *The Rhode Island Campaign*, 148–69; *AR*, 100–103; Ward, *The War of the Revolution*, 2:591–92; Frederick Mackenzie, *Diary of Frederick Mackenzie, Giving a Daily Narrative of His Military Service as an Officer of the Regiment of Royal Welsh Fusiliers During the Years 1775–1781 in Massachusetts, Rhode Island, and New York* (reprint, New York, 1968), 2:391.

21. Lafayette to GW, August 25 [–26], *PGWR* 16:373; GW to Thomas Nelson, August 20, 1778, ibid., 16:341.

22. Clinton to Gloucester, October 10, 1778, series 3: Letterbooks, SHCP (WLCL); Willcox, *Portrait of a General*, 252–53.

23. E. James Ferguson, *The Power of the Purse* (Chapel Hill, NC, 1961), 25–44; GW to John Parke Custis, May 26, 1778, *PGWR* 15:224; GW to Gouverneur Morris, October 4, 1778, ibid., 17:253–54; GW to John Jay, April 23, 1779, ibid., 20:176; GW to Laurens, November 11, 1778, ibid., 18:96.

24. GW to G. Morris, October 4, 1778, *PGWR* 16:253–54; GW to Henry, October 7, 1778, ibid., 16:295; GW to Andrew Lewis, October 15, 1778, ibid., 16:388; GW to Laurens, October 24, 1778, ibid., 16:557–58.

25. GW to G. Morris, May 8, 1779, ibid., 20:385; GW to William Fitzhugh, April 10, 1779, ibid., 20:31; GW to Lund Washington, May 29, 1779, ibid., 20:688.

26. Willcox, "British Strategy in America, 1778," *Journal of Modern History* 19 (1947): 119; Clinton to Germain, October 8, 1778, *DAR* 15:210.

27. Germain to Clinton, July 1, August 5, September 25, November 4, December 3, 1778, *DAR* 15:149, 177–78, 208, 240, 278.

28. Clinton to Germain, October 25, 1778, ibid., 15:232; [Archibald Campbell], *Journal of an Expedition against the Rebels of Georgia in North America*, ed. Colin Campbell (Darien, GA, 1981), ix–x, 29; John Buchanan, *The Road to Charleston: Nathanael Greene and the American Revolution* (Charlottesville, VA, 2019), 4; *AR*, 110; Willcox, *Portrait of a General*, 261, 286.

29. Campbell, *Journal of an Expedition*, 13–20; Campbell to Germain, January 16, 1779, *DAR* 17:33–34; Charles E. Bennett and Donald R. Lennon, *A Quest for Glory: Major General Robert Howe and the American Revolution* (Chapel Hill, NC, 1991), 1–99.

30. Bennett and Lennon, *A Quest for Glory*, 85–99; Campbell to Germain, January 16, 1779, *DAR* 17:34, 36; Campbell, *Journal of an Expedition*, 19–24, 27; David K. Wilson, *The Southern Strategy: Britain's Conquest of South Carolina and Georgia, 1775–1780* (Columbia, SC, 2005), 65–80; Ward, *The War of the Revolution*, 2:679–83. Campbell's quote can be found in Robert L. O'Connell, *Revolutionary: George Washington at War* (New York, 2019), 217. The "astonishing effect" quotation can be found in Jim Piecuch, *South Carolina Provincials: Loyalists in British Service During the American Revolution* (Yardley, PA, 2023), 96.

31. Clinton to Eden, February 5, 1779, *Facsimiles* 12, no. 1258; *AR*, 116–19; Clinton to Germain, May 22, 1779, *DAR* 17:129–30; GW to Lafayette, March 8 [–10], 1779, *PGWR* 19:402; GW to Jay, March 15, 1779, ibid., 19:487; GW to Israel Putnam, March 27, 1779, ibid., 19:629–30.

32. GW to William Smallwood and the Field Officers of the Maryland Line, March 2, 1779, *PGWR* 19:335; GW to Mason, March 27, 1779, ibid., 19:627; GW, Circular to the States, May 22, 1779, ibid., 20:569; GW to G. Morris, May 8, 1779, ibid., 20:385; NG to GW, May 31, 1779, ibid., 20:707.

33. Germain to Clinton, January 23, 1779, *DAR* 17:44–45.

34. Clinton to Germain, May 22, 1779, ibid., 17:129–30; Clinton to Eden, May 20, 1779, *Facsimiles* 9, no. 997.

35. John Selby, *The Revolution in Virginia, 1775–1783* (Williamsburg, VA, 1988), 204–8; Piers Mackesy, *The War for America, 1775–1783* (Cambridge, MA, 1965), 269–70; Clinton to Eden, May 20, 1779, *Facsimiles* 9, no. 997.

36. William Smith, *Historical Memoirs, from 26 August 1778 to 12 November 1783*, ed. William H. W. Sabine (reprint, New York, 1971), 109, 122, 137; Frank Moore, comp., *The Diary of the American Revolution, 1775–1781* (New York, 1967), 374–84; *PGWR* 21:375–76n, 378n, 759–68n; Norwalk Officials to GW, July 9, 1779, ibid., 21:403–4; Jonathan Trumbull to GW, July 10, 1779, ibid., 21:429–30; Clinton to Gloucester, December 10, 1779, Series 3: Letterbooks, vol. 254, SHCP (WLCL).

37. *AR*, 122–26; Clinton to Eden, June 17 and 18, 1779, *Facsimiles* 9, no. 999; Washington to Gates, June 11, 1779, *PGWR* 21:129–31; GW to William Fitzhugh, June 25, 1779, ibid., 21:242.

38. Roger Kaplan, "The Hidden War: British Intelligence During the American Revolution," *William and Mary Quarterly* 47 (1990): 115–38; Gerald C. Stowe and Jac Weller, "Revolutionary West Point: 'The Key to the Continent,'" *Military Analysis of the Revolutionary War: An Anthology by the Editors of "Military Affairs"* (Millwood, NY, 1977), 154–71; GW to Alexander McDougall, November 24, 1778, *PGWR* 18:281; GW to Jonathan Trumbull, July 12, 1779, ibid., 21:459; Knox to GW, March 29, 1780, ibid., 25:223; Knox to Lucy Flucker Knox, June 29, 1779, in *The Revolutionary War Lives and Letters of Lucy and Henry Knox*, ed. Phillip Hamilton (Baltimore, 2017), 149.

39. GW to Wayne, July 9, 14, 1779, *PGWR* 21:410–11, 488; Wayne to GW, July 10, 16, 17, 1779, ibid., 21:432–33, 522, 523, 541–43; GW, Plan of Attack, July 15, 17, 1779, ibid., 21:509–10; GW, General Orders, July 16, 1779, ibid., 21:511; Ward, *War of the Revolution*, 2:596–603; Paul David Nelson, *Anthony Wayne: Soldier of the Early Republic* (Bloomington, IN, 1985), 94–100.

40. GW to Laurens, April 3, 1778, *PGWR* 14:390–91; Ward, *War of the Revolution*, 2:604–10; *AR*, 139.

41. Barbara Graymont, *The Iroquois in the American Revolution* (Syracuse, NY, 1972), 70–72.

42. Colin G. Calloway, *The Indian World of George Washington: The First President, the First Americans, and the Birth of the Nation* (New York, 2018), 242.

43. Jeffers Lennox, *North of America: Loyalists, Indigenous Nations, and the Borders of the Long American Revolution* (New Haven, CT, 2022), 24–29; Max M. Mintz, *Seeds of Empire: The American Revolutionary Conquest of the Iroquois* (New York, 1999), 13–14.

44. Colin G. Calloway, *The American Revolution in Indian Country: Crisis and Diversity in Native American Communities* (Cambridge, UK, 1995), 59–60, 108, 121–24; Isabel T. Kelsay, *Joseph Brant, 1743–1807: Man of Two Worlds* (Syracuse, NY, 1984), 43, 66–67, 109, 113, 115, 134, 155, 160–62, 173, 179, 181–82, 200; Barbara Graymont, *The Iroquois in the American Revolution* (Syracuse, NY, 1972), 25–85, 104–28, 157–91; Alan Taylor, *The Divided Ground: Indians, Settlers, and the Northern Borderland of the American Revolution* (New York, 2006), 3–91; Mintz, *Seeds of Empire*, 48, 64–74.

45. GW to Laurens, November 16, 1778, *PGWR* 18:169; GW to James Duane, January 11 [–12], 1779, ibid., 18: 614; Mintz, *Seeds of Empire*, 76.

46. GW to the Chiefs of the Passamaquoddy Indians, December 24, 1776, *PGWR* 7:433–44. See also Calloway, *The American Revolution in Indian Country*, 190–200; and Jim Piecuch, *Three Peoples, One King: Loyalists, Indians, and Slaves in the Revolutionary South, 1775–1782* (Columbia, SC), 2008, 68–73.

47. GW to Sullivan, May 31, 1779, *PGWR* 20:716–19; GW to Lafayette, October 20, 1779, ibid., 22:769; *JCC* 15:1169–70. On the Sullivan Expedition, see Joseph R. Fischer, *A Well-Executed Failure: The Sullivan Campaign Against the Iroquois, July to September 1779* (Columbia, SC, 1997); and Glenn F. Williams, *Year of the Hangman: George Washington's Campaign Against the Iroquois* (Yardley, PA, 2005). On GW's use of the term "Ohio Territory," and for a succinct and informative piece on the contention over this area, see Jason Edward Anderson, "War and Conflict in the Ohio Country During the American Revolution," *Journal of the American Revolution*, October 19, 2023. For the quotations of soldiers lamenting the terror they spread, see Maeve Kane, " 'She Did Not Open Her Mouth Further': Haudenosaunee Women as Military and Political Targets During and After the American Revolution," in *Women in the American Revolution: Gender, Politics, and the Domestic World*, ed. Barbara B. Oberg (Charlottesville, VA, 2019), 89–90.

48. Samuel Flagg Bemis, *The Diplomacy of the American Revolution* (New York, 1935), 75–80; Thomas F. Chávez, *Spain and the Independence of the United States: An Intrinsic Gift* (Albuquerque, NM, 2002), 127–28; Dull, *The French Navy and American Independence*, 126–35; Piers Mackesy, *The War for America, 1775–1783* (Cambridge, MA, 1965), 149–50.

49. Chávez, *Spain and the Independence of the United States*, 128; Ferreiro, *Brothers at Arms*, 114–15; Dull, *The French Navy and American Independence*, 142–43; Jonathan R. Dull, *A Diplomatic History of the American Revolution* (New Haven, CT, 1985), 107–9; Orville T. Murphy, *Charles Gravier, Comte de Vergennes: French Diplomacy in the Age of Revolution, 1719–1787* (Albany, NY, 1982), 261–77.

50. Dull, *The French Navy and American Independence*, 60, 143–53.

51. A. Temple Patterson, *The Other Armada: The Franco-Spanish Attempt to Invade Britain in 1779* (Manchester, UK, 1960), 96–132.

52. Dull, *The French Navy and American Independence*, 150–58; Patterson, *The Other Armada*, 194–215; Ferreiro, *Brothers at Arms*, 183–88.

53. Patterson, *The Other Armada*, 228.

54. Dull, *The French Navy and American Independence*, 170–79; Chávez, *Spain and the Independence of the United States*, 140–41.

55. Kathleen DuVal, *Independence Lost: Lives on the Edge of the American Revolution* (New York, 2015), 118–25, 147–53; Kathleen DuVal and Gonzalo M. Quintero Saravia, "Bernardo de Gálvez: Friend of the American Revolution, Friend of Empire," in *European Friends of the American Revolution*, ed. Andrew J. O'Shaughnessy, John A. Ragosta, and Marie-Jeanne Rossignol (Charlottesville, VA, 2023), 147–59; Alan Taylor, *American Revolutions: A Continental History, 1750–1804* (New York, 2016), 262–63; Chávez, *Spain and the Independence of the United States*, 10–15, 170–71; *PGWR* 24:503n; Joshua Provan, "La Marcha Galvez: Spanish Planning, Logistics and Grit on the Road to Pensacola, 1779–1780," in *Waging War in America 1775–1783: Operational Challenges of Five Armies During the American Revolution*, ed. Don N. Hagist (Warwick, UK, 2023), 152–62.

56. Juan de Miralles to GW, July 10, October 2, 1779, March 15, 1780, *PGWR* 21:422–23; 22:587–88; 23:487–88n, 537n; 25:52.

57. Provan, "La Marcha Galvez," 163–69; Germain to John Campbell, June 25, 1779, *DAR* 17:153; Campbell to Germain, March 24, 1780, ibid., 18:65–66; DuVal, *Independence Lost*, 154–59, 166–71; Ferreiro, *Brothers at Arms*, 160–64.

58. Selby, *The Revolution in Virginia*, 191–98; Jack M. Sosin, *The Revolutionary Frontier, 1763–1783* (Albuquerque, NM, 1967), 117–20, 137–41.

59. Germain to Frederich Haldimand, June 17, 1779, *DAR* 17:144; Chávez, *Spain and the Independence of the United States*, 178–80; Taylor, *American Revolutions*, 257–63, 344.

60. Chávez, *Spain and the Independence of the United States*, 150–65.

61. Ferreiro, *Brothers at Arms*, 180–81, 198–99; Andrew Jackson O'Shaughnessy, *An Empire Divided: The American Revolution and the British Caribbean* (Philadelphia, 2000), 169–70.

62. *PGWR* 19:132n, 20:294n; GW to Gouverneur Morris, May 8, 1779, ibid., 20:384–85; GW to Gérard, May 1, 1779, ibid., 20:279–80; Gérard to GW, May 5, 1779, ibid., 20:331–32.

63. GW to d'Estaing, September 13, October 4, 1779, ibid., 22:409, 611–15; Planning for an Allied Attack on New York [ca. October 3–7, 1779], ibid., 22:594–601n; GW, Loose Thoughts upon an Attack of New York, [October 3, 1779], ibid., 22:601–3; *AR*, 145–47.

64. Wilson, *The Southern Strategy*, 102–15; Augustine Prevost to Clinton, May 21, 1779, *DAR* 17:127–29; Prevost to Germain, June 10, 1779, ibid., 17:141–43; Piecuch, *South Carolina Provincials*, 99.

65. Alexander A. Lawrence, *Storm over Savannah: The Story of Count d'Estaing and the Siege of the Town in 1779* (Athens, GA 1950), 50, 76–131; Wilson, *The Southern Strategy*, 135–92; Ferreiro, *Brothers at Arms*, 201; *AR*, 150; Piecuch, *South Carolina Provincials*, 106; Benjamin Lincoln to Samuel Huntington, October 22, 1779, *PGWR* 23:232n; David B. Mattern, *Benjamin Lincoln and the American Revolution* (Columbia, SC, 1995), 76–85.

66. Ferreiro, *Brothers at Arms*, 203–4.

67. GW to Schuyler, November 24, 1779, *PGWR* 23:421; Clinton to Eden, November 19, 1779, *Facsimiles* 10, no. 1032.

68. GW to Laurens, November 5, 1779, *PGWR* 23:159.

CHAPTER 9: ARMIES, NAVIES, SOLDIERS, AND SAILORS

1. John Shy, "Charles Lee: The Soldier as Radical," in *George Washington's Generals*, ed. George Athan Billias (New York, 1964), 26–27.

2. Seanegan P. Sculley, *Contest for Liberty: Military Leadership in the Continental Army, 1775–1783* (Yardley, PA, 2019), 15–18; Don Higginbotham, *War and Society in Revolutionary America: The Wider Dimensions of Conflict* (Columbia, SC, 1989), 85–90, 157–59; Caroline Cox, *A Proper Sense of Honor: Service and Sacrifice in George Washington's Army* (Chapel Hill, NC, 2004), 22–29.

3. Robert Wright, *The Continental Army* (Washington, DC, 1983), 46–49, 124–28.

4. Gregory J. W. Urwin, "The Continental Light Dragoons, 1776–1783: 'There Is No Carrying on the War Without Them,'" in *Cavalry of the American Revolution*, ed. Jim Piecuch (Yardley, PA, 2012), 1–10; Lee to GW, December 8, 1776, *PGWR*

7:276; William Maxwell to GW, December 29, 1776, ibid., 7:481; Alexander McDougall to GW, December 30, 1776, ibid., 7:487; GW to Hancock, December 11, 1776, ibid., 7:297.

5. For these three paragraphs, see GW to Richard Henry Lee, August 29, 1775, *PGWR* 1:372; GW to the Delaware Delegates, August 30, 1775, ibid., 1:384; Instructions from the Continental Congress, June 22, 1775, ibid., 1:21; Jonathan Gregory Rossie, *The Politics of Command in the American Revolution* (Syracuse, NY, 1975), 69–74, 136–37; Sculley, *Contest for Liberty*, 21; Wright, *The Continental Army*, 51–52, 77; Paul David Nelson, *Anthony Wayne: Soldier of the Early Republic* (Bloomington, IN, 1985), 41; Harry M. Ward, *Major General Adam Stephen and the Cause of American Liberty* (Charlottesville, VA, 1989), 141; David B. Mattern, *Benjamin Lincoln and the American Revolution* (Columbia, SC, 1988), 23, 36.

6. JA to Abigail Adams, February 21, May 22, 1777, *AFC* 2:6, 165, 245; William Ellery to Nicholas Cooke, October 5, 1776, *LDC* 5:308.

7. Sculley, *Contest for Liberty*, 6–36.

8. GW to William Woodford, November 10, 1775, *PGWR* 2:346–47.

9. GW, General Orders, July 23, 1775, ibid., 1:158.

10. James Kirby Martin and Mark Edward Lender, *A Respectable Army: The Military Origins of the Republic, 1763–1789* (Arlington Heights, IL, 1982), 106–7; Terry Bouton, *Taming Democracy: "The People," the Founders, and the Troubled Ending of the American Revolution* (New York, 2007), 64–65; Don Higginbotham, *The War of American Independence: Military Attitudes, Policies, and Practice, 1763–1789* (New York, 1971), 205.

11. For these three paragraphs, see GW to Hancock, September 25, 1776, *PGWR* 6:394–95; Robert A. Mayers, *The War Man: The True Story of a Citizen-Soldier Who Fought from Quebec to Yorktown* (Yardley, PA, 2009), 19–20; Holly A. Mayer, *Congress's Own: A Canadian Regiment, the Continental Arm, and American Union* (Norman, OK, 2021), 97; Charles Lesser, ed., *The Sinews of Independence: Monthly Strength Reports of the Continental Army* (Chicago, 1976), 32–43; *JCC* 5:854–56; John Resch, *Suffering Soldiers: Revolutionary War Veterans, Moral Sentiment, and Political Culture in the Early Republic* (Amherst, MA, 1999), 19–25, 34; Martin and Lender, *A Respectable Army*, 87–94; Cox, *A Proper Sense of Honor*, 20; Charles Patrick Neimeyer, *America Goes to War: A Social History of the Continental Army* (New York, 1996), 16–24, 27–64.

12. Council of War, July 9, October 8, 1775, *PGWR* 1:79–80; 2:125; GW, General Orders, November 12, 1775, ibid., 2:354–55; GW to Hancock, July 10 [–11], December 31, 1775, ibid., 1:90, 2:623; *JCC* 4:60; Henry Wiencek, *An Imperfect God: George Washington, His Slaves, and the Creation of America* (New York, 2003), 196–205; Judith L. Van Buskirk, *Standing in Their Own Light: African American Patriots in the American Revolution* (Norman, OK, 2017), 52, 61–63.

13. Van Buskirk, *Standing in Their Own Light*, 96–116. JA's comment can be found in Woody Holton, *Liberty Is Sweet: The Hidden History of the American Revolution* (New York, 2021), 364.

14. See Alan Gilbert, *Black Patriots and Loyalists: Fighting for Emancipation in the War of Independence* (Chicago, 2012), 104, 174–75; and Robert Scott Davis, "Black Soldiers of Liberty," *Journal of the American Revolution*, August 31, 2023.

15. Charles Royster, *A Revolutionary People at War: The Continental Army and American Character, 1775–1783* (Chapel Hill, NC, 1979), 35–36, 295–318; Martin and Lender, *A Respectable Army*, 127–28; Bernard Bailyn, *The Ideological Origins of the American Revolution* (Cambridge, MA, 1967), 61–63; Wayne Bodle, *The Valley Forge Winter: Civilians and Soldiers in War* (University Park, PA, 2002), 126.

16. GW to Hancock, October 13 [–14], 1777, *PGWR* 11:499; GW to a Continental Congress Camp Committee, January 29, 1778, ibid., 13:379; John U. Rees, "'The pleasure of their number' 1778: Crisis, Conscription, and Revolutionary Soldiers' Recollections," in *Waging War in America 1775–1783: Operational Challenges of Five Armies During the American Revolution*, ed. Don N. Hagist (Warwick, UK, 2023), 119–21.

17. Rees, "'The pleasure of their number' 1778," 121–29; Sculley, *Contest for Liberty*, 39–63; Martin and Lender, *A Respectable Army*, 77, 88, 93; Mayer, *Congress's Own*, 102, 107; GW to Hancock, September 25, 1776, *PGWR* 6:394–95; Joseph Plumb Martin, *Private Yankee Doodle: Being a Narrative of Some of the Adventures, Dangers and Sufferings of a Revolutionary Soldier*, ed. George F. Scheer (New York, 1962), 61; Royster, *A Revolutionary People at War*, 29–31, 62–69, 131–36; John Shy, *A People Numerous and Armed: Reflections on the Military Struggle for American Independence* (New York, 1976), 173.

18. Martin, *Private Yankee Doodle*, 280.

19. Higginbotham, *The War of American Independence*, 389–90.

20. GW to James Otis, August 7, 1775, *PGWR* 1:264; GW to Ludwig Weltner, December 16, 1780, ibid., 29:515n; GW, General Orders, August 11, 1777, ibid., 10:582; GW to Hancock, January 31, 1777, ibid., 8:202; GW to Reed, April 28, 1780, ibid., 25:514–15; Royster, *A Revolutionary People at War*, 71; Martin and Lender, *A Respectable Army*, 133; Harry M. Ward, *George Washington's Enforcers: Policing the Continental Army* (Carbondale, IL, 2006), 32–33, 108–10.

21. Michael Cecere, ed., *They Behaved like Soldiers: Captain John Chilton and the Third Virginia Regiment, 1775–1778* (Bowie, MD, 2004), 79; Joseph Lee Boyle, "The Journal of Thomas Anderson, Delaware Regiment," *Journal of the American Revolution*, July 25, 27, 2023; Martin, *Private Yankee Doodle*, 288; John Ferling, *A Wilderness of Miseries: War and Warriors in Early America* (Westport, CT, 1981), 94, 100–101.

22. Martin, *Private Yankee Doodle*, 288.

23. Ferling, *A Wilderness of Miseries*, 95–96.

24. R. Arthur Bowler, "Logistics and Operations in the American Revolution," in *War and Society in Revolutionary America: The Wider Dimensions of Conflict*, ed. Don Higginbotham (Columbia, SC, 1989), 55–57; E. Wayne Carp, *To Starve the Army at Pleasure: Continental Army Administration and American Political Culture, 1775–1783* (Chapel Hill, NC, 1984), 55, 220: GW to Fielding Lewis, May 5 [?], 1780, *PGWR* 25:553–56; GW to John Jay, March 15, 1779, ibid., 19:488.

25. These two paragraphs draw on GW, General Orders, July 7, August 1, 22, 1775, *PGWR* 1:73, 207, 347; Ward, *George Washington's Enforcers*, 30–44, 82–91, 102–10, 156–64, 184–97; Sculley, *Contest for Liberty*, 71–95; Cox, *A Proper Sense of Honor*, 80–117, 270.

26. Cox, *A Proper Sense of Honor*, 120–62; John Ferling, *The Ascent of George Washington: The Hidden Political Genius of an American Icon* (New York, 2009), 142–43; Ferling, *A Wilderness of Miseries*, 97.

27. See Edwin G. Burrows, *Forgotten Patriots: The Untold Story of American Prisoners During the Revolutionary War* (New York, 2008); and Holger Hoock, *Scars of Independence: America's Violent Birth* (New York, 2017), 186–223, 487; Robert Clark Morris, *Memoirs of James Morris of South Farms in Litchfield* (New Haven, CT, 1933), 18–19, 24–25; John Settle, "The Eastern Shore Battalion: The Story of the 9th Pennsylvania Regiment," *JAR*, January 19, 2023. On the greater civility extended to American officers—at least those captured in New York in 1776—see Judith L. Van Buskirk, *Generous Enemies: Patriots and Loyalists in Revolutionary New York* (Philadelphia, 2002), 76–81.

28. Many accounts of the haunting memories of war have been left by veterans. Among the best are the works of the journalist Chris Hedges, who saw and was enveloped by the many conflicts he covered as a war correspondent. See Chris Hedges, *The Greatest Evil Is War* (New York, 2022); Hedges, *What Every Person Should Know About War* (New York, 2003); and Hedges, *War Is a Force That Gives Us Meaning* (New York, 2002). Also see Paul Fussell, *Wartime: Understanding and Behavior in the Second World War* (New York, 1989), 267–97. The Martin Luther King Jr. quote can be found in David Brooks, "How America Got Mean," *The Atlantic* 332, September 2023, 71.

29. Mary V. Thompson, "'As if I Had Been a Very Great Somebody': Martha Washington's Revolution," in *Women in the American Revolution: Gender, Politics, and the Domestic World*, ed. Barbara S. Oberg (Charlottesville, VA, 2019), 128–68. The quotations can be found on pages 131 and 132.

30. For this paragraph, see Holly A. Mayer, *Belonging to the Army: Camp Followers and Community During the American Revolution* (Columbia, SC, 1996), 85–185.

31. Piers Mackesy, *Could the British Have Won the War of Independence?* (Worcester, MA, 1976), 5; Higginbotham, *War and Society in Revolutionary America*, 118–19; Shy, *A People Numerous and Armed*, 218; Matthew H. Spring, *With Zeal and with Bayonets Only: The British Army on Campaign in North America, 1775–1783* (Norman, OK, 2008), 16; Van Buskirk, *Generous Enemies*, 4–5.

32. Harry M. Ward, *The War for Independence and the Transformation of American Society* (London, 1999), 111; Spring, *With Zeal and with Bayonets Only*, 15.

33. Burgoyne to Germain, August 20, 1777, *DAR* 14:166; GW to Hancock, September 2, 1776, *PGWR* 6:199; GW to John Augustine Washington, September 22, 1776, ibid., 6:374; NG to Jacob Greene [?], September 28, 1776, *PNG* 1:303; Alexander Hamilton to Aedanus Burke, April 1, 1790, *PAH* 6:333; Cornwallis to Clinton, June 30, 1781, *CP* 5:104–7; Shy, *A People Numerous and Armed*, 216–17.

34. The foregoing paragraphs draw on Don N. Hagist, *British Soldiers, American War* (Yardley, PA 2014), 2–12, 61, 75–78, 153, 186; Hagist, *Noble Volunteers: The British Soldiers Who Fought the American Revolution* (Yardley, PA, 2020), 16, 38, 65, 181; Edward E. Curtis, *The Organization of the British Army in the American Revolution* (New Haven, CT, 1926), 1, 15–16, 24–25, 51, 59–60; Franklin Wickwire and Mary Wickwire, *Cornwallis and the War of Independence* (London, 1971), 49–52; Julie Flavell, *The Howe Dynasty: The Untold Story of a Military Family and the Women Behind Britain's Wars for America* (New York, 2021), 14–33; Sylvia R. Frey, *The British*

Soldier in America: A Social History of Military Life in the Revolutionary Period (Austin, TX, 1981), 27; Christopher Duffy, *The Military Experience in the Age of Reason* (London, 1987), 91; Stephen Conway, "The British Army and the War of Independence," in *The Oxford Handbook of the American Revolution*, ed. Edward G. Gray and Jane Kamensky (New York, 2013), 178, 184; Sarah M. S. Pearsall, "Women in the American Revolutionary War," in ibid., 277; Stephen Brumwell, *Redcoats: The British Soldier and War in the Americas, 1755–1763* (Cambridge, UK, 2002), 84; Richard M. Ketchum, *Decisive Day: The Battle for Bunker Hill* (New York, 1974), 123–26.

35. Curtis, *The Organization of the British Army in the American Revolution*, 125–26; Frey, *The British Soldier in America*, 37.

36. Hagist, *Noble Volunteers*, 141–45; Frey, *The British Soldier in America*, 37–38.

37. R. Arthur Bowler, *Logistics and the Failure of the British Army in America, 1775–1783* (Princeton, NJ, 1975), 14–19, 30, 56; Spring, *With Zeal and with Bayonets Only*, 33; Piers Mackesy, *The War for America, 1775–1783* (Cambridge, MA, 1965), 524–25; Rodney Atwood, *The Hessians: Mercenaries from Hessen-Kassel in the American Revolution* (Cambridge, UK, 1980), 254.

38. Bowler, *Logistics and the Failure of the British Army in America*, 24, 98–99, 118, 127, 148, 149, 151; Piers Mackesy, "The Redcoat Revived," in *The American Revolution: Changing Perspectives*, ed. William M. Fowler and Wallace Coyle (Boston, 1979), 178.

39. Don N. Hagist, "Killed, Imprisoned, Struck by Lightning: Soldiers' Wives on Campaign with the British Army," in *Women Waging War in the American Revolution*, ed. Holly A. Mayer (Charlottesville, VA, 2022), 132–47.

40. Friederike Baer, *Hessians: German Soldiers in the American Revolutionary War* (New York, 2022), 62–63, 79–84, 88, 94, 192–93, 201, 261; Atwood, *The Hessians*, 145, 152–55, 185, 189–91, 193–94.

41. Paul H. Smith, *Loyalists and Redcoats: A Study in British Revolutionary Policy* (Chapel Hill, NC, 1964), 14–31, 33–34, 38, 47–48, 60–61, 64, 76–77; Jim Piecuch, *South Carolina Provincials: Loyalists in British Service During the American Revolution* (Yardley, PA, 2023), xv, 46, 55, 61, 64, 65; John Knight, *War at Saber Point: Banastre Tarleton and the British Legion* (Yardley, PA, 2020), 43–50; Ruma Chopra, *Unnatural Rebellion: Loyalists in New York City During the Revolution* (Charlottesville, VA, 2011), 116–17; Jim Piecuch, *Three Peoples, One King: Loyalists, Indians, and Slaves in the Revolutionary South, 1775–1782* (Columbia, SC, 2008),

176–77, 235, 251. For a comprehensive roster and thumbnail history of Loyalist units, see Thomas B. Allen and Todd W. Braisted, *The Loyalist Corps: Americans in the Service of the King* (Tacoma Park, MD, 2011).

42. Todd W. Braisted, "The Black Pioneers and Others: The Military Role of Black Loyalists in the American War of Independence," in *Moving On: Black Loyalists in the Afro-Atlantic World*, ed. John W. Pulis (New York, 1999), 3–37; Benjamin Quarles, *The Negro in the American Revolution* (Chapel Hill, NC, 1961), 19–32, 111–57; Sylvia R. Frey, *The British Soldier in America*, 18–19; Frey, *Water from the Rock: Black Resistance in a Revolutionary Age* (Princeton, NJ, 1991), 86, 92, 96–97, 121, 124, 128; Edward Countryman, *Enjoy the Same Liberty: Black Americans and the Revolutionary Era* (Lanham, MD, 2012), 47, 56; Gilbert, *Black Patriots and Loyalists*, 117–18, 121–22, 124; Jim Piecuch, "The 'Black Dragoons': Former Slaves as British Cavalry in Revolutionary South Carolina," in Piecuch, *Cavalry of the American Revolution*, 213–23; Ira D. Gruber, *The Howe Brothers and the American Revolution* (New York, 1972), 84; Baer, *Hessians*, 96–97. Sir Henry Clinton is quoted in Braisted's essay, pages 11–12.

43. Ward, *George Washington's Enforcers*, 108; Hagist, *British Soldiers, American War*, 184.

44. Clinton to Admiral Marriot Arbuthnot, n.d., 1780, vol. 118 SHCP (WLCL).

45. Frey, *The British Soldier in America*, 35; "Journal of Surgeon Ebenezer Elmer," *Pennsylvania Magazine of History and Biography* 35 (1911): 105; Wickwire and Wickwire, *Cornwallis and the War of Independence*, 68; Stephen R. Taaffe, *The Philadelphia Campaign, 1777–1778* (Lawrence, KS, 2003), 73; *SOS* 1:441, 575–76, 580, 622; Michael C. Harris, *Brandywine: A Military History of the Battle That Lost Philadelphia but Saved America, September 11, 1777* (El Dorado Hills, CA, 2014), 286; Don N. Hagist, ed., *Roger Lamb's American Revolution: A British Soldier's Story* (Yardley, PA, 2022), 32, 49, 56–58.

46. Colin Jones, *The Great Nation: France from Louis XV to Napoleon, 1715–1799* (New York, 2002), 238; Lee Kennett, *The French Armies in the Seven Years' War: A Study in Military Organization and Administration* (Durham, NC, 1967), 29, 36, 46, 54–55, 67, 72–87, 90, 109; Robert A. Selig, "L'expédition Particulière and the American War of Independence, 1780–1783," in Hagist, *Waging War in America 1775–1783*, 172–73.

47. Rafe Blaufarb, *The French Army, 1750–1820: Careers, Talent, Merit* (Manchester, UK, 2002), 10–37; Robert S. Quimby, *The Background of Napoleonic Warfare: The*

Theory of Military Tactics in Eighteenth-Century France (New York, 1957), 97–100; Duffy, *The Military Experience in the Age of Reason*, 19–21, 37; Christy Pichichero, *The Military Enlightenment: War and Culture in the French Empire from Louis XIV to Napoleon* (Ithaca, NY, 2017), 15, 17, 27, 33, 37, 38, 41; Higginbotham, *War and Society in Revolutionary America*, 88.

48. For the foregoing paragraphs, see Paul Lockhart, *Firepower: How Weapons Shaped Warfare* (New York, 2021), 66–121; Lockhart, *The Drillmaster of Valley Forge: The Baron de Steuben and the Making of the American Army* (New York, 2010), 90–92; Duffy, *The Military Experience in the Age of Reason*, 197, 260; Martin, *Private Yankee Doodle*, 118; Quimby, *The Background of Napoleonic Warfare*, 81. Marshal Saxe's comment can be found in Quimby, page 43.

49. The foregoing draws on N. A. M. Rodger, *The Command of the Ocean: A Naval History of Britain, 1649–1815* (New York, 2004), 127–28, 395–407.

50. Jack Coggins, *Ships and Seamen of the American Revolution: Vessels, Crews, Weapons, Gear, Naval Tactics, and Actions of the War of Independence* (Harrisburg, PA, 1969), 31–42, 147–57.

51. David Syrett, *The Royal Navy in American Waters, 1775–1783* (Altershot, UK, 1989), 35; Brendan Simms, *Three Victories and a Defeat: The Rise and Fall of the First British Empire, 1714–1783* (New York, 2007), 510, 574; Rodger, *The Command of the Ocean*, 369–74; P. J. Marshall, *The Making and Unmaking of Empires: Britain, India, and America c. 1750–1783* (New York, 2005), 275–76.

52. These paragraphs draw on Syrett, *The Royal Navy in American Waters*, 1–87; John A. Tilley, *The British Navy and the American Revolution* (Columbia, SC, 1987), 102–3, 120–21; Andrew Jackson O'Shaughnessy, *The Men Who Lost America: British Leadership, the American Revolution and the Fate of Empire* (New Haven, CT, 2013), 328–29; Eric Jay Dolin, *Rebels at Sea: Privateering in the American Revolution* (New York, 2022), 164.

53. GW to Nicholas Cooke, August 4, 1775, *PGWR* 1:221; John Ferling, *The First of Men: A Life of George Washington* (reprint, New York, 2010), 135; Nathan Miller, *Sea of Glory: The Continental Navy Fights for Independence, 1775–1783* (New York, 1974), 60–61, 184–86; Willard Sterne Randall, *The Founders' Fortunes: How Money Shaped the Birth of America* (New York, 2022), 146–47; Randall, "No Guns, No Glory: The Race to Arm America," *History Net*, April 12, 2022.

54. Barbara W. Tuchman, *The First Salute* (New York, 1988), 45; William M. Fowler Jr., *Rebels Under Sail: The American Navy During the American Revolution* (New York, 1976), 61–78, 212, 215–16.

55. Fowler, *Rebels Under Sail*, 91–134; Marine Committee to John Paul Jones, February 5, 1777, *LDC* 6:221–22; Gardner W. Allen, *A Naval History of the American Revolution* (reprint, New York, 1962), 1:132–38, 256–61, 272; Miller, *Sea of Glory*, 285, 293.

56. Fowler, *Rebels Under Sail*, 256–78.

57. Fowler, *Rebels Under Sail*, 279–301; Coggins, *Ships and Seamen of the American Revolution*, 33–42; Howard Chapelle, *The History of the American Sailing Navy: The Ships and Their Development* (New York, 1949), 56, 60.

58. Miller, *Sea of Glory*, 528–29; Fowler, *Rebels Under Sail*, 96–99; Tuchman, *The First Salute*, 47–48.

59. Samuel Eliot Morison, *John Paul Jones: A Sailor's Biography* (Boston, 1959), 3–76, 186–99, 201–42, 246, 249, 266–68; Evan Thomas, *John Paul Jones: Sailor, Hero, Father of the American Navy* (New York, 2003), 13–66, 168–205.

60. These paragraphs draw on JA to Gates, March 23, 1776, *PJA* 4:59; Kylie A. Hulbert, *The Untold War at Sea: America's Revolutionary Privateers* (Athens, GA, 2022), 4, 9, 16–19, 21, 23, 28, 31, 42, 56, 73, 78, 93; Dolin, *Rebels at Sea*, xviii–xix, 61, 67–69, 92–93, 147, 175, 179, 181–92.

CHAPTER 10: OFF THE BATTLEFIELD

1. These paragraphs draw on David Freeman Hawke, *Everyday Life in Early America* (New York, 1988), 31–71; Mary Beth Norton, *Liberty's Daughters: The Revolutionary Experience of American Women, 1750–1800* (Boston, 1980), 9, 196–205; Steven Elliot, "Neighbors, Land Ladies, and Consorts: New Jersey Women in the Midst of the Continental Army," in *Women Waging War in the American Revolution*, ed. Holly A. Mayer (Charlottesville, VA, 2022), 99, 101; Alisa Wade, "The 'Widowed State': Women's Labor, Sacrifice, and Self-Sufficiency in the American Revolution," ibid., 245–65; Sarah Hodgkins to Joseph Hodgkins, October 9, November 19, December 10, 1775, February 1, 11, May 23, October 19, 1776, April 26, 1778, in *This Glorious Cause: The Adventures of Two Company Officers in Washington's Army*, ed. Herbert T. Wade and Robert A. Lively (Princeton, NJ, 1958), 179, 184, 186, 191, 192, 203, 224, 239–40; Laurel Thatcher Ulrich, *Good Wives: Image and Reality in the Lives of Women in Northern New England, 1650–1750* (New York, 1982), 44;

Abigail Adams to Mercy Otis Warren, August 27, 1775, *AFC* 1:276; Abigail Adams to Isaac Smith Jr., October 30, 1777, ibid., 2:364; Lucy Flucker Knox to Henry Knox, April 13, 1777, in Phillip Hamilton, ed., *The Revolutionary War Lives and Letters of Lucy and Henry Knox* (Baltimore, 2017), 82; Lucy Knox to William Knox, September 4, 1781, ibid., 156; Ray Raphael, *A People's History of the American Revolution: How Common People Shaped the Fight for Independence* (New York, 2001), 107–43; Linda K. Kerber, *Women of the Republic: Intellect and Ideology in Revolutionary America* (Chapel Hill, NC, 1980), 46, 48; Carol Berkin, *Revolutionary Mothers: Women in the Struggle for America's Independence* (New York, 2003), 26–42; Sarah M. S. Pearsall, "Women in the American Revolutionary War," in *The Oxford Handbook of the American Revolution*, ed. Edward G. Gray and Jane Kamensky (New York, 2013), 275, 282; Allan Kulikoff, "The War in the Countryside," ibid., 220–21; Woody Holton, *Abigail Adams* (New York, 2009), 142.

2. Norton, *Liberty's Daughters*, 195–227, 295–99.

3. Berkin, *Revolutionary Mothers*, 135–47; *PGWR* 13:611n; Stuart Gerry Brown, ed., *The Autobiography of James Monroe* (Syracuse, NY, 1959), 26; Mark Edward Lender and Garry Wheeler Stone, *Fatal Sunday: George Washington, the Monmouth Campaign, and the Politics of Battle* (Norman, OK, 2017), 329. On Deborah Sampson, see Alfred F. Young, *Masquerade: The Life and Times of Deborah Sampson, Continental Soldier* (New York, 2005).

4. Woody Holton, *Liberty Is Sweet: The Hidden History of the American Revolution* (New York, 2021), 300; Elliott, "Neighbors, Land Ladies, and Consorts," 108.

5. Holton, *Liberty Is Sweet*, 298, 544; Lauren Duval, "'A Shocking Thing to Tell Of': Female Civilians, Violence, and Rape under British Military Rule," in Mayer, *Women Waging War in the American Revolution*, 76–97.

6. These paragraphs draw on Richard Buel Jr., *Dear Liberty: Connecticut's Mobilization for the Revolutionary War* (Middletown, CT, 1980), 199; Buel, *In Irons: Britain's Naval Supremacy and the American Revolutionary Economy* (New Haven, CT, 1998), 127–28; Dennis Ness, "How Pennsylvania Counties Paid Their Taxes to Congress," *Journal of the American Revolution*, April 13, 2023; Harry M. Ward, *The War for Independence and the Transformation of American Society* (London, 1999), 95; Kulikoff, "The War in the Countryside," 220, 222–23; Mark A. Peterson, "The War in the Cities," 205, in Gray and Kamensky, *The Oxford Handbook of the American Revolution*; Eric Foner, *Tom Paine and Revolutionary America* (New York, 2005), 161. See also Anne Bezanson, *Prices and Inflation During the American Revolution: Pennsylvania, 1770–1790* (Philadelphia, 1951).

7. Ward, *The War for Independence and the Transformation of American Society*, 65–79.

8. JA to Thomas McKean, August 31, 1813, in Charles Francis Adams, ed., *The Works of John Adams, Second President of the United States* (Boston, 1856), 10:62–63; Ruma Chopra, *Choosing Sides: Loyalists in Revolutionary America* (Lanham, MD, 2013), 1, 7, 8, 26, 77, 88. The literature on Loyalism is vast, but good starting points are Robert Calhoon, *The Loyalists in Revolutionary America, 1760–1781* (New York, 1971); and William H. Nelson, *The American Tory* (Oxford, UK, 1961). Wallace Brown, *The King's Friends* (Providence, RI, 1965), remains unsurpassed concerning the numbers of Loyalists in each province.

9. Stephen Mihm, "Funding the Revolution: Monetary and Fiscal Policy in Eighteenth-Century America," in Gray and Kamensky, *The Oxford Handbook of the American Revolution*, 328; E. James Ferguson, *The Power of the Purse: A History of American Public Finance, 1776–1790* (Chapel Hill, NC, 1961), 33–34; Ruma Chopra, *Unnatural Rebellion: Loyalists in New York City During the Revolution* (Charlottesville, VA, 2011), 161; Abigail Adams to JA, June 10, 18, September 29, 1778, June 8, 1779, May 1, November 13, 1780, January 15, April 23, 1781, *AFC* 3:26, 47, 95–96, 200, 336; 4:15, 64, 106, 107n; Jackson Turner Main, *The Sovereign States, 1775–1783* (New York, 1973), 243, 278, 280, 309; Philip Ranlet, *The New York Loyalists* (Knoxville, TN, 1986), 160–62; Marcos Gallo, "Property Rights, Citizenship, Corruption, and Inequality: Confiscating Loyalist Estates During the American Revolution," *Pennsylvania History: A Journal of Mid-Atlantic Studies* 86 (2019): 474–510. Governor Livingston's comment can be found in Gallo, page 497.

10. Mary Beth Norton, *The British-Americans: The Loyalist Exiles in England, 1774–1789* (New York, 1972), 62–95, 235, 236, 245; Nelson, *The American Tory*, 153–69; Chopra, *Unnatural Rebellion*, 136, 143, 145, 148; Maya Jasanoff, *Liberty's Exiles: American Loyalists in the Revolutionary World* (New York, 2011), 29, 30, 32, 56, 70, 72–74, 77; Don Higginbotham, *The War of American Independence: Military Attitudes, Policies, and Practice, 1763–1789* (New York, 1971), 277, 287; Todd W. Braisted, "In Reduced Circumstances: Loyalist Women and British Government Assistance, 1779–1783," Mayer, *Women Waging War*, 213–26. The quotation can be found in the essay by Braisted, page 214.

11. Ward, *The War for Independence and the Transformation of American Society*, 153–55; Elizabeth Cometti, "The Labor Front During the American Revolution," in *The*

American Revolution: The Home Front, West Georgia College Studies in the Social Sciences, ed. John Ferling (1976): 79–90; Eric Foner, *Tom Paine and Revolutionary America* (New York, 2005), 145–82.

12. Jack N. Rakove, *The Beginnings of National Politics: An Interpretive History of the Continental Congress* (Baltimore, 1979), 178, 206, 212, 275; E. James Ferguson, *The Power of the Purse: A History of American Public Finance, 1776–1790* (Chapel Hill, NC, 1961), 40–42, 126.

13. John J. Meng, ed., *Dispatches and Instructions of Conrad Alexandre Gérard, 1778–1780* (Baltimore, 1939), 35–42, 119–20; Benjamin Rush to JA, April 28, 1780, *PJA* 9:248.

14. Conrad Alexandre Gérard to Vergennes, July 16, August 12, 22, September 15, 1778; Meng, *Dispatches and Instructions of Conrad Alexandre Gérard*, 158, 209, 212, 215, 232, 287.

15. *JCC* 13:239–44.

16. Gregg L. Lint, "Preparing for Peace: The Objectives of the United States, France, and Spain in the War of the American Revolution," in *Peace and the Peacemakers: The Treaty of 1783*, ed. Ronald Hoffman and Peter J. Albert (Charlottesville, VA, 1986), 33–40; William C. Stinchcombe, *The American Revolution and the French Alliance* (Syracuse, NY, 1969), 63–74; *JCC*, 14:960–62; Rakove, *The Beginnings of National Politics*, 255–56.

17. John Ferling, *A Leap in the Dark: The Struggle to Create the American Republic* (New York, 2003), 215; Rakove, *The Beginnings of National Politics*, 257; Stacy Schiff, *A Great Improvisation: Franklin, France, and the Birth of America* (New York, 2005), 216–17; H. James Henderson, *Party Politics in the Continental Congress* (New York, 1974), 199–201; Elbridge Gerry to JA, September 29, 1778, *PJA* 8:181.

18. *JCC* 13:363–68; JA to Richard Henry Lee, August 5, 1778, *PJA* 6:354; JA to Samuel Adams, ibid., 7:256; JA to James Lovell, February 20, 1779, ibid., 7:420; JA to Thomas McKean, September 20, 1779, ibid., 8:162; Henry Laurens to JA, October 4, 1779, ibid., 8:189; Gerry to JA, September 29, 1779, ibid., 8:181; John Ferling, "John Adams: Diplomat," *William and Mary Quarterly* 51 (1994): 235.

19. Rakove, *The Beginnings of National Politics*, 135–91.

20. Ibid., 216–39; John Ferling, *John Adams: A Life* (reprint, New York, 2000), 159–60.

21. Troy Bickham, *Making Headlines: The American Revolution as Seen Through the British Press* (DeKalb, IL, 2009), 138–40; Christopher Hobhouse, *Fox* (London, 1934), 86, 91–92.

22. Colin Bonwick, *English Radicals and the American Revolution* (Chapel Hill, NC, 1977), 128, 140; *PH* 20:837, 839, 842, 846, 848–49, 852, 853; Germain to Clinton, September 27, 1779, *DAR* 17:223.

23. The foregoing draws on Stephen Conway, *The British Isles and the War of American Independence* (New York, 2002), 45–107; Alan Valentine, *Lord George Germain* (Oxford, UK, 1962), 405–9; Eliga H. Gould, *The Persistence of Empire: British Political Culture in the Age of the American Revolution* (Chapel Hill, NC, 2000), 163–64, 168; Solomon Lutnick, *The American Revolution and the British Press, 1775–1783* (Columbia, MO, 1967), 146–47; Harry T. Dickinson, "The Impact of the War on British Politics," in Gray and Kamensky, *The Oxford Handbook of the American Revolution*, 357.

24. Richard B. Morris, *The Peacemakers: The Great Powers and American Independence* (New York, 1965), 78–87; Lutnick, *The American Revolution and the British Press*, 160–61; Jesse Norman, *Edmund Burke: The First Conservative* (New York, 2013), 100–101; Alan Valentine, *Lord North* (Norman, OK, 1967), 2:214–18; Christopher Hibbert, *King Mob: The Story of Lord George Gordon and the London Riots of 1780* (New York, 1958), 174.

25. Lee Kennett, *The French Forces in America, 1780–1783* (Westport, CT, 1977), 7–8; Thomas Fleming, *Washington's Secret War: The Hidden History of Valley Forge* (New York, 2005), 5–6; Vergennes to Lafayette, *LSLP* 3:129; Orville T. Murphy, "The View from Versailles: Charles Gravier Comte de Vergennes's Perceptions of the American Revolution," in *Diplomacy and Revolution: The Franco-American Alliance of 1778*, ed. Ronald Hoffman and Peter J. Albert (Charlottesville, VA, 1981), 140; GW to Chevalier de la Luzerne, February 15, 1780, *WW* 18:10.

26. Jeremy D. Popkin, *A New World Begins: The History of the French Revolution* (New York, 2019), 63–71; Paul W. Mapp, "The Revolutionary War and Europe's Great Powers," in Gray and Kamensky, *The Oxford Handbook of the American Revolution*, 317; William V. Wenger, *The Key to American Independence: Quantifying Foreign Assistance to the American Revolution* (El Segundo, CA, 2021), 60, 66, 73; Simon Schama, *Citizens: A Chronicle of the French Revolution* (New York, 1989), 61–62; William Doyle, *The Oxford History of the French Revolution* (New York, 1989), 66; Robert D. Harris, *Necker: Reform Statesman of the Ancien Regime* (Berkeley, CA, 1979), 118.

27. Munro Price, *Preserving the Monarchy: The Comte de Vergennes, 1774–1787* (Cambridge, UK, 1995), 51–52; Morris, *The Peacemakers*, 14, 52, 89–93; H. M. Scott, *British Foreign Policy in the Age of the American Revolution* (Oxford, UK, 1990), 313–14. Britain was indeed unwilling to end the war at the outset of 1780. Lord North, reflecting George III's outlook, said the "moment was not favorable." George III's backbone was stiffened by Necker's brash move toward ending the war. The British king thought it could only mean that there was "some very weighty reason [for France] to wish for peace." See Jeremy Black, *George III: America's Last King* (New Haven, CT, 2006), 239; and David Armitage, "George III and the Law of Nations," *William and Mary Quarterly* 79 (2022): 19.

28. Michael Roberts, *Splendid Isolation* (Reading, UK, 1970).

29. Lafayette to Jean Frédéric Maurepas, January 25, 1780, *LSLP* 2:344–45; Kennett, *The French Forces in America*, 8–10; Louis Gottschalk, *Lafayette and the Close of the American Revolution* (Chicago, 1942), 58–65.

30. Kennett, *The French Forces in America*, 9–14; Jonathan R. Dull, *The French Navy and American Independence: A Study of Arms and Diplomacy, 1774–1787* (Princeton, NJ, 1975), 187–88, 190; Gottschalk, *Lafayette and the Close of the American Revolution*, 65.

31. Gordon S. Wood, *The American Revolution: A History* (New York, 2002), 66; Thomas Paine, *Common Sense* (1776), *CWTP* 1:6, 29. Emphasis added to "*all* men."

32. Paine, *Common Sense*, *CWTP* 1:45; Wood, *The American Revolution*, 91; Gordon S. Wood, *The Radicalism of the American Revolution* (New York, 1992), 169, 179; Thomas Jefferson, First Inaugural Address, March 4, 1801, *PTJ* 33:148–52.

33. Merrill Jensen, *The American Revolution Within America* (New York, 1974), 3, 6, 9, 12, 32–33, 53. The quotation can be found on page 53.

34. Wood, *The American Revolution*, 65–69; Alexander Keyssar, *The Right to Vote: The Contested History of Democracy in the United States* (New York, 2000), 3–20; Jackson Turner Main, *The Upper Houses in Revolutionary America, 1763–1783* (Madison, WI, 1967), 94, 236–37; Jensen, *The American Revolution Within America*, 69, 100. The JA quote is in Jensen, page 69.

35. Main, *The Sovereign States*, 147–50.

36. Wood, *The Radicalism of the American Revolution*, 229–43; Alfred F. Young, *The Shoemaker and the Tea Party: Memory and the American Revolution* (Boston, 1999), 3–4.

37. John Ferling, *Jefferson and Hamilton: The Rivalry That Forged a Nation* (New York, 2013), 50–58; Gordon S. Wood, *Revolutionary Characters: What Made the Founders Different* (New York, 2006), 99; Joyce Appleby, *Liberalism and Republicanism in the Historical Imagination* (Cambridge, MA, 1992), 318.

38. For these two paragraphs, see Thomas Jefferson, *Notes on the State of Virginia*, ed. William Peden (Chapel Hill, NC, 1955), 137–38; Bernard Bailyn, *The Ideological Origins of the American Revolution* (Cambridge, MA, 1967), 235, 239; Gary B. Nash, *Race and Revolution* (Madison, WI, 1990), 9–10, 19; Nash, *The Forgotten Fifth: African Americans in the Age of Revolution* (Cambridge, MA, 2006), 12–13; AH to Jay, March 14, 1779, *PAH* 2:17–19. Not every Continental soldier who was appalled at seeing slavery up close was a convert to abolitionism. Some, in fact, eventually became slave owners. See John A. Ruddiman, "'Is This the Land of Liberty?': Continental Soldiers and Slavery in the Revolutionary South," *William and Mary Quarterly* 79 (2022): 283–314.

39. Nash, *The Forgotten Fifth*, 26–27; Todd Braisted, "The Black Pioneers and Others: The Military Role of Black Loyalists in the American War of Independence," in *Moving On: Black Loyalists in the Afro-American World*, ed. John W. Pulis (New York, 1999), 12–13; Alan Taylor, *The Internal Enemy: Slavery and War in Virginia, 1772–1832* (New York, 2013), 24; Judith L. Van Buskirk, *Generous Enemies: Patriots and Loyalists in Revolutionary New York* (Philadelphia, 2002), 135, 142; Robert G. Parkinson, *The Common Cause: Creating Race and Nation in the American Revolution* (Chapel Hill, NC, 2016), 453–54, 482; Sylvia R. Frey, *Water from the Rock: Black Resistance in the Revolutionary Age* (Princeton, NJ, 1991), 113–15; Douglas R. Egerton, *Death of Liberty: African Americans and Revolutionary America* (New York, 2009), 84–87; Cassandra Pybus, *Epic Journeys of Freedom: Runaway Slaves of the American Revolution and Their Global Quest for Liberty* (Boston, 2006), 40; Lund Washington to GW, December 3, 1775, *PGWR* 2:480; Peter Kolchin, *American Slavery, 1619–1877* (New York, 1993), 73; Billy G. Smith, "Runaway Slaves in the Mid-Atlantic Region During the Revolutionary Era," in *The Transforming Hand of Revolution: Reconsidering the American Revolution as a Social Movement*, ed. Ronald Hoffman and Peter J. Albert (Charlottesville, VA, 1995), 202, 208, 210–11.

40. Kolchin, *American Slavery*, 81; Taylor, *The Internal Enemy*, 30.

41. Taylor, *The Internal Enemy*, 40–41.

42. TJ, Observations on [Jean Nicolas] Démeunier's Manuscript, June 26, 1786, *PTJ* 10:58.

CHAPTER 11: INTO THE SOUTHERN VORTEX

1. Clinton to Germain, May 22, June 18, August 20, 1779, *DAR* 17, 129–30, 146, 188, 189; William Eden to Germain, June 11, 1779, ibid., 17:143–44; *AR*, 148; R. Arthur Bowler, "Logistics and Operations in the American Revolution," in *Reconsiderations on the Revolutionary War*, ed. Don Higginbotham (Westport, CT, 1978), 177; Richard Middleton, *Cornwallis: Soldier and Statesman in a Revolutionary World* (New Haven, CT, 2022), 39; William B. Willcox, *Portrait of a General: Sir Henry Clinton in the War of Independence* (New York, 1962), 86, 230, 281.

2. Germain to Clinton, March 8, 1778, August 28, September 27, 1779, *DAR* 15:61; 17:196, 224.

3. *AR*, 151–53; Clinton to Germain, September 30, November 17, 1779, *DAR* 17:230, 255.

4. Joseph Plumb Martin, *Private Yankee Doodle: Being a Narrative of Some of the Adventures, Dangers and Sufferings of a Revolutionary Soldier*, ed. George F. Scheer (New York, 1962), 169–70; NG to Moore Furman, January 4, 1780, *PNG* 5:230; NG to Jeremiah Wadsworth, January 5, 1780, ibid., 5:236; James Thomas Flexner, *George Washington in the American Revolution* (Boston, 1967), 354–56; Douglas Southall Freeman, *George Washington* (New York, 1948–1957), 5:143–52; *DGW* 3:342–52; GW to Lafayette, March 18, 1780, *PGWR* 25:83; Seanegan P. Sculley, *Contest for Liberty: Military Leadership in the Continental Army, 1775–1783* (Yardley, PA, 2019), 138.

5. Substance of a Conference with Anne-César de La Luzerne, September 16, 1779, *PGWR* 22:438–42, 442–44n; GW to Samuel Huntington, November 29, 1779, ibid., 23:482–83; Lincoln to GW, January 23 [–24], 1780, ibid., 24:235; GW to Friedrich Steuben, April 2, 1780, ibid., 25:288–89; Freeman, *George Washington*, 5:155.

6. GW to Steuben, February 8, 1780, *PGWR* 24:417.

7. John A. Tilley, *The British Navy and the American Revolution* (Columbia, SC, 1987), 173; Clinton to William Eden, December 11, 1779, *Facsimiles* 10, no. 1034.

8. David K. Wilson, *The Southern Strategy: Britain's Conquest of South Carolina and Georgia, 1775–1780* (Columbia, SC, 2005), 203–5; David B. Mattern, *Benjamin Lincoln and the American Revolution* (Columbia, SC, 1995), 88–94. See the correspondence between Lincoln and Commodore Whipple in *Original Papers Relating to the Siege of Charleston, 1780* (Charleston, SC, 1898), 17–33.

9. Mattern, *Benjamin Lincoln and the American Revolution*, 89, 93.

10. Clinton to Germain, May 13, 1780, *DAR* 18:87; Johann Ewald, *Diary of the American War: A Hessian Journal*, ed. Joseph P. Tustin (New Haven, CT, 1979), 235; *AR*, 163.

11. *AR*, 165–66, 169, 171, 177, 189; Clinton to Germain, May 13, 1780, *DAR* 18:87–88; Germain to Clinton, March 15, 1780, ibid., 18:60; Mattern, *Benjamin Lincoln and the American Revolution*, 105–7; John Knight, *War at Saber Point: Banastre Tarleton and the British Legion* (Yardley, PA, 2020), 87–90; Carl P. Borick, *A Gallant Defense: The Siege of Charleston, 1780* (Columbia, SC, 2003), 71–73, 96–108, 121–26, 130–34, 145–60, 204; Wilson, *The Southern Strategy*, 205, 226, 234, 238–39, 246–47; Middleton, *Cornwallis*, 53–56; Willcox, *Portrait of a General*, 305–13.

12. The text of the articles of capitulation can be found in Borick, *A Gallant Defense*, 247–50.

13. Clinton to Eden, May 12, 1780, *Facsimiles* 7, no. 726.

14. Troy Bickham, *Making Headlines: The American Revolution as Seen Through the British Press* (DeKalb, IL, 2009), 155; Stephen Conway, *The British Isles and the War of Independence* (New York, 2009), 304; Alan Valentine, *Lord North* (Norman, OK, 1967), 2:225–36; Jim Piecuch, *Three Peoples, One King: Loyalists, Indians, and Slaves in Revolutionary South Carolina, 1775–1782* (Columbia, SC, 2008), 181; John Pancake, *The Destructive War: The British Campaign in the Carolinas, 1780–1782* (Tuscaloosa, AL, 1985), 148.

15. *PH* 21:809, 811, 818, 821, 833–34, 838, 844, 891, 898.

16. James Simpson to Clinton, May 15, 1780, *DAR* 18:94–95; Robert Stansbury Lambert, *South Carolina Loyalists in the American Revolution* (Columbia, SC, 1987), 96.

17. Walter Edgar, *Partisans and Redcoats: The Southern Conflict That Turned the Tide of the American Revolution* (New York, 2001), 51; Knight, *War at Saber Point*, 58.

18. Knight, *War at Saber Point*, 1–8, 44–45, 88–90, 95–101; Robert D. Bass, *The Green Dragoon: The Lives of Banastre Tarleton and Mary Robinson* (Orangeburg, SC, 1973), 79–83; Thomas B. Allen and Todd W. Braisted, *The Loyalist Corps: Americans in the Service of the King* (Tacoma Park, MD, 2011), 27–28. For an alternative interpretation of the faceoff in the Waxhaws, see Jim Piecuch, *The Blood Be upon Your Head: Tarleton and the Myth of Buford's Massacre* (Charleston, SC, 2010), 23–40.

19. *AR*, 181–82.

20. Germain to Clinton, November 4, 1779, *DAR* 17:250–51; Willcox, *Portrait of a General*, 314–16. The Clinton quote on Cornwallis's unprofessionalism can be found in William B. Willcox, "The British Road to Yorktown: A Study in Divided Command," *American Historical Review* 52 (1946): 5. For a more charitable take on Cornwallis's response, see Middleton, *Cornwallis*, 52.

21. *AR*, 191n; Piers Mackesy, *The War for America, 1775–1783* (Cambridge, MA, 1965), 346; Clinton to Cornwallis, June 1, 1780, *CP* 1:57, 61.

22. Middleton, *Cornwallis*, 57–58.

23. *AR*, 175–76; Clinton, Instructions to Patrick Ferguson, May 22, 1780, *CP* 1:103–5; Ferguson to Cornwallis, June 6, 14, 1780, ibid., 1:102–3, 106–7; Nisbet Balfour to Cornwallis, June 12, 1780, ibid., 1:84; Alexander Innes to Cornwallis, June 8, 1780, ibid., 1:111; Archibald McArthur to Cornwallis, June 13, 1780, ibid., 1:132; Cornwallis to Clinton, June 30, 1780, ibid., 1:161–63; Cornwallis to Germain, August 20, 1780, *DAR* 18:145.

24. Balfour to Cornwallis, June 7, 12, 24, July 20, 1780, *CP* 1:79, 84, 239, 253; Francis Rawdon to Cornwallis, July 12, 1780, ibid., 1:200; Enclosure, George Turnbull to Rawdon, July 12, 1780, ibid., 1:201–2; Cornwallis to Marriot Arbuthnot, July 14, 1780, ibid., 1:166; Cornwallis to Clinton, August 6, 1780, ibid., 1:177; Edgar, *Partisans and Redcoats*, 58–83.

25. Cornwallis to Arbuthnot, June 29, 1780, *CP*, 1:159; editor's note, ibid., 1:149–50; Franklin Wickwire and Mary Wickwire, *Cornwallis and the War of Independence* (London, 1971), 427; Ian Saberton, "Midsummer 1780 in the Carolinas and Georgia—Events Predating the Battle of Camden," *Journal of the American Revolution*, July 15, 2019; Rachel N. Klein, "Frontier Planters and the American Revolution: The Carolina Backcountry, 1775–1782," in *An Uncivil War: The South Carolina Backcountry During the American Revolution*, ed. Ronald Hoffman, Thad W. Tate, and Peter J. Albert (Charlottesville, VA, 1985), 62–63, 78–79; Alan Taylor, *American Revolutions: A Continental History, 1750–1804* (New York, 2016), 223, 234; John Shy, *A People Numerous and Armed: Reflections on the Military Struggle for American Independence* (New York, 1976), 186, 205; Piecuch, *Three Peoples, One King*, 191; Edgar, *Partisans and Redcoats*, 62, 65.

26. Piers Mackesy, *Could the British Have Won the War of Independence?* (Worcester, MA, 1976), 10; Cornwallis to Germain, August 20, 1780, *CP* 2:7; John Buchanan,

The Road to Guilford Courthouse: The American Revolution in the Carolinas (New York, 1997), 116–21, 301; Stanley D. M. Carpenter, *Southern Gambit: Cornwallis and the British March to Yorktown* (Norman, OK, 2019), 103. On Thomas Sumter, see Robert Bass, *Gamecock: The Life and Campaigns of General Thomas Sumter* (New York, 1961). On Francis Marion, see John Oller, *The Swamp Fox: How Francis Marion Saved the American Revolution* (Boston, 2016); and Hugh Rankin, *Francis Marion: The Swamp Fox* (New York, 1973).

27. Russell F. Weigley, *The Partisan War: The South Carolina Campaign of 1780–1782* (Columbia, SC, 1970), 15, 17.

28. Middleton, *Cornwallis*, 66; Edgar, *Partisans and Redcoats*, 61–62; NG to Huntington, December 28, 1780, *PNG* 7:9.

29. Cornwallis to Clinton, August 6, 1780, *CP* 1:176.

30. GW to Johann Kalb, April 2, 4, 1780, *PGWR* 25:281–83; John Armstrong Jr. to Gates, June 6, 15, 1780, *LDC* 15:259, 319; Huntington to Gates, June 13, 1780, ibid., 15:312; Stephen R. Taaffe, *Washington's Revolutionary War Generals* (Norman, OK, 2019), 100.

31. Account of Otho Williams in *The Battle of Camden: A Documentary History*, ed. Jim Piecuch (Charleston, SC, 2006), 28–29; Account of Major Thomas Pinckney, ibid., 39. Also see Robert Orrison and Mark Wilcox, *All That Can Be Expected: The Battle of Camden and the British High Tide In the South, August 16, 1780* (El Dorado Hills, CA, 2023), 13–55; Gates to TJ, July 19, 22, August 3, 1780, *PTJ* 3:495–96, 501, 524–25; TJ to Gates, August 4, 1780, ibid., 3:526–27; Gates to Abner Nash, July 19, 1780, James Gregory and Thomas Dunnings, eds., *Horatio Gates Papers, 1726–1828* (Sanford, NC, n.d.), microfilm, reel 11; Paul David Nelson, *General Horatio Gates: A Biography* (Baton Rouge, LA, 1976), 219–22; Return of the Troops at Camden, August 13, 1780, *CP* 1:233.

32. Account of Sergeant William Seymour, *The Battle of Camden: A Documentary History*, 72.

33. Cornwallis to Clinton, August 10, 1780, *CP* 1:179. Many historians have argued that the manner in which Gates positioned his troops led to his downfall, though that is of course conjectural. See Jim Piecuch, "Repercussions of the Battle of Camden," *Journal of the American Revolution*, May 20, 2013.

34. Orrison and Wilcox, *All That Can Be Expected*, 55–59; Nelson, *General Horatio Gates*, 220–37; Middleton, *Cornwallis*, 63–66; Knight, *War at Saber Point*,

130–31; Carpenter, *Southern Gambit*, 104–16; Account of Gates, *The Battle of Camden: A Documentary History*, 20; Account of Lieutenant C. P. Bennet, ibid., 70; Account of Colonel John Christian Senf, ibid., 29; Account of Major Charles Magill, ibid., 44; Account of Guilford Dudley, ibid., 75; Account of William Gipson, ibid., 90; Account of Charles-Francois, Le Chevalier Du Buysson des Hays, ibid., 46; Account of Anonymous North Carolina Loyalist, ibid., 94; Account of Gates, ibid., 21.

35. Edgar, *Partisans and Redcoats*, 111–13; Knight, *War at Saber Point*, 134–35.

36. Bickham, *Making Headlines*, 153; *PH* 21:888–908. The quotes are in columns 896, 899, and 902.

37. For the foregoing paragraphs, see Eric Sterner, "Britain, Russia, and the Armed Neutrality of 1780," *Journal of the American Revolution*, October 20, 2022; Paul A. Gilje, "Ideology and Interest: Free Trade, the League of Armed Neutrality, and the American Revolution," Andrew J. O'Shaughnessy, John A. Ragosta, and Marie-Jeanne Rossignol, eds., *European Friends of the American Revolution* (Charlottesville, VA, 2023), 45–66; Christopher Lloyd, "Armed Forces and the Art of War," in *The New Cambridge Modern History: The American and French Revolutions, 1763–1793*, ed. A. Goodwin (Cambridge, UK, 1965), 182; Jan Willem Schulte Nordholt, *The Dutch Republic and American Independence* (Chapel Hill, NC, 1982), 19–21, 31–46, 149–52; H. M. Scott, *British Foreign Policy in the Age of the American Revolution* (Oxford, UK, 1990), 277–93, 300–307; John J. Meng, *The Comte de Vergennes: European Phases of His American Diplomacy, 1774–1780* (Washington, DC, 1932), 86; Jonathan R. Dull, *A Diplomatic History of the American Revolution* (New Haven, CT, 1985), 14, 20, 46, 97, 124–26; Andrew Jackson O'Shaughnessy, *An Empire Divided: The American Revolution and the British Caribbean* (Philadelphia, 2000), 216, 221; Orville T. Murphy, *Charles Gravier, Comte de Vergennes: French Diplomacy in the Age of Revolution, 1719–1787* (Albany, NY, 1982), 280–88; Isabel de Madariaga, *Britain, Russia, and the Armed Neutrality of 1780: Sir James Harris's Mission to St. Petersburg during the American Revolution* (New Haven, CT, 1962), 234, 269, 271, 282, 286–87, 302; Alan Valentine, *Lord North* (Norman, OK, 1967), 2:258–59; *PH* 21:1082.

38. *AR*, 186; Cornwallis to Clinton, August 6, 23, 1780, *CP* 1:176–77; 2:16.

39. Cornwallis to Clinton, August 23, 29, September 3, 22, 23, 1780, ibid., 2:16, 41, 43–44, 45; Cornwallis to Germain, September 19, 1780, ibid., 2:37.

40. Cornwallis to Balfour, October 3, 7, 1780, ibid., 2:106–7, 116; Banastre Tarleton, *A History of the Campaigns of 1780 and 1781 in the Southern Provinces of North America* (reprint, New York, 1968), 160.

41. Ferguson to Rawdon, n.d., *CP* 2:142–43; Ferguson to Cornwallis, August 29, 1780, ibid., 2:147; Ferguson, "Declaration," September 9, 1780, ibid., 2:150–52; editor's note, ibid., 2:27; Robert M. Dunkerly, ed., *The Battle of Kings Mountain: Eyewitness Accounts* (Charleston, SC, 2007), 136.

42. Balfour to Cornwallis, June 24, 27, July 12, 1780, *CP*, 1:237, 242, 249; Ferguson to Cornwallis, September 14, 19, 28, October 1, 6, ibid., 2:149, 154–55, 159, 162, 165; Ian Saberton, "George Hanger—His Adventures in the American Revolutionary War," *Journal of the American Revolution*, February 17, 2017; Buchanan, *The Road to Guilford Courthouse*, 229; Middleton, *Cornwallis*, 70–71; Ensign Robert Campbell's Account in Dunkerly, *The Battle of Kings Mountain*, 22.

43. See the following accounts: John Craig's Pension Application in Dunkerly, *The Battle of Kings Mountain*, 39; Statement of Silas McBee, ibid., 64; Isaac Shelby to Evan Shelby, ibid., 68; Thomas Young's Account, ibid., 92; Major Thomas Young's Narrative, ibid., 94; Colonel William Hill's Account, ibid., 50; John Spelts's Accounts, ibid., 84.

44. For detailed accounts of the engagement, see Hank Messick, *King's Mountain: The Epic of the Blue Ridge "Mountain Men" in the American Revolution* (Boston, 1976), 81–155; Wilma Dykeman, *With Fire and Sword: The Battle of Kings Mountain, 1780* (Washington, DC, 1978), 58–76; Christopher Ward, *The War of the Revolution* (New York, 1952), 2:739–45; W. J. Wood, *Battles of the Revolutionary War, 1775–1781* (Chapel Hill, NC, 1990), 196–202; Michael Stephenson, *Patriot Battles: How the War of Independence Was Fought* (New York, 2007), 323–31; Holger Hoock, *Scars of Independence: America's Violent Birth* (New York, 2017), 320–21; Carpenter, *Southern Gambit*, 124–28.

45. Rawdon to Clinton, October 28, 1780, *CP* 2:58; *AR*, 226–28.

CHAPTER 12: THE WAR'S OUTCOME HANGS IN THE BALANCE

1. Editor's note, *PGWR* 28:237.

2. Lee Kennett, *The French Forces in America, 1780–1783* (Westport, CT, 1977), 3–33; Larrie D. Ferreiro, *Brothers at Arms: American Independence and the Men of France and Spain Who Saved It* (New York, 2016), 218–19; Jonathan R. Dull, *The*

French Navy and American Independence: A Study of Arms and Diplomacy, 1774–1787 (Princeton, NJ, 1975), 190; Vergennes to Lafayette, March 5, 1780, *PGWR* 25:501–2n.

3. *AR*, 198.

4. Clinton to Arbuthnot, July 15, 22, 30, 1780, ibid., 443–45, 447; Arbuthnot to Clinton, July 16, 18, 23, 27, 1780, ibid., 444–46; Captain Henry Savage to Clinton, July 30, 1780, ibid., 446–47; Clinton to Eden, August 18, 1780, *Facsimiles* 7, no. 730; William B. Willcox, *Portrait of a General: Sir Henry Clinton in the War of Independence* (New York, 1962), 325–30; *PGWR* 27:412n; GW to Lafayette, July 27, 1780, ibid., 27:324; GW to Huntington, August 3, 1780, ibid., 27:416.

5. Louis-François-Bertrand du Pont d'Aubevoye, comte de Lauberdière, *The Road to Yorktown: The French Campaigns in the American Revolution, 1780–1783*, ed. Norman Desmarais (El Dorado Hills, CA, 2020), 23; Jean-Baptiste-Donatien de Vimeur, Comte de Rochambeau, *Memoirs of the Marshal Count de Rochambeau* (reprint, New York, 1971), 9; Ludwig von Closen, *The Revolutionary Journal of Baron Ludwig von Closen, 1780–1783*, ed. Evelyn M. Acomb (Chapel Hill, NC, 1958), 35.

6. Arnold Whitridge, *Rochambeau* (New York, 1965), 4–64, 87; Kennett, *The French Forces in America*, 12.

7. GW, Memorandum for Concerting a Plan of Operations, July 15, 1780, *WW* 19:174–76; GW to Lafayette, July 15, 16, 1780, *PGWR* 27:134–35, 150–51; Lafayette to GW, July 29, 1780, ibid., 27:347–50; Rochambeau to La Luzerne, August 14, 1780, *LSLP* 3:141; Lafayette to Comte de Rochambeau and Chevalier de Ternay, August 9, 1780, ibid., 3:131–36; Lafayette to the Prince de Poix, September 3, 1780, ibid., 3:165; Rochambeau to Lafayette, August 27, 1780, ibid., 3:155.

8. GW to Huntington, August 20, 1780, *PGWR* 27:563–70.

9. Stephen Brumwell, *Turncoat: Benedict Arnold and the Crisis of American Liberty* (New Haven, CT, 2018), 119–235; Jack Kelly, *God Save Benedict Arnold: The True Story of America's Most Hated Man* (New York, 2023), 250–51, 264–68. See also editor's note, *PGWR* 28:337–56.

10. Clinton to Sir George Brydges (Admiral Rodney), September 18, 1780, in Godfrey B. Mundy, ed., *The Life and Correspondence of the Late Admiral Lord Rodney* (London, 1830), 1:397–400; William B. Willcox, "Rhode Island in British Strategy, 1780–1781," *Journal of Modern History* 17 (1945): 313–14.

11. Summary of the Hartford Conference, September 22, 1780, *LSLP* 3:175–78; editor's note, "The Hartford Conference," *PGWR* 28:235–48.

12. Brumwell, *Turncoat*, 256–94; Douglas Southall Freeman, *George Washington* (New York, 1948–1957), 5:196–222; editor's note, "Major John André's Capture and Execution," *PGWR* 28:255–324.

13. Rawdon to Clinton, October 28, 31, 1780, *CP* 2:57, 60–61; Rawdon to Alexander Leslie, October 31, 1780, ibid., 2:59–60; Clinton to Cornwallis, September 20, 1780, ibid., 2:49; Clinton to Leslie, n.d., ibid., 2:50; Cornwallis to Clinton, December 3, 1780, ibid., 2:24; *AR*, 210, 221, 225, 231.

14. Clinton to Benedict Arnold, December 14, 1780, *AR*, 482–83; Clinton to Germain, December 16, 1780, *DAR* 18:257.

15. NG to GW, October 31, November 3, 1780, *PNG* 6:447–48, 462; NG to Huntington, October 27, 1780, ibid., 6:436; NG to Thomas Sim Lee, November 10, 1780, ibid., 6:473–74; NG to TJ, November 20, 1780, ibid., 6:491–93; Henry Lee to NG, October 25, 1780, ibid., 6:430–31; NG to Alexander McDougall, October 30, 1780, ibid., 6:446; editor's notes, ibid., 5:321n; 6:xvii, 427n, 431, 529.

16. Cornwallis to Clinton, December 4, 1780, January 8, 1781, *CP* 3:27, 35; NG to Edward Stevens, December 1, 1780, *PNG* 6:513; NG to Edward Carrington, December 4, 1780, ibid., 6:516–17; NG to North Carolina Board of War, December 7, 18, 1780, ibid., 6:548, 598; NG to Friedrich Steuben, November 27/28, 1780, ibid., 6:506–7; NG to GW, December 7, 1780, ibid., 6:543; NG to Thomas Sumter, December 12, 1780, January 8, 1781, ibid., 6:563–64; 7:74–15; NG to Francis Marion, December 4, 1780, ibid., 6:519–20; Steuben to NG, December 15, 24, 1780, ibid., 6:584, 609; NG to GW, December 7, 1780, ibid., 6:543; NG to Catherine Greene, December 7, 1780, ibid., 6:542; NG to La Luzerne, December 29, 1780, ibid., 7:19; editor's note, ibid., 6:587n; Theodore Thayer, *Nathanael Greene: Strategist of the American Revolution* (New York, 1960), 290–91; *AR*, 245; Franklin Wickwire and Mary Wickwire, *Cornwallis and the War of Independence* (London, 1971), 274; Richard Middleton, *Cornwallis: Soldier and Statesman in a Revolutionary World* (New Haven, CT, 2022), 75; Stanley D. M. Carpenter, *Southern Gambit: Cornwallis and the British March to Yorktown* (Norman, OK, 2019), 136–37; editor's note, *PNG* 7:200n.

17. For the foregoing, see Don Higginbotham, *Daniel Morgan: Revolutionary Rifleman* (Chapel Hill, NC, 1961); and Lawrence E. Babits, *A Devil of a Whipping: The Battle of Cowpens* (Chapel Hill, NC, 1998). The "squinney well" quote can be found in

Babits, page 87. For an intriguing debate among historians on the engagement, see Wayne Lynch and Jim Piecuch, "Debating Cowpens: How Could Tarleton Lose?" *Journal of the American Revolution*, July 24, 2013.

18. Daniel Morgan to NG, January 23, 1781, *PNG* 7:178, 179n; Cornwallis to Rawdon, January 25, 1781, *CP* 3:252; Cornwallis to Germain, March 17, 1781, ibid., 4:12; editor's note, ibid., 4:3; Wickwire and Wickwire, *Cornwallis and the War of Independence*, 277–83.

19. Cornwallis to Germain, March 17, 1781, *CP* 4:15.

20. Henry Lee to NG, February 25, 1781, *PNG* 7:347–48; Henry Lee, *Memoirs of the War in the Southern Department of the United States* (Philadelphia, 1812), 1:308–11; John Buchanan, *The Road to Guilford Courthouse: The American Revolution in the Carolinas* (New York, 1997), 364.

21. NG to Catherine Greene, March 18, 1781, *PNG* 7:446; NG to Huntington, March 16, 1781, ibid., 7:433–35; editor's note, ibid., 7:436–41n; Cornwallis to Germain, March 17, 1781, *CP* 4:19; Buchanan, *The Road to Guilford Courthouse*, 372–83; Carpenter, *Southern Gambit*, 198–204; Christopher Ward, *The War of the Revolution* (New York, 1952), 2:784–94; Lawrence E. Babits and Joshua B. Howard, *Long, Obstinate, and Bloody: The Battle of Guilford Courthouse* (Chapel Hill, NC, 2009). Colonel Lee's quote can be found in Buchanan, page 381.

22. Return of Casualties in the Battle of Guilford, March 15, 1781, *CP* 4:64–65; Middleton, *Cornwallis*, 83.

23. Cornwallis to Clinton, April 10, 1781, ibid., 4:110; Wickwire and Wickwire, *Cornwallis and the War of Independence*, 314–16.

24. Arnold to Clinton, January 21, 1781, *CP* 5:76–80; Major Edward Brabazon, Return of Captured Arms and Ammunition . . . Taken at Richmond and Westham, n.d., ibid., 5:81–83; Michael Cecere, *The Invasion of Virginia, 1781* (Yardley, PA, 2017), 11–30.

25. Brumwell, *Turncoat*, 314–15; GW to TJ, February 26, 1781, *WW* 21:191; GW to Rochambeau and Ternay, December 15, 1780, *PGWR* 29:527–30; GW, Instructions, February 20, 1781, *LSLP* 3:334–36; GW to Steuben, February 20, 1781, ibid., 3:336n, 342n.

26. GW to Rochambeau, February 15, 19, 1781, *WW* 21:229–32, 246–48; GW to the Officer Commanding the French Squadron in Chesapeake Bay, February 20, 1781, ibid., 21:259–61; Nathaniel Philbrick, *In the Hurricane's Eye: The Genius of George*

Washington and the Victory at Yorktown (New York, 2018), 55–72; Ferreiro, *Brothers at Arms*, 226–31; Kennett, *The French Forces in America*, 94–101.

27. For these two paragraphs, see Richard Henry Lee to JA, September 18, 1780, *PJA* 10:185; TJ to Virginia Delegates to Congress, October 27, 1780, *PTJ* 4:77; GW to Huntington, December 15, 1780, *PGWR* 29:522; GW to BF, December 20, 1780, ibid., 29:572; GW to Edmund Randolph, November 7, 1780, ibid., 29:144; GW to Arthur Lee, November 20, 1780, ibid., 29:301; GW to Sullivan, November 20, 1780, ibid., 29:306; GW to John Cadwalader, October 5, 1780, ibid., 28:468–69; GW to Joseph Reed, May 28, 1780, ibid., 26:220–24; Burke to Hamilton, April 1, 1790, *PAH* 6:336.

28. Editor's note, "The Aborted Attack on the Northern Approaches to New York City," *PGWR* 29:159–79; GW to Gouverneur Morris, December 10, 1780, ibid., 29:477.

29. GW to Wayne, January 3, 1781, ibid., 21:55: Committee on the Pennsylvania Mutiny to Reed, January 8, 1781, *LDC* 16:559–60; Committee on the Pennsylvania Mutiny Draft Proclamation, January 10, 1781, ibid., 16:585; Committee on the Pennsylvania Mutiny to GW, January 10, 13, 15, 1781, ibid., 16:587, 592, 600; *AR*, 240–41; Carl Van Doren, *Mutiny in January* (New York, 1947), 85–86.

30. GW to Howe, January 22, 1781, *WW* 21:128–9; James Thacher, *A Military Journal During the American Revolutionary War, from 1775–1783*, ed. Thomas Bulch (reprint, New York, 1969), 251–53; Charles E. Bennett and Donald R. Lennon, *A Quest for Glory: Major General Robert Howe and the American Revolution* (Chapel Hill, NC, 1991), 133–35.

31. James Lovell to JA, January 2, 1781, *LDC* 16:537; Elbridge Gerry, November 30, 1780, ibid., 16:406; Thomas McKean to JA, December 18, 1780, ibid., 16:459; Sullivan to GW, January 29, 1781, ibid., 16:642; Paine to Blair McClenaghan, May [?], 1780, *CWTP* 2:1184–85; Paine to Reed, June 4, 1780, ibid., 2:1186–88; GW to Esther De Berdt Reed, July 14, August 10, 1780, *PGWR* 27:120–21, 482; *JCC* 18:1080.

32. GW to John Laurens, January 15, 1781, *WW* 21:105–10.

33. Dull, *The French Navy and American Independence*, 169–74, 178–79.

34. Samuel Flagg Bemis, *The Diplomacy of the American Revolution* (New York, 1935), 105–6.

35. Murphy, *Charles Gravier, Comte de Vergennes*, 324–25; William Stinchcombe, *The American Revolution and the French Alliance* (Syracuse, NY, 1969), 88; Richard B.

Morris, *The Peacemakers: The Great Powers and American Independence* (New York, 1965), 93; Munro Price, *Preserving the Monarchy: The Comte de Vergennes, 1774–1787* (Cambridge, UK, 1995), 52; H. M. Scott, *British Foreign Policy in the Age of the American Revolution* (Oxford, UK, 1990), 249–51, 313–14.

36. For these two paragraphs, see Orville T. Murphy, *Charles Gravier, Comte de Vergennes: French Diplomacy in the Age of Revolution, 1719–1787* (Albany, NY, 1982), 330–31; Dull, *The French Navy and American Independence*, 197–98; Price, *Preserving the Monarchy*, 52, 62.

37. Bemis, *The Diplomacy of the American Revolution*, 181–83; Murphy, *Charles Gravier, Comte de Vergennes*, 331; Jonathan R. Dull, *A Diplomatic History of the American Revolution* (New Haven, CT, 1985), 130–31; Isabel de Madariaga, *Britain, Russia, and the Armed Neutrality of 1780: Sir James Harris's Mission to St. Petersburg During the American Revolution* (New Haven, CT, 1962), 266, 283, 285; Laurent Berénger to JA, June 5, 1781, *PJA* 11:352; JA to Berénger, June 8, 1781, ibid., 11:363; Jonathan Singerton, *The American Revolution and the Habsburg Monarchy* (Charlottesville, VA, 2022), 95, 100, 120–35.

38. Austro-Russian Proposal for Anglo-American Peace Negotiations, July 11, 1781, *PJA* 11:408–10; JA to President of Congress, July 11, 14, 15, 1781, ibid., 11:410–11, 318, 419–20; Morris, *The Peacemakers*, 173–90.

39. JA to Vergennes, July 7, 13, 16, 18, 19, 21, 1781, *PJA* 11:405, 413–16, 420–22, 424–25, 425–29, 431–33; JA, Memorandum, July 7, 1781, ibid., 11:405–6; Vergennes to JA, July 18, 1781, ibid., 11:423–24. See also John Ferling, "John Adams, Diplomat," *William and Mary Quarterly* 51 (1994): 227–52.

40. Morris, *The Peacemakers*, 209–10. JA's quotes can be found on pages 209–10.

41. BF to Samuel Cooper, May 15, 1781, *PBF* 35:68; French Loan Certificate, ibid., 35:71–72; editor's note, ibid., 35:28n; JA to BF May 8, 1781, ibid., 35:43; E. James Ferguson, *The Power of the Purse: A History of American Public Finance, 1776–1790* (Chapel Hill, NC, 1961), 110–11).

42. On Spanish interests, see Thomas E. Chávez, *Spain and the Independence of the United States: An Intrinsic Gift* (Albuquerque, NM, 2002), 137–65; Gabriel Paquette and Gonzalo M. Quintero Saravia, "Introduction: Spain and the American Revolution," in *Spain and the American Revolution: New Approaches and Perspectives*, ed. Gabriel Paquette and Gonzalo M. Quintero Saravia (Charlottesville, VA, 2020), 24–25; Larrie D. Ferreiro, "The Rise and Fall of the Spanish-French Bourbon Armada, from Toulon to Pensacola to Trafalgar," ibid., 71–72; Agustín

Guimerá Ravina and José María Blanco Núñez, "Spanish Naval Operations," in *The American Revolution: A World War*, ed. Daniel K. Allison and Larrie D. Ferreiro (Washington, DC, 2018), 79; Dull, *The French Navy and American Independence*, 232–36.

43. North's comment can be found in Piers Mackesy, *The War for America, 1775–1783* (Cambridge, MA, 1965), 385.

CHAPTER 13: ON THE KNIFE'S EDGE

1. Clinton to William Phillips, March 10, April 26–30, 1781, *AR*, 496–97, 515–16; Germain to Clinton, January 3, April 4, 1781, *DAR* 20:30, 99.

2. Germain to Clinton, January 3, 1781, *DAR* 20, 29–30. Emphasis added.

3. Germain to Clinton, January 3, February 7, March 7, 1781, ibid., 20:29–30, 56, 76; Germain to Cornwallis, March 7, 1781, ibid., 20:79; Troy Bickham, *Making Headlines: The American Revolution as Seen Through the British Press* (DeKalb, IL, 2009), 154–55. Emphasis added.

4. Orville T. Murphy, *Charles Gravier, Comte de Vergennes: French Diplomacy in the Age of Revolution, 1719–1787* (Albany, NY, 1982), 312–32; Larrie D. Ferreiro, *Brothers at Arms: American Independence and the Men of France and Spain Who Saved It* (New York, 2016), 235–36; E. James Ferguson, *The Power of the Purse: A History of American Public Finance, 1776–1790* (Chapel Hill, NC, 1961), 126–27.

5. William C. Stinchcombe, *The American Revolution and the French Alliance* (Syracuse, NY, 1969), 155–56.

6. BF to Huntington, August 9, 1780, *PBF* 33:162–63; editor's note, ibid., 33:liii; Huntington to JA, June 20, 1781, *PJA* 11:379–80; Joint Commission to Negotiate a Peace Treaty, June 15, 1781, ibid., 11:371–74; editor's note, ibid., 8:18–19; William Emmett O'Donnell, *The Chevalier de la Luzerne: French Minister to the United States, 1779–1784* (Bruges, Belgium, 1938), 43; Stinchcombe, *The American Revolution and the French Alliance*, 77, 83, 156.

7. These paragraphs draw on GW to John Laurens, January 15, 1781, *WW* 21:105; Thomas Rodney to Caesar Rodney, June 15, 1781, *LDC* 17:325; Huntington to the States, June 1, 1781, ibid., 17:283–85; John Witherspoon Speech to Congress, June 9 [?], 1781, ibid., 17:307; John Sullivan to GW, May 28, 1781, ibid., 17:274; editor's note, ibid., 17:311; New Hampshire Delegates to Meshech Weare, May 29, 1781, ibid., 17:279; Joint Commission to Accept the Mediation of Russia and Austria,

June 15, 1781, *PJA* 11:37–71; Joint Commission to Negotiate a Peace Treaty, June 15, 1781, ibid., 11:371–74; Instructions to the Joint Commission to Negotiate a Peace Treaty, June 15, 1781, ibid., 11:374–76; editor's note, ibid., 11:368–70; O'Donnell, *The Chevalier de la Luzerne*, 56–65; Stinchcombe, *The American Revolution and the French Alliance*, 157–63; James H. Hutson, *John Adams and the Diplomacy of the American Revolution* (Lexington, KY, 1980), 68–74, 99; John Ferling, "John Adams, Diplomat," *William and Mary Quarterly* 51 (1994): 227–52; Richard B. Morris, *The Peacemakers: The Great Powers and American Independence* (New York, 1965), 210–17. Congress's territorial wishes remained the same as in its instructions of 1779, which can be found in *ADA* 4:181–83.

8. Stinchcombe, *The American Revolution and the French Alliance*, 162, 171, 176; Lovell to Abigail Adams, June 26, July 13, 1781, *LDC* 17:352, 406; Lovell to Elbridge Gerry, July 13, 1781, ibid., 17:408; Lovell to JA, July 21, 1781, ibid., 424; Abigail Adams to Lovell, June 30, 1781, *AFC* 4:165; JA to BF, August 25, 1781, *PJA* 11:469. On JA's possible nervous breakdown, see John Ferling, *John Adams: A Life* (reprint, New York, 2010), 237.

9. Jonathan R. Dull, *The French Navy and American Independence: A Study of Arms and Diplomacy, 1774–1787* (Princeton, NJ, 1975), 216–21.

10. Charles Lee Lewis, *Admiral de Grasse and American Independence* (Annapolis, MD, 1945), 95–101, 112; Olivier Chaline, "Season, Winds, and the Sea: The Improbable Route of de Grasse to the Chesapeake," in *European Friends of the American Revolution*, ed. Andrew J. O'Shaughnessy, John A. Ragosta, and Marie-Jeanne Rossignol (Charlottesville, VA, 2023), 103–5; Ferreiro, *Brothers at Arms*, 236, 256–58; Dull, *The French Navy and American Independence*, 216–24, 238–40.

11. Lee Kennett, *The French Forces in America, 1780–1783* (Westport, CT, 1977), 64–91; Louis-François-Bertrand du Pont d'Aubevoye, comte de Lauberdière, *The Road to Yorktown: The French Campaigns in the American Revolution, 1780–1783*, ed. Norman Desmarais (El Dorado Hills, CA, 2020), 85–86 .

12. Kennett, *The French Forces in America*, 102–3; GW to Knox, February 10, 1781, *WW* 21:210; GW to Rochambeau, March 21, April 7, 10, 30, 1781, ibid., 21:351, 426–27, 441–42; 22:12.

13. Thomas E. Chávez, *Spain and the Independence of the United States: An Intrinsic Gift* (Albuquerque, NM, 2002), 176–97; Kathleen DuVal, *Independence Lost: Lives on the Edge of the American Revolution* (New York, 2015), 188–218; Campbell to Germain, May 7, 12, 1781, *DAR* 20:136–37, 139.

14. Chávez, *Spain and the Independence of the United States*, 146–47; Dull, *The French Navy and American Independence*, 232–36; Ferreiro, *Brothers at Arms*, 286–87.

15. Lafayette to Vergennes, October 4, 1780, *LSLP* 3:188–90; editor's note, ibid., 3:192n, 193n.

16. Ferreiro, *Brothers at Arms*, 234–36. On Colonel Laurens's mission to France, see John Ferling, *Apostles of Revolution: Jefferson, Paine, Monroe, and the Struggle Against the Old Order in America and Europe* (New York, 2018), 119–21.

17. Lauberdière, *The Road to Yorktown*, 70, 256.

18. On the Wethersfield conference, see Baron Ludwig von Closen, *The Revolutionary Journal of Baron Ludwig von Closen, 1780–1783*, ed. Evelyn Acomb (Chapel Hill, NC, 1958), 86; Lauberdière, *The Road to Yorktown*, 79; Claude Blanchard, *The Journal of Claude Blanchard*, ed. Thomas Balch (Albany, NY, 1876), 104; *DGW* 3:369–70; Conference with Rochambeau, May 23, 1781, *WW* 22:105–7; GW to NG, June 1, 1781, *PNG* 8:336; Edward Lengel, *General George Washington* (New York, 2005), 331–32; James Thomas Flexner, *George Washington in the American Revolution* (Boston, 1967), 429–30; Douglas Southall Freeman, *George Washington* (New York, 1948–1957), 5:284–90; Ron Chernow, *Washington: A Life* (New York, 2010), 401–2.

19. Ferreiro, *Brothers at Arms*, 238–39. Emphasis added.

20. Kennett, *The French Forces in America*, 108; GW to Rochambeau, June 13, 1781, *WW* 22:208–9.

21. Kennett, *French Forces in America*, 106–12, 114–17; Christopher Ward, *The War of the Revolution* (New York, 1952), 2:881; Itinerary of the Marches of the French Army from Providence to the Camp at Philipsburg, 1781, in *The American Campaigns of Rochambeau's Army, 1780, 1781, 1782, 1783*, ed. Howard C. Rice Jr. and Anne S. K. Brown (Princeton, NJ, 1972), 2:21–107; *DGW* 3:369, 376.

22. Cornwallis to Clinton, January 18, April 10, 1781, *CP* 3:35–36; 4:109–10.

23. *AR*, 306.

24. For these two paragraphs, see ibid., 235, 290; Cornwallis to Clinton, April 10, 1781, *CP* 4:111; Clinton to Germain, April 23–May 1, 1781, *DAR* 20:114; Opinions of

General Sir Henry Clinton on Operations in the Chesapeake, April 26, 1781, ibid., 20:120–22.

25. Clinton to Cornwallis, April 30, 1781, *DAR* 20:129.

26. Cornwallis to Balfour, April 30, 1781, *CP* 4:174.

27. Cornwallis to Clinton, April 23, 1781, ibid., 4:112; Cornwallis to Germain, April 18, 23, 1781, ibid., 4:106, 108.

28. Cornwallis to Clinton, May 20, 1781, ibid., 5:88; Cornwallis to Balfour, April 5, 6, 21, 24, 1781, ibid., 4:43, 44, 121–23.

29. Cornwallis to Germain, January 18, March 17, 1781, ibid., 3:47; 4:11–20; Earl Cornwallis, *An Answer to That Part of the Narrative of Sir Henry Clinton, Which Relates to the Conduct of Lieutenant-General Earl Cornwallis*, in *The Campaign in Virginia: An Exact Reprint of Six Rare Pamphlets on the Clinton-Cornwallis Controversy*, ed. Benjamin F. Stevens (London, 1888), 68–70.

30. Hugh F. Rankin, "Charles Lord Cornwallis: Study in Frustration," in *George Washington's Opponents: British Generals and Admirals in the American Revolution*, ed. George Athan Billias (New York, 1969), 193–232. Also see Ian Saberton, "The Decision That Lost Britain the War: An Enigma Now Resolved," *Journal of the American Revolution*, January 8, 2019.

31. NG to GW, March 18, 29, 1781, *PNG* 7:452, 481; NG to TJ, March 27, 1781, ibid., 7:741–42; NG to Lafayette, March 29, 1781, ibid., 7:748; NG to Abner Nash, May 2, 1781, ibid., 8:190; NG to Huntington, April 27, 1781, ibid., 8:157; NG to Reed, August 6, 1781, ibid., 9:135; NG to Chevalier Anne-Cesar de la Luzerne, April 28, 1781, ibid., 8:168; Balfour to Cornwallis, April 20, May 21, 1781, *CP* 4:171–72; 5:276–77; Balfour to James Wright, July 20, 1781, Historical Manuscripts Commission, *Report on American Manuscripts in the Royal Institution of Great Britain* (London, 1904–1909), 2:303; John Buchanan, *The Road to Charleston: Nathanael Greene and the American Revolution* (Charlottesville, VA, 2019), 138–64.

32. *AR*, 284, 288, 296–97, 300–301, 310–12; Germain to Clinton, November 9, 1780, March 7, May 2, 1781, *DAR* 18:224; 20:76, 132; Clinton to Germain, July 18, August 9, 1781, ibid., 20:193, 214.

33. Clinton to Cornwallis, June 8, 11, 1781, *CP* 5:124, 96; Roger Kaplan, "The Hidden War: British Intelligence Operations During the American Revolution," *William and Mary Quarterly* 47 (1990): 133; *AR*, 304.

CHAPTER 14: THE DECISIVE ALLIED VICTORY IN THE AMERICAN THEATER

1. *DGW* 3:397, 404–5; Conference at Dobbs Ferry, July 19, 1781, *WW* 22:396–97; GW to William Heath, August 19, 1781, ibid., 23:20–33; GW to Robert Morris, August 2, 1781, ibid., 22:450; GW to Samuel Miles, August 27, 1781, ibid., 23:54–55; Jerome Greene, *The Guns of Independence: The Siege of Yorktown, 1781* (New York, 2005), 18.

2. Arnold to Cornwallis, May 12, 16, 1781, *CP* 4:152, 153; Cornwallis to Clinton, May 20, 26, 27, 1781, ibid., 5:87–91; Phillips to Clinton, April 3, 4, 16, 1781, ibid., 5:26, 48; Substance of Conversations Between Clinton and Phillips, April 11, 1781, ibid., 5:56; Clinton to Phillips, March 10, 1781, *DAR* 20:84; Extracts from Information Given to the Commander in Chief, Respecting the Posts in the Chesapeake, ND, in Frederick Mackenzie, *Diary of Frederick Mackenzie, Giving a Daily Narrative of His Military Service as an Officer of the Regiment of Royal Welsh Fusiliers During the Years 1775–1781* (reprint, New York, 1968), 2:457.

3. Lafayette to La Luzerne, May 22, 1781, *LSLP* 4:120; Lafayette to the Vicomte de Noailles, May 22, 1781, ibid., 4:122–23; Lafayette to GW, May 8, 24, 1781, ibid., 4:88, 130–31; James Thacher, *A Military Journal During the American Revolutionary War, from 1775 to 1783*, ed. Thomas Bulch (reprint, New York, 1969), 300; Michael Cecere, *The Invasion of Virginia, 1781* (Yardley, PA, 2017), 22–23, 103–14, 122; Michael Kranish, *Flight from Monticello: Thomas Jefferson at War* (New York, 2010), 283–86; Dumas Malone, *Jefferson and His Time* (Boston, 1948–1981), 1:355–57; Cornwallis to Phillips, April 10, 1781, *CP* 4:114–15; Cornwallis to Clinton, June 30, July 24, 1781, ibid., 5:104, 105–7; 6:12. For the provenance of Cornwallis's alleged "the boy cannot escape me" remark, see Louis Gottschalk, *Lafayette and the Close of the American Revolution* (Chicago, 1942), 431–32. Gottschalk demonstrates that the quotation first appeared in Lafayette's memoirs.

4. Clinton to Cornwallis, May 29 and June 1, July 11, 1781, *CP* 5:118–19; Thomas Graves to Cornwallis, July 12, 1781, ibid., 5:145–46.

5. Clinton to Cornwallis, June 11, 1781, ibid., 5:96; Cornwallis to Clinton, July 8, 1781, ibid., 5:116.

6. Clinton to Cornwallis, July 8, 11, 1781, *DAR* 20:181, 185; Germain to Clinton, May 2, August 2, 1781, ibid., 20:132, 207; Richard Middleton, *Cornwallis: Soldier and Statesman in a Revolutionary World* (New Haven, CT, 2022), 95.

7. Lafayette to Thomas Nelson, July 1, 1781, *LSLP* 4:228; Lafayette to La Luzerne, June 16, 1781, ibid., 4:186.

8. Clinton to Cornwallis, June 8, 11, 19, July 8, 1781, *CP* 5:96, 124, 128, 135, 142; Lee Kennett, *The French Forces in America, 1780–1783* (Westport, CT, 1977), 107; Roger Kaplan, "The Hidden War: British Intelligence Operations During the American Revolution," *William and Mary Quarterly* 47 (1990): 133; Germain to Clinton, April 4, July 7, August 2, 1781, *DAR* 20:99, 175, 206.

9. For these two paragraphs, see Clinton to Cornwallis, June 11, 15, 19, July 11, 15, 1781, *CP* 5:96, 98, 136, 143; 6:20; Cornwallis to Clinton, July 24, August 16, 22, 1781, ibid., 6:15, 24, 27–28; Clinton to Germain, April 5–20, May 18, June 9–13, July 3, 13, 15, 18, 1781, *DAR* 20:104, 146, 156, 170, 186–88, 190, 193; Lafayette to NG, June 20, 21, 1781, *LSLP* 4:198, 203; Clinton to Charles Stuart, October 12, 1781, in Mrs. E. Stuart Wortley, ed., *A Prime Minister and His Son: From the Correspondence of the 3d Earl of Bute and of Lt.-General the Hon. Sir Charles Stuart* (London, 1925), 172; William Smith to Stuart, November 3, 1781, ibid., 173; Thomas B. Allen and Todd W. Braisted, *The Loyalist Corps: Americans in the Service of the King* (Tacoma Park, MD, 2011), 70; *Diary of Frederick Mackenzie*, 2:598–99; Clinton to Rodney, June 28, 1781, *AR*, 533; William B. Willcox, *Portrait of a General: Sir Henry Clinton in the War of Independence* (New York, 1962), 411.

10. Mackenzie, *Diary of Frederick Mackenzie*, 2:581–82, 597–98, 602; Intelligence Report to Clinton, June 29, 1781, vol. 161, SHCP (WLCL); Clinton to Germain, August 20, September 4, 1781, *DAR* 20:217, 221–22; Clinton to Graves, July 6, 1781, *AR*, 539; Graves to Clinton, July 9, 1781, ibid., 542–43; ibid., 320–28; Kaplan, "The Hidden War," 134; John A. Tilley, *The British Navy and the American Revolution* (Columbia, SC, 1987), 244; David Syrett, *The Royal Navy in American Waters, 1775–1783* (Brookfield, VT, 1989), 184–85; William B. Willcox, "Arbuthnot, Gambier, and Graves: 'Old Women' of the Navy," in *George Washington's Opponents: British Generals and Admirals in the American Revolution*, ed. George Athan Billias (New York, 1969), 276–79.

11. Charles Lee Lewis, *Admiral de Grasse and American Independence* (Annapolis, MD, 1945), 119–25.

12. Lafayette to La Luzerne, March 8, April 10, 22, May 9, 22, June 16, 1781, *LSLP* 3:384; 4:23, 55, 89, 121, 186–87; Kennett, *The French Forces in America*, 108–9; William Emmett O'Donnell, *The Chevalier de La Luzerne: French Minister to the United States, 1779–1784* (Bruges, Belgium, 1938), 177–78.

13. Lewis, *Admiral de Grasse and American Independence*, 138–39.

14. Cornwallis to Clinton, August 16, 22, 1781, *CP* 6:24, 27–28; Cornwallis to Charles O'Hara, August 2, 4, 7, 10, 1781, *CP* 6:43, 44, 46, 48; O'Hara to Cornwallis, August 5, 9, 11, 17, 1781, ibid., 6:44–45, 48, 49, 52; Johann Ewald, *Diary of the American War: A Hessian Journal*, ed. Joseph P. Tustin (New Haven, CT, 1979), 325; Clinton to Gloucester, September 20, 1781, Series 3: Letterbooks, vol. 254, SHCP (WLCL).

15. Journal of Jean-Francois-Louis de Clermont-Crèvecoeur, in *The American Campaigns of Rochambeau's Army, 1780, 1781, 1782, 1783*, eds. Howard C. Rice Jr. and Anne S. K. Brown (Princeton, NJ, 1972), 1:33–34, 37–38, 38n; Claude Blanchard, *The Journal of Claude Blanchard, 1780–1781*, ed. Thomas Bulch (reprint, New York, 1969), 107; Louis-François-Bertrand du Pont d'Aubevoye, comte de Lauberdière, *The Road to Yorktown: The French Campaigns in the American Revolution, 1780–1783*, ed. Norman Desmarais (El Dorado Hills, CA, 2020), 107, 118; Ludwig von Closen, *The Revolutionary Journal of Baron Ludwig von Closen, 1780–1783*, ed., Evelyn Acomb (reprint, Chapel Hill, NC, 1958), 91–92; Kennett, *French Forces in America*, 114; Ron Chernow, *Washington: A Life* (New York, 2010), 334, 404; James A. Huston, *Logistics of Liberty: American Services of Supply in the Revolutionary War and After* (Newark, DE, 1991), 267–68; GW to John Augustine Washington, July 15, 1781, *WW* 22:385–86; GW, Instructions for Reconnoitering the Enemy's Posts at the North End of York Island, ibid., 22:370–72; GW to Lafayette, *LSLP* 4:247–48; *DGW* 3:398–99, 408.

16. Lauberdière, *The Road to Yorktown*, 122; GW to Lafayette, August 22, 1781, *LSLP* 4:340; Journal of Clermont-Crèvecoeur, *The American Campaigns of Rochambeau's Army*, 1:40–43; *DGW* 3:414, 413n; GW, General Orders, August 19, 1781, *WW* 23:19; Douglas Southall Freeman, *George Washington: A Biography* (New York, 1948–1957), 5:314; Kennett, *The French Forces in America*, 132.

17. For these paragraphs, see Andrew Jackson O'Shaughnessy, *The Men Who Lost America: British Leadership, the American Revolution and the Fate of the Empire* (New Haven, CT, 2013), 308–11; Olivier Chaline, "Season, Winds, and the Sea: The Improbable Route of de Grasse to the Chesapeake," in *European Friends of the American Revolution*, ed. Andrew J. O'Shaughnessy, John A. Ragosta, and Marie-Jeanne Rossignol (Charlottesville, VA, 2023), 99–122; Nathaniel Philbrick, *In the Hurricane's Eye: The Genius of George Washington and the Victory at Yorktown* (New York, 2018), 145, 161, 305–6; Tilley, *British Navy and the American Revolution*, 241–44; Samuel Hood to Clinton, August 25, 1781, *AR*, 562.

18. Ron Chernow, *Washington: A Life* (New York, 2016), 413; Piers Mackesy, *Could the British Have Won the War of Independence?* (Worcester, MA, 1976), 22; Frederick Wyatt and William B. Willcox, "Sir Henry Clinton: A Psychological Exploration in History," *William and Mary Quarterly* 16 (1959): 3–26.

19. Larrie D. Ferreiro, *Brothers at Arms: American Independence and the Men of France and Spain Who Saved It* (New York, 2016), 181–82; Cornwallis to Clinton, August 31, September 1, 2, 4, 8, 1781, *CP* 6:29–30, 31. Lafayette put the number of French marines that joined him at 3,200. See Lafayette to La Luzerne, September 8, 1781, *LSLP* 4:391.

20. Clinton to Cornwallis, September 6, 1781, *CP* 6:33; *AR*, 328–29, 331; Clinton to Germain, September 7, 1781, *DAR* 20:223.

21. Christopher Lloyd, "Armed Forces and the Art of War," in *The New Cambridge Modern History: The American and French Revolutions, 1763–1793*, ed. A. Goodwin (Cambridge, UK, 1965), 175; Philbrick, *In the Hurricane's Eye*, 179–96; Ferreiro, *Brothers at Arms*, 260–62; Tilley, *British Navy and the American Revolution*, 256–63; Lewis, *Admiral de Grasse and American Independence*, 161–62; Syrett, *Royal Navy in American Waters*, 192–204; Jean-Marie Kowalski, "The Battle of the Chesapeake from the Quarterdeck," *European Friends of the American Revolution*, 123–43; Graves to Clinton, September 9, 1781, *AR*, 567.

22. Extract of Minutes of Councils of War, September 14, 17, 19, 23, 24, 26, 1781, *AR*, 569–70 571–72, 573–74, 576–77; Willcox, *Portrait of a General*, 431, 434; Clinton to Germain, September 12, 26, October 14, 1781, *DAR* 20:230, 232, 241; Cornwallis to Clinton, September 16, 1781, *CP* 6:35; Clinton to Cornwallis, September 24, 1781, ibid., 6:36; *AR*, 339–40; Clinton to Gloucester, October 16, 1781, Series 3: Letterbooks, vol. 254, SHCP (WLCL); Clinton to Stuart, October 12, 1781, Wortley, *A Prime Minister and His Son*, 172.

23. Clinton to Cornwallis, September 2, 4, 6, 1781, *CP* 6:32, 33; Cornwallis to Clinton, September 16, 1781, ibid., 6:35; Middleton, *Cornwallis*, 98–99.

24. Journal of Clermont-Crèvecoeur, *American Campaigns of Rochambeau's Army*, 1:45–46; Journal of Jean-Baptiste-Antoine de Verger, ibid., 1:134; Lauberdière, *The Road to Yorktown*, 139; Thacher, *Military Journal*, 271; Thomas McKean to Rochambeau, September 4, 1781, *LDC* 18:11; Samuel Livermore to Meshech Weare, September 4, 1781, ibid., 18:7; New York Delegates to George Clinton, September 9, 1781, ibid., 18:27; GW to Robert Morris, August 17, 27, September 6, 1781, *WW* 23:12, 52, 89; GW, General Orders, September 6, 1781, ibid., 23:94; Edward G.

Lengel, *General George Washington: A Military Life* (New York, 2005), 335; Kennett, *French Forces in America*, 133–34.

25. Freeman, *George Washington*, 5:321–22; James T. Flexner, *George Washington in the American Revolution* (Boston, 1967), 444; Kennett, *French Forces in America*, 134; Lewis, *Admiral de Grasse and American Independence*, 148.

26. Freeman, *George Washington*, 5:323–24; Journal of Clermont-Crèvecoeur, *American Campaigns of Rochambeau's Army*, 1:52–53, 55; Kennett, *French Forces in America*, 135.

27. Freeman, *George Washington*, 5:325–28; *DGW* 3:419–20, 419n; Lauberdière, *The Road to Yorktown*, 256; GW to Lafayette, September 10, 1781, *LSLP* 4:397; Journal of St. George Tucker, *SOS* 2:1224; Richard M. Ketchum, *Victory at Yorktown: The Campaign That Won the Revolution* (New York, 2004), 186.

28. *DGW* 3:420–22; Questions Proposed by General Washington to Comte de Grasse, September 17, 1781, *WW* 23:122–25; Freeman, *George Washington*, 333–38; Lewis, *Admiral de Grasse and American Independence*, 174; Kennett, *The French Forces in America*, 136.

29. Greene, *The Guns of Independence*, 75, 78, 91–114; GW to George Weedon, September 20, 1781, *WW* 23:126; GW to President of Congress, October 1, 1781, ibid., 23:158; GW to de Grasse, September 25, 1781, ibid., 23:137; GW to McKean, October 6, 1781, ibid., 23:189; Knox to William Knox, September 4, 1781, Phillip Hamilton, ed., *The Revolutionary War Lives and Letters of Lucy and Henry Knox* (Baltimore, 2017), 156.

30. GW to President of Congress, October 1, 1781, *WW* 23:158; George F. Scheer, ed., *Private Yankee Doodle: A Narrative of Some of the Adventures, Dangers and Sufferings of a Revolutionary Soldier* (New York, 1968), 230, 231–32; Thacher, *Military Journal*, 283; Greene, *The Guns of Independence*, 148–91; Middleton, *Cornwallis*, 101; Lewis, *Admiral de Grasse and American Independence*, 184.

31. Thacher, *Military Journal*, 283–84; Cornwallis to Clinton, October 11, 12, 1781, *CP* 6:40; Lauberdière, *The Road to Yorktown*, 158.

32. Greene, *The Guns of Independence*, 240–53; Cornwallis to Clinton, October 15, 1781, *CP* 6:40.

33. Cornwallis to Clinton, October 20, 1781, *CP* 6:127–28; Cornwallis to GW, October 17, 118, 1781, ibid., 6:112, 113, 115; GW to Cornwallis, October 17, 18, 1781, ibid., 6:113, 114–15; Middleton, *Cornwallis*, 365n; Greene, *Guns of Independence*, 283–289.

34. *DGW* 3:430; Articles of Capitulation, October 19, 1781, *CP* 6:117–21.

35. Lewis, *Admiral de Grasse and American Independence*, 186, 188; Thacher, *Military Journal*, 289–90; William Feltman, *The Journal of Lieut. William Feltman, of the First Pennsylvania Regiment, 1781–82* (Philadelphia, 1853), 22; Scheer, *Private Yankee Doodle*, 241; Ewald, *Diary of the American War*, 340; Middleton, *Cornwallis*, 105; Greene, *Guns of Independence*, 290–303; State of the Army in Virginia under the Command of Lt General Earl Cornwallis, October 18, 1781, *CP* 6:116–17. See also Ian Saberton, "Reflections on the Siege and Capitulation of Yorktown and Gloucester," *Journal of the American Revolution*, April 21, 2021.

36. Clinton to Germain, October 29, 1781, *DAR* 20:252; Willcox, *Portrait of a General*, 439; Clinton to Gloucester, December 28, 1781, April 24, 1789, Series 3: Letterbooks, vol. 254, SHCP (WLCL).

37. *DGW* 3:430; Jeffers Lennox, *North of America: Loyalists, Indigenous Nations, and the Borders of the Long American Revolution* (New Haven, CT, 2022), 117; Robert G. Parkinson, *The Common Cause: Creating Race and Nation in the American Revolution* (Chapel Hill, NC, 2016), 521–22; Page Smith, *A New Age Now Begins: A People's History of the American Revolution* (New York, 1976), 2:1711; JA to John Jay, November 26, 1781, *PJA* 12:85; BF to JA, November 26, 1781, ibid., 12:87.

CHAPTER 15: WAR AND PEACE

1. Alan Valentine, *Lord North* (Norman, OK, 1967), 2:274.

2. Francois Van der Kemp to JA, November 26, 1781, *PJA* 12:89; *PH* 22:635–36, 654, 691, 695.

3. Hartley to BF, January 2 [–8], 1782, *PBF* 36:360–64; BF to Hartley, January 15, April 13, 1782, ibid., 36:435; 37:143–44; Orville T. Murphy, *Charles Gravier, Comte de Vergennes: French Diplomacy in the Age of Revolution, 1719–1787* (Albany, NY, 1982), 322; Richard B. Morris, *The Peacemakers: The Great Powers and American Independence* (New York, 1965), 254.

4. Troy Bickham, *Making Headlines: The American Revolution as Seen Through the British Press* (DeKalb, IL, 2009), 160; Valentine, *Lord North*, 2:292, 296, 303–5; Peter D. G. Thomas, *Lord North* (London, 1976), 132; Peter Whiteley, *Lord North: The Prime Minister Who Lost America* (London, 1996), 199–201; Morris, *The Peacemakers*, 253; *PH* 22:1028–48, 1076–80, 1085–90; Christopher Hobhouse, *Fox* (London, 1964), 114.

5. Jonathan Dull, *The French Navy and American Independence: A Study of Arms and Diplomacy, 1774–1787* (Princeton, NJ, 1975), 249–54, 268.

6. Larrie D. Ferreiro, *Brothers at Arms: American Independence and the Men of France and Spain Who Saved It* (New York, 2016), 274–80; Thomas E. Chávez, *Spain and the Independence of the United States: An Intrinsic Gift* (Albuquerque, NM, 2002), 203–9; Dull, *The French Navy and American Independence*, 283–84; Charles Lee Lewis, *Admiral de Grasse and American Independence* (Annapolis, MD, 1945), 208–48, 251; Nathan Miller, *Sea of Glory: The Continental Navy Fights for Independence, 1775–1783* (New York, 1974), 287, 355, 356, 370–71, 529.

7. Lewis, *Admiral de Grasse and American Independence*, 250–52, 260–67.

8. Chávez, *Spain and the Independence of the United States*, 147–49; Dull, *The French Navy and American Independence*, 307–9; Ferreiro, *Brothers at Arms*, 288–91; Larrie D. Ferreiro, "The Rise and Fall of the Spanish-French Bourbon Armada, from Toulon to Pensacola to Trafalgar," in *Spain and the American Revolution: New Approaches and Perspectives*, eds. Gabriel Paquette and Gonzalo M. Quintero Saravia (Charlottesville, VA, 2020), 72–74.

9. Ferreiro, *Brothers at Arms*, 280–84.

10. Editor's notes, *PBF* 37: liii–liv, 102; Hobhouse, *Fox*, 122; H. M. Scott, *British Foreign Policy in the Age of the American Revolution* (Oxford, UK, 1990), 317–20.

11. BF to the Earl of Shelburne, March 22, 1782, *PBF* 37:24; Shelburne to BF, April 6, 1782, ibid., 37:103–4; Charles R. Ritcheson, "Britain's Peacemakers, 1782–1783: 'To an Astonishing Degree Unfit for the Task,'" in *Peace and the Peacemakers: The Treaty of 1783*, ed. Ronald Hoffman and Peter J. Albert (Charlottesville, VA, 1986), 74, 95.

12. Carl Van Doren, *Benjamin Franklin* (New York, 1938), 669; Ritcheson, "Britain's Peacemakers," 79. For Oswald's version of the meeting, see editor's note, *PBF* 37:156–58. For BF's account, see BF to Vergennes, April 15, 1782, ibid., 37:158–59.

13. *PBF* 37:1–3n.

14. Murphy, *Charles Gravier, Comte de Vergennes*, 322, 333.

15. BF to Shelburne, April 18, 1782, *PBF* 37:165–67; Morris, *The Peacemakers*, 268, 273; Jonathan R. Dull, *A Diplomatic History of the American Revolution* (New Haven, CT, 1985), 140.

16. BF to Benjamin Vaughn, July 11, 1782, *PBF* 37:621; Samuel Flagg Bemis, *The Diplomacy of the American Revolution* (New York, 1935), 206–8. The "preposterous chimera" quotation can be found in Eliga H. Gould, *The Persistence of Empire: British Political Culture in the Age of the American Revolution* (Chapel Hill, NC, 2000), 166.

17. Dull, *A Diplomatic History of the American Revolution*, 145.

18. Morris, *The Peacemakers*, 319–20, 328–29, 397.

19. Sarah Livingston Jay to Catherine W. Livingston, August 14, 1782, in Richard B. Morris, ed., *John Jay: The Winning of the Peace: Unpublished Papers, 1780–1784* (New York, 1980), 2:461; John Jay to William Livingston, October 13, 1782, ibid., 2:472; Jay to JA, August 2, 1782, *PJA* 13:215; JA to Jay, August 13, 1782, ibid., 13:238.

20. JA to Robert R. Livingston, September 6, 1782, *PJA* 13:430–31.

21. Resolutions of Congress, November 23, 1781, *LSLP* 4:440; Morris, *The Peacemakers*, 395, 423; *ADA* 3:71; Olivier Bernier, *Lafayette: Hero of Two Worlds* (New York, 1983), 146; Louis Gottschalk, *Lafayette and the Close of the American Revolution* (Chicago, 1942), 408–9, 412–13, 431.

22. Morris, *The Peacemakers*, 306–10; Bemis, *The Diplomacy of the American Revolution*, 218–21; Jay to Robert R. Livingston, November 17, 1782, in Henry P. Johnson, ed., *The Correspondence and Public Papers of John Jay, 1763–1826* (reprint, New York, 1971), 2: No. 372.

23. Jay to Robert R. Livingston, November 17, 1782, Johnson, *Correspondence and Public Papers of John* Jay, 2: 373; Morris, *The Peacemakers*, 310.

24. Dull, *A Diplomatic History of the American Revolution*, 148; Vaughn to BF, September 23, 1782, *PBF* 38:132; BF's Observations on Jay's Draft, July 18, 1782, Morris, *John Jay: The Winning of the Peace*, 2:553. The expression "underhanded bargain" was Benjamin Vaughn's term and conveyed what he believed Jay was thinking. See Morris, *The Peacemakers*, 337.

25. BF to Joseph-Mathias Gérard de Rayneval, September 4, 1782, *PBF* 38:65; ibid., 38:164n; BF to Robert R. Livingston, September 26, 1782, ibid., 38:141–42; Richard Oswald to Thomas Townshend, October 2, 1782, Morris, *John Jay: The Winning of the Peace*, 2:372; Dull, *A Diplomatic History of the American Revolution*, 148.

26. JA to Robert R. Livingston, October 31, November 8, 1782, *PJA* 14:2–3; JA to Jonathan Jackson, November 17, 1782, ibid., 14:61–64; JA to Edmund Jenings, July 20,

1782, ibid., 13:189; JA to Arthur Lee, October 10, 1782, ibid., 13:525; JA to Mercy Otis Warren, August 8, 1807, in Charles Francis Adams, ed., *Correspondence Between John Adams and Mercy Warren*, reprinted in *Collections of Massachusetts Historical Society*, 5th series (1878), 4:427; *ADA* 3:16, 29–38, 40n; *Boston Patriot*, July 27, 1811; Herbert E. Klingelhofer, "Matthew Ridley's Diary During the Peace Negotiations of 1782," *William and Mary Quarterly* 20 (1963): 95–99, 123; R. R. Palmer, *The Age of the Democratic Revolution: A Political History of Europe and America, 1760–1800* (Princeton, NJ, 1959), 251–52.

27. James H. Hutson, *John Adams and the Diplomacy of the American Revolution* (Lexington, KY, 1980), 118.

28. Jeffers Lennox, *North of America: Loyalists, Indigenous Nations, and the Borders of the Long American Revolution* (New Haven, CT, 2022), 128.

29. James H. Hutson, "The American Negotiators: The Diplomacy of Jealousy," in Hoffman and Albert, *Peace and the Peacemakers*, 53.

30. Jonathan R. Dull, "Vergennes, Rayneval, and the Diplomacy of Trust," ibid., 105.

31. Morris, *The Peacemakers*, 362; *PBF* 38:271n; *ADA* 3:48; JA to Robert R. Livingston, November 6, 1782, *PJA* 14:30.

32. *ADA* 3:64–65, 79–81, 81n; JA to Richard Cranch, December 15, 1782, *AFC* 5:47; JA to Francis Dana, December 6, 14, 1782, *PJA* 14:114, 124; JA to Elbridge Gerry, December 14, 1782, ibid., 14:124; Morris, *The Peacemakers*, 375–80.

33. Morris, *The Peacemakers*, 350–51, 361; Jay to Peter Van Schaack, September 17, 1782, Morris, *John Jay: The Winning of the Peace*, 2:467; *ADA* 3:48–49; JA to William Gordon, September 10, 1783, *PJA* 15:278.

34. Draft Peace Treaty Presented by Richard Oswald to the American Peace Commissioners, November 25, 1782, *PJA* 14:86; ibid., 89n; *ADA* 3:80, 82.

35. Jay to BF, September 11, 1783, in Johnston, *The Correspondence and Public Papers of John Jay*, 3:74.

36. *ADA* 3:98; Vergennes to BF, December 15, 1782, *PBF* 38:461–62; BF to Vergennes, February 17, 1782, ibid., 38:465.

37. Jay to Robert R. Livingston, December 12, 1782, Johnston, *Correspondence and Public Papers of John Jay*, 3:6; *ADA* 3:50, 85, 100; JA to Abigail Adams, September 4, 1783, *AFC* 5:234.

38. Jay to Robert R. Livingston, December 14, 1782, Johnston, *Correspondence and Public Papers of John Jay*, 3:8.

39. *PH* 23:410.

40. Dull, *The French Navy and American Independence*, 332–33; Scott, *British Foreign Policy in the Age of the American Revolution*, 335.

41. Scott, *British Foreign Policy in the Age of the American Revolution*, 334.

42. For these two paragraphs, see Dull, *A Diplomatic History of the American Revolution*, 141–43, 145, 151, 152, 157, 158, 159–63; Morris, *The Peacemakers*, 408.

43. *ADA* 3:106; JA to Abigail Adams, January 22, 1783, *AFC* 5:74.

44. JA to Samuel Adams, September 10, 1783, *PJA* 15:271.

45. William Floyd to George Clinton, March 23, 1783, *LDC* 20:75; Theodorick Bland to Frances Tucker, March 24, 1783, ibid., 20:78; John Montgomery to Robert Magaw, February 13, 1783, ibid., 19:694; Hamilton to GW, March 24, 1783, ibid., 20:83.

46. BF to Joseph Banks, July 27, 1783, *PBF* 40:398.

CHAPTER 16: REFLECTIONS ON AMERICA'S REVOLUTIONARY WAR

1. Lee Kennett, *The French Forces in America, 1780–1783* (Westport, CT, 1977), 154–62.

2. William M. Fowler Jr., *American Crisis: George Washington and the Dangerous Two Years After Yorktown, 1781–1783* (New York, 2011), 192.

3. Benjamin Gilbert to James Converse, March 24, 1783, in John Shy, ed., *Winding Down: The Revolutionary War Letters of Lieutenant Benjamin Gilbert of Massachusetts, 1780–1783* (Ann Arbor, MI, 1989), 91; Gilbert to Charles Bruce, June 10, 1783, ibid., 107; Joseph Plumb Martin, *Private Yankee Doodle: Being a Narrative of Some of the Adventures, Dangers and Sufferings of a Revolutionary Soldier*, ed. George F. Scheer (New York, 1962), 283; Thomas Fleming, *The Perils of Peace: America's Struggle for Survival After Yorktown* (New York, 2007), 286–87; Fowler, *American Crisis*, 203; Terry Bouton, *Taming Democracy: "The People," the Founders, and the Troubled Ending of the American Revolution* (New York, 2007), 84–85.

4. GW, Farewell Orders to the Armies of the United States, November 2, 1783, *WW* 27:222–27.

5. Fowler, *American Crisis*, 227–33.

6. John Ferling, *The First of Men: A Life of George Washington* (reprint, New York, 2010), 320–21; GW, Address to Congress, December 23, 1783, *WW* 27:284–85.

7. The figures for Continentals are derived from Howard H. Peckham, ed., *The Toll of Independence: Engagements and Battle Casualties of the American Revolution* (Chicago, 1974), but corrected as a result of new information on the death toll among prisoners of war. See Edwin G. Burrows, *Forgotten Patriots: The Untold Story of American Prisoners During the Revolutionary War* (New York, 2008), 200–201. For an estimate of the number of free Americans at the time of the war, see Don Higginbotham, *The War of American Independence: Military Attitude, Policies, and Practice, 1763–1789* (New York, 1971), 389.

8. Michael Clodfelter, *Warfare and Armed Conflict: A Statistical Reference to Casualty and Other Figures, 1618–1991* (Jefferson, NC, 1992), 1:197–98; Neil Cantlie, *A History of the Army Medical Department* (Edinburgh, UK, 1974), 1:156; Rodney Atwood, *The Hessians: Mercenaries from Hessen-Kassel in the American Revolution* (Cambridge, UK, 1980), 255.

9. Books on the unpredictability of war are limitless. Good starters are John Keegan, *The First World War* (New York, 1999); John Keegan, *The Second World War* (New York, 1990); and Ian Kershaw, *Fateful Choices: Ten Decisions That Changed the World, 1940–1941* (New York, 2007).

10. These paragraphs draw on Eric Robson, *The American Revolution: In Its Political and Military Aspects, 1763–1783* (New York, 1966), 93–122; Stephen Conway, *The British Isles and the War of American Independence* (New York, 2000), 15, 16, 19, 24; Conway, "The British Army and the War of Independence," in *The Oxford Handbook of the American Revolution* (New York, 2013), ed. Edward G. Gray and Jane Kamensky, 183–89; Atwood, *The Hessians* (Cambridge, UK, 1980), 256; Piers Mackesy, *The War for America, 1775–1783* (Cambridge, MA, 1965), 524–25.

11. Piers Mackesy, *Could the British Have Won the War of Independence?* (Worcester, MA, 1976), 26–28.

12. GW, Farewell Orders to the Armies of the United States, November 2, 1783, *WW* 27:223; Thomas Paine, *American Crisis* 13 (1783), *CWTP* 1:230–31.

13. Christopher Lloyd, "Armed Forces and the Art of War," in *The New Cambridge Modern History: The American and French Revolutions, 1763–1793*, ed. A. Goodwin (Cambridge, UK, 1965), 174.

14. JA to Richard Cranch, December 15, 1782, *AFC* 5:47; JA to Abigail Adams, January 22, 1783, ibid., 5:74; JA to Ebenezer Stone, January 25, 1783, *PJA* 14:211; JA to James Warren, March 20, 1783, ibid., 14:348.

15. Thomas Paine, *Common Sense* (1776), *CWTP* 1:30–31.

16. TJ, First Inaugural Address (March 4, 1801), *PTJ* 33:148–52.

17. David S. Reynolds, *John Brown, Abolitionist: The Man Who Killed Slavery, Sparked the Civil War, and Seeded Civil Rights* (New York, 2003), 395.

18. Conway, *The British Isles and the War of American Independence*, 325–45; Eric J. Evans, *The Shaping of Modern Britain: Identity, Industry and Empire, 1780–1914* (Edinburgh, UK, 2011), 42–50, 95–104; Eliga H. Gould, *The Persistence of Empire: British Political Culture in the Age of the American Revolution* (Chapel Hill, NC, 2000), 208–14; Eliga H. Gould, "The Empire That Britain Kept," in Gray and Kamensky, *The Oxford Handbook of the American Revolution*, 465–80; Jeremy Black, *War for America: The Fight for Independence, 1775–1783* (Gloucestershire, UK, 1998), 245. On the fiscal-military state, see John Brewer, *The Sinews of Power: War, Money and the English State, 1688–1783* (London, 1989); and Christopher Storrs, ed., *The Fiscal-Military State in Eighteenth-Century Europe: Essays in Honour of P. G. M. Dickson* (London, 2009). See also Vincent T. Harlow, *The Founding of the Second British Empire, 1763–1793* (London, 1952).

19. Orville T. Murphy, *Charles Gravier, Comte de Vergennes: French Diplomacy in the Age of Revolution, 1719–1787* (Albany, NY, 1982), 397–400; Higginbotham, *The War of American Independence*, 233–34.

20. For these three paragraphs, see TJ, Autobiography, in *The Complete Jefferson: Containing His Major Writings, Published and Unpublished*, ed. Saul K. Padover (Freeport, NY, 1969), 1164, 1176–77; TJ to John de Crevecoeur, August 6, 1787, *PTJ* 11:692; TJ to Jay, June 21, 1787, ibid., 11:489; TJ to James Madison, August 9, 1788, ibid., 13:489; TJ to JA, August 30, 1787, ibid., 12:67–68; TJ to GW, December 4, 1788, ibid., 14:330; TJ to JA, January 11, 1816, September 12, 1821, in Lestor J. Cappon, ed., *The Adams-Jefferson Letters: The Complete Correspondence Between Thomas Jefferson and Abigail and John Adams* (Chapel Hill, NC, 1961), 2:458, 575; TJ to Roger C. Weightman, June 24, 1826, in Paul Leicester Ford, ed., *The Writings of Thomas Jefferson* (New York, 1892–1899), 10:390–92; Louis Gottschalk, "The Place of the American Revolution in the Causal Pattern of the French Revolution," in *Causes and Consequences of the American Revolution*, ed. Esmond Wright (Chicago, 1966), 303–4; Thomas Paine, *Rights of Man, Part the Second* (1792), *CWTP* 1:354. The BF

quotation can be found in Janet Polasky, *Revolutions Without Borders: The Call to Liberty in the Atlantic World* (New Haven, CT, 2015), 14.

21. Thomas Paine, "Reasons for Preserving the Life of Louis Capet," January 15, 1793, *CWTP* 2:551–53.

22. Larrie D. Ferreiro, *Brothers at Arms: American Independence and the Men of France and Spain Who Saved It* (New York, 2016), 319–24.

23. JA to Abigail Adams, August 15, 1782, *AFC* 4:361; TJ to Weightman, June 24, 1826, Ford, *The Writings of Thomas Jefferson*, 10:391–92.

24. JA to Benjamin Waterhouse, October 29, 1805, in Worthington Chauncey Ford, ed., *Statesman and Friend: Correspondence of John Adams and Benjamin Waterhouse, 1784–1822* (Boston, 1927), 31; TJ to JA, January 11, 1816, in Lester J. Cappon, ed., *The Adams-Jefferson Letters: The Complete Correspondence Between Thomas Jefferson and Abigail and John Adams* (Chapel Hill, NC, 1959), 2:459–60.

INDEX

Beaumarchais, Pierre-Augustin
 Caron de, 43–47, 94–95,
 109–10, 359
Bemis Heights, Battle of, 129–30
Bennington, Battle of, 124, 125
Blue Book of Continental Army,
 169
Board of War and Ordnance, 65
Bonhomme Richard (American
 warship), 242–43
Bonvouloir, Achard de, 30–31,
 40, 41, 43, 168–69, 359
Boston, colonial siege of, 16–23
 artillery brought form Fort
  Ticonderoga, 39, 48
 British retreat from Boston to
  Halifax, 50
 colonial disputes over strategy,
  34–35
 colonial fortification of
  heights above city, 17–18,
  48–50
 disease and, 34
 position and number of
  colonial forces, 16–17
 stalemate of war's first year,
  38–39
 Washington's efforts to build
  colonial forces, 31–34
 See also Bunker Hill, Battle of
Boston Massacre, 49
Boston Tea Party, 3
Brandywine, Battle of, 136–40
 Howe's pause following,
  140–41
 Washington's lucky escape
  from sniper in, 138
Brant, Joseph (Thayendanegea),
 189–90, 373
Britain
 aggressive changes in colonial
  policies in 1760s, 1–3
 attacks on Americans, outrage
  in response to, 61–62
 colonies as source of global
  power, 7
 debate on best course for war,
  258, 259
 decision to use force, 8–11
 economic damage from war,
  259–61
 empire, after loss of American
  colonies, 390
 European alliances, history of,
  158–59
 exploration of peace options,
  312–13, 314

French and Spanish plan to
  invade, 194–95
Gordon Riots, 261–62, 318
lack of European ally in war
  with France, 158–61
loss of Minorca, 329, 358
mistakes and missed
  opportunities of war,
  380–82
and Napoleonic wars, 393
obstacles to war success,
  382–83, 386–87
planning for campaign of
  1777, 102–105
postwar economic recovery,
  391
preparations for war, 26
public disenchantment with
  war by 1779, 259
reactions to colonial unrest,
  3–4
refocus of war effort on
  France, 258–59
and Seven Years' War, 5–6
trade with new United States,
  390–91
wartime shortages and taxes,
  56, 102, 260
weak resistance expected from
  colonists, 8–9, 10–11, 13
See also British government;
  peace agreement between
  Britain, France and
  Spain
British Army
 Black freemen and slaves in,
  228–29
 in Boston
  colonists' resentment of, 2
  inexperience of, 14, 28
  number of troops, 14
 campaign of 1776, objectives
  of, 26
 chronic logistical problems,
  68–69, 382
 civilians in entourage of, 226
 departure from America,
  378–79
 and disease, 224
 expansion during
  Revolutionary War, 222
 food, and shortages, 225–26
 in Halifax, prior to attack on
  New York City, 50–52
 logistical problems, 224–26
 Loyalists in, 227–28
 mercenaries hired by, 27

mistakes and missed
  opportunities of war,
  380–82
obstacles to war success,
  382–83, 386
officers' purchasing of
  commissions, 221
recruitment, 223
size of, 222
and southern strategy, 162,
  173–74, 184, 228, 259, 273,
  277, 287, 293, 300–301,
  340–41
total deaths in Revolutionary
  War, 380
as volunteer force, 221
See also mercenaries, German
  ("Hessians")
British Army soldiers
 and American climate, 229
 Americans as, 222–23, 227–28
 daily life of, 224–25
 demographic data on, 222–23
 desertions, 229
 dropping of standards for, 223
 enlistment period, 222
 equipment carried by, 223–24
 reasons for enlisting, 222
 reports on ferocity of fighting,
  229–30
 training, 224
 transport to America, as grim
  ordeal, 224
British government
 Carlisle Commission,
  151, 171
 commissioners sent to receive
  American submission,
  58–60, 75
 debate on war, after Battle of
  Yorktown, 355–57
 efforts to prevent French and
  Spanish intervention,
  148–51
 leak of false plan to divide
  America between Britain,
  France, and Spain, 57
 and peace negotiations, 356,
  359–64, 367–68
 pressure for war results,
  146–47
 Rockingham's ministry,
  359–60, 362
 strategy reset after setbacks of
  1777 campaign, 161–62
 strong support for continuing
  war in 1777, 100–101

INDEX

525

British ships sent to America
in response to, 179, 193
cost of, 264
departure from East Coast,
182
French decision to send,
176–77
lack of accomplishments, 193,
203
return to France, 203
Savannah, attempt to retake,
202–203
secrecy of, 176
size of, 177
souring of relations with
Americans, 326
successes in Caribbean, 200
Washington and, 171, 176,
178–79
window for advantage over
British fleet, 177, 193
See also d'Estaing, Charles-
Hector Théodat, Comte
French officers illegally
commissioned by Deane, 110
French public opinion on war,
263
French Revolution, 392–93

Gage, Thomas
and battles of Lexington and
Concord, 14–15, 16
and Bunker Hill, Battle of, 18,
22
and colonists' trade in military
goods, 32
insufficient troops sent to
reinforce, 10
on necessity of using force on
colonies, 10
and plan to take New York
City, 50
preparations for war, 14
reinforcements sent to, 14, 17,
27
removal from command, 26
and siege of Boston, 17, 18
views on colonial military
capabilities, 9–10
Galloway, Joseph, 137, 142, 145,
168
Gálvez, Bernardo de, 196–98,
327–29, 357
Gates, Horatio
appointment as general, 25
and Bemis Heights, Battle of,
129–30

on Britain's Indian allies'
atrocities, 122–23
on Britain's need to change
course, 161–62
and Burgoyne's campaign
against Albany, 126
as commander of southern
army
Camden, First Battle of,
285–87
rebuilding of forces at
Charleston, 284–85
removal, 301
at Fort Ticonderoga, 82
and Freeman's Farm, Battle of,
126, 127
as head of Northern
Department, 65, 122–23,
126
military background of, 123,
126
and surrender of Burgoyne's
army, 130–31
Washington's suspicions
about, 179
George III (king of England)
as advocate for use of force, 8,
13, 26–27, 258
and Clinton's capture of
Charleston, 277–78
and debate on war after Battle
of Yorktown, 355, 356
on fall of Fort Ticonderoga,
119
hiring of mercenaries as proof
of his perfidy, 63–64
meeting with Mohawk leader,
189
opposition to peace plans, 313,
314
out-of-touch view of American
conflict, 381
refusal to allow peace offers to
colonists, 57–58, 147, 158, 161
support for continuing war in
1777, 100–101
Georgia, British reestablishment
of pre-revolution government,
185
See also Savannah
Gérard, Conrad Alexandre
and American peace envoy,
257
and American peace terms,
254–56
consultation with
Washington, 200–201

and Franklin as minister to
France, 256
as minister to United States,
177–78
negotiations of alliance with
American envoys, 155,
156–57
popularity in America, 254–55
Germain, George
as advocate of aggressive
warfare, 51, 58, 111–12
appointment as American
secretary, 27–28
and British attack in
Carolinas, 52
and Burgoyne's campaign
against Albany, 132
Burgoyne's correspondence
with, 114, 125, 131
and campaign of 1781, orders
for, 340–42
and choice of commissioners
to colonies, 59
and Clinton, support of, 173
Clinton's correspondence
with, 184, 186, 348
and Clinton's Virginia
campaign of 1780–1781,
319–20
controversial background of,
27–28
Cornwallis and, 337
and debate on war, after Battle
of Yorktown, 355
disappointment with
campaign of 1776, 104–105
expectations for taking of Fort
Ticonderoga, 99
and French joining of war, 238
Howe's correspondence with,
79, 85, 86, 111–12
meeting with Mohawk leader,
189–90
and need to close war quickly,
273
opposition to peace proposals,
259
out-of-touch view of American
conflict, 320, 342, 381
Parliament's dissatisfaction
with, 147
plans for attacks on Spanish
assets in America, 198
plans for campaign of 1777,
102–106
public criticism of, 148
removal from cabinet, 356

A NOTE ON THE AUTHOR

JOHN FERLING is professor emeritus of history at the University of West Georgia. He is the author of many books on the American Revolution, including *Jefferson and Hamilton*; *Whirlwind*, a finalist for the 2015 Kirkus Prize; and, most recently, *Winning Independence*. He and his wife, Carol, live near Atlanta.